Shared Representations

Socially situated thought and behaviour are pervasive and vitally important in human society. The social brain has become a focus of study for researchers in the neurosciences, psychology, biology and other areas of behavioural science, and it is becoming increasingly clear that social behaviour is heavily dependent on shared representations. Any social activity, from a simple conversation to a well-drilled military exercise to an exquisitely perfected dance routine, involves information sharing between the brains of those involved. This volume comprises a collection of cutting-edge essays centred on the idea of shared representations, broadly defined. Featuring contributions from established world leaders in their fields and written in a simultaneously accessible and detailed style, this is an invaluable resource for established researchers and those who are new to the field.

SUKHVINDER S. OBHI is Associate Professor in the Department of Psychology, Neuroscience and Behaviour at McMaster University, Canada.

EMILY S. CROSS is Professor of Cognitive Neuroscience in the School of Psychology at Bangor University, Wales.

CAMBRIDGE SOCIAL NEUROSCIENCE

The field of social neuroscience has seen a remarkable rise in recent decades. This series of books, written by internationally known scholars from a variety of disciplines and combining cutting-edge research and theory in the field, provides researchers and students with an in-depth introduction to key topics in social neuroscience.

Titles published in the series:

Shared Representations: Sensorimotor Foundations of Social Life edited by Sukhvinder S. Obhi and Emily S. Cross

Shared Representations

Sensorimotor Foundations of Social Life

Edited by

Sukhvinder S. Obhi

and

Emily S. Cross

CAMBRIDGE
UNIVERSITY PRESS

University Printing House, Cambridge CB2 8BS, United Kingdom

Cambridge University Press is part of the University of Cambridge.

It furthers the University's mission by disseminating knowledge in the pursuit of
education, learning and research at the highest international levels of excellence.

www.cambridge.org
Information on this title: www.cambridge.org/9781107690318

© Cambridge University Press 2016

First published 2016

Printed in the United Kingdom by TJ International Ltd. Padstow Cornwall

A catalogue record for this publication is available from the British Library

Library of Congress Cataloging-in-Publication Data
Names: Obhi, Sukhvinder S., editor. | Cross, Emily, editor.
Title: Shared representations : sensorimotor foundations of social life /
edited by Sukhvinder S. Obhi and Emily S. Cross.
Description: Cambridge, United Kingdom : Cambridge University Press, 2016. |
Includes bibliographical references and index.
Identifiers: LCCN 2016025955 | ISBN 9781107050204 (hardback : alk. paper)
Subjects: LCSH: Social representations. | Social perception. | Social psychology.
Classification: LCC HM1088 .S53 2016 | DDC 302–dc23
LC record available at https://lccn.loc.gov/2016025955

ISBN 978-1-107-05020-4 Hardback
ISBN 978-1-107-69031-8 Paperback

Contents

Colour plates can be found between pages 290 and 291.

Figures

Tables

Boxes

Contributors

CATERINA ANSUINI Department of Robotics, Brain and Cognitive Sciences, Italian Institute of Technology, Genova, Italy

LARA BARDI Department of Experimental Psychology, University of Gent, Belgium

CRISTINA BECCHIO Department of Robotics, Brain and Cognitive Sciences, Italian Institute of Technology, Genova, Italy and Centre for Cognitive Science, Department of Psychology, University of Torino, Torino, Italy

CESARE BERTONE Centre for Cognitive Science, Department of Psychology, University of Torino, Torino, Italy

GEOFFREY BIRD Institute of Psychiatry, King's College London, UK

MARCEL BRASS Department of Experimental Psychology, University of Gent, Belgium

REBECCA BREWER Institute of Psychiatry, King's College London, UK

JOHN T. CACIOPPO University of Chicago, US

STEPHANIE CACIOPPO University of Chicago, US

BEATRIZ CALVO-MERINO Cognitive Neuroscience Research Unit, Psychology Department, School of Arts and Social Science, City University London and Psychology Department, Universidad Complutense de Madrid, Spain

DANA CASPERSEN Forsythe Company, Dresden, Germany

CAROLINE CATMUR Institute of Psychiatry, Psychology and Neuroscience, King's College London, UK

ANDREA CAVALLO Centre for Cognitive Science, Department of Psychology, University of Torino, Torino, Italy

MICHEL-PIERRE COLL School of Psychology, Université Laval, Center for Interdisciplinary Research in Rehabilitation and Social Integration (CIRRIS) and Québec's Institute of Mental Health Research Center (CRIUSMQ), Canada

DAVE COLLINS Institute of Coaching and Performance, University of Central Lancashire, UK

JENNIFER COOK Department of Psychology, School of Arts and Social Sciences, City University, UK

RICHARD COOK Institute of Psychiatry, King's College London, UK

EMILY S. CROSS Wales Institute for Cognitive Neuroscience, School of Psychology, Bangor University, UK and Department of Social and Cultural Psychology, Donders Institute for Brain, Cognition and Behaviour, Radboud University Nijmegen, the Netherlands

JOHN A. DEWEY Department of Cognitive Science, Central European University, Budapest, Hungary

GUILLAUME DEZECACHE Laboratoire de Neurosciences Cognitives (LNC) – INSERM U960, Département des études cognitives, Ecole Normale Supérieure – PSL Research University, Paris

THOMAS DOLK Max Planck Institute for Human Cognitive and Brain Sciences, Leipzig, Germany

TERRY ESKENAZI Laboratoire de Neurosciences Cognitives (LNC) – INSERM U960, Département des études cognitives, Ecole Normale Supérieure – PSL Research University, Paris

EMMA FLYNN Centre for Coevolution of Culture and Biology, School of Education, Durham University, UK

JESSICA A. GRAHN Brain and Mind Institute, Department of Psychology, University of Western Ontario, Canada

MICHAEL S. A. GRAZIANO Department of Psychology, Princeton University, US

JULIE GRÈZES Laboratoire de Neurosciences Cognitives (LNC) – INSERM U960, Département des études cognitives, Ecole Normale Supérieure – PSL Research University, Paris

PAUL L. GRIBBLE Brain and Mind Institute, Department of Psychology, University of Western Ontario, Canada

KRISTA GRIGAITYTE Ahmanson-Lovelace Brain Mapping Cente, Brain Research Institute, Department of Psychiatry and Behavioral Sciences, David Geffen School of Medicine at UCLA, and University of Edinburgh, Scotland

PATRICK HAGGARD Institute of Cognitive Neuroscience, University College London, UK

ANTONIA HAMILTON Institute of Cognitive Neuroscience, University College London, UK

ANDY HILL Institute of Coaching and Performance, University of Central Lancashire, UK

MARCO IACOBONI Ahmanson-Lovelace Brain Mapping Center, Brain Research Institute, Department of Psychiatry and Behavioral Sciences, David Geffen School of Medicine at UCLA, US

PHILIP L. JACKSON School of Psychology, Université Laval, Center for Interdisciplinary Research in Rehabilitation and Social Integration (CIRRIS) and Québec's Institute of Mental Health Research Center (CRIUSMQ), Canada

PETER E. KELLER MARCS Institute, University of Western Sydney, Australia

A. KINGSTONE Department of Psychology, University of British Columbia, Canada

GÜNTHER KNOBLICH Department of Cognitive Science, Central European University, Budapest, Hungary

EDWARD KRAJKOWKSI George Washington University, Department of Anthropology; Center for the Advanced Study of Hominid Paleobiology, Department of Speech and Hearing Science, GW Institute for Neuroscience and Mind-Brain Institute, US

K. E. W. LAIDLAW Department of Psychology, University of British Columbia, Canada

DANIËL LAKENS Department of Industrial Engineering and Innovation Sciences, Eindhoven University of Technology, the Netherlands

JANEEN LOEHR Department of Psychology, University of Saskatchewan, Canada

STERGIOS MAKRIS Department of Psychology, Edge Hill University, UK

HEATHER MCGREGOR Brain and Mind Institute, Department of Psychology, University of Western Ontario, Canada

GIACOMO NOVEMBRE MARCS Institute, University of Western Sydney, Australia

SUKHVINDER S. OBHI Department of Psychology, Neuroscience and Behaviour, McMaster University, Social Brain, Body and Action Lab, Canada

JANINE OOSTENBROEK Department of Psychology, University of York, UK

GUIDO ORGS Department of Psychology, Brunel University and Institute of Cognitive Neuroscience, University College London, UK

HARRIET OVER Department of Psychology, University of York, UK

MARIA-PAOLA PALADINO Department of Social Psychology, University of Trento, Italy

CLARE PRESS Department of Psychological Sciences, Birkbeck, University of London, UK

WOLFGANG PRINZ Max Planck Institute for Human Cognitive and Brain Sciences, Leipzig, Germany

ELIZABETH RENNER George Washington University, Department of Anthropology; Center for the Advanced Study of Hominid Paleobiology, Department of Speech and Hearing Science, GW Institute for Neuroscience and Mind-Brain Institute, US

DANIEL C. RICHARDSON Department of Experimental Psychology, University College London, UK

E. F. RISKO Department of Psychology, University of Waterloo, Canada

LUISA SARTORI Dipartimento di Psicologia Generale, Università di Padova, Italy

THOMAS SCHUBERT Department of Psychology, University of Oslo, Norway

NATALIE SEBANZ Department of Cognitive Science, Central European University, Budapest, Hungary

FRANCYS SUBIAUL George Washington University, Department of Anthropology; Center for the Advanced Study of Hominid Paleobiology, Department of Speech and Hearing Science, GW Institute for Neuroscience and Mind-Brain Institute, US

CAMERON R. TURNER Centre for Coevolution of Culture and Biology, School of Education, Durham University, UK

COSIMO URGESI Laboratorio di Neuroscienze Cognitive, Dipartimento di Scienze Umane, Universita degli Studi di Udine, Italy and Istituto di Ricovero e Cura a Carattere Scientifico 'E. Medea', Italy

CORDULA VESPER Department of Cognitive Science, Central European University, Budapest, Hungary

KRISTINA WACLAWIK Brain and Mind Institute, Department of Psychology, University of Western Ontario, Canada

SARAH WATSON Brain and Mind Institute, Department of Psychology, University of Western Ontario, Canada

JORINA VON ZIMMERMANN Department of Experimental Psychology, University College London, UK

Preface

State-of-the-art knowledge in cognitive neuroscience has emerged largely from the systematic study of individual performance in non-social tasks. Specifically, experimental psychology and human neuroscience have successfully elucidated many of the information-processing elements and neural mechanisms involved in tasks such as visual search, perception and categorisation of objects, memory for words, numbers and objects, and goal-directed actions. Building upon this established work, a significant effort is underway to create a cognitive neuroscience of *socially situated* thought and behaviour – or, in other words, a 'social' cognitive neuroscience. A key characteristic of this endeavour is the combination of psychological and neurophysiological perspectives and levels of analysis. Socially situated thought and behaviour are pervasive and vitally important in human society. Social cognitive neuroscience is a burgeoning field that focuses on key human abilities including, but not limited to, intuiting what others are thinking, empathising with others, understanding and predicting the behaviour of others, identifying the emotions of others, and solving a task jointly with others. The establishment of dedicated journals such as *Social Neuroscience*, *Cognitive, Affective, & Behavioral Neuroscience* and *Social Cognitive & Affective Neuroscience*, as well as the increasing number of books, such as this one, concerned with the neurocognitive bases of social behaviour, is further evidence of the expansion of interest in social information processing.

A central concept in the domain of social cognitive neuroscience is the representation of information in conjunction with, and pertaining to, other people. Common everyday activities such as opening a door to allow someone through, following the gaze of a stranger on a train, moving a piece of furniture together, dancing, and conversing with a colleague, all involve representation of information about, or in concert with, other social agents. Thus, in a broad sense, representations are 'shared' not necessarily because equivalent representations are concurrently activated in two or more individuals, but rather because activated representations across individuals relate to a current task, goal, object, person or process. In this way, representations across individuals are shared as a function of the prevailing circumstance. As such, shared representations would appear to be indispensable for a successful social life.

This book comprises a collection of cutting-edge contributions centred on the idea of shared representations, broadly defined. We are extremely fortunate to have assembled what could be considered a 'dream team' of contributors, all of whom are established and respected leaders in their fields of study. Without these outstanding individuals, this volume could not have become a reality and certainly could not have materialised into the remarkable resource that it is!

The coverage in this volume is quite broad and evolves from a consideration of basic foundations to an examination of applied research in domains such as sport, dance and music. As such, this book will be a useful resource for a wide range of readers. We asked our contributors to write their chapters so that senior undergraduate students or new entrants to the field would be able to understand the content. Inspection of the chapters confirms that contributors succeeded in achieving this goal. To make the task more difficult, we also requested our contributors to write their chapters so that established researchers in the field would find the book a useful resource for their daily work. Again, inspection of the chapters confirms that authors overwhelmingly achieved this goal. Therefore, due to the diligence of our authors, this book will appeal to a wide range of readers, from undergraduate students to established social cognitive neuroscientists and all levels of student and trainee in between.

This book is made up of six parts, each containing four to six chapters: *Foundations, Imitation and Mimicry, Thinking, Perceiving and Acting with Others, Understanding Others, Learning and Development* and *Shared Representations in Applied Contexts*.

Part I, 'Foundations', starts with a thoughtful contribution from Dolke and Prinz, who provide a cogent analysis of what constitutes a shared representation and what task co-representation actually means. Using the joint Simon effect as an example case, these authors put forward arguments for an interpretation of the effect in terms of referential coding in which simultaneous activation of event representations, regardless of the source of their activation, is responsible for interference in different Simon task contexts (i.e. individual and joint). According to this view, joint Simon effects emerge due to concurrent activation of events with shared features, and not due to a socially induced co-representation of another agent's stimulus–response (S–R) mapping.

In the second chapter in Part I, Grigaityte and Iacoboni focus on the human mirror system (HMS) and introduce the idea of the 'merged self', a state in which the intentions, actions and bodies of two interacting individuals become represented within each individual mind. With reference to electrophysiological studies in monkeys, rare single cell recordings in humans, and neuroimaging evidence, they argue that the merged self is induced via the bottom up, automatic functioning of the HMS and that this merged state could support human capacities such as empathy. They note however that this merged self can be influenced and controlled by various forms of top-down input and that such control can be considered preparatory when it is implemented prior to engagement of the HMS, or reactive when it comes online after HMS processing has begun. A dynamic interplay between bottom-up and top-down processes then mediates the merging and unmerging of two individuals, and thereby supports a wide range of social cognition and behaviour.

Following on, in the third chapter of Part I, Graziano provides a superb account of state-of-the-art ideas about the form and function of the primary motor cortex. Situating his chapter in historical context, he argues convincingly that the motor cortex can be usefully considered as an 'action map' as opposed to a homunculus containing a dispersed and discontinuous map of the body (i.e. the textbook description of the motor cortex). Graziano's proposal emerges from consideration of microstimulation studies in monkeys in which stimulation is applied for a (longer) duration that better matches the time- course of certain behaviours. For example, microstimulation applied to the motor cortex for half a second evokes complex movements, such as defensive movements and reach to grasp movements, similar to those seen in the animal's natural repertoire. In the final part of his chapter, Graziano speculates about the links between these defensive reactions, the action map and social behaviour.

In their chapter, Coll and Jackson take us beyond action into consideration of shared representations in non-motor domains. Emphasising the overlap of personally and vicariously activated somatosensory representations, they provide an overview of numerous studies of touch and pain that have used neuroimaging, brain stimulation and behavioural methods. Overall, they present a compelling case that self-experienced sensation and the vicarious experience of sensations share common representational elements. Finally, they point out limitations in current work and advocate for a move to more ecologically valid studies of shared representations in the non-motor domain. They also suggest the tantalising prospect of using brain stimulation approaches to modulate activity in shared representations for therapeutic benefit in a range of patient groups who are afflicted by excessive or impoverished responses to personal and vicariously experienced sensations.

Rounding out Part I, Cacioppo and Cacioppo provide an illuminating discussion of methodological and theoretical considerations in social neuroscience. Starting with a fascinating historical journey, these authors quickly arrive at a contemporary metaphor for the brain that goes beyond the computer metaphor of the last century. Specifically, Cacioppo and Cacioppo suggest the brain can be likened to a mobile, broadband, connected information-processing device. They further highlight the multi-level study of the social brain and discuss methods including psychophysiological measures, functional imaging and epigenetics and gene expression. Finally, they provide five useful considerations for researchers that will help guide thoughtful analyses of data in social neuroscience experiments.

Beginning Part II, 'Imitation and Mimicry', Subiaul, Renner and Krajkowski contribute an excellent chapter on the comparative study of imitation in non-human primates. Pointing out the lack of consensus on whether apes can imitate, they go on to define and operationalise key types of imitation, underlining that imitation is best considered a multi-faceted psychological capacity involving motor and non-motor forms. They distinguish between two types of motor imitation – 'novel' imitation of actions that have not been previously executed and 'familiar' imitation of previously executed actions. After thoughtful consideration of the extant literature, they conclude that, whereas monkeys seem to be capable of some familiar motor imitation and imitation of cognitive rules, they are not capable of novel motor imitation. This is in contrast to apes, which demonstrate both novel and familiar motor imitation. Finally, they suggest that imitation of previously executed actions may be a basic capacity shared by many animals, and is adaptive for life in the hierarchical social structures in which they live.

Moving on from consideration of non-human primates, in the second chapter in this part Oostenbroek and Over focus on cultural and developmental perspectives on notions of imitation. The authors couch their contribution in the broader literature of social learning and cultural transmission, arguing that the importance of imitation extends far beyond learning about the physical world (such as how to use tools), into ideas about how children learn about their group's cultural norms, including values, attitudes, opinions and beliefs. By reviewing the social psychology literature on how children learn about the social world by copying those around them, Oostenbroek and Over provide a compelling and elegant perspective on the utility of studying imitative behaviour beyond the motor domain to understand how we develop shared representations with others in a social world.

In the third contribution to Part II, Bardi and Brass start their chapter by explaining how motor representations can be activated via internal signals like intentions, or external signals such as the observed actions of others. Drawing on a discussion of mirror processing, the authors raise the fundamental question of how an agent can distinguish between an intentionally activated motor representation and an externally activated one, and further how the agent can control activated motor representations such that they do not imitate other agents all the time. This need for self–other control mechanisms forms the main focus of the chapter and Bardi and Brass provide compelling evidence that the areas involved in the control of imitation, namely, the anterior medial prefrontal cortex (aMPFC) and the right temporoparietal junction (rTPJ) overlap with areas associated with theory of mind, mentalising and agency attribution. The authors unpack the likely roles of these brain areas in component processes underlying self–other control with a central idea being that higher order cognitive functions are intimately linked to more basic sensorimotor mechanisms of self–other processing. They close their chapter with a call for more research to better understand this seemingly crucial social cognitive brain network, including an examination of whether the network is in fact domain specific or domain general.

In closing Part II, Obhi provides an integrative account of the possible links between mirroring as studied in action observation and automatic imitation tasks, on the one hand, and more naturalistic social mimicry on the other. He notes that social mimicry, the tendency to copy the bodily movements of an interaction partner, is most often studied by social psychologists, whereas it has mainly been cognitive neuroscientists who have studied the mirror system in laboratory-based action observation and imitation tasks. As a consequence, the link between these two research domains has not been systematically studied. Obhi then provides an overview of recent experiments that have attempted to shed light on whether social mimicry, action observation and automatic imitation 'tasks' share common mechanisms. Using a task analysis, he suggests that caution should be taken when equating laboratory-based imitation tasks and more natural social mimicry. He ends the chapter with speculation on whether social mimicry might usefully be considered an (unconscious) process of action selection, and suggests that future work should focus on how converging inputs interact to produce mimicry.

Part III, 'Thinking, Perceiving and Acting with Others', introduces research examining the cognitive mechanisms underpinning our interactions with others in a social context. Laidlaw, Risko and Kingstone begin this part with a chapter focused on innovative approaches to studying social attention. They explain how the field of social attention is grounded in traditional visual attention research, and call into question whether tried-and-tested laboratory approaches for studying attention enable us to capture important subtleties and nuances involved in how we attend to others in the real world. To overcome these limitations, they discuss how new paradigms evaluating looking behaviour in more realistic social settings shed light on the importance of gaze for acquiring social information and controlling what information is communicated to others. Their contribution builds a strong case for deeper consideration of the 'social' component of social attention, and clearly articulates considerations for future work in this domain.

In the next chapter, Vesper and Sebanz provide a comprehensive overview of the cognitive mechanisms underlying joint action. Sebanz was one of the first researchers to experimentally examine how we coordinate our actions with others, and this contribution reviews the seminal contributions made by her team and others in an attempt to elucidate how it is that two or more people can perform all manner of complex actions together with relative ease. They highlight several mechanisms that support interpersonal coordination, with a focus on the importance of prediction (by both interaction partners) in helping to smooth motor coordination between individuals. Their piece also touches on how joint action research informs verbal communication, development of joint action, as well as human–robot interactions, thus widening the scope for how basic joint action research can apply to related domains.

From joint action, we shift attention to joint perception, with the third piece in this part authored by von Zimmerman and Richardson. In this chapter, the authors challenge the notion that perception is a solitary endeavour, and explore evidence documenting how social forces impact how we interact with the world and respond to incoming perceptual information. They describe ground-breaking work from their laboratory that demonstrates how participants' eye movements when looking at positive, negative or neutral pictures change when they think an interaction partner is looking at the same pictures compared to when they think their interaction partner is looking at a different set of symbols. This work underscores how visual perception is susceptible to what others around us are looking at, and the impact of social influences on basic perceptual processes.

The fourth contribution to this part returns to how we coordinate our actions with others, this time focusing on the antecedents and consequences of interpersonal synchrony. Lakens, Schubert and Paladino review empirical evidence that supports two complementary theoretical proposals: that individuals spontaneously synchronise their behaviour during social interactions, and that when we synchronise our movements with others, we experience stronger social bonding. Taken together, this work builds a compelling case for the interpersonal synchrony establishing or reinforcing social connections between individuals.

The final piece in Part III touches upon ideas introduced in several of the other chapters in this part to examine a special case of joint action: musical ensemble performance. In this piece by Keller, Novembre and Loehr, we learn how successful musical performance requires performers to coordinate their actions across a number of different aspects, including musical dimension, timescale, sensory modality and mode of interaction. Returning to the title of the entire volume, the authors build a compelling case for just how vital shared representations across each of these aspects is during musical performance, and examine behavioural and brain data to show how real-time interpersonal coordination is achieved by performers embodying action outcomes related to the self, others and the ensemble as a whole.

Part IV, 'Understanding Others', begins with a thoughtful contribution from Hamilton, who takes an action-centred perspective, in her words 'a motor chauvinist view', on the functioning of the mirror system. In particular, Hamilton focuses on understanding what, if anything, makes the human mirror system different from the motor system involved in object-directed action, the object motor system. She provides a detailed comparison of these systems in terms of cortical localisation, goals and kinematics, behavioural priming and familiarity, and training and concludes that the mirror system is different from the object motor system primarily because it responds to for observed and executed actions. She asks whether this single distinguishing aspect is sufficient to warrant very different claims about the functional significance of the two systems. In the last part of the chapter, she cycles back to the idea of motor chauvinism and outlines the social responding account of mirror system function, which holds that the system serves response generation above all else.

The following chapter, by Press, focuses on the observed biological tuning of the mirror response in humans. Citing a range of evidence, Press highlights that the mirror response is typically greater for human stimuli than for inanimate stimuli, and seems to be particularly influenced by the form and kinematics of the observed movement. She goes on to suggest two functional implications of this enhanced mirroring for human actions, including the greater likelihood of imitating human rather than robot actions, as a means of skill learning, and potentially greater involvement of the motor system in the perception of human actions compared to robot actions. Press points out that biological tuning is less likely to differ based on discrepancies in higher order inferential processes such as mental state attribution, since evidence for the involvement of mirroring in this function is lacking. The chapter concludes by suggesting that mirroring is a specific example of a domain-general process that links perceptual and motor systems in the service of action control.

In the next chapter dealing with understanding others, Dewey and Knoblich draw upon a diverse range of evidence to address three main themes. First, they consider the effect of action experience on the representation of actions made by the self and others. They emphasise the possible role of mental stimulation on prediction of (self and other) action effects. Second, they consider how action affordances affect the representation of space in relation to self and other. The authors argue that, just as the presence of objects affords actions, so too does the presence of other social agents. They provide evidence that humans spontaneously take the motor capabilities of co-actors into account when working on joint tasks, which results in the construction of joint affordance maps that represent the range of motor possibilities for all agents in a particular action scenario. Third, they go on to consider the fundamental question of how we distinguish self from other. They highlight the importance of multisensory integration of haptic, proprioceptive and visual information in maintaining a sense of body ownership. Finally, they consider the role of motor and external sensory information in the construction of a sense of agency.

Ansuini, Cavallo, Bertone and Becchio discuss the proposition that intentions can be understood from observing the actions of others. Citing the traditional idea that intentions cannot be perceived owing to the fact that they are hidden in someone else's mind, Ansuini et al. go on to highlight a range of experimental findings demonstrating that the intentions that an actor has shape the kinematics of the movements she makes. This initial discussion is followed by a survey of studies showing that observers are actually sensitive to differences in kinematics, such that, among other things, they can decipher whether an action was made in a cooperative, competitive or individual context, simply from videos showing the initial phase (until object contact) of reach to grasp actions. Indeed, even with minimal point-light displays, observers are able to discriminate between these three classes of movement. They end their chapter by considering the possible neural machinery that underlies the intention-from-kinematics ability, and highlight the case of autism as a condition in which intention reading is impaired.

Moving on from intention reading, in the fifth chapter of Part IV Sartori provides an excellent review of studies examining complementary action contexts – situations in which the actions of one individual complete, in some way, the actions of another. Sartori points out that under circumstances where a complementary action is required, motor resonance may not be a useful response and that top-down modulation of the system can facilitate the performance of a non-matching movement. Following on from this, she surveys neuroimaging studies that suggest a role for two distinct systems: one, the mirror system that represents actions in a common code, and the other, an integration system that can flexibly remap actions with respect to task demands. Sartori then provides an overview of neurophysiological studies investigating modulation of corticospinal excitability in complementary action scenarios, including elegant experiments on the time-course of complementary actions. Sartori ends the chapter with a suggestion that the mirror system could serve a working memory function for actions.

In the final chapter of Part IV, Dezecache, Eskenazi and Grèzes focus on whether emotional convergence constitutes a case of contagion. Citing the strong and seemingly natural tendency for humans to imitate the emotional facial expressions of others, Dezecache et al. consider the theoretical assumptions and epistemological consequences of considering this as contagion. Taking us on a historical tour, they survey key models of emotional convergence including social comparison models, conditioning models and the primitive contagion model. They conclude that, whilst there is a case for viewing emotional convergence as contagion, this view is not encompassing of the fact that the response to emotional displays by conspecifics does not always comprise a congruent emotional display. Rather, they propose that fast facial reactions to emotional displays are an evaluation of the emotion portrayed by a conspecific and do not inevitably lead to experiencing a matching emotion. Thus, they end the chapter by suggesting that convergence is an accidental match between the emotional response of an observer and the emotions displayed by a conspecific.

Part V, the penultimate part of this volume, concerns the learning and development of shared representations, with individual chapters exploring how disorders, learning and expertise advance our understanding of social cognition. Catmur begins this part with a chapter that examines how shared representations for actions are acquired. She focuses on the Associative Sequence Learning (ASL) theory, a seminal proposal for how we learn from watching our own actions and actions of others, and presents evidence to demonstrate how mirror neuron properties in the human brain are sensitive to experience in a manner consistent with ASL predictions. She concludes with important considerations for how experience might mitigate damaging effects of disorders of social cognition.

These considerations provide a smooth transition to the next contribution in this part, authored by Cook. In this chapter, Cook examines how individuals with autism spectrum conditions (ASCs) show difficulties with shared representations as demonstrated by their performance on particular types of imitation task. She discusses evidence showing that deficits in action execution or action observation can adversely impact the ability of individuals with ASC to imitate others' actions, and concludes with considerations for how this research might inform how we understand shared representations in other domains beyond action imitation, such as empathy, as well as other conditions beyond ASC, including schizophrenia and alexithymia.

The third chapter in this part continues on the topic of alexithymia to consider how shared representations of emotion vary across individuals. Brewer, Cook and Bird describe how alexithymia, a subclinical phenomenon whereby individuals have difficulty identifying and describing their own emotions, is known to co-occur with several other disorders that are associated with inconsistent reports of emotional impairments, including autism, eating disorders and schizophrenia. The authors present an alexithymia hypothesis, proposing that affective impairments in these disorders (and others) might be best explained by the extent to which a given individual is alexithymic. The noteworthy aspect of this hypothesis is that, if supported, it highlights the necessity of intact representations of one's own emotions to identify those of others, thus providing further evidence underscoring the importance of shared representations in social life.

Turner and Flynn shift the focus in the fourth chapter in Part V to examine how learning by diffusion, a sophisticated type of social observational learning, shapes shared representations. The authors couch their contribution in a broader context of exploring how culture develops, explaining how culture arises from many different individuals interacting with each other, learning from each other, collaborating and sharing knowledge over time. Turner and

Flynn's contribution provides an elegant overview of diffusion experiments, one type of experimental approach used to examine the development of culture, and demonstrate how diffusion experiments show copying behaviour (or observational learning) to fulfil two important roles: information exchange and affiliation.

The next piece, by McGregor and Gribble, picks up on the theme of observational learning, this time with an emphasis on the learning of highly skilled motor tasks in a laboratory environment. McGregor and Gribble delve more deeply into the mechanisms supporting observational motor learning, discussing the importance of action prediction, feedback and error correction. They review empirical evidence demonstrating that observers learn by predicting the upcoming movements of a tutor, and by updating these predictions based on any errors made by the tutor. The authors also highlight neurophysiological and neuroimaging evidence that demonstrates both sensory and motor cortices of the observer's brain are engaged when observing motor learning, and conclude their contribution with considerations for how observational learning interventions might aid in rehabilitation contexts.

The final piece in the learning and development part examines the impact of expertise on shared representations. Cross and Calvo-Merino examine how motor expertise acquired from either long-standing practice where many years are spent honing a physical skill, or laboratory-based learning interventions where participants learn new motor skills in a controlled environment, shapes action perception. The authors examine evidence from their laboratories and others showing that motor expertise in an observer shapes perception of others' actions, and consider broader implications of the malleability of shared representations based on experience.

Much of the work discussed in the piece by Cross and Calvo-Merino focuses on work performed with expert dancers and athletes, which serves as a fitting transition into the final part of the book, 'Shared Representations in Applied Contexts'. This part begins with a chapter by Urgesi and Makris exploring several of the themes from the previous part in the sporting domain. Specifically, the authors focus on how motor expertise among elite athletes refines their ability to predict others' actions, thus demonstrating that expert athletes are experts not only in the motor domain but in the perceptual domain as well. They also discuss how acquired expertise in the sporting domain might help individuals to flexibly inhibit shared representations of one's own and another's actions when such inhibition might be necessary, such as when an opponent is trying to deceive a player. The authors conclude this piece with considerations for how cognitive neuroscience work with expert athletes might inform sports training strategies.

Collins and Hill contribute the next chapter in Part VI with a piece that remains in the sporting domain to consider shared mental models (SMMs) among athletes and referees. Collins and Hill emphasise how important it is for sports team members to both see things in a similar way and make decisions that are similar to or mutually compatible with those of teammates. They describe how an SMM can develop among effective teams, which assists with team play. Moreover, when referees share SMMs, this can also lead to more consistent and coherent refereeing decisions. This chapter concludes with ideas about how research findings concerning SMMs might also benefit interdisciplinary teams and team cultures.

The third chapter in this part shifts from sports to music, with a piece by Waclawik, Watson and Grahn exploring the brain bases of musical synchronisation and social interaction. In this elegant contribution, Waclawik and colleagues discuss why experiencing music with others promotes positive social experiences, with consideration of the evolutionary roots of why music developed in the first place. Touching on some similar themes to those presented in the chapters by Lakens et al. and Keller et al., the authors review data supporting their proposal that links between music and human sociality are mediated by the mirror neuron system as well as brain regions associated with theory of mind. They conclude with broader considerations of the role played by music in social cohesion.

Rounding off the entire volume, the final chapter in this part, by Orgs, Caspersen and Haggard, introduces a revolutionary theoretical proposal concerning shared representations and aesthetic evaluation of dance. Orgs et al. propose that the aesthetic value of dance (and perhaps all performing arts) can be traced to the successful, bidirectional transmission of messages between performer and spectator. Drawing on evidence and theory from the domains of dance, philosophy, communication science, cognitive neuroscience and psychology, the authors build a compelling case for how implicit processing and explicit strategy shape spectators' aesthetic experience of dance, and, in so doing, demonstrate how research into shared representations can inform understanding of domains that extend well beyond the behavioural and brain sciences.

As can be seen when considering each of these contributions as a collective, a lively research community encompassing a range of disciplines, approaches, and questions is engaged in exploring how it is we share representations with others, and why these shared representations help us to thrive in a social world. Our thanks go, first of all, to the contributors themselves, who enthusiastically welcomed the opportunity to contribute original pieces to this volume, delivered manuscripts of outstanding quality in a timely manner, and promptly responded to our requests for revisions. We passionately believe this book will serve as a comprehensive and highly regarded resource for the state-of-the-art research on sensorimotor aspects of socially situated thought and behaviour, and for this we owe a debt of gratitude to our dream team of contributors!

We also offer our sincere thanks to Hetty Marx, Janka Romero and Carrie Parkinson at Cambridge University Press, for their invaluable support, advice, flexibility and, perhaps most of all, patience. Hetty and her team made the entire process of assembling and publishing this book a pleasure, and we are grateful for the opportunity to have worked with such a professional team.

Finally, this volume is dedicated to Pritam Singh Obhi (1936–2014), who sadly passed away before this project came to fruition. He was, and will always be, an inspiration to all who knew him; he is deeply missed.

Part I

Foundations

1   What It Takes to Share a Task: Sharing versus Shaping Task Representations

Thomas Dolk and Wolfgang Prinz

Abstract

In this chapter, we examine task representations in shared task settings like the joint ('social') Simon task. Over the past decade, ideas pertaining to shared representations and co-representation have been advanced to account for performance in such settings. Here, we argue that we can do without these notions. On the one hand, we show that shared representations cannot account for typical findings in shared task settings. This is the negative part. On the other hand, we show that task performance can be explained by the claim that individuals shape their individual task representations according to the needs of the shared task. This is the positive part. Consequentially, we claim that performance in shared task settings relies on shaping individual representations, not sharing common representations. To get there, we take three major steps. First, we examine what it takes to share a task and what the notion of task co-representation entails. Second, we discuss the joint Simon task and the joint Simon effect. Here, we show that the explanation of the effect in terms of shared representations does not work. Instead, we suggest an explanation in terms of referential coding. Finally, in a third step, we come back to the role that social modulators may play in the framework of referential coding.

Task Sharing

Shared Representations

Let us first see what the broad notion of shared representations entails. When do we speak of shared representations and what are they supposed to be good for? To start with, when do we speak of representations at all? Broadly speaking, we invoke representations as hypothetical entities operating in cognitive systems. Their unobservable operation is meant to account for observable segments of (first-person) experience or (third-person) performance. Accordingly, representations are intrinsically individual and private. They can only arise and operate in individual minds, and there is no obvious way in which they could be shared with other minds (Prinz, 2012).

Thus, when we talk about shared representations we do not mean to say that two (or more) individuals share one and the same representation. Instead, what we mean to say is that two or more individuals entertain private representations that refer to one and the same reference object or event. This way they can be both private, i.e. existing in individual minds, and shared, i.e. referring to the same reference. Shared representations may be seen to underlie both shared experience and shared performance. We speak of shared experience when two or more individuals perceive, remember, think, believe or desire certain things and when they do so on the understanding that other individuals do so as well. Likewise, we may speak of shared performance when an individual performs a given task in collaboration and coordination with others. In both cases, we may claim that experience and performance are grounded in shared representations, i.e. representations referring to the same common thoughts, beliefs or desires and the same common task in which the individuals are involved.

The idea that representations can be shared in this way is fundamental for understanding social interaction (Clark, 1996; Tomasello, 2009; Tomasello, Carpenter, Call, Behne, & Moll, 2005). This pertains to both experience and performance. The notion of *shared experience* acknowledges the fact that we are social in the sense that we see the world not only through our own eyes but through others' eyes as well. Likewise, the notion of *shared performance* acknowledges the fact that we can easily collaborate and coordinate with others in many kinds of joint activities. The idea of shared representations thus appears to be a theoretical foundation stone for understanding social communication and interaction that we cannot dispense with (cf., for example, Echterhoff & Higgins, 2010; Higgins, 1981, 1992).

Shared Task Representations

Let us now see how the general notion of shared representations may apply to the special case of shared task settings. We speak of shared task settings when a task is distributed between two (or more) individuals in a division-of-labour mode. Typical examples include playing a piece of music together, carrying a table downstairs or performing the joint Simon task (see below). One of the crucial features of such scenarios is that the involved individuals share the common goal of achieving the task at hand.

It appears to be a natural idea to account for performance in such task settings in terms of shared representations. In order to successfully perform such tasks, individuals must control their own performance in a way that takes their partners' contributions into account. One way of fulfilling this requirement is to co-represent their task shares. If this happens, each participant will form a task representation that represents not only his/her *own share* of the task, but the other participants' *foreign shares* as well. Thus, as a result, each participant will eventually form a representation of the full task.

According to this view, individuals take foreign contributions to the task into account in terms of the way in which others represent their task shares. The notion of task co-representation thus instantiates the idea that individuals look at the task not only through their own eyes but through foreign eyes as well. A claim like this is in functional terms quite demanding. Can we come up with a weaker, less demanding claim? An obvious alternative is to think of others not in terms of their (unobservable) task representations, but rather in terms of the (observable) events that instantiate their performance in the task scenario. This view opens an entirely different perspective for taking foreign contributions into account: not in terms of *tasks* that others have in mind, but rather in terms of *events* through which their performance is instantiated. According to this view, individuals may be entirely ignorant about the others' tasks. Instead, what they share with them are representations of the common scenario of objects, events, actions and agents.

Some would perhaps argue that this can be considered a weaker form of co-representation: event co-representation rather than task co-representation (cf. Dolk et al., 2011). In fact, it is not always clear in the literature what the concept of co-representation is precisely meant to refer to. For instance, it has been suggested that co-representation may refer to actions or agents in the task scenario (e.g. Philipp & Prinz, 2010; Sebanz, Knoblich, & Prinz, 2003, 2005; Wenke et al., 2011). According to this broad reading, the term 'co-representation' would apply to any kind of representation of social facts. Yet, we do not think that broadening the concept this way makes any sense (for further support and discussion of related issues, also see Heyes, 2014). As discussed above, this concept is meant to capture the idea that individuals do not just represent things and events, but also co-represent the way in which others represent them. This is what the concept entails – and this is actually what constitutes the power to explain the emergence of interference in the joint setting.

By contrast, no such claim is entailed in the notion of event representation. When applied to shared task settings, this notion captures two basic ideas. At the descriptive level, it captures the trivial fact that shared task scenarios tend to be richer than regular, unshared scenarios of the same tasks. At the explanatory level, it captures the claim that the social facts that make up these enrichments (i.e. foreign agents, actions, and so on) are taken into account for forming and shaping individual task shares (i.e. the cognitive representation thereof) according to the needs of the task.

The Joint Simon Task

In this section, we examine the joint ('social') Simon effect (JSE) as a test case for studying the relative merits of the ideas of sharing and shaping task representations. As indicated above, the interference effect obtained in the joint Simon task has from the outset been associated with the notion of task co-representation (Sebanz & Knoblich, 2009; Sebanz, Knoblich, & Prinz, 2003; Welsh et al., 2013a, 2013b). In fact, this notion was originally created to account for this effect (Sebanz, Knoblich, & Prinz, 2005).

Findings

Basically, the joint Simon task can be described as a classical Simon task that is divided up between two participants. In the classical (two-choice) Simon task, single participants are required to select one of two keys in response to, for example, the colour of a stimulus patch (e.g. red or green). The patch may appear on the left- or the right-hand side of the screen. Colour is thus relevant for response selection, whereas location is irrelevant in the sense that it plays no role in response selection at all. Yet, on the other hand, the location of the key to be pressed (mounted on the left- versus right-hand side of the table) is a crucial distinctive feature between the two competing responses. The task can thus be seen to instantiate a conflict between two roles of the same feature: while stimulus location is entirely irrelevant, response location is highly relevant for response selection. The pronounced interference effect that is regularly observed in the two-choice Simon task (i.e. smaller RTs in trials with spatial stimulus–response correspondence as compared to trials with noncorrespondence (see, for example, Figure 1.1) indicates that participants in fact find it impossible to effectively ignore the location of the colour patch. The interference effect suggests that the irrelevant stimulus feature (location) is mandatorily processed. It looks as if the strong role that it plays for response selection somehow spills over into stimulus processing.

The joint Simon task combines two participants who are required to perform two independent, complementary *Go/NoGo* tasks. Typically, the two are seated next to each other, with one response key assigned to each of them. Instructions may require, for instance, that one responds to green but withholds from red stimuli and the other does the reverse. Each participant's share of the task is thus completely equivalent to a regular *Single Go/NoGo* task in which a single individual responds to one of the two colors. Accordingly, when looked at from an individual perspective, the *Joint Go/NoGo* task should exhibit the same pattern of interference as the *Single Go/NoGo* task. Surprisingly, however, this is not what the data show. Results from several studies have shown that the Simon effect 'goes away' in the *Single Go/NoGo* task, but 'comes back' in the

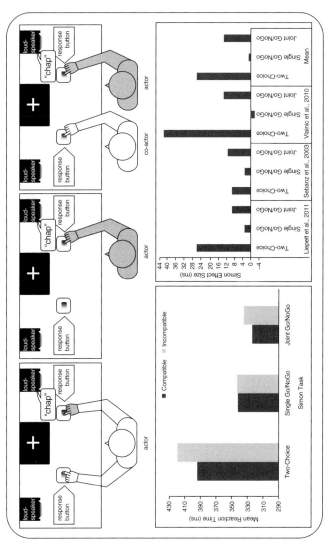

Figure 1.1 Three versions of the Simon task: *two-choice*, *Single Go/NoGo* and *Joint Go/NoGo* (upper row from left to right).

Notes: The lower row prototypically illustrates the result pattern typically observed for all three Simon tasks. On the left: mean reaction time (RT; averaged based on the results of Liepelt et al., 2011; Sebanz et al., 2003; Vlainic et al., 2010) as a function of the Simon task (*two-choice*, *Single Go/NoGo*, *Joint Go/NoGo*) and spatial stimulus–response compatibility (compatible, incompatible). On the right: Simon effect size (i.e. incompatible–compatible trials) as a function of the Simon task version (*two-choice*, *Single Go/NoGo*, *Joint Go/NoGo*) for the study of Liepelt et al. (2011; most left), Sebanz et al. (2003) and Vlainic et al. (2010), as well as the mean of all three studies (far right).

Joint Go/NoGo task (Liepelt, Wenke, Fischer, & Prinz, 2011; Sebanz et al., 2003; Vlainic, Liepelt, Colzato, Prinz, & Hommel, 2010). This finding has been taken to suggest a profound impact of social context on the mechanisms underlying the interference effect (Sebanz et al., 2005; Müller et al., 2011a, 2011b; Tsai & Brass, 2007; Welsh, 2009; Welsh et al., 2013).

Narratives

We may discern two narratives within these findings: *brief* and *extended*. The brief narrative has three major items: (i) the classical Simon task requires the actor to *choose* between two response alternatives. In this two-choice task, a substantial interference effect is obtained. (ii) The interference effect goes away when the *Choice* task is replaced by a *Go/NoGo* task. This task requires selective responses to one kind of stimulus, but no response to the other kind (*Single Go/NoGo*). (iii) The interference effect is back when the *Go/NoGo* task is performed jointly, i.e. when two individuals perform complementary selective responses (*Joint Go/NoGo*; Sebanz et al., 2003, 2005; Welsh, 2009; Welsh et al., 2013).

The brief narrative seems to suggest an obvious conclusion, viz., the *Joint Go/NoGo* task is in functional terms similar, if not equivalent, to the *Choice* task. Moving from description to explanation, it has been assumed that each participant co-represents, on top of his/her own share of the task, also his/her partner's complementary share – to the effect that the two eventually share representations of the full task (Sebanz et al., 2003, 2005; Sebanz & Knoblich, 2009). Since the full task combines two complementary *Go/NoGo* tasks, it exhibits precisely the same functional requirements as the *Choice* task. This elegant move explains why the interference effect is reinstated in the joint task. The idea of co-representation claims that social context leads participants to combine own and foreign task representations into an integrated and shared representation of the full task in an automatic and mandatory fashion (Sebanz & Knoblich, 2009; Welsh et al., 2013).

Yet, one may claim that the brief narrative, on which this interpretation relies, does not cover the full story and may therefore be misleading (Dolk et al., 2011). To cover the full story, it requires two important extensions. (iv) The first extension pertains to response speed: reaction times in the *Joint Go/NoGo* task are at about the same level as in the *Single Go/NoGo* task – far from the substantially higher reaction times in the *Choice* task (see Figure 1.1, lower left panel).

This observation speaks against the idea that the joint task is functionally similar, or even equivalent, to the *Choice* task. (v) The second extension pertains to the size of the interference effect: the Simon effect obtained in the joint task is always much smaller than the classical effect in the *Choice* task (i.e. two-choice Simon task typically > 25 ms; (single/joint) *Go/NoGo* typically ranges between 5 and 15 ms; see, for example, Figure 1.1 lower right panel). This observation speaks against the suggestive account that the original effect from the *Choice* task goes away in the *Single Go/NoGo* task, but comes back in the *Joint Go/NoGo* task.

The extended narrative thus suggests entirely different theoretical conclusions. First, there is no longer any reason to believe that the *Joint Go/NoGo* task carries the functional signature of a *Choice* task. Instead, it exhibits the signature of a selective response task, just like the *Single Go/NoGo* task. Second, there is likewise no reason to believe that social context acts to reinstate a choice-like Simon effect. Instead, the task-demands of selective responding seem to generate a new interference effect which is substantially smaller than the original (two-choice) one (see Figure 1.1).

On the one hand, the extended narrative provides a more complete and more precise account of experimental findings than the original brief one. Yet, on the other hand, it fails to offer an in-built explanation of the joint interference effect. As we have seen, the brief narrative offers such an explanation: if interference is associated with choice, it must be expected to come back when social context acts to instantiate the full choice task for each participant. This is what the action/task co-representation account claims (e.g. Sebanz et al., 2003, 2005). The extended narrative cannot resort to such an in-built automatism. Instead, it needs to come up with new ideas to explain the emergence of interference in the *Joint Go/NoGo* task.

Referential Coding

In what follows, we outline a framework of such ideas. As said above, the framework posits shaping rather than sharing task representations. More specifically, it claims that interference in the *Joint* task arises from shaping and tuning one's own task representation in a way that takes all events in the task scenario into account, including those arising from social context (e.g. events generated by another agent). How can this be possible?

Prominent views theorising about cognitive representations of action events (or the underlying mechanisms thereof; Hommel, 2010; Hommel et al., 2001; Prinz, 1987; see Box 1.1) refer in one way or the other to ideomotor theories of cognitive control (Harleß, 1861; Herbart, 1825; James, 1890; Lotze, 1852; for a review, see Stock & Stock, 2004). According to ideomotor theories, events (perceivable effects) are cognitively represented by codes of their sensory consequences. More precisely, the *theory of event coding* (TEC; Hommel et al., 2001) assumes that the cognitive representation of events consists of networks of codes that represent the features of all perceivable effects, such as the seen, heard or felt location, the direction and the speed, the effectors it involves and the objects it refers to (Figure 1.2; Hommel, 1997). In other words, cognitive control operates on the perceptual representation of events. Hence, these event representations (or the generation thereof) are per se independent of any pre-specified stimulus–response mapping rules.

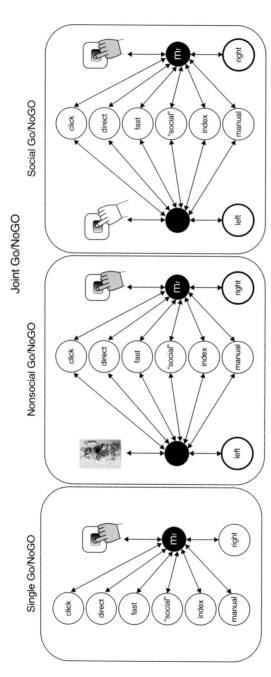

Figure 1.2 Referential coding in the *Single* (upper panel) and *Joint* (i.e. social or nonsocial) *Go/NoGo* version of the Simon task.

Notes: A prototypical agent (i.e. gray shaded hand) operates the right response key, which produces numerous action events. The sensory consequences of these events might be described as something manual, direct and fast, produced by the index finger, 'social' and with a clicking sound that can be coded and are thus cognitively represented by these or any other event-features. Yet, in the *Joint* as opposed to the *Single Go/NoGo* Simon task, these event-features are typically shared between two alternative action events possible in such scenarios, with one exception: the location. Differentiating two (concurrently) activated event representations thus requires emphasising discriminable features, i.e. the corresponding (response) location. This makes the agents' right keypress be represented mainly as 'right' as opposed to the alternative event generated by, for example, another person or Japanese cat. Stimulus events that share the feature 'right' will consequently activate the corresponding action event, leading (typically) to stronger interference effects in the *Joint* (social or non-social) compared to the *Single Go/NoGo* Simon task, as there is simply no alternative event that needs to be differentiated, thus making referential coding in the latter case unnecessary.

Box 1.1 The theory of event coding (TEC)

The theory of event coding (TEC; Hommel, 2004, 2009; Hommel et al., 2001) offers a theoretical framework for the representational basis of inter-actions between perception and action (and thereby an extension of the common coding (CC) theory; Prinz, 1990). In the tradition of ideomotor theorising (Harleß, 1861; Herbart, 1825; James, 1890; Lotze, 1852; for a review, see Stock & Stock, 2004), action and perception are considered as being (i) situated, i.e. tightly connected to on-going – and thereby con-strained by rapid changes of – external or internal processes (Jeannerod, 1994), and (ii) inter-dependent and bi-directional (Hommel et al., 2001).

Common coding theories propose that action and perception share the same coding system, to the effect that the same representational struc-tures (at least in part), which are responsible for the control of one's own action, are also involved in the perception of foreign action (Hommel, 2013; Prinz, 1990). Accordingly, common coding theories can be considered as the theoretical backup of neuronal assemblies that literally share common resources in perceiving and executing actions (known as mirror neurons in the macaque monkey (e.g. Gallese, Fadiga, Fogassi, & Rizzolatti, 1996; di Pellegrino, Fadiga, Fogassi, Gallese, & Rizzolatti, 1992; Rizzolatti, Fadiga, Gallese, & Fogassi, 1996) and a mirroring system in humans (for a review, see Rizolatti & Craighero, 2004).

TEC does not make any distinctions between perceived and produced events (stimuli and responses). Both are cognitively represented by codes of their sensory consequences. According to this reasoning, the cognitive representation of events consists of networks of codes that represent the features of all perceivable effects, such as the seen, heard or felt location, the direction and the speed, the effectors it involves and the objects to which it refers (see Figure 1.2; Hommel, 1997). In other words, the perceptual representations of events constitute the source of cognitive control.

Taking this parity between action and perception seriously, one would expect (i) facilitation of action execution based on direct prior perception and vice versa, and (ii) interference when action and perception recruit shared representations simultaneously. Meanwhile, there is a large amount of behavioural evidence that supports both action facilitation in the case of direct matches between perception and action (e.g. De Maeght & Prinz, 2004; Fagioli, Hommel, & Schubotz, 2007; for a review, see Heyes, 2001) and interference in cases of mismatches (e.g. Brass, Bekkering, & Prinz, 2001; Müsseler & Hommel, 1997; for reviews, see Schütz-Bosbach & Prinz, 2007; Sommerville & Decety, 2006).

As a consequence, and most critical for the extended narrative, this assumption implies that all events – irrespective and independent of their social/non-social nature – in a given task context are basically represented in the same way (i.e. by means of the same kinds of codes; Hommel, 2009, 2011). Hence, simply the assembly of perceivable events causes the *shaping* and *tuning* of one's own cognitive task representation. This in turn clarifies why response conflict (as in the underlying signature of Simon task interference) can be considered to reflect nothing more than the concurrent activation of more than a single action event representation (be it due to endogenous preparation, stimulus-induced activation and/or cross talk). Thus, irrespective of whether representing more than a single action-event alternative (as, for example, in the two-choice Simon task) or the perceivable consequences of another social/non-social entity (as, for example, in the *Joint Go/NoGo* Simon task), the set of action-event alternatives in the task context at hand attunes their cognitive representations. Accordingly, what matters for Simon-like interference is not the source of activation but rather the set of concurrently activated alternatives.

Being able to perform a *Joint* (social/non-social) *Go/NoGo* Simon task requires the actor to select the task-relevant representation from all concurrently activated action event representations. Consequentially, the requirement of selecting the event representation that encodes the corresponding action from a number of activated event representations reflects a discrimination problem. Emphasising features that discriminate task-relevant from task-irrelevant representations (i.e. through an increased 'intentional weighting' of discriminable features; Hommel et al., 2001; Memelink & Hommel, 2013) provides a parsimonious solution to this discrimination problem. In the Simon task the most obvious discriminating feature appears to be the (horizontal/vertical) location on which task-related action event alternatives are arranged (Figure 1.1 upper panel and Figure 1.2 lower panel; also see Dittrich, Dolk, Rothe-Wulf, Klauer, & Prinz, 2013).

Note, however, that any other feature can serve this function too, as long as it enables sufficient discrimination between (stimulus- and/or action-) event alternatives, and thus provides a reference for coding one's own actions. Such feature-based event discrimination is the key principle underlying the *referential coding* account (Dolk et al., 2013; see Sellaro, Dolk, Colzato, Liepelt, & Hommel, 2015, for a feature other than location, i.e. colour). In the case of spatial S–R compatibility paradigms, the spatial coding of one's own actions furnishes the representations of those action events with spatial features that will then interact with spatial features of stimulus events (see Figure 1.2). Consequentially, feature overlap of stimulus and action event codes will facilitate response execution in terms of matches as opposed to mismatches, impairing action execution (Hommel et al., 2001). In other words, feature overlap of S–R codes can be considered a necessary condition for Simon effects to emerge (Dittrich et al., 2013; Kornblum, Hasbroucq, & Osman, 1990).

Hence, as there are simply no alternative action events in the *Single Go/ NoGo* Simon task that have to be distinguished for response coding (Hommel, 1996, 2013), there can be no spatial response coding, and, hence, no longer any Simon effect. Similarly, if co-actors always respond to the same stimulus (Lam & Chua, 2009), the lack of alternative stimulus events (i.e. without assigned responses) does not lead to Simon effects, as there is no spatial stimulus coding required. Finally, in case of a dimensional mismatch between spatial stimulus and action events (horizontal versus vertical or vice versa; Dittrich et al., 2013), the lack of feature overlap between S–R alternatives also leads to the breakdown of the interference effect.

In sum, we claim that interference in the (*Joint*) *Go/NoGo* Simon task does not arise from co-representation of alternative S–R rules of jointly 'interacting' individuals, but rather from the representation of the task scenario as a conglomerate of perceptual events. This is the core claim that distinguishes the task co-representation account from the account of referential coding.

Modulating Self–Other Overlap

The referential coding account (RCA; Dolk et al., 2013) not only provides a compelling alternative to the social interpretation (i.e. idea of task co-representation as the underlying mechanisms), but can also account for a number of previous findings pertaining to social factors modulating the (*Joint*) Go/ NoGo Simon effect.

Consistent with the tradition of ideomotor theorising, the central claim of RCA is that all cognitive representations are commensurate and equivalent – including social and non-social events (Hommel, 2009, 2013; Hommel et al., 2001). However, by coding events alike (i.e. by their perceptual features and the perceivable effect they create), the similarity between action event alternatives and the cognitive representation thereof is not necessarily qualitative but rather gradual (Hommel, 2013). Following this logic, the similarity between self and other, and thus the degree of self–other overlap, can vary as a function of, for example, conceptual, perceptual and/or social features shared between self and other (agents, objects and thus events; see Figure 1.3).

Yet, in the context of performing a *Go/NoGo* Simon task, the requirement of selecting the event representation that encodes the corresponding action from a number of concurrently activated event representations reflects a discrimination problem that is based on and thus challenged by the degree of similarity between those action event alternatives. Consequently, the discrimination of concurrently activated action event alternatives will be more difficult the more

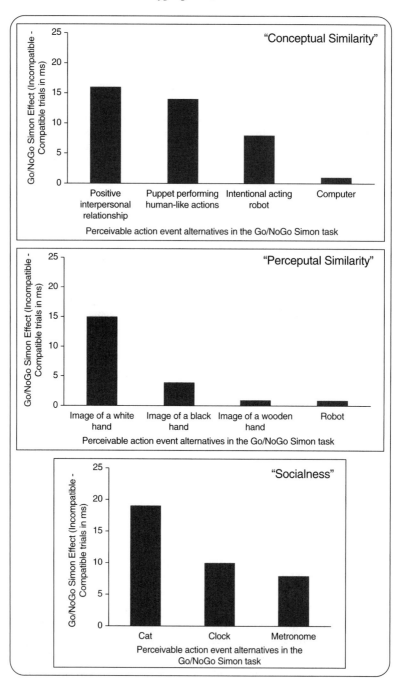

Figure 1.3

Figure 1.3 *(cont.)* According to the referential coding account, the size of *Go/NoGo* Simon effect arises as a function of the similarity between action event alternatives (i.e. the amount of shared features between one's own and other action events) in the given task scenario.

Notes: The more similar these action event alternatives are in terms of, for example, conceptual (see top panel), perceptual (see middle panel) and/or social features (see bottom panel), the harder it is to discriminate them. For example, action event alternatives that share auditory, movement and some social features (Cat) are more similar than those event alternatives that share auditory and movement features (Clock) and those that share only auditory features (Metronome; see lower panel: 'Socialness'). For response coding, however, events have to be discriminated, which can be achieved by focusing on task-relevant features. Due to the typically arranged *Go/NoGo* Simon task workspace (i.e. horizontally or vertically), participants are likely to emphasise the most obvious discriminating features – the location of their responses – and thereby code them as 'left' or 'right'. The spatial coding of one's own actions furnishes the representations of those events with spatial features that will then interact (i.e. match/mismatch) with spatially coded stimulus events. This effect is stronger for more similar event representations and can explain varying *Go/NoGo* Simon effects.

Sources: For conceptual similarity, data are taken from Hommel et al. (2009) for 'Positive interpersonal relationships'; for 'Puppet performing human-like actions' from Müller et al. (2011a);; for 'Intentional acting robot' from Stenzel et al. (2012); for 'Computer' from Tsai et al. (2008). Data for perceptual similarity are taken from Müller et al. (2011b) for 'Image of a black hand' and 'Image of white hand'; for 'Image of a wooden hand' from Tsai and Brass (2007); 'Robot' from Stenzel et al. (2012); and for 'Socialness' from Dolk et al. (2013).

similar they are. Due to typically arranged (joint) workspace (i.e. horizontally or vertically; e.g. Dittrich et al., 2013), however, the discrimination problem can be solved by emphasising features that discriminate between task-relevant and task-irrelevant representations, i.e. the location of action event alternatives. Thus, it appears reasonable that participants will focus on the spatial feature that discriminates their own action from alternative action events, thereby coding their actions as 'left' or 'right'. Hence, this intentional weighing of discriminable features is stronger and even more necessary the more similar are the action event alternatives. As a consequence of feature-based coding in S–R paradigms like the Simon task, these action codes can interact (i.e. match/mismatch) with equally coded stimulus events, leading to and thereby explaining varying degrees of interference. In other words, the challenge of separating concurrently activated action event alternatives impacts the weighting of discriminable features (i.e. the more similar they are, the stronger the feature-based coding), which in turn alters the interaction (match/mismatch) of equivalently (i.e. spatially) coded stimulus and action events and thus modulating the size of (*Joint*) *Go/NoGo* Simon effects (Dolk et al., 2011, 2013; Figure 1.3).

Along these lines, it makes sense that the *Joint Go/NoGo* Simon effect (JSE) is larger as a consequence of genuine human–human interactions compared to interactions with a computer (Tsai, Kuo, Hung, & Tzeng, 2008), a machine-like robot (Stenzel et al., 2012) or a puppet (Tsai & Brass, 2007). This is simply because events produced by non-human, inanimate entities exhibit a lesser degree of (perceptual and/or conceptual) similarity with human events (see Figure 1.3). However, there are measurable JSEs when interacting with a robot that supposedly behave intentionally (implemented via a belief manipulation; Stenzel et al., 2012) or after having observed a puppet performing human-like actions (Müller et al., 2011a), indicating that top-down manipulations can evoke a degree of similarity which would suffice to elicit a JSE.

Moreover, given that interpersonal relations such as attachment style (e.g. Mikulincer, Orbach, & Iavnieli, 1998) and group membership (e.g. Aron, Aron, Tudor, & Nelson, 1991; Avenanti, Sirigu, & Aglioti, 2010) have been shown to increase self–other overlap (Davis, Conklin, Smith, & Luce, 1996) and a more positive evaluation (Brewer, 1979), it is reasonable to assume that a positive relationship between co-acting individuals or a positive mood of individuals engaged in joint action lead to greater perceived similarity (Heider, 1958) and thereby to larger JSEs (Hommel, Colzato, & van den Wildenberg, 2009; Kuhbandner, Pekrun, & Maier, 2010). Consequentially, being in a bad mood during task performance (Kuhbandner et al., 2010), having a negative relationship with the co-actor (Hommel et al., 2009) or interacting with an out-group member (Müller et al., 2011b, Experiment 1) abolishes the JSE. The RCA can explain these phenomena, assuming that (perceived) dissimilarity facilitates discrimination between alternative events. Accordingly, when decreasing the dissimilarity between in- and out-group members (Haslam, 2006), by, for example, instructing participants to take the perspective of an out-group member (Galinsky & Moskowitz, 2000; Galinsky, Ku, & Wang, 2005), the similarity between alternative events (and the representation thereof) increases as indicated by a JSE for out-group members (Müller et al., 2011b, Experiment 2; see Figure 1.3).

This reasoning accords well with a recent study showing that Buddhist practice enhances self–other integration. Individuals with Buddhistic training, who are assumed to have reduced boundaries between themselves and others, demonstrated a larger JSE compared to individuals without such training (Colzato et al., 2012b). Moreover, directly addressing the concept of self–other overlap and its impact on action event representations, a study by Colzato and colleagues (2012a) revealed that the degree of self-construal, a measure expressing how much an individual leans toward personal interdependence (global, context-sensitive) versus independence (local, context-insensitive), mediates the amount of self–other integration, and thus the JSE size is more pronounced for personal interdependence compared to independence. Finally, if we further consider that irrelevant events attract more attention the closer they are to a relevant event (Eriksen & Eriksen, 1974; Miller, 1991), it might also explain why the JSE increases as the distance between actor and co-actor decreases (Guagnano et al., 2010; Sundstrom & Altman, 1976).

In sum, RCA suggests that social modulators affect self–other overlap, i.e. the degree of similarity between concurrently activated event representations pertaining to self and other (Colzato et al., 2012a, 2012b; Dolk et al., 2011, 2013. If this is true, it offers the opportunity to use the Simon effect as a diagnostic tool in pedagogic and/or rehabilitative contexts/circumstances for measuring the degree of similarity between perceivable events (or their influence on cognitive representation) and/or the inter-individual ability to handle these event representations (Dolk, Liepelt, Villringer, Prinz, & Ragert, 2012; Humphreys & Bedford, 2011; Liepelt et al., 2012).

References

Aron, A., Aron, E. N., Tudor, M., & Nelson, G. (1991). Close relationships as including other in the self. *Journal of Personality and Social Psychology*, 60, 241–253.

Avenanti, A., Sirigu, A., & Aglioti, S. M. (2010). Racial bias reduces empathic sensorimotor resonance with other-race pain. *Current Biology*, 20, 1018–1022.

Brass, M., Bekkering, H., & Prinz, W. (2001). Movement observation affects movement execution in a simple response task. *Acta Psychologica*, 106, 3–22.

Brewer, M. B. (1979). In-group bias in the minimal intergroup situation: A cognitive motivational analysis. *Psychological Bulletin*, 86, 307–324.

Clark, H. H. (1996). *Using language*. Cambridge: Cambridge University Press.

Colzato, L. S., de Bruijn, E. R. A., & Hommel, B. (2012a). Up to 'me' or to 'us'? The impact of self-construal priming on cognitive self–other integration. *Frontiers in Psychology*, 3, 341. doi: 10.3389/fpsyg.2012.00341.

Colzato, L. S., Zech, H., Hommel, B., Verdonschot, R., van den Wildenberg, W., & Hsieh, S. (2012b). Loving-kindness brings loving-kindness: The impact of Buddhism on cognitive self–other integration. *Psychonomic Bulletin & Review*, 19, 541–545.

Davis, M. H., Conklin, L., Smith, A., & Luce, C. (1996). Effects of perspective taking on the cognitive representation of persons: A merging of self and other. *Journal of Personality and Social Psychology*, 70, 713–726.

De Maeght, S., & Prinz, W. (2004). Action induction through action observation. *Psychological Research*, 68, 97–114.

Dittrich, K., Dolk, T., Rothe-Wulf, A., Klauer, K. C., & Prinz, W. (2013). Keys and seats: Spatial response coding underlying the joint spatial compatibility effect. *Attention, Perception & Psychophysics*, 75, 1725–1736.

Dolk, T., Hommel, B., Colzato, L. S., Schütz-Bosbach, S., Prinz, W., & Liepelt, R. (2011). How 'social' is the social Simon effect? *Frontiers in Psychology*, 2, 84. doi: 10.3389/fpsyg.2011.00084.

Dolk, T., Hommel, B., Prinz, W., & Liepelt, R. (2013). The (not so) social Simon effect: A referential coding account. *Journal of Experimental Psychology: Human Perception and Performance*, 39, 1248–1260.

Dolk, T., Liepelt, R., Villringer, A., Prinz, W., & Ragert, P. (2012). Morphometric gray matter differences of the medial frontal cortex influence the social Simon effect. *NeuroImage*, 61, 1249–1254.

Echterhoff, G., & Higgins, E. T. (2010). How communication shapes memory: Shared reality and implications for culture. In G. R. Semin & G. Echterhoff (Eds.), *Grounding sociality: Neurons, mind, and culture*. New York: Psychology Press, 115–148.

Eriksen, B. A., & Eriksen, C. W. (1974). Effects of noise letters upon the identification of a target letter in a non-search task. *Perception & Psychophysics*, 16, 143–149.

Galinsky, A. D., Ku, G., & Wang, C. S. (2005). Perspective-taking and self–other overlap: Fostering social bonds and facilitating social coordination. *Group Processes and Intergroup Relations*, 8, 109–124.

Galinsky, A. D., & Moskowitz, G. B. (2000). Perspective-taking: Decreasing stereotype expression, stereotype accessibility, and in-group favoritism. *Journal of Personality and Social Psychology*, 78, 708–724.

Gallese, V., Fadiga, L., Fogassi, L., & Rizzolatti, G. (1996). Action recognition in the premotor cortex. *Brain*, 119, 593–609.

Guagnano, D., Rusconi, E., & Umiltà, C. A. (2010). Sharing a task or sharing space? On the effect of the confederate in action coding in a detection task. *Cognition*, *114*, 348–355.

Harleß, E. (1861). Der Apparat des Willens [The apparatus of will]. *Zeitschrift für Philosophie und philosophische Kritik*, 38, 50–73.

Haslam, N. (2006). Dehumanization: An integrative review. *Personality and Social Psychology Review*, 10, 252–264.

Heider, F. (1958). *The psychology of interpersonal relations*. New York: Wiley.

Herbart, J. F. (1825). *Psychologie als Wissenschaft neu gegründet auf Erfahrung, Metaphysik und Mathematik [Psychology as a science newly based on experience, metaphysics, and mathematics]*. Königsberg: August Wilhelm Unzer.

Heyes, C. (2014). Submentalizing: I am not really reading your mind. *Perspectives on Psychological Science*, 9, 131–143.

Higgins, E. T. (1981). The 'communication game': Implications for social cognition and persuasion. In E. T. Higgins, C. P. Herman & M. P. Zanna (Eds.), *Social cognition: The Ontario symposium* (Vol. I). Hillsdale, NJ: Lawrence Erlbaum, 343–392.

(1992). Achieving 'shared reality' in the communication game: A social action that creates meaning. *Journal of Language and Social Psychology*, 11, 107–131.

Hommel, B. (1996). S–R compatibility effects without response uncertainty. *Quarterly Journal of Experimental Psychology*, 49A, 546–571.

(1997). Toward an action-concept model of stimulus–response compatibility. In B. Hommel & W. Prinz (Eds.), *Theoretical issues in stimulus–response compatibility*. Amsterdam: North-Holland, 281–320.

(2004). Event files: Feature binding in and across perception and action. *Trends in Cognitive Sciences*, 8, 494–500.

(2009). Action control according to TEC (theory of event coding). *Psychological Research*, 73, 512–526.

(2010). Grounding attention in action control: The intentional control of selection. In B. J. Bruya (Ed.), *Effortless attention: A new perspective in the cognitive science of attention and action*. Cambridge, MA: MIT Press, 121–140.

(2011). The Simon effect as tool and heuristic. *Acta Psychologica*, 136, 189–202.

(2013). Ideomotor action control: On the perceptual grounding of voluntary actions and agents. In W. Prinz, M. Beisert & A. Herwig (Eds.), *Action science: Foundations of an emerging discipline*. Cambridge, MA: MIT Press, 113–136.

Hommel, B., Colzato, L. S., & van den Wildenberg, W. P. M. (2009). How social are task representations? *Psychological Science*, 20, 794–798.

Hommel, B., Müsseler, J., Aschersleben, G., & Prinz, W. (2001). The theory of event coding (TEC): A framework for perception and action planning. *Behavioral and Brain Sciences*, 24, 849–878.

Humphrey, G. W., & Bedford, J. (2011). The relations between joint action and theory of mind: A neuropsychological analysis. *Experimental Brain Research*, 211, 357–369.

James, W. (1890). *The principles of psychology* (Vol. II). New York: Holt.

Jeannerod, M. (1994). The representing brain: Neural correlates of motor intention and imagery. *Behavioral and Brain Sciences*, 17, 187–202.

Knoblich, G., Butterfill, S., & Sebanz, N. (2011). Psychological research on joint action: Theory and data. In B. H. Ross (Ed.), *The psychology of learning and motivation* (Vol. LIV). San Diego, CA: Academic Press, 59–101.

Knoblich, G., & Sebanz, N. (2006). The social nature of perception and action. *Current Directions in Psychological Science*, 15, 99–104.

Kornblum, S., Hasbroucq, T., & Osman, A. (1990). Dimensional overlap: Cognitive basis for stimulus–response compatibility – a model and taxonomy. *Psychological Review*, 97, 253–270.

Kuhbandner, C., Pekrun, R., & Maier, M. A. (2010). The role of positive and negative affect in the 'mirroring' of other persons' actions. *Cognition & Emotion*, 24, 1182–1190.

Lam, M. Y., & Chua, R. (2009). Influence of stimulus–response assignment on the joint-action correspondence effect. *Psychological Research*, 74, 476–480.

Liepelt, R., Schneider, J., Aichert, D. S., Wöstmann, N., Dehning, S., et al. (2012). Action blind: Disturbed self–other integration in schizophrenia. *Neuropsychologia*, 50, 3775–3780.

Liepelt, R., Wenke, D., Fischer, R., & Prinz, W. (2011). Trial-to-trial sequential dependencies in a social and non-social Simon task. *Psychological Research*, 75, 366–375.

Lotze, R. H. (1852). *Medicinische Psychologie oder die Physiologie der Seele [Medical psychology or the physiology of the soul]*. Leipzig: Weidmann'sche Buchhandlung.

Memelink, J., & Hommel, B. (2013). Intentional weighting: A basic principle in cognitive control. *Psychological Research*, 77, 249–259.

Mikulincer, M., Orbach, I., & Iavnieli, D. (1998). Adult attachment style and affect regulation: Strategic variations in subjective self–other similarity. *Journal of Personality and Social Psychology*, 75, 436–448.

Milanese, N., Iani, C., Sebanz, N., & Rubichi, S. (2011). Contextual determinants of the socialtransfer-of-learning effect. *Experimental Brain Research*, 211, 415–422.

Miller, J. (1991). The flanker compatibility effect as a function of visual angle, attentional focus, visual transients, and perceptual load: A search for boundary conditions. *Perception & Psychophysics*, 49, 270–288.

Müller, B. C. N., Brass, M., Kühn, S., Tsai, C. C., Nieuwboer, W., et al. (2011a). When Pinocchio acts like a human, a wooden hand becomes embodied: Action corepresentation for non-biological agents. *Neuropsychologia*, 49, 1373–1377.

Müller, B. C. N., Kühn, S., van Baaren, R. B., Dotsch, R., Brass, M., & Dijksterhuis, A. (2011b). Perspective taking eliminates differences in co-representation of outgroup members' actions. *Experimental Brain Research*, 211, 423–428.

Müsseler, J., & Hommel, B. (1997). Blindness to response-compatible stimuli. *Journal of Experimental Psychology: Human Perception and Performance*, 23, 861–872.

Pellegrino, G. di, Fadiga, L., Fogassi, L., Gallese, V., & Rizzolatti, G. (1992). Understanding motor events: A neurophysiological study. *Experimental Brain Research*, 91, 176–180.

Philipp, A. M., & Prinz, W. (2010). Evidence for a role of the responding agent in the joint compatibility effect. *Quarterly Journal of Experimental Psychology*, 63, 2159–2171.

Prinz, W. (1987). Ideo-motor action. In H. Heuer & A. F. Sanders (Eds.), *Perspectives on perception and action*. Hillsdale, NJ: Lawrence Erlbaum, 47–76.

—— (1990). A common coding approach to perception and action. In O. Neumann & W. Prinz (Eds.), *Relationships between perception and action*. Berlin: Springer, 167–201.

—— (2012). *Open minds: The social making of agency and intentionality*. Cambridge, MA: MIT Press.

Rizzolatti, G., & Craighero, L. (2004). The mirror-neuron system. *Annual Review of Neuroscience*, 27, 169–192.

Rizzolatti, G., Fadiga, L., Gallese, V., & Fogassi, L. (1996). Premotor cortex and the recognition of motor actions. *Cognitive Brain Research*, 3, 131–141.

Schütz-Bosbach, S., & Prinz, W. (2007). Perceptual resonance: Action-induced modulation of perception. *Trends in Cognitive Sciences*, 11, 349–355.

Sebanz, N., & Knoblich, G. (2009). Prediction in joint action: What, when, and where. *Topics in Cognitive Science*, 1, 353–367.

Sebanz, N., Knoblich, G., & Prinz, W. (2003). Representing others' actions: Just like one's own? *Cognition*, 88(3), B11–B21.

—— (2005). How two share a task: Corepresenting stimulus–response mappings. *Journal of Experimental Psychology: Human Perception and Performance*, 6, 1234–1246.

Sellaro, R., Dolk, T., Colzato, L. S., Liepelt, R., & Hommel, B. (2015). Referential coding does not rely on location features: Evidence for a non-spatial joint Simon effect. *Journal of Experimental Psychology: Human Perception and Performance*, 41, 186–195.

Sommerville, J. A., & Decety, J. (2006). Weaving the fabric of social interaction: Articulating developmental psychology and cognitive neuroscience in the domain of motor cognition. *Psychonomic Bulletin and Review*, 13, 179–200.

Stenzel, A., Chinellato, E., Tirado Bou, M. A., del Pobil, Á. P., Lappe, M., & Liepelt, R. (2012). When humanoid robots become human-like interaction partners: Co-representation of robotic actions. *Journal of Experimental Psychology: Human Perception and Performance*, 38, 1073–1077.

Stock, A., & Stock, C. (2004). A short history of ideo-motor action. *Psychological Research*, 68, 176–188.

Sundstrom, E., & Altman, I. (1976). Interpersonal relationships and personal space: Research review and theoretical model. *Human Ecology*, 4, 47–67.

Tomasello, M. (2009). *Why we cooperate*. Cambridge, MA: MIT Press.

Tomasello, M., Carpenter, M., Call, J., Behne, T., & Moll, H. (2005). Understanding and sharing intentions: The origins of cultural cognition. *Behavioral and Brain Sciences*, 28, 675–735.

Tsai, C. C., & Brass, M. (2007). Does the human motor system simulate Pinocchio's actions? Coacting with a human hand versus a wooden hand in a dyadic interaction. *Psychological Science*, 18, 1058–1062.

Tsai, C. C., Kuo, W. J., Hung, D. L., & Tzeng, O. J. (2008). Action co-representation is tuned to other humans. *Journal of Cognitive Neuroscience*, 20, 2015–2024.

Vlainic, E., Liepelt, R., Colzato, L. S., Prinz, W., & Hommel, B. (2010). The virtual co-actor: The social Simon effect does not rely on online feedback from the other. *Frontiers in Psychology*, 1, 208. doi: 10.3389/fpsyg.2010.00208.

Welsh, T. N. (2009). When 1+1=1: The unification of independent actors revealed through joint Simon effects in crossed and uncrossed effector conditions. *Human Movement Science*, 28, 726–737.

Welsh, T. N., Kiernan, D., Neyedli, H. F., Ray, M., Pratt, J., et al. (2013). Joint Simon effects in extrapersonal space. *Journal of Motor Behavior*, 45, 1–5.

Wenke, D., Atmaca, S., Holländer, A., Liepelt, R., Baess, P., & Prinz, W. (2011). What is shared in joint action? Issues of co-representation, response conflict, and agent identification. *Review of Philosophy and Psychology*, 2, 147–172.

2   Merged Minds: Integration of Bottom-Up and Top-Down Processes for Social Interactions

Kristina Grigaityte and Marco Iacoboni

Abstract

Social cognition is composed of at least two major types of processes – bottom up and top down. Bottom-up processes are stimulus-driven, fairly automatic and fast. Top-down processes, on the other hand, require effort; they are deliberate and flexible. The mirror neuron system (MNS) is a recently discovered neural system that seems to map fairly well on bottom-up social processes. During social interactions, two individuals internally mirror each other's actions via the MNS, hence connecting their bottom-up processes. At the same time, top-down mechanisms in each interacting person modulate the bottom-up activity. By doing so, each individual's top-down mechanism also influences the other social agent via the bottom-up activity. Here, we discuss the two processes and how they interact with each other. We propose that the interplay between bottom-up and top-down processes creates a strong and dynamic link between the minds of two individuals and suggest a mechanistic model for how these processes may transform two minds into one functional social unit.

Introduction

We spend a vast amount of our time thinking about other people, whether it is a person we socialize with every day in our domestic environments, or a colleague we see at work. The majority of our day involves interacting with other people, trying to understand what they are thinking and how these interactions are going to affect our lives. In addition, we learn from observing other people, and imitating their actions. Taken together, these functional mechanisms form what is generally called social cognition. As for many other types of psychological domain, social cognition consists of two main kinds of subprocess, which we call here bottom up and top down. Bottom-up is fast, reflexive and automatic. The neural system that seems to map well on social bottom-up processes is called the mirror neuron system (MNS) (Rizzolatti & Sinigaglia, 2010). This system is activated by observing actions of other people as well

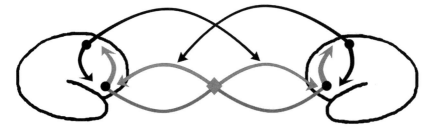

Figure 2.1 Integration of bottom-up and top-down processes between the two minds.

Notes: Bottom-up processes (grey arrows) directly influence the other agent during social interactions creating a connection between the two interacting social agents. Top-down processes (black arrows) in each social agent modulate the bottom-up activity, thus also modulating the connection between the two social agents.

as by executing the same actions ourselves. These properties suggest that the MNS allows the understanding of other people's actions by mapping their perception onto the motor repertoire of the observer. Hence, we consider bottom-up social processing as being what directly connects two socially interacting minds together. Top-down processing, on the other hand, is deliberate and flexible. It modulates the bottom-up activity based on the information and beliefs we have about a person we are interacting with. Since top-down processing modulates the bottom-up activity in each social agent, while the bottom-up processes of two interacting individuals are influencing each other, it follows that the top-down activity is in fact modulating the connections between the two social agents via the bottom-up activity. This scenario is illustrated in Figure 2.1. In this chapter, we will discuss these two subprocesses of social cognition and how the interaction between them influences our social lives.

Bottom-Up Mechanisms at Single-Cell and Neural-System Level

In this section, we will discuss the bottom-up processes that occur via the MNS. Mirror neurons were first discovered in the early 1990s while investigating with single-cell recordings the motor responses of ventral premotor neurons in macaques (di Pellegrino, Fadiga, Fogassi, Gallese, & Rizzolatti, 1992). The recordings of single-cell activity were performed predominantly while the monkey was performing a goal-directed hand action (Rizzolatti et al., 1988). These investigations eventually produced an unexpected observation. Some ventral premotor neurons fired not only when the monkey was executing a goal-directed action, but also when it was observing the same action being executed by somebody else. This phenomenon was the initial discovery regarding mirror neurons, revealing neural mechanisms that could potentially link *the self* with *the other*. One bodily-based way in which mirror neurons seem to link *self* and *other* is by making it fairly simple to imitate others. A mirror neuron can directly match the visual input of the action executed by *the other* to the motor representation of that same action performed by *the self*. This allows for a quick and pre-reflective perception of others' actions and can result in the mimicry of those actions. Such imitative behavior is thought to be crucially important in social learning and cultural development (Hurley & Chater, 2005).

The early observations on mirror neurons in the premotor F5 area of the macaque monkey revealed that some neurons in F5 fired only during observation of grasping hand movements, others fired only for mouth movements, and some fired for both hand and mouth movements (Gallese, Fadiga, Fogassi, & Rizzolatti, 1996). These observations suggest that mirror neurons might be involved in the matching process of the observed and executed actions – a form of action recognition (Rizzolatti, Fadiga, Gallese, & Fogassi, 1996). Nevertheless, many mirror neurons in F5 fire for more than one action, both with the hand and the mouth. This lack of specificity – at the level of the individual action – of some mirror neurons indicates that there must be something more to mirror neurons than just action recognition. Interestingly, the period of time between action observation and execution did not evoke any mirror neuron activity. This suggests that these cells are exclusively active when either *the self* or *the other* move and are not involved in preparation of the observed action (Gallese et al., 1996).

Subsequently, cells with mirror-like properties have been identified in many other neural systems as well. A study reported the presence of mirror neurons in the monkey's rostral part of the intraparietal lobule (IPL) that were selectively activated – at the time of grasping observation – for the action that followed the grasping (Fogassi et al., 2005). A number of neurons fired when the grasping of food was followed by bringing it to the mouth in order to eat. Other neurons fired only when grasping was followed by placing the food into a container. It is important to note that during the experiment monkeys received a food reward after placing the grasped food in the container as well. Therefore, the results cannot be associated with the differences in reward between the two actions. Instead, it appears that mirror neurons in IPL are goal-dependent and thus contribute to the understanding of the intentions of others. In another study, the neurons in the lateral intraparietal (LIP) area of rhesus macaques fired when the monkey was gazing in a particular direction and during observation of another monkey gazing in the same direction (Shepherd, Klein, Deaner, & Platt, 2009). This pattern of neural activity seems relevant to the sharing of attention between individuals, an important building block of social cognition. Similar activity during single-cell recordings was also observed from ventral intraparietal (VIP) neurons of Japanese monkeys that fired when a tactile stimulus was placed on body parts of the monkey. The same neurons also fired when the monkey observed the tactile stimulus being placed on the same body part of the experimenter (Ishida, Nakajima, Inase, & Murata, 2010). This suggests that instead of representing the action of *the other*, as reported in studies that investigated grasping mirror neurons, mirror neurons in VIP map the body parts of *the other* onto the body representation in the brain of *the self*.

Taken together, these studies on parietal mirror neurons provide evidence for a more complex interpretation of the role of neural mirroring, compared to the original idea of action recognition. IPL mirror neurons code for the intention associated with the observed action. Given the similarities at the neuronal population level between F5 and IPL, it is likely that F5 mirror neurons also mirror the goal of the action. On the other hand, mirror neurons in parietal regions (LIP and VIP) seem to add functional properties to the MNS. Indeed, they seem to allow the information from action recognition to be used for joint attention between *the self* and *the other* while also internally perceiving the other's body rather than only the action.

In addition, the physical space between the two interacting social agents also matters. Single-cell recordings of mirror neurons in premotor area F5 demonstrated that some neurons fire differently for actions in peripersonal space and extrapersonal space (Caggiano, Fogassi, Rizzolatti, Thier, & Casile, 2009). Around a quarter of F5 mirror neurons fired when the action was observed in the monkey's peripersonal space, another quarter fired for actions in extrapersonal space, and the remaining half showed no differentiation between observed actions happening in either extrapersonal or peripersonal space. Furthermore, when a graspable object in the peripersonal space of the monkey was made no longer graspable by placing a glass barrier between the monkey and the object, the extrapersonal rather than peripersonal neurons fired. While the distance of the observed action from the monkey had not changed when the glass barrier was placed between the subject and the perceived action, the barrier impeded the monkey's ability to intervene in the action, thus making it an extrapersonal space action. This suggests that some mirror neuron activity codes the possibility of *intervening* on the observed action. These findings further strengthen the hypothesis that mirror neurons indeed contribute to building a code for potential social interactions between social agents. The possibility of interaction determines whether peri- or extrapersonal neurons fire. If an interaction is possible, peripersonal neurons fire and signal other regions responsible for action planning and initiation. If an interaction is impossible, extrapersonal neurons fire and likely suppress the planning of the action.

Up to this point, we discussed different types of mirror neurons in non-human primates. In 2010 a paper reported that cells with mirror neuron properties had successfully been recorded in the human brain as well (Mukamel, Ekstrom, Kaplan, Iacoboni, & Fried, 2010). Such recordings are rare since they involve implanting electrodes through invasive brain surgery. Therefore, these studies could only be done in patients who need brain surgery for medical reasons, as in the case of medication-resistant epilepsy. Obviously only brain sites dictated by medical considerations may be investigated in these studies. In the study by Mukamel and colleagues (ibid), epilepsy patients were instructed to observe or execute facial expressions (smiling and frowning) and hand movements. This was the first study that provided evidence in support of the existence of mirror neurons in the medial frontal cortex, where mirror neurons had never been recorded in the monkey. However, the medial frontal cortex contains areas of motor significance, such as the supplementary motor area and the anterior cingulate cortex. Hence, it is not entirely surprising that mirror neurons were found in these regions. Indeed, the medial frontal cortex is connected to the ventral premotor cortex, where area F5 is located. Furthermore, human imaging studies have suggested that the medial frontal cortex is a major hub for social cognitive processes (Amodio & Frith, 2006), a finding consistent with the existence of mirror neurons in this brain area.

In the study on depth electrode recordings in humans, the majority of the recorded neurons in the medial frontal cortex were selective for action observation or execution. However, some neurons fired during both tasks but crucially not during control tasks. The most unexpected empirical finding, however, was that mirror neurons were also identified in medial temporal lobe structures, namely, in the hippocampus, parahippocampal gyrus and entorhinal cortex. These regions are typically associated with episodic memory and higher-level visual processes, but not with motor functions. Yet, mirror neurons in the medial temporal lobe, as for those in the frontal lobe, fired during observation and execution of action but not during control tasks. How to interpret this unexpected finding? One potential interpretation of the discharge of these cells during action execution is that they encode the memory trace of performing the action. If this interpretation is correct, then the discharge of these cells during action observation likely represents the retrieval of the memory of having previously performed the same action.

The results of both monkey and human studies indicate a diffused MNS that clearly accounts for more than just action recognition. Such pervasive mirroring may allow *the self* to internalize actions of *the other* as if these actions were imitated from within the observer. This neural mechanism provides a functional account as to how we can rapidly perceive intentions of others and how we can learn through imitation, an important human behavior for cultural acquisition and social learning.

However, we do not imitate everybody equally. Interestingly, the extent to which we imitate others depends on the similarity between *the self* and *the other* (Bandura, 1977). The neural correlates of self-similarity in imitative bias have been explored only very recently. When study participants were instructed to observe or imitate hand and arm actions of own and opposite gender while in the MRI scanner, reward-related brain regions (ventral and dorsal striatum, orbitofrontal cortex and left amygdala) were activated during own-gender imitation compared to the opposite gender (Losin, Iacoboni, Martin, & Dapretto, 2012b). However, it is not clear which is the egg and which the chicken here; that is, the cause–effect relationship between brain activity and behavior is not very clear. On the one hand, we may innately perceive our own gender as more similar to us, which in turn may result in a higher level of reward-related brain activity during imitative behavior. On the other hand, children from a very young age may have been praised for behaving according to their own gender-expected social norms, hence resulting in associating the activation of reward-processing brain structures with imitating models of one's own gender.

Furthermore, a study on imitation between same-race and different-race individuals reported that race of the person being imitated in fact modulated the imitation-related neural activity of the imitator (Losin, Cross, Iacoboni, & Dapretto, 2013; Losin, Iacoboni, Martin, Cross, & Dapretto, 2012a). This suggests that imitative racial bias might play an important role in acquisition of culture.

The mirror neuron functions discussed above seem to support functional processes for connecting *self* and *other*. The ability of *the self* to perceive the *other's* body, actions and intentions suggests that two individuals could merge together in each other's minds through the MNS. Since both individuals perceive each other through mirroring, the two sets of actions, intentions and bodies, one set from each of the individuals, diffuse across the two minds to the point where the borders of *the self* and *the other* get temporarily broken. At that point, the two individuals become one *merged self*.

Top-Down Mechanisms for Social Interactions

Nevertheless, we do not stay in this merged state *forever*. Mirror neurons likely facilitate imitative behavior that leads to the perception of *the other*, which ultimately creates social connections between individuals. However, it is clear that we do not automatically imitate all the time. Indeed, successful social interactions are made of orderly and coordinated behavior. There must be a way to distinguish between motor representations triggered during the observation of other's actions and the motor representations activated by *the self* internally. Therefore, control mechanisms are required. Indeed, single-cell recordings have shown that some mirror neurons suppress their activity during action observation.

A study of monkeys using single-cell recordings recorded pyramidal tract neurons (PTNs) while subjects performed and observed grasping actions. Some of these neurons fired during action execution and remarkably suppressed their activity during action observation (Kraskov, Dancause, Quallo, Shepherd, & Lemon, 2009). These neuronal properties in PTNs may be necessary to reduce motor resonance and thus withhold the unwanted imitative action when the observed and intended actions are incompatible. Similar cells were recorded in humans as well. Some mirror neurons in the supplementary motor area and medial temporal lobe increased their firing rate during action execution and decreased it during action observation (Mukamel et al., 2010). This pattern of neuronal activity in the MNS may result in imitation control. While it may be tempting to conclude that these neurons support imitation control from *within* the MNS, we should remember that single-cell recordings cannot indicate the origin of the neural activity determining the recorded firing pattern. Neurons are integrate-and-fire devices in which activity is highly influenced by the pre-synaptic input.

When it comes to imitation control, we can divide it into at least two major forms. One type deals with reactive imitation control, that is, the imitative behavior is inhibited after the action has already been observed. Another type is preparatory imitation control, that is, the imitation control process starts well before the action is observed, as a way of preparing the observer not to imitate.

A recent study investigated reactive imitation control while participants' brain activity was measured with fMRI. The task consisted of two trial types. During congruent trials, participants had to lift their index or middle finger in response to a video depicting an action of the same finger (imitative or biological cues) or a moving dot on that finger (spatial or non-biological cues). In incongruent trials, participants had to lift the finger in response to a video depicting an action of a different finger or a dot moving on a different finger (for instance, moving the index finger while observing middle finger movements or a dot moving on it). Not surprisingly, responses in congruent trials were significantly faster compared to incongruent trials. This is likely due to top-down mechanisms being recruited to control automatic imitation (supported by the bottom-up processes described in the previous section). Indeed, during incongruent trials, fast automatic imitative responses must be inhibited to allow the correct non-imitative response to be executed (Cross, Torrisi, Losin, & Iacoboni, 2013). The neuroimaging data demonstrated that the regions activated more during incongruent than congruent trials in response to imitative, but not spatial cues were the medial prefrontal cortex (mPFC), the anterior cingulate cortex (ACC), the anterior insula (aINS) and the inferior frontal gyrus pars opercularis (IFGpo). This pattern of brain activity suggests that these brain regions may selectively support reactive imitation control. While mPFC and ACC are frontal lobe areas that have been associated with top-down control processes by many studies, and the aINS is a complex integrative area that may well support cognitive processes of control, the involvement of IFGpo is somewhat surprising. Indeed, many studies point to this area as the human homologue of area F5 where mirror neurons in monkeys have been discovered. IFGpo has often been associated with imitative behavior, rather than its control. However, as seen from the single-cell studies discussed above (Kraskov et al., 2009; Mukamel et al., 2010), the MNS contains neurons that suppress their activity during action observation. This neuronal suppression is likely driven by interneuron activity in IFGpo, an activity which in turn may well increase fMRI signals in this region, as was observed in the fMRI study we are discussing.

To further investigate the information flow between mPFC, ACC, aINS and poIFG, this study performed connectivity analyses using dynamic causal modeling (DCM). DCM is used to identify in which direction information flows between regions entered in the model. This method tests a set of potential connectivity models and measures which one fits the empirical data best (Stephan et al., 2010). The analysis revealed that mPFC and ACC might be involved in detecting the incongruence between the observed actions and the intended ones. This information is then passed on to aINS, which in turn modulates the MNS (IFGpo), likely in a top-down manner. Therefore, reactive imitation control seems to be a top-down process that directly controls the mirroring bottom-up activity by interfering with the MNS.

Preparatory imitation control, on the other hand, becomes active before *the self* observes the action, and the action itself is unknown. A recent study used transcranial magnetic stimulation (TMS) to investigate this type of imitation control (Cross & Iacoboni, 2014b). TMS is a non-invasive technique that stimulates a chosen region of the brain to temporarily disrupt its activity. In this study participants had to perform flexion or extension finger movements in response to imitative (green light) or counter-imitative (red light) cues. In the preparatory period of the trial, if the green light is shown, subjects had to prepare to perform the same movement that is eventually shown on the screen (for instance, finger flexion when observing a finger flexion). If the red light is shown during the preparatory period, however, subjects had to perform a finger movement different from the one eventually shown on the screen (for instance, finger flexion when observing a finger extension). Furthermore, in half of the trials, during the preparatory period subjects were shown videos depicting a hand half squeezing a balloon and either squeezing the balloon some more (an action involving finger flexion) or releasing the squeeze (an action involving finger extension). While subjects were observing these videos shown during the preparatory period of an imitative or counter-imitative response, a TMS pulse was delivered to the primary motor cortex in order to induce the first dorsal interosseous (FDI) muscle to twitch, and measure its motor-evoked potential

(MEP). The idea behind this design is that changes in MNS activity may be measured through the changes in *motor resonance* (Fadiga, Fogassi, Pavesi, & Rizzolatti, 1995) while a participant is preparing to imitate or counter-imitate. Motor resonance is a phenomenon that occurs when corticospinal excitability is facilitated specifically for the muscle that is involved in the observed action. Since the FDI muscle is used during the squeeze actions (finger flexion), motor resonance predicts that the MEP should be a bigger size during the observation of squeezing the balloon compared to releasing it. The study found that motor resonance was significantly lower during preparation to counter-imitate compared to preparation to imitate (Cross & Iacoboni, 2014b). Furthermore, motor resonance was not different during preparation to imitate compared to a control condition, while it was reduced during preparation to counter-imitate compared to the control condition. Since motor resonance is considered a marker of MNS activity, these results suggest that MNS activity is suppressed during the preparation to counter-imitate. Therefore, a top-down mechanism must exist that inhibits the MNS even before an action is observed.

A recent fMRI study of preparatory imitation control used an experimental paradigm merging elements of the two studies just discussed (Cross & Iacoboni, 2014a). Indeed, participants had to lift either their index finger or middle finger in response to biological and non-biological cues (as in the previously discussed fMRI study on reactive imitation control). However, in this new study, before each trial there was a preparatory period, as in the TMS study on preparatory imitation control discussed above. The preparatory period signaled whether a participant had to imitate (lift the same finger) or counter-imitate (lift the other finger). The results showed activity in the left dorsolateral prefrontal cortex (DLPFC), left frontal pole, bilateral posterior parietal cortex and early visual areas during the preparation to counter-imitate. In contrast to the reactive imitation control discussed above, there were no significant differences in observed activity between imitative and spatial cues. This suggests that a general top-down mechanism is suppressing imitation during preparatory control. Furthermore, the activity in early visual areas during preparatory control may account for the reduced motor resonance observed in the TMS study previously described. This activity may represent suppression of visual input to motor areas by means of local interneuron inhibition at the level of the visual cortex.

To summarize these complex studies, one can conclude that both specialized and more general top-down processes are involved in modulating the bond between *the self* and *the other* that are directly supported by bottom-up processes like mirroring during social interactions. During reactive control, imitation must be suppressed after we have seen the action, and the MNS has already been activated. Thus, a more specialized top-down process modulates specifically the activity in the MNS (as in the mPFC, a region strongly associated with social cognition). However, during preparatory control imitation suppression is achieved before we see an action. This seems to involve a more generalized top-down process that suppresses visual inputs to motor areas, temporarily making us somewhat 'blind' to all the stimuli that can potentially activate our motor system (including the MNS) in order to prevent us from automatically making actions we do not want to make. While the bottom-up process induces the merging of *the self* and *the other*, the top-down process does not allow the two interacting individuals to get completely lost in each other, thus allowing a well-coordinated interaction.

Self–Other Unity Requires the Merging of Bottom-Up and Top-Down Mechanisms

Having described two of the neural and functional processing streams for imitation and its control, we are now going to turn to how the integration of all these mechanisms can explain specific patterns of interaction between *the self* and *the other*. As a case study for these interactions, we are going to focus on the human capacity to empathize with each other. The ability to understand other people's actions and intentions may also enable us to feel what *the other* is feeling. We express our emotions with our body, our posture and especially our facial expressions. The MNS is likely to contribute to the internal mapping of facial expressions and bodily postures of others, a mapping process that subsequently may facilitate the understanding of how *the other* is feeling, hence making it possible to empathize with other people. The resonance mechanism enabled by the MNS in the case of executed and observed actions, seems at work also in the case of directly experienced pain and pain perceived in other people. Indeed, observing somebody in pain also activates our own pain-associated brain regions (Avenanti, Bueti, Galati, & Aglioti, 2005; Singer et al., 2004).

In cognitive terms, all these neural resonance or neural mirroring mechanisms have been equated with the process of *simulation or emulation* (Grush, 2004; Hurley, 2008). The idea behind simulation is the sharing of neural mechanisms between sensorimotor processes and higher-level cognitive functions. In the specific case of social cognition, we make sense of other people's activity by using simulations of sensorimotor processes through the re-activation of the same neural circuitry we use in bodily perception and action.

The key question, however, is what is the nature of this simulation? Traditionally, there have been two main camps in the simulation literature regarding understanding the mental states of other people. Initially simulation has been framed in a rather intentional way, such that the observer intentionally simulates what the other is doing or feeling (Goldman, 2008; Hurley, 2008). This framing maps well onto top-down neural processing streams, as we have discussed here. Indeed, imitation control need not mean only imitation inhibition, but also voluntary control of what and how to imitate. An alternative view of radical simulation advocates pre-reflective, automatic processes that map well with the bottom-up mechanisms we have described earlier. Somehow, the debate has been framed as if these two alternative frameworks are mutually exclusive. In support of such dichotomy, fairly separate neural systems have frequently been associated with reflective and pre-reflective simulation modes. Yet, an emerging view of the brain is that it is a network of connected nodes and it is unlikely that neural systems are largely independent. Thus, what is more likely is that bottom-up and top-down processing streams interact to subserve flexible and adaptive behavior.

What happens, then, during social interactions? Our hypothesis is that pre-reflective, stimulus-driven, bottom-up activity such as mirroring generally prevails, since interacting agents' bottom-up processes are continuously fed socially relevant information from the other interacting social agents. This reciprocal bottom-up processing makes us feel what the other is feeling, thus facilitating empathy.

Indeed, some behavioral experiments demonstrate clear relationships between automatic imitation during social interactions and empathy (Chartrand & Bargh, 1999). In one of these experiments, the participants had to do some simple task with a confederate present in the room pretending to do the same task. In some cases, the confederate was shaking her foot while in other cases she was rubbing her face. After some time the participants would also start shaking their foot or rubbing their face without being aware of it. This, indeed, suggests that we subconsciously and automatically engage in imitation of *the other*. In the other experiment, the participant had to do the same task with two confederates present in the room. One of the confederates was intentionally imitating some bodily actions of the participants while the other confederate maintained a neutral posture. Later, the participants were asked which other participant they liked more. The responses showed that participants liked the confederates who were imitating their own actions more. This suggests that the liking of *the other* is associated with how much *the other* imitates us. In the third experiment of the same paradigm, participants also had to complete a questionnaire at the end that measured their tendency to empathize. The results showed a correlation between the self-reported level of empathy and the degree of imitative behavior during the task.

These behavioral data suggest that our capacity to empathize might in fact be facilitated by imitation. This concept is consistent with what we proposed at the beginning of this section: that the inner imitation provided by mirror neurons allows for the understanding of the feelings and emotions of other people. The most beautiful thing is that we do this automatically. We do not always try to understand the emotional state of *the other* deliberately or because it is considered the right thing to do. We do this subconsciously as if we are hardwired for empathy. What is even more interesting is that, when people hear about these mirroring cells in our brain that allow us to imitate and thus empathize, they often report that this makes a lot of sense to them, that this is something they can map onto their own phenomenology of social interactions. But what is this self-report, if not a form of reflective processing of previously experienced bottom-up activity?

In the empathy literature, bottom-up and top-down processes are typically framed as fairly independent of each other and often contrasted to each other (Bernhardt & Singer, 2012). However, it is very likely that bottom-up and top-down processes influence each other. For instance, a recent study explicitly investigated how the neural mechanisms associated with bottom-up and top-down forms of empathy interact and might predict prosocial, altruistic behavior (Christov Moore, & Iacoboni, 2014). While inside the MRI scanner, participants had to observe and imitate emotional facial expressions, and watch videos of a human hand being poked by a needle. These tasks have repeatedly activated systems for neural resonance (including the MNS) that we ascribe to pre-reflective, stimulus-driven, bottom-up processing. Outside the MRI scanner, participants also had to play a modified version of the Dictator Game (DG). In DG, each participant had to decide how to divide a sum of money between themself and another person. The game consisted of a number of trials with recipients of either low or high SES. The results showed that the degree of brain activity measured during the bottom-up empathy tasks performed in the scanner could predict participants' decision making during the DG. Participants' offers to both high and low SES recipients were positively correlated with activity in brain regions typically associated with low level, stimulus-driven, bottom-up processing, such as the amygdala (but not the MNS). On the other hand, offers to high SES recipients were negatively correlated with activity typically associated with cognitive control, and therefore top-down processing, such as the dorsolateral and dorsomedial prefrontal cortices, temporoparietal junction and anterior cingulate cortex. The fact that it is possible to predict the degree of an individual's decision-making/pro-social behavior from the level of neural activity during a fairly simple, emotional mirroring/empathy task suggests that these two forms of empathic processing (top-down and bottom-up) indeed interact.

Recall the neural mechanisms of automatic imitation and imitation control discussed in the previous sections. Automatic imitation and the MNS obviously represent bottom-up processing, while imitation control represents the top-down process. The continuous integration of bottom-up and top-down processes allows a fully complete, sophisticated system designed for social interactions. On the one hand, it enables us to understand the actions and intentions of others as well as their feelings and emotions as a result of internal imitation and empathy. On the other hand, top-down control allows us to retain a sense of self and prevent the self from getting lost in a dynamic world where there are so many *others* and just one *self*.

However, when *the self* does find itself interacting with *the other*, and *self* and *other* form this strong yet invisible connection between their minds, it is important to understand that this connection is highly reciprocal. The two individuals imitate and thus empathize with each other in order to remain in this merged state for the period of their interaction. Unfortunately, the whole debate about empathy still suffers from rather entrenched ideas we have about *the self* and our own mind as the starting point of it all. Even low-level, bodily-based empathy is often discussed in terms of mapping the other's actions and intentions onto yourself. Such a viewpoint seems, however, too self-centered. Empathy is not narcissistic. Rather, imitative behavior facilitates empathy and carves out a *world* in space and time between *the self* and *the other* that is physically the world *where empathy happens*. It is the world 'between them'. *The self* and *the other* merged together in this 'empathy world' comprise a *single social unit*. In other words, social interactions require a continuous and dynamic, reciprocal process that connects two people as if they are dancing together. Indeed, when two individuals are dancing with each other they must quickly anticipate each other's movements and body positions in a bottom-up manner while at the same time coordinating their own actions with respect to anticipated movements and positions via top-down processing. Therefore, we propose that such reciprocal behavior while dancing is very close to the concept of empathy we have proposed here. Empathy does not come from just *the self*, and it does not come from just *the other*. Similarly, the two-person dance would not be possible with just one person dancing. *The self* and *the other* constantly exchange empathy within their created *social unit*, where they share it equally with each other. The empathic reciprocity is the key component of these social interactions.

Conclusions

As in many other psychological domains, social cognitive processes can be divided into fairly automatic, stimulus-driven ones and rather effortful but flexible ones. Typically, these types of functional process are called type 1 and type 2 in psychology (Iacoboni, 2009; Kahneman, 2013). However, we have preferred to adopt the terminology of bottom-up and top-down because we think it better captures the dynamic nature of the interactions between these processes. The type 1/type 2 terminology, on the other hand, creates a dichotomy in which these processes are considered as separate and mutually exclusive. Recent descriptions of neural activity from neuroscience clearly reveal the dynamic nature of neural processes. We think it is important to be mindful of the dynamic nature of neural processes when thinking about the psychological processes implemented by the brain. If this is not done, there is the risk of having a rather ambiguous mapping between neuroscience and psychological constructs, as we have discussed in more detail elsewhere.

During social interactions, interacting social agents connect with and influence each other mostly at the level of their bottom-up activity. This activity, however, is modulated by each agent's top-down activity. This allows the creation of a transient social unit in which self and other are both fully merged and yet their individuality is not cancelled.

References

Amodio, D. M., & Frith, C. D. (2006). Meeting of minds: The medial frontal cortex and social cognition. *Nature Reviews Neuroscience*, 7(4), 268–277. doi: 10.1038/nrn1884.

Avenanti, A., Bueti, D., Galati, G., & Aglioti, S. M. (2005). Transcranial magnetic stimulation highlights the sensorimotor side of empathy for pain. *Nature Neuroscience*, 8(7), 955–960. doi: 10.1038/nn1481.

Bandura, A. (1977). *Social learning theory*. Englewood Cliffs, NJ: Prentice Hall.

Bernhardt, B. C., & Singer, T. (2012). The neural basis of empathy. *Annual Review of Neuroscience*, 35, 1–23. doi: 10.1146/annurev-neuro-062111-150536.

Caggiano, V., Fogassi, L., Rizzolatti, G., Thier, P., & Casile, A. (2009). Mirror neurons differentially encode the peripersonal and extrapersonal space of monkeys. *Science*, 324(5925), 403–406. doi: 10.1126/science.1166818.

Chartrand, T. L., & Bargh, J. A. (1999). The chameleon effect: The perception–behavior link and social interaction. *Journal of Personality and Social Psychology*, 76(6), 893–910.

Christov Moore, L., & Iacoboni, M. (2014). Emotions in interaction: Towards a supraindividual study of empathy. In B. Martinovsky (Ed.), *Advances in group decision and negotiation: Emotion in group decision and negotiation*. New York: Springer, pp. 1–32.

Cross, K. A., & Iacoboni, M. (2014a). Neural systems for preparatory control of imitation. *Philosophical Transactions of the Royal Society B: Biological Sciences*, 369(1644). doi: 10.1098/rstb.2013.0176.

(2014b). To imitate or not: Avoiding imitation involves preparatory inhibition of motor resonance. *NeuroImage*. doi: 10.1016/j.neuroimage.2014.01.027.

Cross, K. A., Torrisi, S., Losin, E. A., & Iacoboni, M. (2013). Controlling automatic imitative tendencies: Interactions between mirror neuron and cognitive control systems. *NeuroImage*. doi: 10.1016/j.neuroimage.2013.06.060.

Fadiga, L., Fogassi, L., Pavesi, G., & Rizzolatti, G. (1995). Motor facilitation during action observation: A magnetic stimulation study. *Journal of Neurophysiology*, 73(6), 2608–2611.

Fogassi, L., Ferrari, P. F., Gesierich, B., Rozzi, S., Chersi, F., & Rizzolatti, G. (2005). Parietal lobe: From action organization to intention understanding. *Science*, 308(5722), 662–667. doi: 10.1126/science.1106138.

Gallese, V., Fadiga, L., Fogassi, L., & Rizzolatti, G. (1996). Action recognition in the premotor cortex. *Brain*, 119(2), 593.

Goldman, A. I. (2008). *Simulating minds: The philosophy, psychology, and neuroscience of mindreading*. Oxford and New York: Oxford University Press.

Grush, R. (2004). The emulation theory of representation: Motor control, imagery, and perception. *Behavioral and Brain Sciences*, 27(3), 377–396.

Hurley, S. (2008). The shared circuits model (SCM): How control, mirroring, and simulation can enable imitation, deliberation, and mindreading. *Behavioral and Brain Sciences*, 31(1), 1–22; discussion 22–58. doi: 10.1017/S0140525X07003123.

Hurley, S. L., & Chater, N. (2005). *Perspectives on imitation: From neuroscience to social science*. Cambridge, MA: MIT Press.

Iacoboni, M. (2009). Imitation, empathy, and mirror neurons. *Annual Review of Psychology*, 60, 653–670. doi: 10.1146/annurev.psych.60.110707.163604.

Ishida, H., Nakajima, K., Inase, M., & Murata, A. (2010). Shared mapping of own and others' bodies in visuotactile bimodal area of monkey parietal cortex. *Journal of Cognitive Neuroscience*, 22(1), 83–96. doi:10.1162/jocn.2009.21185

Kahneman, D. (2013). *Thinking, fast and slow*. New York: Farrar, Straus and Giroux.

Kraskov, A., Dancause, N., Quallo, M. M., Shepherd, S., & Lemon, R. N. (2009). Corticospinal neurons in macaque ventral premotor cortex with mirror properties: A potential mechanism for action suppression? *Neuron*, 64(6), 922–930. doi: 10.1016/j.neuron.2009.12.010.

Losin, E. A., Cross, K. A., Iacoboni, M., & Dapretto, M. (2013). Neural processing of race during imitation: Self-similarity versus social status. *Human Brain Mapping*. doi: 10.1002/hbm.22287.

Losin, E. A., Iacoboni, M., Martin, A., Cross, K. A., & Dapretto, M. (2012a). Race modulates neural activity during imitation. *NeuroImage*, 59(4), 3594–3603. doi: 10.1016/j.neuroimage.2011.10.074.

Losin, E. A., Iacoboni, M., Martin, A., & Dapretto, M. (2012b). Own-gender imitation activates the brain's reward circuitry. *Social Cognitive and Affective Neuroscience*. doi: 10.1093/scan/nsr055.

Mukamel, R., Ekstrom, A. D., Kaplan, J., Iacoboni, M., & Fried, I. (2010). Single-neuron responses in humans during execution and observation of actions. *Current Biology: CB*, 20, 750–756. doi: 10.1016/j.cub.2010.02.045.

Pellegrino, G. di, Fadiga, L., Fogassi, L., Gallese, V., & Rizzolatti, G. (1992). Understanding motor events: A neurophysiological study. *Experimental Brain Research*, 91(1), 176–180.

Rizzolatti, G., Camarda, R., Fogassi, L., Gentilucci, M., Luppino, G., & Matelli, M. (1988). Functional organization of inferior area 6 in the macaque monkey. II. Area F5 and the control of distal movements. *Experimental Brain Research*, 71(3), 491–507.

Rizzolatti, G., Fadiga, L., Gallese, V., & Fogassi, L. (1996). Premotor cortex and the recognition of motor actions. *Cognitive Brain Research*, 3(2), 131–141.

Rizzolatti, G., & Sinigaglia, C. (2010). The functional role of the parieto-frontal mirror circuit: Interpretations and misinterpretations. *Nature Reviews Neuroscience*, 11 (4), 264–274. doi: 10.1038/nrn2805.

Shepherd, S. V., Klein, J. T., Deaner, R. O., & Platt, M. L. (2009). Mirroring of attention by neurons in macaque parietal cortex. *Proceedings of the National Academy of Sciences of the United States of America*, 106(23), 9489–9494. doi: 10.1073/pnas.0900419106.

Singer, T., Seymour, B., O'Doherty, J., Kaube, H., Dolan, R. J., & Frith, C. D. (2004). Empathy for pain involves the affective but not sensory components of pain. *Science*, 303(5661), 1157–1162. doi: 10.1126/science.1093535.

Stephan, K. E., Penny, W. D., Moran, R. J., den Ouden, H. E., Daunizeau, J., & Friston, K. J. (2010). Ten simple rules for dynamic causal modeling. *NeuroImage*, 49(4), 3099–3109. doi: 10.1016/j.neuroimage.2009.11.015.

3   A New View of the Motor Cortex and Its Relation to Social Behavior

Michael S. A. Graziano

Abstract

Three main views of the primate motor cortex have been proposed over the 140 years of its study. These views are not necessarily incompatible. In the homunculus view, the motor cortex functions as a rough map of the body's musculature. In the population-code view, populations of broadly-tuned neurons combine to specify hand direction or some other parameter of movement. In the recently proposed action map view, common actions in the movement repertoire are emphasized in different regions of cortex. In the action map view, to fully understand the organization of the motor cortex, it is necessary to study the structure and complexity of the movement repertoire and understand how that statistical structure is mapped onto the cortical surface. This chapter discusses the action map in the primate brain and how some of the complex actions represented there may play a role in social behavior.

Introduction

Since the discovery of motor cortex more than 140 years ago (Fritsch & Hitzig, 1870 [1960]), three prominent views of its function have been proposed. In one view, the motor cortex is a homunculus-like map of muscles, though the map may be partially overlapping and fractured in its somatotopy (e.g. Cheney & Fetz, 1985; Donoghue, Leibovic, & Sanes, 1992; Ferrier, 1874; Foerster, 1936; Fritsch & Hitzig, 1870 [1960]; Fulton, 1938; Gould, Cusick, Pons, & Kaas, 1986; Kwan, MacKay, Murphy, & Wong 1978; Park, Belhaj-Saif, Gordon, & Cheney, 2001; Penfield & Boldrey, 1937; Rathelot & Strick, 2006; Sherrington, 1939; Strick & Preston, 1978; Woolsey, 1952).

   In a second view, the motor cortex functions through a population of spatially tuned neurons. These neurons collectively pool or sum their outputs, thereby specifying an arm movement (Georgopoulos, Kalaska, Caminiti, & Massey, 1982; Georgopoulos, Schwartz, & Kettner, 1986). Whether it is hand direction in particular that is specified, or some other parameter of movement such as speed or force, became controversial and was never fully resolved (e.g. Aflalo & Graziano, 2007; Churchland & Shenoy, 2007; Georgopoulos, Ashe, Smyrnis, & Taira, 1992; Holdefer & Miller, 2002; Kakei, Hoffman, & Strick, 1999; Moran & Schwartz, 1999; Paninski, Fellows, Hatsopoulos, & Donoghue, 2004; Reina, Moran, & Schwartz, 2001; Scott & Kalaska, 1997; Sergio & Kalaska, 2003; Townsend, Paninski, & Lemon, 2006).

In the past decade, a new, third view has been proposed, the action map view of the motor cortex (Graziano, 2006, 2008; Graziano, Taylor, & Moore, 2002). In the action map hypothesis, the motor cortex is organized around the common, useful behaviors performed by the animal. These behaviors extend far beyond the simple reaching and grasping actions typically studied. Different categories of action, such as hand-to-mouth actions, manipulation of objects in central space, reaching, defensive actions, or complex interactions among all four limbs useful for leaping or climbing, are emphasized in different regions in the cortex. In this view, to understand the motor cortex it is necessary to study more than the musculature of the animal's body and more than a few movement parameters such as direction or force. One must study the structure and complexity of the movement repertoire and how that statistical structure is mapped onto the cortical surface.

These three views are not necessarily incompatible. All three could be correct. Certainly the motor cortex contains a rough somatotopy, neurons in it are indeed broadly tuned and would require a population to specify the output, and different highly complex actions tend to be evoked by activity in different subregions of the motor cortex as though the network has become organized around common components of behavior. The following sections describe these three views of motor cortex, emphasizing the most recent action map hypothesis.

The Homunculus

In 1870, Fritsch and Hitzig electrically stimulated the surface of the dog brain and obtained muscle twitches. They noted that these movements could be evoked from a small number of sites or 'centers' in the anterior half of the brain. Shortly after, Ferrier (1874) obtained the first true motor map in monkeys, establishing a systematic map of the body along the precentral gyrus with the legs at the top of the brain and the mouth near the bottom. These early reports emphasized the overlapping and complex nature of the map and the many muscles activated by stimulation of a single site in cortex. Subsequent work, however, emphasized the view of the motor cortex as a roster of muscles laid out in topographic order. A particularly influential report was published by Penfield & Boldrey (1937), nearly 70 years after the initial discovery of motor cortex. Penfield first drew a little distorted man stretched across the surface of

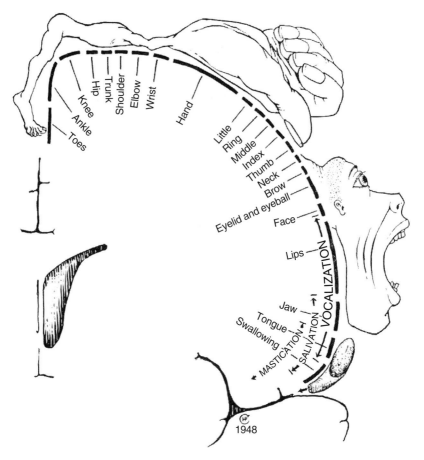

Figure 3.1 The motor homunculus of the human brain, from Penfield and Rasmussen (1950).

Notes: A coronal slice through the motor cortex is shown. Each point in motor cortex was electrically stimulated and the evoked muscle twitch was noted. Although each cortical point could activate many muscles, a rough body plan could be discerned.

the human brain and used the term 'homunculus' to describe it (Penfield & Rasmussen, 1950). Penfield's map is shown in Figure 3.1.

Most researchers who studied the motor map, including Penfield, noted that the map is not precise. It is blurred and overlapping. The organization is not a simple segregation of muscles (e.g. Cheney & Fetz, 1985; Donoghue et al., 1992; Ferrier, 1874; Foerster, 1936; Fritsch & Hitzig 1870 [1960]; Fulton, 1938; Gould et al., 1986; Kwan et al., 1978; Park et al., 2001; Penfield &

Boldrey, 1937; Rathelot & Strick, 2006; Sherrington, 1939; Strick & Preston, 1978; Woolsey, 1952). The argument that a single site in the cortex controls a single muscle, or perhaps a small number of muscles that cross a single joint, was promoted by a few researchers, notably Asanuma (1975). But according to most reports, each cortical locus, and even each cortical neuron, contributes to the activity of a range of muscles that cross a range of joints. This intermingling has been tested most extensively in the case of the arm and hand muscles (e.g. Cheney & Fetz, 1985; Donoghue et al., 1992; Meier, Aflalo, Kastner, & Graziano, 2008; Park et al., 2001; Rathelot & Strick, 2006; Sanes, Donoghue, Thangaraj, Edelman, & Warach, 1995; Schieber & Hibbard, 1993).

One possible explanation for the overlapping nature of the map is that the function of the motor cortex may be to coordinate among muscles and joints that are commonly used together. In support of this view, when cats and monkeys are infants, prior to extensive movement experience, their motor maps have little overlap in the representations of different joints. As the animals gain experience with movement, especially movement that combines the action of more than one joint, the muscle map develops an adult-like pattern of overlap (Chakrabarty & Martin, 2000; Martin, Engber, & Meng, 2005; Nudo, Milliken, Jenkins, & Merzenich, 1996). These results suggest that the complexity and overlap in the cortical map are related to the complexity and overlap in the movement repertoire. While there is clearly a rough somatotopic map in the motor cortex, it is also clear that the motor cortex does not function as a look-up table of muscles or small groups of muscles. Something much more complex is occurring that emerges from the statistics of the animal's natural movement repertoire.

The Population Code

In an attempt to study some of the complexity of natural movement, Georgopoulos and colleagues pioneered the directional reaching paradigm (1982, 1986). In this paradigm, a monkey is trained to reach in many possible directions from an initial central location. During the reach, the activity of motor cortex neurons is recorded. In a now-classic finding, most neurons in the arm region of the motor cortex are active during the reach and are broadly tuned, showing more activity for one preferred direction of reach and progressively less activity for directions that are progressively different from the preferred. These authors noted that a population of such neurons could in effect 'vote', each one voting for its own preferred direction, and once the votes were summed, the result would correspond to a highly specified hand path. Figure 3.2 illustrates the responses of a neuron broadly tuned to the direction of reach.

Over the past 30 years, this account of a population code for the direction of reach has encountered controversy. Motor cortex neurons do not necessarily

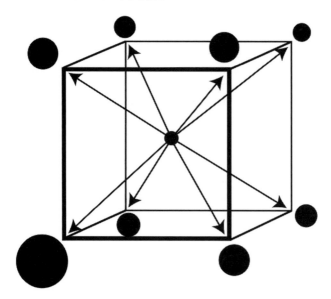

Figure 3.2 Direction tuning of a motor cortex neuron similar to that described in Georgopoulos et al. (1986).

Notes: A monkey was trained to make hand movements from a central location to eight possible surrounding locations forming the vertices of an imaginary cube. Many neurons in motor cortex were broadly tuned to the direction of the reach, firing more during one direction and less during neighboring directions. Here, the size of each black dot represents the firing rate of a hypothetical motor cortex neuron during each direction of reach. This neuron prefers a lower, left direction of reach.

maintain the same preferred direction when different muscle activations or different joint rotations are required to move the hand along the same paths (Scott & Kalaska, 1997). It may be, therefore, that the neurons do not encode the 'extrinsic' variable of hand direction, but instead 'intrinsic' variables such as muscle force or joint rotation. It has been suggested that many motor cortex neurons are better tuned to velocity, joint angle, joint configuration, force or the muscle output itself (e.g. Aflalo & Graziano, 2007; Churchland & Shenoy, 2007; Georgopoulos et al., 1992; Holdefer & Miller, 2002; Kakei et al., 1999; Moran & Schwartz, 1999; Paninski et al., 2004; Reina et al., 2001; Scott & Kalaska, 1997; Sergio & Kalaska, 2003; Todorov, 2000; Townsend et al., 2006). The many hundreds of papers and many thousands of person-hours over 30 years have not resulted in a consensus.

Two general conclusions may be useful to draw from this literature. First, motor cortex neurons are indeed broadly tuned to different movements.

Consistent with the initial insight of Georgopoulos and colleagues, populations of broadly tuned neurons in the motor cortex are likely to control movement.

Second, it is not really correct to think of neurons in motor cortex as 'coding' for movement variables. The concept of 'coding' of specific parameters may have been unwisely borrowed from the domain of sensory physiology, where neurons code for specific stimulus attributes. Neurons in the motor cortex become active and thereby cause movements. Their activity must necessarily ultimately control many aspects of movement such as direction, speed, posture and force, since normal movements vary in those respects. The details of how that control is accomplished remain unclear, arguably because the experiments have focused on correlational methods. Those methods can reveal only so much. Correlation does not imply causation, whereas the fundamental truth of neuronal activity in the motor cortex is that it causes movement.

Box 3.1 Stimulation on a behavioral timescale

The first century of experiments on the motor cortex, from Fritsch and Hitzig's discovery of motor cortex in the dog brain (1870 [1960]) to Woolsey's mapping of the monkey motor cortex (1956), was dominated by the use of electrical stimulation applied to the surface of the brain. Asanuma (1975) and colleagues moved to a more refined method involving small currents (microamps) in brief pulse trains (often less than 10 ms) applied through microelectrodes, sometimes directly to layer 5 of cortex, the output layer. The assumption seems to have been that this punctate stimulation could serve as a method of anatomical tract tracing. It could reveal the pathway of interest from cortex to muscles with a relay in the spinal cord, while avoiding the complication of signals spreading through other connectivity. In retrospect, given the rich, network-like connectivity within the motor system, this hope of picking out a single descending pathway by activating small groups of neurons for short durations seems naïve.

In other neural systems, the use of microstimulation developed along a different tradition. Microstimulation was applied on a longer timescale thereby evoking some aspects of normal behavior. The technique was used successfully in the superior colliculus and frontal eye fields to study saccadic eye movements, in the middle temporal visual area and primary somatosensory area to study perceptual decisions, and in the hypothalamus to study motivated states such as hunger and rage, among other aspects of brain function (e.g. Bruce, Goldberg, Bushnell, & Stanton, 1985; Caggiula & Hoebel, 1966; Hess, 1957; Hoebel, 1969; King & Hoebel, 1968; Robinson, 1972; Robinson & Fuchs, 1969; Romo, Hernandez, Zainos, & Salinas, 1998; Salzman, Britten, & Newsome, 1990; Schiller & Stryker,

1972). None of these experiments involved any assumption about activating one 'correct' pathway while avoiding signal spread through collateral pathways. Instead, the assumption was that the signal, injected in one place in the system would spread according to the natural connectivity, influence related networks and alter behavior in a revealing manner.

Microstimulation on a behavioral timescale was not systematically studied in the motor cortex until recently. Taking a method common in the study of other brain areas and transplanting it into the motor cortex resulted in a new picture radically different from anything that had been described before. Stimulation of the monkey motor cortex on a behavioral timescale, such as for the half-second of a typical reaching movement, evoked complex movements that resembled components of the animal's normal repertoire (Graziano, 2008; Graziano, Aflalo, & Cooke 2005; Graziano et al., 2002). Different movements were evoked from different sites in an 'action map'.

An Action Map in the Motor Cortex

In the past decade, a new view of the motor cortex has begun to emerge. In this view, the function of the motor cortex is not to decompose movement into constituent muscles and joints or into elemental movement parameters such as direction and speed, but instead to help produce some of the most complex components of the movement repertoire. The initial studies to point toward an action map involved applying microstimulation to the motor cortex of monkeys (Graziano et al., 2002). Instead of stimulating on a short timescale, such as for 50 ms or less, as had become traditional in the study of the motor cortex, these experiments involved stimulation for half a second, roughly matching the timescale of a monkey's normal arm movements (see Box 3.1). Figure 3.3 summarizes the results.

Stimulation in different regions of the cortical map evoked different movements that closely resembled common categories of action from the monkey's normal repertoire. For example, when sites within one region of the map were stimulated, a hand-to-mouth movement was evoked (Graziano et al., 2002, 2005). The movement included a closure of the hand into an apparent grip, a turning of the wrist and forearm to direct the hand toward the mouth, a rotation of the elbow and shoulder bringing the hand through space to the mouth, an opening of the mouth, and a turning of the head to align the front of the mouth with the hand. The movement occurred reliably on each stimulation trial and could be replicated even when the monkey was anesthetized. If a lead weight was hung on the hand, the movement compensated and pulled the hand to the correct height to reach the mouth. Yet the movement was in some ways stereotyped. For example, if a barrier was placed between the hand and the mouth,

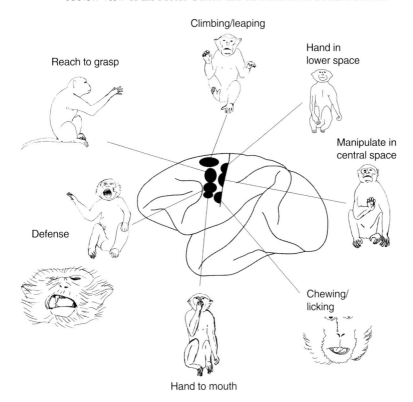

Figure 3.3 Action zones in the motor cortex of the monkey.

Notes: These categories of movement were evoked by electrical stimulation of the cortex on the behaviorally relevant timescale of 0.5 seconds. Images are traced from video frames and each image represents the final posture obtained at the end of the stimulation-evoked movement. Within each action zone in the motor cortex, movements in similar behavioral categories were evoked.

Source: Adapted from Graziano et al. (2002, 2005).

the hand did not move intelligently around the barrier as in normal, motivated behavior. Instead, it crashed into the barrier and remained pressing against it until the stimulation current stopped. Electrical stimulation in this region of the map therefore appeared to generate a stereotyped, average version of a common movement. A large part of a monkey's spontaneous repertoire is composed of complex interactions between the hand and the mouth (Graziano, 2008; Graziano, Cooke, Taylor, & Moore, 2004).

A specific zone in the motor cortex, sometimes called the polysensory zone, contains a high proportion of neurons that respond to tactile and visual stimuli

(Fogassi et al., 1996; Gentilucci et al., 1988; Graziano, Hu, & Gross, 1997; Graziano, Yap, & Gross, 1994, Rizzolatti, Scandolara, Matelli, & Gentilucci, 1981). Each multimodal neuron has a tactile receptive field on the skin and also responds to visual stimuli in the space near the tactile receptive field. Some neurons also have auditory responses that are strongest to sounds near the body. Electrical stimulation of these cortical sites typically evokes a movement that appears to protect the body surface in the area of the tactile receptive field (Cooke & Graziano, 2004a; Graziano et al., 2002, 2005). For example, if a site in the cortex responds to touching the left cheek and to visual stimuli near or approaching the left cheek, then stimulation of that site evokes a squint, a folding back of the left ear, a rightward turning of the head, a lifting of the left shoulder, and a rapid lifting and lateral movement of the left arm as if to block a threat. The movement is fast, reliable across trials, and can be evoked even when the animal is anesthetized. Chemical inhibition of this cortical region results in a temporary reduction of a normal defensive reaction such as to an air puff, and chemical disinhibition results in a hypersensitivity to threats to the face and an exaggerated defensive reaction (Cooke & Graziano, 2004b). In the case of the defensive movements, therefore, the evidence shows corroboration among four different sources of data: the response properties of the neurons, the effect of electrical stimulation, the effect of chemical manipulation, and the animal's natural movement repertoire.

Another region of the map, when stimulated, resulted in reaching movements of the arm into distal space with the palm facing outward and the hand shaped as if to grasp something (Graziano et al., 2005). To compare the effects of electrical stimulation with the response profiles of neurons, we conducted a study in which the monkey was restrained in a chair but free to move its arm spontaneously, grabbing, reaching, scratching and so forth (Aflalo & Graziano 2006a, 2007). These movements of the arm were tracked in three dimensions at high resolution by a set of lights fixed to key points on the arm. Using regression analysis, each neuron could be matched to a preferred posture of the arm, defined not by hand position in space, but by an 8-dimensional joint space. If the arm moved toward that preferred posture, the neuron became more active during that movement. If the arm moved toward other postures, the neuron was less active. The preferred postures obtained at a site in the cortex tended to match the joint configuration of the arm evoked by stimulation of that same site. Although other tuning models were tested, a tuning for preferred posture explained more of the variance in neuronal activity (36 percent) than did direction tuning (8 percent) or speed tuning (3 percent). These results do not in any way discredit the direction-tuning or speed-tuning hypotheses. The neurons did show a significant degree of direction and speed tuning. But the results do suggest that tuning to a single movement variable is unlikely to account for the full pattern of activity in these neurons. Most complex movements require the control of many movement variables simultaneously. Perhaps that is why the neurons that control movement are tuned to so many variables at the same time. Moreover, many common actions of the arm, such as reaching or hand-to-mouth, depend on adjustments or variations round an underlying stabilizing posture, perhaps accounting for why a tuning to posture accounts for so much of the variance in neuronal activity.

Other complex movements, evoked from other regions of the map, included bringing the hand into central space with the fingers gripped or otherwise shaped as if to manipulate an object; putting the hand down into lower lateral space as though bracing the weight of the body on it; and bilateral movements of all four limbs in a pattern that resembled complex locomotion such as climbing or leaping (Graziano et al., 2002, 2005).

Based on these results, we proposed a new hypothesis about the organization of the motor cortex. The complex map might reflect a complex movement repertoire that is flattened onto the cortical sheet. Computational studies showed that, indeed, when a statistical description of a monkey's typical movement repertoire is flattened onto a model of the cortical sheet, subject to a local smoothness constraint in which similar movements are mapped near each other, the resulting map is a close approximation to the actual map obtained by physiology (Aflalo & Graziano, 2006b; Graziano & Aflalo, 2007). In this method, the map begins with an initial state that resembles the discrete somatotopic map imposed on the motor cortex at the outset of development. The map then re-organizes to reflect the complexity of the movement repertoire. The computational method reproduces the standard map of the body, complete with many of its otherwise-puzzling reversals, fractures and overlaps. It also reproduces the arrangement of actions in the action map. Actions that involve coordination among many body parts, such as hand-to-mouth actions or climbing-like actions, tend to gravitate to the anterior edge of the map where the axial muscles are also emphasized, since the axial muscles are necessary to link up different body segments. Actions that focus mainly on individual body parts, such as chewing, or manipulation of an object with the fingers, tend to gravitate to the posterior edge of the map. Actions of the hand tend to cluster in three cortical zones because they play a prominent role in three different types of behavior: manipulation of objects in central space, interactions between the hand and the mouth, and reaching to acquire an object. In these and other ways, the topography predicted by the model closely matched the actual topography in the motor cortex. The model provided a potential explanation for the functional topography spanning a large swath of cortex, including the primary motor cortex, the caudal parts of the premotor cortex, the supplementary motor map, the frontal eye field and the supplementary eye field. A relatively simple underlying principle, a flattening or rendering of the movement repertoire onto the cortical surface, may help explain the seemingly complex organization of the cortical motor system.

Further Studies of Cortical Action Maps

The findings described in the previous section have been corroborated by a range of studies in the primate brain. Stepniewska, Fang, and Kaas (2005, 2009) used electrical stimulation to extensively map the parietal cortex and motor cortex of monkeys and prosimians and found action categories in distinct cortical zones. Overduin, d'Avella, Carmena, and Bizzi (2012) found that stimulation in the motor cortex evoked natural synergistic activations of the hand muscles, and that different synergies were emphasized in different adjacent regions of cortex. Van Acker et al. (2013) obtained complex movements of the limbs, including hand-to-mouth movements, on stimulation of the monkey motor cortex. Caruana, Jezzini, Sbriscia-Fioretti, Rizzolatti, and Gallese (2011) evoked complex social gestures by stimulating the insular cortex of monkeys and found different categories of gesture in adjacent regions of the cortex. Desmurget, Song, Mottolese, and Sirigu (2013) obtained complex, behaviorally relevant movements on stimulation of the human motor cortex.

The rodent motor cortex may share a similar organization. Haiss and Schwarz (2005) evoked different behaviorally relevant whisking actions on stimulating different regions of the rat motor cortex, including exploratory whisking from one cortical region and defensive-like whisker retraction and squinting from another cortical region. Ramanathan, Conner, and Tuszynski (2006) found that stimulation of the rat motor cortex evoked different kinds of forepaw movements from different zones in the cortex. When the reaching zone was lesioned, the rats lost the ability to reach. The ability quickly recovered. When the recovered rats were mapped again, their cortex showed a new zone, near the lesioned site, from which reaching movements could be evoked, and the size of the new reaching zone correlated with the extent of the rat's behavioral recovery. Harrison, Ayling, and Murphy (2012) studied the mouse motor cortex. In order to determine whether the effect of electrical stimulation was somehow artifactual, they compared it to the effect of optogenetic stimulation, which is more precise because it specifically induces action potentials in cell bodies in a small target area. They obtained complex, multi-joint movements of the limbs to specific postures. The more precise optogenetic stimulation matched the results of electrical stimulation at the same sites. Bonazzi et al. (2013) systematically mapped the rat motor cortex using long-train electrical stimulation and found complex, multi-joint movements of the limbs that matched the rat's behavioral repertoire and that were arranged across the cortical surface in an apparent action map.

The evidence is therefore strong and increasing: the motor cortex is organized at least partly as an action map. The bulk of the evidence thus far comes from microstimulation studies, but those studies are now corroborated by optogenetic stimulation, single neuron physiology, chemical inhibition and disinhibition, lesions and recovery from lesions, studies of the natural movement repertoire, and computational studies.

The homunculus – the textbook account of the motor cortex – is not complete and is probably not the fundamental principle of organization. The slightly more subtle, common view of a 'noisy' homunculus is simply a classical homunculus plus the admission that there must be some other, unknown principle influencing the organization. What is that principle? To understand the organization and function of the motor cortex, it may be necessary to understand the movement repertoire of the animal. The movement repertoire is complex and multidimensional. Actions vary in terms of body parts involved, location in space to which actions are directed, broad behavioral significance such as defending the body surface or acquiring objects, and probably many other aspects of movement. Added to that, the cortex tends to self-organize in a manner that optimizes local similarity. It tends to form two-dimensional maps. The squeezing of the multidimensional movement repertoire onto the two-dimensional cortical surface, with an initial bias toward a somatotopic map, appears to result in a complex, but ultimately understandable organization. Many of the quirky details of that organization can be understood through a mathematical analysis, as shown in modeling studies (Graziano & Aflalo, 2007). It is not a simple map in the sense of a map of visual space or a well-ordered map of the body, because the dimensionality of the movement repertoire is too high to be laid out simply on the cortical surface. But it can be understood in a principled manner.

Social Implications of Defensive Movements

Primates, like most animals, have an elaborate set of coordinated behaviors that protect the body surface from damage. We studied these reactions in macaque monkeys, comparing the defensive-like movements evoked from the action map to naturally occurring defensive movements (Cooke & Graziano, 2003, 2004a, 2004b; Cooke, Taylor, Moore, & Graziano, 2003). As these experiments progressed, we noticed a similarity between standard primate defensive movements and many of the actions in human social communication (Graziano, 2008; Graziano & Cooke, 2006).

Evolution works with what it has and as a result follows strange and quirky paths – such as from fish fins to human hands, or from jawbones to inner ear bones. Could many of the social gestures and expressions we consider to be fundamental to human nature, such as smiling, laughing and crying, have evolved from something as specific as defense of the body surface from impending collision? The hypothesis that defensive reactions gave rise to many social displays was proposed by Darwin (1872) and elaborated by Andrew (1962). In this final section, I discuss some speculations based on my own observations of defensive movements in primates.

Three key properties of defensive reactions make them especially likely to evolve into social displays. First, defensive reactions communicate something about the internal state of an animal. Large magnitude defensive reactions suggest stress or a recent startle. More subdued defensive reactions suggest a state of confidence and calm. An animal that is cringing and glancing over its left shoulder broadcasts that it expects a threat from that particular direction. A male and female that allow close body contact with minimal defensive reactions communicate a willingness to mate with each other. Defensive movements are therefore informative.

Second, defensive movements are easily visible to other animals. These actions not only contain information about inner state but also telegraph it to anyone nearby and watching.

Third, an animal cannot safely suppress its defensive reactions or it would expose itself to risk of injury. It therefore cannot help leaking information about its inner state to anyone watching its defensive actions.

Given these properties, animals might evolve brain mechanisms for detecting and taking advantage of the defensive reactions of others. If you can observe and interpret those behaviors, you gain predictive power over other animals. At the same time, animals might evolve mechanisms for modifying their defensive reactions or deploying them in non-defensive situations in order to manipulate the behavior of whoever is watching. In this way, a large and related subset of social signals might have emerged from the more basic need to defend the body from intrusion or attack.

For example, the human smile is thought to have evolved from the 'fear grimace' or 'silent bared teeth display' of non-human primates such as macaques (Andrew, 1962; van Hooff, 1972; Preuschoft, 1992). It may be tempting to think of the silent bared teeth display as solely a facial action. However, that is not correct. In macaque monkeys, it is part of a whole-body display that includes wrinkling the skin around the eyes, lifting the upper lip, folding the ears back against the skull, pulling the head down, hunching the shoulders, curling the body forward, and pulling the arms across the front of the torso. All of these actions are also part of a standard startle and defensive stance. If animal A looms aggressively toward animal B, animal B should engage in a defensive posture to protect itself. The defensive posture, however, accomplishes more than physical protection. As a side effect, it broadcasts information about the degree of submission of animal B. From there, according to the hypothesis, evolution shaped the behavior into a social adaptation, from which humans derive the smile, a signal that says, 'I am not aggressive'. The human smile also sometimes communicates submission. The cringing, servile posture that people use to communicate submission could also be considered a modification of the same original defensive reaction.

A similar story could be constructed about laughter. Human laughter is thought to be homologous to the open-mouthed play display of chimpanzees (van Hooff, 1962, 1972; Preuschoft, 1992; Ross, Owren, & Zimmermann, 2010). Just as for the smile, it may be that too much emphasis in the literature is placed on a limited part of the behavior, in this case the mouth and the voice. Laughter may be much more than just a matter of mouth and voice, and the whole-body context may be useful to consider. Play fighting, a behavior common in mammals, involves attack and defense including all the normal reactions that protect the body and maintain a margin of safety. I previously suggested (Graziano, 2008) that human laughter may have evolved from a ritualized modification of that defensive behavioral set. Consider tickle-evoked laughter. It is caused by intrusions into normally defended personal space. The components go far beyond the mouth and voice. It includes a contraction of musculature around the eye and sometimes eye closure; sometimes tear production; a raising of the upper lip accompanied by a bunching of the cheeks upward toward the eyes; a ducking downward of the head and a shrugging upward of the shoulders; a hunching or forward curving of the torso; a pulling of the arms inward across the vulnerable abdomen; and a series of vocal calls. Point for point, it resembles a ritualized defensive reaction with alarm calls. By hypothesis, the normal defensive behavioral set during a play fight was modified into a social signal. The laughter is effectively a touché signal. It communicates that the tickler has gotten into the most heavily defended parts of the ticklee's personal space. The tickler has won a point in the play fight.

But note how complicated the evolutionary dynamics can become. Each person has control of a social reward, the touché signal that can be dispensed to others to shape their behavior. When you laugh at someone else's joke, could it be that you are providing a signal in response to a display of mental agility? Has the other person gotten the better of you in a mental play fight, and effectively won a point, for which you are providing a social reward? Or suppose someone wins a point by causing discomfort to someone else, and bystanders laugh to reward the win. Is this how ridiculing laughter emerged? In this speculation, laughter is transformed from a defensive reaction, to a component of a play fight, to a touché signal, to a branching bush of quirky social uses, until the behavior is modified into a bizarre and idiosyncratic multiplicity of human behaviors.

Could a similar story be constructed for crying? Again, many previous attempts to understand crying from an evolutionary perspective, such as Darwin's (1872) or Andrew's (1962), focus on the most obvious facial aspects of it, the tear production. But crying may be better understood in the context of a whole-body action. The similarity between crying and laughing was noted 3,000 years ago by Homer, who famously compared the laughter of men at a banquet to the crying they were about to do when Odysseus walked in and killed them all. Crying can include a squinting of the eyes, an excretion of tears, a lifting of the upper lip that results in an upward bunching of the cheeks toward the eyes, a ducking of the head, a shrugging of the shoulders, a forward curving of the torso, a flexion of the hips and knees, a pulling of the arms across the torso or upward over the face, and a series of vocalizations. These components point-for-point resemble or are exaggerations of a defensive reaction, including the copious tear production that normally protects the eyes from dust or other contaminants. Perhaps crying, like laughing, is a modified defensive reaction, but in this case used to solicit help. Other animals give distress cries, such as kittens that cry for their mothers, but as far as I know only humans combine the distress cry with the physical signs of defending the body and especially the eyes against intrusion. Human crying illustrates just how idiosyncratic social signals can become.

Consider the phenomenon of personal space. The zoo curator Hediger (1955) was the first to describe a protective flight zone around animals. When a threatening predator enters this margin of safety, the animal escapes. Other researchers soon noted that humans also have an invisible bubble of protective space surrounding the body, generally larger around the head, extending farthest in the direction of sight (e.g. Dosey & Meisels, 1969; Hall, 1966; Horowitz, Duff, & Stratton, 1964; Sommer, 1959). When that personal space is violated, the person steps away to reinstate the margin of safety. Personal space is fundamentally a protective space that people maintain with respect to each other. It is one of the most basic and obvious ways in which defensive actions intersect with social behavior.

But we cannot always maintain a personal space. The mechanisms that defend personal space must be adjusted in some way to allow for social touching. Not only must the defensive reactions be turned down and personal space shrunk up, but that alteration in the defensive reaction can itself turn into a social signal. A dog rolls on its back and exposes its stomach, a normally heavily defended part of the body, as a gesture of submission and trust. Humans allow themselves to be kissed on the parts of the body that are normally most heavily defended – the face, the neck, the hands – to communicate trust and willingness. Women in fashion magazines tilt their heads and expose their necks, as if offering to let the viewer's teeth onto the one body part most vulnerable to predation. All of these examples show how an overt dropping of your defensive reactions toward somebody else can act as a social signal.

The speculations in this final section may seem far removed from the action map of the motor cortex. Yet the action map as shown in Figure 3.3 has a large zone related to defensive behavior. Neurons in that zone monitor the space around the body using their sensory receptive fields, and that monitored space shares a notable resemblance to personal space (Fogassi et al., 1996; Gentilucci et al., 1988; Graziano & Gandhi, 2000; Graziano et al., 1994, 1997; Rizzolatti et al., 1981). Several other anatomically connected brain regions, such as the ventral intraparietal area, have similar properties and may be part of a larger network that helps to maintain a margin of safety (Graziano & Cooke, 2006). Could this network of brain areas also contribute to social behavior? As unexpected and *non sequitur* as it may seem, could it be that actions that defend the body surface from injury and collision form the evolutionary basis of a great part of our standard social repertoire?

Recent studies suggest that these specific brain areas may indeed play a role in social interaction. Socially relevant stimuli such as faces have an especially strong influence on these neuronal mechanisms, and the same mechanisms may be involved in judging the margins of safety around other people's bodies (Brozzoli et al., 2013; Holt et al., 2014; Sambo & Iannetti, 2013; Teneggi, Canzoneri, di Pellegrino, & Serino, 2013). The emerging story shows how three seemingly unrelated topics – social behavior, defensive reactions and the action map in motor cortex – may overlap in a meaningful way.

References

Aflalo, T. N., & Graziano, M. S. A. (2006a). Partial tuning of motor cortex neurons to final posture in a free-moving paradigm. *Proceedings of the National Academy of Sciences*, 103, 2909–2914.
  (2006b). Possible origins of the complex topographic organization of motor cortex: Reduction of a multidimensional space onto a two-dimensional array. *Journal of Neuroscience*, 26, 6288–6297.
  (2007). Relationship between unconstrained arm movement and single neuron firing in the macaque motor cortex. *Journal of Neuroscience*, 27, 2760–2780.
Andrew, R. J. (1962). The origin and evolution of the calls and facial expressions of the primates. *Behaviour*, 20, 1–107.
Asanuma, H. (1975). Recent developments in the study of the columnar arrangement of neurons within the motor cortex. *Physiological Reviews*, 55, 143–156.
Bonazzi, L., Viaro, R., Lodi, E., Canto, R., Bonifazzi, C., & Franchi, G. (2013). Complex movement topography and extrinsic space representation in the rat forelimb motor cortex as defined by long-duration intracortical microstimulation. *Journal of Neuroscience*, 33, 2097–2107.
Brozzoli, C., Gentile, G., Bergouignan, L., & Ehrsson, H. H. (2013). A shared representation of the space near oneself and others in the human premotor cortex. *Current Biology*, 23, 1764–1768.
Bruce, C. J., Goldberg, M. E., Bushnell, M.C., & Stanton, G. B. (1985). Primate frontal eye fields. II. Physiological and anatomical correlates of electrically evoked eye movements. *Journal of Neurophysiology*, 54, 714–734.

Caggiula, A. R., & Hoebel, B. G. (1966). 'Copulation-reward site' in the posterior hypothalamus. *Science*, 153, 1284–1285.

Caruana, F., Jezzini, A., Sbriscia-Fioretti, B., Rizzolatti, G., & Gallese, V (2011). Emotional and social behaviors elicited by electrical stimulation of the insula in the macaque monkey. *Current Biology*, 21, 195–199.

Chakrabarty, S., & Martin, J. H. (2000). Postnatal development of the motor representation in primary motor cortex. *Journal of Neurophysiology*, 84, 2582–2594.

Cheney, P. D., & Fetz, E. E. (1985). Comparable patterns of muscle facilitation evoked by individual corticomotoneuronal (CM) cells and by single intracortical microstimuli in primates: Evidence for functional groups of CM cells. *Journal of Neurophysiology*, 53, 786–804.

Churchland, M. M., & Shenoy, K. V. (2007). Temporal complexity and heterogeneity of single-neuron activity in premotor and motor cortex. *Journal of Neurophysiology*, 97, 4235–4257.

Cooke, D. F., & Graziano, M. S. A. (2003). Defensive movements evoked by air puff in monkeys. *Journal of Neurophysiology*, 90, 3317–3329.

(2004a). Sensorimotor integration in the precentral gyrus: Polysensory neurons and defensive movements. *Journal of Neurophysiology*, 91, 1648–1650.

(2004b). Super-flinchers and nerves of steel: Defensive movements altered by chemical manipulation of a cortical motor area. *Neuron*, 43, 585–593.

Cooke, D. F., Taylor, C. S. R., Moore, T., & Graziano, M. S. A. (2003). Complex movements evoked by microstimulation of Area VIP. *Proceedings of the National Academy of Sciences*, 100, 6163–6168.

Darwin, C. (1872). *The expression of emotions in man and animals*. London: John Murray.

Desmurget, M., Song, Z., Mottolese, C., & Sirigu, A. (2013). Re-establishing the merits of electrical brain stimulation. *Trends in Cognitive Sciences*, 17, 442–449.

Donoghue, J. P., Leibovic, S., & Sanes, J. N. (1992). Organization of the forelimb area in squirrel monkey motor cortex: representation of digit, wrist, and elbow muscles. *Experimental Brain Research*, 89, 1–19.

Dosey, M. A., & Meisels, M. (1969). Personal space and self-protection. *Journal of Personality and Social Psychology*, 11, 93–97.

Ferrier, D. (1874). Experiments on the brain of monkeys – No. 1. *Proceedings of the Royal Society of London*, 23, 409–430.

Foerster, O. (1936). The motor cortex of man in the light of Hughlings Jackson's doctrines. *Brain*, 59, 135–159.

Fogassi, L., Gallese, V., Fadiga, L., Luppino, G., Matelli, M., & Rizzolatti, G. (1996). Coding of peripersonal space in inferior premotor cortex (area F4). *Journal of Neurophysiology*, 76, 141–157.

Fritsch, G., & Hitzig, E. (1870 [1960]). Uber die elektrishe Erregbarkeit des Grosshirns [On the electrical excitability of the cerebrum]. In G. von Bonin (Ed./ transl.), *Some papers on the cerebral cortex*. Springfield, IL: Charles C Thomas Publisher, 73–96.

Fulton, J. F. (1938). *Physiology of the nervous system*. New York: Oxford University Press, 399–457.

Gentilucci, M., Fogassi, L., Luppino, G., Matelli, M., Camarda, R., & Rizzolatti, G. (1988). Functional organization of inferior area 6 in the macaque monkey.

I. Somatotopy and the control of proximal movements. *Experiments in Brain Research*, 71, 475–490.

Georgopoulos, A. P., Ashe, J., Smyrnis, N., & Taira, M. (1992). The motor cortex and the coding of force. *Science*, 256, 1692–1695.

Georgopoulos, A. P., Kalaska, J. F., Caminiti, R., & Massey, J. T. (1982). On the relations between the direction of two-dimensional arm movements and cell discharge in primate motor cortex. *Journal of Neuroscience*, 2, 1527–1537.

Georgopoulos, A. P., Schwartz, A. B., & Kettner, R. E. (1986). Neuronal population coding of movement direction. *Science*, 233, 1416–1419.

Gould, H. J. III, Cusick, C. G., Pons, T. P., & Kaas, J. H. (1986). The relationship of corpus callosum connections to electrical stimulation maps of motor, supplementary motor, and the frontal eye fields in owl monkeys. *Journal of Comparative Neurology*, 247, 297–325.

Graziano, M. S. A. (2006). The organization of behavioral repertoire in motor cortex. *Annual Review of Neuroscience*, 29, 105–134.

(2008). *The intelligent movement machine: An ethological perspective on the primate motor system*. Oxford: Oxford University Press.

Graziano, M. S. A., & Aflalo, T. N. (2007). Mapping behavioral repertoire onto the cortex. *Neuron*, 56, 239–251.

Graziano, M. S. A., Aflalo, T. N. S., & Cooke, D. F. (2005). Arm movements evoked by electrical stimulation in the motor cortex of monkeys. *Journal of Neurophysiology*, 94, 4209–4223

Graziano, M. S. A., & Cooke, D. F. (2006). Parieto-frontal interactions, personal space, and defensive behavior. *Neuropsychologia*, 44, 845–859.

Graziano, M. S. A., Cooke, D. F., Taylor, C. S. R., & Moore, T. (2004). Distribution of hand location in monkeys during spontaneous behavior. *Experiments in Brain Research*, 155, 30–36.

Graziano, M. S. A., & Gandhi, S. (2000). Location of the polysensory zone in the precentral gyrus of anesthetized monkeys. *Experiments in Brain Research*, 135, 259–266.

Graziano, M. S. A., Hu, X. T., & Gross, C. G. (1997). Visuo-spatial properties of ventral premotor cortex. *Journal of Neurophysiology*, 77, 2268–2292.

Graziano, M. S. A., Taylor, C. S. R., & Moore, T. (2002). Complex movements evoked by microstimulation of precentral cortex. *Neuron*, 34, 841–851.

Graziano, M. S. A., Yap, G. S., & Gross, C. G. (1994). Coding of visual space by premotor neurons. *Science*, 266, 1054–1057.

Haiss, F., & Schwarz, C. (2005). Spatial segregation of different modes of movement control in the whisker representation of rat primary motor cortex. *Journal of Neuroscience*, 25, 1579–1587.

Hall, E. T. (1966). *The hidden dimension*. Garden City, New York: Anchor Books.

Harrison, T. C., Ayling, O. G., & Murphy, T. H. (2012). Distinct cortical circuit mechanisms for complex forelimb movement and motor map topography. *Neuron*, 74, 397–409.

Hediger, H. (1955). *Studies of the psychology and behavior of captive animals in zoos and circuses*. New York: Criterion Books.

Hess, W. R. (1957). *Functional organization of the diencephalons*. New York: Grune and Stratton.

Hoebel, B. G. (1969). Feeding and self-stimulation. *Annals of the New York Academy of Sciences*, 157, 758–778.

Holdefer, R. N., & Miller, L. E. (2002). Primary motor cortical neurons encode functional muscle synergies. *Experiments in Brain Research*, 146, 233–243.

Holt, D. J., Cassidy, B. S., Yue, X., Rauch, S. L., Boeke, E. A., et al. (2014). Neural correlates of personal space intrusion. *Journal of Neuroscience*, 34, 4123–4134.

Hooff, J. van (1962). Facial expression in higher primates. *Symposia of the Zoological Society of London*, 8, 97–125.

(1972). A comparative approach to the phylogeny of laughter and smiling. In R. A. Hind (Ed.), *Non-verbal communication*. Cambridge: Cambridge University Press, 209–241.

Horowitz, M. J., Duff, D. F., & Stratton, L. O. (1964). Body-buffer zone: Exploration of personal space. *Archives of General Psychiatry*, 11, 651–656.

Kakei, S., Hoffman, D., & Strick, P. (1999). Muscle and movemet representations in the primary motor cortex. *Science*, 285, 2136–2139.

King, M. B., & Hoebel, B. G. (1968). Killing elicited by brain stimulation in rats. *Communications in Behavioral Biology*, 2, 173–177.

Kwan, H. C., MacKay, W. A., Murphy, J. T., & Wong, Y. C. (1978). Spatial organization of precentral cortex in awake primates. II. Motor outputs. *Journal of Neurophysiology*, 41, 1120–1131.

Macfarlane, N. B. W., & Graziano, M. S. A. (2009). Diversity of grip in Macaca mulatta. *Experiments in Brain Research*, 197, 255–268.

Martin, J. H., Engber, D., & Meng, Z. (2005). Effect of forelimb use on postnatal development of the forelimb motor representation in primary motor cortex of the cat. *Journal of Neurophysiology*, 93, 2822–2831.

Meier, J. D., Aflalo, T. N., Kastner, S., & Graziano, M. S. A. (2008). Complex organization of human primary motor cortex: A high-resolution fMRI study. *Journal of Neurophysiology*, 100, 1800–1812.

Moran, D. W., & Schwartz, A. B. (1999). Motor cortical representation of speed and direction during reaching. *Journal of Neurophysiology*, 82, 2676–2692.

Nudo, R. J., Milliken, G. W., Jenkins, W. M., & Merzenich, M. M. (1996). Use-dependent alterations of movement representations in primary motor cortex of adult squirrel monkeys. *Journal of Neurosciences*, 16, 785–807.

Overduin, S. A., d'Avella, A., Carmena, J. M., & Bizzi, E. (2012). Microstimulation activates a handful of muscle synergies. *Neuron*, 76, 1071–1077.

Paninski, L., Fellows, M. R., Hatsopoulos, N. G., & Donoghue, J. P. (2004). Spatiotemporal tuning of motor cortical neurons for hand position and velocity. *Journal of Neurophysiology*, 91, 515–532.

Park, M. C., Belhaj-Saif, A., Gordon, M., & Cheney, P. D. (2001). Consistent features in the forelimb representation of primary motor cortex in rhesus macaques. *Journal of Neuroscience*, 21, 2784–2792.

Penfield, W., & Boldrey, E. (1937). Somatic motor and sensory representation in the cerebral cortex of man as studied by electrical stimulation. *Brain*, 60, 389–443.

Penfield, W., & Rasmussen, T. (1950). *The cerebral cortex of man: A clinical study of localization of function*. New York: Macmillan.

Preuschoft, S. (1992). 'Laughter' and 'smile' in Barbary macaques (*Macaca sylvanus*). *Ethology*, 91, 220–236.

Ramanathan, D., Conner, J. M., & Tuszynski, M. H. (2006). A form of motor cortical plasticity that correlates with recovery of function after brain injury. *Proceedings of the National Academy of Sciences USA*, 103, 11370–11375.

Rathelot, J. A., & Strick, P. L. (2006). Muscle representation in the macaque motor cortex: An anatomical perspective. *Proceedings of the National Academy of Sciences USA*, 103, 8257–8262.

Reina, G. A., Moran, D. W., & Schwartz, A. B. (2001). On the relationship between joint angular velocity and motor cortical discharge during reaching. *Journal of Neurophysiology*, 85, 2576–2589.

Rizzolatti, G., Scandolara, C., Matelli, M., & Gentilucci, M. (1981). Afferent properties of periarcuate neurons in macaque monkeys. II. Visual responses. *Behavioural Brain Research*, 2, 147–163.

Robinson, D. A. (1972). Eye movements evoked by collicular stimulation in the alert monkey. *Vision Research*, 12, 1795–1808.

Robinson, D. A., & Fuchs, A. F. (1969). Eye movements evoked by stimulation of the frontal eye fields. *Journal of Neurophysiology*, 32, 637–648.

Romo, R., Hernandez, A., Zainos, A., & Salinas, E. (1998). Somatosensory discrimination based on cortical microstimulation. *Nature*, 392, 387–390.

Ross, M. D., Owren, M. J., & Zimmermann, E. (2010). The evolution of laughter in great apes and humans. *Communicative and Integrative Biology*, 3, 191–194.

Salzman, C. D., Britten, K. H., & Newsome, W. T. (1990). Cortical microstimulation influences perceptual judgements of motion direction. *Nature*, 346, 174–177.

Sambo, C. F., & Iannetti, G. D. (2013). Better safe than sorry? The safety margin surrounding the body is increased by anxiety. *Journal of Neuroscience*, 33, 14225–14230.

Sanes, J. N., Donoghue, J. P., Thangaraj, V., Edelman, R. R., & Warach, S. (1995). Shared neural substrates controlling hand movements in human motor cortex. *Science*, 268, 1775–1777.

Schieber, M. H., & Hibbard, L. S. (1993). How somatotopic is the motor cortex hand area? *Science*, 261, 489–492.

Schiller, P. H., & Stryker, M. (1972). Single-unit recording and stimulation in superior colliculus of the alert rhesus monkey. *Journal of Neurophysiology*, 35, 915–924.

Scott, S. H., & Kalaska, J. F. (1997). Reaching movements with similar hand paths but different arm orientations. I. Activity of individual cells in motor cortex. *Journal of Neurophysiology*, 77, 826–852.

Sergio, L. E., & Kalaska, J. F. (2003). Systematic changes in motor cortex cell activity with arm posture during directional isometric force generation. *Journal of Neurophysiology*, 89, 212–228.

Sherrington, C. S. (1939). On the motor area of the cerebral cortex. In D. Denny-Brown (Ed.), *Selected writings of Sir Charles Sherrington*. London: Hamish Hamilton Medical Books, 397–439.

Sommer, R. (1959). Studies in personal space. *Sociometry*, 22, 247–260.

Stepniewska, I., Fang, P. C., & Kaas, J. H. (2005). Microstimulation reveals specialized subregions for different complex movements in posterior parietal cortex of prosimian galagos. *Proceedings of the National Academy of Sciences USA*, 102, 4878–4883.

(2009). Organization of the posterior parietal cortex in galagos: I. Functional zones identified by microstimulation. *Journal of Comparative Neurology*, 517, 765–782.

Strick, P. L., & Preston, J. B. (1978). Multiple representation in the primate motor cortex. *Brain Research*, 154, 366–370.

Teneggi, C., Canzoneri, E., di Pellegrino, G., & Serino A. (2013). Social modulation of peripersonal space boundaries. *Current Biology*, 23, 406–411.

Todorov, E. (2000). Direct cortical control of muscle activation in voluntary arm movements: A model. *Nature Neuroscience*, 3, 391–398.

Townsend, B. R., Paninski, L., & Lemon, R. N. (2006). Linear encoding of muscle activity in primary motor cortex and cerebellum. *Journal of Neurophysiology*, 96, 2578–2592.

Van Acker, G. M. III, Amundsen, S. L., Messamore, W. G., Zhang, H. Y., et al. (2013). Effective intracortical microstimulation parameters for evoking forelimb movements to stable spatial end-points from primary motor cortex. *Journal of Neurophysiology*, 110, 1180–1189.

Woolsey, C. N., Settlage, P. H., Meyer, D. R., Sencer, W., Hamuy, T. P., & Travis, A. M. (1952). Pattern of localization in precentral and 'supplementary' motor areas and their relation to the concept of a premotor area. In *Association for Research in Nervous and Mental Disease*, Vol. 30. New York: Raven Press, 238–264.

4   Beyond Action: Shared Representations in Non-Motor Domains

Michel-Pierre Coll and Philip L. Jackson

Abstract

With the renewed interest in perception–action coupling at the cerebral level, this idea of shared representations has rapidly been extended to non-motor domains as well, including somatosensory experiences. Indeed, in the last decades, a wealth of evidence has been produced suggesting that experience of somatosensory stimulations such as touch and pain share common neurophysiological and cognitive representations with the perception of the same experiences in others. However, it remains unclear what exactly is shared between an individual experiencing a state and someone observing this individual, and to what extent non-motor shared representations are supported by evidence. Here, we first review the different definitions of shared representations in the somatosensory domain proposed in the cognitive neuroscience literature. We then briefly describe the neurophysiological mechanisms underlying pain and touch perception and provide a critical review of the evidence for and against shared somatosensory representations for the different aspects of pain and touch experiences. Finally, we argue that these shared somatosensory representations can be modulated by individual, relational and contextual characteristics, and while most of these modulations occur implicitly, some can be deliberate, focused and meant to optimize subsequent social interactions.

Introduction

Have you ever felt a sensation akin to pain when witnessing a player being seriously injured during a football game? Have you ever felt embraced when watching friends hug each another? Such vicarious sensations might arise from the close link between our own representations of the sensations and the representation that stems from their perception in others. According to the shared representation hypothesis, actions and sensations in the self and the observation of the same actions or sensations in others share common neural and cognitive codes. One consequence of this overlap could be the constitution of a mechanism by which we can decode and ultimately understand others' actions, sensations and feelings (Decety & Sommerville, 2003). Now imagine that you are working in an emergency room and that you interact with severely injured persons on a regular basis. Your reaction to these sometimes-shocking situations will vary depending on your own state or experience, your relationship with the observed person or the context in which this interaction takes place (Coll, Grégoire, Latimer, Eugène, & Jackson, 2011). The study of how these somatosensory-shared representations can be modulated by physiological, cognitive and social factors, and ultimately, how these representations will prompt our behavior provides crucial insights into how we use our own representations to navigate through our social world.

The concept of shared representation was first developed in the motor domain based on the idea that perception and action share a common link as proposed more than a century ago by American psychologist William James and later refined by Nobel laureate Roger Sperry (1952). However, the discovery of mirror neurons in the macaque monkey (Gallese, Fadiga, Fogassi, & Rizzolatti, 1996; di Pellegrino, Fadiga, Fogassi, Gallese, & Rizzolatti, 1992) and their less convincing and less replicated observation in human subjects (e.g. Mukamel, Ekstrom, Kaplan, Iacoboni, & Fried, 2010) offered a physiological mechanism by which a link between perception and action could arise. Mirror neurons are a type of neurons having the property of firing both when an action is performed and when it is perceived in another individual (Gallese et al., 1996). This new framework and the advancement of cognitive neuroscience gave rise to numerous neuroimaging and behavioral studies offering a wealth of evidence for the perception–action link, including a common neural network recruited during perception and action (Iacoboni & Dapretto, 2006; Chong, Cunnington, Williams, Kanwisher, & Mattingley, 2008; Kilner, Neal, Weiskopf, Friston, & Frith, 2009; Press, Weiskopf, & Kilner, 2012), and the modulation of cortical excitability of the motor cortex by action observation (Baldissera, Cavallari, Craighero, & Fadiga, 2001; Mukamel et al., 2010; Muthukumaraswamy & Johnson, 2004; Strafella & Paus, 2000; Valeriani, Betti, Le Pera, De Armas, & Miliucci, 2008). Although less well established than the perception–action link, the existence of shared mechanisms linking somatosensory experience and perception of somatosensory events in others received considerable attention in the last decade. However, before discussing such evidence, it is important to consider what type of results can constitute evidence for shared somatosensory representations.

Shared Somatosensory Representations: What Exactly Is Shared?

The term *shared representations*, beyond the motor realm, has originally been used to describe how the self is perceived and understood in relation to others and how others are perceived in relation to the self (Decety & Sommerville, 2003). In neuroimaging studies, this term is often synonymous with functional overlap between the neural response to an actual experience and to the observation of this experience in others (e.g. Bufalari, Aprile, Avenanti, Di Russo, & Aglioti, 2007; Lawrence, Shaw, Giampietro, & Surguladze, 2006). Although numerous studies point to a gross overlap in the brain regions activated during perception and somatosensory experience (see Lamm, Decety, & Singer, 2011), currently no neuroimaging studies have been able to conclude on shared neural circuits between perception and sensation with more advanced designs and methods such as adaptation designs or multivariate pattern analyses (see Box 4.1). Furthermore, studies using functional connectivity analyses (Zaki, Ochsner, Hanelin, Wager, & Mackey, 2007) or multivariate pattern analyses (Krishnan et al., 2016) generally observed involvement of different neural networks when perceiving pain in the self and in others (but see Corradi-Dell'Acqua et al., 2012). These findings are of critical importance for the understanding of the cellular mechanisms underlying the social brain and the limits of available neuroimaging techniques. However, we would argue that the demonstration that spatially close, but not identical, neural circuitries subserve the perception of pain or touch in the self and in others is sufficient to support the shared representations framework as a basis for investigating how we perceive and understand others. Indeed, functional overlapping and interactions between somatosensory stimulation in the self and its perception in others is, in our opinion, interesting evidence that we use our own representations of somatosensory states to interpret those of others. It is also evident from our perspective that this sharing between self and other is far from complete: the pain of others can be understood by using our own representations of pain, but it does not become our pain (see Decety, 2010; Jackson, Brunet, Meltzoff, & Decety, 2006). Mechanisms exist in order to distinguish self from other experience, and if such mechanisms are defective, it could lead to certain synesthetic conditions, as discussed in the following sections. The study of the factors that can modulate the extent of this sharing, allowing us to share more or less the somatosensory events we observe in others, is therefore an interesting way in which to reach a better understanding of shared somatosensory representations.

Box 4.1 fMRI analyses and shared representations

Shared neural representations of pain and touch have often been interpreted as the implication of the same neural circuits during experience and observation of pain and touch (e.g. Keysers et al., 2004; Singer, 2004). Most studies reached this conclusion because overlapping patterns of activation in self and others for the experience of a somatosensory experience and its observation in others were observed using functional magnetic resonance imaging

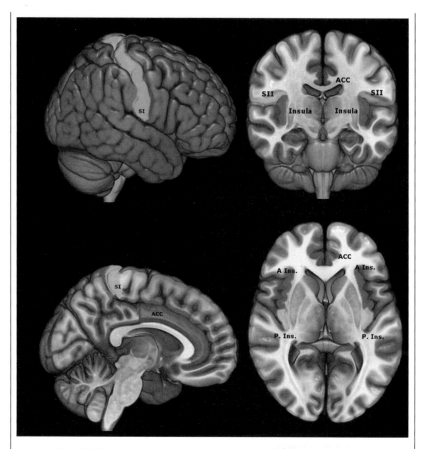

Box 4.1 Illustration of the main brain regions involved in both the experience of pain and touch and their perception in others. *See Plate 1.*

(fMRI). However, it is important to note that traditional mass univariate fMRI analyses are inappropriate to conclude on shared neural networks (Oosterhof, Tipper, & Downing, 2013). Indeed, these types of analyses are based on modeling the hemodynamic responses measured with fMRI in individual voxels and then contrasting the activity map between conditions (e.g. pain facial expressions versus neutral facial expressions) in order to see which voxel show over-threshold activity in one condition compared to another. Depending on different parameters of the acquisition, the hardware used and the experimental design, the size of a voxel is approximately 8 to 27 mm^3 and therefore represents the combined activity of hundreds of thousands of neurons. Furthermore, traditional preprocessing steps involve spatial smoothing of voxels, a technique consisting of averaging contiguous voxels in order to reduce noise and obtain a better signal to noise ratio. Therefore, it is not possible to conclude on the implication of identical neurons or networks in two different conditions based on typical fMRI analyses. Other approaches such as adaptation designs and multivariate pattern analyses (Oosterhof et al., 2013) represent interesting avenues to reach sub-voxel resolution in fMRI studies. Early evidence using multivariate pattern analyses suggests that brain response during pain experience and pain observation in others can be reliably distinguished using this technique (Krishnan et al., 2016), suggesting that they rely on different neural networks. However, some common patterns of activation have also been observed using multivariate pattern analyses during pain sensation and observation (Corradi-Dell'Acqua et al., 2011). These types of analyses should therefore be utilized in future studies of shared representations for pain and touch to help clarify the extent of the neuronal sharing during perception of pain or touch in others.

Here, we thus consider that our own physiological and cognitive representations of a somatosensory state, including semantic and affective representations, share the same patterns of activity with those triggered by the perception of the same state in others. We therefore consider as evidence for shared somatosensory representations any interaction between self and observed somatosensory experiences. This includes demonstrations that observed pain and touch can evoke similar, albeit not identical, physiological responses and neural activity as self-pain or touch as well as demonstrations of influences of self-pain and touch on their perception in others and vice versa. After a brief overview of the mechanisms of self-pain and touch perception, we provide a critical review of the evidence for shared somatosensory representations of pain and touch. Finally, we argue that these shared representations can be modulated by individual, relational and contextual characteristics, and while most of these modulations occur implicitly, some can be deliberate, focused on and fruitful to subsequent social interactions.

Shared Representations of Touch

Tactile information is processed by the somatosensory system, a set of brain regions responsible for receiving, perceiving and interpreting somatosensory information in the self. This system comprises two distinct pathways (Björnsdotter, Löken, Olausson, Vallbo, & Wessberg, 2009; Ebisch et al., 2011). The exteroceptive network, including the primary (SI) and secondary (SII) somatosensory cortices, receives the initial cortical input and processes the physical characteristics of tactile stimulations. The interoceptive network, which includes the posterior insular cortex (pIC) and the rostral cingulate cortex (rCC), processes the internal states evoked by tactile stimulations to produce the affective consequences of this stimulation.

Neuroimaging studies have shown that observing someone else being touched vicariously activates parts of both the exteroceptive and interoceptive networks of the somatosensory system. Within the exteroceptive network, SI, which receives somatosensory input from the motor cortex and the periphery via the thalamus and transfers this information to associative regions, has been shown to be involved in the perception of touch in others (Ebisch et al., 2008; Kuehn, Mueller, Turner, & Schütz-Bosbach, 2014; Kuehn, Trampel, Mueller, Turner, & Schütz-Bosbach, 2013; Rossetti, Miniussi, Maravita, & Bolognini, 2012; Schaefer, Heinze, & Rotte, 2009). Recent studies using high field fMRI suggest that observation of touch in others involves mostly the posterior parts of SI (Kuehn et al., 2013, 2014). This is in line with anatomical considerations indicating that the anterior regions of SI are receiving inputs directly from the periphery and motor regions, while the posterior parts of SI are involved in secondary somatosensory processing and associative processing from other modalities (Keysers, Kaas, & Gazzola, 2010). Bufalari et al. (2007) used the precise temporal resolution of electroencephalography (EEG) to measure which stage of somatosensory processing could be influenced by visual information. They found that observation of a hand being touched did not modulate early somatosensory evoked potentials components following an electrical stimulation associated with anterior SI activity, but modulated components at a later latency associated with activity of the posterior regions of SI. Similarly, Pihko, Nangini, Jousmäki, and Hari (2010) found a modulation of SI activity during touch observation 300 to 600 ms after onset of the visual stimulation. The presence of shared representations for touch in SI are also supported by results showing that SI activation during touch observation is lateralized and somatotopically organized in a manner similar to the experience of the same touch (Blakemore, Bristow, Bird, Frith, & Ward, 2005; Kuehn et al., 2013, 2014; Schaefer, Xu, Flor, & Cohen, 2009). With high field fMRI, Kuehn et al. (2014) found that activation of SI during the observation of touch to an index finger overlapped precisely with activation observed during the experience of touch to the same finger.

The secondary somatosensory cortex is also significantly activated during observation of touch in others (Blakemore et al., 2005; Ebisch et al., 2008, 2011; Keysers et al., 2004; Schaefer et al., 2009). Interestingly, SII also shows increased activation during the observation of objects being touched by other objects compared to observation of objects not being touched (Keysers et al., 2004). This suggests that SII is involved in simulating the quality of the observed touch rather than its social significance (Keysers et al., 2010). Indeed, Keysers and collaborators (2004), as well as others (Ebisch et al., 2008), observed that SII was similarly activated both when the act of touching an inanimate object or touching a human being was observed. However, a distinction in processing observed human versus inanimate touch seems to be present at both the early and later stage of visual processing, as shown by Streltsova and McCleery (2014). By recording event-related potentials over somatosensory areas during observation of human or inanimate touch, these researchers found evidence for a differentiation between these two conditions in early event-related potential components, as well as in later components around 500 ms, indicating preferential processing for human touch in sensory, perceptual and cognitive processing stages.

Oscillatory EEG rhythms have been frequently used to study shared somatosensory representations. The 'mu rhythm' is an alpha (8–13 Hz) rhythm recorded over the sensorimotor areas that is at maximal power during motor rest and that is desynchronized both during action execution and observation (Muthukumaraswamy & Johnson, 2004; Pineda, 2005), but also during touch and pain observation or experience (Cheyne et al., 2003; Gaetz & Cheyne, 2006; Höfle, Pomper, Hauck, & Engel, 2013; Perry, Bentin, Bartal, Lamm, & Decety, 2010). Furthermore, multiple studies suggest that this rhythm originates from somatosensory, rather than motor areas (Arnstein, Cui, Keysers, Maurits, & Gazzola, 2011; Hari et al., 1998; Ritter, Moosmann, & Villringer, 2009; Rossi et al., 2002). Therefore, there is a strong possibility that mu rhythm indexes somatosensory processing during action execution (e.g. touching objects) rather than the motor component of the observed action. Nevertheless, mu rhythm has been a useful tool to show sensorimotor activation during touch and pain observation (Cheyne et al., 2003; Gaetz & Cheyne, 2006; Höfle et al., 2013; Perry et al., 2010).

The brain regions associated with the interoceptive processing of somatosensory information are also found to be significantly activated when the touch observed conveys an affective meaning. Using an elegant manipulation, Morrison, Bjornsdotter, and Olausson (2011a) showed that when subjects observed someone else's arm being stroked by another hand at what was considered a pleasing speed, optimally stimulating the tactile C afferent fibers, the posterior insula (pIC) showed increased activation compared to when they observed the same arm being stroked at a fast non-pleasing speed. In fact, when observing non-pleasing strokes, activity in this region was similar to the level of activity found during actual touch, demonstrating the importance of the pIC in interpreting the affective meaning of stimulation. Furthermore, this change in the pIC activity was not present when observing video-clips in which the strokes were delivered by an object rather than a hand, confirming that insular activity was due to differences in affective meaning rather than simple differences in stimulation velocity. These results are in contradiction with another study that found deactivation in the pIC during the observation of affective touch and increased activation in the same region during the experience of the same touch (Ebisch et al., 2011). According to the authors, these results indicate that the pIC is involved in maintaining self–other distinctions during observation of touch rather than sharing its affective quality. However, some methodological limitations such as absence of control on the touch velocity to produce optimal affective touch could explain these divergent results (Morrison et al., 2011a). Although the affective dimension of touch is traditionally considered to be processed in the pIC and rCC, recent evidence suggests that posterior regions of SI are also involved in processing the affective significance of touch both during the experience (Malinen, Renvall, & Hari, 2014) and the observation of touch (Gazzola, Spezio, Etzel, Castelli, Adolphs, & Keysers, 2012).

Shared Representations of Pain

Pain is defined as, 'An unpleasant sensory and emotional experience associated with actual or potential tissue damage, or described in terms of such damage' (International Association for the Study of Pain, 1994). Pain is therefore a subjective experience resulting from the combination of sensory-discriminative and affective-motivational experiences (Melzack & Casey, 1968). The sensory-discriminative dimension of pain encompasses the physical proprieties of pain, such as location, intensity and quality, while the affective dimension of pain refers to the unpleasantness of felt pain as well as accompanying emotions and implications for future events (ibid). Although pain is traditionally conceptualized as having a physical component, on which we will focus here, some recent work has proposed the hypothesis that 'social pain', resulting from painful social events (e.g. rejection, heartbreak, loneliness), is perceived using similar mechanisms to those for physical pain and has similar consequences for the organism (Eisenberger, 2012; see Box 4.2). Pain experience results from the interaction between a number of cerebral networks comprised of a set of brain regions including SI, SII, the anterior (ACC) and posterior (pCC) cingulate cortex, the insular cortex (IC), the thalamus, the periaqueductal grey matter (PAG), the hypothalamus, the amygdala and parts of the prefrontal cortex (PFC) (Bushnell & Apkarian, 2006; Garcia-Larrea, Frot, & Valeriani, 2003). This network involved in generating the pain experience is often called the 'pain matrix' or 'pain matrices' (e.g. Garcia-Larrea & Peyron, 2013), although some authors question its specificity for pain processing and rather argue that this network is better described as a saliency detection network (Iannetti & Mouraux, 2010). Studies in patients with lesions and using hypnosis in healthy individuals have been able to dissociate the sensory-discriminative and affective dimensions of pain and thus shown that some of these cerebral regions, including SI and SII, are specialized in generating the sensory-discriminative aspect of pain experience, while regions such as the ACC, the aIC and prefrontal structures are involved in generating the affective meaning of pain (Price, 2000; Rainville, 1997, 2002). Pain experience in the central nervous system is also accompanied by an activation of the autonomic nervous system preparing the organism for a fight or flight type response. This autonomic activation is often measured experimentally using skin conductance and heart rate measures. Loggia, Juneau, and Bushnell (2011) found that these two measures correlated with the perceived intensity of a painful stimulation. Another commonly studied peripheral response to pain is the nociceptive reflex, an automatic muscle response causing the limb to move when receiving pain, measured using electromyography (Bromm & Treede, 1980). The amplitude of these reflexes has also been shown to correlate with the intensity of the painful stimulation (Broom & Treede, 1980).

Box 4.2 Shared representations for social pain?

We have all felt emotional pain during difficult social events such as being rejected, the ending of a significant relationship or the death of a loved one. Recent evidence suggests that such 'social pain' might have a strong link to physical pain and have important consequences for one's health. Eisenberger (2012; also see Eisenberger & Cole, 2012) reviewed evidence for the similarity between physical and social pain and suggested that social pain emerges because social ties are fundamental to human survival and that signals indicating threat to these connections tap into the same 'neural alarm system' as physical pain because both represent danger to our survival. Social neuroscience studies on social pain used a variety of paradigms ranging from making participants feel rejected by excluding them from a virtual ball-tossing game (Eisenberger, Lieberman, & Williams, 2003) to displaying pictures of their ex-partner (Kross, Berman, Mischel, Smith, & Wager, 2011). Results show that social pain leads to activation of the ACC, bilateral IC (see Cacioppo et al., 2013 for a meta-analysis) and the SII (Kross et al., 2011), regions involved in both the affective and sensory dimensions of physical pain. Furthermore, witnessing social pain in others has also been shown to activate similar brain regions (Masten, Morelli, & Eisenberger, 2011; Novembre, Zanon, & Silani, 2014), suggesting that we might understand social pain in others using our own representations of social pain (Masten et al., 2011). Although an interesting avenue for future research in social neuroscience, it is important to note that the idea that social pain is experienced as physically painful and that it can be inferred from activation of brain regions involved in pain experience has been criticized (see Iannetti, Salomons, Moayedi, Mouraux, & Davis, 2013). Also, recent fMRI evidence with multivariate pattern analysis suggests that there is no overlap between self-pain perception and perception of social pain in others (Wager et al., 2013).

Evidence for shared representations for pain includes numerous neuroimaging studies showing activations in brain regions involved in self-pain perception when witnessing pain in others (e.g. Bird et al., 2010; Botvinick et al., 2005; Budell, Jackson, & Rainville, 2010; Cheng et al., 2007; Corradi-Dell'Acqua et al., 2011; Costantini, Galati, Romani, & Aglioti, 2008; Danziger, Faillenot, & Peyron, 2009; Jackson et al., 2006; Jackson, Meltzoff, & Decety, 2005; Lamm, Batson, & Decety, 2007; Saarela et al., 2007; Simon et al., 2006; Singer, 2004; Singer et al., 2006). Correlations between activity in these regions, more specifically the IC and the ACC, and the assessment of the intensity or unpleasantness perceived in others suggest that these shared representations are an important step in understanding and assessing pain in others (Cheng et al., 2007; Jackson et al., 2005).

An important question in the study of shared representations for pain is: which dimensions of others' painful experience do we share? Do we only share the negative emotions and affective state of the observed person in pain or do we share the sensory qualities of this pain as well? Conflicted evidence on this issue is offered by fMRI studies of pain perception in others. Indeed, most of these studies support sharing of the affective dimension of pain when witnessing pain in others by showing robust activation of structures involved in the affective dimension of pain experience such as the ACC and the IC (see Lamm et al., 2011 for a meta-analysis). However, evidence for the activation of the brain regions involved in the sensory dimension of pain experience is less common and varies depending on the study design (ibid). One explanation for this discrepancy is the variety of stimuli, task instructions and designs used to study the perception of pain in others (see Figure 4.1). Experimental studies of the perception of pain in others often use different images or video-clips depicting painful events in the form of painful sensory events (e.g. injuries, limbs in painful scenarios; Cheng et al., 2007; Jackson et al., 2005, 2006), socio-affective cues of pain (e.g. facial expressions of pain; Botvinick et al., 2005; Saarela et al., 2007; Simon et al., 2006) or combining both sensory and affective information (Corradi-Dell'Acqua et al., 2011; Loggia, Mogil, & Bushnell, 2008; Osborn & Derbyshire, 2010). Most of these studies aimed to exercise rigorous control over the type of stimuli used in order to differentiate perception of pain from other emotions such as sadness or disgust and

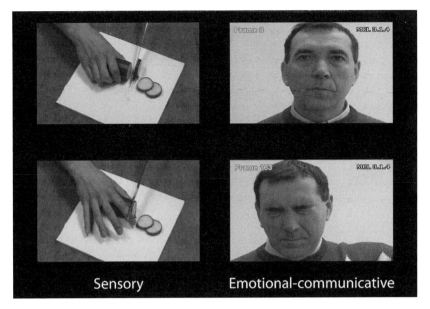

Figure 4.1 Examples of the types of stimuli used for the study of pain perception in others. *See Plate 2.*

Notes: Sensory stimuli depict limbs in painful situations (e.g. Jackson et al., 2005) while the emotional-communicative stimuli show facial expressions of pain without sensory information (e.g. Botvinick et al., 2005). The sensory stimuli shown here were developed by Marcoux et al. (2013) while the emotional-communicative stimuli are from the UNBC-McMaster Shoulder Pain Expression Archive (Lucy, Prkachin, Solomon, & Matthews, 2011).

used controlled stimuli, while others have used a more ecological approach by showing painful events in real-life scenarios (Corradi-Dell'Acqua et al., 2011; Osborn & Derbyshire, 2010) or by showing a live person receiving a painful stimulation (Hein, Silani, Preuschoff, Batson, & Singer, 2010; Jensen et al., 2013). Other studies have relied on the participants' imagination by simply telling them that someone is receiving a painful stimulation when a visual cue is shown (Singer, 2004; Singer et al., 2006). Such variety in the type of stimuli used in these studies might explain some of the discrepancies between the results. In a quantitative meta-analysis of fMRI studies, Lamm et al. (2011) confirmed that witnessing pain in others reliably activates the medial cingulate cortex (mCC), the ACC and the anterior insular cortex (aIC). Furthermore, the authors found that somatosensory areas were activated mostly in experiments using pictures of limbs in painful situations and not in experiments using facial expressions of pain. Vachon-Presseau et al. (2012) directly tested this hypothesis by comparing the same participant's brain activation when observing limbs in pain and facial expressions of pain. They found that, compared to facial expressions, hand and foot in painful scenarios indeed recruited somatosensory regions to a greater extent. This suggests that, while the affective quality of the pain observed in others is consistently shared, we share the sensory qualities only when 'flesh and bone' pain is observed. However, it might be the case that it is not the sensory component of flesh and bone stimuli that triggers somatosensory activation but rather their higher intensity and saliency. Simon et al. (2006) found increased activations in SI and in the amygdala when pain was witnessed in male facial expressions but not in female pain expressions. The authors explained this effect by the fact that male expressions are usually more intense and threatening than female pain expressions.

This sensorimotor activation when witnessing pain in others has also been confirmed by studies using transcranial magnetic stimulation (TMS) and EEG showing that pain observation in others can modulate the excitability of the motor cortex (Avenanti, Bueti, Galati, & Aglioti, 2005; Avenanti, Minio-Paluello, Bufalari, & Aglioti, 2009; Avenanti, Sirigu, & Aglioti, 2010), modulate activity of the somatosensory cortex (Marcoux et al., 2013; Voisin, Marcoux, Canizales, Mercier, & Jackson, 2011) or desynchronize sensorimotor rhythms (Cheng, Yang, Lin, Lee, & Decety, 2008; Yang, Decety, Lee, Chen, & Cheng, 2009).

Another interesting avenue in studying shared representations of pain is the study of how self-pain and the pain perceived in others can influence one another. This interaction can be examined from at least two different perspectives. First, one would expect that one's own experience with pain can be modulated by prior or concomitant exposure to another person's pain. Indeed, studies of this interaction have shown that witnessing pain in others can lower pain threshold (de Wied & Verbaten, 2001), increase the perceived intensity or unpleasantness of a painful stimulation (Godinho et al., 2011; Godinho, Magnin, Frot, Perchet, & Garcia-Larrea, 2006; Loggia et al., 2008; Mailhot, Presseau, Jackson, & Rainville, 2012; Vachon-Presseau et al., 2011), increase automatic withdrawal responses (Mailhot et al., 2012; Vachon-Presseau et al., 2011) and modulate nociceptive evoked brain potentials (Valeriani et al., 2008). Second, one can expect that the assessment of another individual's pain can be influenced by one's own physiological state. It has been shown that being in pain can increase the intensity of the pain perceived in others in some situations (Coll, Budell, Rainville, Decety, & Jackson, 2012; Meng et al., 2013). Furthermore, this increase is accompanied by faster response times in detecting the pain of others and by a modulation of brain-evoked potentials to pain in others, suggesting the use of fewer cognitive resources for processing others' pain when preceded by a self-pain stimulation (Meng et al., 2013). However, the specificity of such interactions can be questioned; it could be the case that any other aversive stimulation in the self or other (sadness, fear, and so on) could lead to such interaction with self or observed pain. More evidence is needed to confirm pain specificity. The available studies comparing the effects of pain compared to other negative emotions suggest that, while other emotional states can influence pain perception in self or others (Meng et al., 2012; de Wied & Verbaten, 2001), self/other pain has been shown to have a preferential influence on self/other pain (Godinho et al., 2006; de Wied & Verbaten, 2001). Together, these studies suggest that witnessing pain in others can influence the representations of our own pain and activate systems involved in the organism's response to self-pain.

Factors Modulating Shared Representations of Pain and Touch

Shared representations of pain and touch are often considered automatic responses stemming from their observation in others. However, the extent of this sharing, (i.e. the strength of the affective and sensory responses generated by the observed state) can vary greatly according to numerous individual, social and contextual factors.

Among individual factors, the level of empathy has often been postulated to be related to the extent of the sharing of others' pain and touch. Empathy can be defined as the capacity to adopt others' perspective and to share part of their experience and discomfort (Davis, 1980; Decety, 2004). Theoretical models distinguish between the cognitive and the affective dimension of empathy (Davis, 1983). The cognitive dimension of empathy refers to the capacity to adopt deliberately other people's perspectives while the affective dimension of empathy refers to feelings of discomfort or concern when witnessing others in distress (ibid). The cognitive and affective dimensions of empathy are usually measured using different subscales of self-reported questionnaires such as the Interpersonal Reactivity Index (IRI; Davis, 1980, 1996). The cognitive dimension of empathy has been shown to correlate with activity in SI during the observation of touch (Schaefer et al., 2012), with activity in SI and SII when participants heard the sound of actions with tactile components (Gazzola, Aziz-Zadeh, & Keysers, 2006) and with the amplitude of sensory-evoked potentials during the observation of pain and touch (Martínez-Jauand et al., 2012). Using transcranial magnetic stimulation to study changes in sensorimotor excitability when observing pain in others, Avenanti et al. (2009) found that individuals reporting higher levels of the cognitive dimension of empathy had increased sensorimotor inhibition when observing pain in others. The affective dimension of empathy has been linked with increased activations in the IC and the CC when participants were told that their loved one was receiving pain (Singer, 2004; Singer et al., 2006), although another study found no relationship between activity in these regions and observation of limbs in pain (Jackson et al., 2005). Vachon-Presseau et al. (2011) found that participants reporting higher levels of the cognitive and affective dimensions of empathy showed increased facilitation of the nociceptive flexion reflex of the leg when witnessing pain in others. Furthermore, more empathic individuals showed reduced hyperalgesia or even hypoalgesia to the nociceptive stimulation when witnessing pain in others. This suggests that empathy increases affective sharing between self and others' pain and that it also allows increased regulation of self-responses, possibly in order to facilitate others oriented empathic responses (ibid). This regulation of shared responses seems to be an important aspect to regulate behavior and could be altered in conditions characterized by empathy deficits such as psychopathy, or individuals with high levels of psychopathic traits (Fecteau, Pascual-Leone, & Théoret, 2008; Marcoux et al., 2013).

Higher levels of empathy have also been found in people with a condition called mirror synaesthesia (Banissy & Ward, 2007). According to a survey carried out with 567 undergraduates in the United Kingdom, Banissy, Kadosh, Maus, Walsh, and Ward (2009) found that 11 percent of this sample reported feeling touch when observing it in others. Laboratory touch observation/ discrimination tasks confirmed that approximately 2.5 percent of the initial sample showed typical mirror–touch symptoms. For mirror-pain synaesthesia, Osborn and Derbyshire (2010) found that approximately a third of the 108 participants they tested reported somatic pain experiences when watching pictures of intense injuries, but they did not use any validation task to verify these reports of mirror-pain synaesthesia, which implies that this proportion is likely inflated. However, it is clear that acquired mirror-pain synaesthesia following traumatic painful events such as amputation is more prevalent than developmental or idiopathic mirror-pain synaesthesia (Fitzgibbon et al., 2010a). One hypothesis commonly proposed to explain this curious phenomenon is that the shared representations system for touch or pain is or becomes hyperactive in these individuals, which leads to above conscious thresholds activation when observing touch or pain in others (Blakemore et al., 2005; Fitzgibbon et al., 2012; Fitzgibbon, Giummarra, Georgiou-Karistianis, Enticott, & Bradshaw, 2010b). This hypothesis received support in an fMRI case study showing that, compared to a control group, the mirror–touch synaesthete participant showed increased activity in SI, SII, the IC and the premotor area during touch observation (Blakemore et al., 2005). Similarly, Osborn and Derbyshire (2010) found increased activation in the IC and SII during pain observation in individuals reporting mirror-pain symptoms compared to a control group. A recent study also added weight to this hypothesis by using transcranial direct current stimulation to increase the excitability of SI in non-synaesthete participants (Bolognini, Miniussi, Gallo, & Vallar, 2013). They found that this stimulation was able to create synaesthesia-like symptoms during a touch observation/discrimination task compared to an inhibitory or sham stimulation or a stimulation to the premotor area.

Acquired mirror-pain synaesthesia can therefore be described as a hyperactivity of the shared representation system following painful experience. Hypoactivity of this system has also been shown in relation to the acquisition of specific experience. Indeed, by comparing physicians experienced in acupuncture to naïve participants during a pain observation task, Cheng et al. (2007) found that, while the naïve group showed typical pain-sharing responses, the physicians group did not show significant activity compared to baseline in multiple regions of the shared representations for pain system, notably the somatosensory cortex, the anterior insula (aI) and the ACC. However, direct group comparisons showed that physicians had increased responses in the media prefrontal cortex (mPFC) and the temporoparietal junction known to be involved in self-regulation and perspective taking. Furthermore, connectivity analyses in this study as well as a replication study using EEG showed that increased activity in the mPFC was associated with decreased insular activity in the physician group and with inferior ratings of the intensity of the pain observed (Cheng et al., 2007; Decety, Yang, & Cheng, 2010). Therefore, it might be the case that regular exposure to the pain of others as experienced by health-care providers leads to increased regulation of shared representations activity (Decety et al., 2010). Although such a mechanism is adaptive in nature and allows these individuals to work with patients without suffering excessive distress (Cheng et al., 2007; Decety et al., 2010), it might be linked to underestimation of the pain of patients and to issues in providing optimal pain treatment in clinical settings (Coll et al., 2011).

Contextual information can also lead to a fluctuation of the shared representation response. Lamm et al. (2007) showed pictures of facial expressions of pain to participants in an fMRI scanner and told participants that some of the patients received a successful treatment for their neurological disease while in others the treatment failed. This manipulation led to increased brain activity in the affective regions of pain perception when participants were told that patients were not in remission. Jacskon, Brunet, Meltzoff, and Decety (2006) directly asked participants to alternate between imagining they were feeling the pain observed on the screen, imagining someone else feeling this pain or to imagine they were watching an artificial limb receiving the painful stimulation. They found that first-person perspective led to more activation in SII, ACC and IC, suggesting increased somatosensory and affective responses. The third-person perspective led to increased activity in the precuneus and the temporoparietal junction, regions involved in adopting the perspective of others and thinking about others' thoughts. These results suggest that shared representations for pain are recruited more extensively when the observation of pain is more closely related to one's own experience and that additional brain regions are necessary to adopt others' perspectives.

The intentionality or motivation behind the observed pain and touch also seems to play an important role in modulating shared somatosensory representations. Ebisch and collaborators (2008) manipulated the intentionality of the observed touch by showing a hand touching objects or a person (intentional condition) or a tree branch moved by the wind touching the same objects/person. They found that the degree of intentionality perceived by the participant was positively correlated with the activation of SI, suggesting that this structure is preferentially involved when observing intentional touching agents. Similarly, Akitsuki and Decety (2009) manipulated the intentionality of pain events in an fMRI experiment by showing participants images of limbs in painful situations where the pain was either self-inflicted or other-inflicted. They found that both self- and other-inflicted pain activated typical regions involved in sharing others' pain, but that compared to self-inflicted pain scenarios, other-inflicted pain scenarios led to higher intensity ratings and increased activity in brain regions involved in representing social interaction and emotional regulation such as the mPFC, the inferior frontal gyrus, the temporoparietal junction and the orbitofrontal cortex. Altogether, these results suggest that shared representations are dependent on the social context in which pain and touch are observed.

Differences in how we perceive touch or pain in ourselves may also be associated with how we perceive them in others. Danziger and collaborators (2009) tackled this question by studying participants presenting congenital insensitivity to pain, a condition leading to a strong decrease in pain sensitivity. Using two fMRI experiments during which patients with congenital insensitivity to pain (CIP) and a control group observed hands in painful situations or facial expressions of pain, they found a similar pattern of brain activations in regions associated with affective processing of pain between CIP patients and control participants such as the ACC and the insula. They also underestimated the intensity of the pain observed compared to controls when observing hands in pain but not when evaluating the intensity of pain facial expressions. This suggests that, despite their inability to experience pain, CIP patients can still share and interpret the affective side of this experience. The interpretation of others' pain in CIP patients might be performed using empathic abilities because pain judgements were correlated with emotional empathy in these patients, which was not the case in control participants (Danziger, Prkachin, & Willer, 2006). Furthermore, significant between-group differences were observed in other regions, notably in the PI, involved in somatosensory processing, suggesting that, although CIP could share the affective aspects of the observed pain, they did not share its sensory component (Borsook & Becerra, 2009).

Using a similar approach, Morrison et al. (2011b) studied touch perception in self and others in individuals with a genetic mutation leading to reduced density of the C-fibers involved in pleasant touch sensation described earlier. Contrary to control participants, these individuals did not show modulation in the pIC when the caressing stimulation was tuned at optimal pleasing speed. Furthermore, although no neuroimaging was performed when they observed caressing stimulation in others, they also rated the pleasantness of the caressing stimulation experienced and observed in others at optimal speed as less pleasant than control participants and also showed an atypical pattern of pleasantness rating modulation when the caressing speed was varied. Pain perception in others has also been studied in patients suffering from fibromyalgia, a condition characterized by chronic widespread pain and decreased pain thresholds with as yet no known cause (Blumenstiel et al., 2011). While previous studies found that fibromyalgia patients showed increased activity in the pain matrix when receiving a painful stimulation compared to controls (Gracely et al., 2003), Lee and collaborators (2013) found that they show decreased brain responses in multiple regions associated with pain processing, such as the ACC and SI, when observing pain in others. This suggests that being regularly in this type of pain leads to less sharing of others' pain, possibly in order to reduce associated arousal or aversive emotions elicited by observing pain in others (ibid).

The extent of the sharing of pain and touch representations can also be modulated by the characteristics of the person receiving pain or touch. Xu, Zuo, Wang, and Han (2009) showed that watching painful stimulation delivered to same-race models led to increased activity in the ACC and IC compared to the same stimulation in other-race models. Avenanti et al. (2010) used transcranial magnetic stimulation in black and white participants to study the influence of this in-group bias on shared responses in sensorimotor regions. Both groups showed typical sensorimotor inhibition when observing in-group pain or purple-colored hands receiving pain, but did not show such modulation when witnessing other-group hands in pain. Using the same paradigm with fMRI and pupil dilatation measures as an index of autonomic reactivity, another group (Azevedo, Macaluso, & Avenanti, 2013) found that same-race pain led to increased activity in the aIC and increased autonomic responses. Furthermore, this race effect is correlated with implicit racial bias measures (Avenanti et al., 2010; Azevedo et al., 2013) and self-reported measures of identification with one's group (Mathur, Harada, & Chiao, 2011).

A few studies have shown how the shared representation for pain and touch can be deliberately changed. The use of a short perspective-taking cognitive intervention was able to lower racial bias during a pain discrimination task in nurses and non-health professionals (Drwecki, Moore, Ward, & Prkachin, 2011). Another study showed a reduction in racial disparities during witnessing pain in others when participants were given intranasal injections of oxytocin, a molecule known to act on the perception of social cues (Shamay-Tsoory et al., 2013). While the use of pharmacological agents represents a simple way to manipulate sharing responses experimentally, the relationship between one molecule and shared representations is no doubt being mediated by countless factors, including individual and contextual factors (Bartz, Zaki, Bolger, & Ochsner, 2011). Another potential way to modulate sharing responses is through the use of non-invasive brain stimulation techniques such as TMS and transcranial direct current stimulation that can be applied to different cortical systems in order to enhance or reduce activity in regions associated with shared representations (see Hétu, Taschereau-Dumouchel, & Jackson, 2012). All of these manipulations, be they cognitive, pharmacological or neurostimulation, could have potential benefits in populations showing deficits in social interactions and social perception. However, with the increasing availability of such techniques, ethical and social questions arise (see Box 4.3).

Box 4.3 Questions for future research

- Do overlapping neural activations during touch and pain experience and observations still hold when using sub-voxel resolution neuroimaging techniques?
- Are shared representations for pain and touch specific to observation of these experiences or can observation of other emotional or sensory experience involve a similar system?
- How does a shared representations system interact with other neural networks to produce adaptive social behavior in real-life interactions?
- Can non-invasive brain stimulation techniques or psychopharmacological interventions be used to increase shared representations activity and provide treatment for disorders showing shared representations deficits?
- Should potential future empathy-enhancing interventions be restricted to people with deficits compared to normative data or could some populations (and society) benefit from increased empathy in 'typical individuals'?

Conclusion

We have shown a wealth of evidence supporting the hypothesis that we use our own representations of pain and touch in order to perceive and understand these same stimulations in others. The study of factors modulating these shared representations allows us to understand which factors can promote or hinder this sharing and that these modulations can represent adaptive or non-adaptive mechanisms.

However, numerous questions remain and future research is needed to improve our understanding of shared representations (see Box 4.3). Indeed, most research on shared representations until now has used controlled, often passive, observation of pain and touch in others. Future studies should therefore aim to increase the ecological validity of those findings by studying shared representations in dynamic social contexts and probe further the pro-social (behavioral) response toward others. Furthermore, with the advent of non-invasive brain stimulations, clinical studies should focus on how this approach could represent a tool to modulate shared representations in conditions where excessive or insufficient sharing can lead to affective and behavioral symptoms (see Box 4.3).

References

Akitsuki, Y., & Decety, J. (2009). Social context and perceived agency affects empathy for pain: An event-related fMRI investigation. *NeuroImage*, 47(2), 722–734.

Arnstein, D., Cui, F., Keysers, C., Maurits, N. M., & Gazzola, V. (2011). μ-suppression during action observation and execution correlates with BOLD in dorsal premotor, inferior parietal, and SI cortices. *Journal of Neuroscience*, 31(40), 14243–14249.

Avenanti, A., Bueti, D., Galati, G., & Aglioti, S. M. (2005). Transcranial magnetic stimulation highlights the sensorimotor side of empathy for pain. *Nature Neuroscience*, 8(7), 955–960.

Avenanti, A., Minio-Paluello, I., Bufalari, I., & Aglioti, S. M. (2009). The pain of a model in the personality of an onlooker: Influence of state-reactivity and personality traits on embodied empathy for pain. *NeuroImage*, 44(1), 275–283.

Avenanti, A., Sirigu, A., & Aglioti, S. M. (2010). Racial bias reduces empathic sensorimotor resonance with other-race pain. *Current Biology*, 20(11), 1018–1022.

Azevedo, R. T., Macaluso, E., & Avenanti, A. (2013). Their pain is not our pain: Brain and autonomic correlates of empathic resonance with the pain of same and different race individuals. *Human Brain Mapping*, 34(12), 3168–3181.

Baldissera, F., Cavallari, P., Craighero, L., & Fadiga, L. (2001). Modulation of spinal excitability during observation of hand actions in humans. *European Journal of Neuroscience*, 13(1), 190–194.

Banissy, M. J., Kadosh, R. C., Maus, G. W., Walsh, V., & Ward, J. (2009). Prevalence, characteristics and a neurocognitive model of mirror–touch synaesthesia. *Experimental Brain Research*, 198(2–3), 261–272.

Banissy, M. J., & Ward, J. (2007). Mirror–touch synesthesia is linked with empathy. *Nature Neuroscience*, 10(7), 815–816.

Baron-Cohen, S., & Wheelwright, S. (2004). The empathy quotient: An investigation of adults with Asperger syndrome or high functioning autism, and normal sex differences. *Journal of Autism and Developmental Disorders*, 34(2), 163–175.

Bartz, J. A., Zaki, J., Bolger, N., & Ochsner, K. N. (2011). Social effects of oxytocin in humans: Context and person matter. *Trends in Cognitive Sciences*, 7, 301–309.

Bird, G., Silani, G., Brindley, R., White, S., Frith, U., & Singer, T. (2010). Empathic brain responses in insula are modulated by levels of alexithymia but not autism. *Brain*, 133(5), 1515–1525.

Björnsdotter, M., Löken, L., Olausson, H., Vallbo, A., & Wessberg, J. (2009). Somatotopic organization of gentle touch processing in the posterior insular cortex. *Journal of Neuroscience*, 29(29), 9314–9320.

Blakemore, S. J., Bristow, D., Bird, G., Frith, C., & Ward, J. (2005). Somatosensory activations during the observation of touch and a case of vision–touch synaesthesia. *Brain*, 128(7), 1571–1583.

Blumenstiel, K., Gerhardt, A., Rolke, R., Bieber, C., Tesarz, J., et al. (2011). Quantitative sensory testing profiles in chronic back pain are distinct from those in fibromyalgia. *Clinical Journal of Pain*, 27(8), 682–690.

Bolognini, N., Miniussi, C., Gallo, S., & Vallar, G. (2013). Induction of mirror–touch synaesthesia by increasing somatosensory cortical excitability. *Current Biology*, 23(10), R436–R437.

Borsook, D., & Becerra, L. (2009). Emotional pain without sensory pain: Dream on? *Neuron*, 61(2), 153–155.

Botvinick, M., Jha, A. P., Bylsma, L. M., Fabian, S. A., Solomon, P. E., & Prkachin, K. M. (2005). Viewing facial expressions of pain engages cortical areas involved in the direct experience of pain. *NeuroImage*, 25(1), 312–319.

Bromm, B., & Treede, R. D. (1980). Withdrawal reflex, skin resistance reaction and pain ratings due to electrical stimuli in man. *Pain*, 9(3), 339–354.

Budell, L., Jackson, P., & Rainville, P. (2010). Brain responses to facial expressions of pain: Emotional or motor mirroring? *NeuroImage*, 53(1), 355–363.

Bufalari, I., Aprile, T., Avenanti, A., Di Russo, F., & Aglioti, S. M. (2007). Empathy for pain and touch in the human somatosensory cortex. *Cerebral Cortex*, 17(11), 2553–2561.

Bushnell, M. C., & Apkarian, A. V. (2006). Representation of pain in the brain. In S. B. McMahon & M. Koltzenburg (Eds.), *Wall and Melzack's textbook of pain*. Philadelphia, PA: Elsevier, 107–124.

Cacioppo, S., Frum, C., Asp, E., Weiss, R. M., Lewis, J. W., & Cacioppo, J. T. (2013). A quantitative meta-analysis of functional imaging studies of social rejection. *Scientific Reports*, 3, 2027.

Cheng, Y., Lin, C.-P., Liu, H.-L., Hsu, Y.-Y., Lim, K.-E., et al. (2007). Expertise modulates the perception of pain in others. *Current Biology*, 17(19), 1708–1713.

Cheng, Y., Yang, C. Y., Lin, C. P., Lee, P. L., & Decety, J. (2008). The perception of pain in others suppresses somatosensory oscillations: A magnetoencephalography study. *NeuroImage*, 40(4), 1833–1840.

Cheyne, D., Gaetz, W., Garnero, L., Lachaux, J.-P., Ducorps, A., et al. (2003). Neuromagnetic imaging of cortical oscillations accompanying tactile stimulation. *Cognitive Brain Research*, 17(3), 599–611.

Chong, T. T. J., Cunnington, R., Williams, M. A., Kanwisher, N., & Mattingley, J. B. (2008). fMRI adaptation reveals mirror neurons in human inferior parietal cortex. *Current Biology*, 18(20), 1576–1580.

Coll, M.-P., Budell, L., Rainville, P., Decety, J., & Jackson, P. L. (2012). The role of gender in the interaction between self-pain and the perception of pain in others. *Journal of Pain*, 13(7), 695–703.

Coll, M.-P., Grégoire, M., Latimer, M., Eugène, F., & Jackson, P. L. (2011). Perception of pain in others: Implication for caregivers. *Pain Management*, 1(3), 257–265.

Corradi-Dell'Acqua, C., Hofstetter, C., & Vuilleumier, P. (2011). Felt and seen pain evoke the same local patterns of cortical activity in insular and cingulate cortex. *Journal of Neuroscience*, 31(49), 17996–18006.

Costantini, M., Galati, G., Romani, G. L., & Aglioti, S. M. (2008). Empathic neural reactivity to noxious stimuli delivered to body parts and non-corporeal objects. *European Journal of Neuroscience*, 28(6), 1222–1230.

Danziger, N., Faillenot, I., & Peyron, R. (2009). Can we share a pain we never felt? Neural correlates of empathy in patients with congenital insensitivity to pain. *Neuron*, 61(2), 203–212.

Danziger, N., Prkachin, K. M., & Willer, J. C. (2006). Is pain the price of empathy? The perception of others' pain in patients with congenital insensitivity to pain. *Brain*, 129(9), 2494–2507.

Davis, M. H. (1980). A multidimensional approach to individual differences in empathy. *JSAS Catalog of Selected Documents in Psychology*, 10, 85.

(1983). Measuring individual differences in empathy: Evidence for a multidimensional approach. *Journal of Personality and Social Psychology*, 44(1), 113–126.

(1996). *Empathy: A social psychological approach*. Madison, WI: Westview Press.

Decety, J. (2004). The functional architecture of human empathy. *Behavioral and Cognitive Neuroscience Reviews*, 3(2), 71–100.

(2010). To what extent is the experience of empathy mediated by shared neural circuits? *Emotion Review*, 2(3), 204–207.

Decety, J., & Sommerville, J. A. (2003). Shared representations between self and other: A social cognitive neuroscience view. *Trends in Cognitive Sciences*, 7(12), 527–533.

Decety, J., Yang, C.-Y., & Cheng, Y. (2010). Physicians down-regulate their pain empathy response: An event-related brain potential study. *NeuroImage*, 50(4), 1676–1682.

Drwecki, B. B., Moore, C. F., Ward, S. E., & Prkachin, K. M. (2011). Reducing racial disparities in pain treatment: The role of empathy and perspective-taking. *Pain*, 152(5), 1001–1006.

Ebisch, S. J. H., Ferri, F., Salone, A., Perrucci, M. G., D'Amico, L., et al. (2011). Differential involvement of somatosensory and interoceptive cortices during the observation of affective touch. *Journal of Cognitive Neuroscience*, 23(7), 1808–1822.

Ebisch, S. J. H., Perrucci, M. G., Ferretti, A., Del Gratta, C., Romani, G. L., & Gallese, V. (2008). The sense of touch: Embodied simulation in a visuotactile mirroring mechanism for observed animate or inanimate touch. *Journal of Cognitive Neuroscience*, 20(9), 1611–1623.

Eisenberger, N. I. (2012). The neural bases of social pain: Evidence for shared representations with physical pain. *Psychosomatic Medicine*, 74(2), 126–135.

Eisenberger, N. I., & Cole, S. W. (2012). Social neuroscience and health: Neurophysiological mechanisms linking social ties with physical health. *Nature Neuroscience*, 15(5), 669–674.

Eisenberger, N. I., Lieberman, M. D., & Williams, K. D. (2003). Does rejection hurt? An fMRI study of social exclusion. *Science*, 302(5643), 290–292.

Fecteau, S., Pascual-Leone, A., & Théoret, H. (2008). Psychopathy and the mirror neuron system: Preliminary findings from a non-psychiatric sample. *Psychiatry Research*, 160(2), 137–144.

Fitzgibbon, B. M., Enticott, P. G., Rich, A. N., Giummarra, M. J., Georgiou-Karistianis, N., & Bradshaw, J. L. (2012). Mirror-sensory synaesthesia: Exploring 'shared' sensory experiences as synaesthesia. *Neuroscience & Biobehavioral Reviews*, 36(1), 645–657. (2010a). High incidence of 'synaesthesia for pain' in amputees. *Neuropsychologia*, 48(12), 3675–3678.

Fitzgibbon, B. M., Giummarra, M. J., Georgiou-Karistianis, N., Enticott, P. G., & Bradshaw, J. L. (2010b). Shared pain: From empathy to synaesthesia. *Neuroscience & Biobehavioral Reviews*, 34(4), 500–512.

Gaetz, W., & Cheyne, D. (2006). Localization of sensorimotor cortical rhythms induced by tactile stimulation using spatially filtered MEG. *NeuroImage*, 30(3), 899–908.

Gallese, V., Fadiga, L., Fogassi, L., & Rizzolatti, G. (1996). Action recognition in the premotor cortex. *Brain*, 119(2), 593–609.

Garcia-Larrea, L., Frot, M., & Valeriani, M. (2003). Brain generators of laser-evoked potentials: From dipoles to functional significance. *Neurophysiologie clinique/Clinical Neurophysiology*, 33(6), 279–292 .

Garcia-Larrea, L., & Peyron, R. (2013). Pain matrices and neuropathic pain matrices: A review. *Pain*, 154, S29–S43.

Gazzola, V., Aziz-Zadeh, L., & Keysers, C. (2006). Empathy and the somatotopic auditory mirror system in humans. *Current Biology*, 16(18), 1824–1829.

Gazzola, V., Spezio, M. I., Etzel, J. A., Castelli, F., Adolphs, R., & Keysers, C. (2012). Primary somatosensory cortex discriminates affective significance in social touch. *Proceedings of the National Academy of Sciences*, 109(25), E1657–E1666.

Godinho, F., Faillenot, I., Perchet, C., Frot, M., Magnin, M., & Garcia-Larrea, L. (2011). How the pain of others enhances our pain: Searching the cerebral correlates of 'compassional hyperalgesia'. *European Journal of Pain*, 16(5), 748–759.

Godinho, F., Magnin, M., Frot, M., Perchet, C., & Garcia-Larrea, L. (2006). Emotional modulation of pain: Is it the sensation or what we recall? *Journal of Neuroscience*, 26(44), 11454–11461.

Gracely, R. H., Geisser, M. E., Giesecke, T., Grant, M. A. B., Petzke, F., et al. (2004). Pain catastrophizing and neural responses to pain among persons with fibromyalgia. *Brain*, 127(4), 835–843.

Hari, R., Forss, N., Avikainen, S., Kirveskari, E., Salenius, S., & Rizzolatti, G. (1998). Activation of human primary motor cortex during action observation: A neuromagnetic study. *Proceedings of the National Academy of Sciences*, 95(25), 15061–15065.

Hein, G., Silani, G., Preuschoff, K., Batson, C. D., & Singer, T. (2010). Neural responses to ingroup and outgroup members' suffering predict individual differences in costly helping. *Neuron*, 68(1), 149–160.

Hétu, S., Taschereau-Dumouchel, V., & Jackson, P. L. (2012). Stimulating the brain to study social interactions and empathy. *Brain Stimulation*, 5(2), 95–102.

Höfle, M., Pomper, U., Hauck, M., & Engel, A. K. (2013). Spectral signatures of viewing a needle approaching one's body when anticipating pain. *European Journal of Neuroscience*, 38(7), 3089–3098.

Iacoboni, M., & Dapretto, M. (2006). The mirror neuron system and the consequences of its dysfunction. *Nature Reviews Neuroscience*, 7(12), 942–951.

Iannetti, G. D., & Mouraux, A. (2010). From the neuromatrix to the pain matrix (and back). *Experimental Brain Research*, 205(1), 1–12.

Iannetti, G. D., Salomons, T. V., Moayedi, M., Mouraux, A., & Davis, K. D. (2013). Beyond metaphor: Contrasting mechanisms of social and physical pain. *Trends in Cognitive Sciences*, 17(8), 371–378.

International Association for the Study of Pain. (1994). *Classification of chronic pain*, 2nd edition. Seattle: IASP Press.

Jackson, P. L., Brunet, E., Meltzoff, A. N., & Decety, J. (2006). Empathy examined through the neural mechanisms involved in imagining how I feel versus how you feel pain. *Neuropsychologia*, 44(5), 752–761.

Jackson, P. L., Meltzoff, A. N., & Decety, J. (2005). How do we perceive the pain of others? A window into the neural processes involved in empathy. *NeuroImage*, 24(3), 771–779.

Jensen, K. B., Petrovic, P., Kerr, C. E., Kirsch, I., Raicek, J., et al. (2013). Sharing pain and relief: Neural correlates of physicians during treatment of patients. *Molecular Psychiatry*, 1–7, 392–398.

Keysers, C., Kaas, J. H., & Gazzola, V. (2010). Somatosensation in social perception. *Nature Reviews Neuroscience*, 11(6), 417–428.

Keysers, C., Wicker, B., Gazzola, V., Anton, J.-L., Fogassi, L., & Gallese, V. (2004). A touching sight. *Neuron*, 42(2), 335–346.

Kilner, J. M., Neal, A., Weiskopf, N., Friston, K. J., & Frith, C. D. (2009). Evidence of mirror neurons in human inferior frontal gyrus. *Journal of Neuroscience*, 29(32), 10153–10159.

Krishnan, A., Woo, CW., Chang, L. J., Ruzic, L., Gu, X., López-Solà, M., et al. (2016). Somatic and vicarious pain are represented by dissociable multivariate brain patterns. *Elife*, Jun 14(5), pii: e15166.

Kross, E., Berman, M. G., Mischel, W., Smith, E. E., & Wager, T. D. (2011). Social rejection shares somatosensory representations with physical pain. *Proceedings of the National Academy of Sciences*, 108(15), 6270–6275.

Kuehn, E., Mueller, K., Turner, R., & Schütz-Bosbach, S. (2014). The functional architecture of S1 during touch observation described with 7 T fMRI. *Brain Structure & Function*, 219(1), 119–140.

Kuehn, E., Trampel, R., Mueller, K., Turner, R., & Schütz-Bosbach, S. (2013). Judging roughness by sight: A 7-tesla fMRI study on responsivity of the primary somatosensory cortex during observed touch of self and others. *Human Brain Mapping*, 34(8), 1882–1895.

Lamm, C., Batson, C. D., & Decety, J. (2007). The neural substrate of human empathy: Effects of perspective-taking and cognitive appraisal. *Journal of Cognitive Neuroscience*, 19(1), 42–58.

Lamm, C., Decety, J., & Singer, T. (2011). Meta-analytic evidence for common and distinct neural networks associated with directly experienced pain and empathy for pain. *NeuroImage*, 54(3), 2492–2502.

Lawrence, E. J., Shaw, P., Giampietro, V. P., & Surguladze, S. (2006). The role of 'shared representations' in social perception and empathy: An fMRI study. *NeuroImage*, 29(4), 1173–1184.

Lee, S. J., Song, H. J., Decety, J., Seo, J., Kim, S. H., et al. (2013). Do patients with fibromyalgia show abnormal neural responses to the observation of pain in others? *Neuroscience Research*, 4, 305–315.

Loggia, M. L., Juneau, M., & Bushnell, M. C. (2011). Autonomic responses to heat pain: Heart rate, skin conductance, and their relation to verbal ratings and stimulus intensity. *Pain*, 152(3), 592–598.

Loggia, M. L., Mogil, J. S., & Bushnell, M. C. (2008). Empathy hurts: Compassion for another increases both sensory and affective components of pain perception. *Pain*, 136(1–2), 168–176.

Lucy, P., Cohn, J. F., Prkachin, K. M., Solomon, P., & Matthrews, I. (2011). Painful data: The UNBC-McMaster Shoulder Pain Expression Archive Database. IEEE International Conference on Automatic Face and Gesture Recognition (FG2011).

Mailhot, J. P., Vachon-Presseau, E., Jackson, P. L., & Rainville, P. (2012). Dispositional empathy modulates vicarious effects of dynamic pain expressions on spinal nociception, facial responses and acute pain. *European Journal of Neuroscience*, 35(2), 271–278.

Malinen, S., Renvall, V., & Hari, R. (2014). Functional parcellation of the human primary somatosensory cortex to natural touch. *European Journal of Neuroscience*, 5, 738–743.

Marcoux, L. A., Michon, P. E., Voisin, J. I., Lemelin, S., Vachon-Presseau, E., & Jackson, P. L. (2013). The modulation of somatosensory resonance by psychopathic traits and empathy. *Frontiers in Human Neuroscience*, 7, 1–13.

Martínez-Jauand, M., González-Roldán, A. M., Muñoz, M. A., Sitges, C., Cifre, I., & Montoya, P. (2012). Somatosensory activity modulation during observation of other's pain and touch. *Brain Research*, 1467, 48–55.

Masten, C. L., Morelli, S. A., & Eisenberger, N. I. (2011). An fMRI investigation of empathy for 'social pain' and subsequent prosocial behavior. *NeuroImage*, 55(1), 381–388.

Mathur, V. A., Harada, T., & Chiao, J. Y. (2011). Racial identification modulates default network activity for same and other races. *Human Brain Mapping*, 33(8), 1883–1893.

Melzack, R., & Casey, K. L. (1968). Sensory, motivational and central control determinants of pain: A new conceptual model. In D. Kenshalo (Ed.), *The skin senses*. Springfield, IL: Charles C Thomas, 423–439.

Meng, J., Hu, L., Shen, L., Yang, Z., Chen, H., et al. (2012). Emotional primes modulate the responses to others' pain: An ERP study. *Experimental Brain Research*, 220(3–4), 277–286.

Meng, J., Jackson, T., Chen, H., Hu, L., Yang, Z., et al. (2013). Pain perception in the self and observation of others: An ERP investigation. *NeuroImage*, 72, 164–173.

Morrison, I., Bjornsdotter, M., & Olausson, H. (2011a). Vicarious responses to social touch in posterior insular cortex are tuned to pleasant caressing speeds. *Journal of Neuroscience*, 31(26), 9554–9562.

Morrison, I., Löken, L. S., Minde, J., Wessberg, J., Perini, I., et al. (2011b). Reduced C-afferent fibre density affects perceived pleasantness and empathy for touch. *Brain*, 134(4), 1116–1126.

Mukamel, R., Ekstrom, A. D., Kaplan, J., Iacoboni, M., & Fried, I. (2010). Single-neuron responses in humans during execution and observation of actions. *Current Biology*, 20(8), 750–756.

Muthukumaraswamy, S. D., & Johnson, B. W. (2004). Changes in rolandic mu rhythm during observation of a precision grip. *Psychophysiology*, 41(1), 152–156.

Novembre, G., Zanon, M., & Silani, G. (2014). Empathy for social exclusion involves the sensory-discriminative component of pain: A within-subject fMRI study. *Social Cognitive and Affective Neuroscience*. doi: 10.1093/scan/nsu038.

Oosterhof, N. N., Tipper, S. P., & Downing, P. E. (2013). Crossmodal and action-specific: Neuroimaging the human mirror neuron system. *Trends in Cognitive Sciences*, 17(7), 311–318.

Osborn, J., & Derbyshire, S. W. G. (2010). Pain sensation evoked by observing injury in others. *Pain*, 148(2), 268–274.

Pellegrino, G., Fadiga, L., Fogassi, L., Gallese, V., & Rizzolatti, G. (1992). Understanding motor events: A neurophysiological study. *Experimental Brain Research*, 91(1), 176–180.

Perry, A., Bentin, S., Bartal, I. B.-A., Lamm, C., & Decety, J. (2010). 'Feeling' the pain of those who are different from us: Modulation of EEG in the mu/alpha range. *Cognitive, Affective & Behavioral Neuroscience*, 10(4), 493–504.

Pihko, E., Nangini, C., Jousmäki, V., & Hari, R. (2010). Observing touch activates human primary somatosensory cortex. *European Journal of Neuroscience*, 31(10), 1836–1843.

Pineda, J. A. (2005). The functional significance of mu rhythms: Translating 'seeing' and 'hearing' into 'doing'. *Brain Research Reviews*, 50(1), 57–68.

Press, C., Weiskopf, N., & Kilner, J. M. (2012). Dissociable roles of human inferior frontal gyrus during action execution and observation. *NeuroImage*, 60(3), 1671–1677.

Price, D. D. (2000). Psychological and neural mechanisms of the affective dimension of pain. *Science*, 288(5472), 1769–1772.

Rainville, P. (1997). Pain affect encoded in human anterior cingulate but not somatosensory cortex. *Science*, 277(5328), 968–971.

(2002). Brain mechanisms of pain affect and pain modulation. *Current Opinion in Neurobiology*, 12(2), 195–204.

Ritter, P., Moosmann, M., & Villringer, A. (2009). Rolandic alpha and beta EEG rhythms' strengths are inversely related to fMRI-BOLD signal in primary somatosensory and motor cortex. *Human Brain Mapping*, 30(4), 1168–1187.

Rossetti, A., Miniussi, C., Maravita, A., & Bolognini, N. (2012). Visual perception of bodily interactions in the primary somatosensory cortex. *European Journal of Neuroscience*, 36(3), 2317–2323.

Rossi, S., Tecchio, F., Pasqualetti, P., Ulivelli, M., Pizzella, V., et al. (2002). Somatosensory processing during movement observation in humans. *Clinical Neurophysiology*, 113(1), 16–24.

Saarela, M. V., Hlushchuk, Y., Williams, A. C., Schürmann, M., Kalso, E., & Hari, R. (2007). The compassionate brain: Humans detect intensity of pain from another's face. *Cerebral Cortex*, 17(1), 230–237.

Schaefer, M., Heinze, H. J., & Rotte, M. (2012). Embodied empathy for tactile events: Interindividual differences and vicarious somatosensory responses during touch observation. *NeuroImage*, 60(2), 952–957.

Schaefer, M., Xu, B., Flor, H., & Cohen, L. G. (2009). Effects of different viewing per-spectives on somatosensory activations during observation of touch. *Human Brain Mapping*, 30(9), 2722–2730.

Shamay-Tsoory, S. G., Abu-Akel, A., Palgi, S., Sulieman, R., Fischer-Shofty, M., et al. (2013). Giving peace a chance: Oxytocin increases empathy to pain in the context of the Israeli–Palestinian conflict. *Psychoneuroendocrinology*, 38(12), 3139–3144.

Simon, D., Craig, K. D., Miltner, W. H. R., & Rainville, P. (2006). Brain responses to dynamic facial expressions of pain. *Pain*, 126(1–3), 309–318.

Singer, T. (2004). Empathy for pain involves the affective but not sensory components of pain. *Science*, 303(5661), 1157–1162.

Singer, T., Seymour, B., O'Doherty, J. P., Stephan, K. E., Dolan, R. J., & Frith, C. D. (2006). Empathic neural responses are modulated by the perceived fairness of oth-ers. *Nature*, 439(7075), 466–469.

Sperry, R. W. (1952). Neurology and the mind–body problem. *American Scientist*, 40, 291–312.

Strafella, A. P., & Paus, T. (2000). Modulation of cortical excitability during action observation: A transcranial magnetic stimulation study. *NeuroReport*, 11(10), 2289–2292.

Streltsova, A., & McCleery, J. P. (2014). Neural time-course of the observation of human and non-human object touch. *Social Cognitive and Affective Neuroscience*, 9(3), 333–341.

Vachon-Presseau, E., Martel, M. O., Roy, M., Caron, E., Jackson, P. L., & Rainville, P. (2011). The multilevel organization of vicarious pain responses: Effects of pain cues and empathy traits on spinal nociception and acute pain. *Pain*, 152(7), 1525–1531.

Vachon-Presseau, E., Roy, M., Martel, M. O., Albouy, G., Chen, J., et al. (2012). Neural processing of sensory and emotional-communicative information associated with the perception of vicarious pain. *NeuroImage*, 63(1), 54–62.

Valeriani, M., Betti, V., Le Pera, D., De Armas, L., & Miliucci, R. (2008). Seeing the pain of others while being in pain: A laser-evoked potentials study. *NeuroImage*, 40(3), 1419–1428.

Voisin, J. I. A., Marcoux, L.-A., Canizales, D. L., Mercier, C., & Jackson, P. L. (2011). I am touched by your pain: Limb-specific modulation of the cortical response to a tactile stimulation during pain observation. *Journal of Pain*, 12(11), 1182–1189.

Wager, T. D., Atlas, L. Y., Lindquist, M. A., Roy, M., Woo, C. W., & Kross, E. (2013). An fMRI-based neurologic signature of physical pain. *New England Journal of Medicine*, 368(15), 1388–1397.

Wied, M. de, & Verbaten, M. N. (2001). Affective pictures processing, attention, and pain tolerance. *Pain*, 90(1–2), 163–172.

Xu, X., Zuo, X., Wang, X., & Han, S. (2009). Do you feel my pain? Racial group mem-bership modulates empathic neural responses. *Journal of Neuroscience*, 29(26), 8525–8529.

Yang, C. Y., Decety, J., Lee, S., Chen, C., & Cheng, Y. (2009). Gender differences in the mu rhythm during empathy for pain: An electroencephalographic study. *Brain Research*, 1251, 176–184.

Zaki, J., Ochsner, K. N., Hanelin, J., Wager, T. D., & Mackey, S. C. (2007). Different cir-cuits for different pain: Patterns of functional connectivity reveal distinct networks for processing pain in self and others. *Social Neuroscience*, 2(3–4), 276–291.

Glossary

Affective-motivational dimension of pain The dimension of pain experience that refers to the unpleasantness of felt pain as well as accompanying emotions and implications for future events.

Empathy The capacity to adopt others' perspectives and to share their emotional state while maintaining a distinction between one's own state and the state observed in others.

Mirror–pain/Mirror–touch synaesthesia A developmental or acquired condition in which individuals report that observing touch (mirror–touch synaesthesia) or pain (mirror–pain synaesthesia) in others automatically triggers the same experience in themselves.

Sensory-discriminative dimension of pain The dimension of the pain experience that encompasses the physical properties of pain, such as localisation, intensity and quality.

5 Cognizance of the Neuroimaging Methods for Studying the Social Brain

Stephanie Cacioppo and John T. Cacioppo

Abstract

A key challenge in the study of the social brain resides not only in determining how psychological states and processes map onto patterns of brain activity but also how this activity is modulated by shared representations, social compositions and social behaviors. The past 20 years have seen the growth of neuroimaging methods for studying neural aspects of shared representations, embodied cognition and the social brain in normal, waking humans. We discuss the intimate relationship between theory and methods; we discuss a set of considerations to guide the interpretation or understanding of data from neuroimaging studies; and we discuss the importance of using converging methods to dissect the social brain.

In 1924, Albert Einstein extended physicist Satyendra Bose's work and predicted that some subatomic particles (bosons) can be attracted to one another in a specific context (below a certain critical temperature), while other subatomic particles (fermions) tend to avoid each other. The requisite methods to produce temperatures low enough to test Einstein's prediction were not available at that time, however. The study of subatomic particles along the attraction-to-repulsion continuum depended on the development of novel techniques (e.g. laser cooling) that did not become available for another seven decades. In 1995, Wieman and Cornell were the first scientists to test and verify Einstein's theory on the Bose–Einstein condensation for which they, along with MIT physicist Ketterle, received the Nobel Prize in 2001.

There are strong, reciprocal ties between theory and methods. The importance of methods and of the development of technology that allow the parsing of component processes and the specification of mechanisms across various levels of organization are critical in all sciences (e.g. physics, chemistry, astronomy and social neuroscience) investigating complex behaviors, such as

Preparation of this chapter was supported by the Defense Medical Research and Development Program Grant No. W81XWH-11-2-0114 to JTC.

those underlying principles of physical and/or social attraction. In addition, the available methods shape the data we collect and therefore affect the information we can gather about a phenomenon. As Einstein demonstrated, however, theory can also permit one to reach beyond the available data, and even beyond the available methods, to depict a phenomenon in ways that motivate the development of new methods.

In addition to rigorous theories, a scientist's intuition or common beliefs about that phenomenon may also shape both the methods used to investigate a phenomenon and the theoretical position that the resulting evidence is said to support. The influence of cultural beliefs and commonsense notions on the methods that scientists use might be thought to be unique to the human sciences, but this issue was first raised in 1939 by astrophysicist Sir Arthur Eddington, in his book, *The Philosophy of the Physical Sciences*. Earlier still, French physician and neuroanatomist Paul Broca (1824–1880) proposed brain size as a scientifically rigorous measure of intelligence, and reportedly found that the skulls of prehistoric hominids had smaller brain capacities than those of contemporary humans. Broca also reported that the brains of women were smaller than those of men (without correcting for body size), which he interpreted as support for the cultural stereotype in France at the time that women were less intelligent than men. Broca's interpretation remained a rooted scientific position until English statistician Francis Galton (1822–1911) and then French psychologist Alfred Binet (1857–1911) pioneered standardized behavioral approaches to intelligence testing.

Both Galton's and Binet's methods had limitations. Galton and Binet had access only to a limited range of technology at that time. As a consequence, when Galton set up his 'anthropometric laboratory' in 1884 to study the inheritance of mental skills and measure character, he first focused on correlational investigations between mental skills and simple physical traits (such as height), as he did not have access to other tools to measure mental skills (Holt, 2005). Over the years, Galton benefited from 'new process of inquiry yearly invented' in the psychometrics of mental skills and emotional temperament. His understanding of mental skills thus grew with the development of technology. Galton moved from mastering methods of observation to studying of twins and to performing introspective research. Theory and methods are intimately connected.

Since the nineteenth century, further advances have been made in the development of methods allowing investigators to better grasp the complexity of brain functions that manifest at very different levels of organization, ranging from networks of computations and information-processing operations (e.g. attention, memory) to behavior in a social context (e.g. mother–infant attachment, communication). The integrative, interdisciplinary field of social neuroscience emerged as electrical neuroimaging procedures were burgeoning, and human lesion studies, comparative research and animal models began to focus more on the biological basis of social structures and processes. For instance, since the first EEG reports in 1929 by the German psychiatrist Hans Berger, who provided a new psychiatric and neurologic diagnostic tool at the time, significant progress has been made in the investigation of brain functions, including several advances in the understanding of a broad variety of social brain functions (Cacioppo et al., 2000; Davidson et al., 2000; Luck, 2005; Ibanez et al., 2012). These advances include (but are not restricted to) (for review, see Ibanez et al., 2012) attitudes and evaluative processes (Cacioppo & Petty, 1979; Cacioppo et al., 1994; Cacioppo, Crites, & Gardner, 1996; Crites & Cacioppo, 1996), emotional processing (e.g. Cacioppo, Petty, & Snyder, 1979; Ekman, Davidson, & Friesen, 1990; Ortigue et al., 2004), persuasion (e.g. Cacioppo, Petty, & Quintanar, 1982), morality (e.g. Decety & Cacioppo, 2012) and love (e.g. Birbaumer et al., 1993; Cacioppo, Grafton, & Bianchi-Demicheli, 2012).

The growth of social neuroscience over the past two decades has been fuelled not only by research using these methods but also by the development of technology and methods such as functional magnetic resonance imaging (fMRI), transcranial magnetic stimulation, and an array of methods from genetics and molecular biology (Cacioppo, Cacioppo, Dulawa, & Palmer, 2014b).

The Perspective of Social Neuroscience on the Brain

When the term 'social neuroscience' was introduced in 1992 and characterized as the study of the transduction pathways between the various biological and social levels of organization (Cacioppo & Berntson, 1992), the dominant perspective for examining the brain was the solitary computer. The human brain, after all, was thought to be an information-processing organ, and the primary information-processing device at the time was the desktop computer. The perspective of cognitive neuroscience, as it emerged at that point in time, reflected the focus on the brain as a solitary computer. The notion of investigating the human brain by stepping back to consider theoretically or investigate empirically how that brain relates to other brains was different and was understandably met with some skepticism. The fact is, though, that members of social species, by definition, create organizations beyond the individual. These superorganismal structures evolved hand in hand with behavioral, neural, hormonal, cellular and molecular mechanisms to support them. In turn, the consequent social behaviors helped these organisms survive, reproduce and – in the case of mammals – care for offspring sufficiently long that they too reproduced, thereby ensuring their genetic legacy. Social neuroscience seeks to specify the neural, hormonal, cellular and genetic mechanisms underlying social behavior, and in so doing to understand the associations and influences between social and biological levels of organization (Cacioppo et al., 2001; Stanley & Adolphs, 2013).

Although social neuroscience and cognitive neuroscience both focus on the relationship between behavior and brain networks, social neuroscience is not simply cognitive neuroscience with social stimuli. Social neuroscience views the social brain as a mobile, broadband connected information-processing device. For instance, from the perspective of cognitive neuroscience, language can be viewed as a system for representation and processing of information; from the perspective of social neuroscience, language is a system for information exchange between brains, a system that promotes connection, communication and coordination across discrete and sometimes distant brains. Accordingly, social neuroscience examines how behavior fits into and is affected by social structures that exist beyond the individual, including the study of shared representations in the social brain (see Box 5.1). Cognitive and social neuroscience utilize many of the same technologies (e.g. fMRI), but the differences in these complementary perspectives manifest in subtle but important differences in paradigms, experimental design and statistical analyses.

Box 5.1 Shared representations

The concept of shared representations rests on the premise that close partners or close mates develop a 'transactive' mental representation of their self while acting together or sharing life experience – a mental representation that calls for cognitive interdependence and includes a structure of stored information across the two individuals (Juan et al., 2013; Ortigue et al., 2010; Wegner, Giuliano, & Hertel, 1985;). Cognitive interdependence in dyads relates to the concept of inclusion of the other in the self-mental representation – a concept that is closely tied to the processes of self-expansion and embodied cognition. Accordingly, individuals can share their feelings and understandings by using verbal and non-verbal cues (Hari & Kujala, 2009), such as kinematics, facial expressions, postures and/or silence. Although many mental representations are not shared, the model of shared representation highlights the extent to which close others may implicitly read and influence our perceptions of their actions, emotions, desires and intentions. Accordingly, cognitive interdependence can provide a processing advantage during anticipatory representations of others' behaviors (Aglioti et al., 2008; Niedenthal, 2007; Niedenthal et al., 2005; Ortigue et al., 2009, 2010; Ruscher, Santuzzi, & Hammer, 2003).

The understanding of shared representations among individuals is challenging because it dives into the hard problem of the mutual influence of biology and social mechanisms– a problem described by Frith and Wolpert (2004) as one of the major problems for the neurosciences to address in the twenty-first century. To help understand the consideration of the methods, paradigms and designs that have been brought to bear on this problem, we summarize in Box 5.2 the doctrine of multi-level analyses proposed by Cacioppo and Berntson (1992).

Box 5.2 Multi-level doctrine of social neuroscience

Principle of multi-level determinism

The *principle of multiple determinism* specifies that behaviors can have multiple antecedents within or across levels of organization. For instance, although immune response was once thought to reflect only physiological responses to pathogens or tissue damage, a more complex picture about immunity has been depicted over the past two decades. Where a person falls on the continuum of social connections (see Box 5.1) may impact inflammation and immunity (e.g. Kiecolt-Glaser, Gouin, & Hantsoo, 2010). Psychosocial stress, operating through the brain's perception of the meaning of events, can also increase pro-inflammatory cytokine production in the absence of infection or injury. Animal research has revealed related findings in mice: exposure of mice to two weeks of isolation enhances tumor liver metastasis in part via its suppressive effect on the immune system of the host (Wu et al., 2000). One implication of this principle is that comprehensive theories of social phenomena require a consideration of *multiple* factors from various levels of organization – e.g. from the biological and individual level to the social level (Cacioppo & Ortigue, 2011). A second implication is that many-to-many mappings between elements across proximal levels of organization become increasingly complex as the number of intervening levels of organization increases. Accordingly, the articulation of these mappings and mechanisms underlying a given multi-level observation may be simpler when working across proximal rather than distal levels of organization, assuming that the transduction pathway has manifestations in each of the intervening levels of organization.

Principle of non-additive determinism

This principle specifies that properties of the whole are not always readily predictable by the simple sum of the (initially recognized) properties of the parts (Cacioppo & Berntson, 1992). For instance, the behavior of non-human primates was examined following the administration of amphetamine or placebo (Haber & Barchas, 1983). No clear pattern emerged until each primate's position in the social hierarchy was considered. When this social factor was taken into account, amphetamines were found to increase dominant behavior in primates high in the social hierarchy and to increase submissive behavior in primates low in the social hierarchy. A strictly bio-logical (or social) analysis, regardless of the sophistication of the mea-surement technology, may not have unraveled the orderly relationship that exists.

Principle of reciprocal determinism

This principle specifies that, 'there can be mutual influences among bio-logical and social factors in determining behavior' (Cacioppo & Bern-tson, 1992). For example, maternal behavior can alter expression of genes through a process of DNA methylation, but genes altered in this way then can affect subsequent maternal behavior (Zhang & Meaney, 2010). One important implication is that comprehensive accounts of human behavior cannot be achieved if the biological, cognitive or social level of organi-zation is considered unnecessary or irrelevant. Different methods, one goal: understanding the biological mechanisms underlying social processes and social behaviors.

Neuroimaging Methods for the Study of Shared Representations

With more than 85 billion brain cells working together in malleable networks to produce our mind, consciousness and behavior, the scientific investigation of the human brain represents one of the most complex and exciting scien-tific frontiers in the twenty-first century. Since Angelo Mosso's discovery of the 'human circulation balance' in the nineteenth century (for review, see Sandrone et al., 2012), significant neuroimaging developments and refine-ments have been made, for instance in terms of neuroimaging power (e.g. from 1T to 3T or 7T for fMRI; from 32 electrodes to 64 and then to 128 elec-trodes or 256 electrodes for surface EEG; Cacioppo et al., 2003; Davidson & Cacioppo, 1992), computational capacities and analytic tools, and statisti-cal approaches (multi-kernel density analyses, multi-voxel pattern analy-ses, network modeling of brain connectivity; graph theoretical analyses; Bullmore & Sporns, 2009; Cacioppo et al., 2013; He & Evans, 2010; Wager et al., 2009;). In addition to traditional physiological measures (e.g. facial electromyography, impedance cardiography and electrocardiography, eye-tracking, electrodermal activity; cf. Cacioppo, Tassinary, & Berntson, 2007), contemporary neuroimaging techniques (such as positron emission tomogra-phy, PET; fMRI; electroencephalogram (EEG) and event-related potentials (ERPs), magneto-encephalography (MEG) or transcranial magnetic stimula-tions, TMS) offer unprecedented access to the human brain during normal waking states.

Also of importance in social neuroscience are the advances made in genetics and molecular biology. For instance, a growing body of research demonstrates that the social environment can modulate gene expression, thereby influencing neural and neuroendocrine functioning. Methods and models are also being developed in social neuroscience to bridge the gap between animal and human research. In line with the fact that most of our human social behavior arises from neurobiological and psychological mechanisms shared with other social species, studies are being performed across phylogeny to understand the neural, hormonal, chemical and genetic bases of social behavior (e.g. Adolphs, 2009; Cacioppo, Cacioppo, Capitanio, & Cole, 2014a). Such interdisciplinary investigations across social species (and across cultures within social species) are becoming more common in the field. Because of space limitations, however, and given shared representations have been investigated primarily in humans, we limit our focus here on the neuroimaging technique most used by social neuroscientists investigating the human brain, i.e. fMRI (Stanley & Adolphs, 2013). Moreover, our discussion of methods is designed to promote the understanding and interpretation of neuroimaging studies in the literature rather than to provide a guide on how to collect or analyze data using these methods.

With high spatial (mm) and intermediate-to-low temporal (seconds) resolution, fMRI has attracted considerable attention as a method for investigating the functional neuroanatomical bases of psychological states and processes. Since its introduction in the 1990s, fMRI has attracted a large number of scientists and led to the discovery of several brain areas involved in various social functions and behaviors (Figure 5.1; Adolphs, 2009; Kennedy & Adolphs, 2012; Stanley & Adolphs 2013). From hundreds of fMRI studies on social cognition and behaviors, a general social brain matrix can be drawn.

Kennedy and Adolphs (2012) identified four core neural networks in the social brain: (1) amygdala network, (2) mentalizing network, (3) empathy network, and (4) mirror simulation/action-perception network. For instance, the functions of the amygdala network range from emotional processing to the detection of socially salient stimuli to social affiliative behaviors, and the functions of the mentalizing network range from thinking about the internal states of self to the thinking about others. The empathy network is activated when individuals empathize with others. Finally, the mirror network is activated during observation of the actions of others, and during the understanding of (emotional and/or motor) intentions of others (Grafton et al., 1996; Rizzolatti & Craighero, 2004). This depiction is illustrative rather than exhaustive, of course, as, for instance, social (e.g. face, gaze) perception involves the fusiform gyrus, middle temporal gyrus, superior temporal sulcus and amygdala (Kanwisher, 2010; Sabatinelli et al., 2011), not to mention the neural circuitry underlying

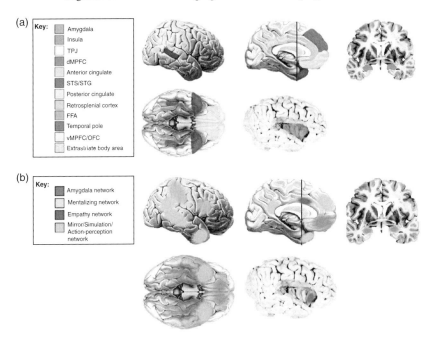

Figure 5.1 The social brain, from Kennedy and Adolphs (2012). *See Plate 3.*

Notes: (a) Brain structures involved in social cognition: amygdala, insula, temporoparietal junction (TPJ), dorsomedial prefrontal cortex (dMPFC), anterior cingulate, superior temporal sulcus/gyrus (STS/STG), posterior cingulate, retrospenial cortex, fusiform face area (FFA), temporal lobe, ventromedial prefrontal cortex/orbitofrontal cortex (vMPFC/OFC) and extrastriate body area (EBA); (b) Four core networks involved in social cognition: amygdala network, mentalizing network, empathy network and mirror/simulation/action observation network.

human speech perception and production (Pinel et al., 2014), attachment and love (Cacioppo et al., 2012) and social rejection (Cacioppo et al., 2013).

According to the theories of simulation and embodied cognition, in addition to verbal descriptions people can share their understanding of the world and of their bodily experiences through nonverbal behavior such as gestures, facial expressions and postures (Hari & Kujala, 2009). The understanding of these nonverbal messages is supported by the 'action observation network' (AON), which is located in an inferior fronto-parietal network (FPN) and includes a subset of areas that are associated within the putative human mirror neuron system (hMNS; a system that is active when one does something or observes someone else acting; Grafton, 2009; Grafton, Arbib, Fadiga, & Rizzolatti, 1996; Ortigue, Thompson, Parasuraman, & Grafton, 2009; Rizzolatti &

Craighero, 2004), which are shaped by individual experience (Hari & Kujala, 2009). The mirror neuron system, first discovered in non-human primates, allows one to grasp others' goals rapidly on the basis of low-level behavioral inputs and past bodily experiences (Cross et al., 2006; Grafton et al., 1996; van Overwalle & Baetens, 2009; Rizzolatti & Craighero, 2004).

Functional MRI provides a wealth of data on how these various neural networks may be selectively activated or co-activated by specific tasks that have been designed (typically through behavioral studies) to isolate one or more information-processing operations underlying a social behavior. There are a few considerations that may be helpful when reading, designing or interpreting fMRI research (Cacioppo et al., 2003; Mather, Cacioppo, & Kanwisher, 2013a, 2013b).

Keep things simple, but not one bit simpler. The current fMRI model of the hemodynamic response posits that a transient increase in neuronal activity within a brain region leads to a relative de-oxygenation of the blood flowing near these cells followed quickly by increased blood flow to the region. As a result, blood near a region of local neural activity can have a higher ratio of oxygenated to deoxygenated hemoglobin than blood in locally inactive areas. The BOLD fMRI provides a measure of these dynamic adjustments and, by inference, the transient changes in neuronal activity in the proximal brain tissues (Raichle, 2000). This makes it possible to investigate the likelihood of one or more neural regions showing changes in activation (increases or decreases in activity level) as a function of experimental tasks that are thought to vary one or more specific psychological states or processes.

No one doubts that the operations underlying behavior emanate from the brain. Early fMRI studies concluding that a particular psychological state or process resulted in brain activation left many wondering what the alternative hypothesis might be. It does not follow necessarily that a particular behavioral function, or even a single psychological operation, is achieved through the operation of a single neural region. More generally, the functional localization of component social processes is not simply (or, at least given the current state of knowledge, even mostly) a search for centers (Cacioppo et al., 2003). The angular gyrus, for instance, is a brain area that has been shown to be activated not only in one social function, but also in a broad variety of social functions, such as bodily self representation, embodied cognition, love, self-esteem, semantic processing, reading, number processing, memory retrieval, attention, spatial cognition, left–right orientation, reasoning, metaphors and abstraction (for review, see Seghier, 2013). This example highlights the importance of investigating neural circuitry/networks, rather than a neural center, when mapping the social brain. Other regions, including the amygdala, medial prefrontal cortex and fusiform gyrus are similarly associated with a variety of putatively different processes. Whether the simple computation being performed by each region has not yet been accurately described or the net effect of the activation of a given region differs as a function of its coupling with one or more of other brain regions has yet to be determined. For instance, think of how different are sodium chloride (a nutrient) and hydrogen chloride (an acid), even though the element, chlorine, is common to both. At this juncture, it is perhaps judicious to keep in mind Einstein's razor, which is to make things as simple as possible, but not one bit simpler. To avoid oversimplified explanations that lead to false conclusions, when designing or interpreting the results of neuroimaging studies a one-to-one mapping between a specific brain region and a specific social state or process should be subjected to strong empirical tests rather than assumed.

Causal inferences are justified from neuroimaging methods only when all plausible alternative interpretations have been eliminated. An image of activated regions of the brain associated with a specific component process may make it appear as if the neural basis for that process has been discovered, but is it sufficient given the correlational nature of current neuroimaging methods? To illustrate the issue, consider a simple physical metaphor in which Φ represents a physical mechanism, a heater (analogous to a neural mechanism in the brain) and ψ represents an invisible but measurable state, the temperature inside a house (analogous to a social state or process). Although the heater and the temperature are conceptually distinct, the operation of the heater represents a physical basis for the temperature in the house. In this case, $\psi = f(\Phi)$. A bottom-up approach – that is, $P(\psi/\Phi)$ – makes clear certain details about the relationship between ψ and Φ, whereas a top-down approach – that is, $P(\Phi/\psi)$ – clarifies others (cf. Cacioppo & Tassinary, 1990). For instance, when the activity of the heater is manipulated (i.e. Φ is stimulated or lesioned), a change in the temperature in the house (ψ) is observed. The fact that manipulating the activity of the heater produces a change in the temperature in the house can be expressed as $P(\psi/\Phi) = E$, where E represents an effect size that differs from zero. Note that the $P(\psi/\Phi)$ need not equal 1 for Φ to be a physical substrate of ψ. This is because in our illustration there are other physical mechanisms that can affect the temperature in the house (ψ), such as the outside temperature (Φ') and the amount of direct sunlight inside the house (Φ''). That is, there is a lack of complete isomorphism specifiable, at least initially, between the functional dimension (ψ) and a physical basis (Φ).

Now consider the indicator light on a thermostat that illuminates when the heater is operating. In this case, the indicator light represents a physical element that would show the same covariation with the temperature in the house as the operation of the heater as long as a top-down (e.g. functional brain imaging) approach was used. If the complementary bottom-up approach were used, it would become obvious that disconnecting (lesioning) the heater can have effects on the temperature in the house whereas disconnecting (or directly activating) the indicator light has none. This simple example should make it clear that a region of differential brain activation that corresponds to a specific information-processing operation does not necessarily mean that this brain region is the neural substrate for the information-processing operation.

To be able to draw causal interpretation (rather than correlational assumptions) about the link between biology and behaviors often requires other methods, such as lesion studies, transcranial magnetic stimulation and pharmacological interventions (e.g. ligands, drugs) in human or non-human animals to elucidate the causal role of any given neural structure, circuit or process in a given task. Any single neuroimaging methodology provides a partial view of brain activity within a very limited range of spatial and temporal levels, and it is the confluence of methods that advances our understanding of the neural mechanisms underlying social and cognitive behaviors.

Consider moderator variables. Social process and behavior are important and interesting in part because they are so complex. Social phenomena, ranging from aggression to discrimination, are multiply determined. The multiply-determined nature of these phenomena calls for the parsing of big research questions into smaller, tractable series of research questions that ultimately constitute systematic and meticulous programs of research. Where to parse a phenomenon may not be obvious without empirical evidence, however. Therefore, the generalizability problem, or the absence of dependence on an originally unmeasured variable, represents a recurring issue in research on human social behavior.

Let's return to the analogy of the heater and temperature described above to illustrate the issue. Let's further assume that a contrast method was used to identify the link between the heater and home temperature. Specifically, the temperature of the test room was found to be higher at noon than at 4 a.m. on a winter day in Chicago, and the contrast between the images of the living room taken with a thermo-imaging camera at 4 a.m. and noon showed the heater to appear in this contrast image. A colleague in southern Florida replicates the procedures precisely, also finding that the temperature of the test room was higher at noon than at 4 a.m. in southern Florida. However, the contrast image failed to reveal any evidence that the heater was involved at all; instead, the curtains covering the large living room windows appeared in the contrast. If room temperature were *only* a function of a heater in a room, then such a result would call into question the replicability of the original observations. However, the multiply-determined nature of room temperature and the differences across contexts in the operation of one or more of these determinants raise the real possibility that both findings are replicable but neither provides a comprehensive account of the phenomenon. Treating such discrepancies as a theoretical question rather than simply noting there were 'methodological differences' should foster the development of testable hypotheses and, ultimately, more comprehensive theories in social neuroscience (see Box 5.2).

Science is cumulative. In addition, several factors (such as sample size) can influence the data. For instance, Button et al. (2013) provide a tutorial on how and why neuroimaging studies with small sample sizes reduce the likelihood of detecting a true effect (due to low statistical power), increase the likelihood that the effect size of a true effect is overestimated (due to the use of $p < 0.05$ to identify when an effect has been 'detected' and the larger sampling error associated with smaller sample sizes) and increase the likelihood that a statistically significant effect is not truly different from zero (due to differences in the base rates for tests of true and untrue effects).

During the past five years, several narrative reviews have tried to address this issue by accumulating evidence from small sample size fMRI studies and grouping them together. Unfortunately, narrative reviews are qualitative rather than quantitative. To better address this question and identify the clusters that are statistically activated beyond chance level, one needs to perform quantitative meta-analyses (Cacioppo et al., 2012, 2013; van Owervalle & Baetens, 2009; Wager et al., 2007, 2009). There are several meta-analysis tools (e.g. activation likelihood estimate, ALE (Eickhoff et al., 2012) and multi-level kernel density analysis, MKDA (Wager et al., 2007, 2009), one can use to test whether peak activations occur randomly throughout the brain or whether they occur statistically above chance in response to some patterns related to an experimental condition. In 2013, we performed such a statistical meta-analysis on the topic of social pain. Contrary to previous narrative reviews on social pain, our MKDA of neuroimaging studies of social pain with 244 participants in the Cyberball paradigm failed to support the prior claims (made exclusively by small sample size studies or narrative reviews) that social rejection operates on the same neural pain matrix as nociceptive stimuli (S. Cacioppo et al., 2013). Rather, our quantitative review indicated that the neural correlates of social rejection were different and more complex than previously thought, questioning whether social pain is figurative rather than literal.

These results emphasize the value of quantitative over narrative reviews of the neuroimaging literature and underscore the importance of treating science as a cumulative rather than an all-or-nothing process. Rather than treating statistical significance testing as a method to determine the likelihood that a given test result would be expected by chance, an arbitrary cutoff such as $p < 0.05$ has often been used to determine the presence or absence of a true effect. This win/lose approach to statistical significance testing has also led to the notion that a successful replication means a previously significant effect is found to again be statistically significant in a replication study. Statistically speaking, however, an initially statistically significant effect means that the confidence interval for this effect in this study does not include zero, and a successful replication means that the effect size detected in the follow-up study falls *within* the confidence interval of the original study. The effect size that is detected in the replication study may or may not differ from zero (i.e. reach $p < 0.05$) depending on the sample size of the replication study. This does not mean that the effect size reported in the original study is true, but only that the original result was replicated – that is, that the effect size detected in the replication study fell within the confidence interval for the effect size reported in the original study. The best estimate of the true effect size is the weighted mean of each of the studies.

Given the small sample size in most neuroimaging research, small but theoretically important effects are likely to go undetected (due to low statistical power), thereby providing at best an incomplete and at worst a misleading depiction of underlying neural mechanisms. Given the cost of fMRI, simply increasing sample size may be a challenge. If the effect sizes and confidence intervals for all regions that reached some minimal threshold of effect size (e.g. $d = 0.1$) were provided in supplementary materials, quantitative reviews and the cumulative nature of science may be fostered.

Consider the time-course within and between brains. Most of the advances in our understanding of the neural basis of the social brain have been based on studies in which people have been considered as isolated, often static entities. For instance, hundreds of studies on action observation and on the understanding of intentions performed by others have examined the kinematics of volunteers (stimuli) performing an action towards an object without the intention to interact with the observer/participant. Although such studies have successfully identified the role of particular functions of the social brain and are reviewed in papers using meta-analysis related to different aspects of social cognition (Adolphs, 2009; Grafton, 2009; Hari & Kujala, 2009; Jeannerod, 1981; Juan et al., 2013; van Overwalle & Baetens, 2009), they do not inform us about real-time interpersonal interactions nor, given the temporal resolution of fMRI, do they provide rich information about the timing of the activation of the associated neural regions that have been identified.

The neural mechanisms underlying shared representations have also tended to focus on single individuals performing tasks that vary aspects of these representations. Although important, the focus on the individual as the unit of analysis may not capture aspects of shared representations that manifest during normal social interactions (for review, see Babiloni & Astolfi, 2012). Neuroimaging methods such as hyperscanning and statistical methods such as multi-level modeling make it possible to investigate the effects of the social aggregate (e.g. dyad) on interacting brains in addition to the effects of the individuals within the social aggregate. Hyperscanning was introduced by Montague and colleagues (2002), who performed an fMRI study using two scanners and pairs of individuals competing against each other in a simple game designed to measure the effect of deception in a competitive context. Montague et al.'s method for hyperscanning uses the internet to allow investigators to synchronize and control two or more scanners to dissect the effects of individual factors, social (relational/interactional) factors and potential interactions among these factors on regional brain activation.

The hyperscanning approach permits investigation of unique aspects of the social brain, but it raises some methodological issues to consider as well. First, the recording parameters and operating characteristics among the linked scanners should be as identical as possible. Even at the same field strength, different scanners may have different gains, different gradient strengths, head coil sensitivities and shimming protocols that may influence the data (Sanger, Lindenberger, & Muller, 2011). Another issue is the accuracy and stability of the synchronization of the scanners across the internet (for review, see Babiloni & Astolfi, 2012; Montague et al., 2002). Finally, multivariate statistical analyses for dependent, multi-level data structures provide useful estimates of the influence of factors at multiple levels of organization.

Since Montague et al.'s demonstration of hyperscanning, other hyperscanning approaches have been developed, including functional near-infrared imaging hyperscanning and EEG hyperscanning (Babiloni & Astolfi, 2012; Scholkmann, Holper, Wolf, & Wolf, 2013). EEG hyperscanning, for instance, provides not only information about where changes in brain activity are observed, but also when they occur. EEG hyperscanning typically uses different devices located in the same laboratory with similar sampling rates, calibration and amplifiers, which simplifies concerns about the synchronization of the different acquisition machines (Babiloni & Astolfi, 2012; Sanger, Lindenberger, & Muller, 2011).

Epigenetic Processes and Gene Expressions of the Social Brains

Two other approaches also of interest in social neuroscience are (1) the study of the modifications of gene expression (transcriptomics), and (2) the study of the alterations of gene activity that can be transmitted to the next cell generation but that occur without changing the genetic code of the DNA (epigenetics; Goossens et al., 2015).[1] In the first approach, labeled transcriptomics, researchers need to have access to RNA, as extracted from blood, to study gene expression. In the second approach, labeled epigenetics (or epigenomics), researchers focus on DNA and study the fundamental differences that make us unique (Goossens et al., 2015; Raddihough & Zahn, 2010). Several epigenetic

---

[1] The Greek preposition 'epi' (meaning 'what goes beyond') is used in the latter approach as these changes occur on top of the genetic code (Goossens et al., 2015; Sweatt et al., 2013).

processes, such as DNA methylation and chromatin modification, can be studied, but DNA methylation is the most studied in neuropsychiatry and neuroscience, as DNA methylation is considered a critical factor influencing gene expression (Kumsta et al., 2013; Moore et al., 2013). Methylation involves the direct chemical modification of the DNA by binding of a methyl molecule to a cytosine basic unit, which then leaves an 'epigenetic' mark and impairs gene transcription (Goossens et al., 2015), with the assumption that patients or persons with a social disorder (such as autism) would show a greater degree of methylation than a control group (Kumsta et al., 2013). Such studies are, as yet, only nascent in social neuroscience.

A popular design in gene expression studies entails that a group of individuals with a specific psychiatric or medical condition is compared to a control group. For instance, in the case of a transcriptomic study of perceived social isolation (loneliness), a group of people with very high scores on a loneliness scale is compared to a group with very low scores on that same measure. Researchers then look for genes whose expression is up-regulated (i.e. relatively overexpressed in lonely individuals) or down-regulated (i.e. relatively overexpressed in non-lonely individuals; Cole, 2009). The complete pattern of up-regulated and down-regulated genes then represents the specific gene expression profile of loneliness. Once such a profile is obtained, researchers check the function of each of the genes involved in a gene database to better understand which biological systems are involved. A germinal study performed by Cacioppo and colleagues (2007) compared six lonely to eight non-lonely individuals, and revealed the up-regulation of expression in 78 genes and down-regulation in 131 genes, including up-regulation of genes bearing response elements for pro-inflammatory NF-κB/Rel transcription factors, and down-regulation of genes bearing anti-inflammatory glucocorticoid response elements, mature B lymphocyte function and type I interferon response (Cole et al., 2007). The authors interpreted the impaired transcription of glucocorticoid response genes and increased activity of pro-inflammatory transcription control pathways as a possible functional genomic explanation for elevated risk of inflammatory disease in individuals who experience chronically high levels of subjective social isolation (Cole, Hawkley, Arevalo, & Cacioppo, 2011; Cole et al., 2007). The overall pattern of results of this discovery was confirmed in a larger replication sample of older adults that compared 25 chronically lonely individuals to 68 controls (Cole et al., 2011). Together, these results helped understand why lonely people show heightened vulnerability to a broad variety of diseases (thought to emerge through excessive non-specific immune activity) and impaired reactions to viral infections (thought to be linked to insufficient specific immune activity; Cacioppo et al., 2015). Further studies need to be done in this field to better understand the transcriptomic and epigenetic of the social brains (Cacioppo et al., 2015; Meloni, 2014).

Conclusion

In sum, significant technological advances over the past few decades have led to the development of new methods and theories for understanding the social brain. These developments have both transformed the nature and amount of data available on brain structure and function at various scales, and expanded the breadth of theories of the social brain. With such advancements come specialized methodological, analytical and conceptual expertise that may benefit from the cumulative expertise of an interdisciplinary team, but also risks increasing subdisciplinary specializations that may make it difficult for non-experts in the field to understand or evaluate research designs and interpretations. Five considerations were discussed that we hope improve cognizance of the neuroimaging methods for studying the social brain.

References

Adolphs, R. (2009). The social brain: Neural basis of social knowledge. *Annual Review of Psychology*, 60, 693–716.

Aglioti, S. M., Cesari, P., Romani, M., & Urgesi, C. (2008). Action anticipation and motor resonance in elite basketball players. *Nature Neuroscience*, 11, 1109–1116.

Babiloni, F., & Astolfi, L. (2012). Social neuroscience and hyperscanning techniques: Past, present and future. *Neuroscience Behavioral Review*, 44, 76–93.

Birbaumer, N., Lutzenberger, W., Elbert, T., Flor, H., & Rockstroh, B. (1993). Imagery and brain processes. In N. Birbaumer & A. Öhmann (Eds.), *The structure of emotion*. Toronto: Hogrefe and Huber, 298–321.

Bullmore, E., & Sporns, O. (2009). Complex brain networks: Graph theoretical analysis of structural and functional systems. *Nature Review Neuroscience*, 10, 186–198. doi: 10.1038/nrn2575.

Button, K. S., Ioannidis, J. P., Mokrysz, C., Nosek, B. A., & Flint, J., et al. (2013). Power failure: Why small sample size undermines the reliability of neuroscience. *Nature Reviews Neuroscience*, 14, 365–376.

Cacioppo, J. T., & Berntson, G. G. (1992). Social psychological contributions to the decade of the brain: Doctrine of multilevel analysis. *American Psychologist*, 47, 1019–1028.

Cacioppo, J. T., Berntson, G. G., Lorig, T. S., Norris, C. J., Rickett, E., & Nusbaum, H. (2003). Just because you're imaging the brain doesn't mean you can stop using your head: A primer and set of first principles. *Journal of Personality and Social Psychology*, 85, 650–661.

Cacioppo, J. T., Cacioppo, S., Capitanio, J. P., & Cole, S. W. (2014a). The neuroendocrinology of social isolation. *Annual Review of Psychology*, 66, 733–767.

Cacioppo, J. T., Cacioppo, S., Dulawa, S., & Palmer, A. (2014b). Social neuroscience and its potential contribution to psychiatry. *World Psychiatry*, 13(2),131–139.

Cacioppo, J. T., Crites, S. L. Jr., & Gardner, W. L. (1996). Attitudes to the right: Evaluative processing is associated with lateralized late positive event-related brain potentials. *Personality and Social Psychology Bulletin*, 22, 1205–1219.

Cacioppo, J. T., & Ortigue, S. (2011). Social neuroscience: How a multidisciplinary field is uncovering the biology of human interactions. *Cerebrum*, 19, 17.

Cacioppo, J. T., & Petty, R. E. (1979). Attitudes and cognitive response: An electrophysiological approach. *Journal of Personality and Social Psychology*, 37, 2181–2199.

Cacioppo, J. T., Petty, R. E., Losch, M. E., & Crites, S. L. (1994). Psychophysiological approaches to attitudes: Detecting affective dispositions when people won't say, can't say, or don't even know. In S. Shavitt & T. C. Brock (Eds.), *Persuasion: Psychological insights and perspectives*. New York: Allyn & Bacon, 43–69.

Cacioppo, J. T., Petty, R. E., & Quintanar, L. R. (1982). Individual differences in relative hemispheric alpha abundance and cognitive responses to persuasive communications. *Journal of Personality and Social Psychology*, 43, 623–636.

Cacioppo, J. T., Petty, R. E., & Snyder, C. W. (1979). Cognitive and affective response as a function of relative hemispheric involvement. *International Journal of Neuroscience*, 9, 81–89.

Cacioppo, J. T., & Tassinary, L. G. (1990). *Principles of psychophysiology: Physical, social, and inferential elements*. New York: Cambridge University Press.

Cacioppo, J. T., Tassinary, L. G., & Berntson, G. G. (2000). *Handbook of psychophysiology*, 2nd edition. New York: Cambridge University Press. (2007). *Handbook of psychophysiology*, 3rd edition. New York: Cambridge University Press.

Cacioppo, S., Bianchi-Demicheli, F., Frum, C., Pfaus, J., & Lewis, J. W. (2012). The common neural bases between sexual desire and love: A multilevel kernel density fMRI analysis. *Journal of Sexual Medicine*, 9, 1048–1054. doi: 10.1111/j.1743-6109.2012.02651.x.

Cacioppo, S., Frum, C., Asp, E., Weiss, R. M., Lewis, J. W., & Cacioppo, J. T. (2013). A quantitative meta-analysis of functional imaging studies of social rejection. *Scientific Reports*, 3, 2027. doi: 10.1038/srep02027.

Cacioppo, S., Grafton, S. T., & Bianchi-Demicheli, F. (2012). The speed of passionate love, as a subliminal prime: A high-density electrical neuroimaging study. *NeuroQuantology*, 10, 715–724.

Cole. S. W. (2009). Social regulation of human gene expression. *Current Directions in Psychological Science*, 18, 132–137.

Cole, S. W., Hawkley, L. C., Arevalo, J. M., & Cacioppo, J. T. (2011). Transcript origin analysis identifies antigen-presenting cells as primary targets of socially regulated gene expression in leukocytes. *Proceedings of the National Academy of Sciences of the United States of America*, 7, 3080–3085.

Cole, S. W., Hawkley, L. C., Arevalo, J. M., Sung, C. Y., Rose, R. M., & Cacioppo, J. T. (2007). Social regulation of gene expression in human leukocytes. *Genome Biology*, 8(9), R189. doi: 10.1186/gb.2007-8-9-r189.

Crites, S. L. Jr., & Cacioppo, J. T. (1996). Electrocortical differentiation of evaluative and nonevaluative categorizations. *Psychological Science*, 7, 318–321.

Cross, E. S., Hamilton, A. F., & Grafton, S. T. (2006). Building a motor simulation de novo: Observation of dance by dancers. *NeuroImage*, 31, 1257–1267.

Davidson, R. J., & Cacioppo, J. T. (1992). New developments in the scientific study of emotion: An introduction to the special section. *Psychological Science*, 3, 21–22.

Davidson, R. J., Jackson, D. C., & Larson, C. L. (2000). Human electroencephalography. In J. T. Cacioppo, L.G. Tassinary, & G. G. Berntson (Eds.), *Handbook of psychophysiology*, 2nd edition. Cambridge: Cambridge University Press, 76–93.

Decety, J., & Cacioppo, S. (2012). The speed of morality: A high-density electrical neuroimaging study. *Journal of Neurophysiology*, 108, 3068–3072. doi: 10.1152/jn.00473.2012.

Eickhoff, S. B., Bzdok, D., Laird, A. R., Kurth, F., & Fox, P. T. (2012). Activation likelihood estimation revisited. *NeuroImage*, 59, 2349–2361.

Ekman, P., Davidson, R. J., & Friesen, W. V. (1990). The Duchenne smile: Emotional expression and brain physiology II. *Journal of Personality and Social Psychology*, 58, 342–353.

Frith, C. D., & Wolpert, D. (2004). *The neuroscience of social interaction: Decoding, influencing and imitating the actions of others.* Oxford: Oxford University Press.

Galton, F. (1884). Measurement of character. *Psychometry*, 36, 179–185.

Grafton, S. T. (2009). Embodied cognition and the simulation of action to understand others. *Annals of the New York Academy of Sciences*, 1156, 97–117. doi: 10.1111/j.1749-6632.2009.04425.x.

Grafton, S. T., Arbib, M. A., Fadiga, L., & Rizzolatti, G. (1996). Localization of grasp representations in humans by positron emission tomography. 2. Observation compared with imagination. *Experimental Brain Research*, 112, 103–111.

Goossens, L., van Roekel, E., Verhagen, M., Cacioppo, J. T., Cacioppo, S., Maes, M., & Boomsma, D. I. (2015). The genetics of loneliness: Linking evolutionary theory to genomics, epigenomics, and social science. *Perspective on Psychological Sciences*, 10(2), 213–226.

Haber, S. N., & Barchas, P. R. (1983). The regulatory effect of social rank on behavior after amphetamine administration. In P. R. Barchas (Ed.), *Social hierarchies: Essays toward a socio-physiological perspective.* Westport, CT: Greenwood, 119–132.

Hari, R., & Kujala, M. V. (2009). Brain basis of human social interaction: From concepts to brain imaging. *Physiological Reviews*, 89, 453–479.

He, Y., & Evans, A. (2010). Graph theoretical modeling of brain connectivity. *Current Opinion in Neurology*, 23, 341–350.

Holt, J. (2005). Measure for measure: The strange science of Francis Galton. *New Yorker*, 72–77.

Huettel, S. A., Song, A. W., & McCarthy, G. (2009). *Functional magnetic resonance imaging*, 2nd edition. Sunderland, MA: Sinauer.

Ibanez, A., Melloni, M., Huepe, D., Helgiu, E., Rivera-Rei, A., et al. (2012). What do event-related potentials (ERPs) bring to social neuroscience? *Social Neuroscience*, 7, 632–649. doi: 10.1080/17470919.2012.691078.

Jeannerod, M. (1981). *The neural and behavioral organization of goal-directed movements.* New York: Oxford Science Publishers.

Juan, E., Frum, C., Bianchi-Demicheli, F., Wang, Y., Lewis, J. W., & Cacioppo, S. (2013). Beyond human intentions and emotions. *Frontiers in Human Neuroscience*, 7, 99. doi: 10.3389/fnhum.2013.00099.

Kanwisher, N. (2010). Functional specificity in the human brain: A window into the functional architecture of the mind. *Proceedings of the National Academy of Sciences of the United States of America*, 25, 11163–11170.

Kennedy, D. P., & Adolphs, R. (2012). The social brain in psychiatric and neurological disorders. *Trends in Cognitive Sciences*, 16, 559–572. doi: 10.1016/j.tics.2012.09.006.

Kiecolt-Glaser, J. K., Gouin, J. P., & Hantsoo, L. (2010). Close relationship, inflammation, and health. *Neuroscience Biobehavioral Review*, 35, 33–38.

Kumsta, R., Hummel, E., Chen, F. S., & Heinrichs, M. (2013). Epigenetic regulation of the oxytocin receptor gene: Implication for behavioral neuroscience. *Frontiers in Neuroscience*, 7, 83.

Luck, S. J. *An introduction to the event-related potential technique*. Cambridge, MA: MIT Press.

Mather, M., Cacioppo, J. T., & Kanwisher, N. (2013a). How fMRI can inform cognitive theories. *Perspectives on Psychological Science*, 8, 108–113.

(2013b). Introduction to the Special Section: 20 years of fMRI – what has it done for understanding cognition? *Perspectives on Psychological Science*, 8, 41–43.

Meloni, M. (2014). The social brain meets the reactive genome: Neuroscience, epigenetics and the new social biology. *Frontiers in Human Neuroscience*, 8, 1–12.

Montague, P. R., Berns, G. S., Cohen, J. D., et al. (2002). Hyperscanning: Simultaneous fMRI during linked social interactions. *NeuroImage*, 16, 1159–1164.

Moore, L. D., Le, T., & Fan, G. (2013). DNA methylation and its basic function. *Neuropsychopharmacology*, 38, 23–38.

Niedenthal, P. M. (2007). Embodying emotion. *Science*, 316, 1002–1005.

Niedenthal, P. M., Barsalou, L. W., Winkielman, P., Krauth-Gruber, S., & Ric, F. (2005). Embodiment in attitudes, social perception, and emotion. *Personality and Social Psychology Review*, 9, 184–211.

Ortigue, S., Michel, C. M., Murray, M. M., Mohr, C., Carbonnel, S., & Landis, T. (2004). Electrical neuroimaging reveals early generator modulation to emotional words. *NeuroImage*, 21, 1242–1251.

Ortigue, S., Sinigaglia, C., Rizzolatti, G., & Grafton, S. T. (2010). Brain dynamics and topography of decoding intentions: A combined event-related EEG/FMRI study. *PLoS ONE*, 5, e12160.

Ortigue, S., Thompson, J. C., Parasuraman, R., & Grafton, S. T. (2009). Spatio-temporal dynamics of human intention understanding in temporo-parietal cortex: A combined EEG/fMRI repetition suppression paradigm. *PLoS ONE*, 4, e6962.

Overwalle, F. van, & Baetens, K. (2009). Understanding others' actions and goals by mirror and mentalizing systems: A meta-analysis. *NeuroImage*, 48, 564–584. doi: 10.1016/j.neuroimage.2009.06.009.

Pinel, P., Lalanne, C., Bourgeon, T., Fauchereau, F., & Poupon, C. (2014). Genetic and environmental influences on the visual word form and fusiform face areas. *Cerebral Cortex*, 25(9), 2478–293.

Raichle, M. E. (2000). A brief history of human functional brain mapping. In A. W. Toga & J. C. Mazziotta (Eds.), *Brain mapping: The systems*. San Diego, CA: Academic Press, 33–75.

Riddihough, G., & Zahn, L. M. (2010). What is epigenetics? *Science*, 330, 611.

Rizzolatti, G., & Craighero, L. (2004). The mirror–neuron system. *Annual Review of Neuroscience*, 27, 169–192.

Ruscher, J. B., Santuzzi, A. M., & Hammer, E. Y. (2003). Shared impression formation in the cognitively interdependent dyad. *British Journal of Social Psychology*, 42, 411–425.

Sabatinelli, D., Fortune, E. E., Li, Q., Siddiqui, A., & Krafft, C. (2011). Emotional perception: Meta-analyses of face and natural scene processing. *NeuroImage*, 54, 2524–2533. doi: 10.1016/j.neuroimage.2010.10.011.

Sandrone, S., Bacigaluppi, M., Galloni, M. R., & Martino, G. (2012). Angelo Mosso (1846–1910). *Journal of Neurology*, 259, 2513–2514. doi: 10.1007/s00415-012-6632-1. PMID 23010944.

Sanger, J., Lindenberger, U., & Muller, V. (2011). Interactive brains, social minds. *Communicative and Integrative Biology*, 4, 655–663.

Scholkmann, F., Holper, L., Wolf, U., & Wolf, M. (2013). A new methodical approach in neuroscience: Assessing inter-personal brain coupling using functional near-infrared imaging (fNIRI) hyperscanning. *Frontiers in Human Neuroscience*, 7, 813.

Seghier, M. L. (2013). The angular gyrus: Multiple functions and multiple subdivisions. *Neuroscientist*, 19, 43–61. doi: 10.1177/1073858412440596.

Stanley, D. A., & Adolphs, R. (2013). Towards a neural basis for social behavior. *Neuron*, 80, 816–826. doi: 10.1016/j.neuron.2013.10.038.

Sweatt, J. D., Meaney, M. J., Nestler, E. J., & Akbarian, S. (Eds.) *Epigenetic regulation in the nervous system: Basic mechanisms and clinical impact.* London: Academic Press.

Wager, T. D., Lindquist, M. A., & Kaplan, L. (2007). Meta-analysis of functional neuroimaging data: Current and future directions. *Social, Cognitive, and Affective Neuroscience*, 2, 150–158.

Wager, T. D., Lindquist, M. A., Nichols, T. E., Kober, H., & Van Snellenberg, J. X. (2009). Evaluating the consistency and specificity of neuroimaging data using meta-analysis. *NeuroImage*, 45, S210–S221.

Wegner, D. M., Giuliano, T., & Hertel, P. (1985). Cognitive interdependence in close relationships. In W. J. Ickes (Ed.), *Compatible and incompatible relationships.* New York: Springer-Verlag, 253–276.

Wu, W., Yamura, T., Murakami, K., Murata, J., Matsumoto, K., et al. (2000). Social isolation stress enhanced liver metastasis of murine colon 26-L5 carcinoma cells by suppressing immuneresponses in mice. *Life Science*, 66, 1827–1838.

Zhang, T. Y., & Meaney, M. J. (2010). Epigenetics and the environmental regulation of the genome and its function. *Annual Review of Psychology*, 61, 439–466.

Part II

Imitation and Mimicry

6 The Comparative Study of Imitation Mechanisms in Non-Human Primates

Francys Subiaul, Elizabeth Renner and Edward Krajkowski

Abstract

Despite more than 100 years of research, there is no agreement among experts as to whether or not primates can imitate. Part of the problem is that there is little agreement as to what constitutes an example of 'imitation'. Nevertheless, recent research provides compelling evidence for both continuities and discontinuities in the psychological faculty that mediates imitation performance. A number of studies have shown that monkeys and apes are capable of copying familiar responses, but it is questionable whether they can also copy novel responses, particularly those involving novel tool-related actions. These results have been interpreted to mean that primates cannot engage in 'imitation learning' or novel imitation. Yet there is some evidence showing that monkeys can imitate novel 'cognitive' rules (i.e. ordinal rules of the form Apple–Boy–Cat) independently of copying specific motor responses. Rather than suggesting that monkeys and other primates are poor imitators, these results suggest that primates can learn novel cognitive rules but not novel motor rules, possibly because such skills require derived neural specializations in the parietal lobe linking social and physical cognitive skills. If true, such evidence represents an important discontinuity between the imitation skills of human and non-human primates with significant implications for human cognitive evolution.

Introduction

The answer to the question, 'Do primates imitate?' depends very much on how 'imitation' is defined. As with all complex questions phrased so simply, the answer inevitably depends on a confluence of factors including how one defines imitation, how one operationalizes this definition, and finally, what evidence counts as an exemplar of the concept. For instance, many have come to the conclusion that, while apes may evidence some limited forms of imitation, monkeys, generally, cannot imitate. This conclusion is based on a variety of studies that required monkeys to copy the use of tools in a specific manner as well as tasks that require individuals to vicariously learn which foods are palatable. In all cases, researchers have argued that any social learning evidenced by monkeys is best explained by mechanisms other than imitation learning, whereby an individual achieves a demonstrated result using the demonstrated means (Adams-Curtis, 1987; Beck, 1976; Fragaszy, & Visalberghi, 2004; Whiten, & Ham, 1992). But it is important to note that doubt has also been cast on the imitation skills of great ape species tested to date (Dean, 2012; Herrmann, 2007; Tennie, 2009; Tomasello, 1997), including those of young human children (Jones, 2009; Subiaul, Anderson, Brandt, & Elkins, 2012). This doubt is perhaps best captured in the titles of well-known publications, which have asked, 'Do apes ape?' (Whiten, Horner, Litchfield, & Marshall-Pescini, 2004), 'Do monkeys ape?'(Visalberghi & Fragaszy, 1990), and even, 'Do humans ape?' (Horowitz, 2003). It is an unfortunate fact that despite more than a century of research, answers to these questions remain controversial and disagreement among experts abounds. The problem stems, in part, from the question itself, which rests on a tangled and complicated concept, imitation.

Various scholars have tried to ameliorate this problem by providing a historical context for the term 'imitation' (Galef, 1988; Subiaul, 2007). Others have offered detailed definitions of common terms used in the social learning literature (Whiten, McGuigan, Marshall-Pescini, & Hopper, 2009b; Zentall, 2006, 2012). Still others have proposed new concepts and alternate social learning mechanisms (e.g. Byrne & Russon, 1998; Lyons, Young, & Keil, 2007; Subiaul, Cantlon, Holloway, & Terrace, 2004; Tennie et al., 2009; Tomasello, 1990). Others have provided a theoretical framework explaining the mechanisms underlying social learning (Carpenter & Call, 2002; Chartrand & Bargh, 1999; Heyes, 2011b; Iacoboni, 2009; Meltzoff & Moore, 1997; Subiaul, 2010). Some of these scholars have even questioned whether there is a specialized imitation or 'social learning' mechanism, independent of universal associative learning processes (Heyes, 2011b). In any case, the success of these various academic approaches remains uncertain. Arguably, many of these ideas and terms have led to greater confusion and disparate usage of what should be standard terminology. But this is by no means a new complaint. At the beginning of the twentieth century, Morgan (1900) expressed the same frustration. He wrote, 'In the face of such apparently diverse usage it is necessary to show within what limits and with what qualifications the word [imitation] may profitably here be used to individuate a factor in social evolution' (p. 180). Given these problems, it seems reasonable to begin a review of the primate faculty for imitation with a conceptual framework that narrowly defines this faculty, providing the reader with the tools to judge for themselves the imitation skills of primates and other animals.

Multiple Imitation Mechanisms: A Model

Here, we argue that it is a mistake to think of imitation as one unitary concept or skill that organisms either have or lack entirely. Rather, we propose that the imitation faculty is likely to be like other vertical cognitive faculties (Fodor, 1983), such as language and executive functions, that are specialized and consist of multiple components with discrete functions. However, it is unlikely that the imitation faculty is as encapsulated as Fodor (1983) proposed for visual systems, for example (Marr, 1982). It is more likely that the imitation faculty consists of rather open or loosely encapsulated modules or systems (Carruthers, 2006) not unlike executive functions such as inhibition, working memory and information processing (Miyake, 2000, 2001). In this conceptualisation, the imitation faculty represents a specialized psychological system with multiple mechanisms. Some of these mechanisms may receive input from a number of domain-general or 'central' systems like attention and reasoning as well as domain-specific 'core knowledge' that includes 'theory of mind' (Leslie, 1994), 'naïve physics' (Spelke & Kinzler, 2007) and 'naïve biology' (Carey, 1985). Nonetheless, the functioning of these mechanisms may be dissociable from the operation of these other skills and processes. Through this kind of domain-specificity, imitation and social learning mechanisms that make up the imitation faculty can copy responses across different domains in a flexible and adaptive fashion (Subiaul, F., Patterson, & Barr, 2016).

Like other faculties, the imitation faculty can be divided by its various functions. These functions are best captured by super-ordinate and sub-ordinate imitation mechanisms associated with the processing of specific types of stimuli (e.g. novel, familiar, auditory, motor, social, and so on). The super-ordinate imitation mechanisms include (1) 'familiar imitation' or the copying of a model's style of problem solving without learning a new action, and (2) 'novel imitation' or the copying of actions or rules not already present in the subject's motor or cognitive repertoire. This is often referred to as 'imitation learning' or 'true imitation' (Boyd & Richerson, 1994; Subiaul, 2010; Thorpe, 1956), which is distinguished from 'familiar imitation' in that it requires observational learning; that is, the ability to learn through vicarious (rather than direct) reinforcement (Bandura, 1977).

Subsumed within those two broad functional concepts – familiar and novel imitation – are sub-ordinate mechanisms of imitation that specify the type of stimulus that is reproduced by either novel or familiar imitation (i.e. auditory, motor, cognitive). All imitation mechanisms grant individuals the ability to flexibly copy specific rules or responses. That is, the behavioral rule that is copied is both deliberate and replicable; not a result of happenstance or trial-and-error learning. In this definition, the term 'rule' is broadly defined as a response involving more than two steps that are hierarchically organised and structured to achieve a matching response. The requirement that any type of imitation be rule-governed and flexible is necessary in order to differentiate imitation from either perceptual or motivational mechanisms associated with rapid trial-and-error learning that may represent an ancestral learning mechanism predating (and potentially scaffolding) the evolution of the imitation faculty. The same is true of narrow species-specific skills such as copying mate preferences (e.g. Bshary & Grutter, 2006) that, while impressive, do not extend beyond a very narrow and specific context (i.e. mating) and stimulus (i.e. females).

Like all psychological faculties, the imitation faculty is adapted to solve a number of problems common among social animals. Besides learning how to operate objects and tools, the imitation faculty is likely involved in solving problems such as (a) dominance relationships (e.g. Bshary, 2010; Bshary & Grutter, 2006; Raihani, Grutter, & Bshary, 2010; deWaal, 1998), where individuals can minimize injury by inferring from observational learning who is likely to be dominant/submissive (Subiaul, Vonk, Okamoto-Barth, & Barth, 2008); (b) what to eat (Jaeggi et al., 2010; van de Waal, Borgeaud, & Whiten, 2013), that is, learning what is edible and what is not or what to eat when; (c) alliances and cooperation (e.g. Melis & Tomasello, 2013; Schneider, Melis, & Tomasello, 2012), where individuals can minimize the risks of bad alliances by inferring from observation who is a reliable/unreliable partner; and, (d) extractive foraging, where individuals can learn from others how to process or acquire protected food products (e.g. Boesch, Marchesi, Fruth, & Joulian, 1994; Wright et al., 2009). And there are certainly other types of problem that can be solved by imitating others. In each instance, specialized mechanisms in the imitation faculty in coordination with other cognitive faculties grant individuals the flexibility to make rapid inferences about the dispositions of others or the causal structure of actions, bypassing the costs associated with trial-and-error learning, which in some instances may be lethal (e.g. the diet problem). Some of these instances require novel imitation (when knowledge is first acquired and reproduced), but others require only the copying of species-typical behaviors – familiar imitation (e.g. social conventions) – wherein previously acquired behaviors (either via imitation or trial and error) are appropriately and adaptively displayed. Below is an outline of the characteristics of this most significant of mental faculties. Table 6.1 summarises these concepts and terms.

Experimental Evidence from 1970 to Present

Novel Motor Imitation

Starting in the early 1970s, Beck (1972, 1973, 1976) published various studies exploring the imitative abilities of baboons and macaques. All of these studies involved the use of a tool (L-shaped and rake-like) to obtain out-of-reach food.

Table 6.1 *Summary of terms and concepts*

Name	Definition	Operationalization	Examples
Super-ordinate category			
Familiar imitation	Copying actions that have been previously executed	Tasks that involve copying one or two actions that have been previously executed or copying the same complex sequence across many trials	Two-action tasks (Bugnyar & Huber, 1997; Caldwell & Whiten, 2004; Dindo et al., 2008; Tennie et al., 2010b; Voekle & Huber, 2000, 2007; van de Waal & Whiten, 2013; Whiten et al., 1996); floating peanut task (Tennie et al., 2010a)
Novel imitation	Copying actions that have not been previously executed	Tasks that involve copying an entirely new response or tasks that involve copying 3 or more familiar actions in a new sequence on the first trial	Tasks requiring novel tools (Beck, 1972, 1973, 1976; Nagell et al., 1993; Tomasello et al., 1987; Fragaszy & Visalberghi, 1989; trap-tube (Herrmann et al., 2007); puzzle boxes involving 3 familiar responses (Adams-Curtis & Fragszy, 1995)
Sub-ordinate category			
Cognitive imitation	Copying abstract, non-observable rules and responses	Tasks that involve copying goals, ordinal rules, abstract conventions or a series of item-specific responses	Touchscreen tasks that require pressing arbitrary items in a specific sequence (Subiaul et al., 2004, 2007a, 2007b); match-to-sample task (Martin et al., 2011); copying specific food preferences (Snowdon & Boe, 2003; van de Waal et al., 2013)
Vocal imitation	Copying auditory, acoustic responses	Tasks that involve copying words or non-words as well as non-linguistic sounds	Matching vocal tone and pitch (Mantell et al., 2013; Stoeger et al., 2012); words (Giret et al., 2009); accent (Subiaul et al., 2015)
Motor imitation	Copying motor actions and responses	Tasks that involve copying motor actions and responses including manual, bodily and oral-facial gestures	Manual gestures, including tool use (Beck, 1972, 1973, 1976; Call & Tomasello, 2004; Nagell et al., 1993; Tomasello et al., 1987; Vasalberghi & Fragaszy, 1990, 1995, 1996); bodily gestures (Custance et al., 1995); oral-facial gestures (Bard, 2007; Ferrari et al., 2006; Myowa-Yamakoshi, & Matzusawa, 2004)

As macaques and baboons (and, in fact, virtually all monkeys) do not habitually use tools in the wild (but see Fragaszy & Perry, 2003; Haslam, Gumert, Biro, Carvalho, & Malaivijitnond, 2013), learning how to operate a tool to procure reinforcement represents an example of novel motor imitation. Beck used a single-cage method (Hall, 1963) to test his subjects. This method resulted in a number of interpretational confounds. Whereas social facilitation may explain the few examples of motor imitation recorded by Beck (1976) in one study, social inhibition likely explains the lack of motor imitation in another (Beck, 1973). The failure of monkeys to learn in this second novel motor imitation task was replicated by Chamove (1974), who reported similar results with rhesus macaques.

In contrast to monkeys, most wild ape species are regular tool users, such as chimpanzees (Whiten et al., 1999) and orangutans (van Schaik et al., 2003). Yet, results across various studies suggest they have significant difficulties (or are incapable of) copying specific tool actions. For example, Tomasello, Davis-Dasilva, Camak, and Bard (1987) used a raking task with a T-shaped rake to explore imitation in captive chimpanzees. Older chimpanzees largely failed at the task, but younger chimpanzees that witnessed an expert chimpanzee raking food items toward itself were more successful at obtaining food items than control individuals that witnessed no such demonstration. Although the chimpanzees were able to learn to manipulate the tool correctly for some placements of the food, they did not copy the demonstrator's idiosyncratic use of the tool in all instances, leading to some failures to retrieve food items.

Nagell and colleagues (1993) performed a similar study with a rake tool that could be used in one of two positions – with the prongs up (optimal) or down (less efficient). Chimpanzees saw either no demonstration, a partial demonstration by a human (prongs up) or a full demonstration by a human (prongs up). All chimpanzees were given the tool in a prongs-down position. The groups viewing different demonstrations did not differ in the proportion of times they used the rake in the prongs-up position. While the chimpanzees that saw some type of demonstration made more attempts and successful attempts than the chimpanzees that saw no demonstration, those seeing the full demonstration did not learn anything extra (e.g. about how to position the tool) compared to those seeing the partial demonstration. Call and Tomasello (1994) performed a similar raking demonstration study with orangutans, and found that the type of demonstration seen by the orangutans (prongs up or prongs down) did not affect the position in which orangutans subsequently used the tool.

Herrmann et al. (2007), as part of the Primate Cognition Test Battery, tested chimpanzees and orangutans on a set of three novel tasks involving extracting a reward item from a tube. Demonstrations were given by a human experimenter. Chimpanzees and orangutans largely failed to solve the tube problems using the demonstrated means (the overall success rate of chimpanzees was 10 percent; that of orangutans, 7 percent).

Adams-Curtis and Fragaszy (1995) used a mechanical puzzle to test the imitative abilities of capuchin monkeys. The use of a mechanical puzzle board with three defences (bolt, hasp and hinge) represents another means of testing novel motor imitation. These researchers allowed their subjects to operate the mechanical puzzle to receive a reward after observing an expert model. Adams-Curtis (1987) and Adams-Curtis and Fragaszy (1995) reported that, while naïve capuchins appeared interested in the task and were attracted to various aspects of the puzzle (i.e. stimulus enhancement), subjects neither discovered the solution nor performed the model's sequence of actions while engaged with the task.

Fragaszy & Visalberghi (1989) and Visalberghi, Fragaszy, and Savage-Rumbaugh (1995b) have been credited with systematically testing capuchins' imitative abilities (Tomasello & Call, 1997). These authors devised a tool-using/tool-making task, which tests specific modes of utilizing a given tool(s) in a given context. Perhaps their most well-known paradigm is the 'trap-tube' task. Tasks such as the trap-tube exclude entirely the possibility of any familiar imitation by virtue of both the novelty of the problem and the fact that in some experiments the tool, while familiar, had to be composed (or decomposed) in a specific and novel fashion in order to be operational. In the course of nearly half a dozen studies, Visalberghi and Fragaszy's results corroborated the conclusions of Adam-Curtis (1987) and Adam-Curtis and Fragaszy (1995). That is, while subjects were motivated to interact with the tool and the experimental task (i.e. stimulus and social enhancement), they were either uninterested or unable to replicate the precise means used by a model to solve the problem or even how to use the tool itself. From this, Fragaszy and Visalberghi (2004) have concluded that monkeys likely learn from individual trial and error and/or stimulus/local enhancement rather than from 'true' imitation. That is, capuchins failed to copy the demonstrated means used to achieve the observed end result. Horner & Whiten (2007) and Herrmann and colleagues (2007) have used the trap tube task with chimpanzees and orangutans. Results have generally replicated those reported by Visalberghi, Fragaszy and colleagues. In general, the great apes tested used idiosyncratic responses in an effort to retrieve the reward inside the tube, rather than the demonstrated tool-using technique.

The work of Tomasello et al. (1987) has generally challenged the notion that great apes are capable of novel motor imitation. It may be that the raking tasks selected by Nagell et al. (1993) and Call and Tomasello (1994) and the tasks of Herrmann et al. (2007) were sufficiently difficult to make imitation unlikely. In contrast, there are various studies by Whiten and colleagues that suggest that chimpanzees may excel in at least some motor imitation tasks (Horner & Whiten, 2005; Horner, Whiten, Flynn, & de Waal, 2006; Whiten, Horner, & de Waal, 2005). Though these tasks, critically, include either relatively familiar objects, actions or responses (Subiaul, 2016). There is much less evidence that monkeys engage in novel motor imitation in the specific tasks used to date.

There are, of course, a number of different reasons why monkeys may have failed to demonstrate learning in these novel motor imitation paradigms. In some instances (e.g. Beck, 1976), learning may have been inhibited by the presence of a dominant conspecific (Fragaszy & Visalberghi, 1989, 1990); in other instances, learning may have been limited by sometimes onerous motor confounds (e.g. Visalberghi et al., 1995a). The latter is a significant concern given that monkeys do not habitually use tools in the wild, with the exceptions of capuchin monkeys (Fragaszy & Visalberghi, 2004) and macaques (Gumert, Hoong, & Malaivijitnond, 2011; Haslam et al., 2013). Indeed, the work of Seed, Call, Emery, & Clayton (2009) with chimpanzees indicates that difficulties with tool use may inhibit primate performance in trap tasks. These limitations have led to the development of paradigms that attempt to assess different facets of the imitation faculty in monkeys: (1) the two-action paradigm (Dawson & Foss, 1965), and (2) the cognitive imitation paradigm (Subiaul et al., 2004). Each will be discussed in turn.

Familiar Motor Imitation

Concern over motor confounds and a limited motor repertoire has led to the use of a bidirectional (Dawson & Foss, 1965) or two-action imitation procedure (Akins & Zentall, 1996). In these paradigms, reinforcement results from the use of two (or more) possible actions (for example, pushing or pulling a door to retrieve a reward). The assumption of such paradigms is that if individuals are sensitive to the actions of others and are capable of copying specific motor movements, they should be more prone to copy the model's technique than an alternative technique, which is also associated with reinforcement. In fact, many animals – from rats to various species of birds – have been shown to copy a model's motor response (Heyes, 2011b; Zentall, 2012). Because the target actions are all familiar to the observers and present in their behavioral repertoire, there is no motor learning per se. However, because in some instances individuals are learning how to apply a familiar rule in a novel context (i.e., contextual imitation, Byrne, 2005). Such behaviors may be achieved by the coordinated activities of a novel cognitive imitation mechanism (see below) and a familiar motor imitation mechanism (e.g., associative learning; see Heyes, 2012).

This procedure markedly differs from those described above where individuals must learn a novel operational rule that does not exist in their behavioral repertoire. The two-action or bidirectional procedure tests subjects' ability to copy a specific but familiar motor response in a purposeful and replicable fashion. As a result, these two-action and bidirectional procedures represent a measure of *familiar* motor imitation, not *novel* motor imitation (for a complementary perspective, characterizing "novelty" in imitation studies, see Byrne, 2005).

Bugnyar and Huber (1997) were among the first to use this paradigm in a monkey species, the common marmoset. In this paradigm, monkeys observed a model use one of two familiar actions to open a door – pulling or pushing

– and retrieve food hidden behind it. Although there were two possible means of opening the door, only one method was demonstrated ('pulling'). The control group did not see any type of interaction with the box; hence, there was no 'enhancement' control. Given these limitations, Bugnyar and Huber (ibid) reported that, during the first phase of the study, two of the five monkeys showed a preference for the modeled 'pull' technique. But in subsequent testing sessions, these monkeys settled upon the alternate 'push' technique, perhaps because it was less motorically complex.

Several other studies suggest that monkeys are capable of familiar motor imitation. In a series of studies, Fragaszy and colleagues devised a two-action task where juvenile capuchin monkeys living in two captive groups could obtain juice in one of two ways: (1) by putting a finger into an opening and turning a wheel that provided juice or (2) by pushing down a lever in order to get a burst of juice. Both of these actions are familiar to animals; as such, they represent examples of familiar motor imitation. Fragaszy et al. (2001, 2002, as cited in Fragaszy & Visalberghi, 2004) report that none of the juveniles solved the problem or learned a specific technique. However, when a different group of immature capuchin monkeys was allowed to watch adult capuchin models, there was some evidence of familiar imitation. Importantly, the authors note that observers tended to adopt the solution style of the adults in their groups. However, because these studies are unpublished it is difficult to evaluate the exact methods used. One potential problem is that the actions used by the models may have been opaque (i.e. inserting a finger in an opening may have occluded the view of an observer) and thus limited motor imitation performance.

Dindo, Thierry, and Whiten (2008) used a more transparent puzzle box experiment where food could be accessed by sliding or lifting a door. They implemented a diffusion chain paradigm with capuchin monkeys wherein each student became the next model, creating an unbroken chain of social learning. Two chains were initiated, one with each opening method, and the monkeys imitated the seeded method with extremely high fidelity. While local or stimulus enhancement could mediate this process, these results provide another piece of evidence for familiar motor imitation in capuchins.

In order to resolve the problem of local enhancement, van de Waal and Whiten (2013) proceeded to design a new puzzle box to further illuminate the imitation faculty in vervets. They used an artificial fruit that could be opened by lifting a door or sliding it left or right using a single handle. Since the same manipulator was used in each type of opening, the spread of a specific type of demonstration would have to be due to copying the actions of the model. Each of these three types of opening spread preferentially in the groups that they were seeded, providing evidence that vervets are not merely spreading information through local or stimulus enhancement.

Caldwell and Whiten (2004), in another familiar motor imitation paradigm, presented common marmosets with a version of an 'artificial fruit', a mechanical puzzle box that was originally developed for the purposes of testing the imitation learning skills of chimpanzees (Whiten et al., 1996). The apparatus used by Caldwell and Whiten (2004) was smaller and had only a single defense; a handle that had to be removed to release a lid in order to obtain the food reward enclosed. Caldwell and Whiten (ibid) report results that are very similar to those reported for capuchin monkeys by Adams-Curtis, Visalberghi, Fragaszy and colleagues reported above. In effect, the marmosets that saw a full demonstration interacted with the apparatus more and were more likely to make contact with the relevant parts of the apparatus (i.e. stimulus enhancement) than control monkeys that saw a partial demonstration (i.e. a monkey eating next to an open apparatus) or those that saw no demonstration.

Two-action tasks have also been used to explore imitation in apes. Whiten, Custance, Gómez, Teixidor, and Bard (1996) created a similar task consisting of an artificial fruit with different possible solutions. After chimpanzees viewed a human demonstrate one of two opening methods (to poke or twist a bolt latch, or to turn or spin a barrel latch), they were more likely to use the method they had seen demonstrated in their first attempt to obtain the reward. However, in a separate study, Tennie, Greve, Gretscher, & Call (2010b) found that apes (bonobos, chimpanzees, gorillas and orangutans) that viewed a full demonstration of solutions to several novel two-action tasks did not copy the target actions from the demonstration on the first trial.

In a variation on the two-action experiment, Voelkl and Huber (2000) gave marmoset subjects a film canister that could be opened using either the mouth or the hand. There were three groups: (1) full-demonstration (mouth or hand opening), (2) no demonstration, and (3) olfactory control (no demonstration, but subjects were presented with the canisters that had been opened by mouth). Voelkl and Huber (ibid) report that, of the six subjects that observed a conspecific using the mouth-opening technique, four used the same technique, whereas none of the subjects that saw the hand-opening technique used the mouth technique. These results are intriguing, but complicated by the fact that the first session of testing included 15 trials (first trial performance is not reported) and, in those 15 trials, only two monkeys used the mouth-opening technique consistently. The other monkeys were either as likely or more likely to use the hand-opening technique. This contrasts with monkeys that saw the hand technique, which used the same technique as the model 100 percent of the time. This pattern of performance is inconsistent with familiar motor imitation (or 'true imitation'). If marmosets are capable of familiar motor imitation, then performance in the mouth-opening group should resemble performance in the hand-opening group and should not be restricted to just one type of action. The fact that it does not suggest that these monkeys are biased to use a particular type of motor response or that individual responses are mediated by motivational and attentional mechanisms that lie outside the imitation faculty.

In another experiment, Voelkl and Huber (2007) focused on the mouth-opening technique and, using detailed motion analysis, evaluated whether observers and non-observers copied not only the global action but also the specific movement patterns associated with the mouth-opening technique. Using a discriminant function analysis, the authors report that the overall movement patterns of observers were more like those of the demonstrators than the movement patterns of the non-observers. They argue that because the movement path to successful opening is rather broad, any similarities cannot be explained by functional constraints alone. However, Voelkl and Huber's (2007) results would be more compelling if individuals could reliably copy movement patterns other than a single species-typical action (i.e. mouthing).

In a study designed to address some of the problems discussed in Voelkl and Huber (2007), van de Waal and Whiten (2012) used a similar canister that could be opened in one of three ways: with the mouth, hands or a rope attached to either side. Since mouth opening seemed to be the default means of opening for monkeys in general, they examined the imitation of the rarer hand and rope openings. In the group of vervet monkeys that saw the hand-opening demonstration, individuals used their hands to open the canister significantly more during first attempts, successful attempts and overall attempts, showing very successful imitation of this method. In the group that saw the rope-opening technique, vervets attempted to use the rope more overall and on successful attempts, but the difference was not significant for first attempts. It is clear that the vervets were using some kind of social learning mechanism, and the fidelity of copying the body part used indicates a focus on the model that is indicative of imitation rather than merely learning the affordances of the container.

Various other tasks can be used to assess familiar motor imitation in primates. Tennie, Call, & Tomasello (2010a) used the 'floating peanut task' to assess imitation in chimpanzees. In the floating peanut task, a buoyant item such as a peanut is placed at the bottom of a tube that is fixed in an upright position; the most common solution is to add enough water to the tube so that the item is retrievable as it floats close to the top of the tube. Chimpanzees were given demonstrations of water being added to the tube by another chimpanzee (using its mouth) or by a human (using a water bottle). Some, but by no means all, chimpanzees successfully solved the problem by spitting water into the tube (5 of 13 who saw a chimpanzee demonstrator and 3 of 14 who saw a human demonstrator).

Some studies have provided evidence that monkeys (Dindo et al., 2008; Voelkl & Huber, 2007; van de Waal & Whiten, 2013) and apes (Tennie et al., 2010a; Whiten, Custance, Gomez, Teixidor, & Bard, 1996) are able to engage in familiar imitation, and the work of Voelkl and Huber and van de Waal and Whiten demonstrates that monkeys are sensitive to specific movement patterns and are capable of familiar motor imitation. However, other studies have provided evidence to the contrary. The results reported by Fragaszy, Visalberghi and their associates are perhaps the best evidence that monkeys have not displayed the ability to copy novel motor responses (such as those that require the use of tools in novel ways). But certainly, more research is needed before we can confidently state that monkeys are capable of familiar imitation or incapable of novel imitation.

Familiar Motor Imitation: Oral-facial Imitation

Marmosets' ability to match opaque facial and head movements parallels reports on human infants copying oral-facial expressions such as mouth openings and tongue protrusions (Meltzoff & Moore, 1977). It has long been believed that the ability to match oral-facial expression represented a human cognitive specialization associated with higher-order cognitive abilities (Meltzoff, 1988, 1999). However, the uniqueness of this ability has been put in doubt by reports showing that chimpanzees (Myowa-Yamakoshi, Tomonaga, Tanaka, & Matsuzawa, 2004) and rhesus monkeys (Ferrari et al., 2006) are also sensitive to such stimuli and copy these expressions in a pattern similar to that present in humans.

However, it is an open question whether the mechanisms mediating the copying of oral-facial responses in infancy are the same as those mediating imitation in older children and adults. This has led some to question the validity of neonatal imitation (e.g., Ray & Heyes, 2011; Jones, 2009). First, an extensive review of the literature revealed that only tongue protrusions are matched by human infants (Anisfeld, 1991, 1996; Anisfeld et al., 2001; Ray & Heyes, 2011). Second, and perhaps most surprisingly, a number of studies have demonstrated that a moving pen (Jacobson, 1979), blinking light(s) (Jones, 1996) and music (Jones, 2006) are all as likely to elicit tongue protrusions in neonates as is watching a model display the same behavior. However, the study by Ferrari and colleagues (2009, 2006) on neonatal imitation in macaques is unique in that the experimental design included non-social controls such as a spinning disk in addition to the typical social stimuli in such experiments (i.e. mouth opening, tongue protrusions, and so on). Ferrari and colleagues reported that lip-smacking and tongue protrusions occurred significantly more often in response to displays of those same actions. However, lip-smacking occurred the most often in response to different types of stimuli, much like tongue protrusions in human infants (Jones, 1996). Ferrari et al. (2006), noting the amount of inter-individual variation and the sensitivity to specific oral-facial movements (e.g. mouth openings and tongue protrusions) in both human and monkey neonatal imitation, pointedly caution that, 'the capacity to respond to the model may not reflect a general imitative skill but rather a sensorimotor sensitivity tuned to specific facial gestures' (p. 1506). At this point, it is impossible to say with any certainty whether these results are mediated by a mechanism independent of the imitation faculty or whether they simply reflect the output of an imitation faculty that is not yet mature.

While, overall, some apes are capable of motor imitation in a variety of situations, the research reviewed above suggests that the motor imitation skills of monkeys are significantly limited. This is certainly more true for novel motor imitation than for familiar motor imitation; at least as measured by the two-action procedure(s). This prompts the question of whether or not monkeys suffer from a novel imitation deficit in general (Ferrari et al., 2006; Visalberghi & Fragaszy, 2004) or whether monkeys are specifically impaired in novel motor imitation. In order to answer that question, however, a test must isolate the copying of novel motor rules from the copying of non-motor (cognitive) rules.

Novel Cognitive Imitation: Copying Serial Rules

Although much has been written about motor imitation as well as vocal imitation in mammals and birds (Janik & Slater, 2000; Zentall, 2006, 2012), little has been written about the imitation of non-motor, non-vocal rules. Subiaul et al. (2004) were the first to demonstrate that the copying of cognitive – serial – rules can be isolated from the imitation of motor rules. The studies conducted on novel cognitive imitation were analogous to learning someone's password at an automated teller machine (ATM) by looking over that person's shoulder. Because the observer already knows how to enter numbers on the keypad, no motor learning is necessary. (In some respects, the actual paradigm that was used was more difficult because, unlike the numbers on a keypad, the pictures on the screen changed spatial position from trial to trial.) Nevertheless, the ATM example illustrates the two different rules that individuals might learn from such an event. For instance, when copying someone's password, observers may copy a motor-spatial rule (e.g. up, down, left, right), ignoring the sequence of numbers being pressed. Conversely, someone might copy the actual numbers pressed (e.g. 2, 8, 4, 6), disregarding the specific motor responses corresponding with each number's location on the touch pad. In both instances the observer is copying a rule; the principal difference is the type of rule that is learned and copied by the observer: motor-spatial versus cognitive/ordinal.

In one experiment (Subiaul et al., 2004, Experiment 1), two rhesus macaques were given the opportunity to execute serial chains involving novel lists of pictures in one of two ways: by trial and error (baseline) or by observing an 'expert' macaque execute the same list in an adjacent chamber (social-learning condition). When the monkeys' performances in the baseline and in the social-learning conditions were compared, results revealed that naïve 'student' macaques who observed an 'expert' executing a new list during the social-learning condition, learned significantly faster than in a baseline condition where they had to learn new lists entirely by trial and error.

In a second experiment (Subiaul et al., 2004, Experiment 2), student macaques were given the opportunity to observe an expert execute a list (e.g. list A). At the end of 20 trials, the student was tested on a *different* list (e.g. list B). Students in this social-facilitation condition could not learn from the expert because both students and experts executed different lists of arbitrary pictures. As in the social-learning condition, performance in the social-facilitation condition was compared to baseline where subjects had to learn new lists entirely by trial and error. In this experiment, any difference between a student's rate of learning in the social-facilitation and baseline conditions would be the result of social facilitation (Zajonc, 1965) rather than novel imitation. Yet, the rate of learning in the social-facilitation and the baseline conditions did not statistically differ.

In all conditions, computer feedback was available to student monkeys. However, in the social-learning condition (Experiment 1) the student could have learned from the computer feedback alone, rather than from the actions of the model, the ordinal position of list items. To test whether performance in the social-learning condition could be replicated by providing naïve students with computer feedback only, in Experiment 3 all features of the social-learning condition were maintained, except that during the computer feedback condition no monkey was present in the adjacent chamber and the computer automatically highlighted the target items in the correct serial order. This control condition is often referred to in the literature as the 'ghost control'. After 20 trials, the student was tested on the same list. As was done in the previous experiments, students' performance in this ghost control was compared with performance in the baseline condition. Results demonstrated that monkeys did not benefit from computer feedback alone, as evidenced by the fact that the rate of learning in the ghost condition did not differ from the rate of learning in the baseline condition. However, a similar test given to human children and individuals with autism showed that children learned in the ghost control (Subiaul et al., 2007); a result that has been replicated in numerous motor imitation studies with children (Huang & Charman, 2005; Subiaul, Vonk, & Rutherford, 2011; Thompson & Russell, 2004) but not other primates, including apes, that have failed to learn in this control condition (Hopper, 2010; Hopper, Lambeth, Schapiro, & Whiten, 2008; Tennie, Call, & Tomasello, 2006). For an excellent review of studies using ghost controls, see Hopper (2010).

What might account for the differences between monkeys and human participants' performance in the ghost condition? One hypothesis is that the difference may rest on the propensity of human subjects (but not non-human animals) to generate percepts of agency, goal-directedness and/or intentionality to aid imitation in the ghost control. This potentially unique human ability has been reported in human infants, who attribute intentionality and/or goal-directedness to a ball that jumps over a barrier and navigates around obstacles (Csibra, 2003). Yet, no comparable evidence exists for monkeys (Cheney & Seyfarth, 1990). However, see Santos and colleagues for possible exceptions (Lyons, Santos, & Keil, 2006; Phillips, Barnes, Mahajan, Yamaguchi, & Santos, 2009).

Using a different paradigm, Martin, Biro, and Matsuzawa (2011) designed an experiment to test whether apes can use 'public information', i.e. information provided by another individual, in order to solve a problem and receive a reward. The task was a match-to-sample paradigm in which one chimpanzee, in response to a hidden cue, initially selected one of two colored panels on their touchscreen; after this, it was the task of the second chimpanzee to select a panel of the same color on a separate screen in order to receive a reward. Both chimpanzees tested were able to use the information gained by watching the other chimpanzee complete their half of the task (Martin et al., 2011). These results indicate that, along with monkeys, apes can imitate another's use of a rule to get a reward.

In sum, the fact that monkeys are capable of flexibly copying novel cognitive rules suggests that monkeys may have a novel motor imitation deficit rather than a general imitation learning deficit. In other words, the fact that monkeys can copy novel cognitive rules from a model demonstrates that monkeys are capable of certain types of novel imitation. Additionally, given that some evidence exists for familiar motor imitation but none for novel motor imitation in monkeys is further evidence that the motor planning and execution systems of apes might be more derived than those of monkeys and other animals, perhaps as a result of apes' long history of using tools (Mercader, Panger, & Boesch, 2002; Mercader et al., 2007). Nevertheless, additional research is necessary in order to better understand monkeys' motor imitation limitations.

Novel Cognitive Imitation: Copying Food Preferences

Given the results of Subiaul and colleagues, what might be the function of cognitive imitation in more ecologically valid settings? One possibility is that novel cognitive imitation is critical for learning and copying social rules that provide individuals with the tools to manage dominance hierarchies, kin relationships and socio-political relationships or alliances at low costs; costs which are too high if not impossible to manage without a social learning mechanism. But in addition to these benefits, novel cognitive imitation may also be critical for learning which foods are palatable. After all, Reader and Laland (2002) note that anecdotal reports of innovation and social learning are most common in foraging. In a number of studies, Visalberghi and colleagues have explored this very question using a captive population of capuchin monkeys. Capuchin monkeys are in many regards an ideal species with which to study the cognitive imitation of novel food preferences because, while they are moderately neophobic of new foods, captive capuchins sit near each other during feeding and closely attend to what others are eating (Fragaszy, Izar, Visalberghi, Ottoni, & de Oliveira, 2004). Capuchins are also very tolerant, allowing conspecifics to take small bits of food they have dropped (Fragaszy & Visalberghi, 2004). Given these characteristics, it seems that their behavioral and motivational states are optimal for observational learning and novel cognitive imitation. Visalberghi and Fragaszy (2004) reason that there are at least three mechanisms by which individuals could acquire novel food preferences. These mechanisms range from (1) a general (arousal/motivational) mechanism that increases feeding overall without regard to particular food items, to (2) a more subtle mechanism where subjects are attracted to novel items in general (e.g. neophilia), to (3) cognitive imitation, where individuals acquire a dietary rule(s) pertaining to the palatability of particular foods.

Visalberghi and Fragaszy (2004) cite a number of studies that suggest that capuchin monkeys use a general (motivational or arousal) mechanism that increases feeding, particularly when presented with novel foods (i.e. neophilia). For Visalberghi and Fragaszy, this precludes any evidence for novel cognitive imitation in the food domain. These conclusions are buttressed by a number of studies showing that monkeys are more likely to eat when in the presence of others than when alone (Galloway, 1998 as cited in Fragaszy & Visalberghi, 2004; Visalberghi & Adessi, 2000). For example, Adessi and Visalberghi (2001) presented capuchins with novel food items (consisting of different food products that were mashed and differentially colored) in three different conditions: (1) alone, (2) in the presence of non-eating group members, and (3) in the presence of eating group members. They reported that, as group size increased, so did the consumption of the novel food product by the observing monkey. Moreover, the sight of a conspecific eating a novel colored food was sufficient to increase food consumption (independently of condition) for two of the three different types of novel food products presented. While these results provide important insights into the feeding behavior of capuchin monkeys, they are not designed as social learning experiments *per se*, as subjects are not provided with a choice, for example between a 'palatable' and a 'non-palatable' food item. However, Visalberghi and Fragaszy (2004) cite unpublished data (i.e. Adessi & Visalberghi, 2002) suggesting that, even when provided with a choice, capuchin monkeys do not show a preference for the 'palatable' food. But in studies that changed the palatability of a familiar food item, there was no difference between a social condition (with a model eating the now-unpalatable food) and an individual learning condition, where subjects discovered the palatability of the food item by happenstance (Visalberghi & Adessi, 2001).

Van de Waal, Borgeaud, and Whiten (2013) conducted a study examining the role of social learning in foraging decisions of vervet monkeys. A group of wild vervets was presented with food of two colors, palatable blue and unpalatable pink. These monkeys were trained to avoid the pink food. During the experimental phase, immigrant males and newborns were presented with a choice between the two types of food, both of which were palatable. All of the newborns imitated the choice of their mother, with 26 choosing the locally-preferred variant and one mother/child pair choosing the other. The preference for the local variant was not as strong in immigrant males, with seven out of ten choosing the local variant; however, when there were no higher-ranking males present this rose to nine out of ten. This provides compelling evidence for two modes of information transfer, one that is vertical, with young vervets extremely faithfully copying their mothers, and one that is horizontal, with information being drawn from conspecifics. In addition, immigrant males seem to be combining this information with dominance hierarchies in order to balance the dangers of the diet problem with the dangers associated with violations of dominance.

Van de Waal, Bshary, and Whiten (2014) went on to study the tendency of newborns to imitate their mothers. Rather than using palatability, where the social information could be coming from a variety of sources, they examined five different approaches to eating grapes: rubbing the grape against hands or a substrate; opening the grape with the hands or mouth; or no cleaning. Again, they found a significant trend for newborns to copy matrilineally-related monkeys. This provides a strong case of ecologically useful information being passed on through a copying – imitative – mechanism.

Similarly, cotton-top tamarins living in a family group avoided palatable food (tuna) that was experimentally manipulated to be unpalatable (excess pepper) after observing a conspecific reject the food (Snowdon & Boe, 2003). In three groups of tamarins, the aversion for the unpalatable food was long lasting. The avoidance and disgust reactions toward tuna were still present after 10 months. These results provide compelling evidence of vicarious learning for which foods are *not* palatable. But, given that tamarins were presented with only one or the other type of food, it is possible that innate mechanisms that lie outside of the imitation faculty could have mediated the avoidance response.

Hopper, Schapiro, Lambeth, and Brosnan (2011) developed a paradigm in which chimpanzees exchanged two types of 'tokens' for food; one token could be traded for a carrot (a medium-value reward) and the other could be traded for a grape (a high-value reward). Two groups of chimpanzees were given both types of token for exchange. When a demonstrator chimpanzee (a high-ranking female) in one group was seen to trade a token for the high-value reward, the others in the group preferred to make the same exchange. Surprisingly, when a demonstrator in the other group was seen to trade a token for the medium-value reward, the other chimpanzees in her group also preferred to make this exchange, rather than trade the other token for a grape. These results indicate that chimpanzees copy (with high fidelity) the food choices of a demonstrator, even when the alternative food may be more desirable.

One concern with most of these studies is that a basic arousal mechanism and/or an attentional mechanism may explain some of these vicariously learned food preferences. An ideal study on cognitive imitation for novel food preferences would have a 'student' see a model eat different types of novel food items that are entirely unknown to the student and whose palatabilities vary along three dimensions: good, bad, neutral. The dependent variable would then be whether the student's response(s) (i.e. latency to approach and expressions of disgust/avoidance) prior to tasting the foods in a forced choice test are consistent with the responses of the model. An alternative approach would be to use a token economy and assess whether primates copy what conspecifics pay for novel food items. Such studies would clarify whether the mechanism(s) mediating food preferences are those of the imitation faculty or some other independent mechanism associated with approach/avoidance responses, arousal or attention alone.

Conclusions

There is no simple answer to the question, 'Do monkeys and apes imitate?' The main reason is that imitation is not a unitary skill. Here, imitation has been conceptualized as a multifaceted psychological faculty whose function is to adaptively and flexibly copy others' knowledge and responses. This faculty has two main functions: the ability to copy familiar skills that are recalled from long-term memory and the ability to copy novel skills that are generated "from scratch", potentially, in working memory. Subsumed within each of these global systems are more specialized imitation mechanisms for copying different types of stimuli: motor (i.e. actions), vocal (sounds) and cognitive (unobservable, abstract representations). Given the behavioral and neurobiological evidence, it has been proposed that the ability to copy familiar responses represents the primitive state of this faculty. The ability to copy novel responses represents a more derived state of the same faculty.

Monkeys appear capable of copying familiar motor rules, as evidenced by studies demonstrating that marmosets and vervets use the same opening technique as a model to open a sealed can, for example (Voelkl & Huber, 2007; van de Waal & Whiten, 2012). Macaques may also possess the ability to copy at least some familiar facial expressions such as lip-smacking (Ferrari et al., 2006). However, monkeys have not evidenced novel motor imitation. This result is in contrast to apes, which have been shown to differentially copy novel or arbitrary motor actions (Horner & Whiten, 2005; Myowa-Yamakoshi &

Matsuzawa, 1999; Whiten, 1998). Yet, despite monkeys' inability to copy novel motor responses, they are capable of copying novel cognitive (non-motor) rules (Subiaul, et al., 2004); a result which demonstrates that, while monkeys may be incapable of novel motor imitation, they are capable of novel cognitive imitation or imitation learning.

So, while novel motor imitation represents a highly advanced cognitive skill that may be unique to the great apes, perhaps due to dietary pressures favoring tool use in apes (but not in monkeys) and resulting in unique cognitive and neural specializations in the parietal lobe, familiar imitation represents a more general yet indispensable skill for social animals that must conform to the vagaries of sometimes strict social hierarchies and coordinated group activities such as feeding and territory defense. These pressures common in social animals likely favored a basic imitation faculty whose primary skill is to adaptively copy familiar rules and responses expressed by conspecifics. Such a skill in response to social pressures is not significantly different from the folk saying among humans that compels us to engage in familiar imitation, 'When in Rome, do as the Romans do'.

References

Adams-Curtis, L. (1987). Social context of manipulative behavior in Cebus apella. *American Journal of Primatology*, 12, 325.

Adams-Curtis, L., & Fragaszy, D. M. (1995). Influence of a skilled model on the behavior of conspecific observers in tufted capuchin monkeys (Cebus apella). *American Journal of Primatology*, 37, 65–71.

Akins, C. K., & Zentall, T. (1996). Imitative learning in male Japanese quail (Coturnix japonica) using the two-action method. *Journal of Comparative Psychology*, 110, 316–320.

Anisfeld, M. (1991). Neonatal imitation: Review. *Developmental Review*, 11(60–97), 4(9), e302.

(1996). Only tongue protrusion modeling is matched by neonates. *Developmental Review*, 16, 149–161.

Anisfeld, M., Turkewitz, G., Rose, S. A., Rosenburg, F. R., Sheiber, F. J., et al. (2001). No compelling evidence that newborns imitate oral gestures. *Infancy*, 2(1), 111–122.

Ankel-Simmons, F. (2000). *Primate anatomy: An introduction*. London: Academic Press.

Bandura, A. (1977). *Social learning theory*. Upper Saddle River, NJ: Prentice Hall.

Bard, K. A. (2007). Neonatal imitation in chimpanzees (Pan troglodytes) tested with two paradigms. *Animal Cognition*, 10(2), 233–242. doi: 10.1007/s10071-006-0062-3.

Bauer, P. J., & Mandler, J. M. (1992). Putting the horse before the cart: The use of temporal order in recall of events by one-year-old children. *Developmental Psychology*, 28(3), 441–452.

Beck, B. B. (1972). Tool use in captive hamadryas baboons. *Primates*, 13, 277–295.

(1973). Observation learning of tool use by captive Guinea baboons (Papio papio). *American Journal of Physical Anthropology*, 38(2), 579–582.

(1976). Tool use by captive pigtailed macaques. *Primates*, 17, 301–310.

Boesch, C., Marchesi, N., Fruth, B., & Joulian, F. (1994). Is nut cracking in wild chimpanzees a cultural behavior? *Journal of Human Evolution*, 26(4), 325–338.

Boinski, S., Quatrone, R. P., Sughrue, K., Selvaggi, L., Henry, M., et al. (2003). Do brown capuchins socially learn foraging skills? In D. M. Fragaszy & S. Perry (Eds.), *The biology of traditions*. Cambridge: Cambridge University Press.

Boyd, R., & Richerson, P. J. (1985). *Culture and the evolutionary process*. Chicago, IL: University of Chicago Press.

(1994). Why does culture increase human adaptability? *Ethology and Sociobiology*, 16, 125–143.

Bshary, R. (2010). Decision making: Solving the battle of the fishes. *Current Biology*, 20(2), R70–R71. doi: S0960-9822(09)02077-6 [pii] 10.1016/j.cub.2009.12.002.

Bshary, R., & Grutter, A. S. (2006). Image scoring and cooperation in a cleaner fish mutualism. *Nature*, 441(7096), 975–978. doi: nature04755 [pii] 10.1038/nature04755.

Bugnyar, T., & Huber, L. (1997). Push or pull: An experimental study on imitation in marmosets. *Animal Behaviour*, 54(4), 817–831. doi: ar960497 [pii].

Byrne, R. W. (2005). Detecting, Understanding, and Explaining Imitation by Animals. In S. Hurley & N. Chater (Eds.), *Perspectives on Imitation: From Neurosciences to Social Science* (Vol. 1: Mechanisms of Imitation and Imitation in Animals, pp. 225–242). Cambridge, MA: MIT Press.

(2005). Social cognition: Imitation, imitation, imitation. *Current Biology*, 15(13), R498–R500. doi: S0960-9822(05)00666-4 [pii] 10.1016/j.cub.2005.06.031.

Byrne, R. W., & Russon, A. E. (1998). Learning by imitation: A hierarchical approach. *Behavioral & Brain Sciences*, 21, 667–721.

Caldwell, C. A., & Whiten, A. (2004). Testing for social learning and imitation in common marmosets, Callithrix jacchus, using an artificial fruit. *Animal Cognition*, 7(2), 77–85. doi: 10.1007/s10071-003-0192-9.

Call, J., & Tomasello, M. (1994). The social learning of tool use by orangutan (Pongo pygmaeus). *Human Evolution*, 9, 297–313.

Carey, S. (1985). *Conceptual change in childhood*. Cambridge, MA: MIT Press.

Carpenter, M., Akhtar, N., & Tomasello, M. (1998). Fourteen- through 18-month-old infants differentially imitate intentional and accidental actions. *Infant Behavior and Development*, 21(2), 315–330.

Carpenter, M., & Call, J. (2002). The chemistry of social learning. *Developmental Science,* 5(1), 22–24.

Carruthers, P. (2006). *The architecture of mind*. Oxford: Oxford University Press.

Chamove, A. S. (1974). Failure to find rhesus observational learning. *Journal of the Behavioral Sciences*, 2, 39–41.

Chartrand, T. L., & Bargh, J. A. (1999). The chameleon effect: The perception–behavior link and social interaction. *Journal of Personality and Social Psychology*, 76(6), 893–910.

Cheney, D. L., & Seyfarth, R. M. (1990). *How monkeys see the world*. Chicago, IL: University of Chicago Press.

Cook, R., Bird, G., Lunser, G., Huck, S., & Heyes, C. (2012). Automatic imitation in a strategic context: Players of rock-paper-scissors imitate opponents' gestures. *Proceedings of the Biological Sciences/Royal Society*, 279(1729), 780–786. doi: 10.1098/rspb.2011.1024.

Csibra, G. (2003). Teleological and referential understanding of action in infancy. *Philosophical Transactions of the Royal Society B: Biological Sciences*, 358(1431), 447–458. doi: 10.1098/rstb.2002.1235.

Custance, D. M., Whiten, A., & Bard, K. A. (1995). Can young chimpanzees (Pan troglodytes) imitate arbitrary actions? Hayes and Hayes (1952) revisited. *Behaviour*, 132, 837–859.

Dawson, B. V., & Foss, B. M. (1965). Observational learning in budgerigars. *Animal Behaviour*, 13, 470–474.

Dindo, M., Thierry, B., & Whiten, A. (2008). Social diffusion of novel foraging methods in brown capuchin monkeys (Cebus apella). *Proceedings of the Biological Sciences/Royal Society*, 275(1631), 187–193. doi: 10.1098/rspb.2007.1318.

Ferrari, P. F., Paukner, A., Ruggiero, A., Darcey, L., Unbehagen, S., & Suomi, S. J. (2009). Interindividual differences in neonatal imitation and the development of action chains in rhesus macaques. *Child Development*, 80(4), 1057–1068. doi: 10.1111/j.1467-8624.2009.01316.x.

Ferrari, P. F., Visalberghi, E., Paukner, A., Fogassi, L., Ruggiero, A., & Suomi, S. J. (2006). Neonatal imitation in rhesus macaques. *PLOS Biology*, 4(9), e302. doi: 10.1371/journal.pbio.0040302.

Fodor, J. A. (1983). *The modularity of mind*. Cambridge, MA: MIT Press.

Fragaszy, D. M., Izar, P., Visalberghi, E., Ottoni, E. B., & de Oliveira, M. G. (2004). Wild capuchin monkeys (Cebus libidinosus) use anvils and stone pounding tools. *American Journal of Primatology*. 64(4), 359–366. doi: 10.1002/ajp.20085.

Fragaszy, D. M., & Perry, S. (2003). *The Biology of Traditions*. Cambridge: Cambridge University Press.

Fragaszy, D. M., & Visalberghi, E. (1989). Social influences on the acquisition of tool-using behaviors in tufted capuchin monkeys (Cebus apella). *Journal of Comparative Psychology*, 103(2), 159–170.

(1990). Social processes affecting the appearance of innovative behaviors in capuchin monkeys. *Folia Primatologica (Basel)*, 54(3–4), 155–165.

(1996). Social learning in monkeys: Primate 'primacy' reconsidered. In B. G. Galef & C. Heyes (Eds.), *Social learning in animals: The roots of culture*. San Diego, CA: Academic Press, pp. 65–84.

(2004). Socially biased learning in monkeys. *Learning & Behavior*, 32(1), 24–35.

Frey, S. H. (2008). Tool use, communicative gesture and cerebral asymmetries in the modern human brain. *Philosophical Transactions of the Royal Society B: Biological Sciences*, 363(1499), 1951–1957. doi: 10.1098/rstb.2008.0008.

Galef, B. G. (1988). Imitation in animals: History, definition, and interpretation of data from the psychological laboratory. In Z. Galef (Ed.), *Social learning: Psychological and biological perspectives*. Hillsdale, NJ: Lawrence Erlbaum, 3–28.

(1996). Social learning and imitation. In G. Heyes (Ed.), *Social learning in animals: The roots of culture*. San Diego, CA: Academic Press.

Giret, N., Peron, F., Nagle, L., Kreutzer, M., & Bovet, D. (2009). Spontaneous categorization of vocal imitations in African grey parrots (Psittacus erithacus). *Behavioural Processes*, 82(3), 244–248. doi: 10.1016/j.beproc.2009.07.001.

Goodall, J. (1986). *The chimpanzees of Gombe: Patterns of behavior*. Cambridge, MA: Belknap Press of Harvard University Press.

Gumert, M. D., Hoong, L. K., & Malaivijitnond, S. (2011). Sex differences in the stone tool-use behavior of a wild population of Burmese long-tailed macaques

(Macaca fascicularis aurea). *American Journal of Primatology*, 73(12), 1239–1249. doi: 10.1002/ajp.20996.

Hall, K. R. L. (1963). Observational learning in monkeys and apes. *British Journal of Psychology*, 54(3), 201–226.

Haslam, M., Gumert, M. D., Biro, D., Carvalho, S., & Malaivijitnond, S. (2013). Use-wear patterns on wild macaque stone tools reveal their behavioural history. *PLoS One*, 8(8), e72872. doi: 10.1371/journal.pone.0072872.

Herrmann, E., Call, J., Hernandez-Lloreda, M. V., Hare, B., & Tomasello, M. (2007). Humans have evolved specialized skills of social cognition: The cultural intelligence hypothesis. *Science*, 317(5843), 1360–1366. doi: 10.1126/science.1146282.

Heyes, C. (1994). Social learning in animals: Categories and mechanisms. *Biological reviews of the Cambridge Philosophical Society*, 69(2), 207–231.

(2011a). Automatic imitation. *Psychological Bulletin*, 137(3), 463–483. doi: 10.1037/a0022288.

(2011b). What's social about social learning? *Journal of Comparative Psychology*, 126(2), 193–202. doi: 10.1037/a0025180.

(2012). What's social about social learning?. *Journal of Comparative Psychology*, 126(2), 193–202. doi: 10.1037/a0025180.

Heyes, C., Bird, G., Johnson, H., & Haggard, P. (2005). Experience modulates automatic imitation. *Cognitive Brain Research*, 22(2), 233–240. doi: S0926-6410(04)00241-1 [pii] 10.1016/j.cogbrainres.2004.09.009.

Hopper, L. M. (2010). 'Ghost' experiments and the dissection of social learning in humans and animals. *Biological reviews of the Cambridge Philosophical Society*, 85(4), 685–701. doi: BRV120 [pii] 10.1111/j.1469-185X.2010.00120.x.

Hopper, L. M., Lambeth, S. P., Schapiro, S. J., & Whiten, A. (2008). Observational learning in chimpanzees and children studied through 'ghost' conditions. *Proceedings of the Royal Society B*, 275(1636), 835–840. doi: JKG55Q617P253P61 [pii] 10.1098/rspb.2007.1542.

Hopper, L. M., Schapiro, S., Lambeth, S. P., & Brosnan, S. (2011). Chimpanzees' socially maintained food preferences indicate both conservatism and conformity. *Animal Behaviour*, 81, 1195–1202.

Horner, V., & Whiten, A. (2005). Causal knowledge and imitation/emulation switching in chimpanzees (Pan troglodytes) and children (Homo sapiens). *Animal Cognition*, 8(3), 164–181. doi: 10.1007/s10071-004-0239-6.

(2007). Learning from others' mistakes? Limits on understanding a trap-tube task by young chimpanzees (Pan troglodytes) and children (Homo sapiens). *Journal of Comparative Psychology*, 121(1), 12–21. doi: 2007-01892-002 [pii] 10.1037/0735-7036.121.1.12.

Horner, V., Whiten, A., Flynn, E., & de Waal, F. B. (2006). Faithful replication of foraging techniques along cultural transmission chains by chimpanzees and children. *Proceedings of the National Academy of Sciences of the United States of America*, 103(37), 13878–13883. doi: 10.1073/pnas.0606015103.

Horowitz, A. C. (2003). Do humans ape? Or do apes human? Imitation and intention in humans (Homo sapiens) and other animals. *Journal of Comparative Psychology*, 117(3), 325–336. doi: 10.1037/0735-7036.117.3.325 2003-07738-013 [pii].

Huang, C. T., & Charman, T. (2005). Gradations of emulation learning in infants' imitation of actions on objects. *Journal of Experimental Child Psychology*, 92, 276–302.

Iacoboni, M. (2009). Neurobiology of imitation. *Current Opinion in Neurobiology*, 19(6), 661–665. doi: Doi 10.1016/J.Conb.2009.09.008.

Jacobson, S. (1979). Matching behavior in the young infant. *Child Development*, 30, 425–430.

Jaeggi, A. V., Dunkel, L. P., Van Noordwijk, M. A., Wich, S. A., Sura, A. A., & Van Schaik, C. P. (2010). Social learning of diet and foraging skills by wild immature Bornean orangutans: Implications for culture. *American Journal of Primatology*, 72(1), 62–71. doi: 10.1002/ajp.20752.

Janik, V. M., & Slater, P. J. (2000). The different roles of social learning in vocal communication. *Animal Behaviour*, 60(1), 1–11. doi: 10.1006/anbe.2000.1410 S0003-3472(00)91410–6 [pii].

Jones, S. S. (1996). Imitation or exploration? Young infants' matching of adults' oral gestures. *Child Development*, 67(5), 1952–1969.

(2006). Exploration or imitation? The effect of music on 4-week-old infants' tongue protrusions. *Infant Behavior and Development*, 29(1), 126–130.

(2009). The development of imitation in infancy. *Philosophical Transactions of the Royal Society B: Biological Sciences*, 364(1528), 2325–2335. doi: 364/1528/2325 [pii] 10.1098/rstb.2009.0045.

Lefebvre, L., & Sol, D. (2008). Brains, lifestyles and cognition: Are there general trends? *Brain, Behavior and Evolution*, 72(2), 135–144. doi: 10.1159/000151473.

Leighton, J., & Heyes, C. (2010). Hand to mouth: Automatic imitation across effector systems. *Journal of Experimental Psychology: Human Perception and Performance*, 36(5), 1174–1183. doi: 2010-17383-001 [pii] 10.1037/a0019953.

Leslie, A. M. (1994). *ToMM, ToBy, and Agency: Core architecture and domain specificity*. New York: Cambridge University Press.

Lyons, D. E., Santos, L. R., & Keil, F. C. (2006). Reflections of other minds: How primate social cognition can inform the function of mirror neurons. *Current Opinion in Neurobiology*, 16(2), 230–234. doi: 10.1016/j.conb.2006.03.015.

Lyons, D. E., Young, A. G., & Keil, F. C. (2007). The hidden structure of overimitation. *Proceedings of the National Academy of Sciences of the United States of America*, 104(50), 19751–19756. doi: 10.1073/pnas.0704452104.

Maier, W. (1984). *Tooth morphology and dietary specialization*. New York: Plenum Press.

Mantell, J. T., & Pfordresher, P. Q. (2013). Vocal imitation of song and speech. *Cognition*, 127(2), 177–202. doi: 10.1016/j.cognition.2012.12.008.

Marr, D. (1982). *Vision: A computational investigation into the human representation and processing of visual information*. San Francisco, CA: W. H. Freeman.

Martin, C. F., Biro, D., & Matsuzawa, T. (2011). Chimpanzees' use of conspecific cues in matching-to-sample tasks: Public information use in a fully automated testing environment. *Animal Cognition*, 14(6), 893–902. doi: 10.1007/s10071-011-0424-3.

Matsuzawa, T., Tomonaga, M., & Tanaka, M. (2006). *Cognitive development in chimpanzees*. Tokyo, New York: Springer.

(2011). *Cognitive development in chimpanzees*. Tokyo, New York: Springer.

Melis, A. P., & Tomasello, M. (2013). Chimpanzees' (Pan troglodytes) strategic helping in a collaborative task. *Biology Letters*, 9(2), 20130009. doi: 10.1098/rsbl.2013.0009.

Meltzoff, A. N. (1988). *The human infant as Homo imitans.* Hillside, NJ: Lawrence Erlbaum.

(1999). Origins of theory of mind, cognition and communication. *Journal of Communication Disorders,* 32(4), 251–269.

Meltzoff, A. N., & Moore, M. K. (1977). Imitation of facial and manual gestures by human neonates. *Science,* 198(4312), 75–78. doi: 198/4312/75 [pii] 10.1126/science.198.4312.75.

(1997). Explaining facial imitation: A theoretical model. *Early Development and Parenting,* 6, 179–192.

Mercader, J., Barton, H., Gillespie, J., Harris, J., Kuhn, S., et al. (2007). 4,300-year-old chimpanzee sites and the origins of percussive stone technology. *Proceedings of the National Academy of Sciences of the United States of America,* 104(9), 3043–3048. doi: 10.1073/pnas.0607909104.

Mercader, J., Panger, M., & Boesch, C. (2002). Excavation of a chimpanzee stone tool site in the African rainforest. *Science,* 296(5572), 1452–1455. doi: 10.1126/science.1070268.

Mitani, J. C., & Watts, D. P. (1999). Demographic influences on the hunting behavior of chimpanzees. *American Journal of Physical Anthropology,* 109(4), 439–454.

Morgan, C. L. (1900). *Animal behaviour.* London: Edward Arnold.

Mulcahy, N. J., & Call, J. (2006). How great apes perform on a modified trap-tube task. *Animal Cognition,* 9(3), 193–199. doi: 10.1007/s10071-006-0019-6.

Myowa-Yamakoshi, M., & Matsuzawa, T. (1999). Factors influencing imitation of manipulatory actions in chimpanzees (Pan troglodytes). *Journal of Comparative Psychology,* 2, 128–136.

Myowa-Yamakoshi, M., Tomonaga, M., Tanaka, M., & Matsuzawa, T. (2004). Imitation in neonatal chimpanzees (Pan troglodytes). *Developmental Science,* 7(4), 437–442.

Nagell, K., Olguin, R., & Tomasello, M. (1993). Processes of social learning in the tool use of chimpanzees (Pan troglodytes) and human children (Homo sapiens). *Journal of Comparative Psychology,* 107, 174–186.

Nehaniv, C., & Dautenhahn, K. (2002). The correspondence problem. In K. Dautenhahn & C. Nehaniv (Eds.), *Imitation in animals and artifacts.* Cambridge, MA: MIT Press, 41–61.

Nguyen, N. H., Klein, E. D., & Zentall, T. R. (2005). Imitation of a two-action sequence by pigeons. *Psychonomic Bulletin & Review,* 12(3), 514–518.

Panger, M., Perry, S., Rose, L. M., Gros-Louis, J., Vogel, E., et al. (2000). Cross-site differences in foraging behavior of white-faced capuchins (Cebus capucinus). *American Journal of Physical Anthropology,* 119(52–66).

Phillips, W., Barnes, J. L., Mahajan, N., Yamaguchi, M., & Santos, L. R. (2009). 'Unwilling' versus 'unable': Capuchin monkeys' (Cebus apella) understanding of human intentional action. *Developmental Science,* 12(6), 938–945. doi: DESC840 [pii] 10.1111/j.1467-7687.2009.00840.x.

Potts, R. (1998). Variability selection in hominid evolution. *Evolutionary Anthropology,* 7, 81–96.

(2004). Paleoenvironmental basis of cognitive evolution in great apes. *American Journal of Primatology,* 62, 209–228.

Povinelli, D. (2000). *Folk physics for apes.* Oxford: Oxford University Press.

Raihani, N. J., Grutter, A. S., & Bshary, R. (2010). Punishers benefit from third-party punishment in fish. *Science*, 327(5962), 171. doi: 327/5962/171 [pii] 10.1126/science.1183068.

Ray, E., & Heyes, C. (2011). Imitation in infancy: the wealth of the stimulus. *Dev Sci*, 14(1), 92–105. doi: 10.1111/j.1467-7687.2010.00961.x.

Reader, S. M., Hager, Y., & Laland, K. N. (2011). The evolution of primate general and cultural intelligence. *Philosophical Transactions of the Royal Society B: Biological Sciences*, 366(1567), 1017–1027. doi: 10.1098/rstb.2010.0342.

Reader, S. M., & Laland, K. N. (2002). Social intelligence, innovation, and enhanced brain size in primates. *Proceedings of the National Academy of Sciences of the United States of America*, 99(7), 4436–4441. doi: 10.1073/pnas.062041299 062041299 [pii].

Schaik, C. P. van, Ancrenaz, M., Borgen, G., Galdikas, B., Knott, C. D., et al. (2003). Orangutan cultures and the evolution of material culture. *Science*, 299(5603), 102–105. doi: 10.1126/science.1078004.

Schneider, A. C., Melis, A. P., & Tomasello, M. (2012). How chimpanzees solve collective action problems. *Philosophical Transactions of the Royal Society B: Biological Sciences*, 279(1749), 4946–4954. doi: 10.1098/rspb.2012.1948.

Seed, A. M., Call, J., Emery, N. J., & Clayton, N. S. (2009). Chimpanzees solve the trap problem when the confound of tool-use is removed. *Journal of Experimental Psychology: Animal Behavior Processes*, 1, 23–34.

Snowdon, C. T., & Boe, C. Y. (2003). Social communication about unpalatable foods in tamarins (Saguinus oedipus). *Journal of Comparative Psychology*, 117(2), 142–148.

Spelke, E. S., & Kinzler, K. D. (2007). Core knowledge. *Developmental Science*, 10(1), 89–96. doi: DESC569 [pii] 10.1111/j.1467-7687.2007.00569.x.

Stoeger, A. S., Mietchen, D., Oh, S., de Silva, S., Herbst, C. T., et al. (2012). An Asian elephant imitates human speech. *Current Biology*, 22(22), 2144–2148. doi: 10.1016/j.cub.2012.09.022.

Subiaul, F. (2007). The imitation faculty in monkeys: Evaluating its features, distribution and evolution. *Journal of Anthropological Sciences*, 85, 35–62.

(2010). Dissecting the imitation faculty: The multiple imitation mechanisms (MIM) hypothesis. *Behavioural Processes*, 83(2), 222–234. doi: 10.1016/j.beproc.2009.12.002.

(2016). What's special about human imitation? A comparison with enculturated apes. *Behavioral Sciences*, 6(16), doi:10.3390/bs6030013.

Subiaul, F., Anderson, S., Brandt, J., & Elkins, J. (2012). Multiple imitation mechanisms in children. *Developmental Psychology*, 48(4), 1165–1179.

Subiaul, F., Cantlon, J. F., Holloway, R. L., & Terrace, H. S. (2004). Cognitive imitation in rhesus macaques. *Science*, 305(5682), 407–410. doi: 10.1126/science.1099136.

Subiaul, F., Lurie, H., Kathryn, R., Klein, T., Holmes, D., & Terrace, H. S. (2007). Cognitive imitation in typically-developing 3- and 4-year olds and individuals with autism. *Cognitive Development*, 22, 230–243.

Subiaul, F., Patterson, E. M.,, Barr, R. (2016). The Cognitive Structure of Goal Emulation in Preschool Age Children: Recruitment of multiple learning processes. *British Journal of Developmental Psychology*, 34, 132–149; doi: 10.1111/bjdp.12111.

Subiaul, F., Vonk, J., Okamoto-Barth, S., & Barth, J. (2008). Do chimpanzees learn reputation by observation? Evidence from direct and indirect experience with generous and selfish strangers. *Animal Cognition*, 11(4), 611–623. doi: 10.1007/s10071-008-0151-6.

Subiaul, F., Vonk, J., & Rutherford, M. D. (2011). The ghosts in the computer: The role of agency and animacy attributions in 'ghost controls'. *PLoS One*, 6(11), e26429. doi: 10.1371/journal.pone.0026429.

Subiaul, F., Winters, K., Krumpak, K., & Core, C. (2015). Vocal overimitation in preschool age children. *Journal of Experimental Child Psychology*, 41, 145–60.

Tennie, C., Call, J., & Tomasello, M. (2006). Push or pull: Imitation versus emulation in human children and great apes. *Ethology*, 112, 1159–1169.

(2009). Ratcheting up the ratchet: On the evolution of cumulative culture. *Philosophical Transactions of the Royal Society B: Biological Sciences*, 364(1528), 2405–2415. doi: 10.1098/rstb.2009.0052.

(2010a). Evidence for emulation in chimpanzees in social settings using the floating peanut task. *PloS One*, 5, e10544.

Tennie, C., Greve, K., Gretscher, H., & Call, J. (2010b). Two-year-old children copy more reliably and more often than nonhuman great apes in multiple observational learning tasks. *Primates: Journal of Primatology*, 4, 337–351.

Tennie, C., Hedwig, D., Call, J., & Tomasello, M. (2008). An experimental study of nettle feeding in captive gorillas. *American Journal of Primatology*, 70(6), 584–593. doi: 10.1002/ajp.20532.

Thompson, D. E., & Russell, J. (2004). The ghost condition: Imitation versus emulation in young children's observational learning. *Developmental Psychology*, 40, 882–889.

Thorndike, E. L. (1898). Animal intelligence: An experimental study of the associative processes in animals. *Psychological Review Monographs Supplement*, 2(8).

(1911). *Animal intelligence*. New York: Macmillan.

Thorpe, W. H. (1956). *Learning and instinct in animals*. London: Methuen.

Tomasello, M. (1990). Cultural transmission in the tool use and communicatory signaling of chimpanzees? In S. Parker & K. Gibson (Eds.), *'Language' and intelligence in monkeys and apes*. Cambridge: Cambridge University Press, 274–311.

(2014). *A natural history of human thinking*. Cambridge, MA: Harvard University Press.

Tomasello, M., & Call, J. (1997). *Primate cognition*. New York: Oxford University Press.

Tomasello, M., Davis-Dasilva, M., Camak, L., & Bard, K. (1987). Observational learning of tool-use by young chimpanzees. *Journal of Human Evolution*, 2, 175–186.

Visalberghi, E., & Addessi, E. (2000). Seeing group members eating a familiar food enhances the acceptance of novel foods in capuchin monkeys. *Animal Behaviour*, 1, 69–76.

(2001). Acceptance of novel foods in capuchin monkeys: Do specific social facilitation and visual stimulus enhancement play a role? *Animal Behaviour*, 62, 567–576.

Visalberghi, E., & Fragaszy, D. M. (1990). Do monkeys ape? In S. Parker & K. Gibson (Eds.), *'Language' and intelligence in monkeys and apes*. Cambridge: Cambridge University Press, 247–273.

Visalberghi, E., Fragaszy, D. M., & Savage-Rumbaugh, S. (1995a). Performance in a tool-using task by common chimpanzees (Pan troglodytes), bonobos (Pan paniscus), an orangutan (Pongo pygmaeus), and capuchin monkeys (Cebus apella). *Journal of Comparative Psychology*, 109(1), 52–60.

(1995b). Performance in a tool-using task by common chimpanzees (Pan troglodytes), bonobos (Pan paniscus), an orangutan (Pongo pygmaeus), and capuchin monkeys (Cebus apella). *Journal of Comparative Psychology*, 109(1), 52–60.

Voelkl, B., & Huber, L. (2000). True imitation in marmosets. *Animal Behaviour*, 60(2), 195–202. doi: 10.1006/anbe.2000.1457 S0003-3472(00)91457-X [pii].

(2007). Imitation as faithful copying of a novel technique in marmoset monkeys. *PLoS One*, 2(7), e611. doi: 10.1371/journal.pone.0000611.

Waal, E. van de, Borgeaud, C., & Whiten, A. (2013). Potent social learning and conformity shape a wild primate's foraging decisions. *Science*, 340(6131), 483–485. doi: 10.1126/science.1232769.

Waal, E. van de, Bshary, R., & Whiten, A. (2014). Wild vervet monkey infants acquire the food-processing variants of their mothers. *Animal Behaviour*, 90, 41–45.

Waal, E. van de, & Whiten, A. (2012). Spontaneous emergence, imitation and spread of alternative foraging techniques among groups of vervet monkeys. *PLoS One*, 7(10), e47008. doi: 10.1371/journal.pone.0047008.

Waal, F. B. M. de. (1998). *Chimpanzee politics, power and sex among apes*. Baltimore, MD: Johns Hopkins University Press.

Whiten, A. (1998). Imitation of the sequential structure of actions by chimpanzees (Pan troglodytes). *Journal of Comparative Psychology*, 112(3), 270–281.

Whiten, A., Custance, D. M., Gomez, J. C., Teixidor, P., & Bard, K. A. (1996). Imitative learning of artificial fruit processing in children (Homo sapiens) and chimpanzees (Pan troglodytes). *Journal of Comparative Psychology*, 1, 3–14.

Whiten, A., Goodall, J., McGrew, W. C., Nishida, T., Reynolds, V., et al. (1999). Cultures in chimpanzees. *Nature*, 399(6737), 682–685. doi: 10.1038/21415.

Whiten, A., & Ham, R. (1992). On the nature and evolution of imitation in the animal kingdom: Reappraisal of a century of research. *Advances in the Study of Behavior*, 21, 239–283.

Whiten, A., Horner, V., Litchfield, C., & Marshall-Pescini, S. (2004). How do apes ape? *Learning and Behavior*, 32, 36–52.

Whiten, A., Horner, V., & de Waal, F. B. (2005). Conformity to cultural norms of tool use in chimpanzees. *Nature*, 437(7059), 737–740. doi: nature04047 [pii] 10.1038/nature04047.

Whiten, A., McGuigan, N., Marshall-Pescini, S., & Hopper, L. M. (2009a). Emulation, imitation, over-imitation and the scope of culture for child and chimpanzee. *Philosophical Transactions of the Royal Society of London B: Biological Sciences*, 364(1528), 2417–2428. doi: 10.1098/rstb.2009.0069.

(2009b). Emulation, imitation, over-imitation and the scope of culture for child and chimpanzee. *Philosophical Transactions of the Royal Society B: Biological Sciences*, 364(1528), 2417–2428. doi: 364/1528/2417 [pii] 10.1098/rstb.2009.0069.

Wright, B. W., Wright, K. A., Chalk, J., Verderane, M. P., Fragaszy, D., et al. (2009). Fallback foraging as a way of life: Using dietary toughness to compare the fallback signal among capuchins and implications for interpreting morphological variation. *American Journal of Physical Anthropology*, 140(4), 687–699. doi: 10.1002/ajpa.21116.

Zajonc, R. B. (1965). Social facilitation. *Science*, 149, 269–274.

Zentall, T. R. (2006). Imitation: Definitions, evidence, and mechanisms. *Animal Cognition*, 9(4), 335–353. doi: 10.1007/s10071-006-0039-2.

(2012). Perspectives on observational learning in animals. *Journal of Comparative Psychology*, 126(2), 114–128. doi: 10.1037/a0025381.

7 The Cultural Transmission of Social Information

Janine Oostenbroek and Harriet Over

Abstract

Human groups differ not only in the types of tools and artifacts they produce, but also in the ways in which they interact with and behave around each other. Social learning is key to explaining these differences between human groups. However, to date, research on cultural transmission has focused predominately on how imitation and other forms of social learning enable children to learn about the physical world. While this research has yielded important insights into the nature of the cultural transmission process, the picture it provides is incomplete. Here, inspired by anthropological perspectives, we adopt a broader view of culture and emphasize that a group's culture is not only composed of the tools and artifacts it produces but also the values, norms, attitudes, opinions and beliefs that it holds dear. Using this broader definition of culture, we review the social psychological literature on how children learn about the social world through copying those around them. We hope this integrative review highlights the importance of the more social aspects of cultural transmission and offers a broader view of human culture that will open up new avenues for future research.

Human culture is special. While there is some cultural variation between neighboring groups of chimpanzees (Luncz, Mundry, & Boesch, 2012; Whiten & Boesch, 2001), this variation is dwarfed by the depth and the breadth of the differences between human groups. Human groups differ not only in the types of tools and artifacts they produce, and in the gestures that they use, but also in the ways in which they think and act socially, in the rituals they perform and in the beliefs they hold about the world.

Social learning is crucial to explaining why human groups differ from each other in these ways. However, developmental and comparative research has

We would like to thank Claudio Tennie for helpful advice and Mark Nielsen for valuable comments on an earlier draft. This research was supported by the ESRC (grant number ES/K006702/1).

tended to focus on explaining a restricted subset of these differences between groups, investigating how social learning enables the transmission of knowledge about the physical world. One goal of this line of work has been to explain why tool and artifact use differs between communities. As we shall outline below, this focus is understandable and has led to important insights into the nature of human cultural transmission (Tennie, Call, & Tomasello, 2009; Tomasello, 1999; Whiten, McGuigan, Marshall-Pescini, & Hopper, 2009). However, it has come at a cost. Neglecting other aspects of culture has meant that our understanding of human cultural transmission is incomplete and perhaps even inaccurate (Heyes, 2013). Here, inspired by anthropological perspectives on culture, we adopt a broader view of culture than that used in previous research. We use this as a basis by which to review, and emphasize, the cultural transmission of social information.

We begin by outlining previous research on social learning and cultural transmission. After this, we move on to offer a broader perspective on culture and discuss research on how children learn about the social world. It is our hope that this integrative review will point the way towards important avenues for future research.

Previous Research on Cultural Transmission

Developmental and comparative research on cultural transmission has focused predominantly on trying to identify the mechanisms underlying social learning about tools and artifacts. In doing so, it has concentrated on how social information helps children and other animals to solve problems such as how to retrieve an out of reach reward or open a complex puzzle box (Flynn & Whiten, 2012, 2013; Horner & Whiten, 2005; Lyons, Young, & Keil, 2007; Nagell, Olguin, & Tomasello, 1993; Turner & Flynn, this volume, Chapter 24).

Research in this tradition has identified social learning processes such as stimulus enhancement, emulation and imitation. In stimulus enhancement, the animal learns to pay attention to an object as a result of watching another animal interact with it (Thorpe, 1956). In emulation, the animal learns about the affordances of objects by reproducing the outcomes of demonstrations but not the particular actions used to produce it (Tomasello, Kruger, & Ratner, 1993). In imitation, the animal learns and reproduces the particular actions in the demonstration (Thorpe, 1956) (see Box 7.1 for definitions of different social learning mechanisms).

Box 7.1 Definitions of cultural transmission mechanisms

Culture Behavior patterns that are shared by members of a group as a result of socially learned and transmitted information (Laland & Hoppitt, 2003).

Cumulative culture The accumulation of modifications to cultural products over time where successful changes are maintained and improved upon by successive generations (Boyd & Richerson, 1985; Caldwell & Millen, 2008).

Emulation When an individual reproduces the outcome of another's behavior on the environment but not the particular actions used to produce it (Tomasello, Kruger, & Ratner, 1993).

Imitation When an individual reproduces the actions of another (Thorpe, 1956).

Mimicry When an individual subconsciously reproduces the mannerisms or gestures of a model (Chartrand & Bargh, 1999).

Overimitation When an individual faithfully reproduces the actions of another, even when those actions have no apparent purpose or causal function (Lyons et al., 2007).

Stimulus enhancement When an individual's attention is drawn to an object in the environment as a result of watching another individual interact with it (Thorpe, 1956).

Of these learning mechanisms, imitation has received by far the most attention (see Nielsen, Subiaul, Whiten, Galef, & Zentall, 2012, Figure 1; also see Subiaul, Renner, & Karjkowski, this volume, Chapter 6). Empirical research by comparative psychologists has shown that children rely on imitation much more than do other primates (Carpenter & Call, 2009; Horner & Whiten, 2005; Tennie et al., 2009; Tomasello, 1999). Indeed, chimpanzees rarely copy the novel actions of a model. Tennie et al. (2009), for example, demonstrated that, when shown a novel action for solving a problem (forming a loop from a piece of material in order to pull a reward within reach), four-year-old children copied it but chimpanzees did not.

Developmental psychologists investigating the nature of children's imitative abilities have shown that children often copy the actions of others surprisingly faithfully, incorporating even causally irrelevant actions into their imitation (Horner & Whiten, 2005; Lyons et al., 2007). Indeed, Lyons and colleagues showed that children copy causally irrelevant actions of a model, for example tapping a feather on a jar before unscrewing the lid, even when they have been explicitly instructed not to do so and when they have previously been trained to identify irrelevant actions. This form of copying is known as overimitation (Lyons et al., 2007; see Box 7.1).

However, other research has shown that children are also capable of selective imitation, incorporating some actions but not others into their behavioral repertoire. In particular, children copy successful actions but not mistakes or failed attempts. Meltzoff (1995), for example, demonstrated that when 18-month-old infants were shown a failed attempt to produce an action (e.g. attempting to pull two halves of a toy apart), they reproduced the intended goal behind the action in their imitation rather than the specific action pattern they observed. In related research, Carpenter, Akhtar, and Tomasello (1998) showed that 14- to 18-month-old infants could discriminate between a model's intentional and accidental actions. Infants in this study imitated the intentional actions of a model (where the demonstration was accompanied by the word 'There!') twice as often as her accidental actions (where the demonstration was accompanied by the word 'Whoops!').

The Social Functions of Imitation

Some researchers within developmental psychology have emphasized the social side of cultural transmission but they have tended to focus on the motivations underlying copying behavior rather than the content of what is copied (Nielsen, 2009; Over & Carpenter, 2012, 2013). These researchers have pointed out that imitation can serve multiple functions in development. Children use imitation as a way to learn about the physical world but also as a way to affiliate with those around them (Eckerman, Davis, & Didow, 1989; Nadel 2002; Uzgiris, 1981). Empirical research has shown that children's imitation is deeply influenced by social factors. For example, Nielsen (2006) showed that 18-month-old children are more likely to copy the specific actions a model performs on a box when she is warm and friendly compared to when she is cold and aloof. Related research with older children has shown that they copy the object-directed actions of a model more faithfully when they have a goal to affiliate (Over & Carpenter, 2009; Watson-Jones, Legare, Whitehouse, & Clegg, 2014) and when the model is present to observe their actions (Nielsen & Blank, 2011).

Research in this tradition has shown that cultural transmission is a deeply social process (Nielsen, 2009) and has helped to explain the apparent paradox that children sometimes copy selectively and sometimes copy faithfully. According to this perspective, children are more likely to copy selectively when their goal is to learn about the physical world and more likely to copy faithfully when their goal is to affiliate with others (Nielsen, 2009; Over & Carpenter, 2012, 2013; Uzgiris, 1981).

However, even this research has concentrated more heavily on how children copy actions with tools and artifacts rather than other aspects of behavior. In this chapter, we also focus on the social side of imitation. However, we approach it from a different perspective. In particular, we investigate how children learn about the social world from copying those around them.

Why Has Social Learning about Tools and Artifacts Received So Much Attention?

Before introducing our broader definition of culture, it is important to consider why so much research attention has been devoted to the question of how children interact with tools and artifacts. The focus of previous research is entirely understandable when considering cultural transmission from a comparative perspective. Chimpanzees produce a range of actions on objects (Horner & Whiten, 2005) and engage in tool use, such as fishing for termites using sticks and cracking nuts using stone and wooden hammers (Luncz et al., 2012). To the extent that these behaviors are similar to young children's interactions with objects, it makes sense to compare them directly.

Furthermore, the focus on children's tendency to imitate faithfully when interacting with the physical world has been critical to understanding the existence of cumulative culture. Human culture accumulates knowledge and innovations over time (see Box 7.1). This so-called ratchet effect is thought to rely on faithful imitation of object-directed actions because innovations must be retained within the population in order to be improved upon later (Caldwell & Millen, 2008; Tomasello, 1994; also see Turner & Flynn, this volume, Chapter 24). Understanding how children interact with tools and artifacts has thus been critical to understanding human uniqueness (Boyd & Richerson, 1985; Tomasello, 1994).

A Broader View of Culture

Human culture, however, is composed of much more than tools and technology. In attempting to outline the cultural transmission of social information, we take our inspiration from anthropology. Anthropologists tend to adopt a much broader view of culture than do psychologists (Bulbulia et al., 2013; Whitehouse & Cohen, 2012). Tools and other technology are but a subset of culture more broadly, which includes artifacts such as ritual objects, the artwork of a community and their sacred mementos. In addition to these products of the group, culture also encompasses the group's values, norms, beliefs, attitudes, morals, customs and religious beliefs.

We contend that the focus on how children interact with tools and artifacts has led researchers to neglect these other aspects of human culture. Although it is sometimes assumed, either explicitly or implicitly, that what we know about action imitation translates to other aspects of culture, this assumption has not been directly assessed. In consequence, it is not yet clear how different forms of copying behavior relate to each other (see Box 7.3).

Furthermore, the focus on tools and artifacts has contributed to an assumption that action imitation is the most important means of cultural transmission in humans. In reality, however, other processes may be just as important (Heyes, 2013). The relative importance of different social learning processes cannot be understood without considering all aspects of human culture.

In outlining the cultural transmission of social information, we attempt to combine insights from previous developmental and comparative research on cultural transmission with recent empirical findings from a more social psychological perspective. In doing so, we hope to provide a basis from which future empirical research can investigate cultural transmission from this broader perspective.

Expanding Our Understanding of Social Learning Mechanisms

Taking this broader perspective on culture moves us beyond the focus on imitation of actions on objects and allows us to consider other forms of cultural transmission as well. Within this broader framework, it becomes possible to view processes such as persuasion and argumentation, social mimicry and normative behavior as examples of cultural transmission.

When considering the many different types of social learning mechanisms, it may be helpful to think of them in terms of their 'chemistry'. Attempting to bring clarity to the literature on how children (and other animals) learn actions on objects, Carpenter and Call (2002) argued that, rather than focusing on social learning types, it would be better to focus on the constituent components, or chemistry, of social learning. They argued that, when children observe a demonstration on an object, they may reproduce the action they observed, the results that action had on the environment or the perceived goals of the model. For example, when observing a demonstration on a box, children may reproduce the specific hand actions the model used, the results of those actions on the environment – the open box, or the perceived goal of the action – retrieving a reward from inside the box.

The same approach can be applied to the social domain (see Box 7.2). A child may copy a particular social action, for example how close to stand to another individual in different social interactions, or how to behave during a ritual, such as when to stand or when to bow. They may also attempt to reproduce the results of another's behavior, for example seeing a social partner happy as a result of one's pro-social behavior. A child may also reproduce the goal behind a model's behavior, for example the goal to be fair to all individuals within an interaction or to be cooperative with other group members in order to achieve a common purpose. In the social domain, the scope for copying is not limited to actions, results and goals, however. A child may also copy the opinions of a model, for example whether a given game is fun to play or not. They may copy the attitudes of a model, for example whether to feel positively or negatively towards a particular social group. They may even copy the beliefs of a model, for example about the existence of a particular deity.

Box 7.2 What is copied?

In the physical domain, children may reproduce:

Actions e.g., the specific actions a model used to open a box
Results e.g., the open box
Goals e.g., retrieving a reward from inside a box (see Carpenter & Call, 2002)

In the social domain, children may reproduce

Actions e.g., how to behave during a ritual, such as when to stand or kneel
Results e.g., seeing a social partner happy as a result of one's pro-social behavior
Goals e.g., to be fair to all individuals within an interaction
Opinions e.g., whether a particular toy is interesting or not
Attitudes e.g., whether to feel positively or negatively towards a particular social group
Beliefs e.g., the existence of a particular deity

Below we outline existing research on these broader aspects of cultural transmission. It is not always possible to determine which of these aspects children are copying, as the reported research was not designed to answer such fine-grained questions. Wherever possible, however, we outline what we think children are learning. Delineating these aspects more carefully is an important priority for future research.

Learning Social Behaviors and Norms

Groups differ from each other in subtle ways, such as in the gestures and mannerisms that characterize their members' nonverbal behavior, as well as in more substantial ways, such as in the rituals they engage in and social norms they adhere to. These behaviors must be transmitted culturally, as the 'correct' way to produce them is typically defined by the way the majority of the group behaves.

Social psychological studies have shown that adults often mimic the gestures and mannerisms of their social partners without even knowing that they are doing so (Chartrand & Bargh, 1999; Lakin & Chartrand, 2003). Aspects of these gestures and mannerisms often differ between social groups (for example, how close individuals stand to each other during conversations). Learning the mannerisms of a particular social group may serve as an important marker of group membership and belonging (Heyes, 2013) and can enhance affiliation and rapport with other group members (Lakin & Chartrand, 2003). A recent study by van Schaik, van Baaren, Bekkering, and Hunnius (2013) demonstrated that three-year-old children also mimic the gestures of their social partners. Van Schaik et al. presented children with a video in which a model performed six different mannerisms and gestures. Children were more likely to produce these behaviors themselves during the video than during a baseline control period.

Other research has investigated how young children learn the rituals of their group. Groups differ in the type of rituals they engage in: whereas individuals in some cultures shake hands to greet each other, individuals in other cultures kiss on the cheek. Whereas individuals in some groups worship their deity, or deities, by burning incense and praying quietly, others do so by singing and dancing in a group. Herrmann, Legare, Harris, and Whitehouse (2013) have argued that children sometimes adopt a 'ritualistic stance' when copying actions. When adopting this stance children copy the actions of others because they believe them to be the conventional actions of their group. For example, when children in their study were led to believe an action on a peg-board toy was ritualistic by being told 'she always does it this way', they copied the action more faithfully than when they were given a more neutral description of the action ('she gets the pegs up').

Rituals of this type are very closely related to social norms (Herrmann et al., 2013). That is, social rules to which individuals typically adhere and to which they believe others ought to adhere as well (Cialdini, 2003). Rakoczy, Warneken, and Tomasello (2008) investigated how children respond to social norms once they have learned them from a social partner. They showed that, once three-year-old children have learned a novel rule game through copying an experimenter, they enforced that novel rule on others. Rakoczy and colleagues introduced children to a novel game (e.g. 'daxing') modeled by the experimenter. A third party (a puppet) then entered and joined the game. Instead of performing actions consistent with the rules of the game previously learned by the child through copying, the puppet performed an action that was clearly a mistake within the rules of the game. Children protested against the puppet's actions, with some children even explaining to the puppet how the game *ought* to be played. Thus, not only do children adhere to the socially learned rules of their group, they expect others to adhere to those rules as well (also see Kenward, 2012; Keupp, Behne, & Rakoczy, 2013).

Learning How to Interact with Other Individuals and Groups

Cultures differ in the ways in which they treat other individuals and other groups. For example, whereas some cultures highly value honor and behave in ways that serve to maintain and protect it at both the individual and group level, other cultures view honor as a private matter and judge its maintenance and protection as less important (Uskul et al., 2014). Whereas some groups value loyalty and hierarchy very strongly, others are more likely to emphasize fairness (Haidt, 2012).

Researchers interested in social development have long suggested that children learn how to interact with people by copying the behaviors of those around them (Bandura, 1997). In particular, they learn what is and is not inappropriate to do within social interactions. In an early demonstration of this, Bandura, Ross, and Ross (1961) tested whether children learn aggressive responses from observing others. They demonstrated that children who observed an experimenter acting aggressively towards a bobo doll (by hitting it with a mallet, punching it, kicking it and throwing it in the air) imitated this behavior when left alone to play in a room containing the doll. Furthermore, these children also engaged in other forms of physical and verbal aggression and directed them towards objects other than the bobo doll. This suggests that children were not only imitating the specific actions of the model, but also reproducing a more general attitude of aggression towards other objects.

Social learning is not only involved in the transmission of interpersonal behaviors but also in the acquisition of intergroup attitudes. Correlational studies have shown that children tend to have similar intergroup attitudes to their parents (e.g. Carlson & Iovini, 1985; Mosher & Scodel, 1960), suggesting a role for cultural transmission. This relation is especially clear in cases where parents explicitly and emotionally discuss their attitudes with their children (Bar-Tal, 1996; Duckitt, 1988) and for children who highly identify with their parents (Sinclair, Dunn, & Lowery, 2005). More recently, experimental research has shown that children aged between three and eleven copied the biased behavior of a model towards different social groups (Olson, Dweck, Spelke, & Banaji, 2011). Children watched a model distribute resources unequally between two arbitrary groups (marked by different colored T-shirts). When asked to distribute resources themselves, children tended to copy the behavior of the model by giving more resources to group members who were previously favored by the model.

Other research has shown that intergroup attitudes can be culturally transmitted through the language parents use when talking about social groups. Rhodes, Leslie, and Tworek (2012) investigated whether hearing generic information about a social group led children to make more generalizations about that group. Results revealed that when four year olds heard generic language about a novel social group (for example, 'Look at this Zarpie! Zarpies love to eat flowers'), they tended to develop essentialist beliefs about that group (for example, that Zarpies are a distinct kind of people, who are different from other kinds of social groups). Furthermore, when parents were led to develop essentialist beliefs about a novel group they produced more generic language when telling their children about that group. The parents led to hold essentialist attitudes also produced more negative evaluative statements about the novel group. This suggests that the transmission of essentialist beliefs might also lead to the transmission of negative evaluations of groups (Haslam, Rothschild, and Ernst, 2002).

Learning Opinions

Groups also differ in their opinions about the world. Whereas some groups hold that marriage ought to be a union between one man and one woman, other groups define marriage differently. Children learn the opinions of their group, at least in part, through copying those around them. Evidence in favor of this claim comes from research on conformity. Haun and Tomasello (2011) tested four-year-old children within a modified version of the Asch conformity paradigm (1956) in which participants are asked whether they agree with the incorrect opinions of a unanimous majority. Children were tested in groups of four, and were asked to make judgments regarding the size of animals in a picture book. The study was set up so that the responses of the first three peers appeared unanimously incorrect to the fourth, target, participant. Results showed that, when the target participants were asked which of the animals was the largest, they gave responses that conformed to the opinion of their peers on approximately one-third of trials. A second experiment tested whether children had internalized the incorrect opinion of their group members or whether they were simply matching their behavior to that of the group in response to perceived social pressure. When children were asked to give their opinion in private, the majority answered correctly. This suggests that similar motivations are in play when children copy actions on objects and the opinions of others (Haun & Tomasello, 2011; Uzgiris, 1981; see Box 7.3). It is also important to note that a minority of children (around 9 percent) still conformed even when they made their judgments in private. Thus, although the majority of the effect seemed to be driven by social concerns, the group still appears to be an important source of information when deciding what to think about the world (Turner, 1991).

Box 7.3 Questions for future research

- What is the relative importance of the different social learning processes described in this chapter for explaining differences between human groups?
- What implications does this broader view of cultural transmission have for our understanding of the cognitive mechanisms underlying copying behavior? For example, how similar is the process of learning and reproducing an action versus an opinion or belief?

- What implications, if any, does this broader view of cultural transmission have for our understanding of the motivations underlying copying behavior?
- What implications, if any, does this broader view of culture have for our understanding of cultural context? Are there cultural differences in how faithfully children reproduce the actions, opinions and beliefs of those around them? (Corriveau & Harris, 2010; Nielsen & Tomaselli, 2010)
- How can the fields of developmental and comparative psychology and social psychology inform each other in order to reach a deeper understanding of cultural transmission?

Learning Beliefs

Groups also differ in the types of belief they hold. One particularly striking example of this is differences in religious beliefs (Bulbulia et al., 2013; Whitehouse, 2012). Whereas some groups believe in a single deity, others believe in multiple deities or indeed in no deities at all. These beliefs are almost certainly developed on the basis of what we hear from others (Guerrero, Enesco, & Harris, 2010).

Research has shown that, at least from the age of five, children accredit superhuman powers to non-human agents (e.g. God) such as omnipotence and eternal life as a result of hearing about these properties from others (e.g. Barrett, Newman, & Richert, 2003; Barrett, Richert, & Driesenga, 2001; Gimenez-Dasi, Guerrero, & Harris, 2005). In related research, Harris and colleagues (2006) have demonstrated that four- to eight-year-old children acquire beliefs about the existence of entities such as Santa Claus, the Tooth Fairy and God from hearing others talk about them. The particular group to which children belong thus plays an important role in determining their beliefs about the world.

Conclusions

To date, research on cultural transmission has focused predominantly on how children learn about tools and artifacts. As a result, imitation of actions on objects has received far more attention than other social learning processes and it is often assumed that this is the primary route through which cultural transmission occurs in humans. This research has led to important insights into the nature of cultural transmission. However, we believe that it is incomplete.

Inspired by anthropological accounts (Bulbulia et al., 2013; Whitehouse & Cohen, 2012), we adopted a broader perspective of culture and pointed out that a group's culture is composed not only of tools and artifacts but also of the values, norms, attitudes, morals, customs and beliefs that they hold dear. Taking this broader view of culture as our guide, we then reviewed the social psychological literature on how children learn about the social world, at least in part, through copying those around them. We hope that this broader perspective, incorporating the more social side of cultural transmission, offers a more complete view of human culture and that it will open up important new avenues for future research.

References

Asch, S. E. (1956). Studies of independence and conformity: A minority of one against a unanimous majority. *Psychological Monographs*, 70, 1–70.

Bandura, A. (1997). *Social learning theory*. Englewood Cliffs, NJ: Prentice Hall.

Bandura, A., Ross, D., & Ross, S. A. (1961). Transmission of aggression through imitation of aggressive models. *Journal of Abnormal and Social Psychology*, 63, 575–582.

Barrett, J. L., Newman, R. M., & Richert, R. A. (2003). When seeing is not believing: Children's understanding of humans' and non-humans' use of background knowledge in interpreting visual displays. *Journal of Cognition and Culture*, 3, 91–108.

Barrett, J. L., Richert, R. A., & Driesenga, A. (2001). God's belief versus mother's: The development of non-human agent concepts. *Child Development*, 72, 50–65.

Bar-Tal, D. (1996). Development of social categories and stereotyping in early childhood: The case of 'the Arab' concept of formation, stereotype, and attitudes by Jewish children in Israel. *International Journal of Intercultural Relations*, 20, 341–370.

Boyd, R., & Richerson, P. (1985). *Culture and the evolutionary process*. Chicago, IL: University of Chicago Press.

Bulbulia, J., Geertz, A. W., Atkinson, Q. D., Cohen, E., Evan, N., et al. (2013). The cultural evolution of religion. In P. J. Richerson & M. H. Christiansen (Eds.), *Cultural evolution*. Cambridge, MA: MIT Press, 381–404.

Caldwell, C. A., & Millen, A. E. (2008). Studying cumulative cultural evolution in the laboratory. *Philosophical Transactions of the Royal Society B: Biological Sciences*, 363, 3529–3539.

Carlson, J. M., & Iovini, J. (1985). The transmission of racial attitudes from fathers to sons: A study of Blacks and Whites. *Adolescence*, 20, 233–237.

Carpenter, M., Akhtar, N., & Tomasello, M. (1998). Fourteen- to 18-month-old infants differentially imitate intentional and accidental actions. *Infant Behavior and Development*, 21, 315–330.

Carpenter, M., & Call, J. (2002). The chemistry of social learning. *Developmental Science*, 5(1), 22–24.

(2009). Comparing the imitative skills of children and nonhuman apes. *Revue de Primatologie*, 1(1), 187–192.

Chartrand, T. L., & Bargh, J. A. (1999). The chameleon effect: The perception–behavior link and social interaction. *Journal of Personality and Social Psychology*, 76(6), 893–910.

Cialdini, R. B. (2003). Crafting normative messages to protect the environment. *Current Directions in Psychological Science*, 12, 105–109.

Corriveau, K. H., & Harris, P. L. (2010). Preschoolers (sometimes) defer to the majority in making simple perceptual judgments. *Developmental Psychology*, 46(2), 437–445.

Duckitt, J. (1988). Normative conformity and racial prejudice in South Africa. *Genetic, Social and General Psychology Monographs*, 114, 413–437.

Eckerman, C., Davis, C., & Didow, S. (1989). Toddlers' emerging ways to achieve social coordination with a peer. *Child Development*, 60, 440–453.

Flynn, E., & Whiten, A. (2012). Experimental 'microcultures' in young children: Identifying biographic, cognitive, and social predictors of information transmission. *Child Development*, 83(3), 911–925.

(2013). Dissecting children's observational learning of complex actions through selective video displays. *Journal of Experimental Child Psychology*, 116, 247–263.

Gimenez-Dasi, M., Guerrero, S., & Harris, P. L. (2005). Intimations of immortality and omni-science in early childhood. *European Journal of Developmental Psychology*, 2, 285–297.

Guerrero, S., Enesco, I., & Harris, P. L. (2010). Oxygen and the soul: Children's conception of invisible entities. *Journal of Cognition and Culture*, 10, 123–151.

Haidt, J. (2012). *The righteous mind. Why good people are divided by politics and religion*. London: Penguin.

Harris, P. L., Pasquini, E. S., Duke, S., Asscher, J. J., & Pons, F. (2006). Germs and angels: The role of testimony in young children's ontology. *Developmental Science*, 9(1), 76–96.

Haslam, N., Rothschild, L., & Ernst, D. (2002). Are essentialist beliefs associated with prejudice? *Behavioral Journal of Social Psychology*, 41, 87–100.

Haun, D. B., and Tomasello, M. (2011). Conformity to peer pressure in preschool children. *Child Development*, 82(6), 1759–1767.

Herrmann, P. A., Legare, C. H., Harris, P. L., and Whitehouse, H. (2013). Stick to the script: The effect of witnessing multiple actors on children's imitation. *Cognition*, 129, 536–543.

Heyes, C. (2013). What can imitation do for cooperation? In K. Sterelny, R. Joyce, B. Calcott, & B. Fraser (Eds.), *Cooperation and its evolution*. Cambridge, MA: MIT Press, 501–523.

Horner, V., & Whiten, A. (2005). Causal knowledge and imitation/emulation switching in chimpanzees (*Pan troglodytes*) and children (*Homo sapiens*). *Animal Cognition*, 8(3), 164–181.

Kenward, B. (2012). Over-imitating preschoolers believe unnecessary actions are normative and enforce their performance by a third party. *Journal of Experimental Child Psychology*, 112, 195–207.

Keupp, S., Behne, T., & Rakoczy, H. (2013). Why do children overimitate? Normativity is crucial. *Journal of Experimental Child Psychology*, 116, 392–406.

Lakin, J., & Chartrand, T. L. (2003). Using nonconscious behavioral mimicry to create affiliation and rapport. *Psychological Science*, 14, 334–339.

Laland, K. N., & Hoppitt, W. (2003). Do animals have culture? *Evolutionary Anthropology*, 12, 150–159.

Luncz, L. V., Mundry, R., & Boesch, C. (2012). Evidence for cultural differences between neighboring chimpanzee communities. *Current Biology*, 22(10), 922–926.

Lyons, D. E., Young, A. G., & Keil, F. C. (2007). The hidden structure of overimitation. *Proceedings of the National Academy of Sciences*, 104, 19751–19756.

Meltzoff, A. N. (1995). Understanding the intentions of others: Re-enactment of intended acts by 18-month-old children. *Developmental Psychology*, 31, 838–850.

Mosher, D. L., & Scodel, A. (1960). Relationships between ethnocentrism in children and the ethnocentrism and authoritarianism rearing practices of their mothers. *Child Development*, 31, 369–376.

Nadel, J. (2002). Imitation and imitation recognition: Functional use in preverbal infants and nonverbal children with autism. In A. N. Meltzoff & W. Prinz (Eds.), *The imitative mind: Development, evolution, and brain bases*. Cambridge: Cambridge University Press, 42–62.

Nagell, K., Olguin, R. S., & Tomasello, M. (1993). Processes of social learning in the tool use of chimpanzees (Pan troglodytes) and human children (Homo sapiens). *Journal of Comparative Psychology*, 107(2), 174–186.

Nielsen, M. (2006). Copying actions and copying outcomes: Social learning through the second year. *Developmental Psychology*, 42, 555–565.

(2009). The imitative behavior of children and chimpanzees: A window on the transmission of cultural traditions. *Revue de Primatology [online]*, 1. doi : 10.4000/primatologie.254.

Nielsen, M., & Blank, C. (2011). Imitation in young children: When who gets copied is more important than what gets copied. *Developmental Psychology*, 47, 1050–1053.

Nielsen, M., Subiaul, F., Whiten, A., Galef, B., & Zentall, T. (2012). Social learning in humans and non-human animals: Theoretical and empirical dissections. *Journal of Comparative Psychology*, 126, 109–113.

Nielsen, M., & Tomaselli, K. (2010). Over-imitation in Kalahari Bushman children and the origins of human cultural cognition. Psychological Science, 21, 729–736.

Olson, K. R., Dweck, C. S., Spelke, E. S., & Banaji, M. R. (2011). Children's responses to group-based inequalities: Perpetuation and rectification. *Social Cognition*, 29(2), 270–287.

Over, H., & Carpenter, M. (2009). Priming third-party ostracism increases affiliative imitation in children. *Developmental Science*, 12, F1–F8.

(2012). Putting the social into social learning: Explaining both selectivity and fidelity in children's copying behavior. *Journal of Comparative Psychology*, 126, 182–192.

(2013). The social side of imitation. *Child Development Perspectives*, 7, 6–11.

Rakoczy, H., Warneken, F., & Tomasello, M. (2008). The sources of normativity: Young children's awareness of the normative structure of games. *Developmental Psychology*, 44(3), 875–881.

Rhodes, M., Leslie, S., & Tworek, C. M. (2012). Cultural transmission of social essentialism. *Proceedings of the National Academy of Sciences*, 109(34), 13526–13531.

Schaik, J. E. van, van Baaren, R., Bekkering, H., & Hunnius, S. (2013). Evidence for nonconscious behavior-copying in young children. In M. Knauff, M. Pauen, N. Sebanz, & I. Wachsmuth (Eds.), *Proceedings of the 35th Annual Conference of the Cognitive Science Society*. Austin, TX: Cognitive Science Society, 1516–1521.

Sinclair, S., Dunn, E., & Lowery, B. (2005). The relationship between parental racial attitudes and children's implicit prejudice. *Journal of Experimental Social Psychology*, 41(3), 283–289.

Tennie, C., Call, J., & Tomasello, M. (2009). Ratcheting up the ratchet: On the evolution of cumulative culture. *Philosophical Transactions of the Royal Society B: Biological Sciences*, 364, 2405–2415.

Thorpe, W. H. (1956). *Learning and instinct in animals*. London: Methuen.

Tomasello, M. (1994). The question of chimpanzee culture. In R. Wrangham et al. (Eds.), *Chimpanzee cultures*. Cambridge, MA: Harvard University Press, 301–317.

(1999). *The cultural origins of human cognition*. Cambridge, MA: Harvard University Press.

Tomasello, M., Kruger, A. C., & Ratner, H. H. (1993). Cultural learning. *Behavioral and Brain Sciences*, *16*, 495–511.

Turner, J. C. (1991). *Social influence*. Buckingham: Open University Press; Pacific Grove, CA: Brooks/Cole.

Uskul, A. K., Cross, S. E., Alozkan, C., Gercek-Swing, B., Ataca, B., et al. (2014). Emotional responses to honor situations in Turkey and the northern USA. *Cognition and Emotion*, 28, 1057–1075.

Uzgiris, I. C. (1981). Two functions of imitation during infancy. *International Journal of Behavioral Development*, 4, 1–12.

Watson-Jones, R. E., Legare, C. H., Whitehouse, H., & Clegg, J. M. (2014). Task-specific effects of ostracism on imitation in early childhood. *Evolution and Human Behavior*, 35, 204–210.

Whitehouse, H. (2012). Religion, cohesion and hostility. In S. Clarke, R. Powell, & J. Savulescu (Eds.), *Religion, intolerance and conflict: A scientific and conceptual investigation*. Oxford: Oxford University Press, 36–47.

Whitehouse, H., & Cohen, E. (2012). Seeking a rapprochement between anthropology and the cognitive sciences: A problem-driven approach. *Topics in Cognitive Science*, 4(3), 404–412.

Whiten, A., & Boesch, C. (2001). The cultures of chimpanzees. *Scientific America*, 284(1), 48–55.

Whiten, A., McGuigan, N., Marshall-Pescini, S., & Hopper, L. M. (2009). Emulation, imitation, overimitaiton and the scope of culture for child and chimpanzee. *Philosophical Transactions of the Royal Society B: Biological Sciences*, 364, 2417–2428.

8 The Control of Shared Representations and Social Cognition

Lara Bardi and Marcel Brass

Abstract

Evidence from cognitive psychology and neuroscience has been accumulated suggesting that perception and execution of action are tightly linked. The observation of an action leads to a direct activation of the corresponding motor representation in the observer, suggesting that perception and action rely on a 'shared representational system'. Moreover, the observation of an action can lead to automatic imitation. However, if perception and action can lead to the concurrent activation of different motor plans, a fundamental problem is how we are able to distinguish between motor representations that have been internally generated by our own intention and those that have been triggered by observing others' actions. In other words, how can we avoid automatic imitation? In the present chapter, we will report recent evidence suggesting that a crucial component of such shared representation systems is self–other distinction and that the control of shared representations involves brain areas that constitute key nodes in high-level socio-cognitive processes such as agency attribution, perspective taking and mentalizing.

Introduction

Almost 10 years ago we proposed a theoretical account that relates the control of shared representations to higher-level social cognitive abilities such as mentalizing and perspective-taking. Ever since, a number of studies have directly or indirectly tested this theoretical account. The aim of the present chapter is to provide an update on the control of shared representations account and to summarize evidence in support of this hypothesis.

Converging evidence from different fields of cognitive psychology and neuroscience strongly suggests that perception and execution of action are tightly linked. The observation of an action leads to a direct activation of the corresponding motor representation in the observer, suggesting that perception and action rely on a 'shared representational system' (Prinz, 1997). The functional role of shared representations has been extensively explored in recent years. It has been argued that a shared representation system forms a basis for imitation, action understanding and social cognition (Bastiaansen, Thioux, & Keysers, 2009; Brass & Heyes, 2005; Gallese, 2003; Gallese & Goldman, 1998; Hurley, 2008; Rizzolatti & Craighero, 2004). However, if perception and action can lead to the concurrent activation of different motor plans, a fundamental problem is how we are able to distinguish between motor representations that have been internally generated by our own intention and those that have been triggered by observing others' actions (Brass & Heyes, 2005; Jeannerod, 1999). In the present chapter we will first briefly summarize empirical support for the concept of shared representations. Furthermore, we will report evidence suggesting that a crucial component of such a shared representation system is self–other distinction. Then, we will review recent data suggesting that the control of shared representations involves brain areas that constitute key nodes in high-level socio-cognitive processes such as agency attribution, perspective-taking and mentalizing (Brass, Derrfuss, & Cramon, 2005; Brass, Ruby, & Spengler, 2009, Santiesteban, Banissy, Catmur, & Bird, 2012a).

Shared Representations

There is evidence from different research fields for the assumption that perception and execution of an action have a common representational basis (Brass & Heyes, 2005). First, it has been demonstrated that the observation of an action primes the corresponding motor representation in the observer (Blakemore & Frith, 2005; Heyes, 2010, 2011; Massen & Prinz 2009). For example, executing an action while concurrently observing an incongruent action leads to interference compared with the observation of a congruent action (Brass, Bekkering, & Prinz, 2001; Craighero, Bello, Fadiga, & Rizzolatti, 2002; Kilner, Paulignan, & Blakemore, 2003). This phenomenon has been referred to as automatic imitation or motor priming and has been extensively investigated over the last 15 years (for a review, see Heyes, 2011). A second line of evidence for shared representations is coming from research in the domain of the 'mirror neuron system' (Rizzolatti, Fogassi, & Gallese, 2001) showing that, in humans, the observation of an action activates brain areas that are also involved in motor planning and execution (Gazzola & Keiser, 2009; Grèzes & Decety, 2001; Keysers & Gazzola, 2010). Furthermore, transcranial magnetic stimulation (TMS) research also provides support for the idea of shared representations. Observing a movement has measurable consequences for the peripheral motor system. When the primary motor cortex of human subjects is stimulated with TMS while subjects observe hand movements, motor-evoked potentials (MEPs) can be recorded from subjects' hand muscles. During action observation and not during observation of control stimuli, researchers found a decrease in the TMS intensity needed to evoke MEPs, or an increase in the MEP amplitude evoked with TMS of the same intensity, in the hand muscles that would be used to make the observed movements. Thus, the peripheral motor system seems to prepare to execute observed movements (e.g. Fadiga, Fogassi, Pavesi, & Rizzolatti, 1995). By the use of this psychophysiological technique, Bardi, Gheza, & Brass et al. (submitted) showed that this muscle-specific response priming also takes place in the context of response execution, thus confirming that this phenomenon is at the origin of action interference previously observed in behavioral studies.

The research we have described above indicates that action observation leads to an activation of an internal motor representation that can be revealed through reaction times, brain activation or motor TMS. There are different research lines, however, showing that shared representations sometimes even lead to overt behavior. For example people spontaneously copy postures, gestures and facial expressions of others (Chartrand & Bargh, 2009) (see Box 8.1). Moreover, clinical neuropsychological research revealed that prefrontal patients sometimes display imitative response tendencies (Brass, Derrfuss, Matthes-von Cramon, & von Cramon, 2003; De Renzi, Cavalleri, & Facchini, 1996; Lhermitte, Pillon, & Serdaru, 1986). Patients with so-called 'imitation behavior' tend to imitate the experimenter, but when asked about the reason for the imitative behavior, most patients claimed that they thought they were supposed to do so. Hence, imitation of the observed behavior seems to turn into their intention, suggesting a problem in distinguishing self-generated motor intentions from externally triggered motor intentions.

Box 8.1 Shared representations and overt behavior

Social psychological research has shown that shared representations can induce overt imitative response tendencies. We all recognize the situation in which we suddenly find ourselves in the same posture as our partner during an interesting conversation. This unconscious tendency to mimic our social interaction partners has been called the 'chameleon effect' and has been investigated systematically in social psychology (Chartrand & Bargh, 1999; Charthand & Lakin, 2013). Research on behavioral mimicry has examined a variety of behaviors, including yawning (Helt, Eigsti, Snyder, & Fein, 2010), body posture (Tiedens & Fragale, 2003), face touching (Chartrand & Bargh, 1999, Lakin & Chartrand, 2003, Genschow & Brass, 2015) but also facial expressions (Bavelas, Black, Lemery, & Mullett, 1986; Dimberg, Thunberg, & Elmehed, 2000). Being imitated increases rapport (Chartrand & Bargh, 1999), altruistic behavior (van Baaren, Holland, Kawakami, & van

Knippenberg, 2004), trust (Bailenson & Yee, 2005) and empathy (De Coster, Verschuere, Goubert, Tsakiris, & Brass, 2013). Furthermore, individuals imitate more when in possession of a positive social attitude (Lakin & Chartrand 2003; Leighton, Bird, & Heyes, 2010). For example, subliminal prosocial, compared to non-social, priming results in significantly higher levels of imitation (Cook & Bird, 2011; Leighton et al., 2010). Thus, imitation is bi-directionally associated with good social interaction and is therefore a key component in building social relationships with others. Crucially, successful social interaction relies on appropriate modulation of the degree of imitation according to the demands of the social situation (Lakin & Chartrand 2003; Wang & Hamilton, 2012).

The Origins of Shared Representations

Recently there has been an intensive debate regarding the origins of shared representations of perception and action (e.g. Cook, Bird, Catmur, Press, & Heyes, 2014). Basically, three accounts have been proposed: (1) an associative learning account, which assumes that shared representations are the result of general associative learning mechanisms, (2) the genetic account, which assumes that shared representations evolve from an innate neural system that is shaped by learning, and (3) ideomotor theory, which can be seen as an extension of the associative learning account. Interestingly, only the associative learning account (ASL) and the ideomotor account (IM) assume that shared representations are a byproduct of motor control (Brass & Heyes, 2005) and are therefore highly compatible with social psychological and cognitive research demonstrating an influence of action observation on action execution. However, while ASL assumes that shared representations of perception and action do not differ from any other kind of associations, IM ascribes a specific status to shared representations by assuming that they play a crucial role in intentional motor control (Greenwald, 1970).

The basic idea that actions are controlled by their perceivable consequences is not a new one and actually goes back to the ideomotor principle (Harleß, 1861; James, 1890; Lotze, 1852). Following up on this idea, Anthony Greenwald further developed a full-blown theory of motor control in the 1970s. From the perspective of ideomotor theory, motor representations are anticipations of the sensory feedback of the action they represent. Because of this inherent property of motor representations, observing a movement automatically activates its corresponding motor plan. While both IM and ASL predict such motor priming by action observation, only IM assumes that action observation activates the very same representation that is used for intentional motor control. This property of ideomotor representations, however, creates the agency problem of shared representations, as will be outlined below.

The Agency Problem of Shared Representations

The assumption of a shared representational system raises a fundamental issue. If the observation of an action leads to the activation of an internal motor representation that is also used for intentional motor control, why does this externally triggered motor representation not always lead to automatic imitative behavior in the observer? In order to avoid imitative behavior, the observer must be able to distinguish between his or her own motor intentions and the externally triggered motor representation (Jeannerod, 1999, 2004; Prinz, 2002). On the representational level, this conflict cannot be solved based on sensory (proprioceptive) input. Rather, the agent must determine whether the motor representation activation originates from a motor intention or the visual input. In other words, the agent must differentiate the self (the agency signal) from the other (the visual input). One possibility is that the conflict is resolved through the interplay of intention signals, originated by the representation of high-level contextual information that specifies the current goal of our behavior, and the analysis of the visual input based on predictions raised by action intention. As we outline above, from the perspective of ideomotor theory, motor plans contain anticipations of the sensory feedback of the action that serve for intentional motor control. By the use of such anticipations, higher-level control functions would not only be able to enforce the intended action (the self) but also to attenuate the effect of sensory inputs that are not compatible with the current goal and its predicted sensory consequences (the other). In the following paragraphs, we will describe an experimental paradigm to investigate self–other distinction in the context of shared representations. Furthermore, we will outline the neural mechanisms that allow us to control shared representations and inhibit automatic imitation tendencies. We will then present evidence supporting the idea that the mechanism and neural structures that are used for self–other distinction in the motor domain are also required for self–other distinction in high-level social-cognitive processes such as perspective-taking and mentalizing.

Overlapping Neural Mechanisms for Control of Imitation, Agency Attribution and Mentalizing

The control of shared representations can best be investigated by inducing conflict on the representational level. We have developed the imitation-inhibition task to investigate such a conflict situation under controlled experimental conditions (Brass et al., 2000). In this task, participants have to respond to a

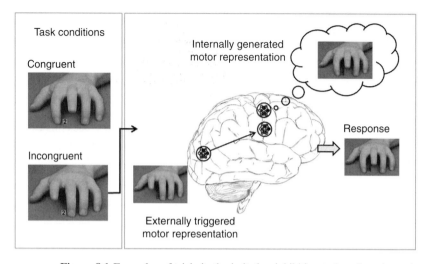

Figure 8.1 Examples of trials in the imitation inhibition task and a schematic representation of the conflict that arises in the incongruent condition. *See Plate 4.*

Notes: Left panel – example of trials in the imitation inhibition task. Participants are instructed to respond to a number displayed on the image of an index or middle finger movement. Participants are required to lift their index finger when a '1' appears and to lift their middle finger when a '2' appears. In the congruent trial, the movement presented on the screen is identical to the instructed movement. In the incongruent condition, the alternative movement is presented. Right panel – a schematic representation of the conflict that arises in the incongruent condition: two representations are concurrently activated and need to be distinguished for response execution.

number by lifting either the index or the middle finger while observing movements of the index or middle finger of a videotaped hand. In congruent trials, participants observe a finger movement of the videotaped hand that is identical to the instructed movement. Because the observed and the intended movement match, no conflict arises. In incongruent trials, the observed movement is different from the instructed movement. Here, participants need to distinguish the externally triggered motor representation from the intended motor representation in order to follow the instruction and avoid imitating the observed behavior. In neutral trials the hand on the computer screen remains still (Figure 8.1). Behaviorally, this paradigm very consistently yields an interference effect, that is, participants are slower in the incongruent than in the congruent condition (Brass et al., 2000, Liebelt, von Cramon, & Brass, 2008). In order to address the question of which brain areas are involved in the control of imitative behavior, we contrasted incongruent trials with congruent trials in an fMRI experiment (Brass et al., 2005). Consistent with the hypothesis that the control of imitative behavior involves brain regions that are related to self–other distinction, activation in the incongruent condition was found in the temporo parietal junction (TPJ) and the anterior medial prefrontal cortex (aMPFC) (Brass, Derrfuss, & von Cramon, 2005; Brass, Ruby, & Spengler, 2009; Brass, Zysset & von Cramon, 2001). Moreover, data suggest that imitative control is different from control employed in classical cognitive control tasks such as the Stroop task (Brass, Derrfuss, & von Cramon, 2005), the flanker task and spatial compatibility tasks, where automatic response tendencies are evoked by non-social, symbolic stimuli (e.g. Botvinick, Cohen, & Carter, 2004). These data strongly suggest that the inhibition of imitative behavior is a special case of response inhibition. Because the observation of an action leads to a direct activation of an internal motor representation, participants have to distinguish their own motor intentions from the externally triggered motor representation.

Notably, brain regions that are found to be involved during the imitation-inhibition task have been implicated in high-level socio-cognitive processes, such as in the sense of agency (i.e. determine who is the cause or initiator of an action or thought; Farrer, Franck, Georgieff, Frith, Decety, & Jeannerod, 2003), perspective-taking (Ruby & Decety, 2003) and self-referential processing (Northoff & Bermpohl, 2004). Moreover, the aMPFC and the TPJ are, in fact, the core brain regions of a network involved in mentalizing or having a 'theory of mind' (ToM), defined as the ability to reflect on other people's mental states (e.g. Amodio & Frith 2006; Frith & Frith, 1999, 2003; Saxe & Kanwisher, 2003; Schurz, Radua, Aichhorn, Richlan, & Pernet, 2014). Spengler, von Cramon, and Brass (2009) directly compared the neural circuits involved in the control of imitative behavior and the brain circuits involved in social-cognitive processes. Participants were asked to perform the imitation-inhibition task, a mentalizing task, a paradigm assessing self-referential judgments and agency processing. Results showed that controlling imitation recruited a region in aMPFC overlapping with activations during mentalizing and self-referential thoughts. A region in the TPJ showed an overlap between imitative control, mentalizing and agency processing. Moreover, performance in the imitation-inhibition task, perspective-taking and mentalizing tasks correlates in brain-damaged patients with lesions around the TPJ and the prefrontal cortex (Spengler, von Cramon, & Brass, 2010).

Consistent evidence for the overlapping hypothesis recently came from studies adopting brain stimulation techniques such as transcranial magnetic stimulation (TMS) and transcranial direct current stimulation (tDCS). These techniques can induce a brief interference/modulation on neural activity within a specific brain area while participants are engaged in a cognitive task. The effect of stimulation on behavioral performance allows us to draw inferences about the causal involvement of the given brain area in a cognitive function. To directly test the role of TPJ and the control of self–other representations, brain stimulation has been applied to the TPJ while participants were performing different social-cognitive tasks (Santiesteban et al., 2012a, 2012b; Sowden & Catmur, 2013). Results revealed that, after anodal tDCS, which enhances cortical excitability, participants' performance was ameliorated in both the imitation-inhibition task and the perspective-taking task. It is important to note that these two tasks require self–other representations to be controlled: the perspective-taking task, which requires the self to be inhibited and the other enhanced, while the control of imitation requires the other to be inhibited and the self enhanced. In the imitation-inhibition task, a reduction of the interference effect was obtained due to a modulation of performance in the incongruent condition. TDCS did not influence performance in a third task (the self-referential task) that did not require on-line self–other control.

Moreover, using TMS, some work has found impairment in different aspects of theory of mind performance following stimulation of the TPJ (Costa, Torriero, Olivieri, & Caltagirone, 2008; Young, Camprodon, Hauser, Pasqual-Leone, & Saxe, 2010). In the study of Sowden and Catmur (2013), a brief TMS pulse delivered to TPJ was sufficient to induce an increase of the congruency effect in the imitation-inhibition task. These results strongly support the idea that TPJ is causally involved in the control of imitation and high-level socio-cognitive functions. How does TPJ mediate the control of shared representations? A potential candidate mechanism is a top-down control over the content of shared representations. Bardi, Gheza, & Brass (submitted) recently tested this hypothesis by combining brain stimulation of the TPJ and the primary motor cortex. In this study, the congruency effect in the imitation-inhibition task was measured by MEPs recorded from the index and the little finger of the participants' hand. Motor cortex excitability was measured after anodal, cathodal and sham tDCS of the TPJ. Results revealed that modulation in cortical excitability within the TPJ directly affect the MEP pattern: increasing activation of TPJ (anodal tDCS) leads to a suppression of MEP differences between congruent and incongruent trials. These data suggest that a top-down control of shared representations is realized through the interaction between TPJ and the primary motor cortex (Bardi, Gheza, & Brass, submitted).

This line of evidence further supports the idea that TPJ plays a critical role in self–other distinction based on sensorimotor information. Finally, neuroimaging data from a different line of research have consistently shown activation of the TPJ during tasks exploring the sense of agency. This area is activated when participants make an external attribution of agency when external attributions are experimentally induced by manipulating the sensorimotor congruency between actual movements and the respective visual feedback (Sperduti, Delaveau, Fossati, & Nadel, 2011). This suggests that TPJ could serve as a mismatch detection mechanism, including detection of a visuo-motor discrepancy

(Spengler, von Cramon, & Brass, 2009; Sperduti et al., 2011), or as a more general system for updating models of environment stimuli or another person's behavior or thoughts (Geng & Vossel, 2013).

In summary, data converge in attributing the control of shared representations to the TPJ and aMPFC. This overlap on the neuroanatomical level raises the question of how the control of shared representation and ToM are related at the functional level. The control of imitation task requires participants to distinguish between their own action intentions and those of the 'other' and to carry out their own motor intention rather than the observed action. On-line control of self and other representations is also crucial in ToM and perspective-taking tasks where one should inhibit one's own point of view and enhance that of the other. In perspective-taking tasks, participants have to separate a first-person perspective from a third-person perspective. Behavioral data has recently lent support to this idea (Santiesteban, White, Cook, Gilbert, Heyes, & Bird, 2012b). In this study, participants underwent a training procedure with either an imitation or a counter-imitation task in which they were asked to watch movies depicting finger movements and to perform the same or the alternative finger movement. On the basis of the control hypothesis, one should expect that the counter-imitation task, training for self–other distinction, rather than imitation task, should positively impact performance in the subsequent task. Results revealed that, after the counter-mirror training only, subjects' performance was enhanced in a perspective-taking task in which participants were asked to take into account the point of view of a character in a scene. Interestingly, this result supports the idea that the control of shared representations involves similar functional-anatomical structures and cognitive mechanisms as more complex sociocognitive skills (the 'functional overlap hypothesis').

From Shared Representations to Social Cognition: The 'Different from Me Hypothesis'

Neuroimaging, patients and brain stimulation studies suggest that TPJ is recruited in situations where on-line control of co-activated self and other representation is crucial for successful task execution. How does this functional–anatomical overlap relate to the proposal that shared representations form the basis for social cognition? The 'like-me hypothesis' of social cognition (Meltzoff & Decety, 2003) maintains that internal simulation of others' actions is critical for action understanding, empathy and mentalizing (Blakemore & Frith, 2005; Gallese & Goldman 1998; Gallese, Fadiga, Fogassi, & Rizzolatti, 1996; Rizzolatti, Fadiga, Fogassi, & Gallese, 1996). However, as outlined above, recent research has identified a network of brain activations in mentalizing tasks that does not include areas with mirror properties (Frith & Frith 1999, 2003; for a review, see Schurz, Radua, Aichhorn, Richlan, & Pernet,

2014). Furthermore, the position that the mirror system is involved in mentalizing has also been criticized on the basis of theoretical arguments (Damasio & Meyer, 2008; Dinstein, Thomas, Behrmann, & Heeger, 2008).

In this chapter, we have presented evidence supporting the idea that common computational processes for the control of shared representations and high-level social-cognitive capacities concern our ability to distinguish the other-perspective from the self-perspective (Brass & Spengler, 2008; Brass et al., 2009; Santiesteban et al., 2012a, 2012b). Interestingly, this proposal is not in contrast with the idea that shared representations form a basis for action understanding and social cognition (Gallese & Goldman, 1998; Rizzolatti & Craighero, 2004). Mirroring the responses of others can contribute to our ability to efficiently and rapidly attribute intention to our interaction partners (Frith & Frith, 2006), but this motor or emotional contagion does not always and unequivocally convey the cause for this action or emotion (Mitchell, Macrae, & Banaji, 2006). Conversely, the formation of higher-level mentalizing capacities may be based on the ability to distinguish the other-perspective from the self-perspective and to form representations of the mental states of others (Decety & Grèzes, 2006). From an ontogenetic perspective, a shared representation system would arise early in development from repeated exposure to associations of a motor program and its perceptual consequences (Brass & Heyes, 2005; Keysers & Perrett, 2004). In the beginning, this system would not differentiate between events in the environment that are produced by other agents or oneself. Shared representations can be considered as a default mode of brain function. Through experience, the system starts to make predictions about the environment and to dissociate events that are contingent with one's action and those that are not. This experience that other people are different from oneself would allow the development of a sense of self and agency and control mechanisms in the motor domain, which would in subsequent development be needed in mental state attribution and could thus be seen as a first precondition for later-developing mental states attribution abilities.

Fascinating indications supporting the idea that self–other distinction has its basis and origin in sensorimotor mechanisms comes from a different field of research concerning the attribution of agency. An influential model, which has been put forward to explain the computational mechanisms underlying the sense of agency, is a predictive forward model of motor control (Wolpert Ghahramani, & Jordan, 1995). During action execution predictions are made about sensory movement consequences. Comparisons of this prediction with the actual sensory feedback contribute to the sense of agency. If prediction matches the actual sensory feedback, the action is perceived as caused by oneself, but if the comparison fails, the action is experienced as other-generated (Frith, Blakemore, & Wolpert, 2000). Although additional evidence is necessary to specify how these predictions are built up, from an ideomotor theory point of view, these anticipations of action-effects are based on action–effect association, acquired through associative ideomotor learning (Spengler, von Cramon, & Brass, 2009).

Hence, this description of cognitive processes implicated in mentalizing overlaps with our conceptualization of imitative control, as a prime example for assigning agency and exerting control over the shared representational system. This suggests that a pivotal precondition for mental state attribution is not the sharing of representations, but rather the building and distinction of representations related to self and other. It further implies that the functional system, which developed to distinguish self and other in the motor domain, subsequently generalized to more abstract representations, such as mental states and higher-level social cognition.

Explicit and Implicit Theory of Mind

Recent research in the domain of ToM may allow us to further specify the functional overlap between the control of imitation and ToM. One idea that emerged in the field of social cognition is that there are different levels of processing. At the lower level, there are fast, relatively inflexible routines that are largely automatic and implicit and may occur without awareness. At the higher level there are slow, flexible routines that are explicit and require the expenditure of mental effort (Frith & Frith, 2008). Recently, implicit and explicit processes have been distinguished in ToM, the former being concerned with on-line and automatic tracking of others' beliefs and the latter involving off-line and deliberate reasoning.

The dominant method to assess ToM abilities is the false-belief task. In this task, typically participants are asked to read stories about a person holding a false belief and then make predictions about his/her behavior. For example, in the Sally–Anne paradigm (Wimmer & Perner, 1983), Sally sees a ball placed in a box and then leaves the room. Anne then hides the ball in a different box. When Sally returns participants are required to identify the box where Sally will look for the ball. Participants are required to predict Sally's behavior on the basis of her false belief and to inhibit the response related to the ball's actual location. Passing this test is achieved by four years of age and requires abilities other than pure mental state attribution, such as inhibition, executive control and language abilities (Perner & Lang, 1999). However, in our everyday life interaction with other people, we are not always concerned with explicit reasoning about others' intentions and beliefs. In effect, rather than deliberate reasoning, efficient social interaction is based on rapid and unconscious interpretation of others' actions. Recently, in order to investigate this implicit form of mentalizing, tasks have been developed that, in contrast to variants of the standard false-belief task, are implicit, make no reference to others' beliefs and require no behavioral predictions of what agents will do on the basis of their beliefs (Kovács, Téglas, & Endress, 2010; Low & Watts, 2013). For example, in the task by Kovács and collaborators (2010) participants are asked to perform the detection of a ball previously positioned behind an occluder in the presence of an agent who can hold a false or true belief about the presence/absence of the ball behind the occluder. Results revealed that participants' reaction times were affected by the content of the agent's belief about the presence of the ball, even if they were never asked to pay attention to the agent's belief. This result revealed that others' mental states have a compelling impact on our own action. Using these methods, it was shown that we continuously undertake a rapid and involuntary tracking of others' beliefs and perspectives (also see Samson, Apperly, Braithwaite, Andrews, & Scott, 2010). Interestingly, eye movement studies suggest that infants as early as 7 to 15 months of age preferentially look at the object location coherent with the false belief of an agent, thus indicating mental state attribution (Kovács et al., 2010; Onishi & Baillargeon, 2005; Southgate, Senju, & Csibra, 2007; Surian, Caldi, & Sperber, 2007). A two-path ToM system has been proposed (Apperly & Butterfll, 2009) consisting of an early developing path, which operates in an implicit manner, allowing efficient monitoring of others' mental states in the social environment, and a late developing path, which involves verbal predictions, inhibition and response selection processes.

Although substantial evidence still needs to be accumulated in support of this distinction, we propose that the functional overlap between the control of motor representation and ToM may be stronger for implicit than for explicit forms of mentalizing. In effect, only in the implicit false-belief task does participants' performance depend on the concurrent activation of different representations of the environment, while explicit ToM includes off-line reasoning. In favor of our prediction, there are indications that the link between imitation control and explicit forms of ToM might be rather weak. Santiesteban and colleagues (Santiesteban, Banissy, Catmur, & Bird, 2012a; Santiesteban et al., 2012b) showed a modulation of performance in a perspective-taking task after counter-mirror training but failed to report any effect in the Strange Stories test, a common task used to measure explicit ToM abilities. Moreover, anodal tDCS of the TPJ improved response execution in the imitation-inhibition task and perspective-taking but did not induce any change in a task testing for mental state judgments (ibid).

Interesting for the current discussion is that studies adopting implicit ToM tasks demonstrated that others' beliefs have a strong impact on our task performance, suggesting that the representation of the content of others' beliefs may interact with our own representations of the state of the environment. This idea raises the interesting hypothesis that representations of others' beliefs have fundamentally similar properties to our own representations of the environment.

Although evidence for this shared representation of the belief content is still lacking, this could lead us to further specify the link between the control of imitation and ToM.

The Control of Imitation and Autism

Finally, the control of shared representation hypothesis of social cognition also generates interesting hypotheses regarding pathologies of social cognition. Autism spectrum conditions (ASCs) are characterized by impairments in social interaction, language and communication. A line of research focused on the integrity of the mirror system in ASCs has related this to poor social abilities and deficits in imitative performance (Dapretto Davies, Pfeifer, Scott, Sigman, Bookheimer, & Iacoboni, 2006; Williams, Waiter, Gilchrist, Perrett, Murray, & Whiten 2006). However, to date, this account is still under debate. A number of studies have demonstrated reduced imitation and mirror system activity in individuals with an ASC compared to control participants (Williams, Whiten, & Singh, 2004). However, experimental evidence does not always support the presence of reduced imitation behavior in ASCs (Bird, Leighton, Press, & Heyes, 2007; Spengler, Bird, & Brass, 2010). Furthermore, clinical observations of high levels of echolalia (automatic repetition of speech patterns) and echopraxia (automatic imitation of observed actions) in individuals with an ASC (Russell 1997; Rutter 1974; Williams et al. 2004) are incompatible with a pure imitation deficit in ASCs. Recently, it has been suggested that, rather than impairment in imitation per se, individuals with an ASC may have difficulties with the control of imitation (Hamilton, 2008; Southgate & Hamilton 2008; Spengler et al. 2010). It is therefore possible that the mirror system is not deficient in ASCs, but that this system is not influenced by mechanisms that distinguish between the self and other agents (Frith, 2003). This would also predict that the control of imitation might be related to social abilities (e.g. performance in ToM tasks) in individuals with an ASC and that the brain areas related to high-level sociocognitive processes, such as aFMC and TPJ, would also show abnormal processing. Studies in ASC individuals reported impairments of mentalizing (for an overview, see Frith, 2003), and also weaker activations of typical 'theory of mind areas' (aFMC and TPJ) in neuroimaging studies (e.g. Castelli, Frith, Happe, & Frith, 2002). In support of this idea, Spengler et al. (2010) investigated spontaneous imitation in high-functioning adults with an ASC while mentalizing was assessed in the same participants using both behavioral measures and fMRI. Individuals with an ASC showed increased imitation compared to controls and this was associated with reduced mentalizing and poorer reciprocal social interaction abilities. Moreover, imaging results support the previous observation that ASC participants with increased imitation showed less brain activation in the aMPFC and TPJ. The 'top-down modulation' account is also supported by the study of Cook and Bird (2012) showing that imitative behavior in ASCs is not modulated by socially relevant priming. Whereas in control participants imitation levels were higher following prosocially relevant priming relative to non-socially relevant priming, there was no difference between pro- and non-socially primed individuals with an ASC. Given the importance of appropriate levels of imitation for positive social interaction, this hypothesis may go some way towards explaining difficulties with social interaction in individuals with an ASC. Finally, this distinction between implicit and explicit forms of ToM may also be critical for the analysis of performance in individuals with an ASC. People at the high-functioning end of the autistic spectrum can show normal performance in standard false-belief tasks. It has been proposed (Frith, 2004) that these people have acquired an explicit form of ToM through teaching and experience, while lack of implicit ToM could be detected in other tasks.

Future Perspectives

Recent years have seen a growing interest in the study of mechanisms involved in the control of imitation and this work has had a substantial impact on the field of social cognition. Common neural mechanisms have been identified for different cognitive functions – namely, the control of shared representations, agency attribution and theory of mind – allowing us to draw connections between partially separate fields of investigation. Starting from this knowledge base, substantial effort still needs to be made to define the computational functions of brain regions involved in the control of shared representations. As outlined above, a timely issue concerns the possible functional and anatomical dissociation of implicit and explicit forms of mentalizing and how these are specifically related to the control of shared representations. Moreover, studies summarized here consistently report activation in the aMPFC and TPJ, both in the control of imitation and ToM. However, from a functional-anatomical point of view, it is very unlikely that both areas serve the same function. Concerning imitation, Brass and colleagues (2009) found indications of a possible dissociation of the two areas. TPJ could be involved in self–other distinction by indicating that the incoming visual information is related to someone else. On the other hand, aMPFC would be required to enforce one's own intention against an externally induced response tendency. A recent model supports the idea that aMPFC is involved in controlling imitation tendencies on the basis of contextual information that defines one's own current goal. Wang and Hamilton (2012) suggest that modulation of mimicry behavior in the social context reflects a social top-down control, which increases one's social advantage. For example, eye contact with the interaction partner facilitates mimicry as compared to averted gaze and this mechanism seems to be mediated by the mPFC. Another open question is whether computations occurring for the control of imitation and ToM are domain-specific or rather extend to other 'non-social' domains of cognition. A recent contribution tried to reconcile models of attention, which widely consider TPJ to be part of a network related to attention control, and models of social cognition. Here, TPJ function has been described as contextual updating: TPJ would be critically involved in updating internal models of the environment (including other people) for the purpose of constructing appropriate expectations and responses. These may occur for attention to simple stimuli as well as for socially relevant information (body movements, actions and intentions) (Geng & Vossel, 2013). Future research should deal with these issues and consequently gain a deeper insight into social cognition.

References

Amodio, D. M., & Frith, C. D. (2006). Meeting of minds: The medial frontal cortex and social cognition. *Nature Reviews Neuroscience*, 7, 268–277.

Apperly, I. A., & Butterfill, S. A. (2009). Do humans have two systems to track beliefs and belief-like states? *Psychological Review*, 116, 753–970.

Baaren, R. B. van, Holland, R. W., Kawakami, K., & van Knippenberg, A. (2004). Mimicry and prosocial behavior. *Psychological Science*, 15, 71–74.

Bailenson, J., & Yee, N. (2005). Digital chameleons: Automatic assimilation of non-verbal gestures in immersive virtual environments. *Psychological Science*, 16, 814–819.

Bardi, L., & Brass, M. (submitted). TPJ-M1 interaction in the control of shared representations: new insights from tDCS and TMS combined.

Bastiaansen, J. A, Thioux, M., & Keysers C. (2009). Evidence for mirror systems in emotions. *Philosophical Transactions of the Royal Society B: Biological Sciences*, 364(1528), 2391–404.

Bavelas, J. B., Black, A., Lemery, C. R., & Mullett, J. (1986). I show how you feel: Motor mimicry as a communicative act. *Journal of Personality and Social Psychology*, 50, 322–329.

Bird, G., Leighton, J., Press, C., & Heyes, C. (2007). Intact automatic imitation of human and robot actions in autism spectrum disorders. *Philosophical Transactions of the Royal Society B: Biological Sciences*, 1628, 3027–3031.

Blakemore, S. J., & Frith, C. (2005). The role of motor contagion in the prediction of action. *Neuropsychologia*, 43(2), 260–267.

Botvinick, M. M., Cohen, J. D., & Carter, C. S. (2004). Conflict monitoring and anterior cingulate cortex: An update. *Trends in Cognitive Sciences*, 12, 539–546.

Brass, M., Bekkering, H., Wohlschläger, A., & Prinz, W. (2000). Compatibility between observed and executed finger movements: Comparing symbolic, spatial, and imitative cues. *Brain & Cognition*, 44(2), 124–143.

Brass, M., Derrfuss, J., & von Cramon, D. Y. (2005). The inhibition of imitative and overlearned responses: A functional double dissociation. *Neuropsychologia*, 43(1), 89–98.

Brass, M., Derrfuss, J., Matthes-von Cramon, G., & von Cramon, D. Y. (2003). Imitative response tendencies in patients with frontal brain lesions. *Neuropsychology*, 17, 265–271.

Brass, M., & Heyes, C. (2005). Imitation: Is cognitive neuroscience solving the correspondence problem? Trends in Cognitive Sciences, 9(10), 489–495.

Brass, M., Ruby, P., & Spengler, S. (2009). Inhibition of imitative behaviour and social cognition. *Philosophical Transactions of the Royal Society B: Biological Sciences*, 364, 2359–2367.

Brass, M., Zysset, S., & von Cramon, D. Y. (2001). The inhibition of imitative response tendencies. *NeuroImage*, 14(6), 1416–1423.

Castelli, F., Frith, C., Happe, F., & Frith, U. (2002). Autism, Asperger syndrome and brain mechanisms for the attribution of mental states to animated shapes. *Brain*, 125, 1839–1849.

Chartrand, T. L., & Bargh, J. A. (1999). The chameleon effect: The perception–behavior link and social interaction. *Journal of Personality and Social Psychology*, 76(6), 893–910.

Chartrand, T. L., & Lakin, J. L. (2013). The antecedents and consequences of human behavioral mimicry. *Annual Review of Psychology*, 64, 285–308.

Chartrand, T. L., & van Baaren, R. (2009). Human mimicry. Advances in Experimental Social Psychology, 41, 219–274.

Cook, J., & Bird, G. (2011). Social attitudes modulate imitation in adolescents and adults. *Experimental Brain Research*, 211(3–4), 1045–1051.

Cook, J. L. & Bird, G. (2012). Atypical social modulation of imitation in autism spectrum conditions. *Journal of Autism and Developmental Disorders*, 42(6), 1045–1051.

Cook, R., Bird G., Catmur, C., Press, C., & Heyes C. (2014). Mirror neurons: From origin to function. *Behavioral Brain Science*, 37(2), 177–192.

Costa, A., Torriero, S., Olivieri, M., & Caltagirone, C. (2008). Prefrontal and temporo-parietal involvement in taking others' perspective: TMS evidence. *Behavioural Neurology*, 19, 71–72.

Craighero, L., Bello, A., Fadiga, L., & Rizzolatti, G. (2002). Hand action preparation influences the responses to hand pictures. *Neuropsychologia*, 40(5), 492–502.

Damasio, A., & Meyer, K. (2008). Behind the looking-glass. *Nature*, 454, 167–168.

Dapretto, M., Davies, M. S., Pfeifer, J. H., Scott, A. A., Sigman, M., et al. (2006). Understanding emotions in others: Mirror neuron dysfunction in children with autism spectrum disorders. *Nature Neuroscience*, 9, 28–30.

Decety, J., & Grèzes, J. (2006). The power of simulation: Imagining one's own and other's behavior. *Brain Research*, 1079(1), 4–14.

De Coster, L., Verschuere B., Goubert L., Tsakiris M., & Brass, M. (2013). I suffer more from your pain when you act like me: Being imitated enhances affective responses to seeing someone else in pain. *Cognitive and Affective Behavioral Neuroscience*, 13(3), 519–532.

De Renzi, E., Cavalleri, F., & Facchini, S. (1996). Imitation and utilisation behaviour. *Journal of Neurology, Neurosurgery and Psychiatry*, 61(4), 396–400.

Dimberg, U., Thunberg, M., & Elmenhed, K. (2000). Unconscious facial reactions to emotional facial expressions. *Psychological Science*, 11, 86–89.

Dinstein, I., Thomas, C., Behrmann, M., & Heeger, D. J. (2008). A mirror up to nature. *Current Biology*, 18, R13–R18.

Fadiga, L., Fogassi, L., Pavesi, G., & Rizzolatti, G. (1995). Motor facilitation during action observation: A magnetic stimulation study. *Journal of Neurophysiology*, 73, 2608–2611.

Farrer, C., Franck, N., Georgieff, N., Frith, C. D., Decety, J., & Jeannerod, M. (2003). Modulating the experience of agency: A positron emission tomography study. *NeuroImage*, 18(2), 324–333.

Frith, C. (2003). What do imaging studies tell us about the neural basis of autism? *Novartis Foundation Symposium*, Discussion 166–176, 281–197.

(2004). Is autism a disconnection disorder? *The Lancet: Neurology*, 10, 577.

Frith, C. D., Blakemore, S. J., & Wolpert, D. M. (2000). Abnormalities in the awareness and control of action. *Philosophical Transactions of the Royal Society of London B: Biological Sciences*, 1404, 1771–1788.

Frith, C. D., & Frith, U. (1999). Interacting minds: Biological basis. *Science*, 286, 1692–1695.

(2006). The neural basis of mentalizing. *Neuron*, 50(4), 531–534.

(2008). Implicit and explicit processes in social cognition. *Neuron*, 6, 503–510.

Gallese, V. (2003). The manifold nature of interpersonal relations: The quest for a common mechanism. *Philosophical Transactions of the Royal Society B: Biological Sciences*, 358, 517–528.

Gallese, V., Fadiga, L., Fogassi, L., & Rizzolatti, G. (1996). Action recognition in the premotor cortex. *Brain*, 119(2), 593–609.

Gallese, V., & Goldman, A. (1998). Mirror neurons and the simulation theory of mind-reading. *Trends in Cognitive Sciences*, 2(12), 493–501.

Gazzola, V., & Keysers, C. (2009). The observation and execution of actions share motor and somatosensory voxels in all tested subjects: Single-subject analyses of unsmoothed fMRI data. *Cerebral Cortex*, 19(6), 1239–1255.

Geng, J., & Vossel, S. (2013). Re-evaluating the role of TPJ in attentional control: Contextual updating? *Neuroscience Behavioral Review*, 37(10), 2608–2620.

Genschow, O., & Brass, M. (2015). The predictive chameleon: Evidence for anticipated social action. *Journal of Experimental Psychology: Human Perception and Performance*, 2, 265–268.

Grèzes, J., & Decety, J. (2001). Functional anatomy of execution, mental simulation, observation, and verb generation of actions: A meta-analysis. *Human Brain Mapping*, 12(1), 1–19.

Hamilton, A. F. (2008). Emulation and mimicry for social interaction: A theoretical approach to imitation in autism. *Quarterly Journal of Experimental Psychology*, 61, 101–115.

Harleß, E. (1861). Der Apparat des Willens [The apparatus of will]. *Zeitschrift für Philosophie und philosophische Kritik*, 38(2), 50–73.

Helt, M. S., Eigsti, I. M., Snyder, P. J., & Fein, D. A. (2010). Contagious yawning in autistic and typical development. *Child Development*, 81(5), 1620–1631.

Heyes, C. (2010). Where do mirror neurons come from? *Neuroscience Behavioral Review*, 34, 575–583.

(2011). Automatic imitation. *Psychological Bulletin*, 137(3), 463–483.

Hurley, S. (2008). The shared circuits model (SCM): How control, mirroring, and simulation can enable imitation, deliberation, and mindreading. *Behavioural Brain Research*, 31(1), 1–22.

James, W. (1890). *The principles of psychology*. New York: Macmillan.

Jeannerod, M. (1999). To act or not to act: Perspectives on the representation of actions. *Quarterly Journal of Experimental Psychology*, 52, 1–29.

(2004). Visual and action cues contribute to the self–other distinction. *Nature Neuroscience*, 7(5), 422–423.

Keysers, C., & Gazzola, V. (2010). Social neuroscience: Mirror neurons recorded in humans. *Current Biology*, 20(8), R354.

Keysers, C., & Perrett, D. I. (2004). Demystifying social cognition: A Hebbian perspective. *Trends in Cognitive Sciences*, 8(11), 501–507.

Kilner, J. M., Paulignan, Y., & Blakemore S. J. (2003). An interference effect of observed biological movement on action. *Current Biology*, 13(6), 522–525.

Kovács, A. M., Téglas, E., & Endress, A. D. (2010). The social sense: Susceptibility to others' beliefs in human infants and adults. *Science*, 330, 1830–1834.

Lakin, J. L., & Chartrand, T. L. (2003). Using nonconscious behavioral mimicry to create affiliation and rapport. *Psychological Science*, 14, 334–339.

Lhermitte, F., Pillon, B., & Serdaru, M. (1986). Human autonomy and the frontal lobes. Part I. Imitation and utilization behavior: A neuropsychological study of 75 patients. *Annals of Neurology*, 19(4), 326–334.

Leighton, J., Bird, G., & Heyes, C. M. (2010). 'Goals' are not an integral component of imitation. *Cognition*, 114, 423–435.

Liepelt, R., von Cramon, D. Y., & Brass, M. (2008). What is matched in direct matching? Intention attribution modulates motor priming. *Journal of Experimental Psychology: Human Perception and Performance*, 34(3), 578–591.

Lotze, R. H. (1852). *Medicinische psychologie oder physiologie der seele Weidmann*. Leipzig: Weidmann.

Low, J., & Watts, J. (2013). Attributing false beliefs about object identity reveals a signature blind spot in humans' efficient mind-reading system. *Psychological Science*, 24(3), 305–411.

Massen, C., & Prinz, W. (2009). Movements, actions and tool-use actions: An ideomotor approach to imitation. *Philosophical Transactions of the Royal Society B: Biological Sciences*, 364(1528), 2349–2358.

Meltzoff, A. N., & Decety, J. (2003). What imitation tells us about social cognition: A rapprochement between developmental psychology and cognitive neuroscience. *Philosophical Transactions of the Royal Society B: Biological Sciences*, 358(1431), 491–500.

Mitchell, J. P., Macrae, C. N., & Banaji, M. R. (2006). Dissociable medial prefrontal contributions to judgments of similar and dissimilar others. *Neuron*, 50, 655–663.

Northoff, G., & Bermpohl, F. (2004). Cortical midline structures and the self. *Trends in Cognitive Sciences*, 8(3), 102–107.

Onishi, K. H., & Baillargeon, R. (2005). Do 15-month-old infants understand false beliefs? *Science*, 308, 255–258.

Perner, J., & Lang, B. (1999). Development of theory of mind and executive control. *Trends in Cognitive Sciences*, 3(9), 337–344.

Prinz, W. (1997). Perception and action planning. *European Journal of Cognitive Psychology*, 9, 129–154.

(2002). Experimental approaches to imitation. In A. N. Meltzoff & W. Prinz (Eds.), In *The imitative mind: Development, evolution, and brain bases.* Cambridge: Cambridge University Press, 143–163.

Rizzolatti, G., & Craighero, L. (2004). The mirror-neuron system. *Annual Review of Neuroscience*, 27, 169–192.

Rizzolatti, G., Fadiga, L., Fogassi, L., & Gallese, V. (1996). Premotor cortex and the recognition of motor actions. *Brain Research: Cognitive Brain Research*, 3, 131–141.

Rizzolatti, G., Fogassi, L., & Gallese, V. (2001). Neurophysiological mechanisms underlying the understanding and imitation of action. *Nature Reviews Neuroscience*, 2(9), 661–670.

Ruby, P., & Decety, J. (2003). What you believe versus what you think they believe: A neuroimagi ng study of conceptual perspective-taking. *European Journal of Neuroscience*, 17(11), 2475–2480.

Russell, J. (1997). *Autism as an executive disorder.* New York: Oxford University Press.

Rutter, M. (1974). The development of infantile autism. *Psychological Medicine*, 4, 147–163.

Samson, D., Apperly, I. A., Braithwaite, J. J., Andrews, B. J., & Bodley Scott, S. E. (2010). Seeing it their way: Evidence for rapid and involuntary computation of what other people see. *Journal of Experimental Psychology: Human Perception and Performance*, 36, 1255–1266.

Santiesteban, I., Banissy, M. J., Catmur, C., & Bird, G. (2012a). Enhancing social ability by stimulating right temporoparietal junction. *Current Biology*, 22(23), 2274–2277.

Santiesteban, I., White, S., Cook, J., Gilbert, S. J., Heyes, C., & Bird, G. (2012b). Training social cognition: From imitation to theory of mind. *Cognition*, 122(2), 228–235.

Saxe, R., & Kanwisher, N. (2003). People thinking about thinking people: fMRI investigations of theory of mind. *NeuroImage*, 9, 1835–1842.

Schurz, M., Radua, J., Aichorn, M., Richlan, F., & Perner, J. (2014). Fractionating theory of mind: A meta-analysis of functional brain imaging studies. *Neuroscience and Biobehavioral Reviews*, 42, 9–34.

Southgate, V., & Hamilton, A. F. (2008). Unbroken mirrors: Challenging a theory of autism. *Trends in Cognitive Sciences*, 12, 225–229.

Southgate, V., Senju, A., & Csibra, G. (2007). Action anticipation through attribution of false belief by 2-year-olds. *Psychological Science*, 18, 587–592.

Sowden, S., & Catmur, C. (2013). The role of the right temporoparietal junction in the control of imitation. *Cerebral Cortex*, 4, 1107–1113.

Spengler, S., von Cramon, D.Y., & Brass, M. (2009a). Control of shared representations relies on key processes involved in mental state attribution. *Human Brain Mapping*, 30(11), 3704–3718.

(2009b). Was it me or was it you? How the sense of agency originates from ideomotor learning revealed by fMRI. *NeuroImage*, 46(1), 290–298.

(2010). Resisting motor mimicry: Control of imitation involves processes central to social cognition in patients with frontal and temporo-parietal lesions. *Social Neuroscience*, 5(4), 401–416.

Sperduti, M., Fossati, P., Delaveau, P., & Nadel, J. (2011). Different brain structures related to self- and external-agency attribution: A brief review and meta-analysis. *Brain Structure and Function*, 216, 151–157.

Surian, L., Caldi, S., & Sperber, D. (2007). Attribution of beliefs to 13-month-old infants. *Psychological Science*, 18, 580–586.

Tiedens, L. Z., & Fragale, A. R. (2003). Power moves: Complementarity in dominant and submissive nonverbal behavior. *Journal of Personality and Social Psychology*, 84, 558–568.

Wang, Y., & Hamilton, A. F de C. (2012). Social top-down response modulation (STORM): A model of the control of mimicry in social interaction. *Frontiers in Human Neroscience*, 6, 153.

Williams, J. H., Waiter, G. D., Gilchrist, A., Perrett, D. I., Murray, A. D., & Whiten, A. (2006). Neural mechanisms of imitation and 'mirror neuron' functioning in autistic spectrum disorder. *Neuropsychologia*, 44, 610–621.

Williams, J. H., Whiten, A., & Singh, T. (2004). A systematic review of action imitation in autistic spectrum disorder. *Journal of Autism and Developmental Disorders*, 3, 285–299.

Williams, J. H., Whiten, A., Suddendorf, T., & Perrett, D. I. (2001). Imitation, mirror neurons and autism. *Neuroscience and Biobehavioral Reviews*, 25(4), 287–229.

Wimmer, H., & Perner, J. (1983). Beliefs about beliefs: Representations and constraining function of wrong beliefs in young children's understanding of deception. *Cognition*, 13, 103–128.

Wolpert, D. M., Ghahramani, Z., & Jordan, M. I. (1995). An internal model for sensorimotor integration. *Science*, 269, 1880–1882.

Young, L., Camprodon, J. A., Hauser, M., Pasqual-Leone, A., & Saxe, R. (2010). Disruption of the right temporoparietal junction with transcranial magnetic stimulation reduces the role of beliefs in moral judgments. *Proceedings of the National Academy of Sciences of the United States of America*, 107(15), 6752–6758.

9 Neurocognitive Explorations of Social Mimicry

Sukhvinder S. Obhi

Abstract

Social mimicry is the ubiquitous tendency to copy the bodily movements, expressions, postures and speech patterns of an interaction partner. Since the 1990s social psychologists have studied this phenomenon intensively and have revealed many interesting findings about the factors that moderate mimicry and its consequences. Recently, social cognitive neuroscientists have also begun to study mimicry, with an emphasis on uncovering its mechanistic underpinnings. In particular, mechanisms that have been studied in tasks such as action observation and automatic imitation have been assumed to play a role in social mimicry. Although intuitive, the notion that these mechanisms are common to both tightly controlled laboratory tasks and more naturalistic social mimicry is an assumption that requires empirical investigation. Here, I present recent work that begins to provide this missing empirical link. I contextualize this work with respect to both the social psychology and the cognitive neuroscience literatures.

Introduction

Modern humans are intensely social, spending a great deal of time every day in the company of others. Humans get feelings of warmth and a general sense of wellbeing from engaging meaningfully with those around them, and good relationships have been identified as a key predictor of human wellbeing (Deiner & Seligman, 2002). Even in the Palaeolithic age when our predecessor, *homo erectus*, first emerged, social interactions were crucial. It has been argued that, during that age, the major cognitive function for *homo erectus* was *mimesis*, which involved the imitation and mimicry of vocalizations, facial expressions, eye movements, body postures and manual signs of conspecifics. Such mimesis served as the basis for communication and allowed for a substantial increase in

Sukhvinder S. Obhi is grateful to Dr. Jeremy Hogeveen and Dr. Geoff Bird for feedback on a portion of this chapter as well as Dr. Emily Cross for valuable feedback.

the range and complexity of, especially emotional, expression (Massey, 2002). Although modern humans possess rich language skills, mimicking the gestures, bodily movements and facial expressions of interaction partners remains ubiquitous in the twenty-first century.

This form of social mimicry is not obviously linked to learning skills, or achieving specific object-oriented goals. Instead, it seems to serve the goal of creating smooth social interactions, which result in feelings of rapport and a prosocial orientation. In the first section of this chapter, I will briefly highlight some important findings from the social psychological study of mimicry. My focus will be limited to behavioural mimicry of bodily movements such as face touching and foot shaking and I will refer to this as 'behavioural mimicry', 'social mimicry' or simply 'mimicry'. In the second section, I will consider how cognitive psychologists and cognitive neuroscientists have attempted to study mimicry under tightly controlled laboratory conditions and I will highlight several challenges associated with linking this work to the social psychological findings. In the third section, I will describe recent experiments that have attempted to integrate the, until now, separate literatures on mimicry from social psychology and cognitive neuroscience. In the fourth section, I will offer speculation about the kinds of mechanism that might be linked with the occurrence of mimicry.

What is Mimicry and What Do We Know about It?

Behavioural mimicry can take many forms, including copying the verbal expressions, accents and speech tones of interaction partners. Due to space limitations, my consideration is restricted to mimicry of bodily movements and does not extend into facial mimicry, or indeed mimicry of body postures.

Mimicry of bodily movements is usually assessed via videorecordings of social interactions between two individuals. It has been defined as the repetition, by one member of a dyad, of a bodily movement made by the other member of the dyad. Typically, the repeated movement must be identical or similar to constitute mimicry and must occur in close temporal proximity to the original movement, and in any case, not longer than 3–5 seconds afterwards (Chartrand & Lakin, 2013). Crucially, if awareness of mimicry does occur during an interaction, this awareness usually arises after the performance of a repeated movement, thus confirming that the mimicry itself occurs automatically and is non-consciously initiated. For this reason, mimicry is often referred to as being *non-conscious*. Box 9.1 highlights some of the key findings from the social psychological literature on behavioural mimicry.

Box 9.1 The social psychology of mimicry

The study of behavioural mimicry increased rapidly after publication of the seminal paper by Chartrand and Bargh (1999) in which the term 'chameleon effect' was used to describe behavioural mimicry. The idea is that, just as a chameleon changes its colour based on its environment, people change their movement behaviour based on their current social environment and who they are interacting with at a particular moment. In that landmark paper, participants were engaged with a confederate who made distinct target movements. For example, sometimes the confederate would touch their own face, whereas at other times, they would shake their foot. The key finding was that participants showed increased face-touching behaviour when the confederate had been performing face touches, and more foot-shaking behaviour when the confederate had been performing foot shakes. Such mimicry manifested despite the fact that participants and confederates did not know each other, the confederate did not perform any welcoming or affiliative behaviours, and participants were unaware of any behavioural patterns on the part of the confederate.

Since that seminal paper, many moderators have been identified that affect the degree of mimicry displayed. For example, friends tend to mimic each other more than strangers (McIntosh, 2006), participants with a conscious or unconscious affiliation goal mimic more than those with no affiliation goal (Lakin & Chartrand, 2003), individuals primed with interdependent self-construal mimic more than those primed with independent self-construal (van Baaren, Maddux, Chartrand, de Bouter, & van Knippenberg 2003) and individuals who have been socially excluded from an in-group tend to mimic members of that in-group more after the exclusion experience (Lakin, Chartrand, & Arkin, 2008). This latter result is thought to be due to exclusion triggering motivation to re-affiliate (also see Over & Oosterbroek, this volume, Chapter 7). In other work, Cheng and Chartrand (2003) found that high self-monitors mimic powerful interaction partners more than powerless partners, and Japanese participants mimic a confederate more than American participants, irrespective of the confederate's ethnicity (van Baaren, Maddux, W. W., Chartrand, 2004). Similarity between interaction partners also increases mimicry whether that similarity refers to opinions (van Swol & Drury, 2006), group membership (Borgeois & Hess, 2008) or even a name (Guégen & Martin, 2009). It has been shown that a happy mood produces more mimicry than a negative mood (van Baaren, Fockenberg, Holland, Janssen, & van Knippenberg 2006). In direct opposition to the finding that affiliation goals facilitate mimicry, goals to disaffiliate lead to less mimicry. In a particularly interesting example, non-Christian women mimicked the face-touching behaviour of obviously Christian confederates less than non-Christian confederates (Yabar, Johnston, Miles, & Peace, 2006).

Social mimicry has myriad consequences for individual information processing. Being mimicked has been found to make people more field dependent, such that they are better at detecting stimuli embedded in a complex background (van Baaren, Maddux, Chartrand, de Bouter, & van Knippenberg, 2003). Being mimicked also encourages more convergent thinking, whereas not being mimicked leads to more divergent thinking (Ashton-James & Chartrand, 2009). Executive resources are affected by expectancy violations relating to mimicry. For example, in one experiment, being mimicked by a powerful individual (an expectation violation because usually powerful people do not mimic the less powerful) led to lower performance on a Stroop task compared to not being mimicked (Dalton, Chartrand, & Finkel, 2010). Social consequences of mimicry include more liking for a confederate who mimicked participants versus a confederate who did not mimic participants (Chartrand & Bargh, 1999). Pro-sociality is also increased by mimicry such that, for example, participants who have just been mimicked in an interaction picked up more pens dropped by the experimenter (i.e. displayed more helping behaviour) than those who had not been mimicked (van Baaren et al., 2003). Correspondingly, mimickers report increased interdependence and this effect on self-construal has even been linked to preferences for liberal political ideas and groups (Redeker, Stel, & Mastop, 2011; Stel & Harnick, 2011). Similarly, feelings of trust increase after being mimicked and lead to greater disclosure of personal information to a stranger (Guéguen, Martin, Meineri, & Simon, 2013). Finally, mimicking an out-group member has been shown to reduce scores on explicit and implicit measures of prejudice compared to mimicking an in-group member (Inzlicht, Gutsell, & Legault, 2012).

This brief account of behavioural mimicry research is obviously not exhaustive, but should provide a flavour of the kinds of finding that have been reported. Of note are the many moderating variables that affect mimicry, and the interesting and largely positive downstream effects, both individual and social, of mimicry.

Studying 'Mimicry' in the Cognitive Neuroscience Laboratory: Motor Resonance and Automatic Imitation

In general, researchers in the domain of cognitive neuroscience have not studied behavioural mimicry, as was discussed in the first section of this chapter. Instead, these researchers have studied the neural correlates of tasks that are

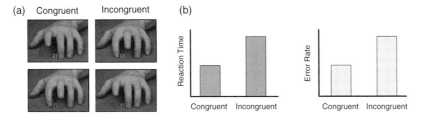

A. In the automatic imitation task (above, AIT), participants respond to numeric cues via a pre-instructed SR-mapping 1=lift index finger, 2=lift middle finger. Incidental actions are presented with the numeric cue that are either congruent or incongruent with the cued response. Form Hogeveen et al. (2013). B. Idealised typical results (not real data) depicting increased reaction times and error rates in incongruent trails. The difference between incongruent and congruent dependents is termed "interference" and reflects the degree to which automatic imitation of the action interfered with production of the cued response. This effect is attributed to motor resonance.

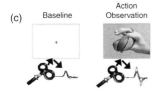

C. In TMS studies of action observation (left) MEPs elicited by single pulse TMS to motor cortical representations during an action observation condition are often normalized to a baseline (non-action observation) condition. The resulting measure reflects MEP facilitation. This measure is often referred to as Motor Resonance (MR) which many believe is brought about by the human mirror system. The first demonstration was provided by Fadiga et al (1995). From Hogeveen, Inzlicht & Obhi (2014).

Figure 9.1 Automatic imitation and action observation tasks.

assumed to be necessary components of social mimicry, including action observation and automatic imitation (see Figure 9.1). There has been an implicit assumption by researchers in this domain that the processes they elucidate from performance on imitative finger-lifting tasks in well-controlled settings, inside and outside of brain scanners, are common to those underlying more naturalistic social mimicry. However, this notion has not been empirically verified (Heyes, 2011). In this section, I will discuss exemplars from the cognitive neuroscience literature in which processes that *might* be involved in behavioural mimicry have been studied. As will be seen, the kind of tasks employed by these researchers bear only limited resemblance to the tasks employed by social psychologists.

Mechanisms of Imitative Behaviour

Given that mimicry involves the production of an identical or similar movement to an interaction partner at a very short latency, minimum information-processing requirements are involved. Mimicry necessitates that the movement of an interaction partner is first registered by the sensory apparatus of the observer and that motor structures in the observer's brain are then activated in such a way as to produce the same or a similar action in short succession. Thus, mimicry fundamentally requires some kind of translation of a sensory event into an identical or nearly identical motor event. Crucial processes therefore should be those that are involved in action observation, action production and the production of specifically imitative responses. In their seminal paper, Chartrand and Bargh (1999) proposed the existence of a perception–behaviour link that underlies the occurrence of mimicry. The ideomotor theory proposes that actions are centrally represented in terms of the effects they produce (Greenwald, 1970; James, 1890; Knuf, Aschersleben, & Prinz, 2001). Hence, by observing action effects, the representation of the action is also activated, thereby facilitating its performance (Greenwald, 1970; Herwig, Prinz, & Waszak, 2007; James, 1890; Knuf et al., 2001). Ideomotor theory provides a plausible conceptual mechanism by which behaviours like imitation and mimicry could occur (Chartrand & Bargh, 1999; Herwig et al., 2007).

At the neural level, the mirror system may provide the neurophysiological machinery for ideomotor mechanisms, thus making it a candidate neural system underlying mimicry and imitation (Frith & Frith, 2006; Iacoboni, 2008; Prinz, 2005). Mirror neurons were first observed in the premotor cortex of macaque monkeys and fire both when an animal performs an action and when it observes another animal performing the same action (Rizzolatti, Fadiga, Gallese, & Fogassi, 1996). Thus neurons that were previously thought to be purely 'motor' also seem to contribute to action perception and, potentially, action understanding (Buccino et al., 2007; Knoblich & Sebanz, 2006). Ideomotor theory and the existence of mirror neurons provide the basis for the activation of corresponding motor representations in actors and observers during action observation. Although the original discovery of mirror neurons occurred in monkeys, the presence of a similar system in humans has been identified by neuroimaging and brain stimulation studies using functional magnetic resonance imaging (fMRI) and transcranial magnetic stimulation (TMS) (Buccino et al., 2007; Fadiga, Fogassi, Pavesi, & Rizzolatti, 1995; Iacoboni & Mazziotta, 2007; Kaplan & Iacoboni, 2006;). Lastly, mirror activation does not always have to mean that a matching action representation is activated. Associative sequence learning (ASL) theory posits that the motor representations that are activated when observing a particular motor act will be those that have been associated with that sensory input in the past (Catmur, Walsh, & Heyes, 2009; Heyes, 2011). Thus, in some cases, a complementary and not matching action is entirely possible.

TMS is an electromagnetic tool that can non-invasively stimulate neurons in cortical motor areas (Hallett, 2007). When body part representations in the motor cortex are stimulated by TMS, a muscle response (measured with electromyography, EMG) can be recorded in the corresponding muscle of the body in the form of a motor-evoked potential (i.e. an MEP; Magistris, Rösler, Truffert, & Myers, 1998). Importantly, MEP amplitudes have been found to increase when someone watches another person performing an action, and this increase is specific to the body part representation(s) in motor cortex corresponding to the observed action(s), although there is mounting evidence of non-specific facilitation as well, dependent on *when* TMS is applied (Fadiga et al., 1995; Fadiga, Craighero, & Olivier, 2005; Obhi, Hogeveen, & Pascual-Leone, 2011; Naish, Houston-price, Bremner, & Holmes, 2014). Hence, MEPs reflect the excitation of motor representations in an observer's brain, providing an indication of the degree of 'motor resonance', and by inference the level of mirror system activity.

Whereas not every motor representation will be activated enough to elicit a movement, some will, and this is what might cause mimicry. Arguably, understanding the relevant factors for pushing one particular motor representation above threshold is the main problem that needs to be solved to fully appreciate how mimicry occurs. For many, it seems almost obvious that mirror mechanisms result in motor activation that can facilitate movement, and therefore, that the mirror system and the 'motor resonance' it produces are causally linked to social mimicry. Despite the temptation to accept this 'mirroring as the cause' intuition, it is important to step back and realize that this is not a fact. Again, as prominent authors in the study of imitation have pointed out, the links between the mirror system, mimicry and imitation have not been empirically verified (Heyes, 2011).

Research Domains as Silos

One obstacle to improving our understanding of whether there is a link between mimicry and the mirror system is the fact that researchers interested in mimicry often work within the social psychology domain, and researchers interested in the mirror system often work within the cognitive neuroscience domain. Historically, then, with the exception of the odd passing reference to the 'other' literature, no concerted effort to integrate these two largely separate bodies of work has occurred. Thankfully, this has begun to change in recent years, with the rising popularity of social neuroscience. In particular, an ever-increasing number of researchers are consulting with and referring to both sets of literature, which enables the creation of a larger, integrated knowledge base. This point should be underlined for new entrants to the field or aspiring new researchers: it is extremely important to consider how a topic has been addressed by researchers in different disciplines, or even different sub-disciplines, as each perspective informs and constrains the other and progress is therefore more encompassing of the extant data.

Task Equivalence or Lack Thereof

Another key challenge in gaining a more holistic understanding of the neural basis of mimicry is that cognitive neuroscientists typically employ very different experimental 'tasks' than social psychologists. As mentioned above, two important components of social mimicry are the processes associated with action observation and production and imitative behaviour (e.g. Buccino, Binkofski, & Fink, 2001; Buccino, Binkofski, & Riggio 2004). The mirror system seems to play a role in each of these task types (Iacoboni et al., 1999a; see Cook, Bird, Catmur, Press, & Heyes, 2014 for a review of mirror system research and theory). Changes in the activity of the mirror system can be tracked as researchers manipulate various situational or other variables, such as the race or cultural background of the model (Losin, Iacoboni, Martin, Cross, & Dapretto, 2012; Losin, Cross, Iacoboni, & Dapretto, 2014). Similarly, in action observation studies, participants typically watch videos of a model making simple actions while brain activity is assessed using neuroimaging, and the effects of various factors such as the expertise of observers in the particular skill can be assessed (e.g. Calvo-Merino, Glaser, Grèzes, Passingham, & Haggard, 2005). This type of work has identified an action observation network in the human brain (Cross, Hamilton, Kraemer, Kelley, & Grafton, 2009a; Cross, Kraemer, Hamilton, Kelley, & Grafton, 2009b). In many of these experiments, stimuli depict only part of a body, such as a hand, or an arm, or perhaps a whole upper body (although there are increasing numbers of exceptions; also see Cross & Calvo-Merino, this volume, Chapter 26). Of course, fMRI is not the only method for investigating action observation. Many action observation experiments utilize TMS to elicit MEPs in the musculature that would be involved if the participant were performing the movements themselves, with the finding of specific facilitation of relevant muscles (Fadiga et al., 1995; Fourkas, Avenanti, Urgesi, & Aglioti, 2006; Sartori, Betti, & Castiello, 2013). Yet other approaches include the assessment of power in the mu-frequency band (8–13 Hz) measured using electroencephalography (EEG) over sensorimotor cortices. Suppression of mu-power has been purported to be an index of human mirror system activity (Hogeveen, Inzlicht, & Obhi, 2013; Oberman, Ramachandran, & Pineda, 2008; Pineda, 2005). These methods have proven illuminating and experiments employing them have aided our understanding of how the brain 'responds' to the actions of others. The automatic imitation paradigm (and its variants) is one laboratory paradigm that does entail some degree of similarity to more naturalistic mimicry in the sense that imitation is incidental to the main task and not instructed (Brass, Bekkering, & Prinz, 2001; Cook & Bird, 2011; Wang, Newport, & Hamilton, 2011).

In stark contrast to the tasks employed by cognitive neuroscientists studying action observation and imitation, social psychologists interested in mimicry typically engage experimental participants in a social interaction with a confederate who executes a target behaviour, or who mimics or does not mimic the participant – depending on the aim of the study. Common 'cover tasks' include a participant and confederate describing photographs or rating music together (Chartrand & Bargh, 1999; van Baaren et al., 2003). Researchers then manipulate specific situational variables to determine the effects on some outcome measure of interest, often a measure of pro-sociality or liking. In other studies, the manipulation takes place prior to the interaction with a confederate and effects of the manipulation on mimicry are assessed (e.g. van Baaren et al., 2003).

Both social psychologists and cognitive neuroscientists often assume that action observation and imitation as studied in 'cognitive' labs tap the same processes that underlie social mimicry as studied in 'social' labs (Chartrand & van Baaren, 2009; Iacoboni, 2009). As even a simple task analysis reveals, this is a questionable assumption. For example, typical action observation tasks often do not involve any specific goals other than to watch the action display. This task set is totally different to the task set involved in social mimicry, which is not explicitly provided by the experimenter, other than perhaps a general instruction to 'get along' with the confederate. Similarly, well-controlled imitation tasks often involve either the explicit intention to imitate or the intention to respond to other cues (i.e. and to therefore suppress imitation), again as a result of explicit instruction by the experimenter. Clearly, the task set involved in these scenarios is very different from that which occurs during a social interaction. The potential fluctuation of goals in a real social interaction, perhaps in response to ongoing contents of conversation, or the presence/absence of mimicry, are completely different from the instructed and more rigid goals in many action observation and imitation tasks. In addition, as mentioned above, there are huge differences in the type of stimulus sets. Finally, there is an affective component inherent in every single real-life interaction that is simply not present or at least is very different in computer-based finger-lifting, or hand-opening and -closing tasks. In view of these large task differences, claims that real mimicry and imitation in a computer-based task are even roughly equivalent seem questionable. Despite this, considering what is common to social mimicry and imitation in the lab – i.e. observing an action and then making it, *seems* to make it obvious that the tasks are very similar and therefore (mirror) mechanisms involved in one are common to the other. I point out the limitation of this conclusion simply to promote consideration of how laboratory tasks that approximate mimicry could be improved.

There is another issue seldom discussed in social mimicry research that further challenges the notion that mimicry and laboratory imitation are the same. That is the issue of the *specificity* of copied actions. Usually, social psychologists use an approximate approach whereby a 'similar' action is coded as mimicry. In a recent preliminary analysis, mimicry was coded in almost 40 participants who had engaged in social interactions as part of an experiment. A large degree of variability was observed in the degree of motor matching that occurred. For example, when the target movement was face touching, situations in which an exact copy of the face-touching movement occurred were very rare. The most common occurrence was the production of a motorically unmatched face touch, with 'similar' face touches being slightly less common but still more common than exact matches. In addition, mimicry was not always matched in terms of the effector used either, with specular and anatomical matching occurring at reasonably similar frequencies. Finally, temporal contingency also varied, with most mimicking occurring after the confederate had made his or her target movement, and only a small proportion of mimicry occurring during the confederate's performance of the target movement. Interestingly, mimicking occurred most often after the confederate had already made 5–10 repetitions of the target movement (Hogeveen & Obhi, unpublished data). What these cursory observations reveal is that mimicry is not necessarily a simple matching of motor actions and that the timing and specificity of movements varies considerably. Furthermore, given that mimicry can be defined differently, for example as the number of movements similar to the target movement or the length of time spent performing similar movements, there is the potential for even more variability in findings. Some of these considerations open up the very important question of whether motor similarity in mimicry matters at all, or whether, for example, contingency is a more important factor. Recent experiments have begun to address these questions and will be discussed later.

With all these concerns, it is important for researchers to be more sceptical about whether imitation as studied in 'cognitive' experiments is the same as social mimicry. Instead of assuming common mechanisms, the emphasis should be on designing experiments that can catalogue what if any mechanisms are shared between these two 'tasks' and what determines whether or not an observed action is mimicked in a social interaction. The reality is that, in experimental settings, many actions made by a confederate are not mimicked, and there is often considerable inter-individual variability in mimicry in these experiments. Explaining these variations is an important research goal.

Recent Attempts to Integrate the Social Psychological Work with the Cognitive Neuroscience Work

Studying naturalistic social mimicry requires two people to interact socially while spontaneous mimicry is recorded. This limits the techniques that can be employed to study the neural basis of the phenomenon and, in particular, it means that functional MRI is quite inappropriate due to the difficulty of participating in a social interaction in a constrained environment, and due to the signal corruption that occurs because of excessive movement. Therefore, researchers interested in shedding light on the neural mechanisms underlying mimicry have used other approaches.

One way to address the issue of whether processes involved in automatic imitation and action observation tasks are also involved in social mimicry, is to determine whether known moderators of mimicry also affect dependent variables measured in these tasks. This 'common-moderators' approach has been taken in a few studies. For example, one study investigated how independence and interdependence affect motor cortical excitability during an action observation task. Specifically, Obhi, Hogeveen, and Pascual-Leone (2011) employed an action observation task in which participants viewed a model's hand squeezing a rubber ball between the forefinger and thumb. In some trials, the videos had an interdependent prime word superimposed over them such as 'together' whereas in other trials prime words like 'individual' that referred to independence were used. In yet other trials, no word was superimposed, and in baseline trials, participants simply viewed a fixation cross. For each trial type, TMS-evoked MEPs were elicited to assess the degree of motor cortical excitability. Motor cortical excitability was higher in interdependent trials than in baseline, no action and independent trials. Why is this result interesting? In a previous study in the social psychology domain, van Baaren et al. (2003) found that individuals primed with interdependence exhibited more behavioural mimicry than individuals who were not primed or who were primed with independence. Thus, a specific moderator variable affects social mimicry and motor resonance in a parallel fashion. While this pattern of results in no way *proves* that motor resonance as indexed by MEPs underlies naturalistic social mimicry, it is highly suggestive that the mechanisms underlying social mimicry and action observation are at least partially common.

In a similar vein, Hogeveen, Inzlicht, and Obhi (2014b) investigated the effects of power on motor resonance in an action observation task. Again, social psychologists have previously shown that powerful individuals do not mimic the less powerful, whereas powerless individuals do mimic the more powerful (Cheng & Chartrand, 2003). Hogeveen et al. (2014b) first primed individuals to feel powerful or powerless by asking them to recall an episode from their own lives where they had power over others or where others had power over them, and then engaged these participants in an action observation task. A third group who were simply asked to write about what they did yesterday were also run through the action observation task. Results showed that motor cortical excitability was lowest for the powerful group and highest for the powerless group, again paralleling the findings of Cheng and Chartrand (2003) for the effects of power on social mimicry.

Other recent studies have used video-based paradigms to address important questions about the factors that drive the rapport-building and liking effects of mimicry. Catmur and Heyes (2013) asked whether it is the matching of motor actions or simply the contingency between the 'mimicker's' action and the other person's action that are important for pro-social outcomes. These authors rightly point out that describing mimicry as an imitative phenomenon emphasizes that reproduction of the original action is key. These authors found that consistently perceiving an action in response to the execution of an action, irrespective of whether the perceived action was motorically identical or not, was associated with enjoyment of the task and feelings of closeness to others.

In other work, Sparenberg, Topolinski, Springer, and Prinz (2012) found that mere effector matching between a participant's movement and observed movements of an on-screen avatar was enough for participants to indicate high pleasantness ratings for the avatar. If this study is generalizable to real-life social interactions, it suggests that mimicry-induced liking may be due to simply observing an interaction partner moving the same effector, and that imitation of the type of movement may not be important. If this were true, the very notion that mimicry is related to specifically imitative processes would be undermined, unless the definition of mimicry is broadened to include effector matching.

It remains for future work to tease out the precise determinants of the rapport-building effects of mimicry, but these two studies provide a useful starting point for this work.

Another study has addressed the potential neural correlates of the positive effects of mimicry. Kühn et al. (2010) asked participants lying in an fMRI scanner to watch an interaction between two individuals under various mimicry conditions. In one condition, one member of the dyad mimicked the other, and in a second condition, they did not mimic the other. Crucially, participants viewed the interaction from a pseudo first-person perspective (over-the-shoulder camera shot) of one of the interaction partners. Results revealed that reward- and emotion-related brain regions such as the medial-orbitofrontal cortex and ventromedial prefrontal cortex were more active in the mimicry condition. Furthermore, the increase in activity in these two areas in mimicry versus non-mimicry conditions was positively correlated with ratings of closeness to the interaction partner. Being mimicked it seems, is more intrinsically rewarding than not being mimicked. This result is an important first step in understanding the reasons why mimicry might be so ubiquitous.

Although all of the above-mentioned studies employed video-based paradigms, they offer important clues as to which aspects of mimicry drive its consequences and how the activity of the brain's reward system is involved. Future work could combine these approaches to manipulate specific aspects of mimicry like motor similarity, effector similarity or temporal contingency within an fMRI environment to ascertain which aspects of mimicry result in the highest levels of reward-related activity. Obviously such approaches suffer from the kind of task equivalence issues mentioned above, not least the fact that they involve watching mimicry not engaging in mimicry, but they offer a promising start, nonetheless. We are working toward experiments of this type.

Taken together, these studies show that moderators that affect mimicry also affect dependent measures of assumed component processes like motor resonance. Although this suggests that mirroring is involved in social mimicry, the degree of imitative matching occurring may not be at the level of exact movements, but rather effectors, or even movement endpoints (i.e. movement goals). Indeed, previous evidence from experiments using the automatic imitation paradigm suggest that imitation is not wholly effector dependent and that movement types are imitated even by a different effector, although to a lesser degree than when the same effector is used (Leighton & Heyes, 2010). More generally, a detailed analysis of the frequency of effector matching, movement matching and timing in social mimicry occurs would be useful in guiding thinking about underlying mechanisms. Whilst experiments employing video-based presentations of a model are useful in providing clues about social mimicry, firm conclusions are limited owing to the aforementioned differences between the contexts of these lab tasks and typical social mimicry experiments.

To more directly address the issue of common mechanisms in tasks such as action observation, on the one hand, and social mimicry, on the other, it is necessary to engage the same participants in both tasks within a single experiment. In a recent study, participants participated in a social interaction with a confederate after which they engaged in an action observation task in which MEPs were recorded. Another group of participants did the action observation task without engaging in a prior social interaction. The fundamental question was whether engaging in social interaction had any effect on the degree of motor resonance occurring in a subsequent action observation task. The results were striking: individuals who had engaged in the social interaction showed significantly more motor resonance than individuals who had not engaged in the social interaction. Furthermore, participants who had shown more mimicry in the social interaction showed even more motor resonance than those who showed less mimicry in the social interaction (Hogeveen & Obhi, 2012). This study was the first to examine social mimicry and motor resonance during action observation in the same participants, and the findings suggest that there is indeed at least some common resource involved. Interestingly, though, unpublished data show that engaging in the action observation task prior to the mimicry task does not affect the degree of mimicry displayed. Therefore, whereas prior mimicry induces more motor resonance in an action observation task, prior participation in an action observation task does not induce more mimicry (Hogeveen & Obhi, unpublished).

Another recent study employed mu-suppression, a common index of mirror activity in conjunction with a mimicry manipulation (Pineda, 2005). In this experiment, Hogeveen, Chartrand, and Obhi (2014a) used EEG to assess mu-suppression over left sensorimotor cortices during an action observation task, before and after engaging in a social interaction with a confederate, or with a computer. Furthermore, in the social interaction some participants were mimicked by the confederate whereas others were not. The results showed that, after the intervening social interaction, only participants who were mimicked by the confederate showed more mu-suppression than in the pre-test. Intriguingly, participants who engaged with a computer actually showed less mu-suppression in the subsequent action observation task, suggesting that mirroring is highly dependent on the recent experience of the individual (Press, Gillmeister, & Heyes, 2007). Other authors have used videos of a model performing subtle face-touches while engaged in a series of clerical tasks and have shown that observers exhibit motor resonance (van Ulzen, Fiorio, & Cesari, 2013).

Perhaps the strongest method to reveal causal mechanisms is to selectively interfere with the normal processing of a node in the processing chain underlying a task and determine the effect on some performance measure. Such interference can take the form of reducing excitability in brain areas, as is often done using low-frequency TMS approaches (e.g. van Honk, Schutter, D'alfonso, Kessels, & de Haan, 2002; Obhi, Haggard, Taylor, & Pascual-Leone, 2002;) or increasing excitability, which is increasingly being achieved via the use of anodal transcranial direct current stimulation (tDCS). In a recent study, Hogeveen et al. (2014c) delivered anodal tDCS to the right inferior frontal cortex (rIFC), which has been implicated in mirroring by previous studies (Heiser, Iacoboni, Maeda, Marcus, & Mazziotta, 2003; Iacoboni, 1999b). Interestingly, increasing excitability of this area resulted in a subsequent increase in social mimicry in a social interaction with a confederate. Although a single study, this is the first to reveal a potentially *causal* link between the human mirror system and the manifestation of social mimicry.

Summary, Speculation and Future Directions

In this short chapter, I have provided a relatively high level and necessarily selective overview of key results from the study of social mimicry and highlighted recent studies that are starting to address the potential mechanisms that underlie social mimicry, using a mixture of cognitive neuroscience and social psychology approaches. Such studies have been successful in revealing the moderating effects of certain variables on the tendency to mimic (or, in lab studies, automatically imitate) and have also shown parallel effects of these variables on presumed component processes of mimicry, including motor resonance in action observation. However, many questions remain about the task equivalence of laboratory approaches such as the automatic imitation paradigm and more naturalistic social mimicry, not least with respect to task goals. Of course, there is almost never a perfect way to balance the need for experimental control and ecological validity, and by pointing out limitations I am not suggesting that researchers should abandon their efforts. Rather, researchers should also work to devise novel experimental paradigms to improve the 'lab–life mapping'.

While there is some evidence for potential mirror system involvement in social mimicry, questions abound about how other signals, both top down and bottom up, interact with mirror mechanisms and the motor system more generally to modulate the degree and type of mimicry exhibited in any given situation. It is interesting to note recent work that reveals that being mimicked is rewarding (Kühn et al., 2010), and another previous study showed that a lack of mimicry was associated with increased levels of salivary cortisol, suggesting that not being mimicked raises stress levels and is perhaps akin to being socially excluded (Kouzakova, van Baaren, & van Knippenberg, 2010). In view of these results, the rewarding and stressful effects of mimicry/lack of mimicry need to be further investigated.

Over recent years, Brass and colleagues have sought to identify self–other control mechanisms, and the purported neural correlates of these mechanisms, mostly in the context of imitation control and often using the automatic imitation task (Brass, Ruby, & Spengler, 2009; Spengler, von Cramon, & Brass, 2009; also see Bardi & Brass, this volume, Chapter 8). These studies have revealed a potential imitation control network with key nodes in the anterior fronto-median cortex and the temporoparietal junction (rTPJ). Both fMRI and neuromodulatory studies support the idea that the rTPJ may play a key role in the control of imitation, and, in general, medial prefrontal cortex is a well-known neural correlate of self-related processing (Hogeveen et al., 2014c; Qin & Northoff, 2011; Santiestiban et al., 2012). Other authors have recently referred to this line of work in the proposal of a top-down regulation model of mimicry called the social top-down regulation model of mimicry (STORM) (Wang & Hamilton, 2012). Models such as this are a welcome development in the study of social mimicry and offer a useful way in which to think about how mimicry unfolds.

Even with these initial contributions, there remains a need to further integrate current state-of-the art research on mimicry with ideas from the study of sensorimotor control. This is vital, as social mimicry is fundamentally a sensorimotor phenomenon. One important and thus far neglected question relates to the role of sensorimotor prediction in social mimicry, but there are other potentially important considerations that I will offer speculation on below.

Speculation: Converging Inputs and Action Selection in Social Mimicry?

A key feature of social mimicry is that, in addition to being variable across individuals, it also fluctuates within and across social interactions for a given individual. That is, mimicry appears to be unconsciously *regulated* and uncovering how this regulation operates is arguably the fundamental question surrounding mimicry. Here, I offer some speculation that may or may not help in thinking about the possible mechanistic underpinnings of mimicry. An interesting idea is that mimicry is schema driven, and that such schemas contain information about the degree of mimicry that can be expected across different social scenarios (e.g. Dalton et al., 2010). Future studies should explore this idea further and determine whether schema violations always incur resource depletion effects and why.

The fact that social mimicry is regulated means that some actions are mimicked while others are not. I propose that mimicry might be well conceptualized as a decision/selection problem for the brain – to act or not to act, and more specifically, *what* action to produce, in response to social input from a partner. Motor resonance might be one relevant factor in this process, but other converging inputs must also play a role, as mimicry does not always consist of a well-matched movement (or from an ASL perspective, a strongly associated movement) and mechanisms are needed that could serve to inhibit a matched (or strongly associated) movement if it is not the best choice, given current goals. Perhaps action selection is achieved via the use of predictions of anticipated reward values of all current motor possibilities? Action selection based on predicted reward has been proposed to involve the orbitofrontal cortex, and, as mentioned above, this area has been shown to be active when observing mimicry (Kühn et al., 2010; Young & Shapiro, 2011). On a related note, what is the role of sensorimotor prediction in mimicry? That is, internal forward models are presumably involved in predicting the sensory consequences of pending actions, and these predictions might include the expected reactions of an interaction partner (Wolpert & Flanagan, 2001; also see Hamilton, this volume, Chapter 15). A fundamental question relates to *how* sensorimotor predictive processes might help regulate motor behaviour during social interactions. Perhaps there is a 'sweet spot' for predictive success such that interactions in which all predictions are accurate or inaccurate would both not yield optimal results in terms of induced rapport and subsequent prosociality? How do stable personality traits interact with state variables like current goals to affect action selection processes in mimicry? In addition, how do real-time changes in goals exert an effect on selection? For example, new information about a social partner that arises during an interaction could change the goal state from an original 'affiliation goal' to a 'disaffiliation goal'. This change in goal state should then exert some effect on activated motor representations and might change the reward values associated with different motor possibilities. That is, under such circumstances the brain may 'see' a non-mimicked action as one associated with the highest reward, thus making it less likely that a matching action is emitted. Specific experiments testing these kinds of ideas in social contexts have not yet been performed. Indeed, if mimicry can be considered as an (unconscious) action selection problem, perhaps invoking ideas from non-socially situated theories of action selection, such as the affordance competition hypothesis, could be useful (Cisek, 2007).

Of course, these speculations in which social input resulting in motor resonance is just one of many converging inputs may be incorrect, and I suggest these ideas merely as food for thought for researchers in the field, and for those who might be considering starting work on social mimicry.

Other issues that might be addressed in future work include understanding what aspects of an action are mimicked in social scenarios. That is, is mimicry related to the end-point of movements, the movements themselves or, more generally, the effector used? What are the conditions that might change what aspects of an action are mimicked (i.e. which aspects of an action become most salient)? Is the temporal relationship between actions and mimicry of those actions important? Specifically, by varying the temporal contingency between an action and mimicry of that action, is it possible to change resulting feelings of rapport and pro-sociality? Is there an optimal degree of mimicry and, if so, what criteria is this optimum based on? What are the key similarities and differences between social mimicry in natural interactions and automatic imitation in laboratory tasks, and what patterns of brain activity are specific to both? Why is mimicry rewarding? What evolutionary processes might be responsible for establishing mimicry as rewarding?

This final section has highlighted just a handful of the many remaining questions surrounding how social mimicry arises. It is noteworthy that the fusion of cognitive neuroscience and social psychological approaches to address questions about mimicry has only begun relatively recently. As such, researchers are in the very early stages of uncovering interesting relationships between ideas from cognitive neuroscience and findings from social psychology. These early results have spawned many more questions, and seeking out answers to these questions should help keep social cognitive neuroscientists and psychologists busy for years to come.

References

Ashton-James, C., & Chartrand, T. L. (2009). Social cues for creativity: The impact of behavioral mimicry on convergent and divergent thinking. *Journal of Experimental Social Psychology*, 45(4), 1036–1040.

Baaren, R. B. van, Fockenberg, D. A., Holland, R. W., Janssen, L., & van Knippenberg, A. (2006). The moody chameleon: The effect of mood on non-conscious mimicry. *Social Cognition*, 24(4), 426–437.

Baaren, R. B. van, Maddux, W. W., Chartrand, T. L., de Bouter, C., & van Knippenberg, A. (2003). It takes two to mimic: Behavioral consequences of self-construals. *Journal of Personality and Social Psychology*, 84(5), 1093–1102.

Bourgeois, P., & Hess, U. (2008). The impact of social context on mimicry. *Biological Psychology*, 77(3), 343–352.

Brass, M., Bekkering, H., & Prinz, W. (2001). Movement observation affects movement execution in a simple response task. *Acta Psychologica*, 106(1–2), 3–22.

Brass, M., Ruby, P., & Spengler, S. (2009). Inhibition of imitative behaviour and social cognition. *Philosophical Transactions of the Royal Society B: Biological Sciences*, 364(1528), 2359–2367.

Buccino, G., Baumgaertner, A., Colle, L., Buechel, C., Rizzolatti, G., & Binkofski, F. (2007). The neural basis for understanding non-intended actions. *NeuroImage*, 36(Suppl. 2), T119–T127.

Buccino, G., Binkofski, F., Fink, G. R., Fadiga, L., Fogassi, L., et al. (2001). Action observation activates premotor and parietal areas in a somatotopic manner: An fMRI study. *European Journal of Neuroscience*, 13(2), 400–404.

Buccino, G., Binkofski, F., & Riggio, L. (2004). The mirror neuron system and action recognition. *Brain and Language*, 89(2), 370–376.

Calvo-Merino, B., Glaser, D. E., Grèzes, J., Passingham, R. E., & Haggard P. (2005). Action observation and acquired motor skills: an FMRI study with expert dancers. *Cerebral Cortex*, 15(8), 1243–1249.

Catmur, C., & Heyes, C. (2013). Is it what you do, or when you do it? The roles of contingency and similarity in pro-social effects of imitation. *Cognitive Science*, 37(8), 1541–1552.

Catmur, C., Walsh, V., & Heyes, C. (2009). Associative sequence learning: The role of experience in the development of imitation and the mirror system. *Philosophical Transactions of the Royal Society B: Biological Sciences*, 364(1528), 2369–2380.

Chartrand, T. L., & Bargh, J. A. (1999). The chameleon effect: The perception–behavior link and social interaction. *Journal of Personality and Social Psychology*, 76(6), 893–910.

Chartrand, T. L., & Lakin, J. L. (2013). The antecedents and consequences of human behavioral mimicry. *Annual Review of Psychology*, 64, 285–308.

Chartrand, T. L., & Van Baaren, R. (2009). Human mimicry. *Advances in Experimental Social Psychology*, 41, 219–274.

Cheng, C. M., & Chartrand, T. L. (2003). Self-monitoring without awareness: Using mimicry as a nonconscious affiliation strategy. *Journal of Personality and Social Psychology*, 85(6), 1170–1179.

Cisek, P. (2007). Cortical mechanisms of action selection: The affordance competition hypothesis. *Philosophical Transactions of the Royal Society B: Biological Sciences*, 362(1485), 1585–1599.

Cook, J., & Bird, G. (2011). Social attitudes differentially modulate imitation in adolescents and adults. *Experimental Brain Research*, 211(3–4), 601–612.

Cook, R., Bird, G., Catmur, C., Press, C., & Heyes, C. (2014). Mirror neurons: From origin to function. *Behavioral and Brain Sciences*, 37(2), 177–192.

Cross, E. S., Hamilton, A. F., Kraemer, D. J., Kelley, W. M., & Grafton, S. T. (2009a). Dissociable substrates for body motion and physical experience in the human action observation network. *European Journal of Neuroscience*, 30(7), 1383–1392.

Cross, E. S., Kraemer, D. J., Hamilton, A. F., Kelley, W. M., & Grafton, S. T. (2009b). Sensitivity of the action observation network to physical and observational learning. *Cerebral Cortex*, 19(2), 315–326.

Dalton, A. N., Chartrand, T. L., & Finkel, E. J. (2010). The schema-driven chameleon: How mimicry affects executive and self-regulatory resources. *Journal of Personality and Social Psychology*, 98(4), 605–617.

Diener, E., & Seligman, M. E. (2002). Very happy people. *Psychological Science*, 13(1), 81–84.

Fadiga, L., Craighero, L., & Olivier, E. (2005). Human motor cortex excitability during the perception of others' action. *Current Opinion in Neurobiology*, 15(2), 213–218.

Fadiga, L., Fogassi, L., Pavesi, G., & Rizzolatti, G. (1995). Motor facilitation during action observation: A magnetic stimulation study. *Journal of Neurophysiology*, 73(6), 2608–2611.

Fourkas, A. D., Avenanti, A., Urgesi, C., & Aglioti, S. M. (2006). Corticospinal facilitation during first and third person imagery. *Experimental Brain Research*, 168(1–2), 143–151.

Frith, C. D., & Frith, U. (2006). The neural basis of mentalizing. *Neuron*, 50(4), 531–534.

Greenwald, A. G. (1970). Sensory feedback mechanisms in performance control: With special reference to the ideo-motor mechanism. *Psychological Review*, 77(2), 73–99.

Guéguen, N., & Martin, A. (2009). Incidental similarity facilitates behavioral mimicry. *Social Psychology*, 40(2), 88–92.

Guéguen, N., Martin, A., Meineri, S., & Simon, J. (2013). Using mimicry to elicit answers to intimate questions in survey research. *Field Methods*, 25(1), 47–57.

Hallett, M. (2007). Transcranial magnetic stimulation: A primer. *Neuron*, 55(2), 187–199.

Heiser, M., Iacoboni, M., Maeda, F., Marcus, J., & Mazziotta, J. C. (2003). The essential role of Broca's area in imitation. *European Journal of Neuroscience*, 17(5), 1123–1128.

Herwig, A., Prinz, W., & Waszak, F. (2007). Two modes of sensorimotor integration in intention-based and stimulus-based actions. *Quarterly Journal of Experimental Psychology*, 60(11), 1540–1554.

Heyes, C. (2011). Automatic imitation. *Psychological Bulletin*, 137(3), 463–483.

Hogeveen, J., Chartrand, T. L., & Obhi, S. S. (2014a). Social mimicry enhances mu-suppression during action observation. *Cerebral Cortex*. doi: 10.1093/cercor/bhu016.

Hogeveen, J., Inzlicht, M., & Obhi, S. S. (2013). Power changes how the brain responds to others. *Journal of Experimental Psychology: General*, 2, 755–762.

(2014b). Power changes how the brain responds to others. *Journal of Experimental Psychology: General*, 143(2), 755–762.

Hogeveen, J., & Obhi, S. S. (2012). Social interaction enhances motor resonance for observed human actions. *Journal of Neuroscience*, 32 (17), 5984–5989.

Hogeveen, J., Obhi, S. S., Banissy, M. J., et al. (2014c). Task-dependent and distinct roles of the temporoparietal junction and inferior frontal cortex in the control of imitation. *Social Cognitive and Affective Neuroscience*, 10(7), 1003–1009.

Honk J. van, Schutter, D. J., D'alfonso, A. A., Kessels, R. P., & de Haan, E. H. (2002). 1 hz rTMS over the right prefrontal cortex reduces vigilant attention to unmasked but not to masked fearful faces. *Biological Psychiatry*, 52(4), 312–317.

Iacoboni, M. (2008). *Mirroring people*. New York: Farrar, Straus & Giroux.

(2009). Neurobiology of imitation. *Current Opinion in Neurobiology*, 19(6), 661–665.

Iacoboni, M., & Mazziotta, J. C. (2007). Mirror neuron system: Basic findings and clinical applications. *Annals of Neurology*, 62(3), 213–218.

Iacoboni, M., Woods, R. P., Brass, M., Bekkering, H., Mazziotta, J. C., & Rizzolatti, G. (1999a). Cortical mechanisms of human imitation. *Science*, 5449, 2526–2528.

(1999b). Cortical mechanisms of human imitation. *Science*, 5449, 2526–2528.

Inzlicht, M., Gutsell, J. N., & Legault, L. (2012). Mimicry reduces racial prejudice. *Journal of Experimental Social Psychology*, 48(1), 361–365.

James, W. (1890). *The principles of psychology*. New York: Holt.

Kaplan, J. T., & Iacoboni, M. (2006). Getting a grip on other minds: Mirror neurons, intention understanding, and cognitive empathy. *Society of Neuroscience*, 1(3–4), 175–183.

Knoblich, G., & Sebanz, N. (2006). The social nature of perception and action. *Current Directions in Psychological Science*, 15(3), 99–104.

Knuf, L., Aschersleben, G., & Prinz, W. (2001). An analysis of ideomotor action. *Journal of Experimental Psychology*, 130, 779–798.

Kouzakova, M., van Baaren, R., & van Knippenberg, A. (2010). Lack of behavioral imitation in human interactions enhances salivary cortisol levels. *Hormones and Behavior*, 57(4–5), 421–426.

Kühn, S., Müller, B. C., van Baaren, R. B., Wietzker, A., Dijksterhuis, A., & Brass, M. (2010). Why do I like you when you behave like me? Neural mechanisms mediating positive consequences of observing someone being imitated. *Society of Neuroscience*, 5(4), 384–392.

Lakin, J. L., & Chartrand, T. L. (2003). Using nonconscious behavioral mimicry to create affiliation and rapport. *Psychological Science*, 14(4), 334–339.

Lakin, J. L., Chartrand, T. L., & Arkin, R. M. (2008). I am too just like you: Nonconscious mimicry as an automatic behavioral response to social exclusion. *Psychological Science*, 19(8), 816–822.

Leighton, J., & Heyes, C. (2010). Hand to mouth: Automatic imitation across effector systems. *Journal of Experimental Psychology: Human Perception and Performance*, 36(5), 1174–1183.

Losin, E. A., Cross, K. A., Iacoboni, M., & Dapretto, M. (2014). Neural processing of race during imitation: Self-similarity versus social status. *Human Brain Mapping*, 35(4), 1723–1739.

Losin, E. A., Iacoboni, M., Martin, A., Cross, K. A., & Dapretto, M. (2012). Race modulates neural activity during imitation. *NeuroImage*, 59(4), 3594–3603.

Magistris, M. R., Rösler, K. M., Truffert, A., & Myers, J. P. (1998). Transcranial stimulation excites virtually all motor neurons supplying the target muscle: A demonstration and a method improving the study of motor-evoked potentials. *Brain*, 121, 437–450.

Massey, D. S. (2002). A brief history of human society: The origin and role of emotion in social life. *American Sociological Review*, 67(1), 1–29.

McIntosh, D. N. (2006). Spontaneous facial mimicry, liking and emotional contagion. *Polish Psychological Bulletin*, 37(1), 31–42.

Naish, K. R., Houston-Price, C., Bremner, A. J., & Holmes, N. P. (2014). Effects of action observation on corticospinal excitability: Muscle specificity, direction, and timing of the mirror response. *Neuropsychologia*, 64C, 331–348.

Oberman, L. M., Ramachandran, V. S., & Pineda, J. A. (2008). Modulation of mu suppression in children with autism spectrum disorders in response to familiar or unfamiliar stimuli: The mirror neuron hypothesis. *Neuropsychologia*, 46(5), 1558–1565.

Obhi, S. S., Haggard, P., Taylor, J., & Pascual-Leone, A. (2002). rTMS to the supplementary motor area disrupts bimanual coordination. *Motor Control*, 6(4), 319–332.

Obhi, S. S., Hogeveen, J., Giacomin, M., & Jordan, C. H. (2014). Automatic imitation is reduced in narcissists. *Journal of Experimental Psychology: Human Perception and Performance*, 40(3), 920–928.

Obhi, S. S., Hogeveen, J., & Pascual-Leone, A. (2011). Resonating with others: The effects of self-construal type on motor cortical output. *Journal of Neuroscience*, 31(41), 14531–14535.

Pineda, J. A. (2005) The functional significance of mu rhythms: Translating 'seeing' and 'hearing' into 'doing'. *Brain Research Reviews*, 50(1), 57–68.

Press, C., Gillmeister, H., & Heyes, C. (2007). Sensorimotor experience enhances automatic imitation of robotic action. *Proceedings of the Royal Society B: Biological Sciences*, 274(1625), 2509–2514.

Prinz, W. (2005). An ideomotor approach to imitation. In S. Hurley, & N. Chater (Eds.), *Perspectives on imitation: From neuroscience to social science* (Vol. 1). Cambridge, MA, US: MIT Press, 141–156.

Qin P., & Northoff, G. (2011). How is our self related to midline regions and the default-mode network? *NeuroImage*, 57(3), 1221–1233.

Redeker, M., Stel, M., & Mastop, J. (2011). Does mimicking others change your self-view? *Journal of Social Psychology*, 151(4), 387–390.

Rizzolatti, G., Fadiga, L., Gallese, V., & Fogassi, L. (1996). Premotor cortex and the recognition of motor actions. *Cognitive Brain Research*, 3(2), 131–141.

Santiesteban, I., Banissy, M. J., Catmur, C., & Bird, G. (2012). Enhancing social ability by stimulating right temporoparietal junction. *Current Biology*, 22(23), 2274–2277.

Sartori, L., Betti, S., & Castiello, U. (2013). Corticospinal excitability modulation during action observation. *Journal of Visualized Experiments*, (82). doi: 10.3791/51001.

Sparenberg, P., Topolinski, S., Springer, A., & Prinz, W. (2012). Minimal mimicry: Mere effector matching induces preference. *Brain and Cognition*, 80(3), 291–300.

Spengler, S., von Cramon, D. Y., & Brass, M. (2009). Control of shared representations relies on key processes involved in mental state attribution. *Human Brain Mapping*, 30(11), 3704–3718.

Stel, M., & Harinck, F. (2011). Being mimicked makes you a prosocial voter. *Experimental Psychology*, 1, 79–84.

Stel, M., van den Bos, K., Sim, S., & Rispens, S. (2013). Mimicry and just world beliefs: Mimicking makes men view the world as more personally just. *British Journal of Social Psychology*, 52(3), 397–411.

Ulzen, N. R. van, Fiorio, M., & Cesari, P. (2013). Motor resonance evoked by observation of subtle nonverbal behavior. *Society of Neuroscience*, 8(4), 347–355.

Van Swol, L. M., & Drury, M. (2006). The effects of shared opinions on nonverbal mimicry. Paper presented at Annual International Communication Association Conference, Dresden, Germany.

Wang, Y., & Hamilton, A. F. (2012). Social top-down response modulation (STORM): A model of the control of mimicry in social interaction. *Frontiers in Human Neuroscience*, 6, 153.

Wang, Y., Newport, R., & Hamilton, A. F. (2011). Eye contact enhances mimicry of intransitive hand movements. *Biology Letters*, 7(1), 7–10.

Wolpert, D. M., & Flanagan, J. R. (2001). Motor prediction. *Current Biology*, 11(18), R729–R732.

Yabar, Y., Johnston, L., Miles, L., & Peace, V. (2006). Implicit behavioral mimicry: Investigating the impact of group membership. *Journal of Nonverbal Behavior*, 30(3), 97–113.

Young, J. J., & Shapiro, M. L. (2011). The orbitofrontal cortex and response selection. *Annals of the New York Academy of Sciences*, 1239, 25–32.

Part III

Thinking, Perceiving and Acting with Others

10 Levels of Complexity and the Duality of Gaze: How Social Attention Changes from Lab to Life

K. E. W. Laidlaw, E. F. Risko and A. Kingstone

Abstract

The field of social attention has its origins in traditional visual attention research, and has largely continued to rely on the same highly controlled, laboratory-based paradigms that are typically used to study basic cognitive processes. There is debate about whether these methods can be applied appropriately to the study of socially-driven behaviors. Indeed, recent evidence from more naturalistic investigations suggests that, while researchers may gain some insight into the mechanisms underlying social attention by relying on more traditionally lab-based approaches, much will be missed. The present chapter focuses on findings from new paradigms sensitive to the social influences on attention, and reviews research demonstrating patterns of looking-behavior in realistic situations that are counter to what is found 'in the lab'. A dual function approach to gaze behavior is described that accommodates these results into a framework that emphasizes the importance of gaze for both acquiring social information and controlling what is communicated to others. Understanding the mechanisms underlying both of these functions and, importantly, their interaction, will lead to a deeper understanding of social attention.

Introduction

In our everyday lives, we are assailed by more information than we can possibly take in. As such, we need to select what information we want to think about, and what information we are going to discard and ignore. Normally when we attend to something, we look at it. Because this shift in our eye gaze can be observed by others, we say that the shift in attention is overt. We can, however, also shift our attention without moving our eyes. That is to say, we can covertly shift our attention, as when we 'look at someone out of the corner of our eye'. This process of selecting and orienting attention to some information to the exclusion of other information can be controlled exogenously (reflexively) or endogenously (volitionally). Understanding the mechanisms that subserve the exogenous and endogenous orienting of overt and covert attention is the bedrock upon which human attention research is built.

This work has routinely been conducted in spartan experimental settings that involve an individual sitting alone in a plain testing room responding to simple flashes of lights, letters, or words that appear on a screen. Hundreds upon hundreds of trials are collected and the isolated individual's behavioral and biological responses to these stimuli are measured. The philosophy behind this experimental simplification is that, by minimizing the complexity of the environment and maximizing experimental control, investigators can create theories that are universally valid. In the words of Broadbent (1971, p. 3), 'A man does not use one brain in the laboratory and another in the rest of his life.' In other words, the working hypothesis is that traditional laboratory research exposes fundamental principles of human thought, attention, and behavior that will generalize to the everyday complex environment of the natural world.

In the last several years researchers have begun to appreciate that attention to stimuli that depict socially meaningful objects, such as the faces of other people, produce biological and behavioral responses that are very different from what findings derived from the classic research approach would predict. For instance, until recently it was held that where people look can largely be explained by the visual primitives that are salient in a scene (e.g. attention goes initially to high contrast regions of a scene; Itti & Koch, 2000). However, simply introducing a person into the scene will result in attention going quickly to the face of that person in a way that cannot be predicted or explained in terms of simple low-level saliency (Birmingham, Bischof, & Kingstone, 2009). Similarly, once that face is selected, attention gets shifted to where it is looking in a way that cannot be predicted or explained by traditional attention paradigms (e.g. Fan, McCandliss, Sommer, Raz, & Posner, 2002; Posner, 1980). In short, classic attention paradigms that routinely exclude biologically relevant stimuli from their tasks fall woefully short in terms of explaining attentional selection and orienting when socially meaningful stimuli are introduced (Kingstone, Smilek, Ristic, Friesen, & Eastwood, 2003; Kingstone, Smilek, & Eastwood, 2008; Risko, Laidlaw, Freeth, Foulsham, & Kingstone, 2012).

The present chapter presents a brief overview of where this interest in attention to biologically relevant stimuli – what we call social attention – has taken the field in general, and our work in particular. We first review recent lab-based findings, before focusing on new research that spans levels of stimulus complexity and situational realism. As we examine the similarities and differences in results generated from lab-based and more naturalistic studies, we highlight what we hypothesize to be fundamental factors that – while traditionally ignored – should be considered if one is to better understand how social attention operates in everyday life.

Selection of Social Stimuli in the Lab

Attention to Eyes in an Isolated Face or Person

When looking at another's face, fixations tend to cluster around the internal features, which include the eyes, mouth and nose (Henderson, Williams, & Falk, 2005; Walker-Smith, Gale, & Findlay, 1977). Of these, the eyes are the most frequently fixated (Henderson et al., 2005; Pelphrey et al., 2002; Walker-Smith, Gale, & Findlay, 1977; Yarbus, 1967). Even when faces are presented within the context of a complex scene, the eyes receive more looks than would be expected given their size and salience (Birmingham, Bischof, & Kingstone, 2008a, 2008b, 2009).

That people show a bias to attend to another's eyes is not altogether surprising. After all, the eyes provide the looker with valuable social information about a person's intentions, emotions and attentional focus. Laidlaw, Risko, and Kingstone (2012) investigated if this bias to look at other people's eyes is automatic or volitional. To discriminate between these two possibilities, the researchers used a 'don't look' paradigm in which participants looked at a series of upright or inverted faces, either without specific task instructions (e.g. free viewing) or while told to avoid either the eyes, or as a control, the mouth.

For both upright and inverted faces, participants showed a strong bias to attend to the eyes and the mouth during free viewing (though the bias was much stronger for the eyes; see Figure 10.1). For upright and inverted faces in the 'Don't Look: Mouth' condition, participants showed active avoidance of the mouth region. For upright faces in the 'Don't Look: Eyes' condition, despite reducing looks to the eye region, participants continued to look at the eyes more than would be expected by chance. Errors (e.g. looks to the eyes or mouth, whichever feature they were told to avoid) were greater within the first second than the last four seconds, but errors to the eyes were nevertheless above chance levels in the latter part of viewing. The same pattern of results was not found for inverted faces, however: when viewed upside down, participants in the 'Don't Look: Eyes' condition were now able to successfully reduce looking at the eyes to levels expected by chance, both during the first second and the last four seconds of viewing. Taken together, these results suggest a sustained non-volitional bias to attend overtly to the eyes of upright faces. As holistic processing is strongest with upright faces and weaker or even absent with inverted faces (Yovel & Kanwisher, 2005), it appears that non-volitional attention to the eyes first requires a holistic face representation to orient overt attention to the eye region.

That there is a bias to look at the eyes when a face is presented in isolation begs the question of whether the bias is still measurable when selection of the feature is made more complex. When looking at faces in isolation, configural

Upright Faces   Inverted Faces

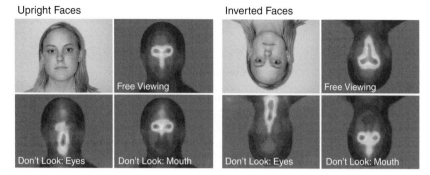

Figure 10.1 Heat maps representing the average location of participant fixations for upright and inverted faces in free viewing Don't Look: Eyes and Don't Look: Mouth conditions. *See Plate 5.*

Note: Participant fixations is presented over faces, with greatest overlap across participant in darker regions that are bordered by lighter-coloured areas of less overlap.

Source: Laidlaw et al. (2012).

face processing may drive fixations to the middle of people's faces, which is where the eyes happen to be located (Andrews, Davies-Thompson, Kingstone, & Young, 2010; Bindemann, Scheepers, & Burton, 2009). Alternatively, eye selection may be so critical to our social lives that others have argued for a distinct neural module (for example, within the superior temporal sulcus; STS) that is uniquely tuned to the eyes of others, regardless of how they are presented (e.g. Akiyama et al., 2006). A study by Levy, Foulsham, and Kingstone (2012) entitled 'Monsters are people too' distinguished between these two accounts. Observers were presented with images of people, non-human creatures with eyes in the middle of their faces ('humanoids') or creatures with eyes positioned in abnormal locations, such as on their hands ('monsters'). There was a profound and significant bias towards looking early and often at the eyes of humanoids. Critically, this bias was also present for looking at the eyes of monsters.

These data strongly support the idea that the human brain is specialized for acquiring social, behaviorally relevant information from others: we can quickly and even non-volitionally select for the gaze of others, even when the location of the eyes is atypical. As gaze selection is the key precursor to gaze following, which is common to both humans and non-human primates, it is reasonable to speculate that this behavior is subserved by a neural system that is shared across primates (Deaner & Platt, 2003; Emery, 2000), with both lesion and functional neuroimaging studies implicating the STS as a likely seat of this ability (for a recent review, see Birmingham & Kingstone, 2009; Calder et al., 2007;

Campbell, Heywood, Cowey, Regard, & Landis, 1990; Heywood, Cowey, & Rolls, 1992; Hoffman & Haxby, 2000; Kingstone, Tipper, Ristic, & Ngan, 2004).

Attention to the Eyes in Complex Static Scenes

If eyes have a privileged status when they are presented as part of an isolated face or person, is it also the case that they will be preferentially selected when scene complexity is increased? Work by Birmingham and colleagues (e.g. 2008a, 2009) addressed this issue directly. Participants were presented with real-world photographs of scenes with people engaged in a variety of natural social situations (e.g. a person sitting alone or with others drinking coffee, people looking at and sharing a menu, and so forth). Despite the increase in stimulus complexity and relatively small size of the eyes in the scene, the results of this work showed that observers looked mostly at the eyes, and looked relatively infrequently at the rest of the scene (e.g. bodies, foreground objects, background objects).

These investigations also found that attention to the eyes of others can be modulated by social factors. For instance, observers selected the eyes more frequently in highly social scenes, that is, scenes containing multiple people doing something together. Additionally, attention to the eyes of others increased when observers were indirectly prompted to focus on social aspects of the scene (e.g. what the people in the scenes are thinking) relative to when performing other less socially focused tasks, such as describing the scenes in general (Birmingham et al. 2008b; also see Smilek, Birmingham, Cameron, Bischof, & Kingstone, 2006).

Finally, and most importantly, Birmingham demonstrated that, when these complex scenes are presented to observers, they quickly fixate the eyes of the people in the scenes independent of their objective stimulus saliency (see Figure 10.2). Collectively, these data indicate a preferential selection of gaze information that is enhanced by a social attention task and by the social content of the scene. Although one might assume that increasing scene complexity might serve to make gaze selection more difficult, embedding a person within a natural scene instead appears to enhance the bias to attend to social stimuli, such as the eyes of others.

Attention to the Eyes in Dynamic Scenes

The studies discussed thus far have involved static displays (i.e. photos). Importantly, the bias to look at faces and eyes extends to displays that are dynamic and include both audio and visual information. In a recent investigation by Foulsham, Cheng, Tracy, Henrich and Kingstone (2010; also see

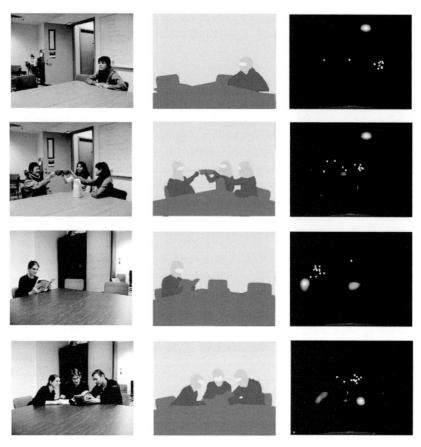

Figure 10.2 Examples of the scenes used by Birmingham et al. (2009; first column), the general regions defined (eyes, heads, bodies, foreground objects and background; second column) and their corresponding saliency maps (third column; larger white areas indicate regions of higher saliency; Itti & Koch, 2000) overlaid with participants' first fixations (small white dots).

Cheng, Tracey, Foulsham, Kingstone, & Henrich, 2013), participants were divided into groups of three and video-recorded while taking part in a cooperative decision-making task. Those video-recordings were then presented to naïve individuals to watch while their eye movements were monitored. The results from these observers indicated that people looked mostly at the eyes of the group members, especially those who were talking, thereby extending to dynamic scenes what has previously been found for static images.

Further research has demonstrated that attention to the faces and eyes of videos of individuals is not an artifact of low-level stimulus saliency, such as sound onsets or visual motion. Foulsham and Sanderson (2013) and Coutrot and Guyader (2014) both investigated whether looks to the faces and eyes of individuals engaged in conversation were significantly affected by whether the audio was present or absent, or if instead looks were driven by changes in visual salience. Their results indicated that the addition of an audio-track increased looks to the faces and eyes of the talkers, and also resulted in greater synchrony for when the observers looked at the speakers (Foulsham & Sanderson, 2013). Critically, whether sound was present or not, and independent of changes in low-level visual saliency (Coutrot & Guyader, 2014), people spent most of their time looking at the faces and eyes of the individuals in the videos.

Based on the data presented here, it would seem that the preferential bias to attend to the eyes of others generalizes across levels of complexity: from static images of faces presented in isolation, to photos of people, to dynamic complex multisensory stimuli composed of people in groups talking amongst themselves and making decisions. This kind of generalization is impressive. The strong implication from this is that the findings are reliable across all levels of stimulus complexity. If what differs between lab and real life is simply an increase in complexity, it suggests that findings from static and dynamic images of people will predict observations from situations involving real people.

Trouble in Paradise: Social Attention is Interactive

Attention in Interactive Contexts

While the evidence for generalization across levels of stimulus complexity hints at a kind of basic principle of social attention, the difference between looking face-to-face at an image of a person versus looking at a real person involves more than just a change in stimulus complexity. One factor is that with a real person there is the possibility to actually interact with the individual. The importance of this factor is not to be dismissed quickly – truly social situations demand a level of behavioral interdependence between the looker and the person being looked at that has not been captured well in traditional computer-based social attention tasks.

Even without interaction, the *possibility* of interacting with others turns out to be critical in how people attend to others. Foulsham, Walker, and Kingstone (2011) investigated whether people distribute their gaze in the same way when they are immersed and moving in the world compared to when they view video-clips taken from the perspective of a pedestrian. Participants wore a mobile eye tracker while walking to buy a coffee, a trip that required a short walk outdoors through the university campus. Later, they returned to the lab and watched first-person videos of the walk. Eye movements to other pedestrians occurred often in both the lab and the real world; however, pedestrians close to

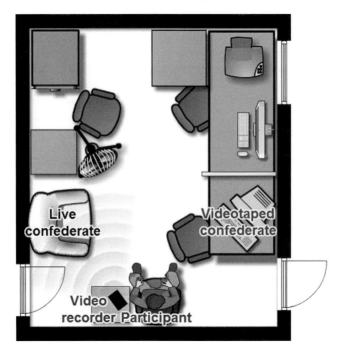

Figure 10.3 Experimental set-up from Laidlaw et al. (2011).

Note: Participants sat in the middle of the room wearing an eye tracker while either a confederate sat to their left or a videotape of the same confederate played to their right.

the walker were fixated more often when they were viewed on video than in the real world. In other words, in real life people looked away from an approaching person, whereas in the lab participants were all too happy to stare at them as they approached and passed the pedestrian in the video. Thus, although the stimulus (a stranger walking toward the participant) is superficially similar in both cases, when the stranger is physically present and is capable of interacting with the participant, the behavior of the participant changes.

To study this point more fully, Laidlaw, Foulsham, Kuhn, and Kingstone (2011) measured participants' looking behavior as they were sitting in a waiting room, either in the presence of a confederate posing as another research participant, or in the presence of a videotape of the same confederate (see Figure 10.3). Thus, the potential for social interaction existed only when the confederate was physically present. While wearing a mobile eye tracker, participants waited in a room for about two minutes, under the guise that the experimenter had stepped out to collect materials necessary for the study to begin. In this way, participants were unaware that the two-minute waiting period was part of the experiment. In the room, there was either a confederate sitting to their left, quietly completing a questionnaire, or a video of the same confederate from a different session playing on a computer screen to the participants' right-hand side. The computer station was set up to look as though a research assistant had left the video playing and stepped out of the room. Participants' eye movements were coded for looks to the confederate (either videotaped or live; coded for looks to the upper body only), or to the baseline object (for those watching the video, baseline was the empty chair that the live confederate would have to sit in during the alternate condition; for those in the room with the confederate, baseline was the blank computer screen that would play the video for other participants).

Although participants frequently looked at the videotaped confederate, they seldom turned toward or looked at the live confederate. In fact, relative to baseline, they were biased *not to look* at the real confederate. This is precisely the opposite behavior observed by researchers for images of people – where participants are preferentially biased to look at the faces of people when they are represented in images (e.g. Birmingham et al., 2009; Levy et al., 2012). In sum, these data demonstrate that the mere opportunity for social interaction can profoundly alter social attention, with participants being biased away from looking at a stranger.

Converging evidence for this conclusion comes from a recent series of studies using naturalistic observation. Gallup et al. (2012) placed an object in a busy hallway and monitored individuals' gaze behavior with respect to that object using a hidden camera. The researchers were interested in the extent to which pedestrians would be influenced by the gaze direction of other pedestrians (i.e. gaze following). Gallup et al. demonstrated that overall looks toward the object increased when other nearby pedestrians looked toward the object. Interestingly, this depended on which way the 'participant' was facing. When the participant was behind a pedestrian, looks to the object increased. When the participant was facing the pedestrian who gazed at the object, however, participants were actually less likely to look at the object than if no one had looked at the object (i.e. the baseline condition). Thus, the gaze of an oncoming pedestrian directed toward a nearby object appeared to inhibit the likelihood of another pedestrian directing their gaze to that object. This behavior is the opposite of what one would expect given the repeated demonstrations in the laboratory that individuals have a strong (and, some have argued, automatic) tendency to follow the gaze of others in a face-to-face situation.

Dual Function of the Eyes: The Role of Signaling Our Attention

The Foulsham, Laidlaw and Gallup work demonstrates that two fundamental social attention behaviors (gaze selection and gaze following) change in a very meaningful way when a participant is embedded in a naturalistic context with real people serving as the stimuli. Indeed, the lab-based effects appear to reverse their direction in the real world. Why should that be?

Our working hypothesis is that the act of looking at the eyes of another person in real-life communicates information to that person, and that we are acutely aware of the dual function of our gaze, both as a way of collecting information and also transmitting it. In short, in real life, attention to another person is a two-way street. But when viewing static images or pre-recorded videos of people, there is no communication – observers can take the information in but nothing is transmitted out. As a result of this awareness, in real life observers may choose to reduce gaze selection and gaze following, not necessarily because there is no bias to attend to real people, but because they weigh the potential gain of attending with the possible cost of revealing their own attention.

While this theory rests on the fundamental idea that humans use their eyes to signal as well as to take in information, empirical studies have until recently focused on the latter side of the equation. In a series of three experiments, Wu, Bischof, and Kingstone (2014) investigated if, and when, humans signal gaze information to other humans in a natural but controlled situation involving eating. Wu et al. established that there is a normative behavior to look away when someone begins to bite into food. This was revealed to depend on a dynamic exchange between the eater and the observer. Participants were significantly more likely to look down at their food before taking a bite when they were eating with another person versus when they were alone, suggesting an awareness of the signaling power of one's own gaze in social situations. Further, when that signal was conveyed, people tended to look away from the eater. In short, the Wu et al. study provides the first clear evidence that people use their eyes systematically to signal to others, and that when read by a conspecific, that signal results in a response behavior that aligns with social norms (i.e. it is rude to look at someone when they open their mouth wide to take a bite and therefore the pro-social behavior is to look away; see Box 10.1).

Box 10.1 Could we have predicted non-transferability from lab to life?

At first blush, the consistency with which we attend to stimuli in the lab is impressive and could lead one to believe that these behaviors are representative of what we do in real life. As we describe, however, this is far from what has been observed. We argue that the way in which people interact with images is dramatically different than how people engage with other individuals, such that the latter involves not only information extraction but also the signaling of one's attention to one or more individuals. Could this disconnect have been predicted from nuances in lab findings?

When Birmingham et al. (2008b) asked participants to describe where attention was directed in the scene versus asking them to simply look at or describe the scene, fixations to the eyes increased. This demonstrates a level of top-down control of attention, suggesting that people are capable of choosing – at least to some extent – the degree to which they attend to social stimuli, and that this social selection varies with task and/or contextual demands. Similarly, in Laidlaw et al.'s (2012) work, even though participants demonstrated a clear non-volitional bias to attend to the eyes of others, looks to the eyes were significantly reduced in the 'don't look' compared to the free-viewing condition. These subtleties from lab-based measures of social attention argue for the view that there is a strong degree of flexibility in how and when people attend to social stimuli. The implication is that how people attend to social stimuli in the real world may bring with it a different set of rules and norms, and accordingly, a change in looking behavior. However, what these non-interactive studies fail to provide is any hint regarding how real life might affect the deployment of attention, and how this might differ from what is observed in the lab. While lab-based studies can be incredibly useful in exploring specific aspects of attention, without committed efforts to characterize social attention within truly social settings, predicting which behaviors are sensitive to social norms and which are stable across levels of complexity and realism would be challenging at best.

This last point regarding social norms turns out to be a critical factor in looking behavior. We argue that not only are we aware of the power of gaze as a signal, as Wu et al. (2014) demonstrate, but that we weigh the benefits and costs associated with signaling one's own attention. The result of this decision often might be contingent on how our signaling behavior aligns with perceived social norms. Recall that recent studies have found that participants consistently look less at people in live situations than one would expect from conventional laboratory experiments (Gallup et al. 2012; Laidlaw et al. 2011). We proposed that this is because people wanted to avoid a negative social interaction – the act of signaling one's own attention to another serves as a social norm related to wanting to engage with that person. An awareness of gaze as a signal should also predict that, in situations where interaction is preferred or is socially appropriate, looking behavior should take on a dynamism not possible when looking at images or videos of other people. By placing participants in a situation (sharing a meal) where looking at a person is congruent with the social norm, Wu, Bischof, and Kingstone (2013) and Wu et al. (2014) found that, although participants looked away when the other person began to bite into their food, overall there was still a significant tendency for participants to look at each other. Indeed, dyads who engaged more in conversation (e.g. were more interactive, and rated as 'high-social' by the authors; 7 dyads) also looked more at the other person than dyads who tended not to engage in conversation (e.g. were rated as 'low-social' by the authors and rarely engaged in conversation during the experimental session; 11 dyads). Thus, visual interaction was modulated by social interaction.

A similar normative effect of gaze was also observed in a study by Freeth, Foulsham, and Kingstone (2013), where eye-tracked participants were interviewed by a live or videotaped interviewer. While looks to the interviewer's face were common in both live and videotaped conditions, when the interviewer made eye contact, participants in the live condition were more likely to look at the face and body of the interviewer than were those in the videotaped condition. In the live condition, participants appeared better able to ascribe the interviewer's eye contact as a signal that accompanied a normative response to return that gaze.

In summary, when in the presence of real people, individuals modify their looking behavior in a pro-social manner consistent with social norms. They look away when they are with strangers and wish to avoid a social interaction (Gallup et al. 2012; Laidlaw et al., 2011), and they look toward people they are interacting with (Freeth et al., 2013; Wu et al., 2014). This communicative complexity is not captured by laboratory studies that use images as stand-ins for real people, although recent efforts to develop interactive methodologies while maintaining more rigorous experimental control have revealed some interesting findings (see Box 10.2). In the real world, one is surrounded by people who are live observers in their own right and this highlights that the act of looking serves two fundamentally different functions: to extract information from the environment (primarily from people if they are present), and to signal information to those people in the environment about oneself.

Box 10.2 Interactive social attention in the lab

While we maintain that the best way to study social attention is with real people in realistic situations, we recognize that this can be more challenging for some research questions than for others. For example, when answers are dependent on particular equipment (e.g. fMRI, ERP), it may not be possible (at least not yet) to create convincingly naturalistic scenarios within which social attention can be studied. That is not to say that efforts cannot be made, however. Recent neuropsychological studies of joint attention highlight the clever ways in which a sense of interaction can be integrated into more traditional lab studies. For instance, findings using gaze-contingent displays that react to the participants' eye movements suggest that people respond differently to others who do or do not follow one's gaze direction. Bayliss et al. (2013) reported that dwell time on a face and time to reorient towards a face are both affected by whether an 'interactive' digital avatar's face followed or looked away from the participant's gaze shift. Further, participants reported more positive affect towards faces that followed their gaze.

Using 'interactive' approaches, one can also delve into differences in neural responses when people follow versus lead a joint attention episode. Schilbach et al. (2010) combined eye-tracking and fMRI methods to study brain responses when a virtual other – supposedly controlled by another eye-tracked participant – either initiated or responded to a shift in gaze. In this way, the authors were able to distinguish effects of reciprocated and rejected shifts of joint attention. They reported that joint attention episodes recruited the medial prefrontal cortex, known to be important in processing intent (Kamp, Frith, & Frith, 2003), implying that in interactive scenarios, participants engage in mentalizing behaviors that might not be engaged in as heavily in non-interactive tasks. In addition, when compared to other-initiated joint attention episodes, there were greater differences in motivation and reward-related brain region activation when a self-initiated shift of attention was reciprocated versus when it was rejected (i.e. the virtual other looked in the opposite direction).

While these studies hint towards ways in which the gap between lab and life can be reduced, we cannot overstate the importance that we feel should be placed on grounding findings on what happens in real life (Kingstone et al., 2003, 2008). Without a more thorough understanding of what people do naturally, one runs the risk of making conclusions based on findings from the lab, which current evidence points to being – at best – a unique and possibly non-representative snapshot of everyday behavior.

Social Presence: Awareness of Signaling Changes Behavior

This dual function framework for understanding social attention places the presence of receptive others in a central position with respect to controlling where we attend. Yet, could our awareness of gaze as a signal be strong enough to change behavior even when the communicative other is not immediately physically present (e.g. the potential for interaction occurs across time), or simply implied? Our labs have leveraged long-standing 'social presence' effects in order to investigate the extent to which we alter our looking behavior in order to adhere to normative social behavior.

It is well known that the physical presence of others can alter people's behavior. For example, the presence of others has been shown to influence people's interactions, self-awareness and performance (Levine, Resnick & Higgins, 1993; Zajonc, 1965) or even alter the way they express their emotions (Buck, Losow, Murphy, & Costanzo, 1992). Walker, Risko, and Kingstone (2014) recently discovered that even the production of fillers ('um's and 'uh's) during a question and answer task increased when a person was in the room (i.e. when people did not know the answer to a question they often feigned knowing the answer but being unable to fully retrieve it). This desire for positive impression management occurred even when the questions and answers were between the participant and a computer, and the experimenter excused herself to sit within earshot. In general, the physical presence of others elevates conformance to social norms, which is argued to be based on our need to attain approval or avoid the disapproval of others (Guerin, 1986).

Interestingly, another individual does not actually need to be physically present to influence behavior (Aiello & Svec, 1993; Putz, 1975; van Rompay, Vonk, & Fransen, 2008). Rather, it appears that the presence simply needs to be implied. For instance, images of eyes can evoke cooperative behavior in people, augmenting the likelihood of individuals cleaning up litter from cafeteria tables (Ernest-Jones, Nettle, & Bateson, 2011) and even influencing people to increase monetary contributions towards an 'honor box' system for consuming drinks (Bateson, Nettle, & Roberts, 2006). Security cameras, which imply the presence of others, also increase pro-social behaviors such that individuals are more likely to provide help to others in a public setting (van Rompay et al., 2008).

Based on these and related findings, Risko and Kingstone (2011) generated the speculative hypothesis that our awareness of gaze as a signal, combined with our desire to adhere to social norms, might lead us to change our looking behavior when we are aware we are being monitored. In other words, simply wearing an eye tracker might be sufficient to imply the presence of another individual and alter our attention. Eye trackers provide a moment-to-moment record of where an individual is looking and thus provide an indispensable tool for studying attention. However, the knowledge that one's eye movements are being recorded – which act as a signal of one's thoughts and intentions – might serve as a particularly powerful form of implied social presence.

In order to determine if a social presence can influence looking behavior, Risko and Kingstone (2011) compared looking behavior when individuals knew their eyes were being watched (via an eye tracker) and when they did not. In all instances, looks were actually recorded using a hidden camera. Participants (mostly female, though male participants were also tested) took part in a 'natural looking' task in which they performed a simple computer task alone in a testing room that contained objects typically found in an office. In addition, Risko and Kingstone mounted a provocative sexy swimsuit calendar in the testing room. After completing the computer task, participants remained alone in the room for a short amount of time. It was participants' looking behavior to the calendar during this free time that was of interest. They predicted that if social presence influences looking behavior, then individuals should alter their behavior to be consistent with social norms when wearing an eye tracker and should be less likely to look at the sexy calendar than individuals not wearing an eye tracker.

The results were unequivocal. Participants who wore an eye tracker were much less likely to look at a provocative stimulus than individuals who were not wearing an eye tracker. Results did not significantly differ based on participant gender. An additional group who wore the eye tracker but were told it was not recording behaved based on whether they believed that their eyes were actually being tracked or not: they modified their looking behavior when they still thought their gaze was signaling their attention. This demonstrates conclusively that eye trackers serve as an implied social presence. Whether participants looked at the sexy calendar or not depended on whether they believed that their looking behavior was being monitored. If they felt that their eyes were being watched, they avoided looking at the calendar, in accordance with the pro-social norm that discourages objectifying women by staring at their bodies. In contrast, if participants felt that their eyes were not being monitored, and therefore their looks at the calendar would not be seen by anyone else, and hence not reflect poorly on them, then they were all too willing to look at the calendar.

Methodologically, the finding that wearing an eye tracker can alter looking behavior serves as an important reminder that the act of experimental observation can influence the behavior being observed. This finding has potentially serious, negative implications for researchers who use eye trackers to understand the mechanisms of human attention and cognition. Briefly, the concern is that, if wearing an eye tracker changes behavior to the extent that people actively avoid looking at things that they would look at in a more natural environment, then researchers run the risk of drawing conclusions regarding human attention and interest that are precisely the opposite to reality. For instance, if Risko and Kingstone (2011) had only run the standard eye-tracking condition, then the data would have supported the conclusion that when left alone in a room the vast majority of people do not look at sexy images of women. In fact, the truth is anything but that.

But what might be bad news for basic eye movement researchers could be good news for people who wear or manufacture wearable computing. Currently, there are profound concerns that wearable computing will record people in places where they expect their personal privacy to be respected (e.g. in a changing room or when sharing a private moment at a restaurant). However, to the extent that wearable computing might reveal the wearer's thoughts and intentions (e.g. Google Glass recording one's head turning to look at an attractive individual) the data from Risko and Kingstone (2011) suggest that people who don such devices might behave in a manner in keeping with pro-social norms.

These methodological (i.e. for eye-tracking research) and social (i.e. for the societal integration of wearable computing) implications are predicated on the assumption that the implied social presence effect of the eye tracker lasts for a prolonged period of time. Nasiopoulos, Risko, Foulsham, and Kingstone (2014) put it to the test. In their study, participants performed a simple sham visual search task outside the lab before bringing people back into a testing room to perform the same task used by Risko and Kingstone (2011).The total testing time took about 10 minutes. The critical manipulation concerned if and when an eye tracker was worn by the participants. There were four groups. In the no eye tracker group, the participants did not wear an eye tracker at any time. In the standard eye tracker group, participants did the visual search task and then were outfitted with the eye tracker. A third group wore the eye tracker both during the visual search task and during the Risko and Kingstone task. The last group also wore the eye tracker for both tasks, but before sitting down to do the Risko and Kingstone task, they were reminded once again of the eye tracker's presence by performing an additional eye tracker calibration.

Replicating Risko and Kingstone (2011), the results showed that people who never wore an eye tracker looked at the sexy swimsuit calendar, while those who put on the eye tracker after the sham visual search task did not. What was surprising is that those who wore the eye tracker during the initial visual search task and then moved straight onto the Risko and Kingstone task were found to behave as if they did not have an eye tracker on at all (i.e. they were very willing to look at the sexy calendar). In other words, using an eye tracker to make participants think of their gaze as a signal did not last in the way one would expect it to when interacting with real people; pro-social effects on looking behavior dissolved rapidly, in about 10 minutes. However, and just as surprisingly, those participants who wore the eye tracker during the initial visual search task and then received an eye-tracker calibration before starting the Risko and Kingstone task behaved as if they had just put on the eye tracker: the implied social presence effect was reactivated and accordingly, they avoided looking at the sexy calendar.

Collectively, these data suggest that the implied social presence effect of an eye tracker is transient, reflecting a shift in attention away from the eye tracker rather than habituation to it (if it were habituation, drawing attention to the tracker would have had little effect). This is good news for basic attention researchers and those studying social attention alike. The implied social presence effect of the tracker can elicit changes consistent with awareness of gaze as a signaling tool, but this effect quickly fades, and individuals who are wearing an eye tracker will soon display eye movements that closely approximate their natural looking behavior when alone. Furthermore, as long as nothing draws a participant's attention to the fact that their eyes are being tracked, natural looking behavior should continue. What do these data mean for manufacturers and users of wearable technologies? The implication is that users of these technologies will likely adapt quickly to the idea that what they see is being recorded and fail to self-monitor in a pro-social manner, although this issue could potentially be mitigated by reminding the wearer that their looking behavior is being documented.

Theoretically, the Nasiopoulos et al. (2014) work reinforces the idea that our looking behavior is strongly influenced by social presence (implied in this case) and begins the critical work of better understanding the mechanism underlying this influence. Namely, in the context of the dual function framework described above, what are the cognitive (and social) mechanisms underlying the 'signaling' function and its interaction with information acquisition in complex social situations? The Nasiopoulos et al. work suggests that the pro-social looking behavior caused by the implied presence of others resembles a kind of controlled or effortful process that requires deliberate monitoring (i.e. without a reminder that their eyes are being monitored individuals quickly fall into a kind of default looking pattern). Such a position is consistent with other recent work on the types of processing underlying self-presentation (e.g. Vohs, Baumeister, & Ciarocco, 2005) and opens the door to new and interesting questions (e.g. how do working memory demands modulate looking behavior in socially complex situations?). Future work exploring these and other questions promises to provide a deeper understanding of social attention in all of its complexity.

Summary and Conclusions

We are fundamentally social beings. As such, understanding social attention will hold a special place within a complete understanding of human attention. That said, simply borrowing paradigms devised to investigate non-social aspects of attention to understand social attention seems limited in important ways. The present review bears this notion out but at the same time provides what might be the beginnings of an alternative framework, one that emphasizes the 'social' in social attention.

References

Aiello, J. R., & Svec, C. M. (1993). Computer monitoring of work performance: Extending the social facilitation framework to electronic presence. *Journal of Applied Social Psychology*, 23, 537–548.

Akiyama, T., Kato, M., Muramatsu, T., Saito, F., Umeda, S., & Kashima, H. (2006). Gaze but not arrows: A dissociative impairment after right superior temporal gyrus damage. *Neuropsychologia*, 44, 1804–1810.

Andrews, T. J., Davies-Thompson, J., Kingstone, A., & Young, A. W. (2010). Internal and external features of the face are represented holistically in face-selective regions of visual cortex. *Journal of Neuroscience*, 30, 3544–3552.

Bateson, M., Nettle, D., & Roberts, G. (2006). Cues of being watched enhance cooperation in a real-world setting. *Biology Letters*, 2, 412–414.

Bayliss, A. P., Murphy, E., Naughtin, C. K., Kritikos, A., Schilbach, L., & Becker, S. I. (2013). 'Gaze leading': Initiating simulated joint attention influences eye movements and choice behavior. *Journal of Experimental Psychology: General*, 142, 76–92.

Bindemann, M., Scheepers, C., & Burton, A. M. (2009). Viewpoint and center of gravity affect eye movements to human faces. *Journal of Vision*, 9(2), 1–16.

Birmingham, E., Bischof, W. F., & Kingstone, A. (2008a). Social attention and real world scenes: The roles of action, competition, and social content. *Quarterly Journal of Experimental Psychology*, 61, 986–998.

(2008b). Gaze selection in complex social scenes. *Visual Cognition*, 16(2/3), 341–355.

(2009). Saliency does not account for fixations to eyes within social scenes. *Vision Research*, 49, 2992–3000.

Birmingham, E., & Kingstone, A. (2009). Human social attention: A new look at past, present and future investigations. *Annals of the New York Academy of Sciences*, 1156, 118–140.

Broadbent, D. E. (1971). *Decision and stress*. New York: Academic Press.

Buck, R., Loslow, J. I., Murphy, M. M., & Costanzo, P. (1992). Social facilitation and inhibition of emotional expression and communication. *Journal of Personality and Social Psychology*, 63, 962–968.

Calder, A. J., Beaver, J. D., Winston, J. S., Dolan, R. J., Jenkins, R., Eger, E., & Henson, R. N. A (2007). Separate coding of different gaze directions in the superior temporal sulcus and inferior parietal lobule. *Current Biology*, 17, 20–25.

Campbell, R., Heywood, C. A., Cowey, A., Regard, M., & Landis, T. (1990). Sensitivity to eye gaze in prosopagnosic patients and monkeys with superior temporal sulcus ablation. *Neuropsychologia*, 28, 1123–1142.

Cheng, J. T., Tracey, J. L., Foulsham, T., Kingstone, A., & Henrich, J. (2013). Two ways to the top: Evidence that dominance and prestige are distinct yet viable avenues to social rank and influence. *Journal of Personality and Social Psychology*, 104(1), 103–125.

Coutrot, A., & Guyader, N. (2014). How saliency, faces, and sound influence gaze in dynamic social scenes. *Journal of Vision*, 14(8), 5.

Deaner, R. O., & Platt, M. P. (2003). Reflexive social attention in monkeys and humans. *Current Biology*, 13, 1609–1613.

Emery, N. J. (2000). The eyes have it: The neuroethology, function and evolution of social gaze. *Neuroscience & Biobehavioral Review*, 24, 581–604.

Ernest-Jones, M., Nettle, N., & Bateson, M. (2011). Effects of eye images on everyday cooperative behavior: A field experiment. *Evolution and Human Behavior*, 32, 172–178.

Fan, J., McCandliss, B. D., Sommer, T., Raz, M., & Posner, M. I. (2002). Testing the efficiency and independence of attentional networks. *Journal of Cognitive Neuroscience*, 14, 340–347.

Foulsham, T., Cheng, J. T., Tracy, J. L., Henrich, J., & Kingstone, A. (2010). Gaze allocation in a dynamic situation: Effects of social status and speaking. *Cognition*, 117, 319–331.

Foulsham, T., & Sanderson, L. A. (2013). Look who's talking? Sound changes gaze behavior in a dynamic social scene. *Visual Cognition*, 21, 922–944.

Foulsham, T., Walker, E., & Kingstone, A. (2011). The where, what and when of gaze allocation in the lab and the natural environment. *Vision Research*, 51, 1920–1931.

Freeth, M., Foulsham, T., & Kingstone, A. (2013). What affects social attention? Social presence, eye contact and autistic traits. *PLoS One*, 8(1), e53286.

Gallup, A. C., Hale, J. J., Sumpter, D. J. T., Garnier, S., Kacelnik, A., Krebs, J. R., & Couzin, I. D. (2012). Visual attention and the acquisition of information in human crowds. *Proceedings of the National Academy of Sciences*, 109, 7245–7250.

Guerin, B. (1986). Mere presence effects in humans: A review. *Journal of Experimental Social Psychology*, 22(1), 38–77.

Henderson, J. M., Williams, C. C., & Falk, R. (2005). Eye movements are functional during face learning. *Memory & Cognition*, 33, 98–106.

Heywood, C. A., Cowey, A., & Rolls, E. T. (1992). The role of the face cell area in the discrimination and recognition of faces by monkeys. *Philosophical Transactions of the Royal Society B: Biological Sciences*, 335, 31–38.

Hoffman, E. A., & Haxby, J. V. (2000). Distinct representations of eye gaze and identity in the distributed human neural system for face perception. *Nature Neuroscience*, 3, 80–84.

Itti, L., & Koch, C. (2000). A saliency-based search mechanism for overt and covert shifts of visual attention. *Vision Research*, 40, 1489–1506.

Kampe, K. K., Frith, C. D., & Frith, U. (2003) 'Hey John': Signals conveying communicative intention toward the self activate brain regions associated with 'mentalizing,' regardless of modality. *Journal of Neuroscience*, 23, 5258–5263.

Kingstone, A., Smilek, D., & Eastwood, J. D. (2008). Cognitive ethology: A new approach for studying human cognition. *British Journal of Psychology*, 99, 317–345.

Kingstone, A., Smilek, D., Ristic, J., Friesen, C. K., & Eastwood, J. D. (2003). Attention, researchers! It is time to take a look at the real world. *Current Directions in Psychological Science*, 12, 176–180.

Kingstone, A., Tipper, C., Ristic, J., & Ngan, E. (2004). The eyes have it! An fMRI investigation. *Brain & Cognition*, 55, 269–271.

Laidlaw, K. E. W., Foulsham, T., Kuhn, G., & Kingstone, A. (2011). Potential social interactions are important to social attention. *Proceedings of the National Academy of Sciences*, 108, 5548–5553.

Laidlaw, K. E. W., Risko, E. F., & Kingstone, A. (2012). A new look at social attention: Orienting to the eyes is not (entirely) under volitional control. *Journal of Experimental Psychology: Human Perception and Performance*, 38, 1132–1143.

Levine, J. M., Resnick, L. B., & Higgins, E. T. (1993). Social foundations of cognition. *Annual Review of Psychology*, 44, 585–612.

Levy, J., Foulsham, T., & Kingstone, A. (2012). Monsters are people too. *Biology Letters*, 9, 20120850.

Nasiopoulos, E., Risko, E. F., Foulsham, T., & Kingstone, A. (2014). Wearable computing: Will it make people prosocial? *British Journal of Psychology*, 106, 109-216.

Pelphrey, K. A., Sasson, N. J., Reznick, S., Paul, G., Goldman, B. D., & Piven, J. (2002). Visual scanning of faces in autism. *Journal of Autism and Developmental Disorders*, 32, 249–261.

Posner, M. I. (1980). Attention and the detection of signals. *Journal of Experimental Psychology: General*, 109, 160–174.

Putz, V. R. (1975). The effects of different modes of supervision on vigilance behavior. *British Journal of Psychology*, 66, 157–160.

Risko, E. F., & Kingstone, A. (2011). Eyes wide shut: Implied social presence, eye tracking and attention. *Attention, Perception, and Psychophysics*, 73, 291–296.

Risko, E. F., Laidlaw, K., Freeth, M., Foulsham, T., & Kingstone, A. (2012). Real vs. Reel: An empirical approach to the equivalence of different 'social' stimuli. *Frontiers in Human Neuroscience*, 6, 143.

Schilbach, L., Wilms, M., Eickhoff, S. B., Romanzetti, S., Tepest, R., Bente, G., Shah, N. J., Fink, G. R., & Vogeley, K. (2010). Minds made for sharing: Initiating joint attention recruits reward-related neurocircuitry. *Journal of Cognitive Neuroscience*, 22, 2702–2715.

Smilek, D., Birmingham, E., Cameron, D., Bischof, W. F., & Kingstone, A. (2006). Cognitive ethology and exploring attention in real world scenes. *Brain Research*, 1080, 101–119.

van Rompay, T. J. L., Vonk, D. J., & Fransen, M. L. (2008). The eye of the camera: Effects of security cameras on prosocial behavior. *Environment and Behavior*, 41(1), 60–74.

Vohs, K. D., Baumeister, R. F., & Ciarocco, N. J. (2005). Self-regulation and self-presentation: Regulatory resource depletion impairs impression management and effortful self-presentation depletes regulatory resources. *Journal of Personality and Social Psychology*, 88, 632–657.

Walker, E., Risko, E. F., & Kingstone, A. (2014). Fillers as signals: Evidence from a question-answering paradigm. *Discourse Processes*, 51, 264–286.

Walker-Smith, G., Gale, A. G., & Findlay, J. M. (1977). Eye movement strategies involved in face perception. *Perception*, 6, 313–326.

Wu, D. W.-L., Bischof, W. F., & Kingstone, A. (2013). Looking while eating: The importance of social context to social attention. *Scientific Reports*, 3, 2356.

    (2014). Natural gaze signaling in a social context. *Evolution & Human Behavior*, 35, 211–218.

Yarbus, A. L. (1967). *Eye movements and vision* (B. Haigh, Trans.). New York: Plenum Press.

Yovel, G., & Kanwisher, N. (2005). The neural basis of the behavioral face-inversion effect. *Current Biology*, 15, 2256–2262.
Zajonc, R. B. (1965). Social facilitation. *Science*, 149, 269–274.

Glossary

Attention signal processing The act of interpreting another's internal states such as their goals, intentions, or emotions based on their overt attentional behavior.

Fixation The maintenance of visual gaze on a specific location to bring the region under focus and allow for processing under high visual acuity.

Gaze following The act of redirecting one's attention in response to the gaze (typically, eye direction, though can broadly refer to head or body orientation) of another to be congruent with the focus of their gaze.

Gaze selection The act of orienting one's attention to the eyes of another.

Holistic processing Often used in reference to processing faces, the analysis of information as a whole or complete set (e.g. a face) as opposed to the processing of its individual features or parts (e.g. two eyes, one mouth, and so on).

Naturalistic observation Monitoring and/or recording of a given behavior in the environment in which it naturally occurs.

Non-volitional attention The orienting of attention that is controlled by external processes independent of the goals of the person who is attending; also referred to as exogenous attention, stimulus-driven or bottom-up attention.

Social attention The processes underlying the allocation of a limited capacity resource (i.e. attention) to socially meaningful stimuli such as but not limited to people, faces and eyes or in accordance with social goals.

Social presence effects Refers to a broad class of phenomenon wherein the actual or implied presence of another person alters behavior.

11 Acting Together: Representations and Coordination Processes

Cordula Vesper and Natalie Sebanz

Abstract

Human life involves and requires joint action. Coordinating our actions with others not only gives rise to cultural products that individuals could not achieve alone, such as the Egyptian pyramids or the performance of a symphony. Rather, everyday life also has us engage in many joint actions, from folding a sheet together to having a conversation. How do people manage to act together in a coordinated way? In this chapter, we consider this question in terms of the cognitive mechanisms underlying joint action, focusing on real-time interactions in dyads or small groups. To illustrate what we are aiming to explore, think of two people who are loading shopping bags into the trunk of a car. At times, they each take a rather light bag from the shopping cart, move towards the trunk and then coordinate who is setting their bag down first, and where. At other moments, they carry heavy bags together, making sure to lift and set these down at the same time. As this shows, performing a joint action often requires adapting one's own actions to what another person is doing. In this chapter, we first introduce some key concepts that have been highlighted in previous accounts of joint action, briefly addressing shared intentions, commitment and representations of joint goals. The main part focuses on coordination mechanisms – cognitive processes and mental representations that make performing joint actions of the kind described above possible. Specifically, we will review findings from experimental studies that shed light on general coordination strategies, representations of joint abilities and tasks, mechanisms of predicting own and others' actions, and non-verbal communication through action. We will conclude by discussing ways in which different coordination mechanisms might be combined to allow co-actors to take on complementary roles.

Shared Intentionality, Commitment and Shared Goals

One way to approach joint action is to think about the intentions that individuals must have in order to be able to act together, and the commitments

216

that may arise in connection with these intentions. For instance, think of two people preparing a meal together: it is unlikely that the two will simply start moving around in the kitchen, chopping up different ingredients and throwing them in a pan. Rather, they might first talk about a recipe, decide on a joint action plan that specifies who will take over which tasks, and both will assume that each will then do what they agreed on. Although this scenario may seem intuitive, there is much debate about the nature of shared intentions, and the role of commitment. Are shared intentions fundamentally different from individual intentions, or should we conceive of them as individual intentions that interlock in particular ways (Bratman, 1992, 2009)? Is commitment a constitutive part of joint action (Gilbert, 1992, 2006)? While these and many related questions have primarily been considered from a theoretical perspective, the notions of shared intentions and commitment have also guided empirical research on language as a coordination device (see Box 11.1) and research on the development of joint action abilities in children (see Box 11.2).

Many researchers would agree that shared intentions and joint commitment are relevant for understanding joint action; however, there is also growing support for the idea that identifying minimal conditions for joint action is useful for understanding basic underlying mechanisms (Butterfill, 2012; Tollefsen, 2005; Vesper, Butterfill, Knoblich, & Sebanz, 2010). Is it possible to perform a joint task without having a shared intention? Could there be minimal commitment that arises from acting together rather than from explicit agreement? Answers to these questions are particularly important for understanding coordinated interactions that happen within split seconds, where there is no time for prior planning – as, for example, when a shopping bag suddenly bursts open and we immediately catch the contents together. One minimal account postulates that, for at least some forms of joint action, it is sufficient for individuals to have a representation of the joint action goal, i.e. the desired outcome of the joint action, in addition to having a representation of their own task and some awareness of the fact that another contribution is needed to achieve the intended outcome (Vesper et al., 2010). Further representations and processes might sometimes provide additional support for smooth and efficient coordination. However, there are other proposals that do not rely on the notion of mental representation at all to explain interpersonal coordination. Specifically, behavioral dynamics accounts explain coordination in terms of coupled oscillators operating in self-organizing biological systems like insect colonies or fish swarms (Marsh, Richardson, & Schmidt, 2009; Schmidt & Richardson, 2008; Schmidt, Fitzpatrick, Caron, & Mergeche, 2011). These accounts imply that groups rather than individuals constitute the appropriate unit of analysis.

For the purpose of this chapter, we assume that a better understanding of the mechanisms underlying joint action can be achieved by focusing on cognitive processes and mental representations within individuals, which we discuss in what follows. To what extent these complement or substitute some of the notions discussed above remains to be addressed elsewhere.

Box 11.1 Verbal communication

Verbal communication is a powerful coordination device because it allows people to build up common ground (Clark, 1996). We talk to generate plans that will guide our joint actions, and we rely on verbal and non-verbal communication to coordinate our actions with others' online during interaction. When common ground is restricted, for instance because a person giving instructions to another cannot see her workspace, language use is adjusted in an attempt to make up for the lack of shared information (Brennan, 2005; Clark & Krych, 2004).

However, dialog is not just a means to facilitate coordination, but also constitutes a paradigm case of joint action in and of itself (Clark, 1996). Does coordination in dialog rely on the same mechanisms as coordination of nonverbal, instrumental actions? A strong candidate for a common mechanism is action prediction through the recruitment of forward models (Pickering & Garrod, 2013). Just as we rely on our own motor repertoire to make predictions about others' (nonverbal) actions, we may also rely on language production processes to comprehend others' utterances. In this view, comprehension is a form of action perception. It follows that other joint action phenomena that rely (at least partially) on action prediction, such as turn-taking and the distribution of efforts, may also be best understood in terms of common underlying mechanisms across dialog and practical action (Enfield, 2013). Moreover, synchronous acting (Vesper, van der Wel, Knoblich, & Sebanz, 2011) and synchronous speaking (Cummins, Li, & Wang, 2013), which can be found in many rituals as well as in educational contexts, may also rely on common mechanisms, such as reducing the variability of one's actions to achieve synchronization. More generally, focusing on commonalities between verbal communication and nonverbal joint action may lead us to re-consider the relation between coordination and communication.

Box 11.2 Development of joint action

Infants gain experience with the timing and structure of dyadic interaction early on, being enveloped in social exchange with their caretakers (Reddy, 2008; Stern, 2002; Trevarthen, 1979). In the second half of their first year, their interactions with adults start to be organized around objects of common interest, which provides opportunities for experiencing the relation between their own and the partner's attention and action (Barresi & Moore, 1996). While much research suggests that children have a special motivation to share attention and to engage in cooperative activities (Carpenter, 2009; Tomasello, Carpenter, Call, Behne, & Moll, 2005), they only gradually become able to contribute actively and independently to joint actions, relying on adults to structure the interaction during much of their first two years (Brownell, 2011).

What cognitive processes must be in place for children to be able to engage in joint action autonomously? A first key ingredient is the ability to understand how others' actions relate to one's own goals and actions (ibid). It may be that children start out with a minimal understanding of others' contributions to joint outcomes. Forming task representations that specify others' actions and the relation between one's own and others' parts allows for more flexible and more coordinated interaction. A second ingredient is the ability to inhibit one's actions, which is important for turn-taking. Toddlers who showed better inhibitory control in an individual task proved better at taking turns during joint action (Meyer, Bekkering, Haartsen, Stapel, & Hunnius, 2015). A third ingredient is being able to predict the timing of others' actions. The better toddlers were at predicting the timing of others' actions in an independent task, the less variable their actions were with respect to a partner's in a joint coordination task (ibid). Important topics for future research include the link between individual motor skills and joint action abilities, the role of scaffolding in the acquisition of individual and joint skills, and the contribution of joint action to cognitive development.

Coordination Strategies

Sometimes, we perform joint actions without having detailed representations about a co-actor or a co-actor's task – be it because actions are performed so fast that there is not enough time to form such representations or because insufficient information is available. An everyday example is a potluck dinner where everyone tries to contribute to a well-balanced meal but where, in the end, there might only be bread and dessert. This situation, in which a group of individuals needs to make decisions without knowing what others will do, is referred to as a 'Schelling game' (Clark, 1996; Schelling, 1960). Further examples are choosing numbers so that the sum matches a given target number (Roberts & Goldstone, 2011) or meeting in a large park without having agreed on an exact location. Commonly, people solve these tasks by referring to saliency (e.g. waiting by a famous monument in the park) and common knowledge (e.g. bringing their favorite dish to the potluck dinner on the assumption that everyone else expects this and will do the same; Clark, 1996).

Recently, joint coordination problems under minimal information have been investigated not only in decision-making tasks where people have to match their choices but also in situations where people perform joint actions together in real time. In contrast to the discrete and explicit response options in Schelling games, real-time interaction is often implicit in the sense that people perform actions without reflecting on what their options are. Take, for instance, a surprise birthday party where all friends want to start singing 'Happy Birthday' at the exact moment the to-be-surprised person has entered the room. This is, in fact, a difficult task because if everyone took their time starting or if everyone waited for the others to begin, the outcome would most likely be a highly uncoordinated performance. Still, people often manage to start singing together in synchrony, even in the dark. How is such synchronized action performance with minimal information about others' actions achieved?

Evidence from experimental studies suggests that, in order to make coordinated behavior without detailed representations of another's task possible, an individual can adapt her own action performance in a way that maximally supports coordination with the task partner. This has been called a coordination strategy or coordination smoother (Vesper et al., 2010). The result of strategically changing one's own behavior is that the likelihood for coordinated action is increased. One such coordination strategy is making oneself predictable (Vesper, van der Wel, Knoblich, & Sebanz, 2011), which is achieved by performing actions as constantly over time as possible, i.e. by reducing the variability of one's own actions. Given that faster actions generally tend to be less variable (Repp, 2005; Wagenmakers & Brown, 2007), making oneself predictable is sometimes achieved by speeding up, that is, by responding as fast as possible after a common event in the environment (Vesper et al., 2011; Vesper, Schmitz, Safra, Sebanz, & Knoblich, 2016). Thus, in order to start singing 'Happy Birthday' at the same time, everyone should start singing as fast as possible after the birthday celebrant has walked in, thereby reducing overall action variability.

Joint Abilities

In many joint actions, more information about others' actions is available than in the situations described in the previous section. We often consider details about our interaction partners, including their features and abilities, and we may be sensitive to the relation between our own and their actions. Several studies have demonstrated that we perceive relations between our own and others' possible actions in a particular context. These joint action affordances constitute or reflect our perception of what we can achieve together with others. For example, when deciding whether to carry an object alone or together with another person (Richardson, Marsh, & Baron, 2007), whether to hold the door open for others (Santamaria & Rosenbaum, 2011) or whether one would fit through a door frame walking next to someone (Davis, Riley, Shockley, & Cummins-Sebree, 2010), people take into account the combined abilities and anatomical characteristics of all agents involved, e.g. combined arm span, or joint distance and speed.

Joint action affordances also change flexibly depending on the characteristics of another person. When judging the weight of boxes that they would later be lifting together, participants systematically underestimated the weight, i.e. heavy boxes were judged to be lighter than they actually were (Doerrfeld, Sebanz, & Shiffrar, 2012). However, if the future co-actor wore a bandage implying a recent arm injury, participants judged the weight of the box as heavier, suggesting that people consider potential co-actors in terms of how much they can contribute to the joint action.

Representing Others' Tasks

In addition to another person's abilities and characteristics, we often have information about another's task. Many studies addressing how we include others' actions and tasks in our planning have focused on situations in which two individuals act independently next to each other. These tasks do not require coordination between people and have been designed to capture incidental, involuntary representations of others' actions and tasks. Therefore, the findings from this line of research possibly 'underestimate' what is being represented during joint action in the sense that people would actually form more detailed representations when coordination is required (see next sections on prediction and non-verbal communication).

If information about a co-actor's task is available, people have a strong tendency to represent aspects of this task, even if it is not relevant for their own performance. Experiments showed that a conflict between two action alternatives arises not only when a single person has to choose between the two alternatives, but also when two co-actors each control one of the two action alternatives, suggesting that each of them is representing the action alternative at the other's disposal (Sebanz, Knoblich, & Prinz, 2003, 2005a; Tsai, Sebanz, & Knoblich, 2011). This was first shown using the Simon task, where a spatial compatibility effect was found in bimanual and joint performance. While alternative accounts of the joint Simon effect have been proposed (Dolk, Hommel, Prinz, & Liepelt, 2013; Guagnano, Rusconi, & Umiltà, 2010), more recent studies provide clear evidence that co-actors form representations of others' tasks that allow them to anticipate when their partner will act (Atmaca, Sebanz, Prinz, & Knoblich, 2008; Böckler, Knoblich, & Sebanz, 2012; Wenke et al., 2011). This can lead to better memory for information that was relevant for one's task partner (Eskenazi, Doerrfeld, Logan, Knoblich, & Sebanz, 2013), and also manifests itself in inhibitory control processes that need to kick in when it is the other's turn to act (Sebanz, Knoblich, Prinz, & Washer, 2006; Tsai, Kuo, Hung, & Tzeng, 2008; Tsai, Kuo, Jing, Hung, & Tzeng 2006).

Do people in these minimally social situations where coordination is not required ever form more elaborate representations of the partner's task? In a picture-naming task, participants showed sensitivity to the lexical frequency of an object to be named by their co-actor, providing perhaps the strongest evidence so far that task partners tend to mentally perform each other's tasks (Baus et al., 2014). Furthermore, recent work shows that co-actors form task representations that specify the relations between their own and their partner's actions, so that, when observing others acting jointly, they find it easier to mimic the observed joint action than to act alone (Tsai et al., 2011).

How do social relations affect task co-representation? Several studies have begun to shed light on this question, showing that the degree to which people show sensitivity to their partner's task varies depending on whether the other is perceived as likable or hostile (Hommel, Colzato, & van den Wildenberg, 2009), and on whether the task partner is perceived as an in-group or out-group member (He, Lever, & Humphreys, 2011; McClung, Jentzsch, & Reicher, 2013; Müller et al., 2011). Findings also suggest that task co-representation depends on the perceived interdependency between the actors (Iani et al., 2011; Ruys & Aarts, 2010). The social nature of task co-representation is further underscored by clinical studies showing deficits in forming representations of others' tasks in neuropsychological patients with brain lesions who have deficits in mental state attribution (Humphreys & Bedford, 2011), as well as in patients with schizophrenia, who may have difficulties relating representations of self and other (Liepelt et al., 2012). Interestingly, high-functioning individuals with autism did show task co-representation effects that were similar to healthy controls (Sebanz, Knoblich, Stumpf, & Prinz, 2005b), indicating that only severe deficits in mental state attribution affect the ability to represent others' tasks.

Motor Prediction

Representing information about another person, her task or the relation of one group to another might not in itself be beneficial for joint action as the representations themselves do not bring about coordinated action. However, they can be used to make predictions about how another person's actions will unfold in the near future and, as a consequence, how one should adapt one's own actions accordingly for smooth and efficient coordination. Action prediction is especially important in fast real-time action coordination where only reacting to what another person is doing would often be too slow. For example, when trying to catch a basketball one does not just follow the ball's trajectory but also predicts the likely target location based on the thrower's action goal (e.g. near the basket) and body movements (e.g. body orientation and arm speed). What is the mechanism underlying this important ability for joint action?

Most of what we know about action prediction comes from tasks in which individuals observe what others are doing. This line of research has identi-fied common representations and processes involved in performing actions and perceiving others' actions. In particular, motor prediction or motor simu-lation involves forward models in the observer's motor system that generate predictions based on the internal motor commands that the observer would use for performing the action herself (Grush, 2004; Wilson & Knoblich, 2005; Wolpert, Doya, & Kawato, 2003). Thus, perception and action are represented in a common representational format (Prinz, 1997) that allows using the same processes underlying individual action planning for predicting others' actions. Motor simulation helps an observer in understanding others' actions (Gallese, Keysers, & Rizzolatti, 2004; Rizzolatti, Fogassi, & Gallese, 2001) and in inferring and interpreting action goals and intentions (Iacoboni et al., 2005). Moreover, expertise and familiarity with an action modulate motor pre-diction such that one's own motor system is more actively engaged in making predictions when one has frequently performed the action oneself (Aglioti, Cesari, Romani, & Urgesi, 2008; Calvo-Merino, Glaser, Grèzes, Passingham, & Haggard, 2005).

However, we cannot always see or hear our interaction partners during joint action. Is action prediction also possible without online sensory information? That is, can task representations alone trigger motor predictions about others' actions? To investigate this question, we studied performance in a coordina-tion task where co-actors did not receive online visual information about each other's actions but knew what the other's exact task was. Dyads coordinated forward jumps of different distances, with the joint goal of synchronizing their landing times (Vesper, van der Wel, Knoblich, & Sebanz, 2013; Figure 11.1). No visual or auditory feedback was given before and during the jumping so that each of them had to time their own action with respect to the predicted tim-ing of their own and the partner's actions. To illustrate, if one person's task was to jump a short distance and the other's task was to jump a large distance, they would only manage to land at the same time if at least one of them modulated their natural jump performance, e.g. by waiting longer before jumping. The results of this study showed that, indeed, participants with the relatively shorter jumps systematically adapted the time of initiating their movement (Figure 11.1C) and the height of their jumps (Figure 11.1D) depending on the specific

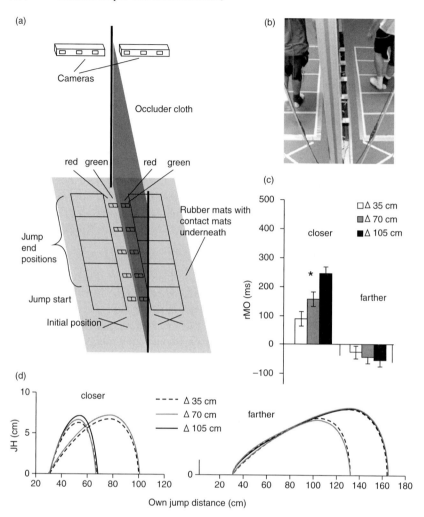

Figure 11.1 Set-up and results of the jumping task used by Vesper et al. (2013).

Notes: The illustration (A) and photograph (B) of the experimental set-up shows that participants were separated by an opaque occluder. In (C), the results of the relative movement onset rMO are shown, i.e. the difference in reaction time in trials in which co-actors jumped different distances relative to a baseline in which they jumped the same distance. The results from jump performance (D) show that only the closer person adapted her jumping height JH to the relative distance between co-actors.

Source: Taken from Vesper et al. (2013).

relation between their own and the partner's jump distance. This shows that even without perceptual information about the interaction partner her actions can be accurately predicted and integrated into one's own action planning and performance.

Importantly, prediction happens not only during an ongoing action performance but also at the planning stage, i.e. before any actual movement is initiated. EEG studies in which dyads handed over objects (Kourtis, Sebanz, & Knoblich, 2013) or were instructed to synchronously lift and clink glasses (Kourtis, Knoblich, Wozniak, & Sebanz, 2014) showed that, already during planning a joint action, motor predictions about the task partner's actions were generated. For example, participants receiving an object from another person showed motor activation preceding the giver's action onset that reflected anticipation of the giver's action. Interestingly, motor prediction even occurs in the complete absence of any movement execution, as when someone only imagines performing a joint action (Vesper, Knoblich, & Sebanz, 2014).

Besides constraining motor simulations, task representations can be useful for monitoring the accuracy of the joint performance and the progress towards the joint goal. If a person throwing a basketball knows where and how the partner should catch it, the actual outcome of the interaction can be compared to the prediction, leading to learning and future adaptations. Moreover, it is useful to immediately notice errors in others' performance to be able to compensate for them. Evidence that co-actors monitor each other's actions comes from a music study (Loehr, Kourtis, Vesper, Sebanz, & Knoblich, 2013) in which expert musicians performed a piano duet together. Crucially, during the pianists' playing some tones were experimentally modulated so that the outcome was not as expected based on their prior experience. An EEG analysis of the pianists' brain responses to such modulations showed that at an early stage of processing these were detected independently of whether the modulation occurred in their own or in the partner's playing; however, modulations that affected the overall musical outcome were later processed as being more relevant than modulations that affected only their individual part. This is consistent with evidence from an fMRI study (Radke, de Lange, Ullsperger, & de Bruijn, 2011) that found different brain activations depending on whether a performance error had consequences for only the participants themselves or also for their partner. Monitoring is also useful to update predictive models about another's actions such that, with training, joint performance can improve (Knoblich & Jordan, 2003). As a consequence, interacting with someone who is maximally similar to oneself such as one's own 'earlier self' should be best in terms of the coordination outcome. This was shown in a study in which pianists performed a musical duet together with a recording of either their own earlier playing or another's, playing most synchronously with their own musical performance (Keller, Knoblich, & Repp, 2007).

Communication through Action

We often explicitly use actions to communicate with others such as when point-ing towards a dangerous object to make another person aware of it (Knudsen & Liszkowski, 2013) or when using co-speech gestures that help clarify the ver-bal content of a message (Goldin-Meadow, 1999; Hostetter, 2011). However, even the way we perform standard, instrumental actions like handing over a cup can be used to communicate information. For instance, moving a cup very slowly while handing it to another person could convey that it has a high per-sonal value (Constable, Kritikos, & Bayliss, 2011).

In joint action, modifying the way actions are performed can be used to make the action or action goal more recognizable for a co-actor. It is known from studies on action observation that people are sensitive to information from oth-ers' action kinematics. For example, one can detect whether an observed action is cooperative or competitive (Georgiou, Becchio, Glover, & Castiello, 2007; Manera, Becchio, Cavallo, Sartori, & Castiello, 2011; Sartori, Becchio, & Castiello, 2011), where the target of an action is (Vesper & Richardson, 2014) and whether an action outcome will be successful or not (Aglioti et al., 2008). When performing actions together, this sensitivity can be further supported by exaggerating relevant information about an action. This is known as signaling and might be especially useful when others need additional information for task performance. As an example, two cyclists moving directly towards each other might prevent a collision if one of them clearly changes her path towards one side of the road. Thus, signaling allows another person to infer important information about one's own action.

Signaling in joint action may presuppose awareness of another's need for information (Pezzulo & Dindo, 2011; Pezzulo, Donnarumma, & Dindo, 2013). Satisfying this need can facilitate coordination. This was demonstrated in a study in which pairs of participants synchronously moved to different tar-gets, while only one person knew where the next targets would be (Vesper & Richardson, 2014). To facilitate coordination, the person having task knowl-edge moved with overall higher amplitude compared to individual performance and also modulated movement amplitude such that it helped disambiguate the targets. These modifications increased the amount of information contained in the action kinematics, as can be inferred from the fact that a new group of participants more accurately predicted the correct target from visual displays of the trajectories. Similar movement exaggeration has been reported in a study showing that a co-actor who knows where to jointly grasp a bottle-shaped object exaggerates her movements such that, compared to individual perfor-mance, her grasp is higher when moving to the top and lower when moving to the bottom (Sacheli, Tidoni, Pavone, Aglioti, & Candidi, 2013). Signaling has also been observed in contexts where two interaction partners both need to compensate for a lack of information about each other's actions, such as when two pianists have to coordinate their playing without receiving auditory information. In this situation, pianists may lift their fingers higher, thereby making it easier for the partner to read the timing of their actions and to play in synchrony (Goebl & Palmer, 2009).

How are Coordination Mechanisms Combined?

The previous sections introduced different coordination mechanisms and described what representations are involved. What are the links between these different mechanisms? How do they interact? Intuitively, people do not always use all coordination mechanisms at the same time but which mechanism(s) most strongly support coordination will change from context to context. As stressed throughout this chapter, the use of coordination mechanisms depends on the availability of information for forming particular representations. For instance, if the partner's task is not known and no perceptual information about her actions is available, it will be difficult to make accurate motor predictions about her behavior, and the best strategy is therefore to make oneself predictable.

A useful way to study the interactions of different coordination mechanisms is to look at asymmetrical joint actions. Asymmetries can arise if co-actors have different tasks, take on different roles or receive different types or amounts of perceptual information. Certain objects (e.g. a seesaw) or situations (e.g. a conductor and an orchestra) also imply asymmetries. In any case, asymmetries may afford people to employ different coordination mechanisms that complement each other. For example, someone carrying a heavy box might just walk straight towards a door and simply expect that another person adapts her actions cooperatively by opening it at the most suitable time. In this case, one person performs her action in a highly predictable way and the other one adapts to this by making predictions about the specific timing of that action.

In some cases, co-actors' tasks might explicitly involve performing different actions that complement each other so that only their combined effort will result in successful joint action (e.g. Bosga & Meulenbroek, 2007; Knoblich & Jordan, 2003; Mottet, Guiard, Ferrand, & Bootsma, 2001). Such cases often demand that co-actors take each other's actions into account and, if necessary, adapt how they perform their own actions to how others perform their actions. For example, in the jumping study described earlier (Vesper et al., 2013; Figure 11.1), the co-actor with the shorter (i.e. relatively easier) jump engages in motor simulation to adapt her movement to the partner's predicted timing, whereas the one with the longer (i.e. the relatively more difficult) jump will generally speed up, consistent with a coordination strategy to make oneself predictable. Furthermore, in the joint target task described above (Vesper & Richardson, 2014), only the person who has information about the upcoming target for a joint movement will engage in signaling while the other will track and possibly predict her actions.

In other cases, co-actors change their own action performance to make otherwise equal actions dissimilar if this is beneficial for coordination. These emergent asymmetries can be seen as cases of role distribution. For example, when acting together in a narrow shared workspace, it might be beneficial for smooth synchronous (Richardson, Harrison, May, Kallen, & Schmidt, 2011) and sequential joint action performance (Vesper, Soutschek, & Schubö, 2009) if at least one person changes her own movement path to prevent collisions with another person's limbs. Similarly, asymmetries in how co-actors perform their tasks can serve to increase efficiency in a joint action, as when people distribute a shared search space among each other to ensure that no part of it is repeatedly searched (Brennan, Chen, Dickinson, Neider, & Zelinsky, 2008). These behaviors could be interpreted as one task partner making herself predictable (i.e. performing her actions in the most efficient way) and the other changing her movements communicatively (i.e. exaggerating her actions to clearly give way).

Differences in perceptual information available to individuals can also influence the use of coordination mechanisms. For instance, modulating who can hear whom in a rhythmic tapping task (Konvalinka, Vuust, Roepstorff, & Frith, 2010) will designate one person as the 'leader' who does not adapt and one a 'follower' who modulates her current action based on the perceptual feedback from the other's actions. In contrast, having symmetric feedback will in the same task make both people adapt to each other, leading to a phenomenon referred to as hyper-following (ibid). Asymmetries can also arise based on differences in individuals' abilities and characteristics, such that people might be better or worse in predicting others' actions (Pecenka & Keller, 2011), reading others' minds (Krych-Appelbaum et al., 2007) or performing at a given tempo (Loehr & Palmer, 2011). Finally, it is important to consider asymmetries when one co-actor is not a human agent but a robot (see Box 11.3).

Summary

This chapter reviewed cognitive mechanisms underlying joint action performance. While there is ongoing debate about what constitutes joint action, it has been possible to pin down specific cognitive mechanisms that are involved when coordinating one's own actions with those of others. These mechanisms span from general coordination strategies in which one modulates one's own action performance in order to make oneself more

Box 11.3 Human–robot interaction

Joint actions are not always performed by humans alone; increasingly often people act together with artificial agents. The fast technological developments in the field of robotics create the possibility that robots will take over many of our everyday tasks, some of which require close interaction between machines and human users. To prevent potential dangers, to make human–robot interaction efficient and enjoyable, and to minimize the time required to train unfamiliar users, a useful approach is to take human behavior as a model for robot design (Hoffman & Ju, 2014). For example, it has been shown that people form representations of a robot's actions only if they believe the robot has been designed in a biologically inspired, human-like way (Stenzel et al., 2012).

Following this human-oriented approach, a variety of successful attempts have been made to implement the coordination mechanisms underlying human joint action into human–robot interaction scenarios. For instance, providing robots with internal forward and inverse models of their own and others' actions allows them to make predictions about a human user's action goals and the respective timing (Bicho, Erlhagen, Louro, & Costa e Silva, 2011). This predictive process can be supported by implementing signaling into a robot's movements (Dragan & Srinivasa, 2013; Dragan, Lee, & Srinivasa, 2013; Pezzulo, Donnarumma, & Dindo, 2013), thereby facilitating the human user in understanding where the robot will move to. Making clear and predictable movements not only allows efficient coordination but also reduces the risk that the human user collides with a robot limb. Finally, research on artificial language processing and production allows increasingly natural interactions with artificial agents that can communicate verbally or with gestures (Kröger, Kopp, & Lowit, 2010; Steels, 2003).

Besides re-creating human joint actions with artificial agents, robots might have additional benefits as interaction partners. In particular, they might inspire new ways of performing actions. One example is the creative process during improvisation in jazz music. A robot impersonating many different styles could help a musician give up often-used stylistic patterns with the effect that something new can be created that might not have emerged individually (Wilf, 2013). Moreover, robots could have particular advantages over humans in clinical applications, e.g. they are more easily accepted as interaction partners by children with autism spectrum disorders (Francois, Powell, & Dautenhahn, 2009).

predictable, to representing others' abilities and tasks in various levels of detail, and from making motor predictions about own and others' future action to modulating actions in order to communicate additional information to co-actors.

Generally, investigating joint action is an important scientific endeavor for cognitive neuroscience as it complements the study of social perception and social cognition by addressing what it is that we do when we fold sheets, cook meals or create music together.

References

Aglioti, S. M., Cesari, P., Romani, M., & Urgesi, C. (2008). Action anticipation and motor resonance in elite basketball players. *Nature Neuroscience*, 11(9), 1109–1116.

Atmaca, S., Sebanz, N., Prinz, W., & Knoblich, G. (2008). Action co-representation: The joint SNARC effect. *Social Neuroscience*, 3(3–4), 410–420.

Barresi, J., & Moore, C. (1996). Intentional relations and social understanding. *Behavioral and Brain Sciences*, 19, 107–154.

Baus, C., Sebanz, N., de la Fuente, V., Branzi, F. M., Martin, C., & Costa, A. (2014). On predicting others' words: Electrophysiological evidence of prediction in speech production. *Cognition*, 133, 395–407.

Bicho, E., Erlhagen, W., Louro, L., & Costa e Silva, E. (2011). Neuro-cognitive mechanisms of decision making in joint action: A human–robot interaction study. *Human Movement Science*, 30(5), 846–868.

Böckler, A., Knoblich, G., & Sebanz, N. (2012). Effects of a coactor's focus of attention on task performance. *Journal of Experimental Psychology: Human Perception and Performance*, 38(6), 1404–1415.

Bosga, J., & Meulenbroek, R. G. J. (2007). Joint-action coordination of redundant force contributions in a virtual lifting task. *Motor Control*, 11, 235–258.

Bratman, M. E. (1992). Shared cooperative activity. *Philosophical Review*, 101, 327–341.

(2009). Modest sociality and the distinctiveness of intention. *Philosophical Studies*, 114(1), 149–165.

Brennan, S. E. (2005). How conversation is shaped by visual and spoken evidence. In J. Trueswell & M. Tanenhaus (Eds.), *Approaches to studying world-situated language use: Bridging the language-as-product and language-as-action traditions*. Cambridge: MIT Press, 95–129.

Brennan, S. E., Chen, X., Dickinson, C. A., Neider, M. B., & Zelinsky, G. J. (2008). Coordinating cognition: The costs and benefits of shared gaze during collaborative search. *Cognition*, 106, 1465–1477.

Brownell, C. A. (2011). Early developments in joint action. *Review of Philosophy and Psychology*, 2, 193–211.

Butterfill, S. (2012). Joint action and development. *Philosophical Quarterly*, 62(246), 23–47.

Calvo-Merino, B., Glaser, D., Grèzes, J., Passingham, R., & Haggard, P. (2005). Action observation and acquired motor skills: An fMRI study with expert dancers. *Cerebral Cortex*, 15, 1243–1249.

Carpenter, M. (2009). Just how joint is joint action in infancy? *Topics in Cognitive Science*, 1(2), 380–392.

Clark, H. H. (1996). *Using language*. Cambridge: Cambridge University Press.

Clark, H. H., & Krych, M. A. (2004). Speaking while monitoring addressees for understanding. *Journal of Memory and Language*, 50, 62–81.

Constable, M. D., Kritikos, A., & Bayliss, A. P. (2011). Grasping the concept of personal property. *Cognition*, 119(3), 430–437.

Cummins, F., Li, C., & Wang, B. (2013). Coupling among speakers during synchronous speaking in English and Mandarin. *Journal of Phonetics*, 41(6), 432–441.

Davis, T., Riley, M., Shockley, K., & Cummins-Sebree, S. (2010). Perceiving affordances for joint actions. *Perception*, 39(12), 1624–1644.

Doerrfeld, A., Sebanz, N., & Shiffrar, M. (2012). Expecting to lift a box together makes the load look lighter. *Psychological Research*, 76, 467–475.

Dolk, T., Hommel, B., Prinz, W., & Liepelt, R. (2013). The (not so) social Simon effect: A referential coding account. *Journal of Experimental Psychology: Human Perception and Performance*, 39(5), 1248–1260.

Dragan, A., Lee, K., & Srinivasa, S. (2013). Legibility and predictability of robot motion. In *8th ACM/IEEE International Conference on Human–Robot Interaction (HRI)*. www.ri.cmu.edu/pub_files/2013/3/legiilitypredictabilityIEEE.pdf.

Dragan, A., & Srinivasa, S. (2013). Generating legible motion. *Proceedings of Robotics: Science and Systems*. www.ri.cmu.edu/pub_ files/2013/6/legibility_analysis.pdf.

Enfield, N. J. (2013). *Relationship thinking: Agency, enchrony, and human sociality*. New York: Oxford University Press.

Eskenazi, T., Doerrfeld, A., Logan, G. D., Knoblich, G., & Sebanz, N. (2013). Your words are my words: Effects of acting together on encoding. *Quarterly Journal of Experimental Psychology*, 66, 1026–1034.

Francois, D., Powell, S., & Dautenhahn, K. (2009). A long-term study of children with autism playing with a robotic pet: Taking inspirations from non-directive play therapy to encourage children's proactivity and initiative-taking. *Interaction Studies*, 10(3), 324–373.

Gallese, V., Keysers, C., & Rizzolatti, G. (2004). A unifying view of the basis of social cognition. *Trends in Cognitive Sciences*, 8(9), 396–403.

Georgiou, I., Becchio, C., Glover, S., & Castiello, U. (2007). Different action patterns for cooperative and competitive behaviour. *Cognition*, 102, 415–433.

Gilbert, M. (1992). *On social facts*. Princeton, NJ: Princeton University Press.
  (2006). Rationality in collective action. *Philosophy of the Social Sciences*, 36(1), 3–17.

Goebl, W., & Palmer, C. (2009). Synchronization of timing and motion among performing musicians. *Music Perception*, 26(5), 427–438.

Goldin-Meadow, S. (1999). The role of gesture in communication and thinking. *Trends in Cognitive Sciences*, 3(11), 419–429.

Grush, R. (2004). The emulation theory of representation: Motor control, imagery, and perception. *Behavioral and Brain Sciences*, 27, 377–442.

Guagnano, D., Rusconi, E., & Umiltà, C. A. (2010). Sharing a task or sharing space? On the effect of the confederate in action coding in a detection task. *Cognition*, 114(3), 348–355.

He, X., Lever, A. G., & Humphreys, G. W. (2011). Interpersonal memory-based guidance of attention is reduced for ingroup members. *Experimental Brain Research*, 211(3), 429–438.

Hoffman, G., & Ju, W. (2014). Designing robots with movement in mind. *Journal of Human–Robot Interaction*, 1(1), 78–95.

Hommel, B., Colzato, L. S., & van den Wildenberg, W. P. M. (2009). How social are task representations? *Psychological Science*, 20, 794–798.

Hostetter, A. B. (2011). When do gestures communicate? A meta-analysis. *Psychological Bulletin*, 137(2), 297–315.

Humphreys, G. W., & Bedford, J. (2011). The relations between joint action and theory of mind: A neuropsychological analysis. *Experimental Brain Research*, 211, 357–369.

Iacoboni, M., Molnar-Szakacs, I., Gallese, V., Buccino, G., Mazziotta, J. C., & Rizzolatti, G. (2005). Grasping the intentions of others with one's own mirror neuron system. *PLoS Biology*, 3(3), 529–535.

Iani, C., Anelli, F., Nicoletti, R., Arcuri, L., & Rubichi, S. (2011). The role of group membership on the modulation of joint action. *Experimental Brain Research*, 211, 439–445.

Keller, P. E., Knoblich, G., & Repp, B. H. (2007). Pianists duet better when they play with themselves: On the possible role of action simulation in synchronization. *Consciousness and Cognition*, 16, 102–111.

Knoblich, G., & Jordan, J. S. (2003). Action coordination in groups and individuals: Learning anticipatory control. *Journal of Experimental Psychology: Learning, Memory, and Cognition*, 29(5), 1006–1016.

Knudsen, B., & Liszkowski, U. (2013). One-year-olds warn others about negative action outcomes. *Journal of Cognition and Development*, 14(3), 424–436.

Konvalinka, I., Vuust, P., Roepstorff, A., & Frith, C. D. (2010). Follow you, follow me: Continuous mutual prediction and adaptation in joint tapping. *Quarterly Journal of Experimental Psychology*, 63(11), 2220–2230.

Kourtis, D., Knoblich, G., Wozniak, M., & Sebanz, N. (2014). Attention allocation and task representation during joint action planning. *Journal of Cognitive Neuroscience*, 26(10), 2275–2286.

Kourtis, D., Sebanz, N., & Knoblich, G. (2013). Predictive representation of other people's actions in joint action planning: An EEG study. *Social Neuroscience*, 8, 31–42.

Kröger, B. J., Kopp, S., & Lowit, A. (2010). A model for production, perception, and acquisition of actions in face-to-face communication. *Cognitive Processing*, 11, 187–205.

Krych-Appelbaum, M., Law, J. B., Jones, D., Barnacz, A., Johnson, A., & Keenan, J. P. (2007). 'I think I know what you mean': The role of theory of mind in collaborative communication. *Interaction Studies*, 8(2), 267–280.

Liepelt, R., Schneider, J. C., Aichert, D. S., Wöstmann, N., Dehning, S., et al. (2012). Action blind: Disturbed self–other integration in schizophrenia. *Neuropsychologia*, 50, 3775–3780.

Loehr, J., Kourtis, D., Vesper, C., Sebanz, N., & Knoblich, G. (2013). Monitoring individual and joint action outcomes in duet music performance. *Journal of Cognitive Neuroscience*, 25(7), 1049–1061.

Loehr, J. D., & Palmer, C. (2011). Temporal coordination between performing musicians. *Quarterly Journal of Experimental Psychology*, 64(11), 2153–2167.

Manera, V., Becchio, C., Cavallo, A., Sartori, L., & Castiello, U. (2011). Cooperation or competition? Discriminating between social intentions by observing prehensile movements. *Experimental Brain Research*, 211, 547–556.

Marsh, K. L., Johnston, L., Richardson, M. J., & Schmidt, R. C. (2009). Toward a radically embodied, embedded social psychology. *European Journal of Social Psychology*, 39, 1217–1225.

McClung, J. S., Jentzsch, I., & Reich, S. D. (2013). Group membership affects spontaneous mental representation: Failure to represent the out-group in a joint action task. *PLoS ONE*, 8(11): e79178.

Meyer, M., Bekkering, H., Haartsen, R., Stapel, J. C., & Hunnius, S. (2015). The role of action prediction and inhibitory control for joint action coordination in toddlers. *Journal of Experimental Child Psychology*, 139, 203–220.

Mottet, D., Guiard, Y., Ferrand, T., & Bootsma, R. J. (2001). Two-handed performance of a rhythmical Fitts task by individuals and dyads. *Journal of Experimental Psychology: Human Perception and Performance*, 27(6), 1275–1286.

Müller, B. C. N., Kühn, S., van Baaren, R. B., Dotsch, R., Brass, M., & Dijksterhuis, A. (2011). Perspective taking eliminates differences in co-representation of out-group members' actions. *Experimental Brain Research*, 211, 423–428.

Pecenka, N., & Keller, P. (2011). The role of temporal prediction abilities in interpersonal sensorimotor synchronization. *Experimental Brain Research*, 211, 505–515.

Pezzulo, G., & Dindo, H. (2011). What should I do next? Using shared representations to solve interaction problems. *Experimental Brain Research*, 211, 613–630.

Pezzulo, G., Donnarumma, F., & Dindo, H. (2013). Human sensorimotor communication: A theory of signaling in online social interactions. *PLoS One*, 8(11), e79876.

Pickering, M. J., & Garrod, S. (2013). An integrated theory of language production and comprehension. *Behavioral and Brain Sciences*, 36, 329–347.

Prinz, W. (1997). Perception and action planning. *European Journal of Cognitive Psychology*, 9(2), 129–154.

Radke, S., de Lange, F., Ullsperger, M., & de Bruijn, E. (2011). Mistakes that affect others: An fMRI study on processing of own errors in a social context. *Experimental Brain Research*, 211, 405–413.

Reddy, V. (2008). *How infants know minds*. Cambridge, MA: Harvard University Press.

Repp, B. H. (2005). Sensorimotor synchronization: A review of the tapping literature. *Psychonomic Bulletin & Review*, 12(6), 969–992.

Richardson, M. J., Harrison, S. J., May, R., Kallen, R. W., & Schmidt, R. C. (2011). Self-organized complementary coordination: Dynamics of an interpersonal collision-avoidance task. *BIO Web of Conferences*, 1, 00075.

Richardson, M. J., Marsh, K. L., & Baron, R. M. (2007). Judging and actualizing intrapersonal and interpersonal affordances. *Journal of Experimental Psychology: Human Perception and Performance*, 33(4), 845–859.

Rizzolatti, G., Fogassi, L., & Gallese, V. (2001). Neurophysiological mechanisms underlying the understanding and imitation of action. *Nature*, 2, 661–670.

Roberts, M. E., & Goldstone, R. L. (2011). Adaptive group coordination and role differentiation. *PLoS One*, 6(7), e22377.

Ruys, K. I., & Aarts, H. (2010). When competition merges people's behavior: Interdependency activates shared action representations. *Journal of Experimental Social Psychology*, 46, 1130–1133.

Sacheli, L., Tidoni, E., Pavone, E., Aglioti, S., & Candidi, M. (2013). Kinematics fingerprints of leader and follower role-taking during cooperative joint actions. *Experimental Brain Research*, 226(4), 473–486.

Santamaria, J. P., & Rosenbaum, D. A. (2011). Etiquette and effort: Holding doors for others. *Psychological Science*, 22(5), 584–588.

Sartori, L., Becchio, C., & Castiello, U. (2011). Cues to intention: The role of movement information. *Cognition*, 119, 242–252.

Schelling, T. C. (1960). *The strategy of conflict*. Cambridge, MA: Harvard University Press.

Schmidt, R., Fitzpatrick, P., Caron, R., & Mergeche, J. (2011). Understanding social motor coordination. *Human Movement Science*, 30, 834–845.

Schmidt, R. C., & Richardson, M. J. (2008). Dynamics of interpersonal coordination. In A. Fuchs & V. K. Jirsa (Eds.), *Coordination: Neural, behavioral and social dynamics*. Berlin: Springer, 281–308.

Sebanz, N., Knoblich, G., & Prinz, W. (2003). Representing others' actions: Just like one's own? *Cognition*, 88, B11–B21.

Sebanz, N., Knoblich, G., Prinz, W., & Wascher, E. (2006). Twin peaks: An ERP study of action planning and control in coacting individuals. *Journal of Cognitive Neuroscience*, 18(5), 859–870.

Sebanz, N., Knoblich, G., Stumpf, L., & Prinz, W. (2005b). Far from action blind: Representation of others' actions in individuals with autism. *Cognitive Neuropsychology*, 22, 433–454.

Sebanz, N. & Prinz, W. (2005a). How two share a task: Corepresenting stimulus–response mappings. *Journal of Experimental Psychology: Human Perception and Performance*, 31(6), 1234–1246.

Steels, L. (2003). Evolving grounded communication for robots. *Trends in Cognitive Sciences*, 7(7), 308–312.

Stenzel, A., Chinellato, E., Bou, M. A. T., del Pobil, Á. P., Lappe, M., & Liepelt, R. (2012). When humanoid robots become human-like interaction partners: Corepresentation of robotic actions. *Journal of Experimental Psychology: Human Perception and Performance*, 38(5), 1073–1077.

Stern, D. N. (2002). *The first relationship: Infant and mother*. Cambridge, MA: Harvard University Press.

Tollefsen, D. (2005). Let's pretend! Children and joint action. *Philosophy of the Social Sciences*, 35, 75–97.

Tomasello, M., Carpenter, M., Call, J., Behne, T., & Moll, H. (2005). Understanding and sharing intentions: The origins of cultural cognition. *Behavioral and Brain Sciences*, 28, 675–735.

Trevarthen, C. (1979). Communication and cooperation in early infancy: A description of primary intersubjectivity. In M. Bullowa (Ed.), *Before speech*. Cambridge: Cambridge University Press, 321–343.

Tsai, C.-C., Kuo, W.-J., Hung, D. L., & Tzeng, O. J. L. (2008). Action co-representation is tuned to other humans. *Journal of Cognitive Neuroscience*, 20(11), 2015–2024.

Tsai, J. C.-C., Kuo, W.-J., Jing, J.-T., Hung, D. L., & Tzeng, O. J.-L. (2006). A common coding framework in self–other interaction: Evidence from joint action task. *Experimental Brain Research*, 175, 353–362.

Tsai, J. C.-C., Sebanz, N., & Knoblich, G. (2011). The GROOP effect: Groups mimic group actions. *Cognition*, 118, 135–140.

Vesper, C., Butterfill, S., Knoblich, G., & Sebanz, N. (2010). A minimal architecture for joint action. *Neural Networks*, 23(8–9), 998–1003.

Vesper, C., Knoblich, G., & Sebanz, N. (2014). Our actions in my mind: Motor imagery of joint action. *Neuropsychologia*, 55, 115–121.

Vesper, C., & Richardson, M. J. (2014). Strategic communication and behavioral coupling in asymmetric joint action. *Experimental Brain Research*, 232(9), 2945–2956.

Vesper, C., Schmitz, L., Safra, L., Sebanz, N., & Knoblich, G. (2016). The role of shared visual information for joint action coordination. *Cognition*, 153, 118–123.

Vesper, C., Soutschek, A., & Schubö, A. (2009). Motion coordination affects movement parameters in a joint pick-and-place task. *Quarterly Journal of Experimental Psychology*, 62(12), 2418–2432.

Vesper, C., van der Wel, R., Knoblich, G., & Sebanz, N. (2011). Making oneself predictable: Reduced temporal variability facilitates joint action coordination. *Experimental Brain Research*, 211, 517–530.

Vesper, C., van der Wel, R. P., Knoblich, G., & Sebanz, N. (2013b). Are you ready to jump? Predictive mechanisms in interpersonal coordination. *Journal of Experimental Psychology: Human Perception and Performance*, 39(1), 48–61.

Wagenmakers, E.-J., & Brown, S. (2007). On the linear relation between the mean and the standard deviation of a response time distribution. *Psychological Review*, 114(3), 830–841.

Wenke, D., Atmaca, S., Holländer, A., Liepelt, R., Baess, P., & Prinz, W. (2011). What is shared in joint action? Issues of co-representation, response conflict, and agent identification. *Review of Philosophy and Psychology*, 2(2), 147–172.

Wilf, E. (2013). Toward an anthropology of computer-mediated, algorithmic forms of sociality. *Current Anthropology*, 54(6), 716–739.

Wilson, M., & Knoblich, G. (2005). The case for motor involvement in perceiving conspecifics. *Psychological Bulletin*, 131(3), 460–473.

Wolpert, D. M., Doya, K., & Kawato, M. (2003). A unifying computational framework for motor control and interaction. *Philosophical Transactions of the Royal Society of London B: Biological Sciences*, 358, 593–602.

12   Joint Perception

Jorina von Zimmermann and Daniel C. Richardson

Abstract

Perception is solitary. After all, it is the individual alone who feels, hears, tastes, smells and sees. Yet, while the phenomenology of engaging with the world through our senses is restricted to subjective sensations, those sensations are often experienced in a social context. Do social forces change how an individual interacts with the environment and responds to incoming information? We present and discuss a recently discovered phenomenon: people's eye movements and focus of attention change with their belief that they are looking at objects alone or together with somebody else. Research on 'joint perception' provides evidence for the pervasive effect of social context, influencing psychological processes from cognition to low-level perception.

Jean-Paul Sartre (1943) is sat in a park. One of the 'objects' he pays attention to is another man, who stands a couple of metres away from him. He starts thinking about that man and realizes that the man is not like the other objects in the environment. He attributes mental states to the man; he ascribes conscious awareness to him. The man experiences the same world that Sartre observes, but he does so on his own terms. Spatial perception, objects in the environment, the colour of the lawn, they are all part of Sartre's universe, but they are also part of the other man's universe. If the man's universe and his universe are the same, Sartre cannot know. However, what he does know is that with the realization that the man, the object, is also a subject, something has changed about the way Sartre looks at his surroundings: '[S]uddenly an object has appeared which has stolen the world from me. ... The appearance of the Other in the world corresponds ... to a fixed sliding of the whole universe, to a decentralization of the world which undermines the centralization which I am simultaneously effecting' (Sartre, 1958, p. 313). Sartre's realization that somebody else is looking, causes him to look at the world differently. The appearance of another subject, with the ability to perceive the world, fundamentally changes Sartre's own perception. Part of the phenomenon Sartre describes has recently received scientific attention. In a series of 'joint perception' studies, researchers found that the knowledge that somebody else is looking at the same stimulus as themselves changed participants' eye movements and focus of attention (Richardson et al., 2012).

Mostly when people think about perception they think about it in individual terms. The phenomenology of perceiving something is a very private and subjective experience that cannot be fully comprehended from an external perspective (Nagel, 1974). The senses exist to allow individuals to experience the world and learn from it. Accordingly, researchers have predominantly studied individual cognition and perception in isolation and removed from any social cues. However, cognition in the real world often takes place in a social context. The real or imagined presence of other people is a ubiquitous influence on human behaviour, emotion and cognition (Allport, 1954). Perceptual processes are not an exception to this and many researchers have adopted the view that cognition is socially situated and needs to be studied accordingly (Smith & Semin, 2007). Biological, cognitive and social scientists have shown that the brain is extremely sensitive to social information (Cacioppo, Berntson, & Decety, 2010). The social aspects of human life do not only manifest themselves in higher-order processes such as language, reasoning or decision making, but are at work in neural, hormonal, cellular and genetic mechanisms (Cacioppo & Cacioppo, 2013).

From the day we are born, we attend to social cues in our environment (Senju & Johnson, 2009). Since we are restricted in our possibilities to experience the world when we are young, we make use of the people around us to learn and pay attention to what might be relevant (Baldwin, 1995; Striano & Reid, 2006). From the very beginning, infants are fascinated by eyes and very quickly come to find that those two oval shapes can be used to access information, to learn the names for objects in the world and to understand other minds (Frischen, Bayliss, & Tipper, 2007). By following the eye gaze of caregivers, infants direct their attention to objects in the environment to learn about the physical world, but simultaneously they also develop social cognition through the mechanisms of joint attention (Shepherd, 2010; Striano & Reid, 2006).

As adults, we continue to be highly sensitive to the gaze of others. Direct eye contact with another is a means to signal attraction (Mason, Tatkow, & Macrae, 2005), establish dominance (Dovidio & Elyson, 1982) and to cue an observer's attention (Kuhn, Tatler, & Cole, 2009). Similarly, when we see other people looking in a particular direction, this serves as a powerful cue to direct our own visual attention (Frischen et al., 2007). In gaze-cueing experiments, however, the participant is looking at the face of another person. Face-to-face contact is perhaps the most immediate and powerful way to experience social context, but it is not the only way that it can arise. Experiments that show participants the face of another person conflate the direct response to a social stimulus with the effect of the presence of another.

We developed the joint perception paradigm to investigate the effects of a *minimal* social context. While we tracked their gaze, participants looked at images in the belief that they were looking alone, as in a typical lab experiment, or with the belief that another person was currently looking at the same stimuli. In these studies, participants did not see each other or interact in any way. This paradigm contrasts with work on gaze coordination, gaze following and the effects of eye contact, in which two people can see each other or interact in some way. Our work draws upon the literature of joint action and coordinated behaviour, which we briefly review here to set the stage for our results.

Acting Together

Human beings are experts at acting together and we can observe successful human interaction every day and everywhere. However, the sensorimotor foundations of social interaction often go unnoticed. Cognitive scientists have started to answer the question of how social structures are manifested. They have begun to study how the perceptual, motor and cognitive activities of two or more individuals become organized into coherently coordinated action (Galantucci & Sebanz, 2009).

As described in Chapter 11, joint action can be defined as any form of social interaction that brings about a change in the environment, due to spatially and temporally coordinated action of two or more individuals (Sebanz, Bekkering, & Knoblich, 2006). Accordingly, joint action studies have looked at the conditions under which joint action emerges, what kind of patterns of behaviour are generated, and how it serves as a basis for social connectedness (Marsh, Richardson, & Schmidt, 2009). These studies have brought forward fascinating patterns of human behaviour and interaction: For example, individuals form shared representations of tasks, even when it would be more effective to ignore one another (Sebanz et al., 2006; see Vesper & Sebanz, this volume, Chapter 11). In the standard version of a spatial compatibility task, participants have to press a left or right button to respond to a stimulus that occurs in a spatial dimension, left or right. In spite of its irrelevance to the task, the spatial location of the stimulus influences reaction times. Participants are slower in responding to stimuli with an incongruent spatial cue.

In the joint action version of the task, two participants are given one response button each. The effect of stimulus location on reaction times should disappear when the task is divided between two people, since the spatial dimension ceases to be important when each individual only needs to attend to one button. Surprisingly, this is not what researchers found in a number of experiments. In the joint condition, the same results as in the individual condition were observed. The congruence or incongruence of the spatial cue paired with the stimulus influences individuals' reaction times during a joint task in spite of separate responsibilities. This suggests that people represent the actions at another person's command as if they were at their own command (Böckler, Knoblich, & Sebanz, 2012; Knoblich & Sebanz, 2006; also see Vesper & Sebanz, this volume, Chapter 11). This means that even when people are formally acting alone, their performance is shaped by others' actions (Atmaca, Sebanz, & Knoblich, 2011).

More evidence for people's inclination to coordinate with others can be found in the literature on interpersonal coordination and behavioural synchrony (see next chapter). Researchers have shown that people temporally coordinate with each other's movements when swinging a pendulum-like stick with a weight at the end (Richardson, Marsh, & Schmidt, 2005), or when they are rocking in a chair (Richardson, Marsh, Isenhower, Goodman, & Schmidt, 2007b). They do so even when coordination is made difficult through a manipulation of the devices used in the coordination task, providing additional support to the idea that individuals strive to be a social unit (Marsh et al., 2009). With ease individuals respond to the movements of an interaction partner and self-organize into an oscillatory system. The social consequences of bodily synchrony are manifold and closely related to those evoked by mimicry (see chapters in Part II of this volume for more detail). They range from enhanced rapport and liking (Miles, Nind, & Macrae, 2009) to increased cooperation (Valdesolo, Ouyang, & DeSteno, 2010; Wiltermuth & Heath, 2009), but can also lead to destructive behaviour and obedience (Wiltermuth, 2012a, 2012b).

In the experiments described, participants are given a task to accomplish, whether it is to classify stimuli or engage in some behaviour such as walking or rocking. The mere presence of a co-acting participant appears to engender coordination in cognitive representations or motor actions. Our joint perception experiments attempted to extend this phenomenon to cases where participants were not performing a task together and could not see each other or directly interact. Their only behaviour was to move their eyes, but they did so out of sight of each other. We hypothesized that, even in this case, participants would respond to the minimal social context of believing that they shared a stimulus with another person. Before we examine the effects of *minimal* social context, we review the ways in which the presence and the sight of other people influence cognition and perception.

Perception in a Social Context

Eyes are inherently social. Before we can engage in any form of joint motor activity, before we can use language, have developed attitudes or explicitly share experiences and memories, we use our eyes and the eyes of others for communication, for retrieving information, and for expressing social affinities (Tomasello, Carpenter, Call, Behne, & Moll, 2005). The human visual system can detect detailed information from only a small region of the visual field, about 2° (Levi, Klein, & Aitsebaomo, 1985). However, by making use not only of their own visual system but also of the eyes of those around them, humans are able to exploit each other's visual systems by being attentive to where conspecifics are looking. Indeed, there is evidence that the white of the sclera in social mammals such as ourselves has evolved so that our gaze direction can be easily perceived by conspecifics (Kobayahsi & Kohshima, 1997). Social attention, as the cognitive process underlying the exploitation of another's visual system, enables humans to learn from others about the environment (Richardson & Gobel, 2015). Like shiner fish (see Box 12.1), human beings exploit each other to perceive the world around them.

Box 12.1 When individuals become a group

Life in a group can compensate for the shortcomings of an individual. For example, individual shiner fish do not have the sensory ability to locate dark areas of water, which provide protection from predators. But the simple mechanics of herd behaviour can overcome this limitation. If individual fish in a shoal slow down whenever they swim into darker water and those in lighter water speed up, then the shoal will turn towards darker areas of water and stay there. Through their local interactions with each other, a sensory ability emerges in the group that is not present in the individual (Berdahl, Torney, Ioannou, Faria, & Couzin, 2013).

Synchronized group behaviour requires that individuals are connected, allowing them to function in the absence of a centralized controller (Couzin, 2007). This convergent social behaviour happens in animals as well as in humans: *herding* refers to the process through which the thoughts and behaviours of individuals become aligned to create coordination through local interactions (Raafat, Chater, & Frith, 2009). The behaviour of the group, however, is not simply the outcome of combined individual behavioural patterns, but a group, herd, flock or swarm can be interpreted as a collective mind, an information-processing system in its own right (Goldstone & Gureckis, 2009; Gureckis & Goldstone, 2006). Through the interaction of many individuals, adaptive, problem-solving structures emerge, which an individual alone could not produce (Gureckis & Goldstone, 2006). It seems therefore very likely that group action will have an effect on the cognitive and perceptual mechanisms typically studied by cognitive scientists. Like shiner fish, human beings use the people around them as cues for their own perception. Members of a group will coordinate their visual attention and shape each other's perception, acting in ways very different from solitary perceivers.

Studies concerned with social influence and conformity have taught us a lot about how our visual perception is shaped by the presence of other people. As early as the 1930s, Muzafer Sherif used a phenomenon called the autokinetic effect to study how people use other people as a source of information when they make judgements under ambiguous circumstances (Sherif, 1937). In his study, Sherif seated individual participants in a dark room and asked them to focus on a dot of light 15 feet away. He then repeatedly wanted to know from his participants how much they thought the light moved in inches. The interesting thing of course is that the light was not moving at all, but all participants were able to arrive at a stable estimate over time. This estimate was entirely different for every person. In the second phase of the experiment, Sherif then created participant groups of three and told them to say their judgements out loud. Although the autokinetic effect is experienced differently by every person, people reached a common estimate and every member of the small group conformed to that estimate. In contrast to studies like the Asch line studies (1951), in which people conformed to social norms to avoid social stigma, people in Sherif's experiment readily accepted other people's judgements as correct. From the experimental data, we cannot conclude that the individuals' actual perception of the seemingly moving dot of light was changed through the presence of others, but Sherif's experiment clearly suggests that the interpretation of the incoming sensory information was altered.

For perception to be influenced by others, it is not necessarily a requirement that people engage in the same task. A number of studies have shown that the mere presence of another person changes an individual's perception of the physical world. One study, for example, showed that the geographical slant of a hill is perceived as less steep whenever a supportive other was imagined or actually present, suggesting that social support lightens an individual's load when facing a physical challenge (Schnall, Harber, Stefanucci, & Proffitt, 2008). Similarly, participants in a series of experiments in which they had to judge the weight of boxes while expecting to either lift the box alone, together with a healthy co-actor or together with an injured co-actor, perceived the box as lighter when they intended to lift it up with a non-injured co-actor (Doerrfeld, Sebanz, & Shiffrar, 2012). Taken together, these studies provide evidence for the idea that how we see the world and how we judge the objects contained in it, hugely depends on context and who is part of that context. While actual physical properties of objects are most likely taken into account, human perception is very susceptible to social factors, which shape how we process information about the environment and the properties of objects (ibid).

The presence of others influences not just how we interpret the world, but also where we look (Gallup, Chong, & Couzin, 2012a). Stanley Milgram instructed groups of people of different sizes to stop and stare into a building window on a crowded street in New York and found that, with an increase in the size of the stimulus group, the gaze-following responses of passersby increased (Milgram, Bickman, & Berkowitz, 1969). Gaze direction seems to be subject to social influence and can be contagious. Recent research has specified in more detail the dynamics of visual attention and information transfer between people in crowded environments (Gallup et al., 2012a, 2012b). The movements and gaze-following behaviours of almost 3,000 pedestrians were quantified in a shopping street in Oxford in the United Kingdom. The mixed-gender stimulus groups varied in size (1, 3, 5, 7, 9, 12 or 15) and were looking up at the camera, which was filming the area, for 60 seconds without moving (Gallup et al., 2012b). What the researchers found was that almost 30 per cent of the passersby adopted the gaze direction of the stimulus group and 14.2 per cent even stopped walking to look up. The proportion of pedestrians copying the gaze direction and the proportion of the individual time spent looking both increased as a function of stimulus group size (ibid). Gaze-following also depended on the spatial location of the pedestrians in relation to the stimulus group: individuals behind and to the side of the group were more likely to follow gaze than individuals who were in front of and within the gaze of the group. This suggests that the gaze-following observed was not caused by social pressure or some form of obedience (ibid).

More evidence for the directional flow of visual information transfer in a natural environment was collected in an experiment in which an attractive stimulus with a hidden camera inside was placed in a trafficked corridor at a university (Gallup et al., 2012a). In this experiment, no confederates were sent out to increase gaze following, but the visual orientation dependence of the passersby was recorded. The baseline rate of gazing at the stimulus was 28.4 per cent, which significantly increased (to 49.4 per cent) whenever another pedestrian had looked at the stimulus within the previous three seconds (ibid). In contrast to cueing paradigms used for laboratory research, individuals were more responsive to changes in the visual orientation of others walking in front of them (57.1 per cent), while attention towards the stimulus even diminished (to 19.8 per cent) in comparison to the baseline rate, when oncoming pedestrians had looked at the stimulus (ibid). The researchers concluded that human beings monitor changes in visual orientation from behind and align with it frequently to be able to relate to cues in an environment that they will shortly experience themselves.

We are accustomed to looking at the same things at the same time when we watch TV, go to a museum, look at lecture slides, posters or shop windows. Often, we talk about the things we observe. One line of research (see Box 12.2) has shown that the degree of gaze coordination between a speaker and listener predicts the success of their communication (Richardson & Dale, 2005). Moreover, people engaged in a conversation coordinate their gaze to accommodate differences in the knowledge and the visual context that they share (Richardson, Dale, & Kirkham, 2007a; Richardson, Dale, & Tomlinson, 2009). These studies and those discussed above demonstrate that social interaction influences how we interpret visual information, how our perception of our immediate environment changes and what stimuli we attend to. Taken together, they suggest that perception in a social context is fundamentally different from perception that takes place under solitary circumstances.

Box 12.2 Gaze coordination

When two people discuss a scene in front of them, their eye movements become coordinated. In a first demonstration of this effect, Richardson and Dale (2005) recorded people speaking about some sitcom characters shown on screen. They played back these monologues to listeners looking at the same set of images. They found that eye movements were coupled with a particular time signature: about two seconds after the speaker fixated a character, the listener was likely to be looking at it too. This gaze coupling was causally linked to the listeners' comprehension. In a second study, the images of characters became brighter at the moment the speaker had been looking at them. These sudden onsets were enough to make the listener's eye movements more closely coupled to the speaker's. As a consequence, the listeners' memory comprehension of the speech improved.

People are able to coordinate their gaze by drawing on the information that they share and the information that they believe they share – what Clark (1996) called their 'common ground'. In a dialogue study, two people discussed a painting after hearing one of two related encyclopaedia entries. If they each had heard the same information, then their gaze was more coordinated in their following conversation (Richardson et al., 2007). Similarly, gaze coordination was influenced by whether two people engaged in a conversation were looking at images or a blank screen, and whether they believed each other to be looking at images or a blank screen (Richardson et al., 2009). These studies reveal that coordinated perception is interwoven with successful communication. However, in the joint perception studies we discuss below, we find that even without any verbal interaction, two people seek to coordinate their gaze when they believe that they share a stimulus.

Joint Perception

We have seen that social context can influence how we move our bodies and how we interpret the world around us. It is not clear, however, exactly what constitutes a social context. Do people have to see each other, or do they have to know

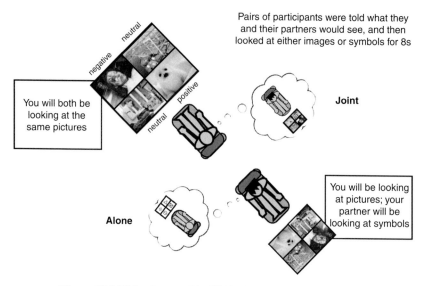

Figure 12.1 Richardson et al.'s (2012) design.

that others see them? Is the potential for social interaction required for effects to emerge? We investigated these questions by stripping down social context to its bare minimum, and measuring how perceptual processes are changed by the mere belief that another person, somewhere, perceives the same thing.

Participants in our experiment (Richardson et al., 2012) entered the laboratory in pairs and sat back to back in opposite corners of a lab room. They viewed sets of four pictures presented on screen, for a short time, as their gaze was tracked. On each trial, two of the pictures were neutral fillers, one picture had a positive valence and another one had a negative valence, as rated by the IAPS norms (Lang, Bradley & Cuthbert, 2005). Before the trials in the joint condition, participants heard the experimenter's voice say, 'You will both be looking at the same set of pictures.' In the alone condition, they heard, 'You will be looking at pictures. Your partner will be looking at symbols.' There were also filler trials in which the participants were looking at symbols while they were told that their interaction partner was looking at pictures (see Figure 12.1). The conditions were randomized within participants.

We found that the minimal social context of the joint condition influenced biases for the positive and negative pictures. As shown in Figure 12.2, when participants believed that their partner was also looking at the pictures, they looked significantly more at the negative images (Richardson et al., 2012, Experiment 1). On a trial-by-trial basis, participants' eye movements were systematically shifted, although they could not see or interact with each other

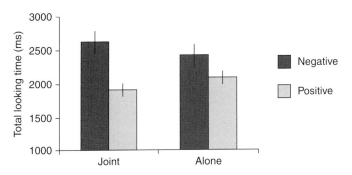

Figure 12.2 Results from Experiment 1.

and had no knowledge of each other's attentional focus. The mere belief that another person is looking at the same images at a given moment changes an individual's gaze patterns.

This result was replicated in a second experiment that tested participants' cognitive memory for the images. Eye movements were not epiphenomenal: participants in the joint condition performed better on a memory test for the negative images (Richardson et al., 2012). The results are in line with the finding that when participants look at stimuli together those that are shared are made more 'psychologically salient' (Shteynberg, 2010), and hence more memorable. However, in the joint perception experiment described, participants were not told what images the other person would be looking at. All they knew was *that* somebody else was looking, too. To investigate more exactly what it was about the minimal social context that brought about the observed attention shifts and what can be counted as 'looking together', a third experiment was conducted (Richardson et al., 2012).

From joint action studies, we know that people only form shared representations and joint action effects only occur when the interaction partner is perceived to be genuinely and intentionally engaging in the same task (Atmaca et al., 2011). Consistent with this knowledge about shared intentionality (see Ansuini, Cavallo, Bertone, & Becchio, this volume, Chapter 18), it was predicted that joint perception effects would be strongest when participants believed that they were acting jointly, rather than just passively sharing an experience (Richardson et al., 2012). To test this hypothesis, participants received instructions for two different tasks. In a memory task, they were told to remember the pictures viewed for a later test, which did not actually take place. In a search task, they were told to find a translucent X superimposed on one of the images and press a mouse button upon detection. They were told that their partner would always look at the same pictures, but that their individual tasks could change from trial to trial. At the beginning of every trial,

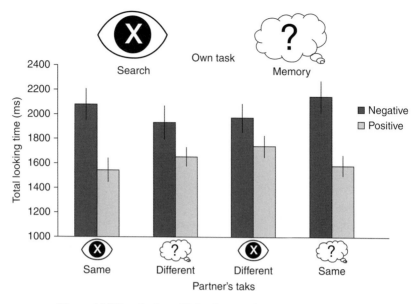

Figure 12.3 Results from Richardson et al. (2012).

participants were told what their task would be and a large icon appeared at the top of the screen, representing the task. A smaller icon below showed their partner's task (see Figure 12.3). In addition to the visual information, participants also heard a voice telling them to search/memorize and what their partner was supposed to do (ibid).

The results confirmed the predictions. Participants only showed a robust preference for negative images when they believed that they and their partner had been assigned to do the same task. These results suggest that the effects of joint perception can only be observed when people believe that they are engaged in the same task (ibid). In the light of the first study, it seems likely that, without instructions, participants assume that they are involved in the same activity by default. Whenever they are made aware of the fact that they are doing something different to their partner, the phenomenon of joint perception diminishes or disappears altogether. Joint perception, like joint action, requires people to believe that they are interacting with an individual who shares similar or the same intentions in a mutually engaging task or environment.

Why Our Eyes Synchronize

Joint perception studies show that even a minimal social context can change perceptual processes. People seem to classify looking together at the same stimuli with another person, who is not even in the same room, as a joint activity. Their gaze patterns and focus of attention change as soon as they think that they are looking together. Participants were not instructed to coordinate their behaviour or act together at any point. In fact, they did not even know where the other person was looking. Yet, the studies revealed that people take each other into account even if the visual task does not require it. This parallels findings from joint action studies in which people pay attention to the task's commands of another person, although their individual task does not demand it. But why is it that, in the joint condition, people specifically look at images of a negative valence?

Some argue that human beings have developed a learnt or evolved priority to detect threats in the environment, which results in a general bias for negative or bad information and stimuli (Baumeister, Bratlavsky, Finkenauer, & Vohs, 2001; Öhman & Mineka, 2001; Rozin & Royzman, 2001). The joint perception studies presented here also found a negativity bias. Across all experiments, people spent more time looking at the images with negative valence than at those with positive or 'neutral' valence, whether they were doing the task alone or together. In the joint conditions, this negativity bias was significantly increased (Richardson et al., 2012). One possible explanation is that, when people collaborate in groups, they tend to align with the group emotion and attitudes (Barsade, 2002; Hatfield, Cacioppo, & Rapson, 1993; Moscovici & Zavalloni, 1969). It is possible that the joint perception condition evoked a minimal, imagined cooperation situation, sufficient to produce an unconscious alignment of group emotional biases, which – in this case – meant a reinforcement of the pre-existing negativity bias. The gaze-coupling mechanisms observed between participants could then be labelled as 'gaze tuning', in the style of social tuning.

Another possibility is that the joint perception effect is driven by salience, a term usually used to denote the remarkable ability of people to resolve ambiguous references during conversations and social interactions (Richardson et al., 2012). People can draw on their knowledge about the context and assumptions that they have in common to coordinate their behaviours effectively and to avoid social disorientation: human beings align their linguistic representations (Garrod & Pickering, 2004); they use each other to store and access memories (Wegner, 1986); they sway their bodies in synchrony (Shockley, Santana, & Fowler, 2003); and they even scratch their noses together (Chartrand & Bargh, 1999). In the absence of any actual communication between participants, some of the mechanisms of coordination may have still been turned on by the simple knowledge that images were viewed together and not alone (Richardson et al., 2012). When participants thought that they were looking at the same images, they may have paid more attention to those ones they thought would be more salient to their partners. Since salience is driven by the valence of the pictures used in the experiment, paying more attention to the most salient pictures meant to pay more attention to the negative pictures (ibid). If this line of reasoning is accepted, one may further argue that the shifts observed in joint perception are the precursors to richer interactive forms of joint activity.

While the specific effects observed during joint perception still await further testing and explanation, the existence of the phenomenon in general is not surprising, given that human beings are conditioned from the very beginning to share representations about the world (Tomasello et al., 2005). Arguably, shared representations are fundamental for the creation of social bonds, which will satisfy the natural human need to belong (Baumeister & Leary, 1995). In accordance with this, Hardin and Higgins (1996) cite George Herbert Mead, who has repeatedly argued that the individual mind exists only among other minds that share understandings. Many authors have since claimed that wanting to share reality with other people is one of four human motives (Higgins & Pittman, 2008). Many concepts that have been and are being studied underline this proposition: empathy and mood contagion, perspective taking, theory of mind, embodied synchrony and mirroring, common ground and interactive alignment in conversation, socially distributed knowledge, and shared cognition in groups, all enable human beings to create and maintain shared representations about the world (Echterhoff, Higgins, & Levine, 2009). Joint perception seems to be an additional mechanism that provides a basis for and serves the emergence of shared reality. Similar to the process of interactive alignment by which people unconsciously align their representations at different linguistic levels at the same time (Garrod & Pickering, 2004), people couple their eye movements with each other as soon as a minimal social context is evoked. Automatically, they seem to transcend their private worlds by responding to the same stimulus in such a way that the foundation for intersubjectivity and common ground is laid (Thompson & Fine, 1999). However, this does not happen under all circumstances, but only whenever there is the prospect of collaborative interaction and the pursuit of a shared goal. Shared intentionality seems to be a binding force for joint perception: the phenomenon of joint perception is strongest when people are engaging in the same task at the same time (Richardson et al., 2012). Effects diminish significantly when they are doing a different task and the only commonality they experience is the set of stimuli.

Internal factors, such as motives and interests, filter the stimuli in our environment (Passer & Smith, 2008). We argue that external factors, such as the social context in which perception takes place, can also act as a filter. Since we find ourselves in social situations all the time, the phenomenon of joint perception is not only of scientific interest, but its existence also has real-world consequences. After all, we like watching movies together, we look at the same lecture slides and speaker together, and we experience the world together when we go to a museum, the countryside or any other new place. If looking together changes our gaze patterns, this means that our visual experiences of the world depend upon the social situation we find ourselves in. In future work, we will investigate the limits and the consequences of this conclusion (see Box 12.3).

Box 12.3 Questions for future research

- Across different cultures, people have a different understanding of the relationship between themselves and others. Will, for example, people from a collectivist culture show a stronger joint perception effect to the mostly individualistic participants in our experiments?
- Does joint perception change according to *who* people share a perception with? Social class and status, for example, have a strong influence in shaping gaze patterns in a wide range of social interactions (Foulsham, Cheng, Tracy, Henrich, & Kingstone, 2010; Dalmaso, Pavan, Castelli, & Galfano, 2012). Will people change their gaze more or less when looking jointly with their superiors, for example?
- In what other ways can minimal social context be manipulated? In our studies, people were told that another person was looking at the same stimuli. In pilot work, we have found that we can obtain the same effect by asking people first to log on to a social network. If they log on under their own identity, rather than anonymously, then they show the same joint perception effects as believing that a real person is looking jointly. It seems that something about social media engages the same sense of social context.
- What neural mechanisms are implicated in joint perception? If our studies are replicated in an fMRI experiment, will we find that certain brain areas are selectively activated by the joint looking condition?
- What is the relationship between joint perception and theory of mind? Specifically, will populations with impaired social cognition such as those with an autism spectrum disorder (ASD) show a reduced joint perception effect?
- What is the phenomenology of looking together? As well as modulating attention, does joint perception change how we experience stimuli? For instance, Fridlund (1991) has shown that people smile and laugh more at comedy when they imagine a friend watching the same show. Similarly, Burum, Karbowicz, and Gilbert (2013) showed that people listening to audio guides in museums had a more enjoyable experience if they believed that others around them were listening to the same recordings.

Summary

Human beings appear to coordinate their actions from the day they are born. Throughout their lives, they jointly pay attention to their social and physical environment to learn from each other and to form shared representations of the world. They share intentional states with others to achieve common goals and synchronize their body movements. Visual perception is not immune to this social pull. People coordinate where they look, even under minimal social conditions, without directly knowing where their interaction partner might look and with little awareness of how social forces are shaping their attention. When we realize that we are not looking alone, our perception changes. As Sartre described in the park, how we perceive the world and what it has in store changes as soon as the 'other' enters the scene. In the experiments presented, we see that something of Sartre's phenomenology can be measured in eye movements.

References

Allport, G. W. (1954). *The nature of prejudice*. Cambridge, MA: Perseus Books.
Asch, S. E. (1951). Effects of group pressure on the modification and distortion of judgments. In H. Guetzkow (Ed.), *Groups, leadership and men*. Pittsburgh, PA: Carnegie Press, 177–190.
Atmaca, S., Sebanz, N., & Knoblich, G. (2011). The joint flanker effect: Sharing tasks with real and imagined co-actors. *Experimental Brain Research*, 211, 371–385.
Baldwin, D. A. (1995). Understanding the link between joint attention and language. In C. Moore & P. J. Dunham (Eds.), *Joint attention: Its origins and role in development*. Hillsdale, NJ: Lawrence Erlbaum, 131–158.
Barsade, S. G. (2002). The ripple effect: Emotional contagion and its influence on group behavior. *Administrative Science Quarterly*, 47(4), 644–675.
Baumeister, R. F., Bratlavsky, E., Finkenauer, C., & Vohs, K. D. (2001). Bad is stronger than good. *Review of General Psychology*, 5(4), 323–370.
Baumeister, R. F., & Leary, M. R. (1995). The need to belong: Desire for interpersonal attachments as a fundamental human motivation. *Psychological Bulletin*, 117(3), 497–529.
Berdahl, A., Torney, C. J., Ioannou, C. C., Faria, J. J., & Couzin, I. D. (2013). Emergent sensing of complex environments by mobile animal groups. *Science*, 339, 574–576.
Böckler, A., Knoblich, G., & Sebanz, N. (2012). Effects of a co-actor's focus of attention on task performance. *Journal of Experimental Psychology: Human Perception and Performance*, 38(6), 1404–1415.
Burum, B., Karbowicz, D., & Gilbert, D. (2013). A good experience is better co-experienced. Meeting of the Society for Personality and Social Psychology, New Orleans, LA, 17–19 January.
Cacioppo, J. T., Berntson, G. G., & Decety, J. (2010). Social neuroscience and its relationship to social psychology. *Social Cognition*, 28(6), 675–685.
Cacioppo, J. T., & Cacioppo, S. (2013). Social neuroscience. *Perspectives on Psychological Science*, 8(6), 667–669.

Chartrand, T. L., & Bargh, J. A. (1999). The chameleon effect: The perception–behavior link and social interaction. *Journal of Personality and Social Psychology*, 76, 893–910.

Clark, H. H. (1996). *Being there: Putting brain, body, and the world together again.* Cambridge, MA: MIT Press.

Couzin, I. (2007). Collective minds. *Nature*, 445, 715.

Dalmaso, M., Pavan, G., Castelli, L., & Galfano, G. (2012). Social status gates social attention in humans. *Biology Letters*, 8, 450–452.

Doerrfeld, A., Sebanz, N., & Shiffrar, M. (2012). Expecting to lift a box together makes the box look lighter. *Psychological Research*, 76, 467–475.

Dovidio, J. F., & Ellyson, S. L. (1982). Decoding visual dominance: Attributions of power based on relative percentages of looking while speaking and looking while listening. *Social Psychology Quarterly*, 45, 106–113.

Echterhoff, G., Higgins, E. T., & Levine, J. M. (2009). Shared reality: Experiencing commonality with others' inner states about the world. *Perspectives on Psychological Science*, 4, 496–521.

Foulsham, T., Cheng, J. T., Tracy, J. L., Henrich, J., & Kingstone, A. (2010). Gaze allocation in a dynamic situation: Effects of social status and speaking. *Cognition*, 117, 319–331.

Fridlund, A. J. (1991). Sociality of solitary smiling: Potentiation by an implicit audience. *Journal of Personality and Social Psychology*, 60, 229–240.

Frischen, A., Bayliss, A. P., & Tipper, S. P. (2007). Gaze cueing of attention: Visual attention, social cognition, and individual differences. *Psychological Bulletin*, 133(4), 694–724.

Galantucci, B., & Sebanz, N. (2009). Joint action: Current perspectives. *Topics in Cognitive Science*, 1, 255–259.

Gallup, A. C., Chong, A., & Couzin, I. D. (2012a). The directional flow of visual information transfer between pedestrians. *Biology Letters*, 8(4), 520–522.

Gallup, A. C., Hale, J. J., Sumpter, D. J. T., Garnier, S., Kacelnik, A., et al. (2012b). Visual attention and the acquisition of information in human crowds. *Proceedings of the National Academy of Sciences*, 109(19), 7245–72506.

Garrod, S., & Pickering, M. J. (2004). Why is conversation so easy? *Trends in Cognitive Sciences*, 8(1), 8–11.

Goldstone, R. L., & Gureckis, T. M. (2009). Collective behaviour. *Topics in Cognitive Science*, 1, 412–438.

Gureckis, T. M., & Goldstone, R. L. (2006). Thinking in groups. *Pragmatics & Cognition*, 14(2), 293–311.

Hardin, C. D., & Higgins, E. T. (1996). *Shared reality: How social verification makes the subjective objective.* In R. M. Sorrentino & E. T. Higgins (Eds.), *Handbook of motivation and cognition*. New York: Guilford Press, 28–84.

Hatfield, E., Cacioppo, J. T., & Rapson, R. L. (1993). Emotional contagion. *Current Directions in Psychological Sciences*, 2, 96–99.

Higgins, E. T., & Pittman, T. S. (2008). Motives of the human animal: Comprehending, managing, and sharing inner states. *Annual Review of Psychology*, 59, 361–385.

Knoblich, G., & Sebanz, N. (2006). The social nature of perception and action. *Current Directions in Psychological Science*, 15(3), 99–104.

Kobayashi, H., & Kohshima, S. (1997). Unique morphology of the human eye. *Nature*, 387, 767–768.

Kuhn, G., Tatler, B. W., & Cole, G. G. (2009). You look where I look! Effect of gaze cues on overt and covert attention in misdirection. *Visual Cognition*, 17, 925–944.

Lang, P. J., Bradley, M. M., & Cuthbert, B. N. (2005). *International affective picture system (IAPS): Digitized photographs, instruction manual, and affective ratings* (Tech. Rep. A-6). Gainesville: University of Florida, Center for Research in Psychophysiology.

Levi, D. M., Klein, S. A., & Aitsebaomo, A. P. (1985). Vernier acuity, crowding and cortical magnification. *Vision Research*, 25(7), 963–977.

Marsh, K. L., Richardson, M. J., & Schmidt, R. C. (2009). Social connection through joint action and interpersonal coordination. *Topics in Cognitive Science*, 1, 320–339.

Mason, M. F., Tatkow, E. P., & Macrae, C. N. (2005). The look of love: Gaze shifts and person perception. *Psychological Science*, 16, 236–239.

Miles, L. K., Nind, L. K., & Macrae, C. N. (2009). The rhythm of rapport: Interpersonal synchrony and social perception. *Journal of Experimental Social Psychology*, 45, 585–589.

Milgram, S., Bickman, L., & Berkowitz, L. (1969). Note on the drawing power of crowds of different size. *Journal of Personality and Social Psychology*, 13(2), 79–82.

Moscovici, S., & Zavalloni, M. (1969). The group as polarizer of attitudes. *Journals of Personality and Social Psychology*, 12(2), 125–135.

Nagel, T. (1974). What is it like to be a bat? *Philosophical Review*, 83(4), 435–450.

Öhman, A., & Mineka, S. (2001). Fears, phobias, and preparedness: Toward an evolved module of fear and fear learning. *Psychological Review*, 108(3), 483–522.

Passer, M. W., & Smith, R. E. (2008). *Psychology: The science of mind and behavior*. New York: McGraw-Hill.

Raafat, R. M., Chater, N., & Frith, C. (2009). Herding in humans. *Trends in Cognitive Sciences*, 13(10), 420–428.

Richardson, D. C., & Dale, R. (2005). Looking to understand: The coupling between speakers' and listeners' eye movements and its relationship to discourse comprehension. *Cognitive Science*, 29, 1045–1060.

Richardson, D. C., Dale, R., & Kirkham, N. Z. (2007a). The art of conversation is coordination: Common ground and the coupling of eye movements during dialogue. *Psychological Science*, 18(5), 407–413.

Richardson, D. C., Dale, R., & Tomlinson, J. M. (2009). Conversation, gaze coordination, and beliefs about visual context. *Cognitive Science*, 33, 1468–1482.

Richardson, D. C., & Gobel, M. S. (2015). Social Attention. In J. M. Fawcett, E. F. Risko, & A. Kingstone (Eds.), *The Handbook of Attention* (pp. 349–367). Cambridge, MA: The MIT Press.

Richardson, D. C., Street, C. N., Tan, J. Y. M., Kirkham, N. Z., Hoover, M. A., & Cavanaugh, A. G. (2012). Joint perception: Gaze and social context. *Frontiers in Human Neuroscience*, 6, 1–8.

Richardson, M. J., Marsh, K. L., Isenhower, R. W., Goodman, J. R. L., & Schmidt, R. C. (2007b). Rocking together: Dynamics of intentional and unintentional interpersonal coordination. *Human Movement Science*, 26, 867–891.

Richardson, M. J., Marsh, K. L., & Schmidt, R. C. (2005). Effects of visual and verbal interaction on unintentional interpersonal coordination. *Journal of Experimental Psychology: Human Perception and Performance*, 31(1), 62–79.

Rozin, P., & Royzman, E. B. (2001). Negativity bias, negativity dominance, and contagion. *Personality and Social Psychology Review*, 5(4), 296–320.

Sartre, J. P. (1958). *Being and nothingness: An essay on phenomenological ontology*. London: Routledge.

Schnall, S., Harber, K. D., Stefanucci, J. K., & Proffitt, D. R. (2008). Social support and the perception of geographical slant. *Journal of Experimental Social Psychology*, 44(5), 1246–1255.

Sebanz, N., Bekkering, H., & Knoblich, G. (2006). Joint action: Bodies and minds moving together. *Trends in Cognitive Sciences*, 10(2), 70–76.

Senju, A., & Johnson, M. H. (2009). Atypical eye contact in autism: Models, mechanisms and development. *Neuroscience & Biobehavioral Reviews*, 33, 1204–1214.

Shepherd, S. V. (2010). Following gaze: Gaze-following behavior as a window into social cognition. *Frontiers in Integrative Neuroscience*, 4, 1–13.

Sherif, M. (1937). An experimental approach to the study of attitudes. *Sociometry*, 1, 90–98.

Shockley, K., Santana, M. V., & Fowler, C. A. (2003). Mutual interpersonal postural constraints are involved in cooperative conversation. *Journal of Experimental Psychology: Human Perception and Performance*, 29, 326–332.

Shteynberg, G. (2010). A silent emergence of culture: The social tuning effect. *Journal of Personality and Social Psychology*, 99(4), 683–689.

Smith, E. R., & Semin, G. R. (2007). Situated social cognition. *Current Directions in Psychological Science*, 16(3), 132–135.

Striano, T., & Reid, V. M. (2006). Social cognition in the first year. *Trends in Cognitive Sciences*, 10(10), 471–476.

Thompson, L., & Fine, G. A. (1999). Socially shared cognition, affect, and behavior: A review and integration. *Personality and Social Psychology Review*, 3, 278–302.

Tomasello, M., Carpenter, M., Call, J., Behne, T., & Moll, H. (2005). Understanding and sharing intentions: The origins of cultural cognition. *Behavioral and Brain Sciences*, 28, 675–735.

Valdesolo, P., Ouyang, J., & DeSteno, D. (2010). The rhythm of joint action: Synchrony promotes cooperative ability. *Journal of Experimental Social Psychology*, 46, 693–695.

Wegner, D. M. (1986). Transactive memory: A contemporary analysis of the group mind. In B. Mullen & G. R. Goethals (Eds.), *Theories of group behavior*. New York: Springer-Verlag, 185–208.

Wiltermuth, S. S. (2012a). Synchronous activity boosts compliance with requests to aggress. *Journal of Experimental Psychology*, 48, 453–456.

(2012b). Synchrony and destructive obedience. *Social Influence*, 7(2), 78–89.

Wiltermuth, S. S., & Heath, C. (2009). Synchrony and cooperation. *Psychological Science*, 20(1), 1–5.

13   Social Antecedents and Consequences of Behavioral Synchrony

*Daniël Lakens, Thomas Schubert and
Maria-Paola Paladino*

Abstract

Behavioral synchronization is one mechanism through which people coordinate their behavior in social interactions. Researchers from a wide range of scientific disciplines have examined the social antecedents and consequences of behavioral synchrony. At the core of this research lies the double assumption that people spontaneously synchronize their behavior during social interactions, and that synchronized movement rhythms transform individuals into a social unit. Recent experimental research has started to offer converging support for these theoretical ideas. In the present chapter, we will first define behavioral synchrony and review early research on movement synchrony. Subsequently, we discuss how behavioral synchrony is measured using frame-by-frame analysis, judgments of synchrony by observers, movement tracking devices or automatic motion analysis. We then provide an overview of recent studies on how synchrony emerges, focusing both on a dynamic systems perspective, as a cognitive perspective based on common coding theory. Finally, we review research on the consequences of behavioral synchrony, on the affective, behavioral and cognitive consequences of moving in synchrony. The research discussed in this chapter points towards the fundamental role synchrony plays in social interaction. The tendency to synchronize, together with the emergence of a social unit when individuals move in synchrony, seems to indicate that people have a predisposition to socially connect to others through mutual adaptation of behavioral rhythms.

Christiaan Huygens noticed something peculiar after inventing the pendulum clock. Pendulums of equal length of two clocks attached to the same wall would reach the leftmost and rightmost points of their swinging motion at the same time. Even if the two pendulums were started at a different moment, their movement rhythms would mutually adapt over time through tiny vibrations passed along through the wall until their movement rhythms became perfectly

Figure 13.1 Military march.
Source: Image courtesy of Jeff on Flickr.

synchronized. A similar tendency to synchronize movement rhythms is present in human beings. When the Millennium Bridge opened in London on 10 June 2000, many of the 90,000 people crossing the bridge experienced difficulties walking across it. A positive feedback loop between the swaying walk of the pedestrians and the tiny sideway oscillations of the bridge caused large groups of people on the bridge to walk in step (Strogatz, Abrams, McRobie, Eckhardt, & Ott, 2005). This synchronized behavior caused the bridge to sway from side to side. The bridge was closed after two days, and construction work to correct these problems took nine months and required an additional investment equaling one-third of the initial building cost.

People display synchronized movement rhythms even when their movements are not directly influenced by an external force. For instance, unintentional synchronized clapping tends to emerge whenever individuals in an audience applaud after a performance for an extended amount of time (Néda, Ravasz, Brechet, Vicsek, & Barabási, 2000). In other situations, people might intentionally decide to move in synchrony or be ordered to synchronize. This happens in military parades in which soldiers march in synchrony (see Figure 13.1), or in certain religious rituals. For instance, in the Madonna of the Arco pilgrimage, which takes place on the Monday after Easter in Naples, Italy, the devoted walk in synchrony in small groups (called Battenti, 'beatings') following the rhythm of drums while they hold statues and other religious symbols. The Zikr (or Dhikr) rituals of Muslim Sufi sects remembering God often involve synchronized movement, dance, singing and even breathing. The important role synchronized behavior plays in social interaction has been observed repeatedly in anthropology (e.g. Birdwhistle, 1970; Chapple, 1940; Fiske, 2004; Hall, 1976).

Early psychological studies established the presence of synchrony between individuals by carefully analyzing films of individuals talking to each other

(Condon & Ogston, 1966). Frame-by-frame micro-analyses of both speech and a wide range of bodily movements revealed synchronous organization of changes in body movements and speech both within and between individuals. When one- to four-day-old babies listened to human speech, micro-analyses revealed similar patterns of synchronization with the human voices (Condon & Sander, 1974). Whereas Condon proposed that interactional synchrony occurs continuously and emerges practically inevitably, Kendon (1970, 1990) did not find sustained synchrony throughout observed social interactions. Kendon (1970) argued that interactional synchrony is a manifestation of attentional and affective attunement, and was one way in which people signal they are paying attention to the other, and thus an indication of whether expectations about each other's behavior are accurate.

In recent years, the amount of experimental research into the social antecedents and consequences of behavioral synchrony has increased in the psychological literature. At the core of this research lies the double assumption that people sometimes spontaneously synchronize their behavior during social interactions, and that synchronized movement rhythms transform individuals into a social unit (Fiske, 2004; Haidt, Seder, & Kesiber, 2008; Semin & Cacioppo, 2008). Researchers from a range of scientific domains – neuroscience, movement sciences, cognitive and social psychology – have started to offer converging support for these theoretical ideas. In the present chapter, we will first define behavioral synchrony, discuss how behavioral synchrony is measured, and then provide an overview of classic and more recent studies on the origins and consequences of behavioral synchrony.

Defining and Measuring Behavioral Synchrony

Behavioral synchronization is one mechanism through which people coordinate their behavior in social interactions. In that respect, it is similar to mimicry (or imitation or mirroring). However, interpersonal adaptation through mimicry can be differentiated from behavioral synchrony (Burgoon, Stern, & Dillman, 1995). Imitation usually refers to copying a specific behavior, also referred to as behavioral matching (Bernieri, Reznick, & Rosenthal, 1988). For example, two people interacting may adopt the same posture. Research on behavioral mimicry focusses on the likelihood that (or frequency with which) a specific behavior is performed by interaction partners. Although some mimicry researchers only count behavior as mimicry when it is performed by one individual within a certain time span after it was performed by the other individual (e.g. within a 10-second window, see Stel & Vonk, 2010), other researchers simply count the number of times a behavior occurred throughout an interaction. Indeed, as Chartrand and Lakin (2013) note, researchers have focused on timing-related issues much less when investigating behavioral mimicry.

The rhythmicity of performed behaviors is central to behavioral synchrony, whether the synchronized behaviors are identical or not (Bernieri et al., 1988). Bernieri and Rosenthal (1991) distinguish between three aspects of synchrony: rhythm, simultaneous movement and the smooth meshing of interaction. Rhythmic movement can lead to simultaneous movements (as in the case of the two pendulum clocks hanging on the same wall) through entrainment. The term 'entrainment' was first used by Condon and Ogston (1966); Bernieri (1988) defined entrainment as the adjustment or moderation of behavior to coordinate or synchronize with another. Thus, when two (or more) individuals perform the same rhythmically recurring action, such as clapping their hands together, setting their foot down while walking, waving their hands, swinging their arms or rocking in a rocking chair, their movement rhythms can entrain and become synchronized, leading to both individuals performing the same rhythmic behavior at the same moment in time. When behaviors entrain spontaneously, periods of synchronized behavior are typically interspersed with periods of asynchronous behavior (Néda et al., 2000; van Ulzen et al., 2008). When rhythmic behaviors are completely entrained, behavioral meshing indicates the situation where the individual behavior rhythms of two individuals have become coordinated into a single, unified and meaningful 'whole' (see Box 13.1).

Box 13.1 Unit of analysis

In work on behavioral synchrony, the unit of analysis is oftentimes the dyad or group, instead of the individual. Condon (1980) regards behavioral synchrony as an emergent phenomenon, not created by any individual, but a holistic organization of co-occurring changes between individuals. This view, where a social unit emerges because individual behaviors become temporarily coordinated, is the dominant perspective in ecological psychology (for a review, see Marsh, Richardson, Baron, & Schmidt, 2006). Instead of considering synchrony as something that occurs 'between' individuals, setting the unit of analysis at the level of the collective recognizes that a social synergy cannot be fully understood by analyzing the individuals. At the same time, research in cognitive psychology often focusses on what individuals in a social interaction feel or think. Capella (1996) highlights the importance of not just analyzing aggregate measures of synchrony (e.g. how similar the movement rhythm of a dyad is) but also how much each individual adapts to the other individual. With the increased popularity of statistical techniques such as multivariate time series analyses and multilevel modeling, researchers can simultaneously examine individual level and group level factors on the affective and cognitive consequences of behavioral synchrony.

Researchers have relied on a range of measurement procedures to determine the extent to which individuals move in synchrony. Fifty years ago, Condon pioneered synchrony research using frame-to-frame analysis of interactions filmed at 48 frames per second (also referred to as *microanalysis*). In this method, each body part that individuals are moving is analyzed together with each speech segment and coded for every video frame (Condon & Ogston, 1966; Condon & Sander, 1974). Central to this measurement procedure is the idea that synchrony provides a holistic description of the organization of behavior as gestalt-like higher-level action structures (Condon, 1980; for a similar view, see Newtson, Hairfield, Bloomingdale, & Cutino, 1987). This approach therefore requires the extensive coding of a wide range of behaviors in an interaction, which makes it very labor intensive. In developmental psychology, this approach has been used to examine how social gaze, co-occurrences of vocalizations and affective matching are correlated to positive developments of social behavior such as self-regulatory skills and the capacity for empathy (for a review, see Feldman, 2007).

A second technique to measure behavioral synchrony, referred to as the *judgment method*, relies on the ability of observers to subjectively quantify the degree of simultaneous movement, similarity in movement rhythm and the amount of coordination between individuals (e.g. Bernieri, 1988; Bernieri et al., 1988; Cappella, 1997). Cappella (1997) correlated the amount of coordination based on the coding of the videotapes following the microanalysis approach with ratings by untrained observers of the amount of coordination in 1-minute excerpts from 30-minute videotaped interactions. He found a high level of agreement among raters, but also found that levels of coordination were strongly related to the amount of smiling between interaction partners (also see Bernieri, Gillis, Davis, & Grahe, 1996). Improving upon these studies, Bernieri, Davis, Rosenthal, and Knee (1994) compared synchrony ratings from standard videos and edited mono-colored pixelated versions of the videos with a much lower resolution (which made it impossible to see smiling behavior), and found strong correlations between the ratings of synchrony made by individuals who watched the original and edited versions. These studies seem to imply that, even though people who rate the level of interpersonal coordination from videotaped interactions rely on multi-modal sources of information when these are available, untrained observers can reliably judge the extent to which individuals are moving in synchrony.

A third technique to measure behavioral synchrony is to determine people's movement rhythm in real time using measurement devices that track the position or angle of limbs or handheld devices over time. For example, magnetic tracking systems can continuously locate the position of sensors attached to individuals, limbs or objects. A benefit of such approaches is that the measurements are truly continuous, and the amount of synchrony between two continuous movement rhythms can be quantified based not just on whether or not movements are performed simultaneously but also on the relative *phase* of the two movement rhythms.

Imagine two pendulums of equal length swinging from the left to the right. If both pendulums swing in the same rhythm and reach the left-most point of their movement trajectory at the same moment in time, they are in-phase, indicated by a phase relation of 0°. If one pendulum reaches the left-most point of its trajectory, and the other reaches the right-most point of the trajectory at the same moment, they are coordinated anti-phase, indicated by a phase relation of 180°. Research has shown that in interpersonal synchronization, the in-phase mode of coordination is most stable (Schmidt, Bienvenu, Fitzpatrick, & Amazeen, 1998). A typical observation when individuals move in synchrony is a relatively large percentage of relative phase angles around 0° (and perhaps some around 180°), whereas all phase angles should occur equally often when there is no movement coordination between individuals (see Figure 13.2, recreated from findings by Richardson, Marsh, & Schmidt, 2005). Although real-time movement tracking provides more detailed information, it is slightly more difficult to collect these measurements in naturalistic settings or without participants' awareness.

A fourth approach to quantify the amount of behavioral synchrony relies on automatic movie analysis. Techniques such as motion energy analysis calculate the difference in grayscales between consecutive frames in a videorecording, which (all else being equal) indicates movement of the videotaped individuals (Grammer, Honda, Schmitt, & Jütte, 1999). This approach has the advantage that it yields an objective, observer-independent score of movement synchrony, and can be measured unobtrusively. Because it is possible that two individuals who are both simply very active and move continuously are incorrectly judged to have a high level of synchrony, researchers have proposed calculating pseudo-synchrony scores (based on randomly shuffling one-minute segments from the interaction, and computing the motion energy for these videos) and analyzing relative differences between synchrony and pseudo-synchrony scores (e.g. Ramseyer & Tschacher, 2011). Such techniques can be considered the starting point of what automated video analysis will be capable of in the future. Delaherche, Chetouani, Mahdhaoui, Saint-Georges, Viaux, and Cohen (2012) outline possible future developments that will allow for a more extensive analysis of interaction dynamics based on an automatic recognition of specific behaviors, as well as the temporal intervals at which these occur.

Causes and Processes of Behavior Synchronization

To be able to synchronize behavior, a minimal requirement is that creatures need to be able to process rhythmicity. This ability is present in many insects,

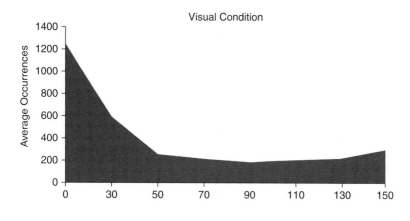

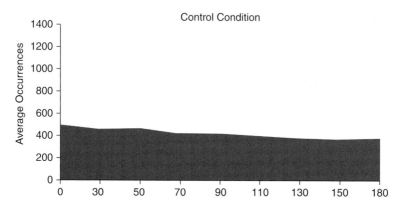

Figure 13.2 The distribution of relative phase angles for a condition in which visual information between partners is present or absent (the control condition).

Source: Based on Richardson et al. (2005).

amphibians and birds, which are known to adjust the timing of acoustic or bioluminescent signals that lead to synchronous flashing in fireflies or choruses in cicadas (for a review, see Greenfield, 1994). The first available evidence that non-human species could synchronize with an external rhythm was provided by a YouTube video that went viral in which the cockatoo Snowball (*Psittacus erithacus*) bobbed his head up and down and stomped its foot to 'Everybody' by the Back Street Boys (https://www.youtube.com/watch?v=N7IZmRnAo6s). Empirical investigations confirmed that the parrot synchronized its movements to external rhythms (Patel, Iversen, Bregman, & Schulz, 2009).

Synchronous behavior can arise through a variety of mechanisms. In the example of the Millennium Bridge in London, individuals synchronized their behavior unintentionally in response to the rhythmically shifting angle of the ground under their feet created by the movement of the bridge as thousands of individuals crossed it and leading to a dangerous accumulation of side to side swaying. In this example, synchrony emerged because individuals adapted to an external requirement, and behavioral synchrony would have occurred even if the people crossing the bridge could not have seen each other. Synchronization of individual behavior with environmental rhythmic stimulation has been extensively studied, including determinants of its occurrence and the extent to which individuals synchronize in specific situations (Dijkstra, Schöner, & Gielen, 1994a; Dijkstra, Schöner, Giese, & Gielen, 1994b; Schmidt, Richardson, Arsenault, & Galantucci, 2007).

When examining the relationship between behavioral synchrony and social behavior, however, researchers are mostly interested in cases where behavior synchronizes as a result of being with another person. In these cases, it is the perception of another individual's actions or their outcomes that leads to synchronization. Such synchronization can occur as entrainment between individuals due to them being mutually aware of their behaviors and rhythms, but it can also occur as adaptation to an external rhythm generated by another person. In many situations, entrainment and adaptation occur in parallel. For instance, synchronization on the dance floor results from adaptation to the external rhythm provided by the music and entrainment to the other dancers (Cross, Hamilton, Kraemer, Kelley, & Grafton, 2009). The same occurs when West African farmers synchronize their hoeing and threshing to a drum providing a rhythm (Fiske, personal communication, 23 June 2014).

To understand synchronization, it is important to realize that the human body is rarely completely at rest. Even when standing still, people's bodies sway in response to and in preparation of movement, including breathing (Shockley, Santana, & Fowler, 2003). Thus, it is probably rarely the case that an external rhythm gets a still body to move, but more typical that an already moving body synchronizes with an external rhythm. When exactly synchronization of behavior will occur and how strong it will be is jointly determined by specifics of the involved agents, dynamics of the movements and the strength of their coupling. On the agent side, important parameters include, for instance, skill in synchronization with an external rhythm in general (which varies by age; Kirschner & Tomasello, 2009; Kleinspehn-Ammerlahn et al., 2011), skill in the executed movements (Schmidt, Fitzpatrick, Caron, & Mergeche, 2011) and constraints of movements (e.g. weight of objects to be moved; Schmidt et al., 2011).

Regarding the dynamics of the movements, amplitude and frequency stand out. The influence of such factors can be understood and modeled based on general models of coupled oscillators (Haken, Kelso, & Bunz, 1985). For instance, the way clapping after a theatrical performance changes from a high intensity uncoordinated initial phase into synchronized applause can be understood as a shift from high to low frequency, decreasing dispersion under a critical value and allowing synchronization at the cost of overall intensity (Néda, et al., 2000). Aspects of agents and their dynamics will interact in modulating synchrony; for instance, synchronization of locomotion of humans to a beat is assumed to peak near 2 Hz (Styns, van Noorden, Moelants, & Leman, 2007).

The coupling describes the flow of information between the involved individuals, and numerous experiments investigate how the coupling moderates the emergence of synchronous behavior between humans. For instance, individuals were found to spontaneously synchronize pendulums swinging from their hands when they could see each other (but not when they were just interacting verbally; Richardson, Marsh, & Schmidt, 2005). Individuals spontaneously synchronize the rhythm with which they swing pendulums if they look at each other compared to when they do not look at each other, even if asked not to synchronize (Schmidt & O'Brien, 1997). Unintended synchronization also occurs for arm movements (Issartel, Marin, & Cadopi, 2007) and for rocking in rocking chairs if the other is attended to (Richardson, Marsh, Isenhower, Goodman, & Schmidt, 2007). Indeed, not synchronizing is difficult when the effectors are the same, the range of possible motions is restricted and informational coupling is provided (Issartel et al., 2007).

Several studies have provided indications that relatively more cognitive resources are available when people perform synchronous movements, compared to asynchronous movements. While rhythmically moving joysticks in-phase, participants responded faster to auditory cues in a simultaneous reaction time task, compared to when participants rhythmically moved the joystick anti-phase (Temprado, 2004), and participants recognized more words presented simultaneously while performing in-phase hand movements, compared to anti-phase or no hand movements (Macrae, Duffy, Miles, & Lawrence, 2008). Together, these studies seem to indicate that people automatically process rhythmic biological movements of conspecifics, and performing rhythmic movements in a different rhythm or phase as an observed movement requires cognitive resources.

Insights from studies on synchronization with environmental stimuli can contribute further insights into the causes of inter-individual synchronization (for a recent review, see Repp & Su, 2013). For instance, rhythms of auditory stimuli may be more entraining than rhythms of visual stimuli (Repp & Penel, 2004). During self-generated rhythmic behavior, only distractor rhythms close in frequency are able to interfere (Repp, 2006). Visual and auditory coupling can be additive (Demos, Chaffin, Begosh, Daniels, & Marsh, 2012). When individuals stand, their postural sway synchronizes in interactions even if the other is only heard but not seen, presumably mediated by synchronization of articulatory actions (Shockley, Baker, Richardson, & Fowler, 2007; Shockley, Richardson, & Dale, 2009; Shockley et al., 2003). See Box 13.2 for deeper consideration of behavioral assimilation.

Box 13.2 Assimilation of observed behavior

Once behavior is synchronized, individuals assimilate aspects of their behavior to the observed model. For instance, when asked to synchronize repeated arm movements in the horizontal or vertical plane with a model facing them, humans tend to align the vector of their movement to the vector of the observed movement (Kilner, Paulignan, & Blakemore, 2003). As a result, if one has to perform horizontal movement while observing synchronous vertical movement, the horizontal movement takes on the shape of a banana, curved in the direction of the observed movement. This alignment occurs strongest if the observed movement one synchronizes with accelerates and decelerates in the way a human hand would. If it does, all kinds of moving agents can cause alignment during synchronized movement: humanoid robots (Chaminade, Franklin, Oztop, & Cheng, 2005; Kupferberg et al., 2011; Oztop, Franklin, & Chaminade, 2005) and also moving dots (Bouquet, Gaurier, Shipley, Toussaint, & Blandin, 2007; but also see Jackson, Brady, Cummins, & Monaghan, 2007, for a failed replication).

If the observed movement is not biologically plausible, for instance if an observed robotic arm jerks back and forth with constant velocity, motor interference in the form of alignment does not occur (Kilner et al., 2003). However, biologically implausible observed movements of a dot can still lead to alignment if they are simply believed to be produced by a human agent (Stanley, Gowen, & Miall, 2007). In sum, behavior that is synchronized to movements of another agent is assimilated to the observed target, especially if the observed behavior is believed or inferred to be that of a mindful being.

Ecological and Cognitive Perspectives on How Synchrony Emerges

As with most psychological phenomena, the best way to understand why one occurs is to understand how it could work. On a micro level, it appears that adaptation to another person's rhythm (and thus also entrainment) is a complex process consisting of reproduction of the central tendency of the last intervals, a copying of the latest interval and an outlier exclusion process (Merker,

Madison, & Eckerdal, 2009). How this is actually achieved by humans, however, is debated. Two general theoretical frameworks are available to explain coordinated joint action in general, and synchronization as one particular case. On the one hand, a focus on the dynamic interaction between the synchronizing agents is offered by a dynamic systems perspective (Marsh, Richardson, & Schmidt, 2009; Schmidt et al., 2011). On the other hand, a cognitive perspective is offered that builds on the common coding theory, supplemented by neurophysiological evidence of mirror neurons (Sebanz & Knoblich, 2009).

The dynamic systems perspective generated a tremendous amount of insights on the conditions and attributes of synchronous behavior (Marsh et al., 2009). It originated from ecological views on perception and action, which concentrate on observable behavior such as timing aspects of interacting individuals. The dynamic systems perspective has in general been less interested in investigating the causal role of mentalistic psychological processes (Marsh et al., 2006; Schmidt et al., 2011). The notion of control by a central executive (i.e. mind and brain) is replaced by the notion of coordination arising 'from the reciprocal interaction among complex systems with many redundant degrees of freedom' (Cummins, 2013, p. 416).

This ecological perspective assumes that the same modeling approach can be used regardless of whether inter-individual synchrony (e.g. the synchronization of two individuals swinging one arm) or intra-individual synchronization (e.g. the synchronization of two swinging arms of the same individual) is studied (Marsh et al., 2009; Schmidt & Turvey, 1994; Schmidt, Carello, & Turvey, 1990). However, the strength of the coupling is thought to be weaker in inter-individual than in intra-individual settings. In this approach, synchrony is seen as an inevitable outcome under some circumstances that are defined by the right properties of dynamics and their coupling, while synchrony is seen as an impossible outcome under other conditions (Marsh et al., 2009a). Even though this line of research has been very productive and achieved a remarkably sophisticated modeling of synchronous behavior itself, it is clear from empirical research that people's goals, expectations and affective response towards others influence whether synchrony will emerge. Although it is possible these factors determine the strength of the coupling in inter-individual synchronization, it is not yet clear how the dynamic systems perspective will be able to incorporate such cognitive and affective factors.

The cognitive perspective on how synchrony emerges is based on a common coding mechanism. According to the common coding theory, actions are mentally represented in terms of the effects they are expected to have. The basic assumption of this theory is that observed actions of others are coded in the same way as actions we perform ourselves (Hommel, Müsseler, Aschersleben, & Prinz, 2001; Prinz, 1990). From this perspective, coordinated joint action, imitation and synchronization are based on an overlapping and integrated coding of the outcomes of one's own actions and the outcomes of others' actions. This approach is now supported by the identification of mirror neuron networks, which respond both when monkeys and humans perform an action, as when they observe the same action, and thereby provide a neural substrate for the common code hypothesis (Gallese, Keysers, & Rizzolatti, 2004).

Note that this emphasis on prediction differs from a common interpretation of the mirror neuron function as being about understanding what just happened. Indeed, when using mirror neuron accounts to explain how synchrony emerges, it seems crucial to acknowledge that imitative processes alone could not suffice (also see Sommerville & Decety, 2006). The generality of the common coding approach places less emphasis on timing aspects; for this reason, it is not yet clear how it can help explain how predictions of own and others' actions may blend into each other and influence own action such that synchronous behavior arises (see Sebanz, Bekkering, & Knoblich, 2006).

One proposal to address timing-related issues in common coding mechanisms is to assume the formation of feed-forward models for the purpose of action control. Such feed-forward models generate predictions of sensory feedback in various modalities, and are an obvious locus of interaction with observing and modeling others (Sebanz & Knoblich, 2009; Wolpert, Doya, & Kawato, 2003). This proposal is compatible with models of sensorimotor synchronization with an external rhythm (Aschersleben, 2002). In a similar vein, the functionality of the mirror neuron system has also been proposed to entail forward models of interactions with objects, which complements this idea (Kilner, Friston, & Frith, 2007; Miall, 2003). Precisely how these processes would work is not yet clear, and several processes may be at work simultaneously. For instance, the lag between action onset and its end may be primed independently of other components (Watanabe, 2008). In a recent example, this view of synchronization as mutual continuous adaptation based on always predicting the next action of the other was called 'hyper-following' (Konvalinka, Vuust, Roepstorff, & Frith, 2010).

Another proposal to solve the timing problem is to assume that when individuals jointly coordinate their behavior, their representation of the outcome of their actions would change. Instead of separately representing own and others' effects on the joint action, individuals may instead represent the total effect on the outcome and regulate that directly (Masumoto & Inui, 2013; Sebanz & Knoblich, 2009). It appears that synchronization can help with that, as it provides a temporal structure to the switching in these tasks.

Social Antecedents and Consequences of Behavioral Synchrony

Behavioral synchrony has been theorized to play an important role in the formation of a social unit (e.g. Condon, 1980; Davis, 1982; Fiske, 2004;

Kendon, 1990; LaFrance, 1985; Marsh, Richardson, Baron, & Schmidt, 2006; Newtson, Hairfield, Bloomingdale, & Cutino, 1987). Durkheim ([1915] 1965) proposed that synchronous rituals increase cooperation. Others have similarly observed how our ancestors may have used music and dancing to form bonds (Freeman, 2000), how movement synchrony is present in courtship patterns (Grammer, Kruck, & Magnusson, 1998), and how historic and contemporary military forces use synchrony during drill and battle to increase group cohesion (McNeill, 1995; McPhail & Wohlstein, 1986; see Figure 13.1).

Researchers have suggested that movement synchrony is an indication of shared feelings of rapport, an affective state of mutual attention and positivity (Bernieri, 1988; Tickle-Degnen & Rosenthal, 1990). LaFrance (1985, 1990) theorizes that movement synchrony is a social gauge by which observers can assess the degree to which individuals are mutually involved with each other. As Marsh and colleagues (2009b, p. 323) summarize: 'Presumably, the pull to such a coordinated state tells us something about the most minimal socioemotional connectedness of a pair.' Whereas the social consequences of behavioral synchrony have traditionally been examined predominantly in correlational studies, more recent research has attempted to experimentally manipulate the amount of behavioral synchrony and examine the consequences on feelings of connectedness, and vice versa.

Bernieri and colleagues (1988) studied mother–infant coordinated behavior and found that movement synchrony was significantly related to a child's positive affect: the happier the child, the greater the synchrony. Replicating these results in a different context, Bernieri (1988) videotaped 19 dyads consisting of students (one assigned to a teacher role, the other to a student role) and found a positive correlation between the amount of movement synchrony (as rated by observers) and self-reported feelings of rapport by the dyad members. Behavior matching (or imitation) did not correlate with self-reported rapport in this study.

Correlational studies are used relatively frequently in domains where experimental manipulation is less feasible, such as in parent–infant interaction, and therapist–patient relationships. For example, Ramseyer and Tschacher (2011) analyzed non-verbal synchrony in 104 videotaped interactions between clients and psychotherapists using motion energy analysis. The amount of behavioral synchrony correlated positively with clients' self-reported evaluations of the quality of the relationship, and with self-reported changes in outcome measures associated with interpersonal behavior, self-efficacy, psychopathology and attachment.

Correlational support has certain limitations, the most important of which is that it remains unclear whether feelings of social connectedness increase synchrony, whether synchrony increases social connectedness or whether this relation is bidirectional. Therefore, researchers have more recently started to examine the relationship between behavioral synchrony and social connect-edness in studies where either the amount of movement synchrony or the extent to which individuals within a dyad feel connected are experimentally manipulated.

Synchrony Influencing Psychological Variables

When the amount of synchrony between individuals is manipulated, the more individuals are synchronized, the more observers perceive these individuals as a social unit (Lakens, 2010). In a series of four studies, Lakens found that stick figures waving in the same rhythm, even if they performed non-identical rhythmic movements, were judged to be a stronger unit (or rated higher on *entitativity*). These findings were replicated in a study using videotaped con-federates performing the same rhythmic waving movements. Furthermore, the larger the difference in movement rhythm between two stick figures (manipu-lated in seven steps in a between-subject design), the less observers judged the stick figures to be a unit.

Miles, Nind, and Macrae (2009b) presented participants with video ani-mations of two stick figures walking in different rhythms or auditory frag-ments of the footsteps of two individuals, and found that the more similar the visual or auditory movement rhythms were, the higher the stimuli were rated on rapport. As noted already, rapport is an affective state of mutual attention and positivity (Bernieri, 1988; Tickle-Degnen & Rosenthal, 1990), and people may assess feelings of rapport in part on the basis of the extent to which they are in sync with their interaction partner (LaFrance, 1985). This should subsequently influence entitativity judgments. Lakens and Stel (2011) provided empirical support for these assumptions. Individuals who wave their hand in synchrony are judged higher on rapport, and rated higher on perceived entitativity. A group of boys walking around a courtyard in synchrony were judged to be a social unit and rated high on rapport, but less so if observers learned that the boys had been instructed to walk in synchrony. These results show that observers use synchrony as a 'tie-sign' (LaFrance, 1985) to judge the extent to which individuals are a social unit, but only when synchrony emerged spontaneously.

Moving from observed to experienced movement synchrony, Hove and Risen (2009) asked participants to perform a rhythmic tapping task side by side with a female experimenter, and found that participants who tapped closer and more consistently with the experimenter rated her as more likable on a sub-sequent questionnaire. A second experiment in which the experimenter either tapped in the same or a different rhythm (or did not tap at all) found that liking of the experimenter was greater in the synchrony condition. This perceived unity is also experienced by individuals: when someone experiences multimodal synchrony with another person (manipulated by stroking participants on the cheek with a paintbrush while watching a video of a stranger being stroked in exact spatio-temporal synchrony, or in asynchrony), self–other distance, measured graphically by two overlapping circles representing self and other, is reduced (Paladino, Mazzurega, Pavani, & Schubert, 2010).

Walking in synchrony with others has been shown to increase the feeling of social unity among individuals, and subsequently leads to more positive outcomes in a cooperative dilemma (Wiltermuth & Heath, 2009). Synchronizing behavior in a simple tapping task increases feelings of similarity with others, and has been shown to subsequently enhance compassionate responses if these individuals are victims of a moral transgression (Valdesolo & DeSteno, 2011). Such increases in perceived similarity after synchronous movements have also been shown to increase helping behavior (Valdesolo, Ouyang, & DeSteno, 2010). The increased cooperation that emerges after moving in synchrony might also have negative consequences. After a task where three group members rhythmically flip a cup in rhythm with the music (either all in synchrony or all in different rhythms) participants were more likely to follow a suggestion by a confederate that would cause discomfort to another group (Wiltermuth, 2012).

Kokal, Engel, Kirschner, and Keysers (2011) have shown that successfully drumming in synchrony leads to activation in brain areas related to the reward system, and participants in the study picked up more pens 'accidentally' dropped by the experimenter (which was actually a test of pro-social helping behavior) when they had been tapping in sync, compared to when they had tapped out of sync. Indeed, the level of success in a synchronization task is an important factor in subsequent cooperative behavior (see Kurzban, 2001; Launay, Dean, & Bailes, 2013). Recent studies by Reddish, Fischer, and Bulbulia (2013) provide an indication that synchrony is especially successful at promoting cooperation when it is framed as a shared goal (i.e. participants entraining to each other's movement rhythms, instead of all individually adapting to a musical rhythm).

The effect of visual and auditory information on movement synchrony and feelings of connection was examined in a study by Demos and colleagues (2012). Dyads rocked back and forth in rocking chairs for 30 seconds, after which they continued rocking while looking at or away from each other. In addition, auditory information was manipulated, by either providing no auditory information about the rocking movements of the other individual (by placing rugs underneath the chairs), providing auditory information (by placing sandpaper underneath the chairs) or playing a song (with approximately 64 bpm). The results indicated that movement synchrony increased with visual information (cf. Richardson, Marsh, Isenhower, Goodman, & Schmidt, 2007) and auditory information about the movements of the other rocking chair.

Interestingly, Demos and colleagues found that self-reported feelings of connectedness with the other individual did not correlate with the extent to which both individuals were synchronized with each other. Instead, feelings of connectedness were related to how much the individual was synchronized to the music. These results suggest that the perceived experience of both moving to the same music (or having a shared goal) might have been a more important source of feeling connected than simply moving in the same rhythm. This parallels findings by Launay and colleagues (2013), whereby perceived synchronization was a better predictor of cooperation than an actual time-based measure of how synchronized individuals were in a task where participants were instructed to synchronize.

Psychological Variables Influencing Synchrony

In the studies discussed so far, manipulating movement synchrony influenced psychological factors, but the relationship between synchrony and psychological factors seems to be bidirectional. Even under biomechanically optimal circumstances (e.g. two individuals with similar leg length), some dyads reveal a stronger tendency to synchronize than other dyads (Nessler, Kephart, Cowell, & De Leone, 2011). One of the personality variables that might underlie differences in the tendency to entrain is the social disposition of an individual. Support for this idea is provided by the work of Lumsden, Miles, Richardson, Smith, and Macrae (2012) who found that 'pro-social' individuals were more likely to spontaneously synchronize arm movements with a video of someone performing similar arm movements than 'pro-self' individuals. Condon (1982, as discussed in Burgoon et al., 1995) observed that the amount of synchrony between people who belong to the same subculture was greater than that between individuals who belonged to different subcultures. At the same time, Miles, Lumsden, Richardson, and Macrae (2011) observed higher levels of interpersonal synchrony when participants and a confederate belonged to different minimal (i.e. blue versus red) groups than when both individuals belonged to the same group. This could be some sort of compensatory mechanism whereby an individual is trying to create a social bond that is not simply present due to group membership, but clearly more work, preferably with larger samples, is needed.

Vacharkulksemsuk and Fredrickson (2012) asked 94 same-sex dyads to either perform a self-disclosure task or (in the control condition) read a scientific article. Two observers rated the amount of behavioral synchrony in each dyad (following Bernieri et al., 1988), which was higher in the self-disclosure condition than in the control condition. Analyses revealed that self-disclosure increased rapport, and that this effect was mediated by the amount of behavioral synchrony. Research has repeatedly revealed that behavioral synchrony is more pronounced in dyads that like each other more (e.g. Paxton & Dale, 2013a), and preliminary findings suggest that the extent to which dyads are synchronized might reduce during arguments (Paxton & Dale, 2013b; see Box 13.3).

Box 13.3 Synchrony and the feeling of 'becoming one'

The pervasiveness of synchronized movements in ancient and modern social rituals suggests that some basic psychological processes might be responsible for the feeling of oneness that typically arises in these circumstances. One possibility is that principles organizing the perception of non-social stimuli would also apply to the social world. Synchrony has been recently proposed as an additional gestalt principle of perceptual organization (Wagemans et al., 2012): visual stimuli that change simultaneously tend to be grouped together. In the case of social stimuli this grouping would transform distinct individuals in a meaningful social unit. Interestingly, this explanation can account both for observing and for being involved in collective synchronous activities.

However, the social effects of acting in synchrony have also been explained in terms of multisensory integration processes (i.e. the ability of the brain to knit together synchronous sensorial stimulations). In many situations synchrony creates the conditions for multisensory synchronous interpersonal stimulations. This is the case when marching or dancing in synchrony: one feels one's feet striking the ground (tactile input) while seeing other people's feet performing exactly the same action (visual input) in close temporal synchrony. Experimental studies have shown that such synchronous visual–tactile stimulation leads to bodily illusory sensations (e.g. 'It feels like it was my body') due to the temporary integration of another body (or body part) in one's own bodily representation (Botvinick & Cohen, 1998). When seeing another person's face being touched in perfect synchrony with one's own face, for instance, participants report the impression of watching oneself in a mirror rather than a stranger (Tsakiris, 2008). Importantly the effects of synchronous multisensory interpersonal stimulations go beyond corporeal aspects. Social outcomes typical of close relationships tend to emerge as well, suggesting that other integration in one's own bodily representation might contribute also to forging a social bond (Paladino, Mazzurega, Pavani, & Schubert, 2010).

Future Questions

The studies reviewed in this chapter have provided promising empirical support for the idea that feeling like a social unit with others can lead to more behavioral synchrony, and that synchrony in turn strengthens social bonds. They point to how entrainment of behavioral rhythms in dyads, or intentionally synchronizing with an external rhythm in larger groups, increases feelings of similarity and social unity, thereby increasing trust, pro-social behavior and self–other overlap. These initial findings confirm the observations from anthropological research that behavioral synchronization is an important mechanism through which individuals transform into a social unit.

At the same time, many of the studies described in this chapter concern exploratory research, often with small sample sizes. Because dyads or groups are often the unit of analysis in these studies, and the studies are complex and labor-intensive, follow-up studies using larger samples are needed to confirm and extend these findings to more naturalistic settings, beyond student populations and across cultures. Where past observational studies analyzed a wide range of behaviors (speech, movements, and so on), more recent work has primarily focused on movement synchrony of individual behaviors. Future work might use the experimental paradigms in which synchrony is manipulated to again broaden the scope and examine multi-modal behavioral synchrony (e.g. Louwerse, Dale, Bard, & Jeuniaux, 2012).

The work that has been done on synchrony relies on a wide range of methodologies and dependent variables. This is both a strength, because it demonstrates the robustness and generalizability of the effects, and a weakness, because it makes it difficult to compare the mechanisms and outcomes between studies. Many questions remain. Synchrony has been manipulated by providing opportunities for spontaneous synchronization or by instructing people to synchronize with an external rhythm or each other. Some initial findings suggest that intentionally synchronizing has additional benefits over spontaneous synchrony in relation to feelings of social unity (Reddish et al., 2013), although it seems likely the relative benefit strongly depends on the task and the context. Similarly, researchers do not strongly differentiate between liking, rapport, entitativity, feelings of connectedness, similarity or self–other overlap. To a large degree, this is because synchrony can have positive effects on any of these experiences in the social context in which synchrony has been examined to date. However, these psychological consequences can be differentiated theoretically, and might be limited to specific contexts or uniquely related to specific ways in which synchronization emerges.

Conclusion

The research discussed in this chapter points towards the fundamental role synchrony plays in social interaction. The tendency to synchronize, together with the emergence of a social unit when individuals move in synchrony, seems to indicate that people have a predisposition to socially connect to others through mutual adaptation of behavioral rhythms. In addition to theoretically intriguing insights into human social behavior, synchrony research has practical consequences ranging from therapeutic settings (Krueger, 2005) to human–computer interaction (Marin, Issartel, & Chaminade, 2009) to crowd control (Strogatz, et al., 2005).

Human bodies are almost always in motion, and many of the actions we perform are rhythmic in nature: breathing, walking or running, talking to each other, rocking young children, making love, physical labor or playing games. The ability to recognize rhythmic behavior that occurs in synchrony with our own actions is a fundamental part of our cognitive system with the goal of recognizing what belongs to our body and what is a consequence of our intentional actions. Humans are by nature extremely social, and constantly motivated to understand the actions, intentions and behavior of other people. It may thus be no surprise that people are sensitive to the amount of synchrony between individuals in social interactions and use it to understand and judge the social environment, and that synchronization can emerge effortlessly and spontaneously if we feel part of a social unit.

References

Aschersleben, G. (2002). Temporal control of movements in sensorimotor synchronization. *Brain and Cognition*, 48(1), 66–79. doi: 10.1006/brcg.2001.1304.

Bernieri, F. J. (1988). Coordinated movement and rapport in teacher–student interactions. *Journal of Nonverbal Behavior*, 12(2), 120–138.

Bernieri, F. J., Davis, J. M., Rosenthal, R., & Knee, C. R. (1994). Interactional synchrony and rapport: Measuring synchrony in displays devoid of sound and facial affect. *Personality and Social Psychology Bulletin*, 20(3), 303–311.

Bernieri, F. J., Gillis, J. S., Davis, J. M., & Grahe, J. E. (1996). Dyad rapport and the accuracy of its judgment across situations: A lens model analysis. *Journal of Personality and Social Psychology*, 71(1), 110–129. doi: 10.1037//0022-3514.71.1.110.

Bernieri, F. J., Reznick, J. S., & Rosenthal, R. (1988). Synchrony, pseudosynchrony, and dissynchrony: Measuring the entrainment process in mother–infant interactions. *Journal of Personality and Social Psychology*, 54(2), 243–253.

Bernieri, F. J., & Rosenthal, R. (1991). Interpersonal coordination: Behavior matching and interactional synchrony. In R. S. Feldman & B. Rime (Eds.), *Fundamentals of nonverbal behavior*. Cambridge: Cambridge University Press, 401–432.

Birdwhistell, R. L. (1970). *Kinesics and context: Essays in body motion communication*. Philadelphia, PA: University of Pennsylvania Press.

Botvinick, M., & Cohen, J. D. (1998). Rubber hand 'feels' what eyes see. *Nature*, 391(6669), 756–756.

Bouquet, C. A., Gaurier, V., Shipley, T., Toussaint, L., & Blandin, Y. (2007). Influence of the perception of biological or non-biological motion on movement execution. *Journal of Sports Sciences*, 25(5), 519–530. doi: 10.1080/02640410600946803.

Burgoon, J. K., Stern, L. A., & Dillman, L. (1995). *Interpersonal adaptation: Dyadic interaction patterns*. Cambridge: Cambridge University Press.

Cappella, J. N. (1996). Dynamic coordination of vocal and kinesic behavior in dyadic interaction: Methods, problems, and interpersonal outcomes. In J. H. Watt & C. A. VanLear (Eds.), *Dynamic patterns in communication processes*. Thousand Oaks, CA: Sage, 353–386.

(1997). Behavioral and judged coordination in adult informal social interactions: Vocal and kinesic indicators. *Journal of Personality and Social Psychology*, 72(1), 119–131.

Chaminade, T., Franklin, D. W., Oztop, E., & Cheng, G. (2005). Motor interference between humans and humanoid robots: Effect of biological and artificial motion. *Proceedings of the 4th International Conference on Development and Learning*, 96–101. doi: 10.1109/DEVLRN.2005.1490951.

Chapple, C. C. (1940). A cabinet cubicle for infants, combining isolation with control of temperature and humidity. *Journal of Pediatrics*, 16(2), 215–219. doi: 10.1016/S0022-3476(40)80122-4.

Chartrand, T. L., & Lakin, J. L. (2013). The antecedents and consequences of human behavioral mimicry. *Annual Review of Psychology*, 64(1), 285–308.

Condon, W. S. (1980). The relation of interactional synchrony to cognitive and emotional processes. In M. R. Key (Ed.), *The relation of verbal and nonverbal behavior*. The Hague: Mouton, 49–65.

(1982). Cultural microrhythms. In M. Davis (Ed.), *Interaction rhythms: Periodicity in communicative behavior*. New York: Human Sciences Press, 53–76.

Condon, W. S., & Ogston, W. D. (1966). Sound film analysis of normal and pathological behavior patterns. *Journal of Nervous and Mental Disease*, 143(4), 338–347.

Condon, W. S., & Sander, L. W. (1974). Neonate movement is synchronized with adult speech: Interactional participation and language acquisition. *Science*, 183(4120), 99–101.

Cross, E. S., Hamilton, A. F. D. C., Kraemer, D. J., Kelley, W. M., & Grafton, S. T. (2009). Dissociable substrates for body motion and physical experience in the human action observation network. *European Journal of Neuroscience*, 30(7), 1383–1392.

Cummins, F. (2013). Social cognition is not a special case, and the dark matter is more extensive than recognized. *Behavioral and Brain Sciences*, 36(4), 415–416.

Davis, M. E. (Ed.) (1982). *Interaction rhythms: Periodicity in communicative behavior*. New York: Human Sciences Press.

Delaherche, E., Chetouani, M., Mahdhaoui, A., Saint-Georges, C., Viaux, S., & Cohen, D. (2012). Interpersonal synchrony: A survey of evaluation methods across disciplines. *IEEE Transactions on Affective Computing*, 3(3), 349–365.

Demos, A. P., Chaffin, R., Begosh, K. T., Daniels, J. R., & Marsh, K. L. (2012). Rocking to the beat: Effects of music and partner's movements on spontaneous interpersonal coordination. *Journal of Experimental Psychology: General*, 141(1), 49–53. doi: 10.1037/a0023843.

Dijkstra, T. M. H., Schöner, G., & Gielen, C. C. A. M. (1994a). Temporal stability of the action–perception cycle for postural control in a moving visual environment. *Experimental Brain Research*, 97(3), 477–486.

Dijkstra, T. M. H., Schöner, G., Giese, M. A., & Gielen, C. C. A. M. (1994b). Frequency dependence of the action–perception cycle for postural control in a moving visual environment: Relative phase dynamics. *Biological Cybernetics*, 71(6), 489–501.

Dumas, G., Nadel, J., Soussignan, R., Martinerie, J., & Garnero, L. (2010). Inter-brain synchronization during social interaction. *PloS One*, 5(8), e12166. doi: 10.1371/journal.pone.0012166.

Durkheim, E. ([1915] 1965). *The elementary forms of the religious life*. New York: Free Press.

Feldman, R. (2007). On the origins of background emotions: From affect synchrony to symbolic expression. *Emotion*, 7(3), 601–611.

Feldman, R., Magori-Cohen, R., Galili, G., Singer, M., & Louzoun, Y. (2011). Mother and infant coordinate heart rhythms through episodes of interaction synchrony. *Infant Behavior and Development*, 34(4), 569–577. doi: 10.1016/j.infbeh.2011.06.008.

Fiske, A. P. (2004). Four modes of constituting relationships: Consubstantial assimilation; space, magnitude, time, and force; concrete procedures; abstract symbolism. In N. Haslam (Ed.), *Relational models theory: A contemporary overview*. Abingdon: Psychology Press, 61–146.

Freeman, W. (2000). A neurobiological role of music in social bonding. In B. Merker, N. L. Wallin, & S. Brown (Eds.), *The origins of music*. Cambridge, MA: MIT Press, 411–424.

Gallese, V., Keysers, C., & Rizzolatti, G. (2004). A unifying view of the basis of social cognition. *Trends in Cognitive Sciences*, 8(9), 396–403. doi: 10.1016/j.tics.2004.07.002.

Grammer, K., Honda, R., Schmitt, A., & Jütte, A. (1999). Fuzziness of nonverbal courtship communication unblurred by motion energy detection. *Journal of Personality and Social Psychology*, 77(3), 487–508.

Grammer, K., Kruck, K. B., & Magnusson, M. S. (1998). The courtship dance: Patterns of nonverbal synchronization in opposite-sex encounters. *Journal of Nonverbal behavior*, 22(1), 3–29.

Greenfield, M. D. (1994). Synchronous and alternating choruses in insects and anurans: Common mechanisms and diverse functions. *American Zoologist*, 34(6), 605–615.

Haidt, J., Seder, J., & Kesebir, S. (2008). Hive psychology, happiness, and public policy. *Journal of Legal Studies*, 37(2), 133–156.

Haken, H., Kelso, J. A. S., & Bunz, H. (1985). A theoretical model of phase transitions in human hand movements. *Biological Cybernetics*, 51(5), 347–356.

Hall, E. T. (1976). *Beyond culture*. Garden City, NY: Anchor Books.

Hommel, B., Müsseler, J., Aschersleben, G., & Prinz, W. (2001). The theory of event coding (TEC): A framework for perception and action planning. *Behavioral and Brain Sciences*, 24(5), 849–878.

Hove, M. J., & Risen, J. L. (2009). It's all in the timing: Interpersonal synchrony increases affiliation. *Social Cognition*, 27(6), 949–960. doi: 10.1521/soco.2009.27.6.949.

Issartel, J., Marin, L., & Cadopi, M. (2007). Unintended interpersonal coordination: 'Can we march to the beat of our own drum?' *Neuroscience Letters*, 411(3), 174–179. doi: 10.1016/j.neulet.2006.09.086.

Jackson, S., Brady, N., Cummins, F., & Monaghan, K. (2007). Interaction effects in simultaneous motor control and movement perception tasks. *Artificial Intelligence Review*, 26(1–2), 141–154. doi: 10.1007/s10462-007-9035-4.

Kendon, A. (1970). Movement coordination in social interaction: Some examples described. *Acta Psychologica*, 32(2), 101–125. doi: 10.1016/0001-6918(70)90094–6

(1990). *Conducting interaction: Patterns of behavior in focused encounters.* New York: Cambridge University Press.

Kilner, J. M., Friston, K. J., & Frith, C. D. (2007). Predictive coding: An account of the mirror neuron system. *Cognitive Processing*, 8(3), 159–166. doi: 10.1007/s10339-007-0170-2.

Kilner, J. M., Paulignan, Y., & Blakemore, S. J. (2003). An interference effect of observed biological movement on action. *Current Biology*, 13(6), 522–525. doi: 10.1016/S0960-9822(03)00165-9.

Kirschner, S., & Tomasello, M. (2009). Joint drumming: Social context facilitates synchronization in preschool children. *Journal of Experimental Child Psychology*, 102(3), 299–314. doi: 10.1016/j.jecp.2008.07.005.

Kleinspehn-Ammerlahn, A., Riediger, M., Schmiedek, F., von Oertzen, T., Li, S.-C., & Lindenberger, U. (2011). Dyadic drumming across the lifespan reveals a zone of proximal development in children. *Developmental Psychology*, 47(3), 632–644. doi: 10.1037/a0021818.

Kokal, I., Engel, A., Kirschner, S., & Keysers, C. (2011). Synchronized drumming enhances activity in the caudate and facilitates prosocial commitment – if the rhythm comes easy. *PLos One*, 6(11), e27272. doi: 27210.21371/journal.pone.0027272.

Konvalinka, I., Vuust, P., Roepstorff, A., & Frith, C. D. (2010). Follow you, follow me: Continuous mutual prediction and adaptation in joint tapping. *Quarterly Journal of Experimental Psychology*, 63(11), 2220–2230. doi: 10.1080/17470218.2010.497843.

Krueger, M. (2005). Four themes in youth work practice. *Journal of Community Psychology*, 33(1), 21–29. doi: 10.1002/jcop.20033.

Kupferberg, A., Glasauer, S., Huber, M., Rickert, M., Knoll, A., & Brandt, T. (2011). Biological movement increases acceptance of humanoid robots as human partners in motor interaction. *AI and Society*, 26(4), 339–345. doi: 10.1007/s00146-010-0314-2.

Kurzban, R. (2001). The social psychophysics of cooperation: Nonverbal communication in a public goods game. *Journal of Nonverbal Behavior*, 25(4), 241–259.

LaFrance, M. (1985). Posture mirroring and intergroup orientation. *Personality and Social Psychology Bulletin*, 11(2), 207–218.

(1990). The trouble with rapport. *Psychological Inquiry*, 1(4), 318–320.

Lakens, D. (2010). Movement synchrony and perceived entitativity. *Journal of Experimental Social Psychology*, 46(5), 701–708. doi: 10.1016/j.jesp.2010.03.015.

Lakens, D., & Stel, M. (2011). If they move in sync, they must feel in sync: Movement synchrony leads to attributions of rapport and entitativity. *Social Cognition*, 29(1), 1–14.

Launay, J., Dean, R. T., & Bailes, F. (2013). Synchronization can influence trust following virtual interaction. *Experimental Psychology*, 60(1), 53–63.

Louwerse, M. M., Dale, R., Bard, E. G., & Jeuniaux, P. (2012). Behavior matching in multimodal communication is synchronized. *Cognitive Science*, 36(8), 1404–1426.

Lumsden, J., Miles, L. K., Richardson, M. J., Smith, C. A., & Macrae, C. N. (2012). Who syncs? Social motives and interpersonal coordination. *Journal of Experimental Social Psychology*, 48(3), 746–751.

Macrae, C. N., Duffy, O. K., Miles, L. K., & Lawrence, J. (2008). A case of hand-waving: Action synchrony and person perception. *Cognition*, 109(1), 152–156. doi: 10.1016/j.cognition.2008.07.007.

Marin, L., Issartel, J., & Chaminade, T. (2009). Interpersonal motor coordination: From human–human to human–robot interactions. *Interaction Studies*, 10(3), 479–504. doi: 10.1075/is.10.3.09mar.

Marsh, K. L., Johnston, L., Richardson, M. J., & Schmidt, R. C. (2009a). Toward a radically embodied, embedded social psychology. *European Journal of Social Psychology*, 39(7), 320–339.

Marsh, K. L., Richardson, M. J., Baron, R. M., & Schmidt, R. C. (2006). Contrasting approaches to perceiving and acting with others. *Ecological Psychology*, 18(1), 1–38.

Marsh, K. L., Richardson, M. J., & Schmidt, R. C. (2009b). Social connection through joint action and interpersonal coordination. *Topics in Cognitive Science*, 1(2), 320–339. doi: 10.1111/j.1756-8765.2009.01022.x.

Masumoto, J., & Inui, N. (2013). Two heads are better than one: Both complementary and synchronous strategies facilitate joint action. *Journal of Neurophysiology*, 109(5), 1307–1314. doi: 10.1152/jn.00776.2012.

McNeill, W. H. (1995). *Keeping together in time: Dance and drill in human history*. Cambridge, MA: Harvard University Press.

McPhail, C., & Wohlstein, R. T. (1986). Collective locomotion as collective behavior. *American Sociological Review*, 51(4), 447–463.

Merker, B. H., Madison, G. S., & Eckerdal, P. (2009). On the role and origin of isochrony in human rhythmic entrainment. *Cortex; a Journal Devoted to the Study of the Nervous System and Behavior*, 45(1), 4–17. doi: 10.1016/j.cortex.2008.06.011.

Miall, R. C. (2003). Connecting mirror neurons and forward models. *Neuroreport*, 14(17), 2135–2137. doi: 10.1097/01.wnr.0000098751.87269.77.

Miles, L. K., Lumsden, J., Richardson, M. J., & Macrae, C. N. (2011). Do birds of a feather move together? Group membership and behavioral synchrony. *Experimental Brain Research*, 211(3–4), 495–503.

Miles, L. K., Nind, L. K., and Macrae, C. N. (2009). The rhythm of rapport: Interpersonal synchrony and social perception. *Journal of Experimental Social Psychology*, 45(3), 585–589.

Néda, Z., Ravasz, E., Brechet, Y., Vicsek, T., & Barabási, A. L. (2000). The sound of many hands clapping: Tumultuous applause can transform itself into waves of synchronized clapping. *Nature*, 403(6772), 849–850. doi: 10.1038/35002660.

Nessler, J. A., Kephart, G., Cowell, J., & De Leone, C. J. (2011). Varying treadmill speed and inclination affects spontaneous synchronization when two individuals walk side by side. *Journal of Applied Biomechanics*, 27(4), 322–329.

Newtson, D., Hairfield, J., Bloomingdale, J., & Cutino, S. (1987). The structure of action and interaction. *Social Cognition*, 5(3), 191–237.

Obhi, S. S., & Sebanz, N. (2011). Moving together: Toward understanding the mechanisms of joint action. *Experimental Brain Research*, 211(3), 329–336.

Oullier, O., de Guzman, G. C., Jantzen, K. J., Lagarde, J., & Kelso, J. A. S. (2008). Social coordination dynamics: Measuring human bonding. *Social Neuroscience*, 3(2), 178–192.

Oztop, E., Franklin, D. W., & Chaminade, T. (2005). Human–humanoid interaction: Is a humanoid robot perceived as a human? *International Journal of Humanoid Robotics*, 2(4), 537–559.

Paladino, M.-P., Mazzurega, M., Pavani, F., & Schubert, T. W. (2010). Synchronous multisensory stimulation blurs self–other boundaries. *Psychological Science*, 21(9), 1202–1207.

Patel, A. D., Iversen, J. R., Bregman, M. R., & Schulz, I. (2009). Experimental evidence for synchronization to a musical beat in a nonhuman animal. *Current Biology*, 19(10), 827–830.

Paxton, A., & Dale, R. (2013a). Frame-differencing methods for measuring bodily synchrony in conversation. *Behavior Research Methods*, 45(2), 329–343.

(2013b). Argument disrupts interpersonal synchrony. *Quarterly Journal of Experimental Psychology*, 66(11), 2092–2102.

Prinz, W. (1990). A common-coding approach to perception and action. In O. Neumann & W. Prinz (Eds.), *Relationships between perception and action: Current approaches*. Berlin: Springer-Verlag, 167–201.

Ramseyer, F., & Tschacher, W. (2011). Nonverbal synchrony in psychotherapy: Coordinated body movement reflects relationship quality and outcome. *Journal of Consulting and Clinical Psychology*, 79(3), 284–295.

Reddish, P., Fischer, R., & Bulbulia, J. (2013). Let's dance together: Synchrony, shared intentionality and cooperation. *PloS One*, 8(8), e71182.

Repp, B. H. (2006). Rate limits of sensorimotor synchronization. *Advances in Cognitive Psychology*, 2(2), 163–181. doi: 10.2478/v10053-008-0053-9.

Repp, B. H., & Penel, A. (2004). Rhythmic movement is attracted more strongly to auditory than to visual rhythms. *Psychological Research*, 68(4), 252–270. doi: 10.1007/s00426-003-0143-8.

Repp, B. H., & Su, Y.-H. (2013). Sensorimotor synchronization: A review of recent research (2006–2012). *Psychonomic Bulletin and Review*, 20(3), 403–452. doi: 10.3758/s13423-012-0371-2.

Richardson, M. J., Campbell, W. L., & Schmidt, R. C. (2009). Movement interference during action observation as emergent coordination. *Neuroscience Letters*, 449(2), 117–122. doi: 10.1016/j.neulet.2008.10.092.

Richardson, M. J., Marsh, K. L., Isenhower, R. W., Goodman, J. R. L., & Schmidt, R. C. (2007). Rocking together: Dynamics of intentional and unintentional interpersonal coordination. *Human Movement Science*, 26(6), 867–891. doi: 10.1016/j.humov.2007.07.002.

Richardson, M. J., Marsh, K. L., & Schmidt, R. C. (2005). Effects of visual and verbal interaction on unintentional interpersonal coordination. *Journal of Experimental Psychology: Human Perception and Performance*, 31(1), 62–79. doi: 10.1037/0096-1523.31.1.62.

Schmidt, R. C., Bienvenu, M., Fitzpatrick, P. A., & Amazeen, P. G. (1998). A comparison of intra- and interpersonal interlimb coordination: Coordination breakdowns and coupling strength. *Journal of Experimental Psychology: Human Perception and Performance*, 24(3), 884–900.

Schmidt, R. C., Carello, C., & Turvey, M. T. (1990). Phase transitions and critical fluctuations in the visual coordination of rhythmic movements between people. *Journal of Experimental Psychology: Human Perception and Performance*, 16(2), 227–247.

Schmidt, R. C., Fitzpatrick, P., Caron, R., and Mergeche, J. (2011). Understanding social motor coordination. *Human Movement Science*, 30(5), 834–845. doi:10.1016/j.humov.2010.05.014

Schmidt, R. C., & O'Brien, B. (1997). Evaluating the dynamics of unintended interpersonal coordination. *Ecological Psychology*, 9(3), 189–206.

Schmidt, R. C., Richardson, M. J., Arsenault, C., & Galantucci, B. (2007). Visual tracking and entrainment to an environmental rhythm. *Journal of Experimental Psychology: Human Perception and Performance*, 33(4), 860–870. doi: 10.1037/0096-1523.33.4.860.

Schmidt, R. C., & Turvey, M. T. (1994). Phase-entrainment dynamics of visually coupled rhythmic movements. *Biological Cybernetics*, 70(4), 369–376.

Sebanz, N., Bekkering, H., & Knoblich, G. (2006). Joint action: Bodies and minds moving together. *Trends in Cognitive Sciences*, 10(2), 70–76.

Sebanz, N., & Knoblich, G. (2009). Prediction in joint action: What, when, and where. *Topics in Cognitive Science*, 1(2), 353–367. doi: 10.1111/j.1756-8765.2009.01024.x.

Semin, G. R., & Cacioppo, J. T. (2008). Grounding social cognition: Synchronization, entrainment and coordination. In G. R. Semin & E. R. Smith (Eds.), *Embodied grounding: Social, cognitive, affective, and neuroscientific approaches.* New York: Cambridge University Press, 119–147.

Shockley, K., Baker, A. A., Richardson, M. J., & Fowler, C. A. (2007). Articulatory constraints on interpersonal postural coordination. *Journal of Experimental Psychology: Human Perception and Performance*, 33(1), 201–208. doi: 10.1037/0096-1523.33.1.201.

Shockley, K., Richardson, D. C., & Dale, R. (2009). Conversation and coordinative structures. *Topics in Cognitive Science*, 1(2), 305–319. doi: 10.1111/j.1756-8765.2009.01021.x.

Shockley, K., Santana, M. V., & Fowler, C. A. (2003). Mutual interpersonal postural constraints are involved in cooperative conversation. *Journal of Experimental Psychology: Human Perception and Performance*, 29(2), 326–332. doi: 10.1037/0096-1523.29.2.326.

Sommerville, J. A., & Decety, J. (2006). Weaving the fabric of social interaction: Articulating developmental psychology and cognitive neuroscience in the domain of motor cognition. *Psychonomic Bulletin & Review*, 13(2), 179–200.

Stanley, J., Gowen, E., & Miall, R. C. (2007). Effects of agency on movement interference during observation of a moving dot stimulus. *Journal of Experimental Psychology: Human Perception and Performance*, 33(4), 915–926. doi: 10.1037/0096-1523.33.4.915.

Stel, M., & Vonk, R. (2010). Mimicry in social interaction: Benefits for mimickers, mimickees, and their interaction. *British Journal of Psychology*, 101(2), 311–323.

Strogatz, S. H., Abrams, D. A., McRobie, A., Eckhardt, B., & Ott, E. (2005). Theoretical mechanics: Crowd synchrony on the Millennium Bridge. *Nature*, 438(7064), 43–44. doi: 10.1038/43843a.

Styns, F., van Noorden, L., Moelants, D., & Leman, M. (2007). Walking on music. *Human Movement Science*, 26(5), 769–785. doi: 10.1016/j.humov.2007.07.007.

Temprado, J.-J. (2004). Attentional load associated with performing and stabilizing a between-persons coordination of rhythmic limb movements. *Acta Psychologica*, 115(1), 1–16. doi: 10.1016/j.actpsy.2003.09.002.

Tickle-Degnen, L., & Rosenthal, R. (1990). The nature of rapport and its nonverbal correlates. *Psychological Inquiry*, 1(4), 285–293.

Tognoli, E., Lagarde, J., DeGuzman, G. C., & Kelso, J. A. S. (2007). The phi complex as a neuromarker of human social coordination. *Proceedings of the National Academy of Sciences of the United States of America*, 104(19), 8190–8195. doi: 10.1073/pnas.0611453104.

Tsakiris, M. (2008). Looking for myself: Current multisensory input alters self-face recognition. *PloS One*, 3(12), e4040.

Ulzen, N. R., Lamoth, C. J. C., Daffertshofer, A., Semin, G. R., & Beek, P. J. (2008). Characteristics of instructed and uninstructed interpersonal coordination while walking side-by-side. *Neuroscience Letters*, 432(2), 88–93. doi: 10.1016/j.neulet.2007.11.070.

Vacharkulksemsuk, T., & Fredrickson, B. L. (2012). Strangers in sync: Achieving embodied rapport through shared movements. *Journal of Experimental Social Psychology*, 48(1), 399–402.

Valdesolo, P., & DeSteno, D. (2011). Synchrony and the social tuning of compassion. *Emotion*, 11(2), 262–266.

Valdesolo, P., Ouyang, J., & DeSteno, D. A. (2010). The rhythm of joint action: Synchrony promotes cooperative ability. *Journal of Experimental Social Psychology*, 46(4), 693–695. doi: 10.1016/j.jesp.2010.03.004.

Wagemans, J., Elder, J. H., Kubovy, M., Palmer, S. E., Peterson, M. A., et al. (2012). A century of Gestalt psychology in visual perception: I. Perceptual grouping and figure–ground organization. *Psychological Bulletin*, 138(6), 1172–1217. doi: 10.1037/a0029333.

Watanabe, K. (2008). Behavioral speed contagion: Automatic modulation of movement timing by observation of body movements. *Cognition*, 106(3), 1514–1524. doi: 10.1016/j.cognition.2007.06.001.

Wiltermuth, S. S. (2012). Synchronous activity boosts compliance with requests to aggress. *Journal of Experimental Social Psychology*, 48(1), 453–456.

Wiltermuth, S. S., & Heath, C. (2009). Synchrony and cooperation. *Psychological Science*, 20(1), 1–5. doi: 10.1111/j.1467-9280.2008.02253.x.

Wolpert, D. M., Doya, K., & Kawato, M. (2003). A unifying computational framework for motor control and social interaction. *Philosophical Transactions of the Royal Society B: Biological Sciences*, 358(1431), 593–602. doi: 10.1098/rstb.2002.1238.

14 Musical Ensemble Performance: Representing Self, Other and Joint Action Outcomes

Peter E. Keller, Giacomo Novembre and Janeen Loehr

Abstract

Musical ensemble performance constitutes a refined form of joint action that involves the non-verbal communication of information about musical structure and expressive intentions via co-performers' sounds and body movements. Successful musical communication requires co-performers to coordinate their actions across multiple musical dimensions (pitch and rhythm), time-scales (expressive micro-timing versus large-scale tempo changes), sensory modalities (auditory and visual) and modes of interaction (unison versus complementary action). From a psychological perspective, ensemble performance necessitates precise yet flexible interpersonal coordination at the level of sensorimotor, cognitive, emotional and social processes. The current chapter addresses how such interpersonal coordination is facilitated by representations of shared performance goals, which are consolidated during preparation for joint musical performance. During actual performance, these shared goal representations interact with online sensorimotor and cognitive processes that allow co-performers to anticipate, attend and adapt to each other's actions in real time. Studies employing behavioral and brain methods provide evidence for three functional characteristics of shared musical representations. First, shared representations involve the integration of information related to one's own part, others' parts and the joint action outcome, while maintaining a distinction between self and other. Second, self, other and joint action outcomes are represented in predictive internal models. Third, internal models recruit the motor system to simulate self- and other-produced actions at multiple hierarchical levels. Shared musical representations thus facilitate exquisite real-time interpersonal coordination by dynamically embodying intended action outcomes related to the self, others and the ensemble as a whole.

Introduction

Human interaction in musical contexts is a vital part of social life in all known cultures. Types of musical interaction range from intimate duets through medium-sized groups to large orchestras, sometimes including more than a hundred performers under the direction of a conductor. Irrespective of size, musical ensemble performance – as a social art form – entails multiple individuals pursuing shared *aesthetic goals*. These goals are typically realized through the non-verbal communication of information about *musical structure* and *expressive intentions* to co-performers as well as audience members. To this end, musical interaction partners engage in mutually coupled, affective exchanges that are mediated by instrumental sounds and body movements (Keller, 2008; MacRitchie, Buck, & Bailey, 2013). From a psychological perspective, musical ensemble performance thus constitutes a highly refined form of joint action that requires real-time interpersonal coordination at the level of sensorimotor, cognitive, emotional and social processes (Keller, Novembre, and Hove, 2014).

A basic requirement in musical joint action is the alignment of information along multiple musical dimensions, including fundamental elements of music such as rhythm, pitch and intensity (loudness), across individuals (Keller, 2014). Rhythm and pitch are fundamental elements of music. Rhythm generally refers to the temporal patterning of sequential events. In music, this patterning is determined by the durations of intervals between sound onsets, which commonly form ratios such as 2:1, 3:1 and 4:1. Pitch is a psychological aspect of sound that is, in music, related mainly to the perceived fundamental frequency of complex tones (ranging from low to high). Pitched tones can be arranged sequentially to produce melodies, while the simultaneous sounding of two or more pitched tones in chords gives rise to harmony.

Rhythm and pitch are typically structured hierarchically: individual tones are concatenated into melodic motives (short sequences of tones perceived as a group, analogous to words in speech) and phrases (short strings of motives, analogous to spoken phrases and sentences). Rhythmic durations can be defined relative to the temporal units of underlying metric frameworks. Metric frameworks are cognitive-motor schemas that comprise hierarchically arranged levels of pulsation that include the beat, beat subdivisions and groupings of beats into bars (Lerdahl & Jackendoff, 1983; London, 2012). Metric pulsations are experienced as regular series of internal events, with every nth event perceived to be accented, i.e. stronger than its neighbors. Regularity at the most salient level of metric pulsation – the beat, with which one might tap along when listening to music – allows it to function as a shared temporal frame of reference that multiple performers use to time their sounds (Nowicki et al., 2013). This function is made explicit in musical contexts that employ a conductor (who provides beat gestures) or a subgroup of instrumentalists who are designated as the 'rhythm section' (e.g. the bass and drums in much standard jazz).

The way in which separate instrumental parts in an ensemble fit together depends largely on the patterning of their rhythmic and pitch elements. On the temporal dimension, separate parts articulate the same rhythm or complementary rhythms that mesh to produce interlocking patterns with varying levels of complexity (defined according to how well the rhythms fit a common metric framework). Similarly, pitch relations between parts can be unison or harmonic (multiple simultaneous pitches), and, in the latter case, consonant or dissonant (depending on the complexity of pitch interval ratios). The more distinguishable are individuals' parts in terms of rhythm and pitch, the more likely they will be perceived to play different roles (e.g. melody versus accompaniment) in a musical texture. Ensemble performance is thus characterized by the hierarchical structuring of musical information and a variety of modes of interpersonal coordination at the level of sounds (Phillips-Silver & Keller, 2012).

Hierarchical structuring and different coordination modes likewise characterize the body movements of ensemble performers. A distinction can be drawn between *instrumental movements*, which are directly related to the production of musical sounds (e.g. the keystrokes of pianists), and *ancillary movements*, which are not technically necessary for sound production but nevertheless accompany performance (e.g. head nods, limb gestures and body sway) (Nusseck & Wanderley, 2009). During ensemble performance, sounds triggered by instrumental movements are coordinated at short timescales in the millisecond range, while ancillary movements such as body sway are aligned at longer timescales associated with higher-order units of musical structure (e.g. phrases). These large-scale movements provide visual cues that, in combination with the auditory cues provided by musical sounds, facilitate the multimodal communication of hierarchical musical structure and expressive intentions (Davidson, 2009). Interpersonal coordination in musical joint action therefore evolves at multiple timescales and across different sensory modalities.

A challenge for ensemble musicians is to achieve precision in basic interpersonal coordination without sacrificing the flexibility required to modulate expressive performance parameters (Keller, 2014; Palmer, 1997). These *expressive variations* may arise spontaneously during performance, though they are also often pre-planned but executed as if spontaneous (Chaffin, Lemieux, & Chen, 2007). Variations in performance timing are a particularly effective means by which performers communicate their intentions concerning musical structure and stylistic expression (Friberg & Battel, 2002; Gabrielsson, 1999; Repp, 2002). Expressive timing variations include micro-timing deviations (delays and advances in sound onset timing in the order of tens of milliseconds) and local *tempo* fluctuations (accelerations and decelerations in the order of hundreds of milliseconds). In ensembles, expressive performance is not merely a matter of individual variation, but rather inter-individual co-variation (Keller, 2014).

To achieve precise yet flexible interpersonal alignment across the multiple dimensions, timescales, sensory modalities and coordination modes described above, ensemble co-performers rely to some degree upon mental representations of each other's parts in the musical texture. This is a specialized form of shared task representation that assists performers in keeping track of who is who (i.e. agency attribution) and dealing with the real-time demands of musical joint action.

Shared Musical Representations

Complex forms of musical joint action require pre-planning. Indeed, musicians in many ensemble traditions spend considerable time preparing for performance through a combination of individual private practice and collaborative group rehearsal. Private practice not only develops the individual's technical skills, but can also facilitate familiarity with co-performers' parts through the study of sound recordings and *musical scores*. Collaborative rehearsal is then typically geared towards establishing a shared performance goal, i.e. a unified conception of the ideal integrated ensemble sound (Keller, 2008; Williamon & Davidson, 2002).

The richness and specificity of performance goals, and the degree to which they are truly shared across ensemble members, vary as a function of the musical context. Members of a symphony orchestra, for example, do not necessarily know the intricacies of each part in the ensemble texture; rather, the conductor functions as a repository of the global performance goal. Moreover, in freely improvised music, co-performers eschew fully preconceived goals in favor of transient shared goals that evolve spontaneously through mimicry and other interactive social processes during live performance. When shared performance goals are strategically pursued during rehearsal, however, ensemble musicians enter into a process of becoming familiar with one another's parts and the manner in which these parts will be played. This process primarily entails non-verbal communication through body movements and musical sounds, though verbal communication usually also takes place (Price & Byo, 2002; Williamon & Davidson, 2002).

Ensemble cohesion is predicated upon the musicians reaching a consensus on how expressive performance parameters should be modulated in order to communicate the goal interpretation of a piece. As musicians coming together to rehearse a piece bring their own preconceptions of the music, this consensus must be negotiated (Ginsborg, Chaffin, & Nicholson, 2006). A mixture of social, conventional and pragmatic considerations govern this process. Social factors – including personality, pre-existing interpersonal relationships, verbal and non-verbal communication styles, and gender and instrument stereotypes – are relevant to the extent that they influence the effectiveness of information exchange during rehearsal (Blank & Davidson, 2007; Davidson & Good, 2002; Davidson & King, 2004; Ginsborg et al., 2006; Goodman, 2002; Williamon & Davidson, 2002). The negotiation of performance goals can also be influenced by how leadership is distributed among ensemble members – ranging from egalitarian piano duos, through democratic mixed chamber groups, to hierarchical regimes where a conductor is expected to impregnate an orchestra with his or her performance goal.

Once shared performance goals are consolidated, they reside in each individual's memory as mental representations of the ideal sounds constituting a musical piece. These representations embody, to varying degrees, the performer's own sound, co-performers' sounds and the overall ensemble sound (Keller, 2008, 2014). Co-performers thus come to co-represent elements of each other's parts (Keller, 2008; Loehr & Palmer, 2011; Sebanz, Bekkering, & Knoblich, 2006). While this process may be grounded in the automatic tendency for individuals engaged in joint action to represent each other's tasks (Knoblich, Butterfill, & Sebanz, 2011; Sebanz et al., 2006), the amount of time that ensemble musicians invest in rehearsal suggests that developing shared performance goals can be effortful.

Shared musical representations ensure that ensemble musicians take each other's actions into account during performance. Research on joint action outside the music domain has demonstrated that individuals behave differently when performing a task alone or with a co-actor (Sebanz, Knoblich, & Prinz, 2005; also see Vesper & Sebanz, this volume, Chapter 11). In tasks requiring interpersonal coordination, individuals increase the salience and regularity of their movements as a strategy to smoothen coordination (Vesper, Butterfill, Knoblich, & Sebanz, 2010). Musicians similarly employ coordination smoothers to facilitate ensemble cohesion. An example is when expressive devices, such as tempo accelerations and decelerations, are dampened during ensemble performance relative to when a musician performs her part alone (Goodman, 2002). Another example is when an ensemble leader sharpens the contrast between rhythmic durations in order to communicate clear expressive intentions (Marchini, Papiotis, & Maestre, 2012), or when the performers exaggerate instrumental movements while simplifying ancillary movements such as head gestures (Glowinski et al., 2010, 2013; Goebl & Palmer, 2009).

Shared representations thus influence the process of planning and executing actions during ensemble performance. Specifically, action plans that guide motor processes involved in translating goal representations into body movements that are appropriate for generating the intended sound (Chaffin, Imreh, & Crawford, 2002; Gabrielsson, 1999; Palmer, 1997) are modified by knowledge of a co-performer's task. Importantly, action plans will differ across co-performers when their parts are complementary (rather than identical), even if the individuals play the same instrument. Ensemble musicians therefore develop systems of shared performance cues to regulate and coordinate their actions (Ginsborg et al., 2006).

Performance cues are features of the music (e.g. phrase boundaries and intensity changes) that group members collectively attend to during performance in order to ensure that things take place as planned (Chaffin & Logan, 2006; Ginsborg et al., 2006). The selected features provide landmarks in a mental map that reflects the hierarchical organization of sections in a piece's formal structure. Hierarchies of performance cues thus serve as retrieval schemes that enable performers to deal with the real-time demands of performance by utilizing domain-specific expert memory processes (Lehmann & Ericsson, 1998). In ensembles, shared performance cues remind co-performers of shared performance goals and link individual performance plans into a common scheme that can be used to regulate the interplay between musicians (Keller, 2014).

Once shared goal representations, performance plans and cues are established, they interact with online sensorimotor and cognitive processes that facilitate precise yet flexible interpersonal coordination by allowing co-performers to anticipate, attend and adapt to each other's actions in real time. The following sections of this chapter deal with how shared representations are formed during preparation for joint musical performance, and how these representations interact with sensorimotor and cognitive processes during actual performance. Our treatment of these topics is organized around three central claims about shared musical representations. First, shared representations involve the integration of information related to one's own part, others' parts and the joint action outcome while maintaining a distinction between self and other. Second, self, other and joint action outcomes are represented in predictive internal models. Third, internal models recruit the motor system to simulate self- and other-produced actions. Studies that employ behavioral and brain methods provide converging evidence for these three claims.

Self–Other Integration and Segregation

While the collective aim of much ensemble performance is to produce a cohesive musical gestalt, the primary responsibility of each individual performer is to produce his or her own part accurately. In other words, the coherence of the whole depends on the integrity of its parts. Therefore, although shared goals are represented and used to guide performance, a distinction between representations of parts produced by the self and others must be maintained in order to allow each performer to retain autonomous control of his or her own movements (cf. De Jaegher & Di Paolo, 2007; Pacherie, 2012). Ensemble musicians thus integrate information related to their own part and others' parts to monitor the joint action outcome while maintaining a distinction between self and other. This balance between self–other merging and self–other distinction entails the simultaneous integration and segregation of information from separate sources (Keller, Novembre, & Hove, 2014).

Generally speaking, the human capacity for segregation relies on the ability to isolate parts that constitute a whole object or event, while the capacity for integration relies on the ability to construct a whole by grouping together a collection of parts. Integration and segregation have been investigated extensively in the domains of visual and auditory perception. In vision, segregation is exemplified by the perception of figure–ground relations in a visual scene, where one object is perceived as a distinct entity against a background, while integration is exemplified by countless demonstrations by gestalt psychologists that the whole is greater than the sum of its parts (Schacter, Gilbert, & Wegner, 2011). In audition, integration and segregation have been studied most thoroughly in the field of *auditory scene analysis*. In particular, research on the phenomenon of auditory streaming has shown how the relationship between concurrent sound sequences in terms of pitch and timing determines the degree to which they are likely to be perceived as separate streams versus an integrated whole (see Snyder & Alain, 2007).

In traditional auditory streaming demonstrations (e.g. Bregman & Campbell, 1971), a sequence of alternating high- and low-pitch tones is perceived by listeners to segregate into a sequence of high tones and a sequence of low tones when the pitch difference between the tones is large and the tempo is fast. Streaming is also influenced by the relationship between tones in terms of their timing, timbre and intensity (see Bregman, 1990). While these features can automatically lead to the segregated or integrated percepts (Müller, Widmann, & Schröger, 2005), the ability to hear sequences as segregated or integrated is nevertheless subject to some degree of control through the allocation of attention (van Noorden, 1975). A classic example of this is the cocktail party effect, which refers to the ability to attend selectively to one stream of information while ignoring others (Cherry, 1953). When listening to ensemble music, it is likewise possible to focus attention locally on a particular instrumental part, or to spread attention across parts and focus more globally on harmonic and rhythmic relationships between them (Bigand, McAdams, & Forêt, 2000; Janata, Tillmann, & Bharucha, 2002).

Furthermore, it has been argued that a mode of attention that is a hybrid of these two extremes may be recruited when listening to, and performing, ensemble music (Keller, 1999). Specifically, in the case of listening, an individual may focus attention on a particular part (e.g. the melody) while simultaneously attending to the interrelationship between parts (e.g. the melody and accompaniment). Similarly, ensemble performance involves concurrently paying attention to one's own actions (high priority) and those of others (lower priority) while monitoring the overall ensemble sound. This form of divided attention has been termed 'prioritized integrative attending' (ibid).

Prioritized integrative attending assists ensemble musicians to integrate their own actions with others' actions while maintaining autonomous control of their own movements (Keller, 2014). This mode of attention facilitates ensemble cohesion by allowing co-performers to adjust their actions based on the online comparison of mental representations of the ideal ensemble sound and incoming perceptual information about the actual sound (Keller, 2008). Performers are thus able to deal with changes in the momentary demands of their own parts and the relationship between their own and others' parts in terms of timing, intensity, intonation, articulation and timbre (Keller, 2014). To the extent that prioritized integrative attending entails simultaneous self–other segregation and integration, it is cognitively demanding and can be seen as an advanced ensemble skill (Keller, 2001).

Keller and Burnham (2005) studied the dynamics of prioritized integrative attending using dual-task paradigms designed to capture a subset of the cognitive and motor demands of ensemble performance. In a listening task, musicians were required simultaneously to memorize a target (high priority) part and the overall aggregate structure (resulting from the combination of two complementary parts) of short percussion duets. Results indicated that recognition memory for both aspects of each duet was influenced by how well the target part and the aggregate structure could be accommodated within the same metric framework.

Analogous results were obtained in a second 'rhythmic canon' study, which required professional percussionists first to listen to a rhythm pattern, and then to reproduce it on a drum while listening to a concurrently presented pattern that also had to be subsequently reproduced. Reproducing the first pattern in time with the second one is essentially a form of sensorimotor synchronization, and as such requires the integration of sensory information associated with the pattern being listened to with motor information related to the pattern being produced (cf. Lakens, Schubert, & Paladino, this volume, Chapter 13). Taken together, Keller and Burnham's (2005) results demonstrate that musicians are able, first, to prioritize one part while monitoring the relationship between parts when listening to or producing multipart patterns and, second, to form memory representations for different levels (part and whole) of the multipart structure. However, the ability for such processing and representation is affected by the temporal compatibility between parts.

Subsequent research has sought to identify the neural correlates of prioritized integrative attending. Recent studies employed fMRI to investigate the simultaneous segregation and integration of melody and accompaniment parts during listening to piano duos (Ragert, Fairhurst, & Keller, 2014; Uhlig et al., 2013). The melody and accompaniment parts were differentiated in terms of both pitch and rhythm, and participants were required to attend to one part while judging its temporal relationship to the other part (leading or following).

The results of these studies suggest that the planum temporale (posterior to the primary auditory cortex) plays a role in segregation, the intraparietal sulcus supports integration, and frontal regions (including dorsolateral prefrontal cortex and frontal gyrus) regulate attentional modulations of the balance between these two processes. By recruiting this fronto–parieto–temporal network, prioritized integrative attending calls upon brain regions that subserve basic forms of auditory attention, including selective, divided and nonprioritized integrative attending (see Janata, Tillmann, & Bharucha, 2002b; Satoh, Takeda, Nagata, Hatazawa, & Kuzuhara, 2001).

In ensemble performance, simultaneous self–other integration and segregation is especially important for the task of monitoring an ongoing performance to determine whether shared performance goals are being met. In a recent study of this process, Loehr et al. (2013) investigated whether pianists are able to monitor their own and their partner's part of a duet in parallel. Pairs of pianists performed duets together while their brain activity was recorded using electroencephalography (EEG). During their performances, the pitches elicited by each performer's keystrokes were occasionally altered (by a computer that controlled the keyboard output) so that an unexpected pitch was produced. Half of the altered pitches occurred in the upper part of the duet (*own part* for the pianist performing the upper part; *partner's part* for the pianist performing the lower part) and half occurred in the lower part of the duet (vice versa). Each unexpected pitch changed either the auditory outcome of one pianist's action (i.e. a single pitch in one pianist's part) or the joint outcome of the pianists' combined actions (i.e. the harmony of the chord produced by the two pianists' combined pitches; see Figure 14.1).

The altered pitches elicited two brain responses that are commonly associated with monitoring action outcomes. First, altered pitches elicited a feedback-related negativity (FRN), a negative-going potential that signals a perceived mismatch between expected and actual action outcomes and peaks approximately 250 ms after the unexpected action outcome (Oliveira, MacDonald, & Goodman, 2007). Equivalent FRNs were elicited whether the altered pitch occurred in the pianist's own part or the partner's part, indicating that pianists monitored their own actions and their partners' actions in parallel. Second, altered pitches elicited a P300 response, a positive-going potential that peaks 300–600 ms after the action outcome. The P300 occurs relatively late in the processing stream and its amplitude is thought to reflect the perceived significance of the unexpected outcome (Nieuwenhuis, Aston-Jones, & Cohen, 2005). As Figure 14.1 shows, the amplitude of the P300 was larger in response to altered pitches that occurred in the pianist's own part compared to the partner's part and in response to altered pitches that changed the joint outcome compared to an individual outcome. Thus, whereas the FRN findings indicate integration of own and others' parts at an early stage of action monitoring, the

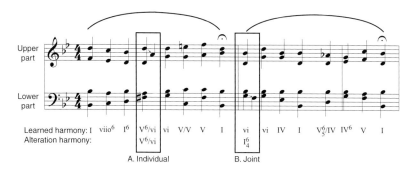

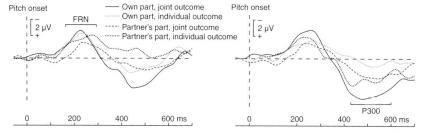

Figure 14.1 Brain responses to unexpected pitches indicate integration and segregation of self and other during action monitoring.

Notes: Upper panel: the first half of a duet, showing two altered pitches. One pianist performed the upper part of the duet and the other performed the lower part. Symbols immediately below chords (labeled 'learned harmony') indicate the harmony given in the score. Symbols labeled 'alteration harmony' indicate the harmony introduced by the altered pitch. (A) *Individual outcome* altered without changing the harmony of the chord. (B) *Joint outcome* altered by changing the harmony of the chord. Lower panel: brain responses to altered pitches. Left side: the feedback-related negativity. The difference between brain responses to expected and unexpected pitches, averaged over five fronto-central electrodes, is shown for each type of altered pitch. Right side: the P300. The difference between brain responses to expected and unexpected pitches, averaged over three parieto-central electrodes, is shown for each type of altered pitch.

Source: Reprinted and modified, with permission, from Loehr et al. (2013).

P300 findings indicate that pianists differentiate between their own and others' action outcomes, and between individual and joint action outcomes, at later stages of processing.

In addition to monitoring joint musical outcomes, the balance between self–other integration and segregation influences the process of maintaining autonomous control of one's own actions. Such autonomous control presumably requires agent-specific representations at the level of the motor system. Novembre, Ticini, Schütz-Bosbach, and Keller (2012) explored the representation of self- and other-related actions in the human motor system in a single-pulse transcranial magnetic stimulation (TMS) study that employed a virtual piano duo paradigm. Skilled pianists were asked to learn several piano pieces bimanually before coming to the laboratory. The right-hand part contained a melody line and the left-hand part contained a complementary bassline. When the pianists were invited to the lab a few days later, they were required to perform the right-hand part of each piece while the left-hand part was either not performed or believed to be played by another pianist hidden behind a screen (this hidden pianist feigned playing while the participant actually heard a recording).

The experiment ran across two sessions, one in which pianists could hear feedback of their actions as well as the recording, and a subsequent session in which the pianists received no auditory feedback (i.e. the piano was muted) but were still aware of the presence of the co-performer behind the screen. In both sessions, single-pulse TMS was applied over the right primary motor cortex to elicit motor-evoked potentials (MEPs), which were measured (with electromyography) from a left forearm muscle that would normally be used to perform the complementary part.

It was assumed that bimanual learning of the piece would lead to a *co*-representation of the left-hand part, which would then be associated either with the self (when the part had been learned but was not performed) or with the other player (behind the screen). Consistent with this, differences in MEP amplitude suggested that distinct patterns of cortico-spinal excitability – inhibition and excitation – were associated with the representation of self and other, respectively (cf. Loehr, 2013; Schütz-Bosbach, Avenanti, Aglioti, & Haggard, 2009; Schütz-Bosbach, Mancini, Aglioti, & Haggard, 2006; Weiss, Tsakiris, Haggard, & Schütz-Bosbach, 2014). Crucially, the results did not change as a function of whether or not the pianists received auditory feedback about their own performance or the 'hidden partner'.

Novembre et al.'s (2012) findings support the hypothesis that musicians form agent-specific forms of motor representations in the context of joint musical tasks. Inhibition and excitation of the motor system might therefore constitute markers of the functional segregation of parts performed by self versus other during musical ensemble performance. The finding that this segregation occurred in the mute session suggests that these agent-specific representations arise in response to the potential for interaction with another, and may therefore be intrinsically social in nature. This 'social' interpretation was buttressed by the additional finding that the degree of excitation in the condition where pianists believed they were performing with another was positively correlated with scores on a subscale of an empathy questionnaire assessing the tendency to adopt others' perspectives in everyday life.

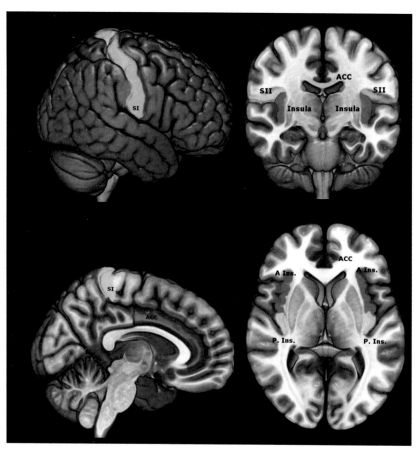

Plate 1 Illustration of the main brain regions involved in both the experience of pain and touch and their perception in others. *See Box 4.1.*

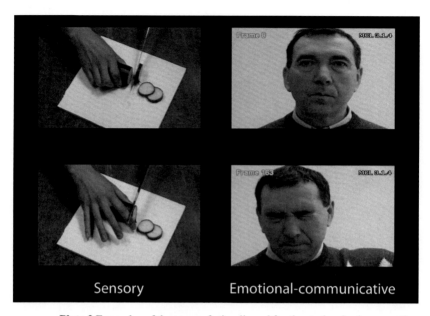

Plate 2 Examples of the types of stimuli used for the study of pain perception in others. *See Figure 4.1.*

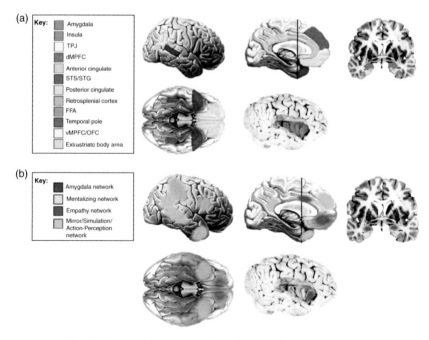

Plate 3 The social brain, from Kennedy and Adolphs (2012). *See Figure 5.1.*

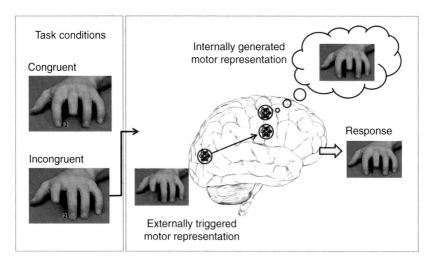

Plate 4 Examples of trials in the imitation inhibition task and a schematic representation of the conflict that arises in the incongruent condition. *See Figure 8.1.*

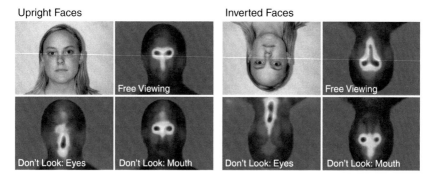

Plate 5 Heat maps representing the average location of participant fixations for upright and inverted faces in free viewing Don't Look: Eyes and Don't Look: Mouth conditions. *See Figure 10.1.*

Plate 6 Individual versus joint affordance maps. *See Figure 17.1.*

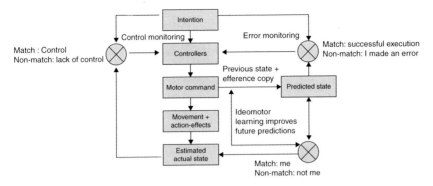

Plate 7 The comparator model of agency. *See Figure 17.2.*

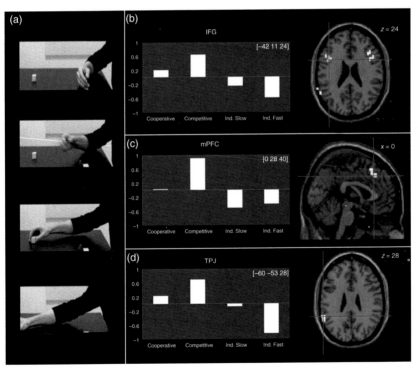

Plate 8 Reading intention from action observation. *See Figure 18.2.*

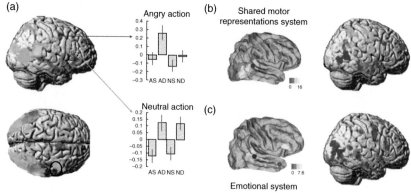

(a)

Angry action

0.4
0.3
0.2
0.1
0
-0.1
-0.2
-0.3
AS AD NS ND

(b) Shared motor representations system

0 16

Neutral action

0.2
0.15
0.1
0.05
0
-0.05
-0.1
-0.15
-0.2
AS AD NS ND

(c)

0 7.6

Emotional system

▇ Neutral dynamic (ND) vs. Neutral static (NS)
■ Fear (bottom) or Anger (top - AD, AS) vs. ND

Plate 9 Statistical parametric maps of brain activation in response to the observation of dynamic versus static emotional expressions, connectivity of two brain areas sustaining shared motor representations, and changes in connectivity pattern of emotion to action brain areas. *See Figure 20.1.*

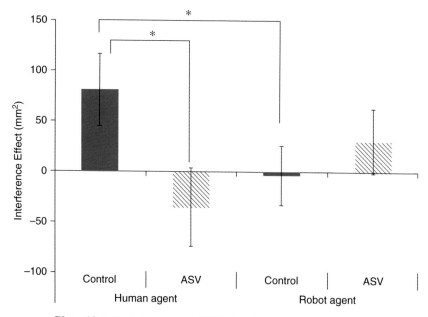

Plate 10 Adjusted mean (+/–SEM) interference effect (incongruent minus congruent variance) is displayed. *See Figure 23.2.*

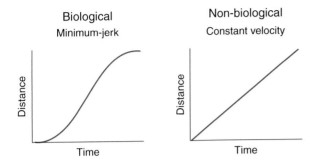

Plate 11 Minimum-jerk and constant velocity profiles. *See Figure 23.3.*

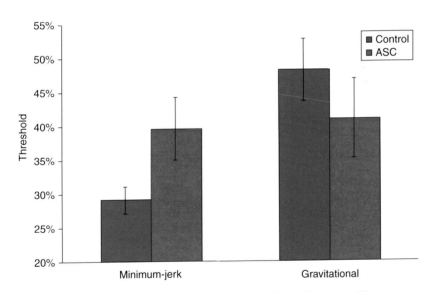

Plate 12 Interaction between group and condition. *See Figure 23.4.*

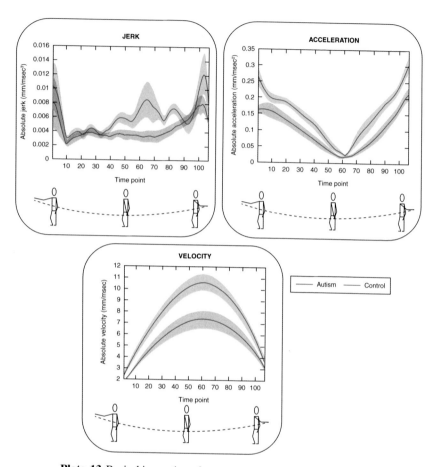

Plate 13 Basic kinematics of arm movements for controls and individuals with ASCs. *See Figure 23.5.*

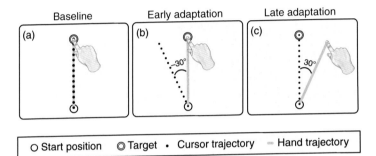

Plate 14 Visuomotor rotation. *See Figure 25.1.*

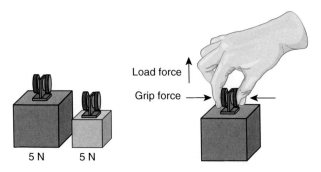

Plate 15 Fingertip force adaptation. *See Figure 25.2.*

5 N   5 N

Load force

Grip force

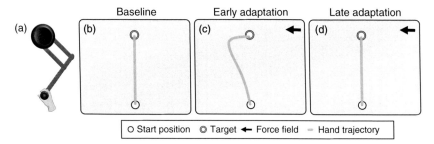

Baseline   Early adaptation   Late adaptation

(a)   (b)   (c)   (d)

○ Start position   ◎ Target   ← Force field   — Hand trajectory

Plate 16 Force field adaptation. *See Figure 25.3.*

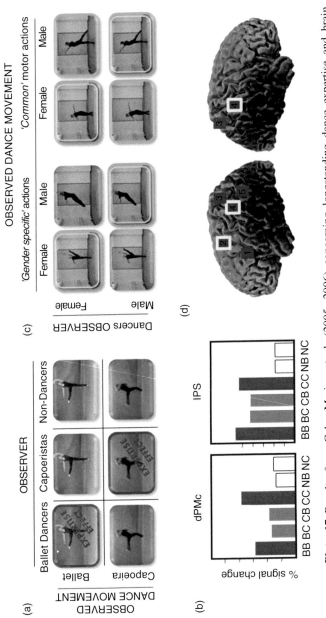

Plate 17 Results from Calvo-Merino et al. (2005, 2006) concerning longstanding dance expertise and brain engagement. *See Figure 26.1.*

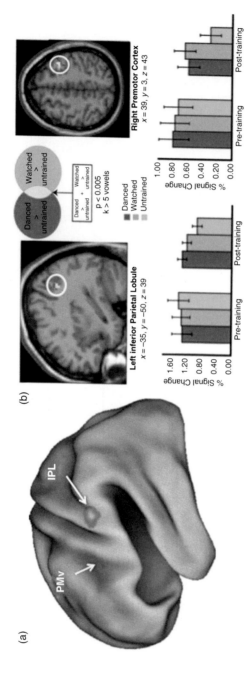

Plate 18 Results from Cross et al. (2006) concerning physical expertise and action embodiment. *See Figure 26.2.*

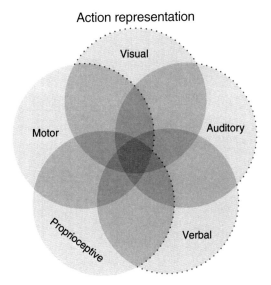

Plate 19 Action representation schema, including information from different sources. *See Box 26.1.*

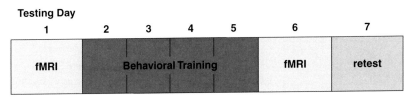

Plate 20 An approach to running training studies where identical fMRI sessions are separated by a period of several days of identical behavioral training sessions. *See Box 26.2.*

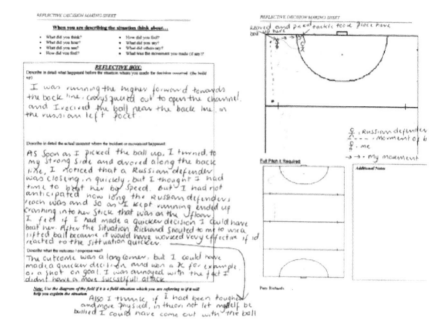

Plate 21 One player's notes on critical moments in field hockey and their perceived key factors. *See Figure 28.1.*

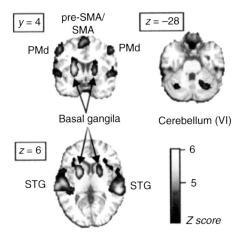

Plate 22 Brain areas activated while listening to rhythms. *See Figure 29.1.*

Plate 23 Snowball, the dancing cockatiel. *See Box 29.2.*

Social factors have also been found to affect the balance of self–other integration and segregation during sensorimotor synchronization with virtual partners that vary in dynamic cooperativity. One relevant study (Fairhurst, Janata, & Keller, 2014) addressed the relationship between leader–follower tendencies, temporal adaptation and locus of control – a dimension of personality related to the degree to which life events are perceived to be a consequence of one's own actions. The study aimed to identify behavioral strategies and patterns of brain activity that distinguish between individuals with different leader–follower dispositions when they interact with synchronization partners with high or low levels of competence. This was examined in an fMRI experiment that required individuals to synchronize finger taps with sounds produced by virtual partners who varied in terms of competence at keeping a steady tempo. For performance to be successful, the human participant must take responsibility for keeping the tempo when the virtual partner cannot.

Results indicated that 'leaders' (individuals who attribute the cause of events to their own actions) generally engaged in less adaptive timing than 'followers' (who attribute events to external factors). In other words, leaders were less likely than followers to adapt the timing of their taps to the virtual partner's timing. This may stem from a difference in the balance of self–other integration and segregation: while followers prioritized the task of synchronizing with their partner (i.e. self–other integration), leaders focused on stabilizing the tempo of their own performance (self–other segregation). This difference was reflected at the level of the brain. Specifically, brain regions implicated in self-initiated action (e.g. pre-supplementary motor area) and the evaluation of agency (e.g. precuneus) were activated more strongly in leaders than followers. More generally, the activation of right lateralized areas (including the inferior frontal gyrus and the inferior parietal lobule) varied as a function of the competence of the virtual partner, suggesting that these areas may be involved in the regulation of degree of self–other integration and segregation based on the skill of an interaction partner.

Internal Models for Self, Other and Joint Action Outcomes

Shared representations of musical goals facilitate ensemble coordination, first, by ensuring that co-performers plan to produce their parts in a manner that is mutually compatible and, second, by assisting co-performers to anticipate each other's action timing via the generation of online predictions during performance. It has been claimed that both of these functions are enabled by 'internal models' instantiated in the central nervous system (see Keller, 2014). Internal models represent sensorimotor associations between motor commands that issue from the brain and the sensory experience of bodily states and events in the immediate environment (Kawato, 1999; Wolpert, Miall, & Kawato, 1998). In the case of music performance, these associations link musical sounds with instrumental and ancillary body movements.

Research in the field of computational movement neuroscience has identified two types of internal model: forward and inverse (ibid). Forward models represent the causal relationship between motor commands (e.g. to lower a finger) and their effects on the body and the environment (the tactile sensation of striking a piano key and the auditory sensation of hearing a tone). Inverse models represent transformations from intended action outcomes (sounds, in the case of music) to the motor commands that produce them. It has been argued that multiple hierarchically nested internal models represent events at multiple timescales in the context of complex action sequences (Pacherie, 2008). Accordingly, music performance recruits models linked to different levels in the music's hierarchical structure, including long-range performance goals and plans (representing musical phrases and ancillary body sway, for example) and models of short-range goals and plans (representing instrumental movements and individual sounds or brief sequences) (Pacherie, 2012; Ragert, Schroeder, & Keller, 2013). Internal models thus represent dynamic processes to the extent that they contain information about movement kinematics and sequential event transitions (Pezzulo, Candidi, Dindo, & Barca, 2013).

It has been proposed that internal models arise from the cerebellum, from where they communicate with other brain regions (see Ito, 2008). Internal models can thus be used to drive simulations of goal-directed actions by recruiting the brain areas that would normally be involved in action execution and action observation, but without causing overt movement and in the absence of corresponding sensory input (Pezzulo et al., 2013). *Action simulation* plays a role in planning one's own actions (Jeannerod, 2001), as well as in predicting the future course of others' actions and understanding their intentions (Schubotz, 2007; Wilson & Knoblich, 2005). Two classes of internal model therefore operate in tandem during ensemble performance, one for simulating one's own actions ('self' models) and the other for simulating co-performers' actions ('other' models) (Keller, 2008; Keller & Appel, 2010; Sänger, Lindenberger, & Müller, 2011).

'Self' models are used to guide the production of one's own part: they facilitate efficient action planning and execution by running slightly ahead of movement, thereby allowing potential errors to be anticipated and corrected before they occur (Wolpert et al., 1998). 'Other' models are used to simulate the observed actions of co-performers: they allow one musician to predict what another will do, how they will do it and when they will do it (Keller, 2008, 2012; Wolpert, Doya, & Kawato, 2003). In the context of joint action, the coupling of 'self' and 'other' models in a 'joint' model facilitates fluent coordination between co-performers by allowing potential interpersonal timing errors (as well as errors affecting other musical dimensions such as pitch and intensity) to be simulated and corrected before they occur (see Box 14.1) (van der Steen and Keller, 2013).

Box 14.1 Internal models

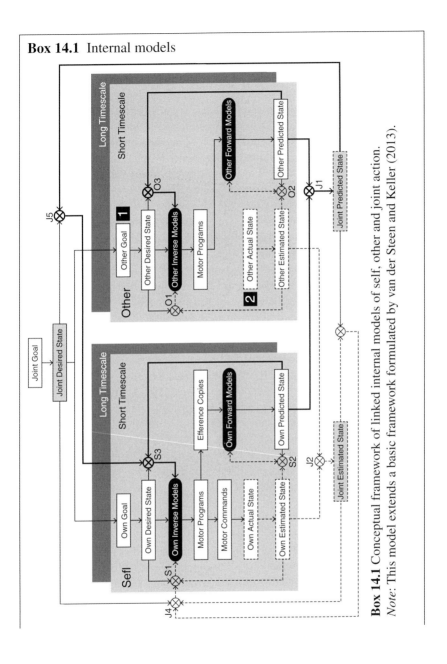

Box 14.1 Conceptual framework of linked internal models of self, other and joint action.
Note: This model extends a basic framework formulated by van der Steen and Keller (2013).

293

Although a number of authors have postulated the existence of internal models that represent 'others' in addition to the 'self', the precise way in which these models are linked is typically not specified. Here, we present a conceptual framework of linked internal models of self, other and joint action that extends a basic framework formulated by van der Steen and Keller (2013) to musical ensemble performance. In this conceptualization, self and other internal models operate at multiple timescales, allowing the simultaneous simulation of instrumental movements at short timescales and ancillary movements at longer timescales. In the schematic diagram, the operations carried out by internal models are illustrated for the short timescale only, but it is assumed that similar operations are performed at long timescales. It is furthermore assumed that hierarchically arranged internal models permit the representation of sequential and temporal relationships between the constituent elements of complex actions, as well as different levels of action specification (see Pacherie, 2008, 2012; Wolpert et al., 2003). The dotted lines in the diagram indicate processes that rely on sensory feedback while unbroken lines indicate feedforward processes.

Self internal models

Internal models that represent sensorimotor transformations related to an individual's own actions (self) facilitate action planning and online control (Ito, 2008; Kawato, 1999; Wolpert et al., 1998). These 'self' internal models may be acquired and refined through musical experience via mechanisms such as Bayesian probabilistic learning (Haruno, Wolpert, & Kawato, 2001; Körding & Wolpert, 2004). During this process, 'own' inverse models, which provide motor programs for achieving action goals, are developed through a process that entails minimizing discrepancies (S1) between the desired state associated with an action goal and estimates of the actual state brought about by executing a motor command. 'Own' forward models receive efference copies of motor programs provided by own inverse models and, based on this information, generate predictions about state changes that would result from the execution of these programs. Own forward models are calibrated during learning by minimizing discrepancies (S2) between predicted and estimated actual states. Once calibrated, own forward models can be used to correct potential errors before they occur by comparing (S3) predicted and desired state during action execution.

Other internal models

'Other' internal models, which represent sensorimotor transformations related to others' actions, allow one individual to predict the actions of co-performers. These predictions may evolve via two routes (cf. Phillips-Silver & Keller, 2012). If an individual has pre-existing knowledge of another's goal (1), then a top-down form of simulation takes place where 'other' inverse models activate motor programs that would be appropriate for achieving the other's (inferred) desired state. 'Other' forward models can generate predictions about the other's likely future state by simulating the execution of these programs. The second 'bottom-up' route (2) proceeds via an automatic process of motor resonance. Incoming perceptual information is used to estimate the other's current state, which is used by an 'other' inverse model to provide a motor program that would be appropriate for bringing about this state. To the extent that the program is linked to higher-level programs representing sequential relations between action elements, an 'other' forward model can be used to predict the future state that would arise if these programs were to be executed.

'Other' inverse models develop with increasing familiarity with particular co-performers through a process involving the minimization discrepancies (O1) between the inferred desired states and estimated actual states. Other forward models are calibrated to co-performers' action styles by minimizing discrepancies (O2) between predicted and estimated states. Following such calibration, other forward models can lead to modifications of other inverse models based on comparisons (O3) between predicted and desired states. In situations where an individual is familiar with neither the structure of co-performer's parts nor their playing style, 'other' internal models may be restricted to representing sensorimotor transformations at long timescales associated with ancillary body movements (e.g. sway) yoked to higher levels in the music's structural hierarchy.

Joint internal models

In the current conceptualization, internal models of self and other interact in a joint internal model. The joint model provides a dynamic representation of the shared performance goal (see the 'Shared Musical Representations' section earlier in this chapter). Joint internal models integrate the outputs of self and other internal models, and then modify 'own' inverse models to compensate for any discrepancies between these outputs. The predicted states for own and other are combined to yield a joint predicted state (J1). Similarly, state estimates based on perceptual information about one's own and another's actions are combined to yield a joint estimated state (J2). Predicted and estimated joint states are compared (J3) and compensatory adaptations made to own internal models to account for discrepancies (J4). Furthermore, inverse models may be modified due to discrepancies arising from comparisons between the joint estimated state and the joint desired state (J4). Finally, interpersonal errors can be corrected before they occur based on comparisons between the joint predicted state and the joint desired state (J5). This is a key component of van der Steen and Keller's (2013) framework.

'Self', 'other' and 'joint' internal models for complex skills such as music performance require training. Specifically, the sensorimotor transformations represented in internal models must be acquired, strengthened and refined through active experience and observational learning (Cross et al., 2009; Schubotz, 2007; Wolpert et al., 2003). Representations of these transformations may develop in tandem with the strengthening of links between sensory and motor cortical regions, notably, the auditory–motor coupling that develops with musical experience (Herholz & Zatorre, 2012; Zatorre, Chen, & Penhune, 2007). Practicing instrumental technique thus leads to the development of internal models that assist in producing the desired sounds, while observing and listening to co-performers allows one individual to learn to simulate another's idiosyncratic playing style via the calibration of internal models to the other's action system (Repp & Keller, 2010). Reliable and efficient 'self', 'other' and 'joint' internal models can be viewed as a hallmark of expertise as an ensemble musician.

In music performance, action simulation is experienced (in phenomenological terms) as anticipatory auditory and motor imagery of musical sounds and related movements (Keller, 2012; Keller & Appel, 2010). It is through such mental imagery that ensemble musicians activate internal representations of shared goals, plans and cues during performance (Keller, 2014). Anticipatory imagery thus steers action simulation while internal models provide the motor that drives it. The importance of imagery in ensemble performance is highlighted by self-reports of elite musicians. A member of the renowned brass section of the Chicago Symphony Orchestra states: 'If I don't hear it [the ideal sound] or conceptualize it in my brain, there's no way I'm going to get it' (Trusheim, 1991, p. 146). The performer is referring to the use of anticipatory auditory imagery to recruit 'self' inverse models that assist in achieving the level of motor control required to produce the ideal sound. Another Chicago brass player alludes to the use of auditory imagery of co-performers' parts during private practice for ensemble performance:

The sound of what is going on in the rest of the orchestra is always in my imagination … you're training yourself to think of what else is happening. You're hearing the whole picture…. (ibid, pp. 145–146)

Here, the performer refers to the use of 'other' and 'joint' models even when playing in the absence of co-performers. Clearly, the effectiveness of such a strategy would depend upon knowledge of the structure of co-performers' parts and their playing style.

Evidence that self, other and joint action outcomes are represented in predictive internal models comes from behavioral, neuroimaging and brain stimulation studies addressing the effects of familiarity with a co-performer's part on the performance of an individual's own part, as well as on overall ensemble coordination.

A specific piece of evidence supporting the claim that musicians form internal models of their partner's part of a duet is the finding that knowledge of the partner's part influences how the pianist's own part is performed. Loehr and Palmer (2011) and Palmer and Loehr (2013) compared pianists' performances of a right-hand melody when paired with a left-hand accompaniment produced by themselves or by a partner. The left-hand accompaniment was either simple (repetitive, arpeggiated pitch changes and repeating harmonies) or complex (scalar pitch changes with less repetitive harmony). When the pianists performed both parts themselves, the right-hand melody was produced differently (e.g. more slowly and with a more pronounced temporal grouping structure) than when paired with a simple compared to complex left-hand accompaniment. The same pattern of differences occurred when the left-hand accompaniment was produced by a partner. Thus, pianists' internal models of the partner's part modified the production of their own part of a joint performance.

In another study (Ragert et al., 2013), pairs of unacquainted pianists came to the lab after practicing either one part or both parts of several piano duets at home. The complementary parts of the duets were therefore familiar in one condition and unfamiliar in the other. Pianists' keystroke timing was recorded on digital pianos and their body movements were tracked with a motion-capture system as they played repeat performances across six takes in each condition. It was assumed that, in the unfamiliar condition, each pianist would develop performance goals, plans and cues for his own part during private practice, whereas shared goals, plans and cues that take both parts into account would not be consolidated. Internal models for simulating the co-performer's part would therefore not be initially available when the part was unfamiliar. However, increasing exposure to the co-performer's part and playing style across takes was expected to lead to the formation of shared performance goals, plans and cues, and to the acquisition of internal models that generate temporal predictions based on simulations that are consistent with the co-performer's expressive style.

Ragert et al.'s results pointed to a partial dissociation between interpersonal coordination at the level of keystrokes and body sway. Variability in keystroke asynchronies decreased across the takes, and was generally lower in the unfamiliar condition than the familiar condition. This indicates that coordination started out better, and remained so, when pianists had *not* rehearsed their co-performer's part. By contrast, body sway coordination was high throughout the takes in the familiar condition, while it started out low and improved across takes in the unfamiliar condition. These findings suggest that knowledge affects interpersonal coordination by influencing predictions at different timescales. Familiarity with a co-performer's part, but not their playing style, engenders predictions about expressive micro-timing variations that are based instead upon one's own personal playing style, leading to a mismatch between predictions and actual events at short timescales. As knowledge about a co-performer's stylistic idiosyncrasies is acquired, however, the individual learns – through the calibration of internal models – to simulate the other's action style. Familiarity with the structure of a co-performer's part, on the other hand, facilitates predictions at longer timescales related to high-level metric units and musical phrases, and is reflected in ancillary body sway movements.

Another study (Novembre, Ticini, Schütz-Bosbach, & Keller, 2014) examined how disrupting (via double-pulse TMS) the cortical brain network underlying action simulation affects the ability of pianists to adapt to tempo changes in familiar and unfamiliar parts during virtual duet performance. The task (see Figure 14.2A) required participants to play the right-hand part of piano pieces in synchrony with a recording of the complementary left-hand part, which had (trained) or had not (untrained) been practiced beforehand. The recordings of the left-hand part contained occasional tempo changes, to which the pianists had to adapt in order to maintain synchrony. In critical conditions, these tempo changes were preceded by double-pulse TMS delivered over the right primary motor cortex (to interfere with simulation of the left-hand part). It was hypothesized that practicing the left-hand part would lead to the development of internal models for performing the part, thereby enhancing the ability to simulate it and assisting with adaptation to the tempo changes. To test this hypothesis, the accuracy of tempo adaptation following TMS or sham stimulations was compared across trained and untrained conditions (Figure 14.2B).

It was found (Figure 14.2C) that TMS impaired tempo adaptation when the left-hand part had been previously trained, but not when the part was untrained (suggesting that tempo adaptation may have been underpinned by a different, possibly subcortical, brain network in this case). These results extend previous research on the role of training in developing the capacity for (cortical) motor simulation (see the 'Motor Simulation of Self and Other' section below; cf. D'Ausilio, 2007; Haueisen & Knösche, 2001; Lahav, Saltzman, & Schlaug, 2007) by demonstrating that motor representations of others' actions support interpersonal coordination. Consistent with the results of Novembre et al. (2012), the social implications of such co-representation at the level of the motor system were borne out by the additional finding that the pianists who were particularly susceptible to TMS-induced interference with tempo adaptation scored highly on the perspective-taking subscale of an empathy questionnaire (Figure 14.2D).

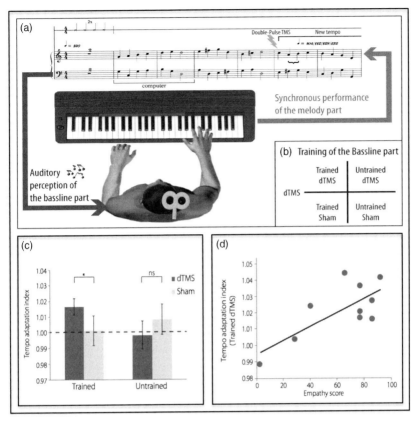

Figure 14.2 Schematic summary of the study by Novembre et al. (2014).
Notes: A. Experimental task. B. Experimental design. C. Tempo adaptation index across conditions (the dashed horizontal line indicates perfect adaptation, values above or below indicate deceleration or acceleration, respectively, of the produced melody with respect to the bassline part presented by the computer). D. Correlation between TMS-interference to motor simulation and the perspective-taking (empathy) score of each participant.
Source: Reprinted and modified, with permission, from Novembre et al. (2014).

Motor Simulation of Self and Other

The proposal that internal models recruit an ensemble musician's motor system to simulate co-performers' actions is consistent with embodied accounts of social cognition more generally (e.g. Hurley, 2008). A corollary of such motor involvement is that representations of co-performers' actions may be influenced by one's own action repertoire and action style. *Action repertoire*

refers to the set of musical structures that an individual performer is potentially able to produce given her technical mastery of her instrument. *Action
style* refers to idiosyncratic ways of producing these structures (in terms of
fluctuations in event micro-timing and intensity). Action style may vary due to
a mixture of factors, including learning history, aesthetic preferences (Repp,
1997, 1998), level of expertise (e.g. expert pianists play with more idiosyncratic expressive timing profiles than novices; Repp, 1995) and biomechanical
properties related to individuals' physical characteristics (see Keller, 2014).
Here, we consider how the effects of action simulation on interpersonal coordination in ensembles are moderated by the degree of overlap in co-performers'
action repertoires and the similarity of their preferred action styles.

Synchronizing with a recording of one's own performance presents a special case of perfect overlap in action repertoire and action style, because the
sensorimotor system engaged in action simulation is the same system that
produced the action in the first place. In a study of such self-synchronization
(Keller, Knoblich, & Repp 2007), pianists were asked to record one part from
several duets and then, several months later, to play the complementary part
in synchrony with either their own or others' recordings. As expected, synchronization was best when the pianists played with their own recordings.
This finding was taken as support for the hypothesis that pianists predicted
the timing of sounds in the recordings by engaging in online simulation of the
performances. On this account, such simulation led to a self-synchronization
advantage because the match between simulated event timing and actual timing in a complementary part was best when both were products of the same
sensorimotor system. Additional analyses (examining correlations between
timing profiles of duet parts recorded separately by the same pianist) indicated
that the self-synchronization advantage was not merely due to *a priori* self-
similarity in performance technique. This reinforces the claim that overlap in
action repertoire and action style facilitates interpersonal coordination by enabling the accurate simulation of other co-performers' actions.

The self-synchronization advantage found by Keller et al. (2007) invites the
hypothesis that ensemble musicians with similar action styles (when they perform alone) should be better able to simulate each other's actions and therefore better able to coordinate with each other when they perform together. In a
study on this topic, Loehr and Palmer (2011) investigated whether performers
who are more similar to each other in terms of their preferred solo performance tempi are better able to coordinate with each other during duet performance. Each pianist in a randomly assigned pair was first asked to perform a
simple melody alone, from which her preferred performance tempo was calculated. The pairs then performed duets together, and the degree to which the
pianists were able to synchronize with each other and mutually adapt to fluctuations in each other's timing was measured. Pairs who were better matched

in solo performance tempi were better able to synchronize with each other and displayed mutual adaptation, whereas pairs who were less well-matched produced larger asynchronies and displayed a tendency for one person to track the other's timing but not vice versa. Importantly, coordination between partners was predicted by the degree of similarity between their preferred solo tempi, but not by either partner's solo tempo considered alone. These findings suggest that performers who are better matched are better able to generate predictions about each other's timing, resulting in improved coordination.

Compatibility in action style may therefore occur at multiple timescales, ranging from local micro-timing to global tempo. The way in which similarity in action style influences motor simulation and the process of generating predictions at these different timescales depends to some degree on the amount of overlap in action repertoire. Movements that produce sounds on a particular musical instrument (such as a pianist's keystrokes) can be simulated accurately only when these actions are in the observer's behavioral repertoire (e.g. when a pianist sees or hears another pianist). Indeed, neurophysiological studies of music listening have revealed that the strength and anatomical specificity of brain activations associated with motor simulation is modulated by the degree to which an individual is experienced at producing the movements required to produce the heard sounds (D'Ausilio, 2007; Haueisen & Knösche, 2001; Lahav, Saltzman, & Schlaug, 2007). For example, regions of the primary motor cortex that represent specific fingers (thumb and little finger) become especially active when pianists listen to sounds that would be played by those particular fingers in the context of a specific musical piece (Haueisen & Knösche, 2001). Without such specific knowledge, simulation is limited to more general, instrument-independent movements (body sway, rocking, and expressive gesturing with the head and hands), as well as vocal and articulatory activity that could potentially approximate others' sounds (Keller, 2008; Schubotz, 2007). Overlap in action repertoire thus affects the specificity of the movements that are simulated, ranging from instrumental movements at short timescales to ancillary movements that evolve at longer timescales.

Conclusions

Ensemble performance is a refined form of joint action that entails the non-verbal communication of information about musical structure and expressive intentions via sounds and body movements produced collectively by co-performers. For such communication to be successful, precise yet flexible interpersonal coordination is required across multiple musical dimensions (including pitch and rhythm), timescales (expressive micro-timing versus large-scale tempo changes), sensory modalities (auditory and visual) and modes of interaction (unison versus complementary action). Furthermore, the real-time demands and aesthetic goals of ensemble coordination necessitate interpersonal alignment at the level of sensorimotor, cognitive, emotional and social processes.

In the current chapter, it was claimed that such alignment is facilitated by representations of performance goals that are shared across ensemble members. These shared musical representations facilitate ensemble cohesion by interacting with sensorimotor and cognitive processes during performance, thereby allowing ensemble musicians to anticipate, attend and adapt to each other's actions in real time.

We presented evidence that shared musical representations consist of integrated information related to an ensemble performer's own part, other performers' parts and the joint ensemble sound, while maintaining a distinction between self and other. Such simultaneous integration and segregation of self and other allows each performer to retain autonomous control of his own actions, while the ensemble itself attains a form of autonomy that signals cohesive social interaction (Keller et al., 2014; cf. De Jaegher & Di Paolo, 2007). The balance between group integration and individual segregation may be especially critical in small ensembles. For instance, a member of the renowned *Trio Wanderer* describes the ensemble as follows: 'It's like a holy trinity. It's three individuals in a group. Both things [individuality and group] are equal and very important' (Interviewed by Peter Keller, 9 September 2011, Leipzig).

Finally, we argued that self, other and joint action outcomes are represented in internal models that recruit a performer's motor system to simulate actions at multiple hierarchical levels, ranging from movements that produce sounds on an instrument to ancillary body movements (e.g. sway) that are linked to higher levels of musical structure. Shared musical representations are thus dynamic in the way in which they embody action outcomes related to the self, others and the ensemble as a whole. Investigating open questions on shared musical representations (see Box 14.2) will potentially further our understanding of how humans achieve exquisite real-time interpersonal coordination in complex forms of communicative joint action.

Box 14.2 Questions for future research

- What form do shared representations take when performance goals cannot be fully specified in advance (e.g. during improvisation) or distributed equally among all ensemble members (e.g. in a symphony orchestra)?
- What factors determine the quality of interpersonal coordination at short timescales where instrumental movements occur versus longer timescales associated with co-performers' ancillary movements?

- How do joint internal models develop over the course of training or rehearsal? Are joint internal models of higher hierarchical levels (e.g. tempo changes at the phrase level) developed sequentially or simultaneously with models at lower levels (e.g. micro-timing deviations)?
- What factors determine the balance between self–other integration and segregation, and how does this balance change dynamically over the course of a musical joint action?
- How is the balance between self–other integration and segregation regulated in the brain?
- How do shared representations influence performers' sense of agency or control over a performance?
- To what degree does the accuracy of joint internal models contribute to feelings of 'flow' or positive affect that arise during musical interactions?

References

Bigand, E., McAdams, S., & Forêt, S. (2000). Divided attention in the listening of polyphonic music. *International Journal of Psychology*, 35, 270–278.

Blank, M., & Davidson, J. W. (2007). An exploration of the effects of musical and social factors in piano duo collaborations. *Psychology of Music*, 35(2), 231–248.

Bregman, A. S. (1990). *Auditory scene analysis*. Cambridge, MA: MIT Press.

Bregman, A. S., & Campbell, J. (1971). Primary auditory stream segregation and perception of order in rapid sequences of tones. *Journal of Experimental Psychology*, 89, 244–249.

Chaffin, R., Imreh, G., & Crawford, M. (2002). *Practicing perfection: Memory and piano performance*. Mahwah, NJ: Lawrence Erlbaum.

Chaffin, R., Lemieux, A. F., & Chen, C. (2007). 'It is different each time I play': Variability in highly prepared musical performance. *Music Perception*, 24(5), 455–472.

Chaffin, R., & Logan, T. (2006). Practicing perfection: How concert soloists prepare for performance. *Advances in Cognitive Psychology*, 2(2), 113–130.

Cherry, E. C. (1953). Some experiments on the recognition of speech, with one and two ears. *Journal of the Acoustic Society of America*, 25, 975–979.

Cross, E. S., Kraemer, D. J., Hamilton, A. F., Kelley, W. M., & Grafton, S. T. (2009). Sensitivity of the action observation network to physical and observational learning. *Cerebral Cortex*, 19(2), 315–326.

D'Ausilio, A. (2007). The role of the mirror system in mapping complex sounds into actions. *Journal of Neuroscience*, 27(22), 5847–5848.

Davidson, J. W. (2009). Movement and collaboration in musical performance. In S. Hallam, I. Cross, & M. Thaut (Eds.), *The Oxford handbook of music psychology*. Oxford: Oxford University Press, 364–376.

Davidson, J. W., & Good, J. M. M. (2002). Social and musical co-ordination between members of a string quartet: An exploratory study. *Psychology of Music*, 30(2), 186–201.

Davidson, J. W. & King, E. C. (2004). Strategies for ensemble practice. In A. Williamon (Ed.), *Enhancing musical performance.* Oxford: Oxford University Press, 105–122.

De Jaegher, H., & Di Paolo, E. (2007). Participatory sense-making: An enactive approach to social cognition. *Phenomenology and the Cognitive Sciences,* 6, 485–507.

Fairhurst, M. T., Janata, P., & Keller, P. E. (2014). Leading the follower: An fMRI investigation of dynamic cooperativity and leader–follower strategies in synchronization with an adaptive virtual partner. *NeuroImage,* 84, 688–697.

Friberg, A., & Battel, G. U. (2002). Structural communication. In R. Parncutt & G. E. McPherson (Eds.), *The science and psychology of music performance: Creative strategies for teaching and learning.* New York: Oxford University Press, 1–16.

Gabrielsson, A. (1999). The performance of music. In D. Deutsch (Ed.), *The psychology of music.* San Diego, CA: Academic Press, 501–602.

Ginsborg, J., Chaffin, R., & Nicholson, G. (2006). Shared performance cues in singing and conducting: A content analysis of talk during practice. *Psychology of Music,* 34, 167–192.

Glowinski, D., et al. (2010). Multi-scale entropy analysis of dominance in social creative activities. *Proceedings of the ACM Multimedia International Conference,* Firenze, Italy, 1035–1038.

(2013). The movements made by performers in a skilled quartet a distinctive pattern, and then the function it serves. *Frontiers in Psychology,* 4, 841.

Goebl, W., & Palmer, C. (2009). Synchronization of timing and motion among performing musicians. *Music Perception,* 26(5), 427–438.

Goodman, E. (2002). Ensemble performance. In J. Rink (Ed.), *Musical performance: A guide to understanding.* Cambridge: Cambridge University Press, 153–167.

Haruno, M., Wolpert, D., & Kawato, M. (2001). Mosaic model for sensorimotor learning and control. *Neural Computation,* 13(10), 2201–2220.

Haueisen, J., & Knösche, T. R. (2001). Involuntary motor activation in pianists evoked by music perception. *Journal of Cognitive Neuroscience,* 13, 786–792.

Herholz, S. C., & Zatorre, R. J. (2012). Musical training as a framework for brain plasticity: Behavior, function, and structure. *Neuron,* 76(3), 486–502.

Hurley, S. (2008). The shared circuits model (SCM): How control, mirroring, and simulation can enable imitation, deliberation, and mindreading. *Behavioral and Brain Sciences,* 31(1), 1–58.

Idil, K., Engel, A., Kirschner, S., & Keysers, C. (2011). Synchronized drumming enhances activity in the caudate and facilitates prosocial commitment – if the rhythm comes easily. *PloS One,* 6(11), e27272.

Ito, M. (2008). Control of mental activities by internal models in the cerebellum. *Nature Reviews: Neuroscience,* 9(4), 304–313.

Janata, P., Tillmann, B., & Bharucha, J. J. (2002). Listening to polyphonic music recruits domain-general attention and working memory circuits. *Cognitive, Affective & Behavioral Neuroscience,* 2(2), 121–140.

Jeannerod, M. (2001). Neural simulation of action: A unifying mechanism for motor cognition. *NeuroImage,* 14, S103–S109.

Kawato, M. (1999). Internal models for motor control and trajectory planning. *Current Opinion in Neurobiology,* 9, 718–727.

Keller, P. E. (1999). Attending in complex musical interactions: The adaptive dual role of meter. *Australian Journal of Psychology,* 51, 166–175.

(2001). Attentional resource allocation in musical ensemble performance. *Psychology of Music*, 29, 20–38.

(2008). Joint action in music performance. In F. Morganti, A. Carassa, & G. Riva (Eds.), *Enacting intersubjectivity: A cognitive and social perspective to the study of interactions*. Amsterdam: IOS Press, 205–221.

(2012). Mental imagery in music performance: Underlying mechanisms and potential benefits. *Annals of the New York Academy of Sciences*, 1252, 206–213.

(2014). Ensemble performance: Interpersonal alignment of musical expression. In D. Fabian, R. Timmers, & E. Schubert (Eds.), *Expressiveness in music performance: Empirical approaches across styles and cultures*. Oxford: Oxford University Press, 260–282.

Keller, P. E., & Appel, M. (2010). Individual differences, auditory imagery, and the coordination of body movements and sounds in musical ensembles. *Music Perception*, 28(1), 27–46.

Keller, P. E., & Burnham, D. K. (2005). Musical meter in attention to multipart rhythm. *Music Perception*, 22, 629–61.

Keller, P. E., Knoblich, G., & Repp, B. H. (2007). Pianists duet better when they play with themselves: On the possible role of action simulation in synchronization. *Consciousness and cognition*, 16(1), 102–111.

Keller, P. E., & Repp, B. H. (2008). Multilevel coordination stability: Integrated goal representations in simultaneous intra-personal and inter-agent coordination. *Acta Psychologica*, 128(2), 378–386.

Keller, P. E., Novembre, G., & Hove, M. J. (2014). Rhythm in joint action: Psychological and neurophysiological mechanisms for real-time interpersonal coordination. *Philosophical Transactions of the Royal Society B: Biological Sciences*, 369, 20130394.

Knoblich, G., Butterfill, S., & Sebanz, N. (2011). Psychological research on joint action. In B. H. Ross (Ed.), *Advances in research and theory*. London: Academic Press, 59–101.

Körding, K. P., & Wolpert, D. M. (2004). Bayesian integration in sensorimotor learning. *Nature*, 427(6971), 244–247.

Lahav, A., Saltzman, E., & Schlaug, G. (2007). Action representation of sound: Audiomotor recognition network while listening to newly acquired actions. *Journal of Neuroscience*, 27(2), 308–314.

Lehmann, A. C., & Ericsson, K. A. (1998). Preparation of a public piano performance: The relation between practice and performance. *Musicae Scientiae*, 2, 69–94.

Lerdahl, F., & Jackendoff, R. (1983). *A generative theory of tonal music*. Cambridge, MA: MIT Press.

Loehr, J. D. (2013). Sensory attenuation for jointly produced action effects. *Frontiers in Psychology*, 4, 172.

Loehr, J. D., Kourtis, D., Vesper, C., Sebanz, N., & Knoblich, G. (2013). Monitoring individual and joint action outcomes in duet music performance. *Journal of Cognitive Neuroscience*, 25(7), 1049–1061.

Loehr, J. D., & Palmer, C. (2011). Temporal coordination between performing musicians. *Quarterly Journal of Experimental Psychology*, 64(11), 2153–2167.

London, J. (2012). *Hearing in time: Psychological aspects of musical meter*. New York: Oxford University Press.

MacRitchie, J., Buck, B., & Bailey, N. J. (2013). Inferring musical structure through bodily gestures. *Musicae Scientiae*, 17(1), 86–108.

Marchini, M., Papiotis, P., & Maestre, E. (2012). Timing synchronization in string quartet performance: A preliminary study. In M. Barthet & S. Dixon (Eds.), *Proceedings of the 9th International Symposium on Computer Music Modeling and Retrieval (CMMR)*. London: Queen Mary University of London, 177–185.

Müller, D., Widmann, A., & Schröger, E. (2005). Auditory streaming affects the processing of successive deviant and standard sounds. *Psychophysiology*, 42(6), 668–676.

Nieuwenhuis, S., Aston-Jones, G., & Cohen, J. D. (2005). Decision-making, the P3, and the locus coeruleus-norepinephrine system. *Psychological Bulletin*, 131, 510–532.

Noorden, L. van. (1975). *Temporal coherence in the perception of tone sequences*. Eindhoven: Institute for Perception Research.

Novembre, G., Ticini, L. C. F., Schütz-Bosbach, S., & Keller, P. E. (2012). Distinguishing self and other in joint action: Evidence from a musical paradigm. *Cerebral Cortex*, 22(12), 2894–2903.

(2014). Motor simulation and the coordination of self and other in real-time joint action. *Social Cognitive and Affective Neuroscience*, 9, 1062–1068.

Nowicki, L., Prinz, W., Grosjean, M., Repp, B. H., & Keller, P. E. (2013). Mutual adaptive timing in interpersonal action coordination. *Psychomusicology: Music, Mind, and Brain*, 23(1), 6–20.

Nusseck, M., & Wanderley, M. M. (2009). Music and motion: How music-related ancillary body movements contribute to the experience of music. *Music Perception*, 26(4), 335–353.

Oliveira, F. T. P., MacDonald, J. J., & Goodman, D. (2007). Performance monitoring in the anterior cingulate cortex is not all error related: Expectancy deviation and the representation of action–outcome associations. *Journal of Cognitive Neuroscience*, 19, 1994–2004.

Pacherie, E. (2008). The phenomenology of action: A conceptual framework. *Cognition*, 107(1), 179–217.

(2012). The phenomenology of joint action: Self-agency vs. joint-agency. In A. Seemann (Ed.), *Joint attention: New developments*, Vol. 93. Cambridge, MA: MIT Press, 343–389.

Palmer, C. (1997). Music performance. *Annual Review of Psychology*, 48, 115–138.

Palmer, C., & Loehr, J. D. (2013). Meeting of two minds in duet piano performance. In L. F. Bernstein & A. Rozin (Eds.), *Musical implications: Essays in honor of Eugene Narmour*. Hillsdale, NY: Pendragon Press, 323–338.

Pezzulo, G., Candidi, M., Dindo, H., & Barca, L. (2013). Action simulation in the human brain: Twelve questions. *New Ideas in Psychology*, 31(3), 270–290.

Phillips-Silver, J., & Keller, P. E. (2012). Searching for roots of entrainment and joint action in early musical interactions. *Frontiers in Human Neuroscience*, 6, 26.

Price, H. E., & Byo, J. L. (2002). Rehearsing and conducting. In R. Parncutt & G. E. McPherson (Eds.), *The science and psychology of musical performance: Creative strategies for teaching and learning*. Oxford: Oxford University Press, 335–351.

Ragert, M., Fairhurst, M. T., & Keller, P. E. (2014). Segregation and integration of auditory streams when listening to multi-part music. *PloS One*, 9(1), e84085.

Ragert, M., Schroeder, T., & Keller, P. E. (2013). Knowing too little or too much: The effects of familiarity with a co-performer's part on interpersonal coordination in musical ensembles. *Frontiers in Psychology*, 4, 368.

Repp, B. H. (1995). Expressive timing in Schumann's 'Träumerei:' An analysis of performances by graduate student pianists. *Journal of the Acoustical Society of America*, 98(5), 2413–2427.

(1997). The aesthetic quality of a quantitatively average music performance: Two preliminary experiments. *Music Perception*, 14(4), 419–444.

(1998). A microcosm of musical expression. I. Quantitative analysis of pianists' timing in the initial measures of Chopin's Etude in E Major. *Journal of the Acoustical Society of America*, 104(2), 1085–1100.

(2002). The embodiment of musical structure: Effects of musical context on sensorimotor synchronization with complex timing patterns. In W. Prinz & B. Hommel (Eds.), *Common mechanisms in perception and action: Attention and Performance XIX*. Oxford: Oxford University Press, 245–265.

Repp, B. H., & Keller, P. E. (2010). Self versus other in piano performance: Detectability of timing perturbations depends on personal playing style. *Experimental Brain Research*, 202(1), 101–110.

Sänger, J., Lindenberger, U., & Müller, V. (2011). Interactive brains, social minds. *Communicative and Integrative Biology*, 4, 655–663.

Satoh, M., Takeda, K. Nagata, K. Hatazawa, J., & Kuzuhara, S. (2001). Activated brain regions in musicians during an ensemble: A PET study. *Cognitive Brain Research*, 12, 101–108.

Schacter, D. L., Gilbert, D. T., & Wegner, D. M. (2011). *Psychology*, 2nd edition. New York: Worth.

Schubotz, R. I. (2007). Prediction of external events with our motor system: Towards a new framework. *Trends in Cognitive Sciences*, 11(5), 211–218.

Schütz-Bosbach, S., Avenanti, A., Aglioti, S. M. & Haggard, P. (2009). Don't do it! Cortical inhibition and self-attribution during action observation. *Journal of Cognitive Neuroscience*, 21(6), 1215–1227.

Schutz-Bosbach, S., Mancini, B., Aglioti, S. M., & Haggard, P. (2006). Self and other in the human motor system. *Current Biology*, 16(18), 1830–1834.

Sebanz, N., Bekkering, H., & Knoblich, G. (2006). Joint action: Bodies and minds moving together. *Trends in Cognitive Sciences*, 10(2), 70–76.

Sebanz, N., Knoblich, G., & Prinz, W. (2005). How two share a task: Corepresenting stimulus–response mappings. *Journal of Experimental Psychology: Human Perception and Performance*, 31(6), 1234–1246.

Snyder, J. S., & Alain, C. (2007). Toward a neurophysiological theory of auditory stream segregation. *Psychological Bulletin*, 133(5), 780–799.

Steen, M.C. van der, & Keller, P. (2013). The ADaptation and Anticipation Model (ADAM) of sensorimotor synchronization. *Frontiers in Human Neuroscience*, 7, 253.

Trusheim, W. H. (1991). Audiation and mental imagery: Implications for artistic performance. *Quarterly Journal of Music Teaching and Learning*, 2, 138–147.

Uhlig, M., Fairhurst, M. T., & Keller, P. E. (2013). The importance of integration and top-down salience when listening to complex multi-part musical stimuli. *NeuroImage*, 77, 52–61.

Vesper, C., Butterfill, S. Knoblich, G., & Sebanz, N. (2010). A minimal architecture for joint action. *Neural Networks*, 23(8–9), 998–1003.

Weiss, C., Tsakiris, M., Haggard, P., & Schütz-Bosbach, S. (2014). Agency in the sensorimotor system and its relation to explicit action awareness. *Neuropsychologia*, 52, 82–92.

Williamon, A., & Davidson, J. W. (2002). Exploring co-performer communication. *Musicae Scientiae*, 6, 53–72.

Wilson, M., & Knoblich, G. (2005). The case for motor involvement in perceiving conspecifics. *Psychological Bulletin*, 131(3), 460–473.

Wolpert, D. M., Doya, K., & Kawato, M. (2003). A unifying computational framework for motor control and social interaction. *Philosophical Transactions of the Royal Society B: Biological Sciences*, 358(1431), 593–602.

Wolpert, D. M., Miall, R. C., & Kawato, M. (1998). Internal models in the cerebellum. *Trends in Cognitive Sciences*, 2, 338–347.

Zatorre, R. J., Chen, J. L., & Penhune, V. B. (2007). When the brain plays music: Auditory–motor interactions in music perception and production. *Nature Reviews: Neuroscience* 8(7), 547–558.

Glossary

Action repertoire The set of goal-directed actions that an individual is potentially able to execute. These sets are developed through the implicit learning and deliberate practice of motor skills. In music, a performer's action repertoire includes movements that are necessary to meet the technical requirements of producing sound on an instrument, as well as specific movement sequences required to play a particular musical piece.

Action simulation The activation of sensory and movement-related brain areas in a manner that does not necessarily follow from exogenous stimulation or lead to overt movement. Such covert simulation, which may be experienced phenomenologically as mental imagery, can assist in action planning and online motor control, as well as in understanding the goals and predicting the outcomes of observed actions performed by others.

Action style An individual's idiosyncratic way of doing things. Action style is determined by a mixture of factors, including anatomical constraints, learning history, level of expertise, personality and aesthetic preferences. While individuality in action style is valued in music performance, ensemble co-performers may seek to transcend their individual musical identities to achieve a group identity.

Aesthetic goals The artistic ideals of ensemble performance. These ideals may vary as a function of musical piece, genre, socio-cultural context and performers' predilections. Nevertheless, ensemble musicians commonly aim to interact during performance in a manner that is conducive to producing a cohesive sound in which the whole is perceived to be greater than the sum of its parts. This general goal is expressed in different forms of behavior. Multiple performers may seek to sound as one voice, to establish leader–follower relations or to engage in turn-taking analogous to conversation. These forms of interaction require shared artistic goals to be agreed upon (explicitly or implicitly) by the group.

Ancillary movements Movements that are not technically necessary for sound production but nevertheless accompany music performance. Examples include head nods, body sway and limb gestures (e.g. shoulder, elbow and hand motion). Ancillary movements function to regulate performance tempo and to provide visual cues that assist basic interpersonal coordination and the communication of expressive intentions.

Auditory scene analysis Ensemble music presents a complex auditory scene characterized by streams of sound emanating from multiple instruments, each representing a separate sound source. The human auditory system recovers individual sounds from the mixtures of sounds that arrive at the ear based on auditory cues related to pitch, timbre, intensity, timing and spatial localization, as well as perceptual grouping cues that operate according to gestalt principles of organization. Auditory scene analysis facilitates the perception and production of ensemble music by allowing sounds from different instruments to be simultaneously segregated and integrated by listeners and performers.

Expressive intentions The impression that a performer wishes to convey to a listener about musical structure, meaning, mood and emotion. Ensemble musicians express their intentions to co-performers and audience members through musical sounds and body movements. Musical expression thus entails non-verbal communication via auditory and visual cues.

Expressive variations Variations in musical sound parameters that are introduced deliberately by the performer to convey her expressive intentions. These variations may affect the timing, intensity (loudness), articulation (length), intonation (tuning) and timbre (tone color) of musical sounds. A common expressive device is deceleration of performance tempo at the end of musical phrases, especially those ending major sections in the formal structure of a piece. In ensemble performance, such expressive devices need to be aligned across individuals.

Instrumental movements Movements that a performer is required to execute in order to produce sounds on a particular musical instrument (e.g. keystrokes of pianists; bowing actions of violinists; articulation and fingering of wind players).

Musical scores Systems of notation that specify elements of musical structure (pitch and rhythm) and expression (tempo, articulation and intensity changes) as intended by a composer. Scores provide ensemble musicians and orchestral conductors with an overview of all instrumental parts and how they fit together, thus forming a potential basis for shared musical representations.

Musical structure The patterning of musical sounds in pitch and time to produce melody, rhythm, harmony and higher-order forms of organization. Melodic structure is determined by the way in which the sequential ordering of tones encourages perceptual grouping into motives and phrases that constitute a melody. Rhythmic structure is influenced by temporal relations between sounds within and between instrumental parts. Harmonic structure refers to sequential progressions of chords (simultaneously sounding tones) that are governed by genre-specific syntactic rules. Formal structure stems from the organization of melodic, rhythmic and harmonic structural units into sections (e.g. verse and chorus in songs) that combine to form the narrative of a musical piece.

Tempo Musical speed or pace. In music where rhythms are structured relative to a regular underlying beat, tempo can be specified in terms of beats per minute, as produced by a metronome. Musical tempi typically fall within a range that corresponds to rates at which human locomotion is possible. Performance tempo (unless electronically controlled) is not strictly regular but contains unintentional fluctuations due to perceptual and motor limitations as well as intentional variations introduced for expressive purposes.

Part IV

Understanding Others

15 The Social Function of the Human Mirror System: A Motor Chauvinist View

Antonia Hamilton

Abstract

Many different claims have been made concerning the function and role of the human mirror system. This chapter first examines the question of what makes the mirror system special, and whether this particular network can be clearly distinguished from visuomotor systems in the brain. Current studies suggest it is surprisingly hard to draw clear distinctions between mirroring and visuomotor systems. The second part then distinguishes between models for understanding, predicting and responding to social stimuli. I suggest that responding theories have been somewhat neglected, and that social responding should be considered as an important function of the mirror system, in the same way that grasping objects is an important function of the visuomotor system.

The humble sea squirt provides an excellent example of motor chauvinism – after an early period of active swimming, it settles on a rock and assumes a passive lifestyle of waiting for food to drift by. At this point, it digests its own brain, because a body that does not move has no need for a brain. The motor chauvinist makes the claim that the primary function of the human brain is to move – to decide what actions to perform and then implement those actions in an efficient manner. In this chapter, I examine how this view can help us understand the functioning of the human mirror system.

Mirror neurons were first discovered in the premotor cortex of the macaque monkey in the context of studies of motor physiology (Gallese, Fadiga, Fogassi, & Rizzolatti, 1996; di Pellegrino, Fadiga, Fogassi, Gallese, & Rizzolatti, 1992). These neurons respond when a monkey picks up an object, but also when it sees a person pick up an object. However, the macaque monkey's abilities to engage socially and to imitate are somewhat limited. Neuroimaging studies allow us to examine equivalent brain systems in humans to test their role in human social behaviour. A large number of studies have now documented activation of the human premotor cortex and inferior parietal cortex when participants observe actions, perform actions and imitate actions (Caspers, Zilles, Laird, & Eickhoff, 2010; Molenberghs, Cunnington, & Mattingley, 2012). In this chapter, I focus on the properties of the brain systems that respond when typical

313

adults observe actions – the mirror neuron system (MNS) – and consider what role this plays in human behaviour. In particular, I draw comparisons between the MNS and other cortical motor systems for object use (object–motor system – OMS). This comparison aims to highlight which features are similar between the MNS and OMS, and which differ. Then, I consider different theories of the function of the MNS.

What Might Make the Human Mirror System Special?

Since mirror neurons were first discovered, many claims have been made for the special function of this brain network, that it can provide a unified model of social cognition (Gallese, Keysers, & Rizzolatti, 2004) and transform our understanding of psychology (Ramachandran, 2000). However, before examining the function of the MNS in human behaviour, it is useful to consider if this network has any special properties – is it unique in localization, or in what category of stimuli drive its responses, or how it is modulated by experience or by other brain networks? In particular, I address this question in comparison to cortical motor systems for object use (OMSs), which allow people to interact with tools and other objects in everyday life. The aim of this review is to determine if there is anything unique about the MNS that is not true for the rest of the object–motor system.

Cortical Localisation

Mirror neurons themselves are not easy to localise in humans, because fMRI operates at a much grosser resolution than single-unit recordings. However, multiple studies have tested which brain regions are active when participants observe actions and perform actions. Both at the single-subject level (Gazzola & Keysers, 2009) and the level of meta-analyses (Caspers, Zilles, Laird, & Eickhoff, 2010; Molenberghs et al., 2012), these studies reveal networks in the inferior frontal, premotor and inferior parietal cortex (see Box 15.1). These areas are engaged when participants see hand actions and also when they perform hand actions. Imitation of hand actions (Molenberghs, Cunnington, & Mattingley, 2009) and imagination of actions (Grèzes & Decety, 2001) engage similar areas. Though it is not possible to record single-cell activity within these regions, detailed studies using multivoxel pattern analysis (Oosterhof, Wiggett, Diedrichsen, Tipper, & Downing, 2010) and repetition suppression (Kilner, Neal, Weiskopf, Friston, & Frith, 2009) give a clear indication that these regions contain neuronal populations with mirror properties.

Studies of the cortical motor control system have shown that very similar brain areas are engaged when participants perform hand actions without any social context. The basic circuitry for grasping actions includes premotor cortex, supplementary motor area and inferior parietal cortex (Grafton,

Fagg, Woods, & Arbib, 1996). This frontoparietal network is strongly engaged when participants plan tool use actions (Johnson-Frey, Newman-Norlund, & Grafton, 2005), plan familiar gestures (Króliczak & Frey, 2009) and imagine actions (Johnson et al., 2002). The critical role of premotor and inferior parietal cortex in performing object-directed actions is best illustrated by studies of damage to these regions, which results in apraxia (Buxbaum, Johnson-Frey, & Bartlett-Williams, 2005) and difficulty in tasks requiring planning and execut-ing of hand–object interactions as well as imitation. An influential model of the cortical motor system (Cisek & Kalaska, 2010) suggests that the frontoparietal motor system operates by specifying possible actions in the word (i.e. object affordances) and the prefrontal and subcortical regions help in selecting which actions to perform.

Box 15.1 Brain regions involved in visuomotor tasks

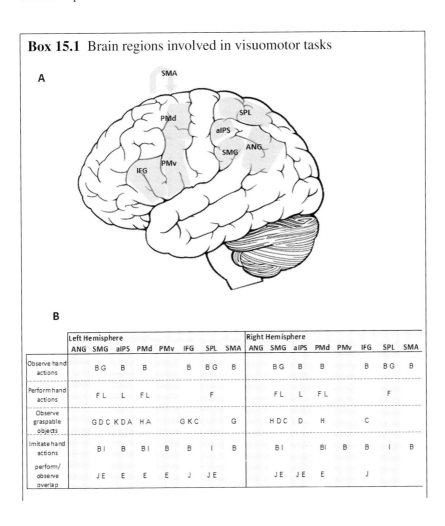

	Left Hemisphere								Right Hemisphere							
	ANG	SMG	aIPS	PMd	PMv	IFG	SPL	SMA	ANG	SMG	aIPS	PMd	PMv	IFG	SPL	SMA
Observe hand actions	B G	B	B		B	B G	B		B G	B	B			B	B G	B
Perform hand actions	F L	L	F L			F			F L	L	F L				F	
Observe graspable objects	G D C	K D A	H A		G K C		G		H D C	D	H			C		
Imitate hand actions	B I	B	B I	B	B	I	B		B I		B I	B	B	I		B
perform/ observe overlap	J E	E	E	E	J	J E			J E	J E	E			J		

Box 15.1 A. Sketch of brain regions involved in visuomotor tasks. *Notes*: IFG – inferior frontal gyrus; PMv – ventral premotor cortex; PMd – dorsal premotor cortex; aIPS – anterior intraparietal sulcus; SMG – supramarginal gyrus; ANG – angular gyrus; SPL – superior parietal lobe; SMA – supplementary motor area.

B. Table showing the involvement of these regions in different tasks. *Notes*: Letters show which paper provides this evidence, from the following list. Note that meta-analyses have been cited where possible. **A** Buxbaum, Kyle, Tang, and Detre (2006) *Brain Research*; **B** Caspers, Zilles, Laird, and Eickhoff (2010) *NeuroImage*; **C** Creem-Regehr et al. (2007) *Journal of the International Neuropsychological Society*; **D** Gallivan, Cavina-Pratesi, and Culham (2009) *Journal of Neuroscience*; **E** Gazzola & Keysers (2009) *Cerebral Cortex*; **F** Grèzes & Decety (2002) *Neuropsychologia*; **G** Grèzes & Decety (2001) *Human Brain Mapping*; **H** Handy et al. (2003) *Nature Neuroscience*; **I** Molenberghs, Cunnington, and Mattingley (2009) *Neuroscience and Biobehavioral Reviews*; **J** Molenberghs, Cunnington, and Mattingley (2012) *Neuroscience and Biobehavioral Reviews*; **K** Valyear et al. (2007) *NeuroImage*; van Overwalle and Baetens (2009) *NeuroImage*.

It is particularly useful to compare brain activation when participants observe human actions (i.e. the MNS) to activation when participants observe graspable objects or other non-social cues to action. The theory of affordances (Gibson, 1977) suggests that seeing an object leads to an immediate percept of the way that object can be grasped – its affordance. In cognitive terms, this might mean that observing a graspable object automatically engages motor systems for grasping. Several neuroimaging studies suggest that, when participants see graspable objects, they engage premotor and parietal cortices (Grèzes & Decety, 2002; Grèzes, Tucker, Armony, Ellis, & Passingham, 2003). This is also true for tools (Grafton, Fadiga, Arbib, & Rizzolatti, 1997; Kellenbach, Brett, & Patterson, 2003). Note that photographs of objects or objects that are out of reach do not engage the frontoparietal network in such a robust fashion (Gallivan, Culham, & Cavina-Pratesi, 2009). These studies suggest that observing objects, which afford actions, can robustly engage the frontoparietal network in the human brain.

To illustrate more closely the specific regions engaged in different tasks, the table in Box 15.1 presents an overview of recent literature. Both observation and performance of hand actions reliably engage SMG, aIPS and PMd. These summary data are taken from recent meta-analyses to ensure robustness (Caspers et al., 2010; Grèzes & Decety, 2001; Molenberghs et al., 2009, 2012). In the case of observation of graspable objects, a formal meta-analysis was not available so the citations represent an informal survey of the available literature. A full meta-analysis of this neglected area would be valuable in future. The data so far indicate that, again, SMG, aIPS, PMd and also IFG are the regions most reliably activated by the observation of graspable objects. Performed actions, observed actions and observed objects did not engage PMv or ANG in this summary. The results here highlight that performing actions, observing actions and observing action cues all engage the same regions of the frontoparietal network. The same conclusion is clear in the macaque studies, where mirror neurons are intermingled with canonical neurons and other visuomotor neurons in the same brain areas (Murata et al., 1997; Rizzolatti et al., 1988). Thus, the conclusions here are not novel, but do sometimes seem to be forgotten in the excitement to attribute engagement of the FPN to mirror neurons. Finally, the overlap of motor and mirror systems highlights that cortical localisation cannot be considered as a feature that makes the MNS unique.

Goals and Kinematics

What features of the visual world drive the responses of the MNS? It is a requirement that the MNS be tuned to human actions, but several studies suggest this tuning is not tight – the MNS responds equally to human and robotic actions (Cross et al., 2012; Gazzola, Rizzolatti, Wicker, & Keysers, 2007). Beyond this, it is also possible to distinguish different types of human action. One key debate concerns different levels of representation of action. Any single action can be described at multiple different hierarchical levels. For example, the action depicted in Figure 15.1 (top) could be described as 'take the mug' (goal level) or as a 'whole-hand grasp' (kinematic level) or as a set of dynamic muscle movements. Both goal-level and kinematic-level representations of actions are present in the MNS, with some debate concerning their precise localisations. A series of studies using repetition suppression methods suggest that left aIPS represents the goal of an action (Hamilton & Grafton, 2006; Ramsey & Hamilton, 2010), while IFG represents actions at a kinematic level (Hamilton & Grafton, 2007; Kilner et al., 2009). In other studies, parietal cortex is sensitive to the relationship between hand and object (pull versus push) while premotor cortex is sensitive to the effector used (Jastorff et al., 2010).

The same distinction can be found in studies of visuomotor control. Performed actions that differ in terms of kinematic features can be distinguished in inferior frontal cortex (Kilner et al., 2009), while actions which differ in terms of object-goal can be differentiated in aIPS (Oosterhof et al., 2010). Both premotor cortex and aIPS show repetition suppression when participants perform the same tool-use action twice in a row (Valyear, Gallivan, McLean, & Culham, 2012), but not when they perform arbitrary actions with the same tools. Grasping the same object twice in a row leads to adaptation in aIPS and left SMG (Króliczak, McAdam, Quinlan, & Culham, 2008),

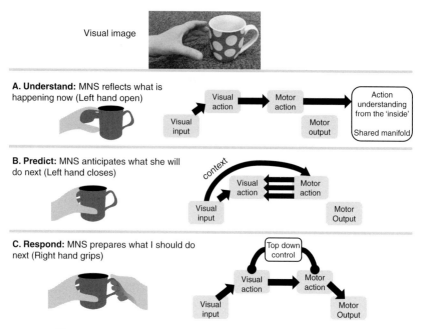

Figure 15.1 Theories of MNS function.

Notes: A. Understanding theories suggest that the MNS provides a motor representation of what the other person is doing, which can be used to understand the action 'from the inside'. B. prediction theories emphasise the role of top-down signals in predicting what action another will perform next. C. Responding theories connect the MNS to motor outputs and suggest that the primary role of the MNS is to produce socially appropriate responses.

indicating that these regions are sensitive to object identity as well as the kinematic parameters of grasping. In another study, both premotor cortex (PMv and PMd) and aIPS are selective to different types of performed grasp (Fabbri, Strnad, Caramazza, & Lingnau, 2014).

Overall, these studies suggest that both the MNS and the OMS are tuned to similar dimensions of action. For both observed actions and observed objects, studies can distinguish goal-related action representations (e.g. those sensitive to object identity) and also kinematic action representations. There are hints in both datasets that the parietal components of the frontoparietal network have a stronger role in encoding action goals, while the premotor regions are more relevant for action kinematics. However, it is likely that there is overlap in this classification for both social and non-social cues.

Behavioural Response Priming

Automatic imitation is a behavioural effect which arises when participants view an action and are instructed to perform another action, which could be congruent or incongruent (Brass, Bekkering, & Prinz, 2001). Responses are faster for congruent actions, and this robust behavioural effect can be taken as a measure of the link between a performed and observed action (Heyes, 2011). Similar priming effects can be observed for other visuomotor phenomena, such as object affordances. For example, responses to an image of a tool are faster when the responding hand is on the same side as the graspable part of the tool (Tucker & Ellis, 2004) and this effect depends upon the FPN (Grèzes et al., 2003). Recent work shows the effect is stronger for grasps related to the object's function, showing that even basic priming can be influenced by action goals (Masson, Bub, & Breuer, 2011). Together, these studies suggest that similar processes govern priming of imitative responses and priming of responses to objects.

Familiarity and Training

Many studies have shown that familiarity with actions is a key factor influencing responses in the MNS. Blood-oxygen-level-dependent (BOLD) signals during action observation are larger when participants view actions they are familiar with and can perform themselves, compared to novel actions (Calvo-Merino et al., 2005). Familiarity is also a key driver of activation in the OMS. Responses to familiar tools and stimuli, which are linked to motor responses, are much stronger than those to unfamiliar or novel objects (Valyear et al., 2012). These studies all suggest that viewing familiar stimuli that are linking to motor responses, either action stimuli or object stimuli, can robustly drive engagement of the MNS or OMS.

However, contrary to these results, there are also cases where unfamiliar actions elicit a greater BOLD signal in the MNS. Viewing unfamiliar, robotic dancing leads to more engagement than viewing familiar, smooth dancing (Cross et al., 2012). Planning novel actions can also lead to greater BOLD activation than planning familiar actions (van Elk, Viswanathan, van Schie, Bekkering, & Grafton, 2012). Explaining these different patterns of activation is not entirely straightforward – in some context, increases in familiarity may lead to increased neural recruitment, but in other cases learning may lead to more efficient encoding and less recruitment (Wiestler and Diedrichsen, 2013). One solution to this difficulty is to use MVPA approaches that reveal a clearer distinction between different motor patterns after learning (ibid) but this has not yet been applied to observed actions.

Another approach to understanding the role of stimulus familiarity in driving responses in the MNS or OMS is to train participants to make new stimulus–response associations, thus achieving complete control of the level of familiarity with experimental and control stimuli. In an early study, Cross, Hamilton, and Grafton (2006) showed increases in MNS activity when participants viewed learnt dance sequences compared to matched novel sequences. Using training, it is also possible to induce responses that run counter to the common mirror neuron principle that observed and performed actions should match. If participants learn to make a hand action every time they see a foot action, and to make a foot action every time they see a hand action, then BOLD signal when viewing hand actions is strongest in 'foot'-related parts of the premotor cortex, while BOLD signal when viewing foot actions is strongest in 'hand'-related parts of the premotor cortex (Catmur et al., 2008).

Training is also critically important in the responsiveness of cortical motor systems to objects. In a detailed study, Creem-Regehr, Dilda, Vicchrilli, Federer, & Lee (2007) trained participants to use novel objects as tools in different ways. Observation of the trained tools during fMRI led to engagement of bilateral IPL and IFG, while observation of novel objects that had not been trained as tools did not. Different types of training differentially affect activation of the OMS. If participants are trained to manipulate novel objects, they later activate left IFG and left IPL when viewing the objects, but this pattern is not seen for objects that are trained in a purely visual manner (Bellebaum et al., 2013). These results emphasise that activation of the FPN when viewing objects is driven by links between the objects and possible actions.

Training methods have also been used to directly test whether the MNS behaves in the same way as the OMS. Data suggest that, if participants are trained to respond to arbitrary visual cues (coloured circles) with finger movements, then viewing these cues leads to engagement of the same regions (aIPS and premotor cortex) as observing or performing the actions (Landmann, Landi, Grafton, & Della-Maggiore, 2011). Another study directly contrasted arbitrary cues and observed action cues (Cross, Hamilton, Kraemer, Kelley, & Grafton, 2009). Participants were trained over the course of a week to perform novel dance sequences in response to arrow cues in a video game. During fMRI scanning, they observed sequences of arrow cues associated with both trained dances and untrained dances, and each of these could include a human dancer behind the arrows or not. This gives a 2x2 factorial design crossing the factors *training* and *human action observation*. The results show that PMv was more robustly activated when participants viewed trained sequences compared to untrained, but was not sensitive to the presence or absence of a human dancer. The converse pattern was seen in superior temporal sulcus, with greater activation when viewing sequences with a human dancer regardless of training status. This suggests that engagement of PMv is driven by motoric familiarity with a particular sequence, and not by the requirement to observe or understand another person.

A stronger test of similarity between the MNS and OMS is to use methods that give a more detailed measure of sensorimotor links. For example, one of the best demonstrations of mirror neuron responses in the human MNS used a cross-modal repetition suppression method (Kilner et al., 2009). In this approach, participants execute an action (e.g. ring-pull) and in the next trial see an action (e.g. twist *or* ring-pull). In cases where the performed action matches the observed action, repetition suppression means that a smaller BOLD signal should be expected from mirror neurons (but not from visual-only or motor-only neurons). Such a pattern was found in the inferior frontal gyrus. Recently, Press and colleagues (2012) trained participants to make new sensorimotor associations (e.g. see purple square → do thumbs-up sign) and then used a repetition suppression approach to search for brain regions showing cross-modal visual–motor links. For example, if participants had been trained to link a purple square to a thumb action, and then performed a thumb action in the scanner followed by viewing a purple square, one would predict a suppressed response to the visual stimulus as part of a trained link. In contrast, if a performed thumb action was followed by an untrained stimulus (orange circle), no suppression would be expected. The predicted pattern of BOLD was found in both PMv and IPL. These results suggest that both visual action–motor links and visual cue–motor links can be found in similar brain regions with similar methods, and that the latter can be induced with simple training procedures.

Overall, these studies of training and familiarity suggest that both the MNS and OMS are strongly engaged by observing stimuli that are linked to motor responses. Furthermore, patterns of BOLD response following training are very similar for familiar observed actions and trained symbolic cues. The implication of such studies is that the same associative, sensorimotor processes underlie both responses to observed actions and responses to other visual cues. Detailed discussion of what this means for our understanding of the origins of the MNS can be found elsewhere (Cook, Bird, Catmur, Press, & Heyes, 2014).

Summary

The data reviewed so far aimed to summarise the properties of the human mirror system, and to determine if any of these are unique and unlike other sensorimotor systems. These studies suggest that the MNS and OMS are located in the same cortical regions. Both are sensitive to action goal and action kinematics, with a preference for goals in parietal regions. Responses to both observed actions and observed objects are substantially modulated by familiarity. Training seems to be able to generate new sensorimotor links that are indistinguishable from the links between performed and observed actions. This means that the only 'special' feature of the MNS that distinguishes it from the OMS is that the MNS responds to observed human actions while the OMS responds to objects. Is this distinction enough to attribute very different cognitive and functional properties to the MNS? The remainder of the present chapter instead focuses on theories of MNS function, and considers how our knowledge of the MNS and OMS can inform these theories.

What is the Function of the MNS?

While many different theories of MNS function have been proposed, here I distinguish between three major types, as illustrated in Figure 15.1. All three consider the same four basic components: visual inputs, visual representations of actions, motor representations of actions and motor outputs. More subtle distinctions between goal and kinematic representations or other categories are found in these models, but the present summary glosses over these for simplicity. The models differ primarily in how the four basic components are connected and process information. To introduce each, I provide a little historical background.

When mirror neurons were first discovered in the premotor cortex of the macaque monkey (Gallese et al., 1996; di Pellegrino et al., 1992), it was important to distinguish 'motor' activation of these neurons from perceptual activation. A key aim of these early studies was to demonstrate that these patterns of neural activation were not 'just' sub-threshold motor activation, as the monkey prepared to perform an action, but rather reflected some level of understanding of the observed action. Thus, early studies showed that the monkey did not move its own hands at the time of mirror neuron activation, and emphasised explanations in terms of recognising or understanding the observed actions.

Similar to the macaque studies, early studies of the human MNS focused on explaining MNS activation in terms of understanding actions (Buccino et al., 2001) and aimed to rule out motor involvement (Rizzolatti & Craighero, 2004). Research focused on the contribution of the human MNS to imitating actions (Buccino et al., 2004b; Iacoboni et al., 1999) and understanding action goals. Similarly, theories of MNS function emphasised the novel idea that basic motor systems could make an important contribution to cognitive and even perceptual functions within the social domain. Important data here showed how the MNS is active when people observe meaningful (Buccino et al., 2004a) and familiar (Calvo-Merino et al., 2005) actions, and is essential for judging action kinematics (Pobric & Hamilton, 2006). From these studies, the theory that mirror neurons are for *action understanding* was developed. This model places an emphasis on the idea that motor representations allow an observer to feel an action 'from the inside' (Rizzolatti & Sinigaglia, 2010) and are important in understanding why other people perform actions (Figure 15.1a). Thus, motor systems could make a contribution to social and cognitive processes. This was a very novel idea and generated substantial research. However, it was also debated whether the MNS alone could provide action understanding or whether other cognitive processes were needed (Csibra, 2007; Jacob & Jeannerod, 2005).

In considering how actions might be understood, researchers realised that for an individual observer, reflecting on why an action was performed after it is complete (retrodicting) is often less useful than *predicting* what action will be performed next. ERP data demonstrate that premotor cortical regions are activated in anticipation of a future action (Kilner, Vargas, Duval, Blakemore, & Sirigu, 2004; Southgate, Johnson, Osborne, & Csibra, 2009) and eye gaze while observing actions is also predictive (Flanagan & Johansson, 2003). Building on these ideas, the *predictive* theory of the mirror neuron system emerged (Kilner, Friston, & Frit, 2007; Wilson & Knoblich, 2005). Under this model, the primary purpose of the MNS is to predict what actions another person will perform, drawing strongly on top-down processes. For example, contextual information and prior knowledge can be used to generate a set of possible actions a person might perform and then to make more detailed predictions about the visual input should those actions occur. The predicted visual patterns can then be compared to the incoming visual information to determine what action was actually performed (Figure 15.1b). This model fits within a broader Bayesian predictive framework (Friston, Mattout, & Kilner, 2011), which attempts to explain the function of the brain in terms of a need to minimise prediction error in visual and motor systems. Bayesian predictive models are fairly well established in sensory systems, but it is not yet clear if they provide a useful account of motor systems.

The New Social Prediction Account

Both the action understanding and action prediction accounts of the MNS are problematic in two ways. First, they largely ignore the parallels between the MNS and OMS highlighted above, and thus do not take into account what models of motor control might be able to tell us. If the MNS and OMS are entirely intertwined and seem to operate on similar principles, it would be odd to suggest that the primary function of the MNS (understanding/prediction) is entirely unrelated to the OMS. Second, it is clear that both the predictive and understanding frameworks are largely concerned with passive observation. If you watch a familiar movie, you might be able to predict what will happen in every scene, but you still cannot be part of the action. In real-life situations, it is critical to respond to others in a timely fashion, and to dynamically interact (Pfeiffer, Timmermans, Vogele, Frith, & Schilbach, 2013a). Such dynamic interaction is rarely studied in the lab because it is hard to control and experimentally manipulate. New methods such as virtual reality (Pfeiffer, Vogeley, &

Schilbach, 2013b; Zanon, Novembre, Zangrando, Chittaro, & Silani, 2014) are gradually reducing this problem. This approach is sometimes termed 'second-person neuroscience' (Schilbach et al., 2013), and it suggests that when using realistic and interactive tasks, we may engage more and/or different cognitive and neural resources, compared to traditional passive observation studies.

Here, I present a social responding account of the MNS (Figure 15.1c), which builds on previous work (Dezecache et al., 2013; Hamilton, 2013; Schilbach et al., 2013; Wang & Hamilton, 2012) and sets out in more detail how considering social responses can help us understand the function of the MNS. Key to this discussion is the idea that situations can contain *social affordances*, that is, 'possibilities for interaction provided by others' (Schilbach et al., 2013). An object may have a particular motor affordance (a pencil affords drawing), and similarly a social situation may have a particular social affordance (an outstretched hand affords a hand-shake response). There is evidence that being in a joint action context can change the perceived affordances of objects (Richardson, Marsh, & Baron, 2007). However, social affordances can go beyond this and comprise a purely social response to another – seeing a smiling face might afford a smile in return. In this context, the role of the MNS is not just to observe and understand the situation, but rather is to produce the appropriate motor response. A similar position has been set out from a philo-sophical point of view (Brincker, 2011), suggesting that the MNS and OMS together represent an affordance space of the possible social and non-social actions available to allow action planning.

Building on the idea of social affordances, I suggest that the implementation and use of social affordance in the MNS directly parallels the implementation and use of object affordances in the OMS (Cisek & Kalaska, 2010). Following Cisek and Kalaska's motor model, it seems likely that the parietal cortex can specify the possible social responses afforded by the other people in the current environment, passing this information forward to premotor cortex. Evaluative processing in prefrontal cortex and subcortical areas can then select which of the plausible motor responses should actually be implemented. This scheme can work for social stimuli (MNS) in just the same way as it works for non-social stimuli (objects), with response specification and selection in each case being strongly influenced by past experience and associative learning. The primary difference between social and non-social affordances is that social stimuli are more dynamic and likely to change faster than objects.

There are several lines of evidence hinting that social responding is impor-tant in determining the behaviour of the MNS, though this idea has not yet been tested directly. In a study of automatic imitation, Liepelt, Prinz, & Brass (2010) asked participants to respond with a left- or right-hand action to an image of a left or right hand performing a grasping action. In these trials, participants respond faster to a left-hand image with a right-hand action, because the visual stimulus provides a mirror image of the response hand, similar to the effect typically found in automatic imitation studies (Heyes, 2011). However, when participants see an image of a left or right hand outstretched to shake hands with the participant, they respond faster with the complementary hand (left hand to left image, right hand to right image). This reflects the socially learnt way to shake hands, rather than being a mirror image of the visual stimulus. Thus, response-priming effects reflect social affordances rather than just mirroring.

Another study measured the excitability of primary motor cortex during observation of actions using TMS (Sartori, Bucchioni, & Castiello, 2013). This is commonly considered a measure of mirror neuron system activation (Fadiga, Fogassi, Pavesi, & Rizzolatti, 1995). In this case, participants observed a video of an actor grasping a coffee thermos with a whole-hand grasp, and the participant showed motor facilitation consistent with performing a whole-hand grasp, as an action-understanding account of the MNS would suggest. However, the video stimulus then showed the actor reaching towards the viewer to pour coffee into a small cup. The socially appropriate response at this point would be for the viewer (the participant) to pick up the small cup and move it toward the actor. At this point, the motor facilitation seen in the participant switched to that appropriate for grasping a small cup, that is, for the appropriate motor response. This key study suggests that the MNS can engage in understanding actions when a participant is in a passive context, but switches to active responding when that option becomes useful.

A different approach is to examine the timing of social responding. Conty, Dezecache, Hugueville, & Grèzes (2012) showed participants images of neutral or angry actors pointing or gazing at or away from the participant. Using ERP and fMRI, they report that seeing an angry person pointing towards the participant led to a robust premotor effect only 210 msec after stimulus onset. This early response to emotion and gesture would not be predicted in a purely action-understanding account because anger is not normally imitated (Bourgeois & Hess, 2008). However, it makes sense if the premotor activation reflects response preparation – an anger gesture towards the participant is a potent cue to do something, and premotor cortex is a good candidate for activation of possible social responses.

It is also worth considering the brain systems linked to social affordances. In reviewing the study of anger perception described above, Dezecache et al. (2013) point out that this social responding requires brain systems both within and beyond the MNS. Specifically, the amygdala is critical to the detection of the emotional facial expression in the stimuli. Other studies also suggest that social responding draws on more than just the MNS. Wang and Hamilton (2013) and Wang, Newport, and Hamilton (2011a) have shown that eye gaze rapidly enhances the automatic imitation of hand actions ; and that this effect is implemented by a top-down control system in the medial prefrontal cortex (Wang, Ramsey, & Hamilton, 2011b). The idea that control signals from outside the frontoparietal network influence action selection in that network closely parallels Cisek and Kalaska's (2010) object–motor control model in which object affordances in the frontoparietal network are subject to control and selection processes from the prefrontal cortex and subcortical regions.

To summarise, the social responding theory of MNS function is a relatively new approach which makes testable claims: that the MNS is engaged by the possible actions which a participant can perform in response to a social stimulus (social affordances); that other cortical regions work with the MNS to select and implement these actions; and that the MNS is most strongly driven by familiar stimuli for which robust likely motor responses exist. This model implies close parallels between the MNS and the object–motor system, with both having very similar selectivity, cortical localisation and functioning. The review of object–motor systems and mirror neuron systems in the first half of this chapter provides evidence for these claims.

The social responding model goes beyond our traditional, passive approach to social cognition where participants in a lab observe stimuli. In this context, understanding or predicting the visual information might be appropriate. But in the real world, understanding or prediction of actions is a secondary function to the more important requirement to respond appropriately to others. This means that the social responding theory of the MNS is a motor chauvinist theory, which focuses on the need to perform a motor response. If, like the mature sea squirt, people just watched the world drift by, we might not need a motor system (or a brain). As active, engaged interactors in the world, we need both a mirror system and motor system together to find, plan and execute the social and non-social actions that change our world.

References

Bellebaum, C., Tettamanti, M., Marchetta, E., Della Rosa, P., Rizzo, G., et al. (2013). Neural representations of unfamiliar objects are modulated by sensorimotor experience. *Cortex*, 49, 1110–1125.

Bourgeois, P., & Hess, U. (2008). The impact of social context on mimicry. *Biological Psychology*, 77, 343–352.

Brass, M., Bekkering, H., & Prinz, W. (2001). Movement observation affects movement execution in a simple response task. *Acta Psychologica*, 106, 3–22.

Brincker, M. (2011). Moving beyond mirroring: A social affordance model of sensorimotor integration during action perception. PhD thesis, City University of New York.

Buccino, G., Binkofski, F., Fink, G.R., Fadiga, L., Fogassi, L., et al. (2001). Short communication action observation activates premotor and parietal areas in a somatotopic manner: An fMRI study. *European Journal of Neuroscience*, 13, 400–404.

Buccino, G., Lui, F., Canessa, N., Patteri, I., Lagravinese, G., et al. (2004a). Neural circuits involved in the recognition of actions performed by nonconspecifics: An FMRI study. *Journal of Cognitive Neuroscience*, 16, 114–126.

Buccino, G., Vogt, S., Ritzl, A., Fink, G. R., Zilles, K., et al. (2004b). Neural circuits underlying imitation learning of hand actions: An event-related fMRI study. *Neuron*, 42, 323–334.

Buxbaum, L. J., Johnson-Frey, S. H., & Bartlett-Williams, M. (2005). Deficient internal models for planning hand–object interactions in apraxia. *Neuropsychologia*, 43, 917–929.

Calvo-Merino, B., Glaser, D. E., Grèzes, J., Passingham, R. E., & Haggard, P. (2005). Action observation and acquired motor skills: An FMRI study with expert dancers. *Cerebral Cortex*, 15, 1243–1249.

Caspers, S., Zilles, K., Laird, A. R., & Eickhoff, S. B. (2010). ALE meta-analysis of action observation and imitation in the human brain. *NeuroImage*, 50(3), 1148–1167.

Catmur, C., Gillmeister, H., Bird, G., Liepelt, R., Brass, M., & Heyes, C. (2008). Through the looking glass: Counter-mirror activation following incompatible sensorimotor learning. *European Journal of Neuroscience*, 28, 1208–1215.

Cisek, P., & Kalaska, J. F. (2010). Neural mechanisms for interacting with a world full of action choices. *Annual Review of Neuroscience*, 33, 269–298.

Conty, L., Dezecache, G., Hugueville, L., & Grèzes, J. (2012). Early binding of gaze, gesture, and emotion: Neural time course and correlates. *Journal of Neuroscience*, 32, 4531–4539.

Cook, R., Bird, G., Catmur, C., Press, C., & Heyes, C. (2014). Mirror neurons: From origin to function. *Behavioral and Brain Sciences*, 37, 177–192.

Creem-Regehr, S. H., Dilda, V., Vicchrilli, A. E., Federer, F., & Lee, J. N. (2007). The influence of complex action knowledge on representations of novel graspable objects: Evidence from functional magnetic resonance imaging. *Journal of the International Neuropsychological Society*, 13, 1009–1020.

Cross, E. S., Hamilton, A. F. de C., & Grafton, S. T. (2006). Building a motor simulation de novo: Observation of dance by dancers. *NeuroImage*, 31, 1257–1267.

Cross, E. S., Hamilton, A. F. de C., Kraemer, D. J. M., Kelley, W. M., & Grafton, S. T. (2009). Dissociable substrates for body motion and physical experience in the human action observation network. *European Journal of Neuroscience*, 30, 1383–1392.

Cross, E. S., Liepelt, R., Hamilton, A. F. de C., Parkinson, J., Ramsey, R., Stadler, W., & Prinz, W. (2012). Robotic movement preferentially engages the action observation network. *Human Brain Mapping*, 33, 2238–2254.

Csibra, G. (2007). Action mirroring and action understanding: An alternative account. In P. Haggard, Y. Rossetti, & M. Kawato (Eds.), *Sensorimotor foundations of higher cognition*. Oxford: Oxford University Press, 435–459.

Dezecache, G., Conty, L., & Grèzes, J. (2013). Social affordances: Is the mirror neuron system involved? *Behavioral and Brain Sciences*, 36, 417–418.

Elk, M. van, Viswanathan, S., van Schie, H. T., Bekkering, H., & Grafton, S. T. (2012). Pouring or chilling a bottle of wine: an fMRI study on the prospective planning of object-directed actions. *Experimental Brain Research*, 218, 189–200.

328   *Antonia Hamilton*

Fabbri, S., Strnad, L., Caramazza, A., & Lingnau, A. (2014). Overlapping representations for grip type and reach direction. *NeuroImage*, 94, 138–146.

Fadiga, L., Fogassi, L., Pavesi, G., & Rizzolatti, G. (1995). Motor facilitation during action observation: A magnetic stimulation study. *Journal of Neurophysiology*, 73, 2608–2611.

Flanagan, J. R., & Johansson, R. S. (2003). Action plans used in action observation. *Nature*, 424, 769–771.

Friston, K. J., Mattout, J., & Kilner, J. M. (2011). Action understanding and active inference. *Biological Cybernetics*, 104, 137–160.

Gallese, V., Fadiga, L., Fogassi, L., & Rizzolatti, G. (1996). Action recognition in the premotor cortex. *Brain*, 3, 593–609.

Gallese, V., Keysers, C., & Rizzolatti, G. (2004). A unifying view of the basis of social cognition. *Trends in Cognitive Sciences*, 8, 396–403.

Gallivan, J. P., Culham, J. C., & Cavina-Pratesi, C. (2009). Is that within reach? fMRI reveals that the human superior parieto-occipital cortex encodes objects reachable by the hand. *Journal of Neuroscience*, 29, 4381–4391.

Gazzola, V., & Keysers, C. (2009). The observation and execution of actions share motor and somatosensory voxels in all tested subjects: Single-subject analyses of unsmoothed fMRI data. *Cerebral Cortex*, 19, 1239–1255.

Gazzola, V., Rizzolatti, G., Wicker, B., & Keysers, C. (2007). The anthropomorphic brain: The mirror neuron system responds to human and robotic actions. *NeuroImage*, 35, 1674–1684.

Gibson, J. J. (1977). The theory of affordances. In R. E. Shaw & J. Bransford (Eds.), *Perceiving, acting, knowing: Toward an ecological psychology*. Hillsdale, NJ: Lawrence Erlbaum, pp. 127–142.

Grafton, S. T., Fadiga, L., Arbib, M. A., & Rizzolatti, G. (1997). Premotor cortex activation during observation and naming of familiar tools. *NeuroImage*, 6, 231–236.

Grafton, S. T., Fagg, A. H., Woods, R. P., & Arbib, M. A. (1996). Functional anatomy of pointing and grasping in humans. *Cerebral Cortex*, 6, 226–237.

Grèzes, J., & Decety, J. (2001). Functional anatomy of execution, mental simulation, observation, and verb generation of actions: A meta-analysis. *Human Brain Mapping*, 12, 1–19.

(2002). Does visual perception of object afford action? Evidence from a neuroimaging study. *Neuropsychologia*, 40, 212–222.

Grèzes, J., Tucker, M., Armony, J. L., Ellis, R., & Passingham, R. E. (2003). Objects automatically potentiate action: An fMRI study of implicit processing. *European Journal of Neuroscience*, 17, 2735–2740.

Hamilton, A. F. de C. (2013). The mirror neuron system contributes to social responding. *Cortex*, 49, 2957–2959.

Hamilton, A. F. de C., & Grafton, S. T. (2006). Goal representation in human anterior intraparietal sulcus. *Journal of Neuroscience*, 26, 1133–1137.

(2007). The motor hierarchy: From kinematics to goals and intentions. In P. Haggard, Y. Rosetti, & M. Kawato (Eds.), *Sensorimotor foundations of higher cognition: Attention and performance XXII*. Oxford: Oxford University Press, 1–29.

Heyes, C. (2011). Automatic imitation. *Psychological Bulletin*, 137, 463–483.

Iacoboni, M., Woods, R. P., Brass, M., Bekkering, H., Mazziotta, J. C., & Rizzolatti, G. (1999). Cortical mechanisms of human imitation. *Science*, 286(5449), 2526–2528.

Jacob, P., & Jeannerod, M. (2005). The motor theory of social cognition: A critique. *Trends in Cognitive Sciences*, 9, 21–25.

Jastorff, J., Begliomini, C., Fabbri-Destro, M., Rizzolatti, G., & Orban, G. A. (2010). Coding observed motor acts: Different organizational principles in the parietal and premotor cortex of humans. *Journal of Neurophysiology*, 104, 128–140.

Johnson, S. H., Rotte, M., Grafton, S. T., Hinrichs, H., Gazzaniga, M. S., & Heinze, H. J. (2002). Selective activation of a parietofrontal circuit during implicitly imagined prehension. *NeuroImage*, 17, 1693–1704.

Johnson-Frey, S. H., Newman-Norlund, R., & Grafton, S. T. (2005). A distributed left hemisphere network active during planning of everyday tool use skills. *Cerebral Cortex*, 15, 681–695.

Kellenbach, M. L., Brett, M., & Patterson, K. (2003). Actions speak louder than functions: The importance of manipulability and action in tool representation. *Journal of Cognitive Neuroscience*, 15, 30–46.

Kilner, J. M., Friston, K. J., & Frith, C. (2007). Predictive coding: An account of the mirror neuron system. *Cognitive Processes*, 8, 159–166.

Kilner, J. M., Neal, A., Weiskopf, N., Friston, K. J., & Frith, C. (2009). Evidence of mirror neurons in human inferior frontal gyrus. *Journal of Neuroscience*, 29, 10153–10159.

Kilner, J. M., Vargas, C., Duval, S., Blakemore, S.-J., & Sirigu, A. (2004). Motor activation prior to observation of a predicted movement. *Nature Neuroscience*, 7, 1299–1301.

Króliczak, G., & Frey, S. H. (2009). A common network in the left cerebral hemisphere represents planning of tool use pantomimes and familiar intransitive gestures at the hand-independent level. *Cerebral Cortex*, 19, 2396–2410.

Króliczak, G., McAdam, T. D., Quinlan, D. J., & Culham, J. C. (2008). The human dorsal stream adapts to real actions and 3D shape processing: A functional magnetic resonance imaging study. *Journal of Neurophysiology*, 100, 2627–2639.

Landmann, C., Landi, S. M., Grafton, S. T., & Della-Maggiore, V. (2011). fMRI supports the sensorimotor theory of motor resonance. *PLoS One*, 6, e26859.

Liepelt, R., Prinz, W., & Brass, M. (2010). When do we simulate non-human agents? Dissociating communicative and non-communicative actions. *Cognition*, 115, 426–434.

Masson, M. E. J., Bub, D. N., & Breuer, A. T. (2011). Priming of reach and grasp actions by handled objects. *Journal of Experimental Psychology: Human Perception and Performance*, 37, 1470–1484.

Molenberghs, P., Cunnington, R., & Mattingley, J. B. (2009). Is the mirror neuron system involved in imitation? A short review and meta-analysis. *Neuroscience & Biobehavioral Reviews*, 33, 975–980.

(2012). Brain regions with mirror properties: A meta-analysis of 125 human fMRI studies. *Neuroscience & Biobehavioral Reviews*, 36, 341–349.

Murata, A., Fadiga, L., Fogassi, L., Gallese, V., Raos, V., & Rizzolatti, G. (1997). Object representation in the ventral premotor cortex (area F5) of the monkey. *Journal of Neurophysiology*, 78, 2226–2230.

Oosterhof, N. N., Wiggett, A. J., Diedrichsen, J., Tipper, S. P., & Downing, P. E. (2010). Surface-based information mapping reveals crossmodal vision: Action representations in human parietal and occipitotemporal cortex. *Journal of Neurophysiology*, 104, 1077–1089.

Pellegrino, G. di, Fadiga, L., Fogassi, L., Gallese, V., & Rizzolatti, G. (1992). Understanding motor events: A neurophysiological study. *Experimental Brain Research*, 91, 176–180.

Pfeiffer, U. J., Timmermans, B., Vogeley, K., Frith, C. D., & Schilbach, L. (2013a). Towards a neuroscience of social interaction. *Frontiers in Human Neuroscience*, 7, 22.

Pfeiffer, U. J., Vogeley, K., & Schilbach, L. (2013b). From gaze cueing to dual eye-tracking: Novel approaches to investigate the neural correlates of gaze in social interaction. *Neuroscience & Biobehavioral Reviews*, 37, 2516–2528.

Pobric, G., & Hamilton, A. F. de C. (2006). Action understanding requires the left inferior frontal cortex. *Current Biology*, 16, 524–529.

Press, C., Catmur, C., Cook, R., Widmann, H., Heyes, C., & Bird, G. (2012). fMRI evidence of 'mirror'responses to geometric shapes. *PloS One*, 7(12), e51934.

Ramachandran, V. S. (2000). Mirror neurons and imitation learning as the driving force behind 'the great leap forward' in human evolution. http://edge.org/3rd_culture/ramachandran/ramachandran_index.html.

Ramsey, R., & Hamilton, A. F. de C. (2010). Triangles have goals too: Understanding action representation in left aIPS. *Neuropsychologia*, 48, 2773–2776.

Richardson, M. J., Marsh, K. L., & Baron, R. M. (2007). Judging and actualizing intrapersonal and interpersonal affordances. *Journal of Experimental Psychology: Human Perception and Performance*, 33, 845–859.

Rizzolatti, G., & Craighero, L. (2004). The mirror-neuron system. *Annual Review of Neuroscience*, 27, 169–192.

Rizzolatti, G., & Sinigaglia, C. (2010). The functional role of the parieto-frontal mirror circuit: Interpretations and misinterpretations. *Nature Reviews Neuroscience*, 11, 264–274.

Rizzolatti, G., Camarda, R., Fogassi, L., Gentilucci, M., Luppino, G., & Matelli, M. (1988). Functional organization of inferior area 6 in the macaque monkey. I. Somatotopy and the control of proximal movements. *Experimental Brain Research*, 71, 475–490.

Sartori, L., Bucchioni, G., & Castiello, U. (2013). When emulation becomes reciprocity. *Social Cognitive and Affective Neuroscience*, 8, 662–669.

Schilbach, L., Timmermans, B., Reddy, V., Costall, A., Bente, G., et al. (2013). Toward a second-person neuroscience. *Behavioral and Brain Sciences*, 36, 393–414.

Southgate, V., Johnson, M. H., Osborne, T., & Csibra, G. (2009). Predictive motor activation during action observation in human infants. *Biology Letters*, 5, 769–772.

Tucker, M., & Ellis, R. (2004). Action priming by briefly presented objects. *Acta Psychologica*, 116, 185–203.

Valyear, K. F., Gallivan, J. P., McLean, D. A., & Culham, J. C. (2012). fMRI repetition suppression for familiar but not arbitrary actions with tools. *Journal of Neuroscience*, 32, 4247–4259.

Wang, Y., & Hamilton, A. F. de C. (2012). Social top-down response modulation (STORM): A model of the control of mimicry in social interaction. *Frontiers in Human Neuroscience*, 6, 1–10.

(2013). Why does gaze enhance mimicry? Placing gaze-mimicry effects in relation to other gaze phenomena. *Quarterly Journal of Experimental Psychology*, 67(4), 747–762.

Wang, Y., Newport, R., & Hamilton, A. F. de C. (2011a). Eye contact enhances mimicry of intransitive hand movements. *Biology Letters*, 7, 7–10.

Wang, Y., Ramsey, R., & Hamilton, A. F. de C. (2011b). The control of mimicry by eye contact is mediated by medial prefrontal cortex. *Journal of Neuroscience*, 31, 12001–12010.

Wiestler, T., & Diedrichsen, J. (2013). Skill learning strengthens cortical representations of motor sequences. *Elife*, 2, e00801.

Wilson, M., & Knoblich, G. (2005). The case for motor involvement in perceiving conspecifics. *Psychological Bulletin*, 131, 460–473.

Zanon, M., Novembre, G., Zangrando, N., Chittaro, L., & Silani, G. (2014). Brain activity and prosocial behavior in a simulated life-threatening situation. *NeuroImage*, 98,134–146.

16   Biological Tuning of Mirror Mechanisms: Evidence and Functional Implications

Clare Press

Abstract

A range of behavioural and neuroimaging evidence demonstrates that we mirror observed human action in our motor systems to a greater extent than similar non-biological movement. This chapter reviews such evidence, considering the form and kinematic features of observed stimuli to which mirror mechanisms are sensitive. It subsequently considers the role of this biological tuning in our interactions with, and processing of, humans relative to inanimate devices, in the context of functions likely to be supported by mirror mechanisms. It notes that in contrast with common assumptions, biological tuning is unlikely to reflect increased inferential processing about mental states of observed humans. It considers that biological tuning is more likely to influence our imitation and perception of human and inanimate movements. The final section examines how biological tuning can be integrated with evidence that mirror mechanisms are part of a wider domain-general system adapted for action control, mapping motor codes onto observed events from both our social and inanimate environments.

Introduction

Observation of action activates the motor codes required for performance. For example, we automatically imitate others when there is no intention to have done so and no reported awareness of matching behaviour (e.g. Chartrand & Bargh, 1999). Consistent with these behavioural data, neuroimaging studies demonstrate that observing action activates an 'action observation network' (AON), including motor structures such as ventral and dorsal premotor cortices, posterior regions of the inferior frontal gyrus and primary motor cortex (Rizzolatti & Craighero, 2004). In homologous areas, 'mirror neurons' have been found in the macaque that discharge not only when the monkey executes an action of a certain type (e.g. precision grip), but also when it

I am grateful to Jennifer Cook for comments on an earlier draft of this chapter.

observes the experimenter or another monkey performing that action (Cisek & Kalaska, 2004; Dushanova & Donoghue, 2010; Gallese, Fadiga, Fogassi, & Rizzolatti, 1996; di Pellegrino, Fadiga, Fogassi, Gallese, & Rizzolatti, 1992). Furthermore, neuroimaging adaptation techniques demonstrate that populations of cells with mirror properties are likely to exist in these areas in humans (Kilner, Neal, Weiskopf, Friston, & Frith, 2009; Lingnau, Gesierich, & Caramazza, 2009; Press et al., 2012a; Press, Cook, Blakemore, & Kilner, 2012b). Motor mirror mechanisms (hereafter, simply mirror mechanisms) have been proposed to support a wide range of social and non-social functions, from intention reading (Iacoboni et al., 2005) through to aesthetic experience (Di Dio & Gallese, 2009).

Concurring with some of these hypothesised functions, studies investigating the properties of mirror mechanisms typically demonstrate biological tuning, such that human actions activate corresponding motor codes to a greater extent than non-biological movements. This chapter will begin by reviewing behavioural and neuroimaging studies that demonstrate biological tuning, considering the form and kinematic features of observed stimuli to which mirror mechanisms are sensitive. It will define mirror mechanisms functionally – that they support the activation of corresponding, or mirroring, motor codes during action observation. According to this definition, the cardinal features of mirror mechanisms are (1) that a motor code is activated during action observation, and (2) that it is the code required for performing *that specific* action. Both behavioural and neuroimaging studies can demonstrate that motor codes are activated during action observation, but behavioural methods are often superior for demonstrating specificity. For example, the classic studies conducted by Chartrand and & Bargh (1999) demonstrate that observation of a confederate scratching their head elicits head scratching, rather than foot-shaking behaviour, and observation of foot shaking elicits foot shaking. In contrast, neuroimaging studies rarely provide evidence of specificity, often simply demonstrating that motor structures are active when observing action (unless employing adaptation or multivariate pattern classification techniques; Oosterhof, Tipper, & Downing, 2013). Despite these limitations, neuroimaging studies will be reviewed in the present chapter given that they largely concur with the behavioural data. Functional magnetic resonance imaging (fMRI) and positron emission tomography (PET) studies demonstrating observation-related activation in motor circuits will be outlined, alongside magnetoencephalography (MEG) studies examining attenuation of central beta (15–30 Hz) oscillations. Alpha (7–14 Hz) oscillatory studies will not be included, due to recent evidence that these effects relate to tactile, rather than motor, mirroring (Coll et al., 2015). This section will conclude that there is evidence for tuning with respect to both the form and kinematic profile of observed movements.

The chapter will subsequently consider the role of biological tuning in our interactions with, and processing of, humans relative to inanimate devices, in the context of functions likely to be supported by mirror mechanisms. First, it will establish that there is little evidence for a role of mirror mechanisms in inferential sociocognitive functions required to support a theory of mind, and therefore that, in contrast with common assumptions, biological tuning is unlikely to reflect inferential processing about mental states of humans, but not inanimate entities. Second, it will outline preliminary evidence that mirror mechanisms support various types of imitation and action perception, and consider how biological tuning may influence our imitation and perception of human and inanimate movements. Third, it will examine how biological tuning can be integrated with the view that mirror mechanisms are part of a wider domain-general system adapted for action control, thereby mapping motor codes to observed events from both our social and inanimate environments.

Evidence of Biological Tuning

Behavioural Evidence

Kilner, Paulignan, and Blakemore (2003) showed that the execution of sinusoidal arm movements in a vertical or horizontal plane was subject to interference from simultaneous observation of another human performing arm movements in the opposite plane; if participants executed vertical arm movements while observing horizontal movements, there was greater variance in the horizontal dimension, compared with conditions where they observed vertical movements (Figure 16.1a). This 'interference effect' is thought to be a result of the automatic activation of motor codes that correspond to observed action, and an interaction between these motor codes and those required for executing the intended action. When the observed movements were made by a robotic arm, there was no interference effect. However, there were at least two differences between the human and non-human stimuli presented in this experiment. First, the stimuli differed in form. Namely, the human stimuli were a flesh colour, rounded, and had a certain joint configuration, whereas the non-biological stimuli were more geometric and with fewer joints. Second, the stimuli differed in kinematics. The human arms followed an approximately minimum-jerk trajectory, where the movement is slow at turning points and faster on straight trajectories (Hogan, 1984), whereas the robotic stimulus moved with constant velocity. A number of studies have controlled for one of these factors while measuring the effect of the other, to investigate whether one or both of form and kinematics generate the biological tuning within mirror mechanisms (see Box 16.1 for related studies that investigate the top-down influence of belief about stimulus identity on biological mirror mechanism activation).

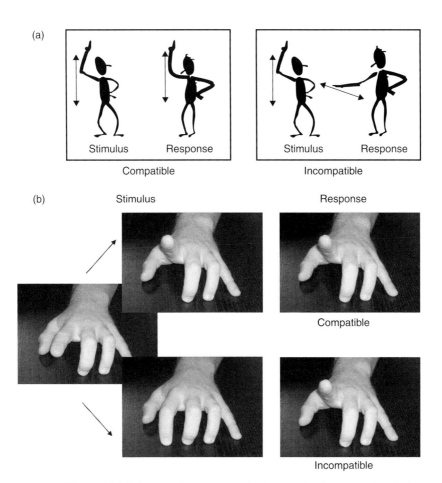

Figure 16.1 Behavioural measures of mirror mechanism operation during action observation.

Notes: (a) The interference procedure used by Kilner et al. (2003). Participants must execute sinusoidal vertical or horizontal arm actions at the same time as observing vertical or horizontal actions in phase with the executed actions. The observed actions (e.g. horizontal) can be in either the same or opposite direction as executed actions. Variance in the dimension perpendicular to intended motion in the executed actions is recorded. This variance is higher when observing actions perpendicular to the intended execution direction. (b) The automatic imitation procedure used by Brass et al. (2001). In a simple RT task, participants are presented with a hand in a neutral position. After a certain amount of time, the stimulus hand moves (e.g. the finger lifts). Participants are instructed to execute a pre-specified response upon movement of the stimulus hand. This pre-specified response can be either compatible (finger lifting) or incompatible (finger tapping) with the observed movement. The automatic imitation effect is calculated by subtracting RT on compatible trials from RT on incompatible trials.

Box 16.1 Beliefs about stimulus identity

Stanley, Gowen, and Miall (2007) examined effects of instructing participants that stimuli were human or computer generated, when the stimuli were
in fact identical, to test effects of belief about stimulus identity on mirror
activation. They found a larger interference effect when participants were
instructed that dot stimuli were generated by a human rather than a computer, regardless of whether the dots moved with a human or constant velocity profile. However, in contrast, Press, Gillmeister, and Heyes (2006) found
no evidence of effects of belief. In an automatic imitation factorial design,
participants saw human or robotic hand movements, and were instructed in
one session that these were human generated, and in another, that they were
performed by a robot. There was no effect of instruction on automatic imitation, either when the stimuli had physically human or robotic properties.
Instead, the effects were determined by the stimulus perceptual properties,
with a larger automatic imitation effect for human relative to robotic hands.
This lack of instruction effect was observed despite questionnaire measures
indicating that beliefs about identity had been successfully manipulated.

There are at least two possible explanations for the discrepancy between
findings in these studies. First, there was arguably more perceptual information about animacy in Press et al. (2006) than in Stanley et al. (2007) and
belief about identity may have an impact only when there is little perceptual
information upon which to base inferences. This 'perception hypothesis'
is consistent with an fMRI experiment conducted by Stanley, Gowen, and
Miall (2010), where 15 points, rather than 1 (Stanley et al., 2007), consti-
tuted the perceptual information. There was no difference in activation in
any motor, premotor or pIFG cortical areas regardless of whether participants were told that the stimulus was human or computer generated (note,
however, that this study also did not find any motor effects that correlated
with the level of actual human motion in the stimulus). Second, participants
had more control over the locus of their spatial attention in Stanley et al.
(2007) than Press et al. (2006), and greater attention to stimuli believed to
be human may generate belief effects. More attention to stimuli has been
found to lead to larger automatic imitation effects (Chong, Cunnington,
Williams, & Mattingley, 2009; also see Gowen, Bradshaw, Galpin, Lawrence, & Poliakoff, 2010; Longo & Bertenthal, 2009), and in Stanley et al.'s
study (2007) participants were not required to devote high attention to the
stimuli; they only needed to pace their actions with observed stimuli and the
pace was constant. In contrast, Press et al. (2006) required participants to
respond on the basis of stimulus movement, where this movement happened
at a variable point in the trial, and the task was to respond as quickly as possible. Therefore, attention towards stimuli may have been high regardless

of belief. This 'attention hypothesis' – that greater attention paid to stimuli believed to be human rather than inanimate generates belief effects – is supported by a study that found effects of belief on automatic imitation when there was high perceptual information, but the response was not signalled by the observed action meaning that attention was free to shift (Liepelt & Brass, 2010; also see Klapper, Ramsey, Wigboldus, & Cross, 2014).

If the perception hypothesis is correct, beliefs may indeed exert direct top-down influence on the operation of mirror mechanisms. In contrast, if the attention hypothesis is found to provide a better account of the data, beliefs would not directly determine the operation of mirror mechanisms – beliefs act upon mechanisms determining spatial attention, and level of perceptual processing therefore impacts upon the operation of mirror mechanisms (as well as many other sociocognitive processes). Hence, given the uncertainty about the nature of differences between studies, there is currently no evidence that beliefs about identity play a direct role in biological tuning.

In a simple reaction time (RT) task, Brass, Bekkering, & Prinz (2001) found evidence of greater activation of corresponding motor codes when stimuli had a human, rather than point, form, and were matched for kinematics. Participants were required to make a pre-specified index finger lifting or tapping movement whenever they saw the index finger of an observed hand move. They were faster to execute this movement (e.g. finger lifting) in response to observed compatible (lifting) than to incompatible (tapping) movements. This effect has been termed the 'automatic imitation' effect, given that it signifies primed imitative, relative to non-imitative, responses (see Figure 16.1b) and, for similar reasons to the interference effect, is considered to reflect automatic activation of motor codes that correspond to observed actions. (Note, however, that automatic imitation and interference effects are not thought to be differentially dependent upon priming versus inhibition, respectively – both effects are likely driven by both processes – but the common nomenclature is used in this chapter to differentiate the paradigms.) Brass and colleagues (2001) found no evidence of an automatic imitation effect when responses were made to a point that moved up or down with the same kinematic profile as the observed finger actions. Gowen et al. (2010) replicated this finding of a form x compatibility interaction when comparing automatic imitation of index/middle finger lifting movements relative to similar movement of geometric shapes. Likewise, in a paradigm akin to that employed by Kilner et al. (2003), Gowen, Stanley, and Miall (2008) found a greater interference effect when participants observed a real human model performing movements that were incongruent with their own, relative to a point on a computer monitor moving with a similar kinematic profile.

Influences of form on motor activation have also been found when the non-human stimuli are structurally more similar to the human stimuli. Press, Bird, Flach, and Heyes (2005) investigated differences in processing of human and robotic form, while controlling for kinematics, by removing kinematic information and simply presenting end state postures of movement. Using a simple RT procedure, they required participants to execute a pre-specified hand opening or closing response whenever an observed stimulus hand in a neutral posture was replaced by a hand in an open (fingers splayed) or closed (fist) posture. Participants were faster to execute the action (e.g. hand opening) in response to observed compatible (open) than to incompatible (closed) postures. This automatic imitation effect was larger when observing human hands than robotic hands (Figure 16.2a; also see Bird, Leighton, Press, & Heyes, 2007; Press et al., 2006, 2007 for the same effect). Similarly, Cook, Swapp, Pan, Bianchi-Berthouze, and Blakemore (2014) found greater interference effects when participants observed human avatar form stimuli compared with robotic form stimuli. These studies therefore indicate that stimuli with human form activate corresponding motor codes to a greater degree than stimuli with closely matched non-biological form. Interestingly, Kupferberg et al. (2012) found that interference effects with a robotic arm were similar to those with a human arm if the joint configurations matched those of a human arm (Figure 16.2b). Similarly, there was no evidence of greater automatic imitation of finger movements made by an avatar hand than of inanimate blocks with the same 'joints' (Klapper et al., 2014). Therefore, form effects may be determined solely by configural joint features, not other stimulus properties such as skin tone, concurring also with the finding that biological tuning remains when all stimuli are presented in the same – inanimate – tone (Press et al., 2005).

Other behavioural studies have examined the effects of kinematics on processing in mirror mechanisms. These studies have indicated that, when stimuli are matched for form, movements with human kinematics sometimes generate greater motor activation than movements with non-biological kinematics. For example, Chaminade, Franklin, Oztop, and Cheng (2005) found larger interference effects when a humanoid robot form stimulus moved with human kinematics rather than an artificially generated trajectory, and Kilner et al. (2007) found more interference when participants observed human form stimuli that moved with human kinematics rather than constant velocity. However, the same effect was not found by Kilner et al. (2007) when watching a point move with the two kinematic profiles, and both Gowen et al. (2008) and Cook et al. (2014) failed to find evidence that the kinematic profile influenced the magnitude of an interference effect. Therefore, kinematic manipulations sometimes generate a biological bias, although these effects are not detected in all studies.

Neuroimaging Evidence

A number of imaging studies support these behavioural findings. For example, a PET study found that the observation of human grasping actions activates premotor cortex to a greater degree than the observation of similar robotic actions (Tai, Scherfler, Brooks, Sawamoto, & Castiello, 2004). Additionally, in three fMRI studies, stronger premotor and pIFG activation was found when participants observed meaningless human hand movements relative to the movements of yellow objects (Engel, Burke, Fiehler, Bien, & Rösler, 2008; BA6), human finger actions relative to scissor movements (Costantini et al., 2005; BA44), and humans rather than robots dancing (Miura et al., 2010; BA44 and BA6).

Neuroimaging studies have also demonstrated influence of either form or kinematics, while controlling for the other stimulus variable. For example, Saygin, Wilson, Hagler, Bates, & Sereno (2004) found that observing human motion represented by points of light attached to each joint resulted in greater premotor activation than when points with the same kinematic trajectories were scrambled such that a human form was no longer implied. Additionally, a virtual reality near-infrared spectroscopy study found evidence of biological tuning according to kinematic features; demonstrating greater sensorimotor activation when a human form model grasped objects with human, rather than constant velocity, kinematics (Shimada, 2010); note that there was not the same effect of kinematics in a robotic form condition). An MEG study reached a similar conclusion: Press, Cook, Blakemore, and Kilner (2011) presented participants with human form or point form vertical sinusoidal arm actions, which moved with human or constant velocity kinematics. When observing movements with human kinematics, beta oscillations changed across time in a manner that would be expected if executing the actions. No such dynamic modulations were seen when observing movements with constant velocity kinematic profiles. These dynamic modulations were observed regardless of whether the stimulus had a human or point form.

Effects of kinematics have also been demonstrated when the non-biological kinematic profile is matched to the human profile for complexity. One PET study (Stevens, Fonlupt, Shiffrar, & Decety, 2000) showed greater primary motor cortex activation when participants observed an arm movement video that was played at a rate that made it biologically plausible, compared with when it was played more rapidly. Two fMRI studies have similarly indicated that, both when stimuli are of point (Dayan et al., 2007; BA6 and BA44) and human (Casile et al., 2010; dorsal BA6) form, observing movements obeying the two-thirds power law (Lacquaniti, Terzuolo, & Viviani, 1983) – that slow down at curved relative to straight parts of motion, which broadly speaking corresponds to a minimum-jerk trajectory – activates premotor

(a)   (b)   (c)

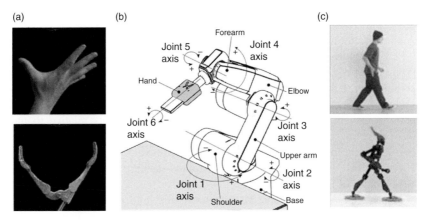

Figure 16.2 Form manipulations. (a) Human and robot form stimuli used in Press et al. (2005). (b) Humanoid robot form stimulus used in Kupferberg et al. (2012). (c) Human and Lego form stimuli used in Cross et al. (2012). Note that biological tuning was only observed in (a) where the joint configurations of the robotic stimulus are different from a human hand.

and pIFG structures to a greater extent than observing movements with the inverted kinematic profile. These studies therefore indicate that stimuli with human kinematics consistently activate motor areas to a greater extent than stimuli with non-biological kinematics when the two profiles are matched for complexity.

One fMRI study observed equal motor activation when observing human and constant velocity robotic grasping actions (Gazzola, Rizzolatti, Wicker, & Keysers, 2007; although if applying a $p < 0.001$ uncorrected threshold, some of the human actions generated greater activation than some of the robotic actions at BA6 coordinates). Additionally, Gobbini et al. (2011) found similar premotor activation when observing human and humanoid emotional facial expressions (in fact, there was a larger response for humanoid actions at some coordinates). Given that the humanoid robot in this study was matched so closely in form to the human stimuli, including joint configurations, these findings concur with those of Kupferberg et al. (2012) – that human joint configurations are the important form feature that determines mirror activation. Similarly, Cross et al. (2012) found that, when the joint configurations of a Lego figure were matched to those of human whole-body stimuli (see Figure 16.2c), typical biological tuning effects were not obtained.

Therefore, most neuroimaging studies support the behavioural data by demonstrating greater motor activation when observing human relative to non-biological movement, in structures such as the dorsal and ventral premotor cortex, and posterior regions of the IFG. As non-biological stimuli become more human-like, for example, by exhibiting human joint configurations, biological tuning effects disappear. Therefore, despite the poorer demonstration of specificity in these studies, the evidence concurs with the behavioural data.

Biological Tuning Evidence: Conclusion

In summary, there have been a number of studies indicating greater operation of mirror mechanisms when observing human action, relative to similar non-biological movement. There are observable influences both of the form and the kinematics of the stimuli.

Functional Implications of Biological Tuning

It has long been hypothesised that mirror mechanisms allow us to 'understand' others' actions 'from within' (Gallese & Sinigaglia, 2011; Rizzolatti, Fadiga, Gallese, & Fogassi, 1996). Under this hypothesis, biological tuning reflects greater 'understanding' of humans compared to inanimate devices. Indeed, it has been suggested that, when mirror mechanisms are active during the observation of non-human agents like humanoid robots, it is a sign of ascription of human properties such as mental states to these agents (e.g. Chaminade & Cheng, 2009; Gazzola et al., 2007; Oberman, McCleery, Ramachandran, & Pineda, 2007). For example, Oberman et al. (2007) claim 'the implication is that the human mirror neuron system may be activated as a result of the human interactant anthropomorphising these robots. Indeed, by activating the human mirror neuron system humanoid robots could potentially tap into the powerful social motivation system inherent in human life, which could lead to more enjoyable and longer lasting human-robot interactions' (p. 2195). Similarly, Gazzola et al. (2007) say, 'now we know that our mirror neuron system may be part of the reason why, when in *Stars Wars*, C3PO taps R2D2 on the head in a moment of mortal danger, we cannot help but attribute them human feelings and intentions, even if their physical aspect and kinematics are far from human' (p. 1683). Furthermore, Chaminade and Cheng (2009) state, 'the underlying assumption is that the measure of … [motor activation] indicates the extent to which an artificial agent is considered as a social inter-actor' (p. 289).

The term 'action understanding' was introduced by Rizzolatti and colleagues to characterise the function of mirror neurons (Rizzolatti & Fadiga, 1998; Rizzolatti et al., 1996). However, there is still no consensus about exactly what is meant by 'action understanding', and how it differs from inferential mentalising, perceptual or motoric functions (Gallese et al., 2011). Therefore, the following section will first consider the potential role of mirror mechanisms in distinct, operationally established, functions involved in understanding and interacting with others. These functions are mentalising, imitation and action perception. In each case it will consider what biological tuning can tell us about processing of humans and inanimate devices. Second, it will examine how biological tuning can be integrated with the view that mirror mechanisms are part of a wider domain-general system adapted for action control, thereby mapping motor codes onto observed events from both our social and inanimate environments.

Mentalising, Imitation and Action Perception

Initial investigations have suggested that mirror mechanisms are unlikely to be involved in inferential processes required for intention understanding. For example, Brass et al. (2007) found no changes in motor activation when manipulating the difficulty of intention inference associated with observed actions. Similarly, de Lange, Spronk, Willems, Toni, & Bekkering (2008) found that requiring participants to attend to the intention underlying an action did not increase activation in motor circuits relative to attention to the means by which an action was executed. Instead, these manipulations generated differences in other regions such as the medial prefrontal cortex, which have been classically associated with social inferential functions. Therefore, claims that operation of mirror mechanisms – when observing either human or inanimate models – reflects the extent to which we 'attribute them human feelings and intentions' (Gazzola et al., 2007, p. 1683) are premature, if not inaccurate.

There is better evidence that mirror mechanisms are involved in imitation, and therefore that biological tuning influences the nature of imitated events. Automatic imitation is considered a demonstration of the operation of mirror mechanisms (defined functionally as in the present chapter, rather than anatomically – remember that this functional definition relies solely upon demonstration that action observation activates motor codes for performing that action). Therefore, by definition, mirror mechanisms are involved in such imitation. There are known positive effects of automatic imitation, for example interactions are perceived as smoother, and interactees are rated more positively (Chartrand & Bargh, 1999), and humans may typically benefit from these effects to a greater extent than their inanimate counterparts such as robots. For these reasons, stimulus variables are often tuned to equate automatic imitation of humanoid robots with that of humans to enhance the 'social competence' of robots (Marin, Issartel, & Chaminade, 2009). There is also evidence that we rely upon the same mechanisms during intentional imitation. For example, damage to the inferior frontal cortex results in impaired imitation of finger movements (Goldenberg & Karnath, 2006), and transcranial magnetic stimulation (TMS) studies have demonstrated that stimulation of premotor/

pIFG regions disrupts both intentional and automatic imitation of simple finger and hand actions (Catmur, Walsh, & Heyes, 2009; Heiser, Iacoboni, Maeda, Marcus, & Mazziotta, 2003; Newman-Norlund, Ondobaka, van Schie, van Elswijk, & Bekkering, 2010). Therefore, biological tuning of mirror mechanisms likely contributes to greater intentional imitation of humans than inanimate devices. Intentional imitation is likely to facilitate acquisition of skills and behaviours (Heyes, 1993), and therefore we will be able to learn a number of skills from conspecifics in a way that we do not with inanimate devices.

Finally, a handful of studies have considered whether activation of mirror representations aids perception of action. Patient and TMS studies suggest that a top-down contribution of mirror mechanisms to perception is likely, given that lesions to motor regions can impair perception (for a review, see Cook, Swapp, Pan, Bianchi-Berthouze, & Blakemore, 2014). Therefore, the motor system may contribute to perception of human actions to a greater extent than that of inanimate movement. Some initial investigations support this possibility. For example, Candidi, Urgesi, Ionta, & Aglioti (2008) demonstrated that TMS of pIFG (BA44) impaired the ability of participants to discriminate two kinematically possible arm and leg actions, but had no effect on their performance in distinguishing two kinematically impossible movements.

In summary, biological tuning within mirror mechanisms may have at least two functional implications. First, we will likely imitate humans more than inanimate devices. Therefore, we will be able to learn a number of skills from conspecifics in a way that we do not with inanimate devices, and humans may benefit from the effects of automatic imitation to a greater extent. Second, the motor system may contribute to perception of human actions more than non-human movements. However, biological tuning is less likely to reflect processing about mental states of an observed entity because there is no evidence that mirror mechanisms are involved in such processing.

Biological Tuning within a Domain-General Perception–Action Mapping Mechanism

There is emerging evidence that mirror mechanisms are not genetic adaptations specifically for mirroring the actions of others, but rather, emerge through domain-general processes of sensorimotor associative learning within a system adapted for action control (see Catmur, present volume, Chapter 22). It may seem counterintuitive that biological tuning is seen within such a system that is not specifically designed for social functions. However, in fact biological tuning is predicted under this account given that we have had more correlated experience of observing human action – rather than inanimate movement – while executing action (Press, 2011). It is also worth noting that stimulus generalisation is a ubiquitous feature of associative learning (Pearce, 1987), which can explain the situations where inanimate movements activate mirror mechanisms (see Press et al., 2005), even to the same extent as human action. For example, as discussed in the behavioural evidence provided in the 'Evidence of Biological Tuning' section, when a mechanical stimulus presents similar joint configurations to a human body, tuning according to form may not be observed because all stimuli equally activate the sensory representation of action.

This account makes two predictions about biological tuning. First, correlated sensorimotor experience with inanimate movement should eliminate the tuning. Two studies support this hypothesis. Press et al. (2007) measured automatic imitation effects with human and robotic hand movements before any training, and, supporting previous findings (Press et al., 2005, 2006), found that the human stimuli generated larger automatic imitation effects than the robotic stimuli. Participants were subsequently trained with the robotic hands in a compatible (requiring performance of actions, which matched those observed) or incompatible (requiring non-matching actions) fashion. Following such training, the group that had received incompatible training still exhibited greater automatic imitation of the human than of robotic hands. However, the group that had received compatible training displayed equal automatic imitation of the two stimulus types. Cross et al. (2009) similarly found evidence that motor cortical areas were not biologically tuned following training with non-biological stimuli. During training, participants were required to perform dance step movements in response to an observed sequence of arrows. The arrows were accompanied (human present) or not (human absent) by a video of a human executing these actions. The cortical response was subsequently measured with fMRI while participants observed the human present and human absent videos. This study demonstrated greater right premotor and pIFG (BA6 and BA44) cortical activation when participants observed the sequences with which they had associated actions during training, but no effect of whether there was a human present in the video or not. Therefore, presenting correlated sensorimotor experience with non-biological stimuli appears to eliminate the bias.

The second prediction states that the same representations in motor regions both mirror observed actions *and* respond to any other stimuli that have been paired predictively with action, i.e. the *same* mechanisms both mediate action observation–execution mapping and arbitrary stimulus observation–execution mapping. We are exposed to a plethora of sensorimotor experience within our sensory world that does not relate to perceived action, or even perceived movement. For example, we swing a cricket bat on the right of our body, hear the sound of the ball contacting the bat in our right ear, and observe the ball rapidly appearing from the right. Additionally, we observe objects such as teacups and learn to perform precision grips in their presence. We are also exposed to apparently arbitrary relationships between action and the physical sensory environment, for example stamping on a brake pedal with our right foot when we see a red traffic light. After events have been paired systematically, we will automatically activate motor codes for grasping when we observe cups, or right-foot movement in the presence of red lights, demonstrated by priming/interference effects with object–action pairs similar to those with observed–executed actions (Tucker & Ellis, 1998). Additionally, patients with prefrontal lesions who are impaired in top-down control exhibit utilisation behaviours with objects, whereby they will brush their teeth whenever they see a toothbrush, as well as imitate actions in a way that is typically inhibited (Lhermitte, Pillon, & Serdaru, 1986).

Press et al. (2012a) conducted an fMRI study to test the hypothesis that the same mechanisms mediate action observation–execution mapping and arbitrary stimulus observation–execution mapping. During training, arbitrary shapes such as hexagons, circles and squares were paired with executed manual intransitive actions such as hand splaying and thumb extension. There was no meaningful relationship between actions and shapes with which they were paired, and the specific shape–action combinations were counterbalanced between participants to control for any arbitrary pre-existing relationships not evident to the experimenters. After training, this study used adaptation techniques to demonstrate that shapes activated, not only motor but specifically mirror representations of the actions with which they had been paired in training in right pIFG (BA44). The authors reached this conclusion via the following logic: first, participants could not observe their actions during training, therefore if common representations are activated when simply observing actions and shapes with which the actions have been paired, it must be due to the shapes activating mirror (not purely motor) representations of actions. Second, adaptation logic specifies that repeated activation of the same population of cells results in a decline in responsivity (Grill-Spector, Henson, & Martin, 2006), and observation of a shape just after observation of the action with which the shape had been paired in training resulted in a reduced blood-oxygen-level-dependent (BOLD) signal in BA44. Therefore, this study confirmed the hypothesis that the mechanisms involved in mirroring human action are not distinct from those that retrieve motor codes to other sensory events with which a predictive relationship has been established.

In conclusion, according to the domain-general associative account and a handful of recent findings, the same mechanisms that mediate mirroring of observed human action support retrieval of motor codes linked with other physical events in the environment. Therefore, mirror mechanisms must be considered one component of a domain-general system mapping between perceptual and motor domains to support a range of functions for action control. Under this hypothesis, biological tuning is not an intrinsic property of mirror mechanisms, but simply reflects the nature of an individual's sensorimotor experience.

Conclusion

A range of behavioural and neuroimaging studies demonstrate that we mirror observed human action to a greater extent than similar non-biological movement; tuning sensitive both to the form and the kinematic profile of observed movement. Biological tuning of mirror mechanisms may contribute to greater imitation of human action than inanimate movement, and a greater role of the motor system in perception of conspecifics. However, current evidence suggests that mirror mechanisms are one component of a domain-general system mapping between perception and action to support action control, and biological tuning reflects simply the nature of an individual's sensorimotor experience rather than an intrinsic property of the mechanism.

References

Bird, G., Leighton, J., Press, C., & Heyes, C. (2007). Intact automatic imitation of human and robot actions in autism spectrum disorders. *Proceedings of the Royal Society B: Biological Sciences*, 274, 3027–3031. doi: 10.1098/rspb.2007.1019.

Brass, M., Bekkering, H., & Prinz, W. (2001). Movement observation affects movement execution in a simple response task. *Acta Psychologica*, 106, 3–22. doi: 10.1016/S0001-6918(00)00024-X.

Brass, M., Schmitt, R. M., Spengler, S., & Gergely, G. (2007). Investigating action understanding: Inferential processes versus action simulation. *Current Biology*, 17, 2117–2121. doi: 10.1016/j.cub.2007.11.057.

Candidi, M., Urgesi, C., Ionta, S., & Aglioti, S. M. (2008). Virtual lesion of ventral premotor cortex impairs visual perception of biomechanically possible but not impossible actions. *Society for Neuroscience*, 3, 388–400. doi: 10.1080/17470910701676269.

Casile, A., Dayan, E., Caggiano, V., Hendler, T., Flash, T., & Giese, M. A. (2010). Neuronal encoding of human kinematic invariants during action observation. *Cerebral Cortex*, 20, 1647–1655. doi: 10.1093/cercor/bhp229.

Catmur, C., Walsh, V., & Heyes, C. (2009). Associative sequence learning: The role of experience in the development of imitation and the mirror system. *Proceedings of the Royal Society B: Biological Sciences*, 364, 2369–2380. doi: 10.1098/rstb.2009.0048.

Chaminade, T., & Cheng, G. (2009). Social cognitive neuroscience and humanoid robotics. *Journal of Physiology – Paris* 103, 286–295. doi: 10.1016/j.jphysparis.2009.08.011.

Chaminade, T., Franklin, D. W., Oztop, E., & Cheng, G. (2005). Motor interference between humans and humanoid robots: Effect of biological and artificial motion. In *Proceedings of the 4th International Conference on Development and Learning*, 96–101. doi: 10.1109/DEVLRN.2005.1490951.

Chartrand, T. L., & Bargh, J. A. (1999). The chameleon effect: The perception–behavior link and social interaction. *Journal of Personality and Social Psychology*, 76, 893–910. doi: 10.1037/0022-3514.76.6.893.

Chong, T. T.-J., Cunnington, R., Williams, M. A., & Mattingley, J. B. (2009). The role of selective attention in matching observed and executed actions. *Neuropsychologia, 47*, 786–795. doi:10.1016/j.neuropsychologia.2008.12.008

Cisek, P., & Kalaska, J. F. (2004. Neural correlates of mental rehearsal in dorsal premotor cortex. *Nature, 431*, 993–996. doi: 10.1038/nature03005.

Coll, M. P., Bird, G., Catmur, C., & Press, C, (2015). Cross-modal repetition effects in the mu rhythm indicate tactile mirroring during action observation. *Cortex, 63*, 121–131.

Cook, J., Swapp, D., Pan, X., Bianchi-Berthouze, N., & Blakemore, S.-J. (2014). Atypical interference effect of action observation in autism spectrum conditions. *Psychological Medicine, 44*, 731–740. doi: 10.1017/S0033291713001335.

Cook, R., Bird, G., Catmur, C., Press, C., & Heyes, C. (2014). Mirror neurons: From origin to function. *Behavioral and Brain Sciences, 37*(02), 177–192.

Costantini, M., Galati, G., Ferretti, A., Caulo, M., Tartaro, A., et al. (2005). Neural systems underlying observation of humanly impossible movements: An fMRI study. *Cerebral Cortex, 15*, 1761–1767. doi: 10.1093/cercor/bhi053.

Cross, E. S., Hamilton, A. F. de C., Kraemer, D. J. M., Kelley, W. M., & Grafton, S. T. (2009). Dissociable substrates for body motion and physical experience in the human action observation network. *European Journal of Neuroscience, 30*, 1383–1392. doi: 10.1111/j.1460-9568.2009.06941.x.

Cross, E. S., Liepelt, R., Hamilton, A. F. de C., Parkinson, J., Ramsey, R., et al. (2012). Robotic movement preferentially engages the action observation network. *Human Brain Mapping, 33*, 2238–2254. doi: 10.1002/hbm.21361.

Dayan, E., Casile, A., Levit-Binnun, N., Giese, M. A., Hendler, T., & Flash, T. (2007). Neural representations of kinematic laws of motion: Evidence for action–perception coupling. *Proceedings of the National Academy of Sciences, 104*, 20582–20587. doi: 10.1073/pnas.0710033104.

Di Dio, C., & Gallese, V. (2009). Neuroaesthetics: A review. *Current Opinion in Neurobiology, 19*, 682–687.

Dushanova, J., & Donoghue, J. (2010). Neurons in primary motor cortex engaged during action observation. *European Journal of Neuroscience, 31*, 386–398. doi: 10.1111/j.1460-9568.2009.07067.x.

Engel, A., Burke, M., Fiehler, K., Bien, S., & Rösler, F. (2008. How moving objects become animated: The human mirror neuron system assimilates non-biological movement patterns. *Society for Neuroscience, 3*, 368–387. doi: 10.1080/17470910701612793.

Gallese, V., Fadiga, L., Fogassi, L., & Rizzolatti, G. (1996). Action recognition in the premotor cortex. *Brain, 119*, 593–609. doi: 10.1093/brain/119.2.593.

Gallese, V., Gernsbacher, M.A., Heyes, C., Hickok, G., & Iacoboni, M. (2011). Mirror neuron forum. *Perspectives on Psychological Science, 6*, 369–407. doi: 10.1177/1745691611413392.

Gallese, V., & Sinigaglia, C. (2011). What is so special about embodied simulation? *Trends in Cognitive Sciences, 15*, 512–519. doi: 10.1016/j.tics.2011.09.003.

Gazzola, V., Rizzolatti, G., Wicker, B., & Keysers, C. (2007). The anthropomorphic brain: The mirror neuron system responds to human and robotic actions. *NeuroImage, 35*, 1674–1684. doi: 10.1016/j.neuroimage.2007.02.003.

Gobbini, M. I., Gentili, C., Ricciardi, E., Bellucci, C., Salvini, P., et al. (2011). Distinct neural systems involved in agency and animacy detection. *Journal of Cognitive Neuroscience*, 23, 1911–1920. doi: 10.1162/jocn.2010.21574.

Goldenberg, G., & Karnath, H.-O. (2006). The neural basis of imitation is body part specific. *Journal of Neuroscience*, 26, 6282–6287. doi: 10.1523/jneurosci.0638-06.2006.

Gowen, E., Bradshaw, C., Galpin, A., Lawrence, A., & Poliakoff, E. (2010). Exploring visuomotor priming following biological and non-biological stimuli. *Brain and Cognition*, 74, 288–297. doi: 10.1016/j.bandc.2010.08.010.

Gowen, E., Stanley, J., & Miall, R. C. (2008). Movement interference in autism-spectrum disorder. *Neuropsychologia*, 46, 1060–1068. doi: 10.1016/j.neuropsychologia.2007.11.004.

Grill-Spector, K., Henson, R., & Martin, A. (2006). Repetition and the brain: Neural models of stimulus-specific effects. *Trends in Cognitive Sciences*, 10, 14–23. doi: 10.1016/j.tics.2005.11.006.

Heiser, M., Iacoboni, M., Maeda, F., Marcus, J., & Mazziotta, J.C. (2003). The essential role of Broca's area in imitation. *European Journal of Neuroscience*, 17, 1123–1128. doi: 10.1046/j.1460-9568.2003.02530.x.

Heyes, C. M. (1993). Imitation, culture and cognition. *Animal Behaviour*, 46, 999–1010. doi: 10.1006/anbe.1993.1281.

Hogan, N. (1984). An organizing principle for a class of voluntary movements. *Journal of Neuroscience*, 4, 2745–2754.

Iacoboni, M., Molnar-Szakacs, I., Gallese, V., Buccino, G., Mazziotta, J. C., & Rizzolatti, G. (2005). Grasping the intentions of others with one's own mirror neuron system. *PLoS Biology*, 3, e79. doi: 10.1371/journal.pbio.0030079.

Kilner, J., Hamilton, A. F. de C., & Blakemore, S.-J. (2007). Interference effect of observed human movement on action is due to velocity profile of biological motion. *Society for Neuroscience*, 2, 158–166. doi: 10.1080/17470910701428190.

Kilner, J. M., Neal, A., Weiskopf, N., Friston, K. J., & Frith, C. D. (2009). Evidence of mirror neurons in human inferior frontal gyrus. *Journal of Neuroscience*, 29, 10153–10159. doi: 10.1523/JNEUROSCI.2668-09.2009.

Kilner, J. M., Paulignan, Y., & Blakemore, S. (2003). An interference effect of observed biological movement on action. *Current Biology*, 13, 522–525. doi: 10.1016/S0960-9822(03)00165-9.

Klapper, A., Ramsey, R., Wigboldus, D., & Cross, E. S. (2014). The control of automatic imitation based on bottom-up and top-down cues to animacy: Insights from brain and behavior. *Journal of Cognitive Neuroscience*, 1–11. doi: 10.1162/jocn_a_00651.

Kupferberg, A., Huber, M., Helfer, B., Lenz, C., Knoll, A., & Glasauer, S. (2012). Moving just like you: Motor interference depends on similar motility of agent and observer. *PLoS One*, 7, e39637. doi: 10.1371/journal.pone.0039637.

Lacquaniti, F., Terzuolo, C., & Viviani, P. (1983). The law relating the kinematic and figural aspects of drawing movements. *Acta Psychologica*, 54, 115–130. doi: 10.1016/0001-6918(83)90027-6.

Lange, F. P. de, Spronk, M., Willems, R. M., Toni, I., & Bekkering, H. (2008). Complementary systems for understanding action intentions. *Current Biology*, 18, 454–457. doi: 10.1016/j.cub.2008.02.057.

Lhermitte, F., Pillon, B., & Serdaru, M. (1986). Human autonomy and the frontal lobes. Part I: Imitation and utilization behavior: A neuropsychological study of 75 patients. *Annals of Neurology*, 19, 326–334. doi: 10.1002/ana.410190404.

Liepelt, R., & Brass, M. (2010). Top-down modulation of motor priming by belief about animacy. *Journal of Experimental Psychology: Human Perception and Performance*, 57, 221–227. doi: 10.1027/1618–3169/a000028.

Lingnau, A., Gesierich, B., & Caramazza, A. (2009). Asymmetric fMRI adaptation reveals no evidence for mirror neurons in humans. *Proceedings of the National Academy of Sciences*, 106, 9925–9930. doi: 10.1073/pnas.0902262106.

Longo, M. R., & Bertenthal, B. I. (2009). Attention modulates the specificity of automatic imitation to human actors. *Experimental Brain Research*, 192, 739–744. doi: 10.1007/s00221-008-1649-5.

Marin, L., Issartel, J., & Chaminade, T. (2009). Interpersonal motor coordination: From human–human to human–robot interactions. *Interaction Studies*, 10, 479–504. doi: 10.1075/is.10.3.09mar.

Miura, N., Sugiura, M., Takahashi, M., Sassa, Y., Miyamoto, A., et al. (2010). Effect of motion smoothness on brain activity while observing a dance: An fMRI study using a humanoid robot. *Society for Neuroscience*, 5, 40–58. doi: 10.1080/17470910903083256.

Newman-Norlund, R. D., Ondobaka, S., van Schie, H. T., van Elswijk, G., & Bekkering, H. (2010). Virtual lesions of the IFG abolish response facilitation for biological and non-biological cues. *Frontiers in Behavioral Neuroscience*, 4, 5. doi: 10.3389/neuro.08.005.2010.

Oberman, L. M., McCleery, J. P., Ramachandran, V. S., & Pineda, J. A. (2007). EEG evidence for mirror neuron activity during the observation of human and robot actions: Toward an analysis of the human qualities of interactive robots. *Neurocomputing*, 70, 2194–2203. doi: 10.1016/j.neucom.2006.02.024.

Oosterhof, N. N., Tipper, S. P., & Downing, P. E. (2013). Crossmodal and action-specific: Neuroimaging the human mirror neuron system. *Trends in Cognitive Sciences*, 17, 311–318. doi: 10.1016/j.tics.2013.04.012.

Pearce, J. M. (1987. A model for stimulus generalization in Pavlovian conditioning. *Psychological Review*, 94, 61–73. doi: 10.1037/0033-295X.94.1.61.

Pellegrino, G. di, Fadiga, L., Fogassi, L., Gallese, V., & Rizzolatti, G. (1992). Understanding motor events: A neurophysiological study. *Experimental Brain Research*, 91, 176–180. doi: 10.1007/BF00230027.

Press, C. (2011). Action observation and robotic agents: Learning and anthropomorphism. *Neuroscience & Biobehavioral Reviews*, 35, 1410–1418.

Press, C., Bird, G., Flach, R., & Heyes, C. (2005). Robotic movement elicits automatic imitation. *Cognitive Brain Research*, 25, 632–640. doi: 10.1016/j.cogbrainres.2005.08.020.

Press, C., Catmur, C., Cook, R., Widmann, H., Heyes, C., & Bird, G. (2012a). fMRI evidence of 'mirror' responses to geometric shapes. *PLoS One*, 7, e51934. doi: 10.1371/journal.pone.0051934.

Press, C., Cook, J., Blakemore, S.-J., & Kilner, J. (2011). Dynamic modulation of human motor activity when observing actions. *Journal of Neuroscience*, 31, 2792–2800. doi: 10.1523/JNEUROSCI.1595-10.2011.

Press, C., Gillmeister, H., & Heyes, C. (2006). Bottom-up, not top-down, modulation of imitation by human and robotic models. *European Journal of Neuroscience*, 24, 2415–2419. doi: 10.1111/j.1460-9568.2006.05115.x.

(2007). Sensorimotor experience enhances automatic imitation of robotic action. *Proceedings of the Royal Society B: Biological Sciences*, 274, 2509–2514. doi: 10.1098/rspb.2007.0774.

Press, C., Weiskopf, N., & Kilner, J. M. (2012b). Dissociable roles of human inferior frontal gyrus during action execution and observation. *NeuroImage*, 60, 1671–1677. doi: 10.1016/j.neuroimage.2012.01.118.

Rizzolatti, G., & Craighero, L. (2004). The mirror-neuron system. *Annual Review of Neuroscience*, 27, 169–192. doi: 10.1146/annurev.neuro.27.070203.144230.

Rizzolatti, G., & Fadiga, L. (1998). Grasping objects and grasping action meanings: The dual role of monkey rostroventral premotor cortex (area F5). *Novartis Foundation Symposium*, 218, 81–95.

Rizzolatti, G., Fadiga, L., Gallese, V., & Fogassi, L. (1996). Premotor cortex and the recognition of motor actions. *Cognitive Brain Research*, 3, 131–141. doi: 10.1016/0926-6410(95)00038-0.

Saygin, A. P., Wilson, S. M., Hagler, D. J., Bates, E., & Sereno, M. I. (2004). Point-light biological motion perception activates human premotor cortex. *Journal of Neuroscience*, 24, 6181–6188. doi: 10.1523/jneurosci.0504-04.2004.

Shimada, S. (2010). Deactivation in the sensorimotor area during observation of a human agent performing robotic actions. *Brain and Cognition*, 72, 394–399. doi: 10.1016/j.bandc.2009.11.005.

Stanley, J., Gowen, E., & Miall, R. C. (2007). Effects of agency on movement interference during observation of a moving dot stimulus. *Journal of Experimental Psychology: Human Perception and Performance*, 33, 915–926. doi: 10.1037/0096-1523.33.4.915.

(2010). How instructions modify perception: An fMRI study investigating brain areas involved in attributing human agency. *NeuroImage*, 52, 389–400. doi: 10.1016/j.neuroimage.2010.04.025.

Stevens, J. A., Fonlupt, P., Shiffrar, M., & Decety, J. (2000). New aspects of motion perception: Selective neural encoding of apparent human movements. *Neuroreport*, 11, 109–115.

Tai, Y. F., Scherfler, C., Brooks, D. J., Sawamoto, N., & Castiello, U. (2004). The human premotor cortex is 'mirror' only for biological actions. *Current Biology*, 14, 117–120. doi: 10.1016/j.cub.2004.01.005.

Tucker, M., & Ellis, R. (1998). On the relations between seen objects and components of potential actions. *Journal of Experimental Psychology: Human Perception and Performance*, 24, 830–846. doi: 10.1037/0096-1523.24.3.830.

17 Representation of Self versus Others' Actions

John A. Dewey and Günther Knoblich

Abstract

In many social settings, people are expected to respond to and anticipate the actions of others. Everyday examples include team sports, card games and normal conversations. Clearly, an important aspect of social cognition is thinking about and planning for other agents' actions. But what processes are involved in thinking about others' actions, as opposed to one's own actions? This chapter introduces some broad ideas about the possible sensorimotor foundations of action representation in both self and other, drawing on recent findings from the fields of cognitive psychology and cognitive neuroscience. The chapter is organized around three themes: (1) how action experience shapes the representation of others' actions; (2) action affordances and the representation of space in relation to self and other; and (3) distinguishing self and other.

As social animals, humans have much to gain from observing the behavior of others. For example, we can learn from the success and failures of others' actions, infer intentions and other mental states, and anticipate what others will do next in order to prepare an appropriate response. A growing body of evidence suggests observed actions are represented in functionally similar ways to one's own actions, yet we rarely confuse our own intentions and actions with what other people think or do. This raises fundamental questions: how are mental representations of others' actions similar to and different from mental representations of one's own actions? If they are similar, what is the basis for the self-other distinction? In recent decades, significant strides have been made towards answering these questions. The answers help shed light on how we understand others' actions, how others' actions influence mental representations of shared social environments, and why we feel a sense of agency for our own actions but not for others' actions.

How Action Experience Shapes the Representation of Others' Actions

The last few decades in cognitive science have seen an increased emphasis on theories that postulate overlap between motor and perceptual processes. According to *common coding theory*, actions are represented in terms of their contingent sensory consequences, or *action-effects* (Hommel, Müsseler, Aschersleben, & Prinz, 2001; Prinz, 1997). When individuals perform actions, they acquire bidirectional associations between motor patterns and action-effects. As a result, motor processes influence perception and vice versa (Blaesi & Wilson, 2010; Elsner & Hommel, 2001). An implication of common coding theory is that perceiving others' actions should activate motor patterns in the mind of the observer. This has been confirmed in many experiments where observing others' actions leads to activation in many of the same areas of the brain involved in preparing and executing one's own actions (for reviews, see Rizzolatti & Craighero, 2004; Rizzolatti & Sinigaglia, 2010). Motor activity during action observation, often referred to as *motor resonance*, might serve several functions, including supporting imitation and understanding others' intentions.

An idea which has gained traction over the last decade is that the close overlap between motor and perceptual processes enables observers to perform *mental simulations* of other agents' actions, and thereby predict upcoming action-effects (Wilson & Knoblich, 2005). Perception is strongly influenced by prior expectations, and accurate predictions make the job of interpreting incoming sense data more efficient. Predicting the sensory consequences of one's own actions is one of the motor system's major functions, so it makes sense that it would be re-purposed in this way to predict others' actions, as opposed to relying on an entirely different system. The mental simulation hypothesis is consistent with the fact that familiar actions are easier to predict than unfamiliar actions. For example, observers watching movies of people throwing darts are more accurate in predicting where the darts will land when viewing a movie of themselves compared to a stranger (Knoblich & Flach, 2001). In this way, first-hand action experience plays an important role in the representation and understanding of others' actions.

The ability to map observed actions onto one's own action repertoire emerges early in life. Infants develop the ability to imitate others during the first two years (Jones, 2009), and some researchers argue that even new-born infants show a rudimentary ability to imitate adults' facial expressions (Meltzoff & Moore, 1983). Infants also begin to recognize other people's actions as goal-directed during the first year (Sommerville & Woodward, 2005). Infants' sensitivity to goals in the actions of others is modulated by their own experiences performing similar actions. For example, a study by Sommerville, Woodward, and Needham (2005) addressed three-month-old infants' sensitivity to other people's action goals by measuring their eye gaze while an actor reached for an object. Infants with previous experience reaching for the same object showed greater surprise (longer looking time) when the actor reached for a different-than-expected object compared to infants with no prior experience reaching for the object. Similarly, infants show increased surprise when observing an actor reaching for an object in an inefficient manner if they have previous experience reaching for the same object (Skerry, Carey, & Spelke, 2013). These findings suggest that the experience of performing goal-directed actions provides scaffolding for predicting similar goal-directed actions in others.

Action experiences also influence how adults perceive others' actions. In a study by Casile and Giese (2006) participants were blindfolded and learned novel upper-body movements based on haptic and verbal feedback. This motor training selectively improved visual recognition of biological motion in point-light stimuli which contained the learned movement, indicating that motor learning without vision influences visual action perception. Similarly, expertise in a particular action domain influences how easy it is to predict similar actions performed by others. For example, skilled basketball players show greater motor resonance and are better at predicting if another person's shot will go through the basket compared to novices (Aglioti, Cesari, Romani, & Urgesi, 2008). One might question whether athletes are better than average at predicting action-effects in general. However, the effects of expertise appear to be domain specific. In a study comparing older and younger figure skating experts with age-matched novices, experts at all ages showed superior prediction performance for figure skating moves, but were no better than novices at predicting simple movement exercises. There was also a main effect of age on both tasks, indicating that the ability to predict others' actions declines in old age (Diersch, Cross, Stadler, Schütz-Bosbach, & Rieger, 2012).

Action expertise also has implications for memory. In a study comparing novice and expert rock climbers, both groups were shown displays of easy, difficult and impossible rock-climbing paths. Following a distraction task, the groups were tested on their memory for the position of the climbing holds. While there was no difference between groups on the easy and impossible paths, expert rock climbers showed a better memory for the difficult paths. A plausible interpretation is that the experts were able to mentally simulate the difficult path more easily than the novices, and this improved their recall (Pezzulo, Barca, Bocconi, & Borghi, 2010).

Mental simulation is not the only possible strategy for predicting others' actions. An alternative is to rely on rule-based inferences, reasoning about others' mental states by deduction or rules-of-thumb. To revisit an earlier example, an observer might predict that a basketball player's shot will go into the basket, not as a result of a mental simulation, but simply because the observer believes that the player is highly skilled. The conceptual distinction between rule-based inference and simulation in social cognition is supported by neurophysiological experiments (Van Overwalle & Baetens, 2009). Neurons involved in action simulation are located in the pre-motor area of the frontal cortex, an area involved in planning movements, and in parts of parietal cortex, particularly the anterior intraparietal sulcus. By contrast, rule-based inferences and attributions involve the temporoparietal junction, precuneous, and medial prefrontal cortex. Both systems play important roles in reasoning about others' actions, and likely work together in a complementary fashion. One such proposal is that simulation is the primary means by which people understand other actors' perspectives, whereas rule-based approaches develop as shortcuts when a particular task becomes sufficiently familiar (Mitchell, Currie, & Ziegler, 2009). The rule-based inference could also come into play when observed actions are not suitable for simulation. For example, an fMRI study on human participants found that observing actions belonging to the motor repertoire of the observer (e.g. biting) activated the motor system even when they were performed by a different species (dog or monkey). A movie of a barking dog, however, did not produce any frontal activation. This is presumably because humans do not bark, so there was no prior motor experience to associate with the visual properties of the stimulus (Buccino et al., 2004). See Box 17.1.

Box 17.1 Motor contributions to the perception of music

Production and enjoyment of music is a near universal aspect of human culture, which plays an important role in many people's daily lives. The human mirror neuron system is known to respond to visual and auditory stimuli associated with particular actions, and playing a musical instrument is an excellent example of a multisensory experience, which involves associating specific motor and auditory patterns. For this reason, it has been proposed that the mirror neuron system mediates certain effects of expertise on music perception (Lahav, Saltzman, & Schlaug, 2007; Molnar-Szakacs & Overy, 2006).

Similar to the findings that action experience leads to increased motor resonance during action observation, the experience of producing music leads to increased motor activation when a familiar piece of music is presented. For example, Lahav and colleagues (2007) trained non-musicians to play a simple melody by ear, and then monitored brain activity while participants listened to the learned melody as well as unfamiliar melodies. The learned melodies were associated with greater activation across a fronto-parietal network of regions associated with action observation and the human mirror neuron system, suggesting the participants mentally simulated the motor component of the familiar melodies. In another study, musicians showed greater activation in action planning areas of the brain compared to non-musicians when they viewed musical notation, indicating that visual stimuli can also induce mental simulations (Behmer & Jantzen, 2011).

The ability to simulate the motor component of musical performances has implications for musical perception and production. For example, in a study in which jazz musicians listened to piano melodies and were asked to judge whether the performances were improvised or imitated, judgment accuracy correlated with musical experience, and performances judged to be improvised were associated with greater activation in areas associated with action simulation (Engel & Keller, 2011). In another study, pianists were asked to play the complementary part of a piano duet in synchrony with pre-recorded performances of their own or other pianists' earlier performances. Participants recognized and achieved better synchrony with their own recordings (Keller, Knoblich, & Repp, 2007). Taken together, these results suggest that action experience fundamentally alters the representation of music via the coupling of motor and perceptual codes. As in other domains, action experience enables more accurate mental simulations, which contributes to musical recognition and synchronization.

Action Affordances and the Representation of Space in Relation to Self and Other

The possibility of action is a function of the environment an organism finds itself in as well as its capabilities. Many actions are directed toward particular objects or people whose properties must be taken into account for the action to succeed. Properties of an environment which support the possibility of action are called *affordances* (Gibson, 1977).

One particularly important property of objects from an action-oriented perspective is their spatial location. To effectively guide the body through space, it is obviously necessary to track the position of nearby objects. However, the spatial coordinates of an object with respect to a sense organ (e.g. eyes or ears) may be very different from the spatial coordinates of the object with respect to a motor effector (usually the hands). This presents a problem: how does the brain represent the spatial location of objects? An early and influential theory of the relation of visual space to motor space was posited by Hermann Lotze (1817–1881). Lotze's Theory of Local Signs proposed that our visual sense of the position of objects in a scene depends on the same mechanisms that move the eyes and hands, as opposed to two distinctive systems. In the 1990s, neuroscientists discovered neurons in the ventral premotor cortex of the macaque monkey which specifically responded to visual stimuli adjacent to the hand or arm (Graziano, Yap, & Gross, 1994). The neurons' firing changed when the animal moved its arm, but not when it moved its eyes. Thus, these neurons seemed to provide a representation of space near the body (*peripersonal space*) related to the visual control of reaching movements.

For convenience, we will refer to populations of neurons that show sensitivity to the position of objects in peripersonal space as *affordance maps*, because the nearby objects they respond to afford the possibility of action. Importantly, affordance maps are flexible and can be altered by action experience. Specifically, there is evidence from both behavioral and neurophysiological studies that affordance maps are re-shaped by tool use. For example, Jessica Witt and colleagues (2005) asked participants to estimate distances to targets while they either did or did not hold a reaching tool. Estimates of perceived distance were shorter when participants held the tool and intended to reach with it, suggesting that participants' representation of space was influenced by the action affordances provided by the tool. Similarly, neuroscientists have discovered neurons in monkeys whose firing patterns take tools into account (Iriki, Tanaka, & Iwamura, 1996; Ishibashi, Hihara, & Iriki, 2000). For example, they would fire if an object was within arm's reach, or within reach using a rake provided a rake was present.

Just as tools can alter the range of actions available to an organism, so too can the presence of other agents. Two or more individuals acting together have a greater set of behavioral possibilities compared to either individual acting alone. A classic example is a heavy object, which is only liftable by cooperating with a second person. Furthermore, different people may have different capabilities, spatial perspectives and relationships with the objects they intend to interact with. All of this raises the question of how the brain represents not just actions, but also the potential for action, for the self as well as other agents.

As one might expect, humans are generally very good at taking the properties of potential co-actors into account when planning actions. For example, people account for the combined shoulder width of themselves and another person when estimating whether a door is sufficiently wide for both to walk through simultaneously, although their ability to do so depends on the perspective from which they view the other (Davis, Riley, Shockley, & Cummins-Sebree, 2010). In another study, dyads worked together to move planks from a conveyor belt onto a drop-off ramp. The planks could be moved either individually (for short planks) or with the partner (for longer planks). Interestingly, the plank length at which the dyads transitioned from solo to joint lifting was determined by the arm span of the partner with shorter arms (Isenhower, Richardson, Carello, Baron, & Marsh, 2010). This illustrates how the capabilities of co-actors are spontaneously taken into account during joint actions. In line with the assumption of action simulation, the perception of other agents' action affordances may be influenced by first-hand action experiences. For example, tall people tend to slightly overestimate the reaching capabilities of shorter people (Ramenzoni, Riley, Shockley, & Davis, 2008).

Given that co-actors influence action affordances, it is natural to wonder what effects other people may have on affordance maps and the representation of peripersonal space. To investigate this question, Costantini and colleagues (2011a) tested whether observation of tool-use impacts perceived distances similarly to active tool-use. They found that it did, so that both performing and observing tool actions extended the range of peripersonal space. On this basis, one could argue that the brain represents other agents similarly to tools which offer extended opportunities for interacting with shared environments (Figure 17.1). A caveat is that this effect only occurred when observers shared action potentialities in common with the observed agent (both were holding a tool). Further studies have shown that both response times and motor-evoked potentials are influenced by the spatial alignment of an object's handle with respect to a hand (congruent or incongruent), regardless of whether the hand belongs to the participant or a computer avatar (Cardellicchio, Sinigaglia, & Costantini, 2012; Costantini, Committeri, & Sinigaglia, 2011b). Together, these studies provide evidence that action affordances are represented similarly for self and other. It has been proposed that representing objects in a shared-action space may help support coordinated joint actions, particularly when there is some disparity between the perspectives of self and other (Pezzulo, Iodice, Ferraina, & Kessler, 2013).

Distinguishing Self and Other

The previous sections emphasized similarities between the representations of executed and observed actions. This overlap may be useful for predicting others' actions and representing action affordances in a shared action space. However, it is also important that actors know how to distinguish their own actions from others' actions. Distinguishing the actions of self and others involves recognizing one's own body as distinct from others' bodies, as well as an ability to causally attribute action-effects to their correct source. In this section we discuss two phenomenological qualities of self-action that support this distinction: the sense of body ownership and the sense of agency.

Sense of Body Ownership

The *sense of body ownership*, that is, awareness and identification with one's own body, is fundamental to the self–other distinction (Gallagher, 2000). Recognizing one's body may be a precondition for knowing what action the self is performing. But what is the basis for the sense of body ownership? On

Figure 17.1 Individual versus joint affordance maps. *See Plate 6.*

Notes: The red ovals indicate areas which afford the possibility of action (raking or lifting hay). Neuroscientists first discovered neurons which responded to objects within reach of an individual's arm or tool. The single red oval in the top panel indicates a hypothetical receptive field for such a neuron belonging to the worker on the far right. More recent studies suggest that action affordances available to self and others are represented in a functionally similar way, so the receptive field of the hypothetical neuron might actually respond to objects within reach of his own rake, or his co-workers' rakes, as depicted by the multiple red ovals in the bottom panel.

the surface it may seem axiomatic that one's own body is part of the self, or that the body in some way belongs to the self. However, the sense of body ownership can be disrupted in patients with particular kinds of brain damage, and even in healthy individuals under certain circumstances.

Brain lesions occasionally produce dramatic changes in individuals' sense of body ownership. For example, somatoparaphrenia is a delusion where one denies ownership of a limb or even an entire side of one's body (Vallar & Ronchi, 2009). The following dialog is an excerpt from a clinical examination of patient AR, an 84-year-old woman who suffered a right-hemisphere stroke (Bisiach, Rusconi, & Vallar, 1991); the examiner points to the patient's left arm and begins asking questions:

EXAMINER: Whose arm is this?
A. R.: It's not mine.
EXAMINER: Whose is it?
A.R: It's my mother's.
EXAMINER: How on earth does it happen to be here?
A.R: I don't know. I found it on my bed.
EXAMINER: How long has it been there?
A.R: Since the first day. Feel, it's warmer than mine. The other day too, when the weather was colder, it was warmer than mine…

As in this example, most reported cases of somatoparaphrenia involve lesions to the right hemisphere of the brain, particularly the parietal lobe, and the associated delusional beliefs are usually felt towards the contralateral (left) side of the body. The right parietal lobe is generally involved in any task which involves integrating motor and perceptual information, and many distortions of body image involve damage to this area (Vallar & Ronchi, 2009). However, in many cases of somatoparaphrenia the brain damage is widespread, resulting in a constellation of symptoms including spatial neglect (i.e. chronic inattention to a particular region of space), a loss of control over parts of the body, and the aforementioned feeling of estrangement from one's own body. For this reason, brain lesion studies are not ideal for isolating the anatomical regions that give rise to the sense of body ownership.

The delusional beliefs which characterize somatoparaphrenia, such as AR's feeling that her arm actually belonged to her mother, are not easy to reproduce in a controlled laboratory environment with healthy individuals. However, with clever experimental designs it is possible to manipulate one major component of the sense of body ownership: the feeling that one's body occupies a particular location in space. There is strong evidence that this phenomenology depends on an integration of signals from different sensory modalities. The point is demonstrated convincingly by experiments in which individuals are induced to feel a sense of ownership over objects external to their body or to have out-of-body experiences. These phenomena are collectively known as *body-transfer illusions*. For example, in the famous rubber hand illusion, participants view an artificial hand being stroked with a paint brush while brush strokes are simultaneously applied to their own hand which is hidden from view (Botvinick & Cohen, 1998). This often leads to a convincing illusion that the participant's real hand occupies the space where the rubber hand sits – that is, the sense of body position (proprioception) shifts to reconcile with the visual and tactile information. The rubber hand illusion is now being exploited to help amputees with prosthetic limbs experience the artificial limb as a part of their body (D'Alonzo & Cipriani, 2012).

A similar principle may also explain out-of-body experiences. For example, Henrik Ehrsson (2007) induced body-transfer illusions by showing participants images from cameras placed behind their head (thus giving them the visual perspective of another), while using plastic rods to simultaneously touch the participant's actual chest and the chest of the illusory body just below the camera's view. This gave participants the sensation of sitting behind their physical bodies. Body-transfer illusions are strongly dependent on the compatibility of multisensory information. Ehrsson, Spence, and Passingham (2004) took advantage of this to investigate the neural correlates of the rubber hand illusion. Synchronous visual and tactile stimulation paired with a non-rotated view of the hand (which induced the rubber hand illusion) was associated with increased activity in the premotor cortex compared to asynchronous and/or visually rotated conditions, suggesting that this area is involved in the multisensory integration processes underlying the sense of body ownership.

In body-transfer illusions, the integration of visual and tactile signals influences the sense of proprioception. In much the same way, the integration of tactile and proprioceptive signals can also influence judgments of visual stimuli. The enfacement illusion refers to an effect where an observer incorporates another person's facial features into the representation of their own face (Tsakiris, 2008). This is achieved by touching the face of a participant while they view simultaneous touching of a partner's face. Synchronous, but not asynchronous stimulation leads to a shift in the representation of facial identities, so that the partner's face is judged to be more similar to the participant's own face. This indicates that correlations between multisensory signals are used to update visual representations of one's face.

There is considerable variability in individuals' susceptibility to the rubber hand and enfacement illusions. For example, the strength of the rubber hand illusion is modulated by interoceptive sensitivity (awareness of internal body states such as heart rate) (Tsakiris, Tajadura-Jiménez, & Costantini, 2011), and the enfacement illusion correlates with personality variables and with the perceived attractiveness of the partner (Sforza, Bufalari, Haggard, & Aglioti, 2010). In extreme cases, synchronous stimulation to one's own face is not necessary to achieve the enfacement illusion. Mirror–touch synesthesia is a rare condition in which observing touch or pain in others evokes a conscious haptic sensation on the synesthete's own body (Banissy, Cohen Kadosh, Maus, Walsh, & Ward, 2009). Mirror–touch synesthetes show the enfacement effect after simply viewing touch to others, suggesting the self–other distinction may be unusually blurred in these individuals (Maister, Banissy, & Tsakiris, 2013).

The sense of body ownership may allow individuals to recognize their own body as distinct from other bodies. However, many actions have consequences that are not directly related to the body. Thus, the sense of body ownership alone is not sufficient to distinguish between actions of self and other.

The Sense of Agency

The term *sense of agency* refers to a subjective awareness that one is initiating an action or some other event (Gallagher, 2000; Tsakiris, Schütz-Bosbach, & Gallagher, 2007). This cuts to the heart of the self–other distinction, as individuals normally experience a sense of agency for their own thoughts and actions but not for others' actions. For example, a voluntary movement would normally elicit a sense of agency, whereas having one's body pushed around by another person would not.

The sense of agency seems to emerge from a combination of motor, perceptual and higher-order conceptual information. In the nineteenth century, Hugo Münsterberg (1888) argued that perceived causality of the self depends on two things: the ability to foresee consequences before they occur and the feeling of activity. In recent decades, a particularly influential hypothesis has been that the sense of agency originates with forward models, which predict and monitor action-effects produced by voluntary movements (Blakemore, Wolpert, & Frith, 2002; Feinberg, 1978; Frith, 2005; Frith & Done, 1989). This is referred to as the central monitoring hypothesis, or comparator model. The idea that efferent motor signals enable sensory predictions has a long history (Festinger & Canon, 1965; von Holst, 1954; Sperry, 1950). As a theory of agency, the comparator model has seen numerous adaptations and updates over the years, but the central idea is that a match between predicted and observed action-effects allows actors to recognize actions as self-generated (Figure 17.2). Frith and Done (1989) proposed that the normal operations of this system may be damaged or compromised somehow in schizophrenic populations, which might help explain passivity delusions during which patients experience their own actions as caused by someone else. Thus, the central monitoring hypothesis emphasizes prediction of action-effects by the motor system as the primary means by which we recognize our own actions.

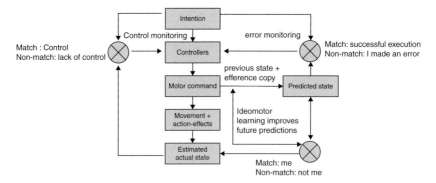

Figure 17.2 The comparator model of agency. *See Plate 7.*

Notes: According to the central monitoring hypothesis, motor commands produce movements while a corollary discharge or 'efference copy' of the motor command is processed in parallel to predict the future state of the system. These predictions include upcoming body position and the sensory consequences of the movement. The sense of agency depends on the degree of match between the predicted and actual states (in the lower right of the figure). Additional comparators may exist to monitor consistency between intended and estimated states (upper left), and intended and predicted states (upper right).

Consistent with the central monitoring hypothesis, many studies have confirmed that judgments of self-agency are influenced by the predictability of action-effects. For example, introducing spatial and temporal discrepancies between executed movements and the visual feedback of those movements can cause participants to misidentify their own movements as belonging to another person (Farrer, Bouchereau, Jeannerod, & Franck, 2008), while coincidental agreement between self-generated actions and sensory feedback can produce a misleading sense of agency for action-effects produced by others (Sato & Yasuda, 2005).

The sensory predictions, which accompany voluntary movements, may give self-generated action-effects a unique subjective quality compared to other types of stimuli. *Sensory attenuation* is a phenomenon whereby self-generated action-effects are perceived to be less intense, or attenuated, compared to identical but externally generated stimuli. The most well-known example is that it is impossible to tickle oneself (Blakemore, Wolpert, & Frith, 1998; Claxton, 1975). Similarly, the perception of forces applied to a finger are reduced by about a half when the forces are self-generated (Shergill, Bays, Frith, & Wolpert, 2003), tones triggered by voluntary button presses are perceived to be less loud than equivalent tones triggered by a computer (Sato, 2008; Weiss, Herwig, & Schütz-Bosbach, 2011), and moving objects triggered by voluntary key presses are perceived to be slower than computer-triggered movements (Dewey & Carr, 2013a). Interestingly, sensory attenuation can also occur when intended movements are disrupted via transcranial magnetic stimulation (Voss, Ingram, Haggard, & Wolpert, 2005). This suggests that preparation for movement, rather than movement itself, may be the critical component driving the effect. Some investigators have wondered if mental simulation of observed actions could also lead to sensory attenuation. On this question the evidence is mixed, but the sensory attenuation effect appears to be most reliable for the consequences of voluntary, self-generated movements (Sato, 2008; Weiss & Schütz-Bosbach, 2012; Weiss et al., 2011). In fact, merely believing that an action-effect is *not* self-generated (when in fact it is) can prevent attenuation (Desantis, Weiss, Schütz-Bosbach, & Waszak, 2012a; Desantis, Weiss, & Waszak, 2012b), which suggests a relationship between sensory attenuation and explicit agency beliefs. Self- and externally generated stimuli may also differ with respect to the perceived temporal interval between movements and action-effects. This is described in detail in Box 17.2.

The central monitoring hypothesis has motivated several investigators to study the neural correlates of the sense of agency by manipulating the degree of match or mismatch between predicted and actually observed action-effects. Mismatches are typically associated with increased activation in several areas of a frontal-parietal network, but particularly the right inferior parietal lobule, suggesting that this area is involved in representing the intended consequences of actions (Chaminade & Decety, 2002; Farrer et al., 2008b; Fink et al., 1999; Leube et al., 2003; Schnell et al., 2007; Spengler, von Cramon, & Brass, 2009). Breakdowns in the normal sense of agency may occur when areas involved in computing action awareness are damaged, or when areas involved in planning and executing movements do not communicate. For example, anarchic hand syndrome is a neurological disorder in which a person's hand moves without conscious will. The causes are still uncertain, but one proposal is that the primary motor cortex which executes the hand movement remains intact but is isolated from the planning influences of the premotor cortex (Assal, Schwartz, & Vuilleumier, 2007; Della Sala, Marchetti, & Spinnler, 1991).

Although there is strong evidence that sensorimotor predictions do influence the sense of agency, individuals can adapt to minor discrepancies between their movements and the resulting action-effect without conscious awareness of doing so (Knoblich & Kircher, 2004). It should also be pointed out that it is possible to experience a sense of agency in the absence of movement. For example, in one study individuals were induced to experience a vicarious sense of agency over arm movements performed by another person when those movements are preceded by valid verbal descriptions of the action (Wegner, Sparrow, & Winerman, 2004). Simulation theory offers one alternative to a purely motor-based account of agency (Jeannerod, 2003; Jeannerod &

Pacherie, 2004). According to this hypothesis, the motor system is employed to predict both self-generated and observed actions. Because the predictions are more precise for self-generated actions than for other agents (e.g. Daprati, Wriessnegger, & Lacquaniti, 2007; Knoblich & Flach, 2001), the degree of prediction error serves as a useful cue to agency. In this view, motor information may help disambiguate the sense of agency, but the predictions which give rise to a sense of agency need not be accompanied by an efferent motor signal.

Beyond body movements, individuals can also experience a sense of agency for more distal events, such as the sound produced by ringing a doorbell. In this type of situation, perceptual cues and inferences play important roles in determining whether an event is causally attributed to the self or to another source. In general, two events A and B are much more likely to be perceived as causally related if they occur close together in space and time (Michotte, 1963). The same is true of agency judgments. For example, when two individuals each press a button and then a tone plays, the tone is most likely to be attributed to whomever pressed their button last (Dewey & Carr, 2013b). The sense of agency may also be stronger when a self-generated movement appears to be the only explanation for a subsequent perception, as causal explanations may be viewed with greater skepticism when plausible alternatives are provided (Einhorn & Hogarth, 1978; Khemlani & Oppenheimer, 2011; Wegner & Wheatley, 1999).

When actions are goal-directed, success or failure to achieve the desired outcome can strongly influence judgments of agency and control. B. F. Skinner's (1948) documentation of 'superstitious' behavior in pigeons (caused by coincident reinforcement of behaviors that were, in reality, unrelated to outcome probabilities) is an important precursor to work in this area. For example, when people are led to believe that the outcome in a game of chance is actually skill dependent, positive outcomes often lead to illusions of control (Langer, 1975; Langer & Roth, 1975). Similarly, when individuals rate their control over moving cursors in videogame-like environments, judgments of control are influenced by whether or not the goal is achieved (Dewey, Seiffert, & Carr, 2010; Metcalfe & Greene, 2007).

There is an emerging consensus that the sense of agency depends on both internal motor signals and external sensory evidence, possibly involving an optimal integration of internal and external cues (Moore, Wegner, & Haggard, 2009; Synofzik, Vosgerau, & Voss, 2013). The extent to which one influence or another dominates is context dependent, and may rely on the perceived reliability of the cues. For example, action-effect predictability seems to have a larger influence on agency judgments when action goals are not achieved (Kumar & Srinivasan, 2013). Schizophrenic individuals, who show impairment on tasks involving monitoring for discrepancies between executed movements and their visual consequences, are more reliant on external cues to performance when judging their control (Metcalfe, Van Snellenberg, DeRosse, Balsam, & Malhotra, 2012). Hierarchical models attempt to explain how motor, perceptual and inferential processes combine to influence the sense of agency (Gallagher, 2003; Kumar & Srinivasan, 2014; Moore & Haggard, 2008; Pacherie, 2008; Synofzik, Vosgerau, & Newen, 2008). These models imply that the sense of agency is not a unitary phenomenon that relies on one source of information, but rather a complex construct that arises from the interplay of perception, action and cognition.

Box 17.2 Temporal binding and the sense of agency

Temporal binding is a temporal attraction in the perceived times of actions and their effects. For example, the delay between a voluntary keypress and a tone triggered by the keypress is typically underestimated (Haggard, Clark, & Kalogeras, 2002; Wohlschläger, Haggard, Gesierich, & Prinz, 2003). In recent years, increasing numbers of investigators have used temporal binding as an implicit measure of the sense of agency (e.g. Enbert, Wohlschläger, & Haggard, 2008; Moore, Dickinson, & Fletcher, 2011; Moore et al., 2009). This has been justified by findings which suggest temporal binding and the sense of agency may be governed by overlapping sensorimotor processes (for a review, see Moore & Obhi, 2012). For example, temporal binding is stronger for intervals following active movements compared to passive movements (Engbert, Wohlschläger, & Haggard, 2008).

On the other hand, some studies have found comparable temporal binding for self- and externally generated action-effects (Buehner, 2012; Poonian & Cunnington, 2013), suggesting that action-effect anticipation may lead to temporal binding regardless of self-agency. There have also been experiments where explicit agency judgments and temporal binding were dissociated (Ebert & Wegner, 2010; Kumar & Srinivasan, 2013; Obhi & Hall, 2011; Strother, House, & Obhi, 2010). For example, in a study on temporal binding in the context of joint action, two individuals sat side-by-side and performed key presses at either end of a space bar to produce tones. Participants pressed the space bar at a time of their own choosing, and if their partner pressed it first, were instructed to let their finger move up and down with the key without exerting any force. Participants only felt causally responsible for the tones in the active condition, but surprisingly, temporal binding was present for both active and passive movements (Strother, House, & Obhi, 2010).

The view that temporal binding is a unique marker of intentional action has also been challenged. Marc Buehner (2012) has argued that temporal binding is a general feature of causal perception, rather than intentional action per se. He proposes that causes and their effects are normally close together in time, and temporal binding reflects this bias when people must perform temporal judgments under uncertainty. To investigate the respective contributions of causality and intentionality to temporal binding, Cravo, Claessens, and Baldo (2009) used a variation of Michotte's famous 'launching effect' where object A appears to collide with object B, setting object B into motion. Intentionality was manipulated by having participants control the launching object during some blocks but not others. The perception of causality was manipulated by altering the timing and spatial arrangement of the objects in the display. Temporal binding was only found on trials with both high perceived causality and voluntary action, suggesting that interval estimations are influenced by both causality and intentionality.

Caveats aside, a recent review article described the relationship between temporal binding and the sense of agency as 'compelling' (Moore & Obhi, 2012). It remains an important task for future investigation to precisely delineate the uses and limitations of temporal binding as an implicit measure of agency.

Summary

Action representations are fundamentally grounded in sensorimotor experiences. There is now strong evidence that people predict and understand others' actions with the same neural machinery used for planning and executing their own actions. From this perspective, to understand an action means to form a sensorimotor representation of what it would be like to actually perform the action. Likewise, to understand an object means to form a representation of what it would be like to perform an action in relation to the object. Thus, familiarity with observed actions leads to increased motor resonance and more precise predictions. In addition to representing others' observed actions, the potential for others to act is also mapped onto an observer's own motor repertoire. Recent findings show that action affordances available to other people extend the reach of an observer's peripersonal space.

Despite widespread overlap in the functional and neurophysiological representations of executed and observed actions, self-generated actions and their sensory consequences have a unique experiential quality which allows us to distinguish what we do from what is passively done to us. The sense of body ownership seems to emerge from a multisensory integration of haptic, proprioception and visual information, while the sense of agency depends on an integration of internal motor and external sensory evidence. The sense of body ownership and sense of agency allow individuals to recognize their own actions and to make proper causal attributions to self and other.

References

Aglioti, S. M., Cesari, P., Romani, M., & Urgesi, C. (2008). Action anticipation and motor resonance in elite basketball players. *Nature Neuroscience*, 11(9), 1109–1116.

Assal, F., Schwartz, S., & Vuilleumier, P. (2007). Moving with or without will: Functional neural correlates of alien hand syndrome. *Annals of Neurology*, 62(3), 301–306.

Banissy, M. J., Cohen Kadosh, R., Maus, G. W., Walsh, V., & Ward, J. (2009). Prevalence, characteristics and a neurocognitive model of mirror-touch synaesthesia. *Experimental Brain Research*, 198(2–3), 261–272.

Behmer, L. P. J., & Jantzen, K. J. (2011). Reading sheet music facilitates sensorimotor mu-desynchronization in musicians. *Clinical Neurophysiology*, 122(7), 1342–1347.

Bisiach, E., Rusconi, M. L., & Vallar, G. (1991). Remission of somatoparaphrenic delusion through vestibular stimulation. *Neuropsychologia*, 29(10), 1029–1031.

Blaesi, S., & Wilson, M. (2010). The mirror reflects both ways: Action influences perception of others. *Brain and Cognition*, 72(2), 306–309.

Blakemore, S., Wolpert, D., & Frith, C. (2002). Abnormalities in the awareness of action. *Trends in Cognitive Sciences*, 6(6), 237–242.

Blakemore, S. J., Wolpert, D. M., & Frith, C. D. (1998). Central cancellation of self-produced tickle sensation. *Nature Neuroscience*, 1(7), 635–640.

Botvinick, M., & Cohen, J. (1998). Rubber hands 'feel' touch that eyes see. *Nature*, 391(6669), 756–756.

Buccino, G., Lui, F., Canessa, N., Patteri, I., Lagravinese, G., Benuzzi, F., Porro, C. A., & Rizzolatti, G. (2004). Neural circuits involved in the recognition of actions performed by nonconspecifics: An fMRI Study. *Journal of Cognitive Neuroscience*, 16(1), 114–126.

Buehner, M. J. (2012). Understanding the past, predicting the future: Causation, not intentional action, is the root of temporal binding. *Psychological Science*, 23(12), 1490–1497.

Cardellicchio, P., Sinigaglia, C., & Costantini, M. (2012). Grasping affordances with the other's hand: A TMS study. *Social Cognitive and Affective Neuroscience*, 8(4), 455–459.

Casile, A., & Giese, M. A. (2006). Nonvisual motor training influences biological motion perception. *Current Biology*, 16(1), 69–74.

Chaminade, T., & Decety, J. (2002). Leader or follower? Involvement of the inferior parietal lobule in agency. *Neuroreport*, 13(15), 1975–1978.

Claxton, G. (1975). Why can't we tickle ourselves? *Perceptual and Motor Skills*, 41, 335–338.

Costantini, M., Ambrosini, E., Sinigaglia, C., & Gallese, V. (2011a). Tool-use observation makes far objects ready-to-hand. *Neuropsychologia*, 49(9), 2658–2663.

Costantini, M., Committeri, G., & Sinigaglia, C. (2011b). Ready both to your and to my hands: Mapping the action space of others. *PLoS One*, 6(4), e17923.

Cravo, A., Claessens, P. E., & Baldo, M. C. (2009). Voluntary action and causality in temporal binding. *Experimental Brain Research*, 199(1), 95–99.

D'Alonzo, M., & Cipriani, C. (2012). Vibrotactile sensory substitution elicits feeling of ownership of an alien hand. *PLoS One*, 7(11), e50756.

Daprati, E., Wriessnegger, S., & Lacquaniti, F. (2007). Kinematic cues and recognition of self-generated actions. *Experimental Brain Research*, 177(1), 31–44.

Davis, T. J., Riley, M. A., Shockley, K., & Cummins-Sebree, S. (2010). Perceiving affordances for joint actions. *Perception*, 39(12), 1624–1644.

Della Sala, S., Marchetti, C., & Spinnler, H. (1991). Right-sided anarchic (alien) hand: A longitudinal study. *Neuropsychologia*, 29(11), 1113–1127.

Desantis, A., Weiss, C., Schütz-Bosbach, S., & Waszak, F. (2012a). Believing and perceiving: Authorship belief modulates sensory attenuation. *PLoS One*, 7(5), e37959.

Desantis, A., Weiss, C., & Waszak, F. (2012b). Believing and perceiving: Authorship belief modulates sensory attenuation. *PLoS One*, 7(5), e37959.

Dewey, J. A., & Carr, T. H. (2013a). Predictable and self-initiated visual motion is judged to be slower than computer generated motion. *Consciousness and Cognition*, 22(3), 987–995.

(2013b). When dyads act in parallel, a sense of agency for the auditory consequences depends on the order of the actions. *Consciousness and Cognition*, 22(1), 155–166.

Dewey, J. A., Seiffert, A. E., & Carr, T. H. (2010). Taking credit for success: The phenomenology of control in a goal-directed task. *Consciousness and Cognition*, 19(1), 48–62.

Diersch, N., Cross, E., Stadler, W., Schütz-Bosbach, S., & Rieger, M. (2012). Representing others' actions: The role of expertise in the aging mind. *Psychological Research*, 76(4), 525–541.

Ebert, J. P., & Wegner, D. M. (2010). Time warp: Authorship shapes the perceived timing of actions and events. *Consciousness and Cognition*, 19(1), 481–489.

Ehrsson, H. H. (2007). The experimental induction of out-of-body experiences. *Science*, 317(5841), 1048.

Ehrsson, H. H., Spence, C., & Passingham, R. E. (2004). That's my hand! Activity in premotor cortex reflects feeling of ownership of a limb. *Science*, 305(5685), 875–877.

Einhorn, H. J., & Hogarth, R. M. (1978). Confidence in judgment: Persistence of the illusion of validity. *Psychological Review*, 85(5), 395–416.

Elsner, B., & Hommel, B. (2001). Effect anticipation and action control. *Journal of Experimental Psychology. Human Perception and Performance*, 27(1), 229–240.

Engbert, K., Wohlschläger, A., & Haggard, P. (2008). Who is causing what? The sense of agency is relational and efferent-triggered. *Cognition*, 107(2), 693–704.

Engel, A., & Keller, P. E. (2011). The perception of musical spontaneity in improvised and imitated jazz performances. *Frontiers in Psychology*, 2, 83.

Farrer, C., Bouchereau, M., Jeannerod, M., & Franck, N. (2008a). Effect of distorted visual feedback on the sense of agency. *Behavioural Neurology*, 19(1–2), 53–57.

Farrer, C., Frey, S., Van Horn, J., Tunik, E., Turk, D., et al. (2008b). The angular gyrus computes action awareness representations. *Cerebral Cortex*, 18(2), 254–261.

Feinberg, I. (1978). Efference copy and corollary discharge: Implications for thinking and its disorders. *Schizophrenia Bulletin*, 4(4), 636–640.

Festinger, L., & Canon, L. K. (1965). Information about spatial location based on knowledge about efference. *Psychological Review*, 72(5), 378–384.

Fink, G. R., Marshall, J. C., Halligan, P. W., Frith, C. D., Driver, J., et al. (1999). The neural consequences of conflict between intention and the senses. *Brain*, 122(3), 497–512.

Frith, C. (2005). The self in action: Lessons from delusions of control. *Consciousness and Cognition*, 14(4), 752–770.

Frith, C., & Done, J. (1989). Experiences of alien control in schizophrenia reflect a disorder in the central monitoring of action. *Psychological Medicine*, 19, 359–363.

Gallagher, S. (2000). Philosophical conceptions of the self: Implications for cognitive science. *Trends in Cognitive Sciences*, 4(1), 14–21.

——— (2003). Sense of agency and higher-order cognition: Levels of explanation for schizophrenia. *Cognitive Semiotics*. http://kfil.upol.cz/hpo2003/gall03.html.

Gibson, J. J. (1977). The theory of affordances. In R. E. Shaw & J. Bransford (Eds.), *Perceiving, acting, and knowing: Toward an ecological psychology*. Hillsdale, NJ: Lawrence Erlbaum, pp. 127–142.

Graziano, M., Yap, G., & Gross, C. (1994). Coding of visual space by premotor neurons. *Science*, 266(5187), 1054–1057.

Haggard, P., Clark, S., & Kalogeras, J. (2002). Voluntary action and conscious awareness. *Nature Neuroscience*, 5(4), 382–385.

Holst, E. von. (1954). Relations between the central nervous system and the peripheral organs. *British Journal of Animal Behavior*, 2, 89–94.

Hommel, B., Müsseler, J., Aschersleben, G., & Prinz, W. (2001). The theory of event coding (TEC): A framework for perception and action planning. *Behavioral and Brain Sciences*, 24(05), 849–878.

Iriki, A., Tanaka, M., & Iwamura, Y. (1996). Coding of modified body schema during tool use by macaque postcentral neurones. *Neuroreport*, 7(14), 2325–2330.

Isenhower, R. W., Richardson, M. J., Carello, C., Baron, R. M., & Marsh, K. L. (2010). Affording cooperation: Embodied constraints, dynamics, and action-scaled invariance in joint lifting. *Psychonomic Bulletin & Review*, 17(3), 342–347.

Ishibashi, H., Hihara, S., & Iriki, A. (2000). Acquisition and development of monkey tool-use: Behavioral and kinematic analyses. *Canadian Journal of Physiology and Pharmacology*, 78(11), 958–966.

Jeannerod, M. (2003). The mechanism of self-recognition in humans. *Behavioural Brain Research*, 142(1–2), 1–15.

Jeannerod, M., & Pacherie, E. (2004). Agency, simulation, and self-identification. *Mind and Language*, 19(2), 113–146.

Jones, S. S. (2009). The development of imitation in infancy. *Philosophical Transactions of the Royal Society B: Biological Sciences*, 364(1528), 2325–2335. doi: 10.1098/rstb.2009.0045.

Keller, P., Knoblich, G., & Repp, B. (2007). Pianists duet better when they play with themselves: On the possible role of action simulation in synchronization. *Consciousness and Cognition*, 16(1), 102–111.

Khemlani, S. S., & Oppenheimer, D. M. (2011). When one model casts doubt on another: A levels-of-analysis approach to causal discounting. *Psychological Bulletin*, 137(2), 195–210.

Knoblich, G., & Flach, R. (2001). Predicting the effects of actions: Interactions of perception and action. *Psychological Science*, 12(6), 467–472.

Knoblich, G., & Kircher, T. (2004). Deceiving oneself about being in control: Conscious detection of changes in visuomotor coupling. *Journal of Experimental Psychology: Human Perception and Performance*, 30(4), 657–666.

Kumar, D., & Srinivasan, N. (2013). Hierarchical control and sense of agency: Differential effects on control on implicit and explicit measure of agency. In *Proceedings of the 35th Annual Meeting of the Cognitive Science Society*, Berlin.

(2014). Naturalizing sense of agency with a hierarchical event-control approach. *PLoS One*, 9(3), e92431.

Lahav, A., Saltzman, E., & Schlaug, G. (2007). Action representation of sound: Audiomotor recognition network while listening to newly acquired actions. *Journal of Neuroscience*, 27(2), 308–314.

Langer, E. J. (1975). The illusion of control. *Journal of Personality and Social Psychology*, 32(2), 311–328.

Langer, E. J., & Roth, J. (1975). Heads I win, tails it's chance: The illusion of control as a function of the sequence of outcomes in a purely chance task. *Journal of Personality and Social Psychology*, 34, 191–198.

Leube, D., Knoblich, G., Erb, M., Grodd, W., Bartels, M., & Kircher, T. (2003). The neural correlates of perceiving one's own movements. *NeuroImage*, 20(4), 2084–2090.

Maister, L., Banissy, M. J., & Tsakiris, M. (2013). Mirror-touch synaesthesia changes representations of self-identity. *Neuropsychologia*, 51(5), 802–808.

Meltzoff, A. N., & Moore, M. K. (1983). Newborn infants imitate adult facial gestures. *Child Development*, 54(3), 702–709.

Metcalfe, J., & Greene, M. (2007). Metacognition of agency. *Journal of Experimental Psychology: General*, 136(2), 184–199.

Metcalfe, J., Van Snellenberg, J. X., DeRosse, P., Balsam, P., & Malhotra, A. K. (2012). Judgements of agency in schizophrenia: An impairment in autonoetic metacognition. *Philosophical Transactions of the Royal Society B: Biological Sciences*, 367(1594), 1391–1400.

Michotte, A. (1963). *The perception of causality* (T. R. Miles & E. Miles, Trans.). New York: Basic Books.

Mitchell, P., Currie, G., & Ziegler, F. (2009). Two routes to perspective: Simulation and rule-use as approaches to mentalizing. *British Journal of Developmental Psychology*, 27(3), 513–543.

Molnar-Szakacs, I., & Overy, K. (2006). Music and mirror neurons: From motion to 'e'motion. *Social Cognitive and Affective Neuroscience*, 1(3), 235–241.

Moore, J. W., & Haggard, P. (2008). Awareness of action: Inference and prediction. *Consciousness and Cognition*, 17(1), 136–144.

Moore, J. W., & Obhi, S. S. (2012). Intentional binding and the sense of agency: A review. *Consciousness and Cognition*, 21(1), 546–561.

Moore, J. W., Wegner, D. M., & Haggard, P. (2009). Modulating the sense of agency with external cues. *Consciousness and Cognition*, 18(4), 1056–1064.

Münsterberg, H. (1888). *Die Willenshandlung [The Voluntary Action]*. Freiburg: Mohr.

Obhi, S. S., & Hall, P. (2011). Sense of agency and intentional binding in joint action. *Experimental Brain Research*, 211(3–4), 655–662.

Pacherie, E. (2008). The phenomenology of action: A conceptual framework. *Cognition*, 107(1), 179–217.

Pezzulo, G., Barca, L., Bocconi, A. L., & Borghi, A. M. (2010). When affordances climb into your mind: Advantages of motor simulation in a memory task performed by novice and expert rock climbers. *Brain and Cognition*, 73(1), 68–73.

Pezzulo, G., Iodice, P., Ferraina, S., & Kessler, K. (2013). Shared action spaces: A basis function framework for social re-calibration of sensorimotor representations supporting joint action. *Frontiers in Human Neuroscience*, 7, 800.

Poonian, S. K., & Cunningham, R. (2013). Intentional binding in self-made and observed actions. *Experimental Brain Research*, 229(3), 419–427.

Prinz, W. (1997). Perception and action planning. *European Journal of Cognitive Psychology*, 9(2), 129–154.

Ramenzoni, V. C., Riley, M. A., Shockley, K., & Davis, T. (2008). An information-based approach to action understanding. *Cognition*, 106(2), 1059–1070.

Rizzolatti, G., & Craighero, L. (2004). The mirror-neuron system. *Annual Review of Neuroscience*, 27, 169–192.

Rizzolatti, G., & Sinigaglia, C. (2010). The functional role of the parieto-frontal mirror circuit: Interpretations and misinterpretations. *Nature Reviews Neuroscience*, 11(4), 264–274. doi: 10.1038/nrn2805.

Sato, A. (2008). Action observation modulates auditory perception of the consequences of others' actions. *Consciousness and Cognition*, 17(4), 1219–1227.

Sato, A., & Yasuda, A. (2005). Illusion of sense of self-agency: Discrepancy between the predicted and actual sensory consequences of actions modulates the sense of self-agency, but not the sense of self-ownership. *Cognition*, 94(3), 241–255.

Schnell, K., Heekeren, K., Schnitker, R., Daumann, J., Weber, J., et al. (2007). An fMRI approach to particularize the frontoparietal network for visuomotor action monitoring: Detection of incongruence between test subjects' actions and resulting perceptions. *NeuroImage*, 34(1), 332–341.

Sforza, A., Bufalari, I., Haggard, P., & Aglioti, S. M. (2010). My face in yours: Visuo-tactile facial stimulation influences sense of identity. *Social Neuroscience*, 5(2), 148–162.

Shergill, S. S., Bays, P. M., Frith. C. D., & Wolpert, D. M. (2003). Two eyes for an eye: The neuroscience of force escalation. *Science*, 301(5630), 187.

Skerry, A. E., Carey, S. E., & Spelke, E. S. (2013). First-person action experience reveals sensitivity to action efficiency in prereaching infants. *Proceedings of the National Academy of Sciences*, 110(46), 18728–18733.

Skinner, B. F. (1948). 'Superstition' in the pigeon. *Journal of Experimental Psychology*, 38, 168–172.

Sommerville, J. A., & Woodward, A. L. (2005). Pulling out the intentional structure of action: The relation between action processing and action production in infancy. *Cognition*, 95(1), 1–30.

Sommerville, J. A., Woodward, A. L., & Needham, A. (2005). Action experience alters 3-month-old infants' perception of others' actions. *Cognition*, 96(1), B1–B11.

Spengler, S., von Cramon, D. Y., & Brass, M. (2009). Was it me or was it you? How the sense of agency originates from ideomotor learning revealed by fMRI. *NeuroImage*, 46(1), 290–298.

Sperry, R. W. (1950). Neural basis of the spontaneous optokinetic response produced by visual inversion. *Journal of Comparative and Physiological Psychology*, 43(6), 482–489.

Strother, L, House, K. A., & Obhi, S. S. (2010). Subjective agency and awareness of shared actions. *Consciousness and Cognition*, 19(1), 12–20.

Synofzik, M., Vosgerau, G., & Newen, A. (2008). Beyond the comparator model: A multifactorial two-step account of agency. *Consciousness and Cognition*, 17(1), 219–239.

Synofzik, M., Vosgerau, G., & Voss, M. (2013). The experience of agency: An interplay between prediction and postdiction. *Frontiers in Psychology*, 4. doi.org/10.3389/fpsyg.2013.00127.

Tsakiris, M. (2008). Looking for myself: Current multisensory input alters self-face recognition. *PLoS One*, 3(12), e4040.

Tsakiris, M., Schütz-Bosbach, S., & Gallagher, S. (2007). On agency and body-ownership: Phenomenological and neurocognitive reflections. *Consciousness and Cognition*, 16(3), 645–660.

Tsakiris, M., Tajadura-Jiménez, A., & Costantini, M. (2011). Just a heartbeat away from one's body: Interoceptive sensitivity predicts malleability of body-representations. *Proceedings of the Royal Society B: Biological Sciences*, 278(1717), 2470–2476.

Vallar, G., & Ronchi, R. (2009). Somatoparaphrenia: A body delusion. A review of the neuropsychological literature. *Experimental Brain Research*, 192(3), 533–551.

Van Overwalle, F., & Baetens, K. (2009). Understanding others' actions and goals by mirror and mentalizing systems: A meta-analysis. *NeuroImage*, 48(3), 564–584.

Voss, M., Ingram, J. N., Haggard, P., & Wolpert, D. M. (2005). Sensorimotor attenuation by central motor command signals in the absence of movement. *Nature Neuroscience*, 9(1), 26–27.

Wegner, D., Sparrow, B., & Winerman, L. (2004). Vicarious agency: Experiencing control over the movements of others. *Journal of Personality and Social Psychology*, 86(6), 838–848.

Wegner, D., & Wheatley, T. (1999). Apparent mental causation. Sources of the experience of will. *American Psychologist*, 54(7), 480–492.

Weiss, C., Herwig. A., & Schütz-Bosbach, S. (2011). The self in action effects: Selective attenuation of self-generated sounds. *Cognition*, 121(2), 207–218.

Weiss, C., & Schütz-Bosbach, S. (2012). Vicarious action preparation does not result in sensory attenuation of auditory action effects. *Consciousness and Cognition*, 21(4), 1654–1661.

Wilson, M., & Knoblich, G. (2005). The case for motor involvement in perceiving conspecifics. *Psychological Bulletin*, 131(3), 460–473.

Witt, J. K., Proffitt, D. R., & Epstein, W. (2005). Tool use affects perceived distance, but only when you intend to use it. *Journal of Experimental Psychology: Human Perception and Performance*, 31(5), 880–888.

Wohlschläger, A., Haggard, P., Gesierich, B., & Prinz, W. (2003). The perceived onset time of self- and other-generated actions. *Psychological Science*, 14(6), 586–591.

Glossary

Action-effect The contingent sensory consequences of an action.

Affordance A property of the environment which supports or enables an action.

Affordance maps Populations of neurons which show sensitivity to the position of objects in peripersonal space (relative to self or others).

Common coding theory The theory that there is a shared representational format (a common code) for perception and action.

Mental simulation The mind's ability to imagine performing a specific action and to anticipate its consequences.

Motor resonance Increased excitability in the motor system associated with observing others' actions.

Peripersonal space The space immediately surrounding the body.

Sense of agency The feeling of initiating a thought, action or other event in the world.

Sense of body ownership A feeling of awareness and identification with one's own body.

Sensory attenuation A reduction in the perceived intensity of self-generated sensations.

Temporal binding A subjective shortening of the interval between an action and its sensory consequences.

18   Reading Intention in Action

*Caterina Ansuini, Andrea Cavallo, Cesare Bertone
and Cristina Becchio*

Abstract

The human ability to predict and interpret others' intentions is crucial
to social life. The purpose of this chapter is to consider the proposition
that intentions can be understood from observing others' movements. To
this end, we first focus on experimental evidence showing that individual,
social and communicative intentions 'shape' movement kinematics. Next,
we review recent work suggesting that during action observation humans
are capable of picking up intention information and using it to predict others' behavior. In the third section, we address the neural mechanisms that
mediate the ability to read intention from movement observation. Based on
preliminary data, we argue that mirror neuron areas are sensitive to intention information conveyed by movement kinematics. Finally, we discuss the
hypothesis that a deficit in this ability might account for the difficulties in
social interaction reported in autism spectrum disorders.

Introduction

The ability to interpret and predict the behavior of other people hinges crucially on judgments about the intentionality of their actions – whether they act
purposefully (with intent) or not – as well as on judgments about the specific
intentions guiding their actions – whether they performed a given action with
an individual, a social or a communicative intent. Until recently, direct investigation of these skills has been rare (Baldwin & Baird, 2001). One obstacle
to such investigation has been the framing of the problem of intention understanding as a problem of access to mental states which are hidden away in the
other person's mind and therefore inaccessible to perception. The supposition,

This work received funding from the European Research Council under the European Union's
Seventh Framework Programme (FP7/2007-2013)/ERC grant agreement n. 312919. The authors
would like to thank Laura Taverna for her help in figure preparation.

as noted by Gallagher (2008), has been that intentions are not 'things that can be seen'.

Recent findings challenge this perspective by positing that intentions shape movement and are thus specified at a tangible and quantifiable level in the movement kinematics (Becchio, Sartori, & Castiello, 2010). This raises the intriguing possibility that *covert* mental state dispositions may become 'visible' in a person's *overt* motor behavior (Runeson & Frykholm, 1983).

The purpose of this chapter is precisely to consider the proposition that our cognitive system has the ability to use intention-from-movement information to understand others' behavior. The chapter is organized in four sections. The first examines the relationship between prior intention and action planning/ execution. Following the demonstration that prior intention does indeed influence action kinematics, the second section reviews recent work investigating the ability to pick up intention information from movement patterns. The third section addresses the neural mechanisms that mediate the ability to read intention from movement observation, while the fourth and final section deals with the hypothesis that a deficit in the ability to understand intention from movement might account for the difficulties in social interaction reported in autism spectrum disorders.

Executing Intention

Individual Prior Intention

To address the question of whether intentions might be inferred or simply perceived from movement kinematics (e.g. Gallagher 2008), it is first necessary to establish how performed movements relate to intentions during action execution. In their pioneering work, Marteniuk, MacKenzie, Jeannerod, Athenes, and Dugas (1987) first demonstrated that reach-to-grasp movements are differently executed depending on the type of action following the object grasp (i.e. fit the object into a similarly sized opening or throw it away). Notably, though the context requirements and the object to-be-grasped were identical in the two conditions, participants spent more time in deceleration and had a lower hand peak velocity in view of a fitting than a throwing action.

Since this seminal work, a plethora of studies have investigated how intentions influence the execution of reach-to-grasp movements. For example, Armbruster and Spijkers (2006) demonstrated that the deceleration peak of the wrist during the reaching phase was higher when the grasp was followed by either a throwing or a placing movement compared to when it was followed by a lifting movement. Similar results have also been reported by Schuboe, Maldonado, Stork, and Beetz (2008). In this study, participants were asked to grasp and pick up a bottle either to place it in a different location or to pour its contents into a glass. Kinematics inspection revealed that both the acceleration and the deceleration peak of the grasping movement were reached earlier in time when the intention was to pour than when it was to place.

Continuing this research, Ansuini, Santello, Massaccesi, and Castiello (2006) added a level of complexity to the topic by considering whether the entire shaping of the hand would reflect the nature of the upcoming action. To this end, in addition to reaching variables such as movement duration and speed, they recorded and analyzed angular excursion of all five fingers together with adduction/abduction angles using sensors embedded in a glove. This new methodological approach confirmed that, similar to the reaching component, the shaping of the hand was affected by the nature of the upcoming task. In particular, although all experimental conditions required grasping the same object, different co-variation patterns among finger joint angles were observed depending on whether the task was to place the object in a tight or a large niche.

Building on these results, a subsequent study showed that not only accuracy constraints but also functional properties of the intended goal have an effect on action kinematics (Ansuini, Giosa, Turella, Altoè, &, Castiello, 2008). By asking participants to reach towards, grasp a bottle and accomplish one of four possible actions (i.e. pouring, displacing, throwing or passing), Ansuini and colleagues (ibid) demonstrated that, when the bottle was grasped with the intent to pour, both the middle and the ring finger were more extended than for all the other considered goals.

Besides hand shaping during hand transport, the selection of hand placement on the object has been shown to adapt to the upcoming task demands. A few studies reported the existence of a functional link between action intention and how/where the hand is placed on the object. For instance, Crajè, Lukos, Ansuini, Gordon, and Santello (2011) showed that – when grasping a bottle – participants placed their thumb and index finger in a higher position when the grasping was performed with the intention to pour than when it was performed with the intention to lift. Using a similar setting in which the upcoming task was either pouring or moving, Sartori, Straulino, and Castiello (2011b) found that the ring and the little finger were functionally modulated so that they were higher on the object when the intention was to pour. Furthermore, in line with Crajé and colleagues' (2011) results, it was observed that the 3D distance between the index finger and the other fingers increased when the task was pouring rather than moving (Sartori et al. 2011b).

Social and Communicative Prior Intention

Using the reach-to-grasp experimental window, variations in the kinematic patterning have also been demonstrated when comparing movements subserving individual and social intentions. For example, when asked to reach and grasp an object to either move it to a different location or pass it to another person, participants' maximal finger aperture has been shown to be smaller in the social than in the individual condition (Becchio, Sartori, Bulgheroni, & Castiello, 2008a). Furthermore, the grip-closing velocity peak decreased when the intention was to pass the object to a partner (ibid).

Extending the task employed by Becchio and colleagues (ibid), subsequent studies (Becchio, Sartori, Bulgheroni, & Castiello, 2008b; also see Georgiou, Becchio, Glover, & Castiello, 2007) showed that the kinematics of grasping movements differed depending on whether the movements were performed with the intent to cooperate or compete. In the cooperative condition, participants were required to reach towards and grasp a wooden block with the intent to cooperate with a partner in building a tower in the middle of the working surface. The competitive condition was similar, except that they had to compete against an opponent to place their own object in the middle of the working surface first. Results revealed different reach-to-grasp patterns for cooperative and competitive movements. Strikingly, these patterns were distinct from those of reach-to-grasp movements performed individually at a similar speed (i.e. slow versus fast speed).

In a recent experiment, Quesque, Lewkowicz, Delevoye-Turrell, and Coello (2013) investigated the effects of the social context on kinematic characteristics of sequential actions consisting in placing an object on an initial pad (i.e. preparatory action), before reaching and grasping the object as fast as possible to move it to another location (i.e. main action). Reach-to-grasp actions were performed either in isolation or in the presence of a partner who could act on the object. Results showed the influence of the social contexts on both the preparatory and the main action. More specifically, during the preparatory action, the wrist displacement was higher and the reaching movement slower when the object was placed for a partner than when it was placed for self-use.

Further support for the idea that the social nature of an intention influences kinematics comes from a study investigating communicative prior intention (Sartori, Becchio, Bara, & Castiello, 2009). In this study, two different contexts were operationalized through an individual task and a communicative task. The individual task required participants to reach towards, grasp and lift either a blue or a green spherical object according to one of five sequences. The communicative task was identical except that each sequence was associated with a different meaning. Participants were asked to select a meaning, and thus a sequence, and to communicate it to a partner by lifting the object in the predetermined order. Although the to-be-grasped object remained the same, approach movements to the object in the communicative task were more careful than those in the individual task, suggesting that participants adapted the shaping of the hand so as to optimize the viewing of the object by the partner. This conclusion was confirmed by the results obtained in a second experiment in which the partner was blindfolded; under these circumstances, in which adaptation to the partner was clearly pointless, no 'communicative effect' on movement was observed.

Observing Intention

The above findings suggest that intentions influence action planning and control so that, although the to-be-grasped object is the same, different kinematic features are selected depending on the remote goal to be achieved. Yet, the question remains whether observers are sensitive to these differences. Perceptual sensitivity requires that not only discriminant information is available, but also that the perceptual system is attuned to this information. To what extent are observers sensitive to intention information conveyed by action kinematics? Are they able to pick up and use early differences in visual kinematics to discriminate between other people's intentions in grasping an object? In the following, we briefly summarize action observation studies in which this ability appears or fails to. As the question of whether observers are sensitive to intention information conveyed by visual kinematics presupposes that intention related differences are available in the observed movements, only studies providing quantitative evidence of kinematic differences are considered.

One approach to investigate the contribution of visual kinematics to intention understanding is progressive temporal occlusion (Abernethy & Russell, 1987). Using this approach, multiple occlusion points are characteristically used so as to form a progressive series of viewing periods (or time windows) within the event of interest (Farrow, Abernethy, & Jackson, 2005). Studies using the progressive temporal occlusion paradigm in sport settings have consistently demonstrated that experts – but not novices – are capable of picking up useful anticipatory information from early events in their opponent's movement pattern (Abernethy & Zawi, 2007; Abernethy, Zawi, & Jackson, 2008).

Naish, Reader, Houston-Price, Bremner, and Holmes (2013) adapted this approach to test how much of the action participants needed to see to correctly predict the outcome of a reach-to-grasp movement – either eating or placing. The duration of the movement viewed by participants in each trial was determined by their (correct or incorrect) response in the previous trial according to an adaptive staircase procedure. This procedure revealed that participants needed to see at least part of the post-grasp to correctly distinguish between grasp-to-eat and grasp-to-place movements. This seems to suggest that observers were not sensitive to the pre-grasp kinematic differences or that they did not use them to discriminate reach-to-grasp movements performed with different individual intentions. The validity of this conclusion, however, should be viewed with caution. First, although the authors report kinematic differences between grasp-to-eat and grasp-to-place movements in a separate movement execution experiment, these differences do not refer to the movements that were actually used as stimuli in the observation experiment. It is thus not possible to determine whether pre-grasp kinematics actually differed between grasp-to-eat and grasp-to-place movements. Second, movements were displayed from three different viewpoints: 'above', 'side' and 'front'. As intention information available from one viewpoint (e.g. the side view) may not be available from other viewpoints (e.g. the front view; see Sebanz & Shiffrar, 2009), it is plausible that the three views were not equally informative. Unfortunately, the experimental design makes impossible to determine whether viewpoint-dependency contributed to the poor discrimination performance.

Data bearing on discrimination of intention from visual kinematics were provided by Sartori, Becchio, and Castiello (2011a) in a study investigating the ability to detect the intentional content of a social action. These authors first analyzed the kinematics of reach-to-grasp movements performed with the intent to cooperate with a partner, compete against an opponent, or performing an individual action at natural or fast speed. Next, to assess attunement to kinematic information, they presented participants with video-clips of the same grasping movements in an intention discrimination task. To ensure that only advanced sources of information were made available to judge the model's intention, videos were temporally occluded at the time the fingers contacted the object so that neither the second part of the movement nor the interacting model, when present, were visible. The results revealed that observers were able to discriminate cooperative, competitive and individual movements (ibid). But *what* specific kinematic cue did participants use to make these anticipation judgments?

To determine whether arm/hand information could be used in isolation to discriminate intention, in a second experiment, Sartori et al. (ibid) spatially occluded the video-clips so that only the arm and forearm of the model were visible. As the spatial occlusion procedure had no substantial impact on the accuracy of the discrimination performance, these findings suggest that arm kinematics were sufficient to discriminate between movements performed with different intentions. This conclusion was further confirmed by Manera, Becchio, Cavallo, Sartori, and Castiello (2011) using the point-light technique. Point-light displays, which consist of disconnected points of light corresponding to the key joint centered on the body of the person being observed, lack contour, texture, shape and color cues present in video displays, but preserve the essential kinematic information provided in the movement pattern of the agent (e.g. Vanrie & Verfaillie, 2004). To examine whether, based on this information, observers would be able to discern the prior intention in grasping an object, Manera and colleagues (2011) presented participants with point-light

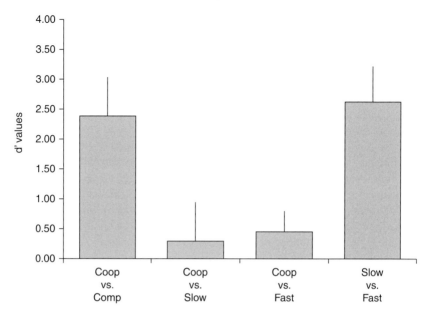

Figure 18.1 Executing different intentions.

Notes: Histograms represent d′ values across experimental conditions. Please note that a value of zero indicates an inability to discriminate between signal and no signal, whereas larger values indicate a correspondingly greater ability to discriminate between signal and no signal. Bars represent standard errors.

Source: Data adapted from Manera et al. (2011).

displays of cooperative, competitive and individual reach-to-grasp movements. Despite the fact that displays were reduced to only three disconnected points of light, participants were nonetheless able to discriminate between intentions (see Figure 18.1).

These results challenge the view that, in the absence of contextual information, observers are not able to differentiate between movements performed with different intentions (Kilner, 2011). Even when no contextual information is available, kinematics may provide a sufficient basis for understanding others' intentions.

Neural Basis for the Ability to Read Others' Actions

All in all, the studies reviewed so far suggest that: (1) movement kinematics convey information about intentions; and (2) observers are able to pick up and use this information to discriminate between movements performed with different social and individual intentions.

But what neural mechanism may mediate this ability to understand intentions from movements? Ever since their discovery in the ventral premotor cortex of a macaque (Gallese, Fadiga, Fogassi, & Rizzolatti, 1996; di Pellegrino, Fadiga, Fogassi, Gallese, & Rizzolatti, 1992), mirror neurons have been proposed to underlie the ability to understand what others are doing (for a review, see Rizzolatti & Sinigaglia, 2010). The general idea behind this hypothesis is that, while observing someone acting on an object, an internal motor representation of the observed motor act is activated in the observer's brain, enabling the transformation of 'visual information into knowledge' about others' goals and intentions (Gallese & Goldman, 1998).

Studies on monkeys indicate that frontal and parietal mirror neurons are involved in encoding not only the goal of the specific motor act (e.g. grasping a peanut), but also the entire action in which the observed motor act is embedded. In a series of experiments, Fogassi et al. (2005; also see Bonini et al., 2010) recorded the activity of parietal and ventral premotor neurons during both the execution and observation of grasp-to-eat or grasp-to-place actions. Although the recorded neurons were all activated during the grasping observation, the intensity of their discharge varied strongly according to the prior intention of the observed action. Noteworthy, their visual selectivity for grasp-to-eat or grasp-to-place matched their motor (execution) selectivity for the same action (Bonini, Ferrari, & Fogassi, 2013). However, because in these studies the presence/absence of a container acted as a contextual cue, the possibility that pre-contact modulation reflected context, rather than early differences in visual kinematics, cannot be ruled out.

In humans, evidence that *how* an object is grasped may influence intention processing within mirror circuits was first provided by Kaplan and Iacoboni (2006). In this fMRI experiment, participants watched precision grips and whole-hand grasps embedded in a drinking or a cleaning context. Activity within the right inferior frontal gyrus (IFG), a mirror neuron area, was higher when the type of grasp (e.g. precision grip) and the context (drinking context) conveyed the same intention, suggesting that the IFG is sensitive to the level of congruency among 'intention cues'. However, as the effect was not observed for actions performed within the cleaning context, it is not clear whether it generalizes to other intentions.

Adopting a somehow different approach, Vingerhoets and colleagues (2010) employed stimuli consisting of single-tool objects that were grabbed by an actor who intended either to use or to displace the tool. By viewing the way in which the object was seized, participants had to decide what the intention of the actor was. As no context was provided, participants had to base their decision entirely on the movement kinematics. Results revealed that discriminating between the actor's intention to move or use an object involved multifocal activations within the intraparietal sulcus, a region also involved in planning of grasp-related actions (Tunik, Rice, Hamilton, & Grafton, 2007).

Further evidence that human mirror areas are sensitive to intention information conveyed by movement kinematics was provided by Becchio and colleagues (2012). In this study, participants observed isolated prehensile movements performed with the intent to cooperate, compete or perform an individual movement. The action videos were all followed by a static test picture and participants were required to judge whether this picture depicted or not a continuation of the movement they had just observed. Despite the lack of contextual information, observing prehensile movements performed with a social intent relative to prehensile movements performed with an individual intent activated mirror areas, including the IFG and the inferior parietal lobule (see Figure 18.2).

Interestingly, comparison of social (i.e. cooperative and competitive) versus individual movements also revealed differential activations at the temporoparietal junction (TPJ) and within the dorsal medial prefrontal cortex (dmPFC) (Figure 18.2). Since these two regions are traditionally associated with explicitly thinking about the state of mind of other individuals (i.e. 'mentalizing'), it is plausible to suggest that activity in these regions can be driven in a bottom-up manner by intentionally salient kinematic features. Both the mirror and the mentalizing circuits (as far as social intentions are concerned) seem thus to be sensitive to intention information conveyed by movement kinematics.

Difficulties in Reading Others' Intention: The Case of Autism

Damage to parietal and premotor regions impacts on the ability to reproduce/recognize gestures (Buxbaum, Kyle, & Menon, 2005; Pazzaglia, Smania, Corato, & Aglioti, 2008). However, whether patients with lesions in these regions also experience difficulty understanding others' intentions remains unknown.

In recent years, a few studies have reported difficulties in tracking the intentions of others in children with autism spectrum disorder (ASD). ASDs affect a variety of nervous structures ranging from the brainstem to the cerebellum and the cerebral cortex. Furthermore, recent studies report a marked disorder of intrahemispheric connections at the level of both white and gray matter (Casanova et al., 2006; Minshew & Williams, 2007). There is also evidence that ASD adults exhibit structural abnormalities in cortical thickness in fronto-parietal areas and that thinning of these areas correlates with the severity of autistic impairment (Hadjikhani, Joseph, Snyder, & Tager-Flusberg, 2006).

At a functional level, abnormalities in the neural mechanism matching action observation and execution in ASD have been reported using electroencephalography (EEG; Martineau, Cochin, Magne, & Barthelemy, 2008; Oberman et al., 2005; Oberman, Ramachandran, & Pineda, 2008), magnetoencephalography

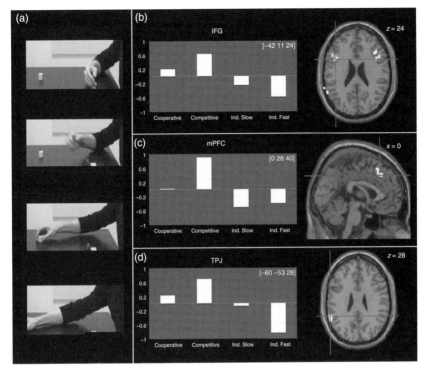

Figure 18.2 Reading intention from action observation. *See Plate 8.*

Notes: (A) Exemplar schematic representation of event sequencing during a competitive action sequence. A trial started with a video-clip depicting the model's arm and forearm reaching towards and grasping for an object. The last visible frame of each clip showed the model's hand disappearing behind a black screen after grasping the object. Then a test picture showing the model's hand placing the object in its final position was presented. Participants were instructed to decide whether or not the test picture was a continuation of the observed action. Observing reach-to-grasp movements performed with a social intent [(competitive+cooperative)>(individual fast+individual slow)] increased activity in the left IFG (B), in the dorsal sector of the medial prefrontal cortex (mPFC) (C), and within the supramarginal gyrus (D), extending inferiorly to encompass the TPJ.

Source: Data adapted from Becchio et al. (2012).

(MEG; Nishitani, Avikainen, & Hari, 2004) and fMRI (Martineau, Andersson, Barthélémy, Cottier, & Destrieux, 2010; Williams et al., 2006). For example, Oberman et al. (2005) found that in comparison to typically developing controls, mu wave suppression – an index of mirror neuron activity – is reduced in ASD during action observation. Similarly, using fMRI, Martineau and colleagues (2010) showed atypical activation in ASD during observation of human movement in various cerebral areas, including the motor cortex, the IFG and the parietal lobule.

Clinical evidence suggests that a deficit in understanding the prior intention of the actions is present in children with autism. An example is the classical finding that, whereas typically developing (TD) children respond to the arm extension toward them with a similar gesture, children with autism fail to do so, possibly not understanding the 'why' of the mother's gesture (Kanner, 1943). Surprisingly, although several studies investigated the link between mirror neuron mechanism and ASD symptoms (Iacoboni & Dapretto, 2006), only a few specifically tackled the issue of altered recognition of prior intentions in ASD.

In a behavioral study, Boria and colleagues (2009) explored ASD children's ability to understand the goal and the prior intention of motor acts in an action observation task. To this end, in a first experiment, they asked TD and ASD children to watch hand–object interactions (e.g. a hand on a phone) and to identify the observed goal (e.g. grasping) as well as the underlying prior intention (e.g. phoning). The results showed that children with ASD had no difficulties in reporting the goals of individual motor acts. In contrast, however, they made several errors when requested to identify the prior intention of the observed action. In order to disentangle the role played by the contextual cues, in a second experiment, the authors asked the same two groups of children to watch pictures showing a hand grip congruent with the object use (e.g. cutting by using a pair of scissors), but within a context suggesting either the use of the object or its placement into a container. Here, children with ASD performed as well as TD children, correctly indicating the agent's prior intention. These results suggest that ASD children fail to understand others' prior intentions when they have to rely exclusively on the agent's motor behavior, but are able to do so when additional information from objects surrounding the object acted upon is available.

In another study, Cattaneo and colleagues (2007) studied a group of TD children and a group of children with ASD while they observed an experimenter grasping an object with two different prior intentions: to eat or to place it into a container. The electromyographic (EMG) activity of the mylohyoid muscle (MH), a muscle involved in mouth opening, was recorded. The results showed that, in TD children, the observation of grasping-to-eat determined an activation of the MH muscle, while such activation was not present in children with ASD (Figure 18.3).

In a second experiment, both ASD and TD children were asked to perform the same actions. In TD children, the activation of the MH muscle started as soon as the reaching movement began, much before the object was grasped. In children with ASD, the MH muscle activation appeared only much later,

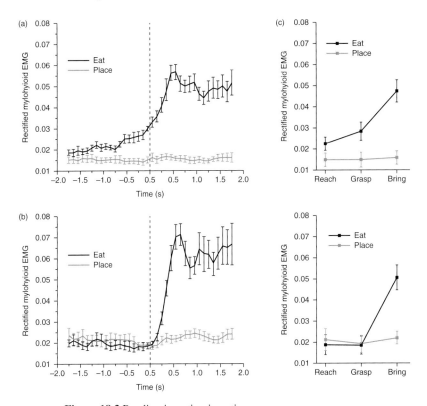

Figure 18.3 Reading intention in autism.

Notes: Time-course of the rectified EMG activity of mylohyoid muscle (MH) during execution of the bringing-to-the-mouth (black) and placing actions (gray) in typically developing children (A) and children with autism (B). Vertical bars indicate the standard error. All curves are aligned with the moment of object lifting from the touch-sensitive plate used as starting position (t = 0, dashed vertical lines). (C) Mean EMG activity of MH muscle in the three epochs of the two actions, i.e. bringing to the mouth and placing actions. Vertical bars indicate 95 percent confidence intervals.

Source: Data adapted from Cattaneo et al. 2007; © National Academy of Science, USA (2007).

i.e. approximately when they started bringing food to the mouth. These data have been interpreted to suggest that the difficulties in reading others' intentions in ASD may depend on a severe impairment in motor organization that includes a deficit in chaining motor acts into intentional actions. If confirmed, this discovery would have important clinical and diagnostic implications.

Summary and Conclusion

The view that the motor is separated from the mental has long been dismissed, yet traces of it remain in the way the problem of intention understanding is addressed in psychology and cognitive neuroscience (Schilbach et al. 2013). Disconnecting intention and movement, current accounts of intention understanding assume, either explicitly or implicitly, that visual kinematics provides an insufficient basis for discerning others' intentions. In contrast to this view, recent findings indicate that during action execution intentions shape movement kinematics. Furthermore, observers appear to be attuned to early differences in visual kinematics and may use these differences to discriminate between movements performed with different intentions. Although far from being conclusive, the current state of art suggests that the human ability to read intention from movement is mediated by a fronto-parietal network. That intention reading deficits are evident in the ASD clinical population corroborates this conclusion and suggests that disabilities in the social domain characteristic of ASD may be related to difficulties in the ability to understand intentions from movement (see Box 18.1).

Box 18.1 Predictive coding account

The predictive coding account provides a mechanistic description of how responses in the visual and motor systems are organized and explains how the cause of an action can be inferred from its observation. The essence of the predictive coding account is that, given an a priori expectation about the goal/intention of the person we are observing, we can predict their motor commands. Given their motor commands, we can predict the kinematics on the basis of our own action system. The comparison of the predicted kinematics with the observed kinematics generates a prediction error (PE) that can be used to update our representation of the other's motor commands. Similarly, the inferred goals are updated by minimizing the PE between the predicted and inferred motor commands. By minimizing the PE at all levels of a cortical hierarchy engaged when observing actions, the most likely cause of the action will be inferred (Kilner et al., 2007). Please note that within this model the intention attribution process requires an a priori expectation about the action intention. This expectation, according to the model, would be derived from the context in which the observed action takes place. Evidence reviewed in this chapter and elsewhere (also see Ansuini, Cavallo, Bertone, & Becchio, 2014), however, indicates that intentions can not only be inferred from the context, but can also be *read* in the visual kinematics. Further investigation is needed to shed light on the differential contribution of kinematics and context to intention-from-movement understanding (see Box 18.2).

Box 18.2 Questions for future research

- Are observers sensitive to early differences connoting movements performed with a communicative intent?
- What role does context play? How is information from different sources (e.g. situational context, target objects, movement kinematics) integrated?
- How does the ability to read intentions from movement observation develop? Are infants able to use the movement kinematics to extract information concerning the intention with which an action is performed?
- Do observers with ASD have difficulties in reading other people's intentions from the way they move?
- Could human–robot interaction benefit from intention-specific kinematics programming? If humanoid robot systems were capable of taking early motor cues to intentions into account, would human–robot interaction improve?

References

Abernethy, B., & Russell, D. G. (1987). The relationship between expertise and visual search strategy in a racquet sport. *Human Movement Science*, 6, 283–319.

Abernethy, B., & Zawi, K. (2007). Pickup of essential kinematics underpins expert perception of movement patterns. *Journal of Motor Behavior*, 39, 353–367.

Abernethy, B., Zawi, K., & Jackson, R. C. (2008). Expertise and attunement to kinematic constraints. *Perception*, 37, 931–948.

Ansuini, C., Cavallo, A., Bertone, C., & Becchio, C. (2014). Prior-intention in the brain: The unveiling of Mister Hyde. *The Neuroscientist*, 21(2), 126–135.

Ansuini, C., Giosa, L., Turella, L., Altoè, G. M., & Castiello, U. (2008). An object for an action, the same object for other actions: Effects on hand shaping. *Experimental Brain Research*, 185, 111–119.

Ansuini, C., Santello, M., Massaccesi, S., & Castiello, U. (2006). Effects of end-goal on hand shaping. *Journal of Neurophysiology*, 95, 2456–2465.

Armbrüster, C., & Spijkers, W. (2006). Movement planning in prehension: Do intended actions influence the initial reach and grasp movement? *Motor Control*, 10, 311–329.

Baldwin, D. A., & Baird, J. A. (2001). Discerning intentions in dynamic human action. *Trends in Cognitive Sciences*, 5, 171–178.

Becchio, C., Cavallo, A., Begliomini, C., Sartori, L., Feltrin, G., & Castiello, U. (2012). Social grasping: From mirroring to mentalizing. *NeuroImage*, 61, 240–248.

Becchio, C., Sartori, L., Bulgheroni, M., & Castiello, U. (2008a). Both your intention and mine are reflected in the kinematics of my reach to grasp movement. *Cognition*, 106, 894–912.

(2008b). The case of Dr. Jekyll and Mr. Hyde: A kinematic study on social intention. *Consciousness and Cognition*, 17, 557–564.

Becchio, C., Sartori, L., & Castiello, U. (2010). Toward you: The social side of actions. *Current Directions in Psychological Science*, 19, 183–188.

Bonini, L., Ferrari, P. F., & Fogassi, L. (2013). Neurophysiological bases underlying the organization of intentional actions and the understanding of others' intention. *Consciousness and Cognition*, 22, 1095–104.

Bonini, L., Rozzi, S., Serventi, F. U., Simone, L., Ferrari, P. F., & Fogassi, L. (2010). Ventral premotor and inferior parietal cortices make distinct contribution to action organization and intention understanding. *Cerebral Cortex*, 20,1372–1385.

Boria, S., Fabbri-Destro, M., Cattaneo, L., Sparaci, L., Sinigaglia, C., et al. (2009). Intention understanding in autism. *PLoS One*, 4, e5596.

Buxbaum, L. J., Kyle, K. M., & Menon, R. (2005). On beyond mirror neurons: Internal representations subserving imitation and recognition of skilled object-related actions in humans. *Cognitive Brain Research*, 25, 226–239.

Casanova, M. F., van Kooten, I. A., Switala, A. E., van Engeland, H., Heinsen, H., et al. (2006). Minicolumnar abnormalities in autism. *Acta Neuropathologica*, 112, 287–303.

Cattaneo, L., Fabbri-Destro, M., Boria, S., Pieraccini, C., Monti, A., et al. (2007). Impairment of action chains in autism and its possible role in intention understanding. *Proceedings of the National Academy of Sciences*, 104, 17825–17830.

Crajé, C., Lukos, J. R., Ansuini, C., Gordon, A. M., & Santello, M. (2011). The effects of task and content on digit placement on a bottle. *Experimental Brain Research*, 212, 119–124.

Farrow, D., Abernethy, B., & Jackson, R. C. (2005). Probing expert anticipation with the temporal occlusion paradigm: Experimental investigations of some methodological issues. *Motor Control*, 9, 332–351.

Fogassi, L., Ferrari, P. F., Gesierich, B., Rozzi, S., Chersi, F., & Rizzolatti, G. (2005). Parietal lobe: From action organization to intention understanding. *Science*, 308: 662–667.

Gallagher, S. (2008). Direct perception in the intersubjective context. *Consciousness and Cognition*, 17, 535–543.

Gallese, V., Fadiga, L., Fogassi, L., & Rizzolatti, G. (1996). Action recognition in the premotor cortex. *Brain*, 119, 593–609.

Gallese, V., & Goldman, A. (1998). Mirror neurons and the simulation theory of mind-reading. *Trends in Cognitive Sciences*, 2, 493–501.

Georgiou, I., Becchio, C., Glover, S., & Castiello, U. (2007). Different action patterns for cooperative and competitive behavior. *Cognition*, 102, 415–433.

Hadjikhani, N., Joseph, R. M., Snyder, J., & Tager-Flusberg, H. (2006). Anatomical differences in the mirror neuron system and social cognition network in autism. *Cerebral Cortex*, 16, 1276–1282.

Iacoboni, M., & Dapretto, M. (2006). The mirror neuron system and the consequences of its dysfunction. *Nature Reviews Neuroscience*, 7, 942–951.

Kanner, L. (1943). Autistic disturbances of affective contact. *Nervous Child*, 2, 217–250.

Kaplan, J. T., & Iacoboni, M. (2006). Getting a grip on other minds: Mirror neurons, intention understanding, and cognitive empathy. *Social Neuroscience*, 1, 175–183.

Kilner, J. M. (2011). More than one pathway to action understanding. *Trends in Cognitive Science*, 15, 352–357.

Kilner, J. M., Friston, K. J., & Frith, C. D. (2007). Predictive coding: An account of the mirror neuron system. *Cognitive Processing*, 8, 159–166.

Manera, V., Becchio, C., Cavallo, A., Sartori, L., & Castiello, U. (2011). Cooperation or competition? Discriminating between social intentions by observing prehensile movements. *Experimental Brain Research*, 211, 547–556.

Marteniuk, R. G., MacKenzie, C. L., Jeannerod, M., Athenes, S., & Dugas, C. (1987). Constraints on human arm movement trajectories. *Canadian Journal of Psychology*, 41, 365–378.

Martineau, J., Andersson, F., Barthélémy, C., Cottier, J. P., & Destrieux, C. (2010). Atypical activation of the mirror neuron system during perception of hand motion in autism. *Brain Research*, 1320, 168–175.

Martineau, J., Cochin, S., Magne, R., & Barthelemy, C. (2008). Impaired cortical activation in autistic children: Is the mirror neuron system involved? *International Journal of Psychophysiology*, 68, 35–40.

Minshew, N. J., & Williams, D. L. (2007). The new neurobiology of autism: Cortex, connectivity, and neuronal organization. *Archives of Neurology*, 64, 945–950.

Naish, K. R., Reader, A. T., Houston-Price, C., Bremner, A. J., & Holmes, N. P. (2013). To eat or not to eat? Kinematics and muscle activity of reach-to-grasp movements are influenced by the action goal, but observers do not detect these differences. *Experimental Brain Research*, 225, 261–275.

Nishitani, N., Avikainen, S., & Hari, R. (2004). Abnormal imitation-related cortical activation sequences in Asperger's syndrome. *Annals of Neurology*, 55, 558–562.

Oberman, L. M., Hubbard, E. M., McCleery, J. P., Altschuler, E. L., Ramachandran, V. S., & Pineda, J. A. (2005). EEG evidence for mirror neuron dysfunction in autism spectrum disorders. *Cognitive Brain Research*, 24, 190–198.

Oberman, L. M., Ramachandran, V. S., & Pineda, J. A. (2008). Modulation of mu suppression in children with autism spectrum disorders in response to familiar or unfamiliar stimuli: The mirror neuron hypothesis. *Neuropsychologia*, 46, 1558–1565.

Pazzaglia, M., Smania, N., Corato, E., & Aglioti, S. M. (2008). Neural underpinnings of gesture discrimination in patients with limb apraxia. *Journal of Neuroscience*, 28, 3030–3041.

Pellegrino, G. di, Fadiga, L., Fogassi, L., Gallese, V., & Rizzolatti, G. (1992). Understanding motor events: A neurophysiological study. *Experimental Brain Research*, 91, 176–180.

Quesque, F., Lewkowicz, D., Delevoye-Turrell, Y. N., & Coello, Y. (2013). Effects of social intention on movement kinematics in cooperative actions. *Frontiers in Neurorobotics*, 7, 14.

Rizzolatti, G., & Sinigaglia, C. (2010). The functional role of the parieto-frontal mirror circuit: Interpretations and misinterpretations. *Nature Reviews Neuroscience*, 11, 264–274.

Runeson, S., & Frykholm, G. (1983). Kinematic specification of dynamics as an informational basis for person-and-action perception: Expectation, gender recognition, and deceptive intention. *Journal of Experimental Psychology: General*, 112, 585–615.

Sartori, L., Becchio, C., Bara, B. G., & Castiello, U. (2009). Does the intention to communicate affect action kinematics? *Consciousness and Cognition*, 18, 766–772.

Sartori, L., Becchio, C., & Castiello, U. (2011a). Cues to intention: The role of movement information. *Cognition*, 119, 242–252.

Sartori, L., Straulino, E., & Castiello, U. (2011b). How objects are grasped: The interplay between affordances and end-goals. *PloS One*, 6, e25203.

Schilbach, L., Timmermans, B., Reddy, V., Costall, A., Bente, G., et al. (2013). Toward a second-person neuroscience. *Behavioral and Brain Sciences*, 36, 393–414.

Schuboe, A., Maldonado, A., Stork, S., & Beetz, M. (2008). Subsequent actions influence motor control parameters of a current grasping action. *In Robot and Human Interactive Communication, RO-MAN. Presented at the 17th IEEE International Symposium*, Yokohama, Japan, 389–394.

Sebanz, N., & Shiffrar, M. (2009). Detecting deception in a bluffing body: The role of expertise. *Psychonomic Bulletin & Review*, 16, 170–175.

Sherrington, C. S. (1947). *The integrative action of the nervous system*. New Haven, CT: Yale University Press.

Tunik, E., Rice, N. J., Hamilton, A., & Grafton, S. T. (2007). Beyond grasping: Representation of action in human anterior intraparietal sulcus. *NeuroImage*, 36, T77–T86.

Vanrie, J., & Verfaillie, K. (2004). Perception of biological motion: A stimulus set of human point-light actions. *Behavior Research Methods, Instruments, & Computers*, 36, 625–629.

Vingerhoets, G., Honoré, P., Vandekerckhove, E., Nys, J., Vandemaele, P., & Achten, E. (2010). Multifocal intraparietal activation during discrimination of action intention in observed tool grasping. *Neuroscience*, 169, 1158–1167.

Weiss, P. (1941). Autonomous versus reflexogenous activity of the central nervous system. *Proceedings of the American Philosophical Society*, 84, 53–64.

Williams, J. H., Waiter, G. D., Gilchrist, A., Perrett, D. I., Murray, A. D., & Whiten, A. (2006). Neural mechanisms of imitation and 'mirror neuron' functioning in autistic spectrum disorder. *Neuropsychologia*, 44, 610–621.

Glossary

Action context The environment in which the action takes place, including the objects in the scene and, depending on whether the objects are familiar or unfamiliar, the knowledge about their use and associated actions.

Goal (or immediate goal) The immediate and intended outcome of a given action. In simple, object-oriented actions (e.g. reaching towards and grasping an object), the goal is the target toward which the action is directed. In everyday life, immediate goals are often embedded in action sequences (see **Prior intention**).

Kinematics or movement kinematics Detailed analysis of the hand's behavior in terms of position and displacement (angular and linear), as well as acceleration and velocities of the hand or hand segments.

Motor functional hierarchy Kinematics, goals and intentions have been proposed to represent different levels within a functional hierarchy. The notion that the motor system is hierarchically organized was first advanced by Sherrington (1947) and implies that the motor system can be viewed as a system of systems (Weiss, 1941). In such a system, higher levels of the hierarchy can modulate the activity in lower levels. With respect to motor functional hierarchy, this would result in higher levels that generate commands to achieve an action goal, while lower-level mechanisms translate the motor commands into movement kinematics.

Prior-intention (or intention) The intention representing the projected action sequence as a unified whole. For instance, grasping an object as a glass is usually the initial component (i.e. the immediate goal) of a broader action sequence in which the grasped object is used to achieve a distal goal (e.g. drinking).

Visual kinematics Movement kinematics as they are visually perceived by an observer.

19   Complementary Actions

Luisa Sartori

Abstract

Human beings come into the world wired for social interaction. At the fourteenth week of gestation, twin fetuses already display interactive movements specifically directed towards their co-twin. Readiness for social interaction is also clearly expressed by the newborn who imitates facial gestures, suggesting that there is a common representation mediating action observation and execution. While actions that are observed and those that are planned seem to be functionally equivalent, it is unclear if the visual representation of an observed action inevitably leads to its motor representation. This is particularly true with regard to *complementary* actions (from the Latin *complementum*; i.e. that fills up), a specific class of movements which differ, while interacting, with observed ones. In geometry, angles are defined as complementary if they form a right angle. In art and design, complementary colors are color pairs that, when combined in the right proportions, produce white or black. As a working definition, complementary actions refer here to any form of social interaction wherein two (or more) individuals complete each other's actions in a balanced way. Successful complementary interactions are founded on the abilities: (1) to simulate another person's movements; (2) to predict another person's future action/s; (3) to produce an appropriate congruent/ incongruent response that completes the other person's action/s; and (4) to integrate the predicted effects of one's own and another person's actions. It is the neurophysiological mechanism that underlies this process which forms the main theme of this chapter.

Introduction

As has been observed in mimicry, priming and automatic imitative actions (Heyes, 2011), humans are remarkably efficient at resonating with one another (Box 19.1). In specific contexts that require incongruent, complementary rather than imitative forms of interaction, motor resonance with action observation can, nevertheless, be an unsuitable response (for review, see Knoblich, Butterfill, & Sebanz, 2011). In the case, for example, that someone hands us a mug by its handle, we will automatically, without thinking, grab the mug using a whole-hand grasp (the most appropriate grasping gesture in this particular situation). The types of grasp adopted here by the two interacting agents are incongruent, but in this case they are appropriate and complementary. This example illustrates the functional importance of complementary actions in the context of the action–perception domain (Graf, Schütz-Bosbach, & Prinz, 2009), and it encourages us to take a look at what is taking place behind the scenes and to question the mechanisms involved in producing this outcome. Preliminary data addressing this question have been provided by recent studies utilizing different research methods.

The first part of the chapter will be dedicated to providing behavioral and neuroimaging data illustrating the processes and specific activation underlying complementary actions. The focus of the second, neurophysiologic part, will be to specifically describe, in spatial and temporal terms, the shift from imitative to reciprocal forms of interaction. Additionally, these processes will be explained in computational terms, and a novel theoretical framework will be proposed to elucidate this kind of social interaction.

Box 19.1 Motor resonance

In humans, a large number of neurophysiological studies have demonstrated that a *motor resonance* mechanism in the motor, premotor and the posterior parietal cortices is at work when individuals observe goal-directed actions being executed by other persons (for review, see Fadiga, Craighero, & Olivier, 2005; Heyes, 2011; Rizzolatti, Cattaneo, Fabbri-Destro, & Rozzi, 2014). Gallese (2001), in fact, explained that: 'when we observe actions performed by other individuals our motor system "resonates" along with that of the observed agent' (pp. 38–39). The discovery of mirror neurons in the monkey provided the physiological model for the basic perception–action coupling mechanism (Rizzolatti & Craighero, 2004). Located in the ventral premotor cortex (area F5) and posterior parietal cortex, it was seen that mirror neurons fire *both* when a monkey carries out a goal-directed action and when it observes that same action being performed by another subject (di Pellegrino, Fadiga, Fogassi, Gallese, & Rizzolatti, 1992). Neuroimaging studies have likewise provided evidence that a fronto-parietal perception–action system is implicated in coupling the representations of executed and observed actions in humans (for review, see Fabbri-Destro & Rizzolatti, 2008; Giorello & Sinigaglia, 2007; Keysers, 2009; Molenberghs, Cunnington, & Mattingley, 2012; Rizzolatti & Sinigaglia 2010; Turella, Tubaldi, Erb, Grodd, & Castiello, 2012). Taken together, monkey and human data have been interpreted to favor the *direct matching hypothesis*, which states that we understand observed actions by mapping their visual representation onto our motor representation (Rizzolatti, Fogassi, & Gallese 2001), and that the similarity between the observer's and the agent's action representations determines the degree to which motor resonance occurs in the former. Motor resonance seems to pre-activate our own motor system in order to represent and interpret the movements of someone else even when the go signal is not given and pre-activation remains unconscious (Costantini, Committeri, & Sinigaglia 2011b).

Behavioral Studies of Complementary Actions

The British evolutionary biologist John Napier (1956), who pioneered the modern study of human hand movements, explained that how our hands interact with objects depends not only on the object's features but also on the intentions guiding the action. Capitalizing on this insight, reach-to-grasp actions have been utilized as an experimental window in a variety of behavioral and neurophysiologic studies (Box 19.2). Available evidence indicates that different kinds of social object-oriented actions (e.g. passing an object to someone else) involve specific and often distinct movement parameterizations depending on whether the situation implies manipulating an object in order to cooperate or to compete against an opponent (Becchio, Sartori, Bulgheroni, & Castiello, 2008a, 2008b; Georgiou, Becchio, Glover, & Castiello, 2007; Sacheli, Tidoni, Pavone, Aglioti, & Candidi, 2013; Sartori, Becchio, Bara, & Castiello, 2009a; Sartori, Becchio, Bulgheroni, & Castiello, 2009b; Sartori, Becchio, & Castiello, 2011a). According to this perspective, direct perception of intentions underlying actions seems to afford specific action plans (Gangopadhyay & Schilbach, 2012). Moving an empty hand to unexpectedly ask for an object, for instance, possesses the power to override an observer's initial motor plan and to induce a complementary response, regardless of any previously imparted instructions (Sartori et al., 2009b). Evidence that the action context plays a pivotal role in shaping complementary actions has also been provided by a series of studies (Newman-Norlund, van Schie, van Zuijlen, & Bekkering, 2007b; Poljac, van Schie,& Bekkering, 2009; van Schie, van Waterschoot, & Bekkering, 2008b) in which participants were explicitly instructed to imitate or complement a virtual actor's grasp on a manipulandum using either a precision or a whole-hand grasp (grips are defined by the position of the thumb and the fingers; see Box 19.2). As expected, within the context of an imitation task, participants were faster at initiating a predefined action if their own action was congruent with the observed behavior, and their response was relatively delayed when they observed dissimilar actions. But the reverse pattern was found during complementary action tasks: the participants responded with greater rapidity when they observed dissimilar rather than similar actions. The need to maintain a task representation (imitative versus complementary) temporarily overruled existing long-term stimulus–response (S–R) associations, influencing the way that action–perception coupling took place. Further evidence on this flexible perception–action coupling came from a motion capture study (Ocampo & Kritikos, 2010) in which reaching and grasping parameters of identical responses were improved in imitative contexts, but the opposite was true for complementary contexts. Consistent with these findings, Longo, Kosobud, and Bertenthal (2008) reported that automatic imitation is modulated by top-down influences. They demonstrated that the level of action coding can be changed (e.g. towards coding in terms of movements) depending on task requirements. Taken together, these data challenge the idea that action observation automatically leads to imitation in the observer (i.e. direct matching hypothesis) and suggest that observed actions can prime non-identical responses depending on the context.

Box 19.2 Prehensile actions as an experimental window

Throughout any ordinary day we routinely reach for objects, grasp, lift and manipulate them while interacting with others. Reaching to grasp an object is, in fact, probably one of the most common human manual activities. Classic kinematic studies have distinguished and defined two main types of grasping action depending on intrinsic properties (e.g. the size and shape) of the object to be grasped: precision grip (PG; i.e. opposition between the index finger and thumb; see top right of panel (a) in the figure below) and whole-hand grasp (WHG; i.e. opposition of the thumb with the other fingers; (a), bottom left). Precise actions towards small objects are typically associated with lower wrist velocity profiles than whole-hand prehension movements due to the extra time needed to control accurate hand shaping in relation to a small object (Gentilucci et al., 1991; (b) in figure). The maximum amplitude of the index finger–thumb distance (maximum grip aperture, MGP) is also related to the object size, allowing the careful and smooth positioning of the fingers as the hand approaches the target. MGP is significantly larger when grasping is being performed to carry out whole-hand with respect to precision tasks ((c) in figure). Capitalizing on the differences between hand postures, neurophysiologic studies have demonstrated how observing different muscular activations leads to specific motor facilitation effects in the onlooker's corresponding muscles (Cavallo,

Becchio, Sartori, Bucchioni, & Castiello, 2012; Cavallo, Sartori, & Casti
ello, 2011; Fadiga, Craighero, & Olivier, 2005; Fadiga, Fogassi, Pavesi, &
Rizzolatti, 1995; Sartori & Castiello, 2013; Sartori, Bucchioni, & Castiello, 2012a; Urgesi, Candidi, Fabbro, Romani, & Aglioti, 2006). In particular, observing another person grasping a large object induces motor facilitation in both the first dorsal interosseus (FDI; the muscle serving index
finger flexion/extension) and the abductor digiti minimi (ADM; the muscle
serving little finger abduction) because those are the muscles involved in
a WHG. Conversely, only motor-evoked potentials (MEPs; (d) in figure)
recorded from the FDI muscle show a markedly increased activation when
an individual observes someone grasping a small object, because the ADM
muscle is not implicated in a PG grasp.

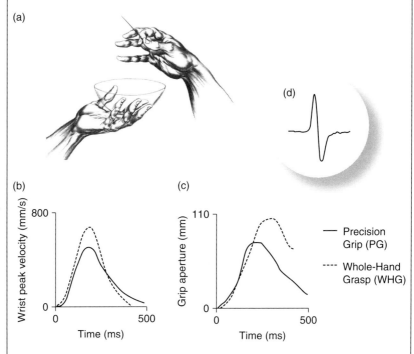

Box 19.2 Precision grip and whole-hand grasp characterization.
Notes: (a) Graphic drawing of an WHG (left) and a PG (right). (b) Wrist
peak velocity profile for PG and WHG actions. (c) Grip aperture profile for
PG and WHG actions. (d) TMS-induced MEP recorded in a hand muscle.

Neuroimaging Studies of Complementary Actions

Very few studies have examined the circuitry behind joint actions, and in particular the human mirror neuron system's (hMNS; Box 19.1) involvement in complementary forms of social interaction. In a pioneering experiment, the response of the hMNS was specifically investigated in imitative and complementary action contexts using fMRI (Newman-Nordlund et al., 2007b). Signals were recorded while the participants prepared to grasp a manipulandum in one of two ways (with a WHG or a PG) after they viewed an actor doing it (Figure 19.1a). With respect to imitative actions, preparation of complementary ones resulted in an increased blood-oxygen-level-dependent (BOLD) signal in the right inferior frontal gyrus (IFG) and bilateral inferior parietal lobule (IPL), two core components of the mirror system (Figure 19.1b). This has been explained in terms of different kinds of mirror neuron: strictly congruent mirror neurons, which respond to identical observed and executed actions, and broadly congruent mirror neurons, which respond to non-identical observed and executed actions upon the same object, possibly involving complementary actions (Fogassi & Gallese, 2002). Alternatively, another explanation could be that in the complementary condition, the participants observed an action that drew attention to an object eliciting a different action. This might have determined an interplay between mirror and canonical neurons: the latter type of neuron responds both during action execution and during the perception of the objects that are related to those behaviors (Rizzolatti & Craighero, 2004). Canonical motor neurons that become active during PG movements are, for instance, also activated when a small object that can be grasped using a PG is simply presented. Conversely, canonical neurons that become active during a WHG are selectively activated when a large object is shown (Murata et al., 1997). The need to perform a complementary action involving a different object might then imply a combination of mirror and canonical neurons coding for different types of action at different times. The hypothesis that different sets of mirror neurons might serve to integrate observed and executed actions during complementary kinds of social interaction is indeed an appealing one. Moreover, Newman-Norlund et al. (2007b) and Newman-Norlund, Bosga, Meulenbroek, and Bekkering (2008) hypothesized that a joint action could preferentially recruit right lateralized components of the mirror system since right inferior frontal activations are linked to inhibition processes (Brass, Derrfuss, & von Cramon, 2005). Planning and executing complementary actions in this framework would mean, first of all, actively inhibiting the natural tendency to imitate observed actions. It is also possible that right hemisphere components of the mirror system serve to integrate information regarding actions being generated by multiple actors and to determine an appropriate response, which is then forwarded to left hemisphere areas which are better suited to support

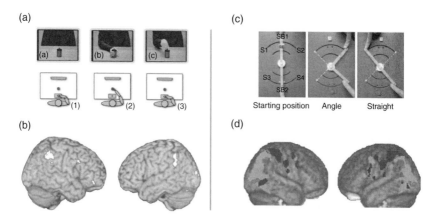

Figure 19.1 Brain structures that are involved in imitative and complementary actions.

Notes: (a) Investigations into the neural basis of joint actions have yielded partially converging results from functional imaging studies in normal individuals. Subjects participated in an 'imitation' and a 'complementary' action task with a manipulandum that could be grasped in two ways. The top-side of the object allowed a PG from above; the bottom side afforded a full-grip from the side. During the imitation task, subjects imitated the grasping behavior of a virtual actor viewed on a computer screen; during the complementary action condition, subjects performed the opposite action. In some (40%) of the trials a color cue indicated that the subjects were to execute a predefined grasp of the manipulandum (either WHG or PG), regardless of the actor's behavior. (b) Brain areas with a greater BOLD signal for complementary actions include the right IFG (pars opercularis) and bilateral IPL. (c) Participants were engaged in real-time joint actions with an experimenter who was standing next to them by performing an action similar or opposite to the one observed to achieve a common goal on a response box (the experimenter's and the participant's finger could either form an angle or a straight line). Participants also performed the same actions individually (execution) and observed the experimenter's actions (observation). (d) Rendering of the average brain of participants with hMNS (blue), superadditive voxels in joint actions (green) and overlap between hMNS and JA (red). Voxels common to both networks were restricted to the superior parietal lobule and higher-level visual areas.

Sources: (a) Set up and procedures adapted from Newman-Norlund et al. (2007b). (c) Set up and procedures adapted from Kokal and Keysers (2010) and Kokal et al. (2009).

execution of specific movement trains (Newman-Norlund et al., 2008). In the light of recent debates concerning the interpretation of the mirror mechanism (de Bruin & Gahhagher, 2012; Gallese & Sinigaglia, 2011), some have theorized that mirror neurons would transform perceptual information regarding an intentional action in terms of the observer's own action possibilities. In the case of aplasic patients born without arms or hands, observation of hand actions activated regions generally attributed to the hMNS, but involved in the execution of foot or mouth actions (Gazzola et al., 2007).

The idea that the hMNS would link perceived actions with appropriate motor plans was confirmed by an fMRI study carried out by Ocampo, Kritikos, and Cunnington (2011), who investigated if performing actions that are dissimilar to ones we observe activates core regions of the hMNS (namely, IPL and IFG) or general control mechanisms responsible for selecting and preparing conflicting responses. Consistent with the direct matching hypothesis, activity within right IPL and right IFG regions in the imitative context was greatest when participants responded with similar actions to observed hand actions. Interestingly, activity within these regions increased also when performing dissimilar responses, reflecting increased demands in the remapping of stimulus–response associations. In a similar way, Shibata, Inui, and Ogawa (2011) found that the right IFG was involved in mediating higher-order action understanding linked to a requested complementary action. Overall, these findings seem to suggest that there are two separate processes both supported by fronto-parietal brain regions. The first process operates at a simple motor level within contexts that require similar responses. The second process allows an observer to inhibit those responses and prepare the most compatible with task demands.

A more integrated account of the neural circuits underlying joint actions (both imitative and complementary) was recently proposed by Kokal, Gazzola, and Keysers (2009) and Kokal and Keysers (2010). Participants in an interactive fMRI study were required to carry out complementary and imitative actions in real-time cooperation with an experimenter ('joint action'), to perform the same actions individually ('execution'), or to simply observe the experimenter's actions (observation; Figure 19.1c).

This experiment brought our understanding of social interactions to a new level by specifically mapping the contribution of the hMNS (i.e. common voxels for both execution and observation) together with the areas specifically involved in the joint actions (i.e. voxels exceeding the sum of execution and observation). The areas responsible for this integration process were located bilaterally in the IFG, IPL, precentral gyrus, superior parietal lobule, middle and temporal occipital gyri and cerebellum (Figure 19.1d).

Two anatomically separate networks were thus delineated: one that would transform observed and executed actions into a single code (Etzel, Gazzola, & Keysers, 2008) and another that would integrate this information to achieve common goals. These findings show that, although the hMNS plays a critical role in coordinating two-party efforts by translating all actions into a common code, the flexible remapping of these actions seems to be performed somewhere else.

Neurophysiologic Studies of Complementary Actions

Action observation automatically activates corresponding motor representations in an observer, and this seems to be an essential step in coordinating actions with others. A direct way to examine this link is by using single-pulse transcranial magnetic stimulation (spTMS) over the primary motor cortex (M1) and concomitant electromyography (EMG) (e.g. Fadiga et al., 1995). This method allows for the investigation of modulations of the observer's corticospinal (CS) excitability while he watches an agent performing an action. A statistically significant modulation of TMS-induced MEP amplitudes in the corresponding muscles indicates that observers are specifically attuned to the observed action.

The CS facilitation phenomenon provided the first physiological evidence for a direct matching in humans between action perception and action execution (for a review, see Fadiga et al., 2005), and made it possible to explore motor system reactions in interactive contexts. A series of recent neurophysiologic studies were indeed designed to assess CS facilitation while participants observed video-clips evoking imitative and incongruent complementary gestures (Sartori, Betti, & Castiello, 2013b, 2013c, 2013d; Sartori, Cavallo, Bucchioni, & Castiello, 2011b, 2012b).

CS Excitability is Specifically Modulated by the Social Dimension of Observed Actions

In order to investigate whether the CS facilitation phenomenon is modulated depending on contextual factors, TMS-induced MEPs were recorded from participants' right hand muscles in response to either an observed action *explicitly* calling for a complementary response or the same action performed in a context which did not imply any social interaction (Sartori et al., 2011b). As the participants were instructed to remain motionless throughout the task, the degree to which the motor system was activated provided an index of the CS activity elicited by action preparation. In the experimental condition, seeing an actor in a frontal position with an open hand signaling a request near a salient object strategically placed out of her reach induced a modulation in the observer's MEP amplitudes that was consistent with the intention to accept the request (i.e. reaching for and grasping the object in question) rather than with the tendency to resonate with the observed action (Figure 19.2a). Notably, placing the object in the observer's peripersonal space is a crucial factor for inducing a function-related affordance (Costantini, Ambrosini, Scorolli, & Borghi, 2011a; Costantini, Ambrosini, Tieri, Sinigaglia, & Committeri, 2010; De Stefani et al., 2014; see Box 19.3). In this case, the type of grasp observed and the one that was planned were crucially mismatched (i.e. an open hand versus a WHG).

(a)   (b)

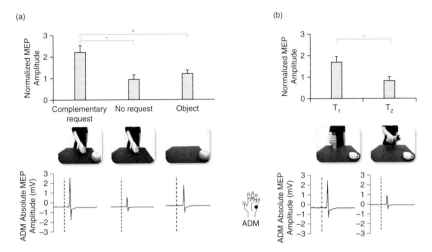

Figure 19.2 Experimental stimuli and TMS-induced mean MEP amplitude recorded in a participant's right ADM muscle.

Notes: (a) Three frames extracted from the experimental video-clips show: an actor extending an arm toward the viewer and unfolding her hand as if to explicitly request an out-of-reach apple ('complementary request'), the same actor extending her arm toward the viewer and unfolding her hand without the apple ('no-request') and the out-of-reach apple alone ('object'). Notably, only in the first condition is the out-of-reach apple present in the direction of the extended hand and the actor's open hand can readily be interpreted as a request addressed to the viewer to hand over the object. The normalized (top panel) and absolute (low panel) mean MEP amplitude indicates a significant pre-activation of ADM muscle in the 'complementary request' condition with respect to the other control conditions. This suggests that the complementary action disposition is contingent on perceiving the social gesture in connection to an object. (b) Two frames extracted from one of the experimental video-clips show an actor grasping a thermos with a whole-hand grasp (T_1), and then extending her arm toward the viewer as she attempts to pour something into the out-of-reach coffee cup (T_2). Notably, the gesture can readily be interpreted as a request to move the cup closer to the actor. The normalized (top panel) and absolute (low panel) mean MEP amplitude indicates an imitative pattern during the first part of the video (T_1) followed by a disposition toward executing the complementary grip in the second part (T_2), in preparation to hand the object over.

Sources: (a) Visual stimuli and results adapted from Sartori et al. (2011b). (b) Visual stimuli and results adapted from Sartori et al. (2012b).

As no explicit instructions were imparted to the participants, the effect uncovered spontaneous tendencies to fulfill the request embedded in a social interaction. This experiment was indeed particularly enlightening in view of the fact that most studies typically ask participants to perform actions that are *not* associated with any meaningful behavior in real life or tasks that are likely to uncover dispositions formed during the execution of the experimental task itself (e.g. in imitation versus complementary blocks), rather than spontaneous tendencies.

To further strengthen these data, another experiment was designed to ascertain if the effect was intrinsically social or might be elicited even by nonsocial cues (i.e. an arrow cue pointing towards the object). It is well known, indeed, that the mere sight of an object activates the representation of the action that can be performed on it even in the absence of explicit intentions to act (Craighero, Fadiga, Rizzolatti, & Umilta, 1998; Jeannerod, 1994; Tucker & Ellis, 1998; Box 19.3). The results showed that the presence of either the object or the arrow had the ability to determine MEP activation, but to a lesser extent than when the context was characterized by a request gesture toward the object. Taken together, these findings corroborate the idea that it is the social nature of an observed gesture along with the coding of object affordances (Box 19.3) that determine the observed effect. This was the first neurophysiologic evidence that the mechanisms underlying action observation are flexible, and spontaneously respond to contextual factors guiding social interactions above and beyond imitation.

The Functional Shift of Complementary Actions

A fundamental requirement for successful complementary actions is the capacity to smoothly and efficiently switch from observing another person's gestures to planning a corresponding reciprocal action, the so-called *functional shift* (Sartori et al., 2012b). Observed actions embedding a complementary request were studied in experimental trials to investigate the succession of these mechanisms. TMS-induced MEPs were recorded from participants' hand muscles in response to observing an actor grasping an object and then trying vainly to fulfill a task (e.g. pouring coffee) in a cup that was strategically placed out of her reach but in the video foreground, close to the observer's right hand (Figure 19.2b). The movement of the actor's hand was interpreted as a request to move the out-of-reach cup closer to the actor, so that she could complete the action. The type of grasp observed and the one that was required to carry out what was requested were reciprocally mismatched in all the videos (i.e. a WHG performed by the actor versus a PG requested of the observer, and vice versa). Results showed that a matching mechanism at the beginning of the action sequence turned into a complementary one as long as the request for a reciprocal action became evident (functional shift). The muscle-specificity of MEP amplitude highlighted an interplay between the initial tendency to resonate with what was observed and the implicit preparation for a dissimilar complementary action. This functional switch generated a modulation in grasp

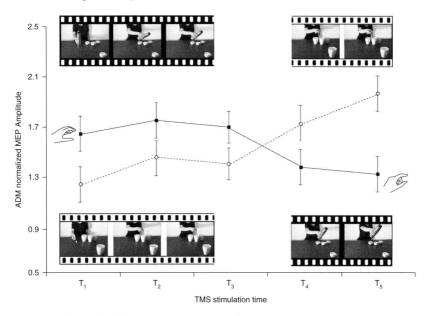

Figure 19.3 The time-course of complementary actions.

Notes: Visual stimuli and corresponding mean MEP amplitude recorded in a participant's ADM muscle show the time-course of the functional shift from motor resonance to reciprocity. spTMS was delivered at: T1 (the time the hand made contact with the object), T2 (when the model finished pouring), T3 (when the model raised her hand from the third cup/mug), T4 (the onset of the complementary request gesture) and T5 (the end of the complementary request gesture). Social precision grip movements requiring a WHG (white) and social whole-hand grasp movements requiring a PG (black) are illustrated. Bars represent the standard error of means. Note that a measurable variation in the observer's MEP amplitude occurred 240 ms after the actor completed the first of a two-step sequence (T4), at a time when it was still difficult to predict the course of action the actor would take.

Source: From Sartori et al. (2013d).

planning, immediately reflected in the activation of different hand muscles (Chinellato & del Pobil 2009).

Interestingly, the observer's handedness also seems to shape complementary interactions (Sartori, Begliomini, Panozzo, Garolla, & Castiello, 2014). In particular, observers tend to translate the complementary motor activation to their most functional effector (i.e. left-handers pre-activate the left hand and right-handers the right hand). These results confirm the hypothesis of a functional tuning of the action observation–execution system enabling left-handers living in a right-handed world to correctly plan movements in a highly efficient action-specific modality (Sartori, Begliomini, & Castiello, 2013a).

The Time-Course of Complementary Actions

The functional shift, as previously shown, indicates the ability to untie the automatic tendency to mirror another's actions and prepare for appropriate, complementary movements. The next question was then at what point this phenomenon occurs. A new experiment was then designed in which TMS was delivered at *five* different time points corresponding to five kinematic landmarks characterizing the observed action (Sartori et al., 2013c, 2013d; Figure 19.3). The most important was the fourth (T_4) time point when the actor's hand trajectory began to significantly move towards the out-of-reach object. A TMS pulse was specifically delivered at that time to investigate whether participants were able to predict the moment's trajectory relevance even before the action became explicit. The results showed that the participants were able to quickly discriminate between an action driven by a social goal and one that was not, simply by observing the kinematic cues signaling the direction of the actor's hand (Figure 19.3). Interestingly, the control condition consisted of the actor bringing her hand back to its initial position – with the out-of-reach object still visible in the foreground (Figure 19.3). This control condition made it possible to disentangle the role of *complementary affordances* (see Box 19.3).

These findings have direct implications with regard to action representation theories as they suggest that intention attribution (i.e. social versus individual) is sensitive to kinematic constraints. As different types of intentional actions have different motion signatures, observers seem to take note of precocious differences in kinematics during action observation to predict the actor's intentions (Becchio, Manera, Sartori, Cavallo, & Castiello, 2012a; Becchio, Sartori, & Castiello, 2010; Becchio et al., 2012b; Kilner et al., 2007; Manera, Becchio, Cavallo, Sartori, & Castiello, 2011; Sartori et al., 2009b, 2011a). Advance information gained while an action sequence is being observed allows observers not only to mirror an observed action but also to see behind the what and the why of an action and how to interact appropriately. It would seem, then, that any potential discrepancy between an observed action and a non-identical, complementary response is resolved flexibly in a two-step manner by the system itself. During the first step, the observed action is processed in order to predict its goal. During the second step, associations are made between the observed action and an appropriate action needed to accomplish a complementary goal. In line with this, it is tempting to assume that the motor system can mediate both automatic and flexible action–perception coupling. Erlhagen et al. (2006) recently proposed a model implementing both a direct (automatic) and a flexible route. The model involves four interconnected brain areas, namely, the superior temporal sulcus (STS), area PF, area F5 and the prefrontal cortex (PFC). The STS–F5 connection, allowing for the matching between a visual description of an action and its motor representation, would represent the neural basis of the direct route for the automatic imitation of an observed action. More importantly, when required, the flexible action–perception coupling is realized in the model by the connection between the PF area and the PFC through which goal representations from the PFC can modulate and set the coupling between visual (STS) and motor (F5) representations (ibid).

Box 19.3 Complementary affordances

Perception is an active process that highlights particular properties of the environment called 'affordances' (Gibson, 1979). Affordances can be defined as action possibilities, associations between environmental properties and abilities (Chemero, 2003). Crucially, some affordances are more relevant than others. *Complementary affordances* are a specific subcategory, referring to all those possibilities for interaction provided by others that activate appropriate motor programs aiming to bring a common goal to completion. We are selectively responsive to a world of relevant affordances, including complementary ones. We directly perceive, for instance, the 'meaning' of a cup's handle, which, of course, is used to pick it up, and this perception results from past experience. In a similar way, complementary requests can be understood in terms of the potential for the interactive involvement they elicit, even in situations in which the involvement does not take place. Complementary affordances depend on a number of variables, such as the presence of objects in a space that are necessary for an action to occur, gaze information (the relational orientation between the actor and the perceiver allowing for joint action; i.e. facing rather than behind or to the side), and the willingness to engage in a collaborative task. The concept of *readiness to interact* describes the disposition to engage in socially meaningful situations (Di Paolo & De Jaegher, 2012). The readiness to interact has been identified in the increased CS excitability of M1 as an index of a covert disposition to respond to a social gesture (Sartori et al., 2011b, 2012b, 2013b, 2013c, 2013d). In those studies, the functional shift from imitative to complementary action inclinations was contingent on perceiving a social gesture in connection to an object and was not likely to be mediated by inferential mechanisms. In this respect, *social signals* (e.g. instrumental gestures), whose function is to alter a recipient's behavior by triggering a range of opportunities for action, deserve special attention (Dezecache, Conty, & Grèzes, 2013; Gallagher & Frith, 2004). Depending on its posture and context, for example, an extended open hand can lead to a handshake or other actions (see figure). As demonstrated by social interactive paradigms, engaging in complementary actions is made possible by

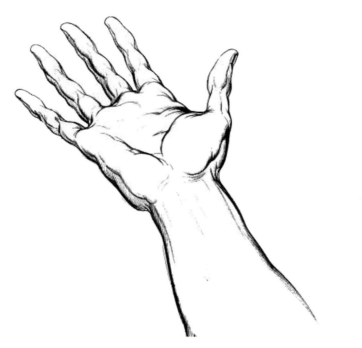

Box 19.3 Social signals such as an extended open hand can alter a recipient's behavior by triggering a range of opportunities for actions.

immediate apprehension of another person's goals (Sartori et al., 2009b). The activation of a complementary affordance is extremely powerful, and suggests that in our everyday interactions the automatic and rapid decoding of social cues influences our intentional behavior, maximizing the efficiency of our responses.

Predictive Simulation in Social Contexts Calling for Reciprocity: A Computational Model

One of the motor system's basic functions is to predict another person's actions (Blakemore & Frith, 2005; Prinz, 2006; Wilson & Knoblich, 2005). Some evidence suggests that motor resonance would indeed support action prediction (Kilner, Vargas, Duval, Blakemore, & Sirigu, 2004), allowing individuals to extend the temporal horizon of their motor planning and anticipating another person's actions rather than simply responding to them.

The simulation theory (Gallese & Goldman, 1998) specifically argues that our ability to predict the actions of others depends on our capacity to simulate (i.e. to internally reproduce) their actions. From this perspective, the same predictive mechanisms used to anticipate the sensory consequences of one's own movement/s may be employed to predict what others will do next (Wolpert & Flanagan, 2001). Indeed, observing another person's action is not simply a post-hoc reconstruction of visual input but an intrinsically predictive activity. When we observe another person's actions, we automatically anticipate their future ones. At the most basic level, humans can predict how a movement will evolve simply by watching how it was begun (Aglioti, Cesari, Romani, & Urgesi, 2008; Knoblich & Flach, 2001). In this vein, motor simulation seems to be called into play to solve fundamental computational dilemmas posed by action perception in those cases where information is missing or ambiguous (Aglioti & Pazzaglia, 2011; Avenanti & Urgesi, 2011; Schütz-Bosbach & Prinz, 2007; Wilson & Knoblich, 2005). Notably, predicting another person's behavior has immediate implications for one's own action selection system because, depending on the output of action simulation, a suitable action can be selected from a multiplicity of possible alternatives (Bekkering et al., 2009; Sartori et al., 2012c).

In contexts calling for complementary responses, the initially observed motor act must be coded from the very beginning in terms of the subsequent steps required to fulfill the action goal. This issue has been tackled in computational terms. Kinematic data linked to videos filmed by Sartori and colleagues (2013d) were utilized to implement a model identifying the switching point from the resonance to the social response phases (Chinellato, Ognibene, Sartori, & Demiris, 2013). Depending on the actor's hand trajectory, the model is capable of detecting a changeover even before the movement has come to an end. Once validated, one of the research project's long-term goals is to provide an artificial system, such as a humanoid robot, with more advanced social skills as it interacts with human partners.

In general terms, these studies have proposed a novel framework for modeling social interactions. The functional switch that has been previously described (Sartori et al., 2013c, 2013d) would be part of a dynamic interplay between the Action Observation System (AOS) and the Action Planning System (APS). The AOS is in charge of monitoring the actions of the person being observed, mainly by matching them to the observer's own motor repertoire. The APS is, instead, the neural system that plans and monitors the execution of all types of action. In social scenarios requiring non-identical joint actions, the APS takes control over the AOS, overriding automatic imitation behavior with a complementary social response (Chinellato et al., 2013). Notably, when the APS takes control over the AOS, monitoring the other person's actions is still performed by the AOS, and could directly affect on-line action execution. The process of selecting the appropriate action, therefore, does not necessarily bypass resonating behavior but seems to proceed in an intermingled way. The following section focuses on this process.

Temporal Coupling of Congruent and Non-Congruent Motor Resonance during Action Observation

What are the basic mechanisms facilitating complementary actions? At first glance, it would seem that complementary actions can be successfully performed by an observer only if activation of motor representations of observed actions is suppressed. Brass, Zysset, and von Cramon (2001) pointed out that the automatic tendency to imitate needs, first of all, to be inhibited if we want to generate a response that is different from the one that was observed. Recent computational and electrophysiological data seem, however, to suggest that motor resonant and associative processes can work side-by-side (Chinellato et al., 2013; Sartori, Bulgheroni, Tizzi, & Castiello, 2015b). Motor simulation of another person's actions during complementary interactions is particularly critical to success. An experiment combining spTMS and EMG recordings from multiple effectors was designed to examine if observing another person's actions priming for an incongruent reaction can lead to a motor-resonant response in the observer's corresponding muscles as well as a predictive activation and a simultaneous preparation of effectors necessary for a non-congruent response (Sartori, Betti, Chinellato, & Castiello, 2015a; Figure 19.4). CS modulation was assessed in the upper and lower limb muscles of participants observing a soccer player performing: (1) a penalty kick straight in their direction and then coming to a full stop, (2) a penalty kick straight in their direction and then continuing to run, (3) a penalty kick to the side and then continuing to run. The results showed a modulation of the observer's CS excitability in different effectors at different times, reflecting a multiplicity of motor coding: the internal replica of the observed action, the predictive activation and the adaptive integration of congruent and non-congruent responses to the actions of others.

A Working Memory Hypothesis

Taking the findings described a step further raises another interesting question: if observing an action performed using a specific effector can trigger responses in different ones, what mechanism selects the effectors needing to be activated for an appropriate response? A dual process seems to lie behind joint actions: a low-level motor resonance would store and analyze information on observed actions (allowing the onlooker to experience what is being observed), while a high-level simulation would flexibly integrate the individual's actions with those of others and select the most appropriate course to achieve joint

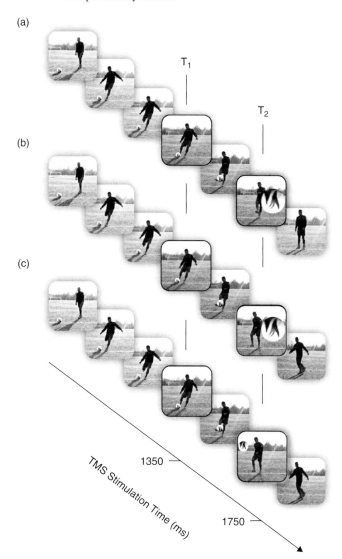

Figure 19.4 Video-clips and timing of TMS pulses.

Notes: The continuous oblique line represents the entire presentation of the three video-clips: (a) still, (b) running, (c) side. The vertical lines denote the time points when single TMS pulses were delivered: at T1 (when the player's foot makes contact with the ball) and at T2 (when the ball trajectory reaches its highest peak).

Source: From Sartori et al. (2013d).

goals (van Schie et al., 2008a). It can be hypothesized, then, that the hMNS' function is similar to that of a working memory, but specifically tailored for action. The hMNS's primary role is, as demonstrated by studies outlining its multisensory nature, to keep the neuronal activation linked to the visual, auditory or imaging aspects of motor actions (Kohler et al., 2002) on hold. As in the case of the working memory, distinct elements are kept on-line while others are being processed (Gibson, 2000).

Complementary actions are the ideal way to test this hypothesis. During complex social interactions, an individual needs to keep information relative to the observed action available while the attempt is being made to process its relative response. The working memory permits an individual to manipulate distinct components of a scene to extract meaning from it in view of a final goal. In the same way, during social interactions, the mirror system may be involved in keeping action-related information on hold to enable other brain areas to extract the meaning of an observed action to achieve a joint goal. The relation between observed and executed actions could be coordinated by a *social associative memory*, which would match certain actions to their natural social responses, irrespective of who is actually performing the action (Chinellato et al., 2013). If action B (e.g. take) usually follows action A (e.g. give), observing an actor executing A elicits pre-planning of B in the observer. If, instead, an actor executes A, she expects to see the observer perform B in response. A response that differs from the expected one could either be classified as an anomaly to discard or be considered an important new reaction that needs to be kept in our filing system. It is the comparison between predicted and observed stimuli, both with regard to individual and social movements, which directs the use and plastic modification of action components and their relations. The nature of the linkage between perception and action continues to be debated: is learning how to interact with other persons treated in the same way as stimulus–response (S–R) associations, or is it treated as a special way? Notably, there is a huge difference between basic and complex forms of complementary action. The former involve coordination without representation of the other persons' intentions and may be sub-served by the hMNS. The latter require a specific form of interdependence of the individual's intentions, as described by Bratman (1992), and the supplementary intervention of specific brain networks. Future research on complementary action may prove critical in clarifying how humans learn to interact with other persons.

Summary

The basic idea behind the research outlined here is that motor resonance elicited by action observation is modulated depending on the context: when an observed gesture is socially relevant (i.e. there is an implicit or explicit request), anticipatory complementary activations follow. The theory that observing an action automatically triggers an inclination to execute it was largely based on the fact that most studies did not explicitly challenge the automaticity and flexibility of the visuomotor transformation process. It is nevertheless undeniable that successful interactions often require complementary rather than imitative actions. A series of neurophysiologic studies have, in fact, demonstrated that an observed action characterized by a complementary request evokes a shift from motor resonance to reciprocity in the observer's motor system (Sartori et al., 2011b, 2012b, 2013b, 2013c, 2013d).

The data outlined here have contributed to shedding light on the functioning of the human motor system in social contexts and have increased knowledge on forms of social behavior frequently occurring in daily life situations. Defining the conditions and the modalities by which motor-resonant responses to action observation can be modulated may prove to have specific translational implications leading to the development of novel neuro-rehabilitation protocols for patients with localized lesions to cortical motor areas (e.g. ischemic stroke) and for pathologies such as autism. More distant horizons may include developing models of brain mechanisms underlying social interactions in view of endowing artificial agents such as robots with the ability to perform meaningful responses to observed actions.

References

Aglioti, S. M., Cesari, P., Romani, M., & Urgesi, C. (2008). Action anticipation and motor resonance in elite basketball players. *Nature Neuroscience*, 11, 1109–1116.

Aglioti, S. M., & Pazzaglia, M. (2011). Sounds and scents in (social) action. *Trends in Cognitive Sciences*, 15 (2011), 47–55.

Avenanti, A. & Urgesi, C. (2011). Understanding 'what' others do: Mirror mechanisms play a crucial role in action perception. *Social Cognitive and Affective Neuroscience*, 6, 257–259.

Becchio, C., Cavallo, A., Begliomini, C., Sartori, L., Feltrin, G., & Castiello, U. (2012b). Social grasping: From mirroring to mentalizing. *NeuroImage*, 61, 240–248.

Becchio, C., Manera, V., Sartori, L., Cavallo, A., & Castiello, U. (2012a). Grasping intentions: From thought experiments to empirical evidence. *Frontiers in Human Neuroscience*, 6, 1–6.

Becchio, C., Sartori, L., Bulgheroni, M., & Castiello, U. (2008a). The case of Dr. Jekyll and Mr. Hyde: A kinematic study on social intention. *Consciousness and Cognition*, 17, 557–564.

(2008b). Both your intention and mine are reflected in the kinematics of my reach to grasp movement. *Cognition*, 106, 894–912.

Becchio, C., Sartori, L., & Castiello, U. (2010). Towards you: The social side of actions. *Current Directions in Psychological Science*, 19, 183–188.

Bekkering, H., de Bruijn, E., Cuijpers, R., Newman-Norlund, R., van Schie, H., & Meulenbroek, R. (2009). Joint action: Neurocognitive mechanisms supporting human interaction. *Topics in Cognitive Science*, 1, 340–352.

Blakemore, S. J., & Frith, C. (2005). The role of motor contagion in the prediction of action. *Neuropsychologia*, 43, 260–267.

Brass, M., Derrfuss, J., & von Cramon, D. Y. (2005). The inhibition of imitative and overlearned responses: A functional double dissociation. *Neuropsychologia*, 43, 89–98.

Brass, M., Zysset, S., & von Cramon, D. Y. (2001). The inhibition of imitative response tendencies. *NeuroImage*, 14, 1416–1423.

Bratman, M. E. (1992). Shared cooperative activity. *Philosophical Review*, 101, 327–341.

Bruin, L. de, & Gallagher, S. (2012). Embodied simulation, an unproductive explanation: Comment on Gallese and Sinigaglia. *Trends in Cognitive Sciences*, 16, 98–99.

Castiello, U., Becchio, C., Zoia, S., Nelini, C., Sartori, L., et al. (2010). Wired to be social: The ontogeny of human interaction. *PLoS One*, 5, e13199.

Cavallo, A., Becchio, C., Sartori, L., Bucchioni, G., & Castiello, U. (2012). Grasping with tools: Corticospinal excitability reflects observed hand movements. *Cerebral Cortex*, 22, 710–716.

Cavallo, A., Sartori, L., & Castiello, U. (2011). Corticospinal excitability modulation to hand muscles during the observation of appropriate versus inappropriate actions. *Cognitive Neuroscience*, 2, 83–90.

Chemero, A. (2003). An outline of a theory of affordances. *Ecological Psychology*, 15, 181–195.

Chinellato, E., & del Pobil, A. P. (2009). The neuroscience of vision-based grasping: A functional review for computational modeling and bio-inspired robotics. *Journal of Integrative Neuroscience*, 8, 223–254.

Chinellato, E., Ognibene, D., Sartori, L., & Demiris, Y. (2013). Time to change: Deciding when to switch action plans during a social interaction. In N. F. Lepora, A. Mura, H. G. Krapp, P. F. M. J. Verschure, & T. J. Prescott (Eds.), *Biomimetic and biohybrid systems*. London: Springer, 47–58.

Costantini, M., Ambrosini, E., Scorolli, C., & Borghi, A. M. (2011a). When objects are close to me: Affordances in the peripersonal space. *Psychonomic Bulletin and Review*, 18, 302–308.

Costantini, M., Ambrosini, E., Tieri, G., Sinigaglia, C., & Committeri, G. (2010). Where does an object trigger an action? An investigation about affordances in space. *Experimental Brain Research*, 207, 95–103.

Costantini, M., Committeri, G., & Sinigaglia, C. (2011b). Ready both to your and to my hands: Mapping the action space of others. *PLoS One*, 6, e17923.

Craighero, L., Fadiga, L., Rizzolatti, G., & Umilta, C. (1998). Visuomotor priming. *Visual Cognition*, 5, 109–125.

De Stefani, D., Innocenti, A., De Marco, D., Busiello, M., Ferri, F., et al. (2014). The spatial alignment effect in near and far space: A kinematic study. *Experimental Brain Research*, 1–8.

Dezecache, G., Conty, L., & Grèzes, J. (2013). Social affordances: Is the mirror neuron system involved? *Behavioral and Brain Sciences*, 36, 417–418.

Di Paolo, E., & De Jaegher, H. (2012). The interactive brain hypothesis. *Frontiers in Human Neuroscience*, 6, 1–16.

Erlhagen, W., Mukovskiy, A., Bicho, E., Panin, G., Kiss, A., et al. (2006). Goal-directed imitation for robots: A bio-inspired approach to action understanding and skill learning. *Robotics and Autonomous Systems*, 54, 353–360.

Etzel, J. A., Gazzola, V., & Keysers, C. (2008). Testing simulations theory with cross-model multivariate classification of fMRI data. *PLoS One*, 3, 1–6.

Fabbri-Destro, M., & Rizzolatti, G. (2008). Mirror neurons and mirror systems in monkeys and humans. *Physiology*, 23, 171–179.

Fadiga, L., Craighero, L., & Olivier, E. (2005). Human motor cortex excitability during the perception of others' action. *Current Opinion in Neurobiology*, 15, 213–218.

Fadiga, L., Fogassi, L., Pavesi, G., & Rizzolatti, G. (1995). Motor facilitation during action observation: A magnetic stimulation study. *Journal of Neurophysiology*, 73, 2608–2611.

Fogassi, L., & Gallese, V. (2002). The neural correlates of action understanding in non-human primates. *Advances in Consciousness Research*, 42, 13–36.

Gallagher, H. L., & Frith, C. D. (2004). Dissociable neural pathways for the perception and recognition of expressive and instrumental gestures. *Neuropsychologia*, 42, 1725–1736.

Gallese, V. (2001). The shared manifold hypothesis. From mirror neurons to empathy. *Journal of Consciousness Studies*, 8, 5–7.

Gallese, V., & Goldman, A. (1998). Mirror neurons and the simulation theory of mind-reading. *Trends in Cognitive Sciences*, 2, 493–501.

Gallese, V., & Sinigaglia, C. (2011). What is so special about embodied simulation? *Trends in Cognitive Sciences*, 15, 512–519.

Gangopadhyay, N., & Schilbach, L. (2012). Seeing minds: A neurophilosophical investigation of the role of perception–action coupling in social perception. *Social Neuroscience*, 7, 410–423.

Gazzola, V., van der Worp, H., Mulder, T., Wicker, B., Rizzolatti, G., & Keysers, C. (2007). Aplasics born without hands mirror the goal of hand actions with their feet. *Current Biology*, 17, 1235–1240.

Gentilucci, M., Castiello, U., Corradini, M. L., Scarpa, M., Umiltà, C., & Rizzolatti, G. (1991). Influence of different types of grasping on the transport component of prehension movements. *Neuropsychologia*, 29, 361–378.

Georgiou, I., Becchio, C., Glover, S., & Castiello, U. (2007). Different action patterns for cooperative and competitive behaviour. *Cognition*, 102, 415–433.

Gibson, E. (2000). The dependency locality theory: A distance-based theory of linguistic complexity. In Y. Miyashita, A. Marantz, & W. O'Niel (Eds.), *Image, language, brain*. Cambridge, MA: MIT Press, 95–126.

Gibson, J. J. (1979). *The ecological approach to visual perception*. Boston, MA: Houghton Mifflin.

Giorello, G., & Sinigaglia, C. (2007). Perception in action. *Acta Biomedica*, 78, 49–57.

Graf, M., Schütz-Bosbach, S., & Prinz, W. (2009). *Motor involvement in action and object perception: Similarity and complementarity.* New York: Psychology Press.

Heyes, C. (2011). Automatic imitation. *Psychological Bulletin*, 137, 463–483.

Jeannerod, M. (1994). The representing brain: Neural correlates of motor intention and imagery. *Behavioral Brain Sciences*, 17, 187–245.

Keysers, C. (2009). Mirror neurons. *Current Biology*, 19, R971–R973.

Kilner, J. M., Friston, K. J., & Frith, C. D. (2007). Predictive coding: An account of the mirror neuron system. *Cognitive Processes*, 8, 159–166.

Kilner, J. M., Vargas, C., Duval, S., Blakemore, S. J., & Sirigu, A. (2004). Motor activation prior to observation of a predicted movement. *Nature Neuroscience*, 7, 1299–1301.

Knoblich, G., Butterfill, S., & Sebanz, N. (2011). Psychological research on joint action: Theory and data. In B. Ross (Ed.), *The psychology of learning and motivation*. Burlington, VT: Academic Press, 59–101.

Knoblich, G., & Flach, R. (2001). Predicting the effects of actions: Interactions of perception and action. *Psychological Science*, 2, 467–472.

Kohler, E., Keysers, C., Umiltà, M. A., Fogassi, L., Gallese, V., & Rizzolatti, G. (2002). Hearing sounds, understanding actions: Action representation in mirror neurons. *Science*, 297, 846–848.

Kokal, I., Gazzola, V., & Keysers, C. (2009). Acting together in and beyond the mirror neuron system. *NeuroImage*, 47, 2046–2056.

Kokal, I., & Keysers, C. (2010). Granger causality mapping during joint actions reveals evidence for forward models that could overcome sensory-motor delays. *PLoS One*, 5, e13507.

Longo, M. R., Kosobud, A., & Bertenthal, B. I. (2008). Automatic imitation of biomechanically possible and impossible actions: Effects of priming movements versus goals. *Journal of Experimental Psychology: Human Perception and Performance*, 34, 489–501.

Manera, V., Becchio, C., Cavallo, A., Sartori, L., & Castiello, U. (2011). Cooperation or competition? Discriminating between social intentions by observing prehensile movements. *Experimental Brain Research*, 211, 547–556.

Meltzoff, A. N. (2005). Imitation and other minds: The 'like me' hypothesis. In S. Hurley & N. Chater (Eds.), *Perspectives on imitation: From cognitive neuroscience to social science,* Volume 2. Cambridge, MA: MIT Press, 55–77.

Molenberghs, P., Cunnington, R., & Mattingley, J. B. (2012). Brain regions with mirror properties: A meta-analysis of 125 human fMRI studies. *Neuroscience and Biobehavioral Reviews*, 36, 341–349.

Murata, A., Fadiga, L., Fogassi, L., Gallese, V., Raos, V., & Rizzolatti, G. (1997). Object representation in the ventral premotor cortex (area F5) of the monkey. *Journal of Neurophysiology*, 78, 2226–2230.

Napier, J. R. (1956). The prehensile movements of the human hand. *Journal of Bone and Joint Surgery*, 38, 902–913.

Newman-Norlund, R. D., Bosga, J., Meulenbroek, R. G., & Bekkering, H. (2008). Anatomical substrates of cooperative joint-action in a continuous motor task: Virtual lifting and balancing. *NeuroImage*, 41, 169–177.

Newman-Norlund, R. D., Noordzij, M. L., Meulenbroek, R. G., & Bekkering, H. (2007a). Exploring the brain basis of joint action: Co-ordination of actions, goals and intentions. *Social Neuroscience*, 2, 48–65.

Newman-Nordlund, R. D., van Schie, H. T., van Zuijlen A. M., & Bekkering, H. (2007b). The mirror neuron system is more activated during complementary compared with imitative action. *Nature Neuroscience*, 10, 817–818.

Ocampo, B., & Kritikos, A. (2010). Placing actions in context: Motor facilitation following observation of identical and non-identical manual acts. *Experimental Brain Research*, 201, 743–751.

Ocampo, B., Kritikos, A., & Cunnington, R. (2011). How frontoparietal brain regions mediate imitative and complementary actions: An fMRI study. *PLoS One*, 6, e26945.

Pellegrino, G. di, Fadiga, L. Fogassi, L., Gallese, & Rizzolatti, G. (1992). Understanding motor events: A neurophysiological study. *Experimental Brain Research*, 91, 176–180.

Poljac, E., van Schie, H. T., & Bekkering, H. (2009). Understanding the flexibility of action–perception coupling. *Psychological Research*, 73, 578–586.

Prinz, W. (2006). What re-enactment earns us. *Cortex*, 42, 515–517.

Rizzolatti, G., Cattaneo, L., Fabbri-Destro, M., & Rozzi, S. (2014). Cortical mechanisms underlying the organization of goal-directed actions and mirror neuron-based action understanding. *Physiological Reviews*, 94, 655–706.

Rizzolatti, G., & Craighero, L. (2004). The mirror-neuron system. *Annual Review of Neuroscience*, 27, 169–192.

Rizzolatti, G., Fogassi, L., & Gallese, V. (2001). Neurophysiological mechanisms underlying the understanding and imitation of action. *Nature Review Neuroscience*, 2, 661–670.

Rizzolatti, G., & Sinigaglia, C. (2010). The functional role of the parieto-frontal mirror circuit: Interpretations and misinterpretations. *Nature Reviews Neuroscience*, 11, 264–274.

Sacheli, L. M., Tidoni, E., Pavone, E. F., Aglioti, S. M., & Candidi, M. (2013). Kinematic fingerprints of leader and follower role-taking during cooperative joint actions. *Experimental Brain Research*, 226, 473–486.

Sartori, L., & Castiello, U. (2013). Shadows in the mirror. *Neuroreport*, 24, 63–67.

Sartori, L., Becchio, C., Bara, B. G., & Castiello, U. (2009a). Does the intention to communicate affect action kinematics? *Consciousness and Cognition*, 18, 766–772.

Sartori, L., Becchio, C., Bulgheroni, M., & Castiello, U. (2009b). Modulation of the action control system by social intention: Unexpected social requests override preplanned action. *Journal of Experimental Psychology: Human Perception and Performance*, 35, 1490–1500.

Sartori, L., Becchio, C., & Castiello, U. (2011a). Cues to intention: The role of movement information. *Cognition*, 119, 242–252.

Sartori, L., Begliomini, C., & Castiello, U. (2013a). Motor resonance in left- and right-handers: Evidence for effector-independent motor representations. *Frontiers in Human Neuroscience*, 13, 7–33.

Sartori, L., Begliomini, C., Panozzo, C., Garolla, A., & Castiello, U. (2014). The left side of motor resonance. *Frontiers in Human Neuroscience*, 8, 702.

Sartori, L., Betti, S., & Castiello, U. (2013b). When mirroring is not enough: That is, when only a complementary action will do (the trick). *Neuroreport*, 24, 601–604.

(2013c). Corticospinal excitability modulation during action observation. *Journal of Visualized Experiments*, 82, e51001.

Sartori, L., Betti, B., Chinellato, E., & Castiello, U. (2015a). The multiform motor cortical output: Kinematic, predictive and response coding. *Cortex*, 70, 169–178.

Sartori, L., Bucchioni, G., & Castiello, U. (2012a). Motor cortex excitability is tightly coupled to observed movements. *Neuropsychologia*, 50, 2341–2347.

(2013d). When emulation becomes reciprocity. *Social Cognitive and Affective Neuroscience*, 8, 662–669.

Sartori, L., Bulgheroni, M., Tizzi, R., & Castiello, U. (2015b). A kinematic study on (un)intentional imitation in bottlenose dolphins. *Frontiers in Human Neuroscience*, 5(9), 446.

Sartori, L., Cavallo, A., Bucchioni, G., & Castiello, U. (2011b). Corticospinal excitability is specifically modulated by the social dimension of observed actions. *Experimental Brain Research*, 211, 557–568.

Sartori, L., Cavallo, A., Bucchioni, B., & Castiello, U. (2012b). From simulation to reciprocity: The case of complementary actions. *Social Neuroscience*, 7, 146–158.

Sartori, L., Xompero, F., Bucchioni, G., & Castiello, U. (2012c). The transfer of motor functional strategies via action observation. *Biology Letters*, 8, 193–196.

Schütz-Bosbach, S., & Prinz, W. (2007). Perceptual resonance: Action-induced modulation of perception. *Trends in Cognitive Sciences*, 11, 349–355.

Sebanz, N., Bekkering, H., & Knoblich, G. (2006). Joint action: Bodies and minds moving together. *Trends in Cognitive Sciences*, 10, 70–76.

Shibata, H., Inui, T., & Ogawa, K. (2011). Understanding interpersonal action coordination: An fMRI study. *Experimental Brain Research*, 211, 569–579.

Schie, H. T. van, Koelewijn, T., Jensen, O., Oostenveld, R., Maris, E., & Bekkering, H. (2008a). Evidence for fast, low-level motor resonance to action observation: An MEG study. *Social Neuroscience*, 3, 213–228.

Schie, H. T. van, Waterschoot, B. M., & Bekkering, H. (2008b). Understanding action beyond imitation: Reversed compatibility effects of action observation in imitation and joint action. *Journal of Experimental Psychology: Human Perception and Performance*, 34, 1493–1500.

Tucker, M., & Ellis, R. (1998). On the relations between seen objects and components of potential actions. *Journal of Experimental Psychology: Human Perception and Performance*, 24, 830–846.

Turella, L., Tubaldi, F., Erb, M., Grodd, W., & Castiello, U. (2012). Object presence modulates activity within the somatosensory component of the action observation network. *Cerebral Cortex*, 22, 668–679.

Urgesi, C., Candidi, M., Fabbro, F., Romani, M., & Aglioti, S. M. (2006). Motor facilitation during action observation: Topographic mapping of the target muscle and influence of the onlooker's posture. *European Journal of Neuroscience*, 23, 2522–2530.

Wilson, W., & Knoblich, G. (2005). The case for motor involvement in perceiving conspecifics. *Psychological Bulletin*, 131, 460–473.

Wolpert, D. M. & Flanagan, J. R. (2001). Motor prediction. *Current Biology*, 11, R729–R732.

20 Emotional Convergence: A Case of Contagion?

Guillaume Dezecache, Terry Eskenazi and Julie Grèzes

Abstract

Because they are likely to trigger convergent emotional reactions in observers, it has become extremely common to refer to emotions as 'contagious' elements. While it could have simply remained a metaphor, the concept of contagion has become central to account for situations of emotional convergence between individuals. In this respect, the primitive emotional contagion model introduced by Hatfield and colleagues in 1994 assumes that we have a strong tendency to mimic the facial, postural and vocal motor behaviour of the people we interact with. This claim resembles the shared representations framework, according to which we make use of our own motor resources to access and share others' states. This chapter consists of a critical review of the primitive emotional contagion model and further discusses the legitimacy of considering emotions as contagious elements to describe situations of affective or emotional convergence.

Introduction

Behaviours are typically termed 'contagious' if they tend to elicit the adoption of a similar behaviour in others. In this respect, emotions, moods and feelings are conceived as particularly contagious behaviours in humans (Hatfield, Cacioppo, & Rapson, 1994) and other social mammals (Langford et al., 2006). The perception of emotional signals in others (expressed by facial, bodily, vocal, verbal or chemosensory signals) is thought likely to cause the unintentional and involuntary adoption of congruent emotional states in the observers. These emotional signals need not be fully explicit to the observers (Dezecache et al., 2013a; Hsee, Hatfield, & Chemtob, 1992) for emotional convergence to occur. For that reason, it has long been thought a dangerous process for its apparent automaticity (Bargh & Williams, 2006; Chartrand & Bargh, 1999), irrepressible character (Uchino, Hsee, Hatfield, Carlson, & Chemtob, 1991)

Parts of this chapter were adapted from an article published in *Neuropsychologia* (Grèzes & Dezecache, 2013). GD, JG and TE are supported by ANR-10-LABX-0087 IEC, ANR-10-IDEX-0001-02 PSL and INSERM.

417

and the potential social consequences it could have at a collective level (Le Bon, 1896; Sighele, 1901).

The idea that one makes use of his own motor and emotional resources to access and share others' affective states (an idea which has further been developed within the shared representations framework) is at the heart of the 'primitive emotional contagion' model introduced by Hatfield et al. (1994). If observers come to 'catch' so readily the emotions, moods and feelings of the persons they interact with, Hatfield and colleagues argue, it is because of a strong and natural tendency humans have to mimic and synchronize with others' motor behaviours. When observing somebody expressing anxiety, for instance, motor mimicry (the subtle, dynamic and fine-tuned adoption of the observed individuals' facial, postural and vocal behaviour – see Box 20.1) and its physiological consequences (notably, the muscle afferent feedback) would naturally lead the observer to converge emotionally with the individual being observed.

Box 20.1   Key concepts and definitions

Contagion Behaviours are termed 'contagious' if they tend to elicit a strong motivation to adopt a similar behaviour in uninvolved third parties. Many behaviours are contagious in humans, including emotions, yawning (Provine, 2005), laughter (Provine, 2001) and gaze-following (Gallup et al., 2012). The concept of contagion (just like the transmission of germs and diseases) supposes that such process is fast, rapid, unintentional and largely irrepressible.

Emotions/moods Affective convergence encompasses the experience of various kinds of contents, such as moods (which are long-lasting and diffuse phenomena with no obvious physiological signature) and emotions (which are briefer phenomena with a somewhat specific physiological signature) (Ekman & Davidson, 1994). Scholars often focus on convergence of emotional states: their duration and physiological signatures make them easier to study in laboratory settings.

Empathy Unlike emotional convergence, empathy involves the capacity to attribute the source of our emotional state to others (de Vignemont & Jacob, 2012). Phylogenetically speaking, it is thought to be more recent as it involves the capacity to override the first emotional contagion response and increased neural and cognitive resources in executive control (Bartal, Decety, & Mason, 2011; Decety & Jackson, 2006). However, this capacity is likely shared with rodents and primates.

Motor mimicry (also termed the Chameleon effect; Chartrand & Bargh, 1999) The spontaneous and unintentional adoption of the muscular behaviour (facial, postural or vocal) of the person we interact with. Although thought to be automatic and spontaneous, this behaviour can be inhibited (Spengler, von Cramon, & Brass, 2010).

Primitive emotional contagion A model introduced by Hatfield et al. (1994), which states that emotional convergence relies on a two-step process. First, emotional displays are mimicked, leading to the adoption of a muscular behaviour congruent to that of the observed individual. Second, the feedback afferents of the newly adopted muscular configuration alter the affective state of the mimicker, further leading to the adoption of an affective state similar to that of the observed individual. Although remarkable in details, such models (and notably the causality between the different steps) lack strong empirical evidence.

However, recent empirical results and theoretical advances suggest that if shared motor and emotional representations may help us access and interpret others' emotions, the selection of one's own adaptive motor and emotional responses (which can drastically differ in kind and intensity to those of the observed individual, and may not necessarily result in emotional convergence) may ultimately rely on different cognitive or neural processes (Jeannerod, 2006).

After having introduced the phenomenon of emotional convergence and the historical models which have been proposed to account for it, we will focus on the scope and the limits of the primitive emotional contagion framework (Hatfield et al., 1994). We will then propose that convergence with others' affective experience, often labelled 'emotional contagion', does not result from the fundamental tendency to catch others' motor and emotional representations, but from an accidental match between the behaviour of the observed individual, and our own adaptive motor and emotional response. We argue that the function of the shared representations system is not to ensure congruence between people's affective states. Rather, this system can be used to predict the immediate outcomes of the observed behaviour.

Emotional Convergence as a Ubiquitous Phenomenon

Emotional convergence is so ubiquitous in human affairs that, as argued by Hatfield et al. (1994; also see Hsee et al., 1992), one might even gain the most valuable information about a target's affective states by focusing on one's own feelings during an ongoing social interaction rather than by pursuing explicit and conscious reasoning about the target's own account of his affective state. Supporting the view that emotional convergence constitutes an ineluctable process when interacting with someone, an experiment carried out by Hatfield's research team (Uchino et al., 1991) showed that prior expectations about a target's emotional states do not alter participants' subsequent susceptibility to experience similar emotions, as revealed by their emotional self-reports, as well as by their facial emotional responses during exposure to the target displays.

Emotional Convergence as a *Primitive* Phenomenon

Emotional convergence appears only in ontogeny: new-born babies are allegedly highly sensitive to the distress of their fellows, crying in response to others' cries (Dondi, Simion, & Caltran, 1999; Simner, 1971). It is also thought to be widely distributed in phylogeny. Evidence remains scarce (due notably to the difficulty of assessing affective responses in non-humans) but studies reporting emotional convergence in social mammals can be found in the literature. In this respect, a study by Miller, Banks, & Ogawa (1963) showed that monkeys witnessing conspecifics being presented with aversive stimuli display avoidance-related behaviours. Also, rodents are known to be sensitive to the pain of their conspecifics (Langford et al., 2006). Rats were notably found to show pro-social behaviour towards their conspecifics in distress, further revealing a capacity to override emotional convergence (Bartal et al. 2011). The fact that emotional convergence is precocious and the suggestion that it is a phylogenetically well-distributed phenomenon support the idea that it is primitive, and that it might therefore be largely irrepressible.

The 'Contagion' Metaphor: Theoretical Presuppositions and Epistemological Consequences

It is common to conceptualize affective states as highly contagious elements: at no stage in the contagion process would agents intend either to emit or to react to others' affective states (Hatfield et al., 1994). Therefore, emotions, moods and feelings have been thought to operate just like diseases (Hill, Rand, Nowak, & Christakis, 2010). In fact, the idea that affective states can be contagious is not a novel one. Early social psychologists of the nineteenth and twentieth centuries, such as Gustave Le Bon (L1896), Gabriel Tarde (1890) or Scipio Sighele (1901) were already warning their fellows of the danger of others' emotions. As termed by Gustave Le Bon (1896), emotions were thought to possess a contagious power 'as intense as that of microbes'. As a consequence, 'a panic that [would have] seized on a few sheep [could] soon extend to the whole flock', making any rational being behave like 'a slave of his impulses' (ibid). Such historical retour on the concept of contagion and its application in the understanding of human social cognition could be perceived as superfluous. However, the use of this metaphor has dramatically shaped the way in which we understand the process behind emotional convergence. Emotional convergence is thought to be primitive, fast, passive, unintentional, irrepressible and somewhat dangerous, as it cannot be inhibited, and it can lead to dramatic consequences, such as fatal stampedes in panicking crowds (Brown, 1954). As a consequence, the spread of emotions can be analysed in a way similar to that applied to the spread of disease. The epistemological impact of the introduction of this metaphor of the contagion process is clear when considering the works of Nicholas A. Christakis and colleagues (Coviello et al., 2014; Fowler & Christakis, 2008; Hill et al., 2010), which have treated the spread of moods by explicitly using a disease epidemiology model. Within this type of model, moods are transmitted in large networks, from node to node, through social contact, over a long period of time, and in a spontaneous and irrepressible fashion. The use of this metaphor is, in itself, interesting to analyse. The contagion metaphor strongly presupposes that agents are passive in the process of converging emotionally, not that this process is irrepressible. In fact, many factors are known to modulate emotional convergence. Similarity, in particular, between the sender and the receiver of the signal is notably an important moderator of the response to emotional signals (for a review of the evidence, see Dezecache, Mercier, & Scott-Phillips, 2013b). For example, Lanzetta and Englis (1989) have showed that the misfortune of an opponent could lead to a process termed 'counter-empathy' rather than to the experience of empathy, suggesting that considering emotional convergence as a default response to others' emotion could be counterfactual. In a similar vein, facial mimicry, a phenomenon thought to be at the basis of emotional convergence (Hatfield et al., 1994) and, supposedly automatic, can be repressed when facing individuals toward whom we have a negative attitude (Likowski, Mühlberger, Seibt, Pauli, & Weyers, 2008). In sum, as we do not share the happiness of a person we consider bad, emotions cannot be said to spread automatically and in an irrepressible fashion.

The Many Media of Emotional Convergence

Affective states can be signalled in many ways: emotional facial behaviour, which presumably originated for intrapersonal sensory regulation (Lee, Susskind, & Anderson, 2013; Susskind et al., 2008; Vermeulen, Godefroid, & Mermillod, 2009), is one of the major media selected for social coordination and communication of adaptive-value to our conspecifics (Chovil, 1991, 1997; Fridlund, 1994). Exposure to fear expressions is, for example, known to enhance vision of contrast (Phelps, Ling, & Carrasco, 2006) or of low spatial frequencies in the observer but not exposure to disgust (Nicol, Perrotta, Caliciuri, & Wachowiak, 2013), showing that emotional facial expressions can affect observers in emotion-specific ways. Additionally, postural behaviour can signal one's affective state (de Gelder, 2006; de Gelder, Snyder, Greve, Gerard, & Hadjikhani, 2004; Grèzes, Pichon, & de Gelder, 2007). Affective states can also be signalled via verbal expressions. More surprisingly, emotions can also be transmitted through chemosensory signals (Mujica-Parodi et al., 2009; Prehn-Kristensen et al., 2009). As evidence for this, Mujica-Parodi and colleagues (2009) have shown that smelling the sweat of skydiving beginners can trigger activation in resting participants' amygdala (AMG), a key emotional centre in the human brain. Finally, the massive use of internet-based communication nowadays would also call for a thorough examination of emotional convergence through emoticons (Derks, Fischer, & Bos, 2008).

Emotional Convergence at the Cognitive Level

What are the other models that have been proposed to account for emotional convergence?

Social Comparison Models

The first broad class of models historically proposed can be said to rely on a process of 'social comparison' whereby observers adopt affective states similar to those of the target by consciously reasoning and imagining being in the same situation. Such a model can be traced back to Adam Smith's (1759 [2010]) observation that when 'our brother is upon the rack … our senses will never inform us of what he suffers … and it is by the imagination only that we form any conception of what are his sensations. More recent accounts of this model do exist (e.g. Bandura, 1969), but they share the similar problematic assumption that some sort of deliberation is at the core of the process of emotional convergence. Yet, such a costly cognitive process may be problematic in accounting for the fact that emotional convergence can be rapid.

Conditioning Models

Other models that rely on associative processes have been proposed to account for the primitive character of emotional convergence. They argue that emotional responses can be conditioned and unconditioned and account for most cases of emotional contagion (Aronfreed, 1970). For instance, one may generalize situations where smiles are expressed in response to situations of pro-sociality and well-being, or learn that fearful expressions are associated with stressful situations (conditioning). Also, one could well be unconditioned to react to joyful and fearful expressions with joy and fear, respectively. Those models are appealing in virtue of their simplicity, but they are so simple that they remain mechanistically unspecified. They may rely on associative cognitive processes but they do not account for the fact that new-borns are sensitive to the distress of their fellows and that emotional convergence is an ontogenetically precocious phenomenon.

Overall, the theoretical limits of both models probably explain why the 'primitive emotional contagion' model, which is causally very explicit, has been the most popular over recent years to explain how people may rapidly converge at the emotional level.

The Primitive Contagion Model

Through their work on the processing of social cues, John Bargh and his colleagues have consistently showed that we have a natural tendency to spontaneously and unconsciously mimic the postures of individuals we are interacting with (Chartrand & Bargh, 1999). This 'mimicry' would not be restricted to postures as the perception of facial expressions of emotion is also known to induce, in observers, slight activity in the target facial muscle within the first second after exposure to the stimulus (Dimberg, 1982; Dimberg & Thunberg, 1998). Such behavioural mimicry effects are, for Hatfield et al. (1994), at the basis of 'primitive emotional contagion'. It is a two-step process: (1) first, people tend to mimic and synchronize their motor behaviour (facial expressions, body postures, vocal behaviour) with that of those with whom they interact; (2) doing so, they adopt a muscular configuration, which, through muscular feedback, alters the emotional experience in a way congruent with the adopted muscular configuration. Consequently, observers and the target individual converge emotionally.

Each of these two steps has been documented extensively in the literature. People indeed tend to precisely and rapidly mimic and synchronize with the facial expressions (Dimberg, 1982; Dimberg, Thunberg, & Elmehed, 2000; Moody, McIntosh, Mann, & Weisser, 2007), bodily postures (Bernieri, 1988; Bernieri & Rosenthal, 1991) and vocal behaviour (Cappella, 1981, 1997) of the people they interact with. Conversely, there is also some evidence that facial (Bush, Barr, McHugo, & Lanzetta, 1989; Duclos et al., 1989; Hennenlotter et al., 2009; Laird, 1984; Lanzetta & Orr, 1980; Soussignan, 2002; Strack, Martin, & Stepper, 1988), postural (Duclos et al., 1989; Stepper & Strack, 1993) and vocal feedback (Hatfield & Hsee, 1995) can alter the subjective emotional experience. In sum, these two steps, when causally combined, could indeed allow for the transmission of emotion between two interacting agents.

This model suffers from four main limitations. First, there is no definitive evidence that those two steps are indeed causally linked in the process of emotional convergence as it occurs in real social interactions.

Second, although the capacity for motor mimicry is to a certain extent linked to a capacity to recognize others' emotional expressions (blocking facial mimicry is thought to selectively impair recognition of certain emotional expressions; Oberman, Winkielman, & Ramachandran, 2007), motor mimicry might facilitate emotion recognition rather than simply allow for it (Schnall & Laird, 2007). Emotion recognition is indeed not impaired in people with Möbius syndrome, who suffer from a congenital bilateral facial paralysis and are therefore incapable of producing facial mimicry (Calder, Keane, Cole, Campbell, & Young, 2000).

Third, rapid facial reactions similar to those observed in response to the perception of emotional facial expressions were obtained in response to arousing pictures (e.g. snakes; Dimberg, Hansson, & Thunberg, 1998), bodily (Grèzes et al., 2013; Magnée, Stekelenburg, Kemner, & de Gelder, 2007; Tamietto et al., 2009) or vocal expressions (Hietanen, Surakka, & Linnankoski, 1998) showing that rapid facial reactions can occur even in the absence of observed facial movements. These studies suggest that rapid facial reactions are not merely a result of motor mimicry but rather reflect the evaluation of the emotional dimension of a given stimulus (Grèzes et al., 2013; Moody et al., 2007; Soussignan et al., 2013).

Fourth, and finally, the primitive emotional contagion model presupposes that the emotional reaction of an observer should match that of the observed individual, even when certain social contexts might not favour the sharing of emotional experience between two agents ('Shall I really catch the joy of my competitor, or the fear of my enemy?'). This fourth problem, though acknowledged by Hatfield and colleagues, is totally incompatible with the view that motor mimicry is at the basis of emotional transmission. Recently, Hess and Fisher (2013) distinguished two types of possible behaviour prompted by others' emotional displays: an emotional mimicry response in an affiliative context and an emotional reactive response in a non-affiliative social context. These two behaviours are the consequence of emotional appraisal (the interpretation of signals as emotions in context), and thus do not rely on non-affective motor matching of the perceived expressions. However, and surprisingly, the authors persist in using the term 'mimicry', which posits that one strictly replicates others' motor behaviour.

More generally speaking, the motor mimicry model is based on the equation between the process of emotional convergence and that of emotional contagion (see Box 20.1). The latter is a process whereby observers are thought to be passive and where they mandatorily catch the various emotions of the target. Yet, accounting for emotional convergence requires an explanation of how humans can flexibly respond to others' emotional signals, sometimes in a congruent or convergent way (by adopting an emotional experience similar to that of the observer), sometimes in incongruent ways.

Emotional Convergence as a Corollary Result of Emotional Communication Processes

One of the most important assumptions of the primitive emotional contagion is that emotional convergence is a special process, which relies on dedicated psychological mechanisms. This is particularly the case for the primitive emotional contagion model: proposers of this model assume that, following emotional convergence, emotions of A and B are shared and therefore are replicas. In turn, they typically restrict their investigation to psychological processes that allow for a mirroring between agents A and B. Yet, it does not follow that B's reactions to A's emotional displays rely on mechanisms whose function are to ensure congruence between emotional states of A and B. In fact, emotional convergence could be a corollary result of emotional communication processes: confronted by emotional signals, observers may coincidentally react in a congruent manner (thus leading to emotional convergence), but they may equally react in an incongruent manner (leading to incongruent emotional reactions or counter-contagion; Lanzetta & Englis, 1989). In sum, emotional convergence would merely be a case where B's emotional reaction to A's emotional display happens to be similar. Therefore, explaining emotional convergence brings us back to the wider issue of what the psychological mechanisms that allow humans to react to others' emotional displays are, be they congruent or incongruent with the emotions observed in others. This also rules out the possibility that shared motor and emotional representations alone could account for our emotional reactions (whether they are congruent or not with those of the observed individual) to others' emotional displays. In this respect, considering the neural involvement of regions associated with emotion processing and those with motor preparation during perception of emotional displays similarly suggests that emotional convergence may not rely on dedicated and specific cognitive and neural resources, but could rather be a corollary result of emotional communication processes.

Emotional Convergence at the Neural Level

Emotional displays are communicative signals, and as such, they have evolved to influence the behaviour of those receiving the signals (Dezecache et al., 2013b). Accordingly, emotional signals we perceive prompt an appropriate response behaviour given the constraints of the present social context. For instance, an appropriate response to a display of anger could be fear, and not anger, so the agent can generate the necessary action steps to avoid a confrontation (Jeannerod, 2006). This necessarily involves an appraisal process that relies on a neural mechanism extending beyond shared action and emotion representations. Indeed, a growing body of literature strongly suggests a functional and anatomical link between neural systems that sustain emotional appraisal and those that underlie action preparation, which are fundamental for the production of an appropriate response to the evaluated signal.

Anatomical studies indicate that the amygdala (AMG), a key centre of the emotion-processing circuitry, plays a pivotal role in emotion-related functions and context-appropriate social behaviour (Adolphs, 2010). Animal and human studies show that the AMG increases vigilance and facilitates perceptual processing (Davis & Whalen, 2001; Vuilleumier, Richardson, Armony, Driver, & Dolan, 2004; Whalen, 1998) and is particularly sensitive to threatening stimuli (LeDoux, 1995; Morris, Iansek, Matyas, & Summers, 1996; Hoffman, Gothard, Schmid, & Logothetis, 2007; Phelps & LeDoux, 2005; Whalen, 1998). In addition to facilitating perceptual processing, threat signals also trigger physiological reflexes and influence ongoing behaviour of the observer (for review, see Pessoa, 2008).

In humans, several functional neuroimaging (fMRI) studies reveal a co-activation of the AMG and motor-related areas, notably the premotor cortex (PM) known for its role in action preparation, during the perception of emotional displays (Carr, Iacoboni, Dubeau, Mazziotta, & Lenzi, 2003; Decety & Chaminade, 2003; de Gelder et al., 2004; Grèzes et al., 2007; Grèzes, Adenis, Pouga, & Armony, 2012; Grosbras & Paus, 2006; Hadjikhani, Hoge, Snyder, & de Gelder, 2008; Isenberg et al., 1999; Pichon, de Gelder, & Grèzes, 2008, 2009, 2012; Pouga, Berthoz, de Gelder, & Grèzes, 2010; Sato, Kochiyama, Yoshikawa, Naito, & Matsumura, 2004; Van den Stock, Tamietto, Sorger, Pichon, Grèzes, & de Gelder, 2011; Warren et al., 2006; Whalen, Shin, McInerney, Fischer, Wright, & Rauch, 2001). Functional connectivity between the AMG and motor system has also been suggested (Ahs et al., 2009; Grèzes et al., 2009; Qin, Young, Supekar, Uddin, & Menon, 2012; Roy et al., 2009; Voon et al., 2010). Also, transcranial magnetic stimulation (TMS) studies demonstrated that perception of negative stimuli or emotional displays such as fear and anger, both of which are threat signals, primes the motor system and facilitates action readiness (Balconi & Bortolotti, 2013; Baumgartner, Matthias, & Lutz, 2007; Coelho, Lipp, Marinovic, Wallis, & Riek, 2010; Coombes et al., 2009; Oliveri et al., 2003; Schutter, Hofman, & van Honk, 2008). There is thus ample evidence that the AMG works in concert with cortical motor-related areas, mainly in response to fearful and angry expressions (for a review, see Grèzes & Dezecache, 2013).

For example, in a first set of fMRI studies carried out by our research team, we investigated the interplay between the shared action-representation and the emotion appraisal systems in response to emotional displays through the use of static and dynamic stimuli. As expected, the comparison between dynamic and static stimuli triggered a differential neural activity in brain areas associated with the shared action-representation system (premotor cortex, intraparietal lobule and the superior temporal sulcus – see Figure 20.1A, bottom panel, indicated in green); whereas the comparison between emotional and neutral expressions recruited brain areas that are a part of, what we call, the emotion-to-action system (i.e. fusiform gyrus and STS, AMG and PM – see Figure 20.1A, top panel, indicated in red) (Grèzes et al., 2007, 2009; Pichon et al., 2008; Pouga et al., 2010). The functional connectivity (PPI – psychophysiological interaction) analyses we conducted further suggest that shared action-representation and emotion-to-action systems work in parallel when facing emotional displays of others. The shared action-representation system allows for the activation of the motor representation that corresponds to the perceived action and associated predicted somatosensory consequences to anticipate the unfolding of the action (Figure 20.1B), while the emotion-to-action system could underlie the preparation of potential adaptive responses in the observed, triggered by the emotional signal (Figure 20.1B) (Grèzes & Dezecache, 2013).

The actions prompted in the observing agent of an emotional display are constrained by their significance relative to the observer's current state and goals (Rietveld, De Haans, & Denys, in press). The precise perceived intention associated with the emotional display, and thus the evoked behavioural reaction in the observer, can vary significantly depending on how relevant the signal is judged to be by the observer. This is particularly evident in the case of anger, where the direction of gaze and body posture determines if one is the intended target of the display or simply an observer. When coupled with direct gaze, angry expressions tend to be more accurately and quickly recognized, and are judged to be more intense (Adams & Kleck, 2003, 2005; Cristinzio, N'Diaye, Seeck, Vuilleumier, & Sander, 2010; Hess, Adams, & Kleck, 2007; Sander, Grandjean, Kaiser, Wehrle, & Scherer, 2007). In contrast, fearful faces are perceived to express more fear when gaze is averted as they inform the observer about the source of a potential threat in their immediate environment (N'Diaye, Sander, & Vuilleumier, 2009; Sander et al., 2007).

We combined functional magnetic resonance imaging (fMRI) with electroencephalography (EEG) to explore the temporal dynamics underlying the combination of multiple co-emitted social cues; i.e. gaze, pointing and emotional displays (Conty, Dezecache, Hugueville, & Grèzes, 2012). The results of this study revealed that the emotional content of a perceived action was first processed by the AMG (170 ms) before being integrated with other social cues (i.e. gaze direction and pointing gestures) by the premotor cortex (200 ms). Importantly, premotor cortex was most active in response to an expression of

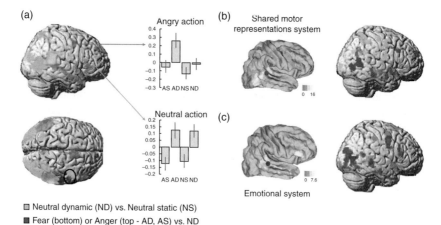

☐ Neutral dynamic (ND) vs. Neutral static (NS)
■ Fear (bottom) or Anger (top - AD, AS) vs. ND

Figure 20.1 Statistical parametric maps of brain activation in response to the observation of dynamic versus static emotional expressions, connectivity of two brain areas sustaining shared motor representations, and changes in connectivity pattern of emotion to action brain areas. *See Plate 9.*

Notes: A. (left) Dynamic versus static emotional expressions (red, top: anger (Pichon et al., 2008), bottom: fear (Pouga et al., 2010)) and dynamic versus static neutral expressions (green); (right) parameter estimates (arbitrary units, mean centred) of the PMv/PMd border (top: xyz = 50 2 48) and of the posterior part of the inferior frontal gyrus IFG44 (bottom: xyz = 52 16 32). AS: Anger Static; AD: Anger Dynamic; NS: Neutral Static; ND: Neutral Dynamic. B. Using psychophysiological interaction (PPI), we (Grèzes and Pouga, unpublished data) address changes in the connectivity pattern of two brain areas sustaining shared motor representations (black circles in the middle image – the pSTS (xyz = 54 − 46 8) and inferior frontal cortex IFG44 (xyz = 46 12 26)) when an action becomes emotional. Middle image: statistical maps showing brain activations in the right hemisphere in response to the perception of dynamic body expressions versus static ones, irrespective of the emotional content, rendered on a partially inflated lateral view of the human PALS-B12 atlas. Right image: statistical maps showing increased functional connection with the STS (purple) or IFG44 (green). C. Changes in the connectivity pattern of emotion-to-action brain areas (STS (xyz = 50 −40 −2) and amygdala (xyz = 18 −6 −24)) when a static fearful stimulus becomes dynamic. Middle image: statistical maps showing brain activations in the right hemisphere in response to the perception of fearful expressions versus neutral ones, irrespective of their nature (static or dynamic), rendered on a partially inflated lateral view of the human PALS-B12 atlas. Right image: statistical maps showing increased functional connection with the STS (purple) or the amygdala (Red).

anger accompanied by both gaze and pointing directed at the observer. We proposed that only a combination of two complementary mechanisms explains the highest level of activity observed in the PM for the highest level of potential threat: (1) the estimation of prior expectations about the perceived agent's immediate intent, which relies on the shared action-representation system (Kilner et al., 2007); and (2) the evaluation of the emotional content and the selection of the appropriate action for the observer to deal with the immediate situation. The dynamic interaction between the two systems underlies the appraisal of the emotional signal, which gives rise to a response behaviour that is either congruent or incongruent with the observed emotional displays, a response optimal for a given situation.

Conclusion

The observation of anxiety in our conspecifics may lead us to feel anxious. Similarly, the perception of joy in others is likely to make us joyful. Generalization of such cases can lead us to think that we always react congruently to others' affective states, and that we are equipped with mechanisms whose function is to ensure the congruency of our own affective states with those of our conspecifics (Dezecache, G., Jacob, P., & Grèzes, J., 2015). In this respect, the primitive emotional contagion model provides a mechanistic explanation of how we can come to converge emotionally, with particular reliance on the process of motor mimicry, i.e. the spontaneous and fine-tuned replication of others' muscular movements. In this chapter, we have argued that such a framework, however elegant, is inadequate given recent discoveries. In particular, it appears that rapid facial reactions to emotional displays (which according to Hatfield and colleagues is motor mimicry) reflect the evaluation of the emotional dimension of a given stimulus. As a consequence, the perception of an emotion in others, rather than triggering only the experience of a similar emotion in ourselves, can give rise to a variety of behavioural responses. Such behavioural responses can be congruent with those of the observed individual (thus giving the impression that the affective state of the target has contaminated the observer) or not. Emotional convergence, we conclude, consists of an accidental match between the emotions of an individual, and the emotional response of the observer. See Box 20.2.

Box 20.2 Questions for future research

- Are all emotions likely to be shared? Are emotions linked to direct survival (e.g. fear, disgust) more likely to lead to congruent emotional behaviour (accidental emotional contagion) in observers than emotions which are less directly linked to danger in the environment (e.g. sadness)?

- Why should certain emotions (e.g. fear, disgust) lead to congruent emotional behaviour while others (e.g. sadness) preferentially call for empathetic or complementary reaction in observers?
- What are the links between emotional convergence and empathy? Does empathy necessarily rely on a capacity to override emotional convergence?
- Can non-basic social emotions be shared (e.g. pride, shame)? Can such convergence processes rely on the primitive processes involved in fear convergence, as such complex affective states might be characteristic of humans alone?
- When emotional convergence is blocked or overridden (e.g. when having to do with a competitor), are emotional convergence processes inhibited at an early or late processing stage? In other words, is emotional convergence a default response (that can later be inhibited) or not?

References

Adams, R. B. Jr, & Kleck, R. E. (2003). Perceived gaze direction and the processing of facial displays of emotion. *Psychological Science*, 14(6), 644–647.
    (2005). Effects of direct and averted gaze on the perception of facially communicated emotion. *Emotion*, 5(1), 3–11.
Adolphs, R. (2010). What does the amygdala contribute to social cognition? *Annals of the New York Academy of Sciences*, 1191, 42–61.
Ahs, F., Pissiota, A., Michelgard, A., Frans, O., Furmark, T., et al. (2009). Disentangling the web of fear: Amygdala reactivity and functional connectivity in spider and snake phobia. *Psychiatry Research: Neuroimaging*, 172, 103–108.
Aronfreed, J. (1970). The socialization of altruistic and sympathetic behavior: Some theoretical and experimental analyses. In J. Macaulay & L. Berkowitz (Eds.), *Altruism and Helping Behavior*. New York: Academic Press, pp. 103–126.
Balconi, M., & Bortolotti, A. (2013). Emotional face recognition, empathic trait (BEES), and cortical contribution in response to positive and negative cues. The effect of rTMS on dorsal medial prefrontal cortex. *Cognitive Neurodynamics*, 7(1), 13–21. doi: 10.1007/s11571-012-9210-4.
Bandura, A. (1969). Principles of behavior modification. http://psycnet.apa.org/psycinfo/1971-10097-000.
Bargh, J. A., & Chartrand, T. L. (1999). The unbearable automaticity of being. *American Psychologist*, 54(7), 462.
Bargh, J. A., & Williams, E. L. (2006). The automaticity of social life. *Current Directions in Psychological Science*, 15(1), 1–4.
Bartal, I. B.-A., Decety, J., & Mason, P. (2011). Empathy and pro-social behavior in rats. *Science*, 334(6061), 1427–1430.
Baumgartner, T., Matthias, W., & Lutz, J. (2007). Modulation of corticospinal activity by strong emotions evoked by pictures and classical music: A transcranial magnetic stimulation study. *NeuroReport*, 18, 261–265.
Bernieri, F. J. (1988). Coordinated movement and rapport in teacher–student interactions. *Journal of Nonverbal Behavior*, 12(2), 120–138.

Bernieri, F. J., & Rosenthal, R. (1991). Interpersonal coordination: Behavior matching and interactional synchrony. *Fundamentals of Nonverbal Behavior*, 401.

Brown, R. W. (1954). Mass phenomena. *Handbook of Social Psychology*, 2, 833–876.

Bush, L. K., Barr, C. L., McHugo, G. J., & Lanzetta, J. T. (1989). The effects of facial control and facial mimicry on subjective reactions to comedy routines. *Motivation and Emotion*, 13(1), 31–52.

Calder, A. J., Keane, J., Cole, J., Campbell, R., & Young, A. W. (2000). Facial expression recognition by people with Möbius syndrome. *Cognitive Neuropsychology*, 17(1–3), 73–87.

Cappella, J. N. (1981). Mutual influence in expressive behavior: Adult–adult and infant–adult dyadic interaction. *Psychological Bulletin*, 89(1), 101.

(1997). Behavioral and judged coordination in adult informal social interactions: Vocal and kinesic indicators. *Journal of Personality and Social Psychology*, 72(1), 119.

Carr, L., Iacoboni, M., Dubeau, M. C., Mazziotta, J. C., & Lenzi, G. L. (2003). Neural mechanisms of empathy in humans: A relay from neural systems for imitation to limbic areas. *Proceedings of the National Academy of Sciences of the USA*, 100, 5497–502.

Chartrand, T. L., & Bargh, J. A. (1999). The chameleon effect: The perception–behavior link and social interaction. *Journal of Personality and Social Psychology*, 76(6), 893.

Chovil, N. (1991). Social determinants of facial displays. *Journal of Nonverbal Behavior*, 15(3), 141–154. doi: 10.1007/BF01672216.

(1997). Facing others: A social communicative perspective on facial displays. *Psychology of Facial Expression*, 25, 321.

Coelho, C. M., Lipp, O. V., Marinovic, W., Wallis, G., & Riek, S. (2010). Increased corticospinal excitability induced by unpleasant visual stimuli. *Neuroscience Letters*, 481, 135–138.

Coombes, S. A., Tandonnet, C., Fujiyama, H., Janelle, C. M., Cauraugh, J. H., & Summers, J. J. (2009). Emotion and motor preparation: A transcranial magnetic stimulation study of corticospinal motor tract excitability. *Cognitive, Affective and Behavioral Neuroscience*, 9, 380–388.

Conty, L., Dezecache, G., Hugueville, L., & Grèzes, J. (2012). Early binding of gaze, gesture, and emotion: Neural time course and correlates. *Journal of Neuroscience*, 32(13), 4531–4539.

Coviello, L., Sohn, Y., Kramer, A. D. I., Marlow, C., Franceschetti, M., et al. (2014). Detecting emotional contagion in massive social networks. *PLoS One*, 9(3), e90315. doi: 10.1371/journal.pone.0090315.

Cristinzio, C., N'Diaye, K., Seeck, M., Vuilleumier, P., & Sander, D. (2010). Integration of gaze direction and facial expression in patients with unilateral amygdala damage. *Brain*, 133(Pt 1), 248–261.

Decety, J., & Chaminade, T. (2003). When the self represents the other: A new cognitive neuroscience view on psychological identification. *Consciousness and Cognition*, 12, 577–596.

Decety, J., & Jackson, P. L. (2006). A social-neuroscience perspective on empathy. *Current Directions in Psychological Science*, 15(2), 54–58. doi: 10.1111/j.0963-7214.2006.00406.x.

Derks, D., Fischer, A. H., & Bos, A. E. (2008). The role of emotion in computer-mediated communication: A review. *Computers in Human Behavior*, 24(3), 766–785.

Dezecache, G., Conty, L., Chadwick, M., Philip, L., Soussignan, R., et al. (2013a). Evidence for unintentional emotional contagion beyond dyads. *PLoS One*, 8(6), e67371. doi: 10.1371/journal.pone.0067371.

Dezecache, G., Jacob, P., & Grèzes, J. (2015). Emotional contagion: its scope and limits. *Trends in Cognitive Sciences*, 19(6), 297–299. http://doi.org/10.1016/j.tics.2015.03.011.

Dezecache, G., Mercier, H., & Scott-Phillips, T. C. (2013b). An evolutionary approach to emotional communication. *Journal of Pragmatics*, 59, 221–233.

Dimberg, U. (1982). Facial reactions to facial expressions. *Psychophysiology*, 19(6), 643–647.

Dimberg, U., Hansson, G. Ö., & Thunberg, M. (1998). Fear of snakes and facial reactions: A case of rapid emotional responding. *Scandinavian Journal of Psychology*, 39(2), 75–80.

Dimberg, U., & Thunberg, M. (1998). Rapid facial reactions to emotional facial expressions. *Scandinavian Journal of Psychology*, 39(1), 39–45. doi: 10.1111/1467-9450.00054.

Dimberg, U., Thunberg, M., & Elmehed, K. (2000). Unconscious facial reactions to emotional facial expressions. *Psychological Science*, 11(1), 86–89. doi: 10.1111/1467-9280.00221.

Dondi, M., Simion, F., & Caltran, G. (1999). Can newborns discriminate between their own cry and the cry of another newborn infant? *Developmental Psychology*, 35(2), 418–426.

Duclos, S. E., Laird, J. D., Schneider, E., Sexter, M., Stern, L., & Van Lighten, O. (1989). Emotion-specific effects of facial expressions and postures on emotional experience. *Journal of Personality and Social Psychology*, 57(1), 100.

Ekman, P. E., & Davidson, R. J. (1994). *The nature of emotion: Fundamental questions*. Oxford: Oxford University Press.

Fowler, J. H., & Christakis, N. A. (2008). Dynamic spread of happiness in a large social network: Longitudinal analysis over 20 years in the Framingham Heart Study. *British Medical Journal*, 337. doi: 10.1136/bmj.a2338.

Fridlund, A. J. (1994). *Human facial expression: An evolutionary view* (Vol. 38). San Diego, CA: Academic Press.

Gallup, A. C., Hale, J. J., Sumpter, D. J. T., Garnier, S., Kacelnik, A., et al. (2012). Visual attention and the acquisition of information in human crowds. *Proceedings of the National Academy of Sciences*, 109(19), 7245–7250. doi: 10.1073/pnas.1116141109.

Gelder, B. de. (2006). Towards the neurobiology of emotional body language. *Nature Reviews Neuroscience*, 7(3), 242–249. doi: 10.1038/nrn1872.

Gelder, B. de, Snyder, J., Greve, D., Gerard, G., & Hadjikhani, N. (2004). Fear fosters flight: A mechanism for fear contagion when perceiving emotion expressed by a whole body. *Proceedings of the National Academy of Sciences of the United States of America*, 101(47), 16701–16706.

Grèzes, J., Adenis, M. S., Pouga, L., & Armony, J. L. (2012). Self-relevance modulates brain responses to angry body expressions. *Cortex*, 49(8), 2210–2220.

Grèzes, J., & Dezecache, G. (2014). How do shared-representations and emotional processes cooperate in response to social threat signals? *Neuropsychologia*, 55, 105–114. doi: 10.1016/j.neuropsychologia.2013.09.019.

Grèzes, J., Philip, L., Chadwick, M., Dezecache, G., Soussignan, R., & Conty, L. (2013). Self-relevance appraisal influences facial reactions to emotional body expressions. *PLoS One*, 8(2), e55885. doi: 10.1371/journal.pone.0055885.

Grèzes, J., Pichon, S., & de Gelder, B. (2007). Perceiving fear in dynamic body expressions. *NeuroImage*, 35(2), 959–967. doi: 10.1016/j.neuroimage.2006.11.030.

Grèzes, J., Wicker, B., Berthoz, S., & de Gelder, B. (2009). A failure to grasp the affective meaning of actions in autism spectrum disorder subjects. *Neuropsychologia*, 47, 1816–1825.

Grosbras, M. H., & Paus, T. (2006). Brain networks involved in viewing angry hands or faces. *Cerebral Cortex*, 16, 1087–1096.

Hadjikhani, N., Hoge, R., Snyder, J., & de Gelder, B. (2008). Pointing with the eyes: The role of gaze in communicating danger. *Brain and Cognition*, 68, 1–8.

Hatfield, E., Cacioppo, J. T., & Rapson, R. L. (1994). *Emotional contagion*. Cambridge: Cambridge University Press.

Hatfield, E., & Hsee, C. K. (1995). The impact of vocal feedback on emotional experience and expression. *Journal of Social Behavior and Personality*, 10, 293–313.

Hennenlotter, A., Dresel, C., Castrop, F., Ceballos-Baumann, A. O., Wohlschläger, A. M., & Haslinger, B. (2009). The link between facial feedback and neural activity within central circuitries of emotion: New insights from Botulinum toxin-induced denervation of frown muscles. *Cerebral Cortex*, 19(3), 537–542.

Hess, U., Adams, R., & Kleck, R. (2007). Looking at you or looking elsewhere: The influence of head orientation on the signal value of emotional facial expressions. *Motivation & Emotion*, 31(2), 137–144.

Hess, U., & Fischer, A. (2013). Emotional mimicry as social regulation. *Personality and Social Psychology Review*. doi: 10.1177/1088868312472607.

Hietanen, J. K., Surakka, V., & Linnankoski, I. (1998). Facial electromyographic responses to vocal affect expressions. *Psychophysiology*, 35(5), 530–536. doi: 10.1017/S0048577298970445.

Hill, A. L., Rand, D. G., Nowak, M. A., & Christakis, N. A. (2010). Emotions as infectious diseases in a large social network: The SISa model. *Proceedings of the Royal Society B: Biological Sciences*. doi: 10.1098/rspb.2010.1217.

Hoffman, K. L., Gothard, K. M., Schmid, M. C., & Logothetis, N. K. (2007). Facial-expression and gaze-selective responses in the monkey amygdala. *Current Biology*, 17(9), 766–772.

Hsee, C. K., Hatfield, E., & Chemtob, C. (1992). Assessments of the emotional states of others: Conscious judgments versus emotional contagion. *Journal of Social and Clinical Psychology*, 11(2), 119–128. doi: 10.1521/jscp.1992.11.2.119.

Isenberg, N., Silbersweig, D., Engelien, A., Emmerich, S., Malavade, K., et al. (1999). Linguistic threat activates the human amygdala. *Proceedings of the National Academy of Sciences*, 96, 10456–10459.

Jeannerod, M. (2006). *Motor cognition: What actions tell the self*. Oxford: Oxford University Press.

Kilner, J., Friston, K., & Frith, C. (2007). Predictive coding: An account of the mirror neuron system, *Cognitive Processes*, 8(3), 159–166.

Laird, J. D. (1984). The real role of facial response in the experience of emotion: A reply to Tourangeau and Ellsworth, and others. http://psycnet.apa.org/journals/psp/47/4/909/.

Langford, D. J., Crager, S. E., Shehzad, Z., Smith, S. B., Sotocinal, S. G., et al. (2006). Social modulation of pain as evidence for empathy in mice. *Science*, 312(5782), 1967–1970.

Lanzetta, J. T., & Englis, B. G. (1989). Expectations of cooperation and competition and their effects on observers' vicarious emotional responses. *Journal of Personality and Social Psychology*, 56(4), 543.

Lanzetta, J. T., & Orr, S. P. (1980). Influence of facial expressions on the classical conditioning of fear. *Journal of Personality and Social Psychology*, 39(6), 1081.

Le Bon, G. (1896). *Psychologie des foules*. London: Macmillan.

LeDoux, J. E. (1995). Emotion: Clues from the brain. *Annual Review of Psychology*, 46, 209–235.

Lee, D. H., Susskind, J. M., & Anderson, A. K. (2013). Social transmission of the sensory benefits of eye widening in fear expressions. *Psychological Science*. doi: 10.1177/0956797612464500.

Likowski, K. U., Mühlberger, A., Seibt, B., Pauli, P., & Weyers, P. (2008). Modulation of facial mimicry by attitudes. *Journal of Experimental Social Psychology*, 44(4), 1065–1072. doi: 10.1016/j.jesp.2007.10.007.

Magnée, M. J. C. M., Stekelenburg, J. J., Kemner, C., & de Gelder, B. (2007). Similar facial electromyographic responses to faces, voices, and body expressions. *Neuroreport*, 18(4), 369–372.

Miller, R. E., Banks J. H. Jr, & Ogawa, N. (1963). Role of facial expression in 'cooperative-avoidance conditioning' in monkeys. *Journal of Abnormal and Social Psychology*, 67(1), 24.

Moody, E. J., McIntosh, D. N., Mann, L. J., & Weisser, K. R. (2007). More than mere mimicry? The influence of emotion on rapid facial reactions to faces. *Emotion*, 7(2), 447–457. doi: 10.1037/1528-3542.7.2.447.

Mujica-Parodi, L. R., Strey, H. H., Frederick, B., Savoy, R., Cox, D., et al. (2009). Chemosensory cues to conspecific emotional stress activate amygdala in humans. *PLoS One*, 4(7), e6415. doi: 10.1371/journal.pone.0006415.

N'Diaye, K., Sander, D., & Vuilleumier, P. (2009). Self-relevance processing in the human amygdala: Gaze direction, facial expression, and emotion intensity. *Emotion*, 9(6), 798–806.

Nicol, J. R., Perrotta, S., Caliciuri, S., & Wachowiak, M. P. (2013). Emotion-specific modulation of early visual perception. *Cognition & Emotion*, 27(8), 1478–1485. doi: 10.1080/02699931.2013.793654.

Oberman, L. M., Winkielman, P., & Ramachandran, V. S. (2007). Face to face: Blocking facial mimicry can selectively impair recognition of emotional expressions. *Social Neuroscience*, 2(3–4), 167–178.

Oliveri, M., Babiloni, C., Filippi, M. M., Caltagirone, C., Babiloni, F., et al. (2003). Influence of the supplementary motor area on primary motor cortex excitability during movements triggered by neutral or emotionally unpleasant visual cues. *Experimental Brain Research*, 149, 214–221.

Pessoa, L. (2008). On the relationship between *emotion* and cognition. *Nature Reviews Neuroscience*, 9(2), 148–158. doi: 10.1038/nrn2317.

Phelps, E. A., & LeDoux, J. E. (2005). Contributions of the amygdala to emotion processing: From animal models to human behavior. *Neuron*, 48(2), 175–187.

Phelps, E. A., Ling, S., & Carrasco, M. (2006). Emotion facilitates perception and potentiates the perceptual benefits of attention. *Psychological Science*, 17(4), 292–299. doi: 10.1111/j.1467-9280.2006.01701.x.

Pichon, S., de Gelder, B., & Grèzes, J. (2008). Emotional modulation of visual and motor areas by dynamic body expressions of anger. *Social Neuroscience*, 3, 199–212.

(2009). Two different faces of threat: Comparing the neural systems for recognizing fear and anger in dynamic body expressions. *NeuroImage*, 47, 1873–1883.

(2012). Threat prompts defensive brain responses independently of attentional control. *Cerebral Cortex*, 22, 274–285.

Pouga, L., Berthoz, S., de Gelder, B., & Grèzes, J. (2010). Individual differences in socioaffective skills influence the neural bases of fear processing: The case of alexithymia. *Human Brain Mapping*, 31, 1469–1481.

Prehn-Kristensen, A., Wiesner, C., Bergmann, T. O., Wolff, S., Jansen, O., et al. (2009). Induction of empathy by the smell of anxiety. *PLoS One*, 4(6), e5987.

Provine, R. R. (2001). *Laughter: A scientific investigation.* London: Penguin.

(2005). Yawning: The yawn is primal, unstoppable and contagious, revealing the evolutionary and neural basis of empathy and unconscious behavior. *American Scientist*, 93(6), 532–539.

Qin, S., Young, C. B., Supekar, K., Uddin, L. Q., & Menon, V. (2012). Immature integration and segregation of emotion-related brain circuitry in young children. *Proceedings of the National Academy of Sciences*, 109, 7941–7946.

Rietveld, E., De Haans, S., & Denys, D. (2013). Social affordances in context: What is it that we are bodily responsive to? *Behavioral and Brain Sciences*, 36(4), 436.

Roy, A. K., Shehzad, Z., Margulies, D. S., Kelly, A. M. C., Uddin, L. Q., et al. (2009). Functional connectivity of the human amygdala using resting state fMRI. *NeuroImage*, 45, 614–626.

Sander, D., Grandjean, D., Kaiser, S., Wehrle, T., & Scherer, K. R. (2007). Interaction effects of perceived gaze direction and dynamic facial expression: Evidence for appraisal theories of emotion. *European Journal of Cognitive Psychology*, 19, 470–480.

Sato, W., Kochiyama, T., Yoshikawa, S., Naito, E., & Matsumura, M. (2004). Enhanced neural activity in response to dynamic facial expressions of emotion: An fMRI study. *Brain Research*, 20, 81–91.

Schnall, S., & Laird, J. D. (2007). Facing fear: Expression of fear facilitates processing of emotional information. *Social Behavior & Personality: An International Journal*, 35(4), 513–524.

Schutter, D. J. L. G., Hofman, D., & van Honk, J. (2008). Fearful faces selectively increase corticospinal motor tract excitability: A transcranial magnetic stimulation study. *Psychophysiology*, 45, 345–348.

Sighele, S. (1901). *La foule criminelle: Essai de psychologie collective.* F. Alcan.

Simner, M. L. (1971). Newborn's response to the cry of another infant. *Developmental Psychology*, 5(1), 136–150. doi: 10.1037/h0031066.

Smith, A. (1759 [2010]). *The theory of moral sentiments.* London: Penguin.

Soussignan, R. (2002). Duchenne smile, emotional experience, and autonomic reactivity: A test of the facial feedback hypothesis. *Emotion*, 2(1), 52.

Soussignan, R., Chadwick, M., Philip, L., Conty, L., Dezecache, G., & Grèzes, J. (2013). Self-relevance appraisal of gaze direction and dynamic facial expressions: Effects on facial electromyographic and autonomic reactions. *Emotion*, 13(2), 330–337. doi: 10.1037/a0029892.

Spengler, S., von Cramon, D. Y., & Brass, M. (2010). Resisting motor mimicry: Control of imitation involves processes central to social cognition in patients with frontal and temporo-parietal lesions. *Social Neuroscience*, 4, 401–416.

Stepper, S., & Strack, F. (1993). Proprioceptive determinants of emotional and non-emotional feelings. *Journal of Personality and Social Psychology*, 64(2), 211–220. doi: 10.1037/0022-3514.64.2.211.

Strack, F., Martin, L. L., & Stepper, S. (1988). Inhibiting and facilitating conditions of the human smile: A nonobtrusive test of the facial feedback hypothesis. *Journal of Personality and Social Psychology*, 54(5), 768.

Susskind, J. M., Lee, D. H., Cusi, A., Feiman, R., Grabski, W., & Anderson, A. K. (2008). Expressing fear enhances sensory acquisition. *Nature Neuroscience*, 11(7), 843–850.

Tamietto, M., Castelli, L., Vighetti, S., Perozzo, P., Geminiani, G., et al. (2009). Unseen facial and bodily expressions trigger fast emotional reactions. *Proceedings of the National Academy of Sciences*, 106(42), 17661–17666.

Tarde, G. (1890). *Les lois de l'imitation: étude sociologique*. Félix Alcan.

Uchino, B., Hsee, C. K., Hatfield, E., Carlson, J. G., & Chemtob, C. (1991). The effect of expectations on susceptibility to emotional contagion. Unpublished manuscript, University of Hawaii, Hawaii. www2.hawaii.edu/~elaineh/83.pdf.

Van den Stock, J., Tamietto, M., Sorger, B., Pichon, S., Grèzes, J., & de Gelder, B. (2011). Cortico-subcortical visual, somatosensory, and motor activations for perceiving dynamic whole-body emotional expressions with and without striate cortex (V1). *Proceedings of the National Academy of Sciences of the USA*, 108, 16188–16193.

Vermeulen, N., Godefroid, J., & Mermillod, M. (2009). Emotional modulation of attention: Fear increases but disgust reduces the attentional blink. *PLoS One*, 4(11), e7924. doi: 10.1371/journal.pone.0007924.

Vignemont, F. de, & Jacob, P. (2012). What is it like to feel another's pain? *Philosophy of Science*, 79(2), 295–316.

Voon, V., Brezing, C., Gallea, C., Ameli, R., Roelofs, K., et al. (2010). Emotional stimuli and motor conversion disorder. *Brain*, 133, 1526–1536.

Vuilleumier, P., Richardson, M. P., Armony, J. L., Driver, J., & Dolan, R. J. (2004) Distant influences of amygdala lesion on visual cortical activation during emotional face processing. *Nature Neuroscience*, 7(11), 1271–1278.

Warren, J. E., Sauter, D. A., Eisner, F., Wiland, J., Dresner, M. A., et al. (2006). Positive emotions preferentially engage an auditory-motor mirror system. *Journal of Neuroscience*, 26, 13067–13075.

Whalen, P. J., Rauch, S. L., Etcoff, N. L., McInerney, S. C., Lee, M. B., & Jenike, M. A. (1998). Masked presentations of emotional facial expressions modulate amygdala activity without explicit knowledge. *Journal of Neuroscience*, 18(1), 411–118.

Whalen, P. J., Shin, L. M., McInerney, S. C., Fischer, H., Wright, C. I., & Rauch, S. L. (2001). A functional MRI study of human amygdala responses to facial expressions of fear versus anger. *Emotion*, 1, 70–83.

in ASD has been mixed, however. While many studies have reported impaired recognition of others' facial emotion (Ashwin, Chapman, Colle, & Baron-Cohen, 2006; Humphreys, Minshew, Leonard, & Behrmann, 2007; Rump, Giovannelli, Minshew, & Strauss, 2009) and atypical AI and ACC function in these individuals (Di Martino et al., 2009; Uddin & Menon, 2009), a considerable amount of research has found no evidence for such deficits (Adolphs, Sears, & Piven, 2001; Castelli, 2005; Grossman, Klin, Carter, & Volkmar, 2000; Jones et al., 2011). Indeed, Harms et al. (2010) concluded from a review of the literature that 'behavioral studies are only slightly more likely to find facial emotion recognition deficits in autism than not' (p. 317). Similarly, studies of vocal emotion recognition in ASD have produced equivocal results (Golan, Baron-Cohen, Hill, & Rutherford, 2007; Jones et al., 2011; Loveland et al., 1997). The ability of individuals with ASD to identify others' affective states has therefore been a topic of great contention.

While the equivocal findings on emotion recognition impairments may be due, in part, to methodological differences (Harms et al., 2010), the co-occurrence of alexithymia with ASD may be of more use in disambiguating the literature. Although the incidence of alexithymia in the general population is thought to be at most 10 per cent (Linden, Wen, & Paulus, 1995; Salminen, Saarija, & Rela, 1999), severe degrees of alexithymia are suggested in approximately 50 per cent of individuals with ASD (Berthoz & Hill, 2005; Hill, Berthoz, & Frith, 2004; Lombardo, Barnes, Wheelwright, & Baron-Cohen, 2007). Importantly, despite their co-occurrence, alexithymia and autism are independent constructs; alexithymia is neither necessary nor sufficient for an autism diagnosis, nor is it universal among individuals with ASD. Similarly, many individuals with no diagnosis of ASD suffer severe alexithymia. The elevated levels of alexithymia in individuals with ASD are likely, however, to have meant that alexithymia and autism have been confounded in many studies comparing autistic and typical samples. It is therefore possible that group differences have been observed purely due to the fact that ASD groups are likely to comprise more individuals with severe levels of alexithymia than typical control groups.

In order to determine the independent contributions of alexithymia and autism symptom severity to emotion recognition abilities, Cook, Brewer, Shah, and Bird (2013) matched ASD and control groups according to alexithymia severity, eliminating the confound between ASD and alexithymia. Findings indicated that alexithymia, rather than autistic symptom severity itself, predicted ability to attribute emotion to facial expressions. ASD and alexithymia-matched control groups did not, therefore, differ in their emotion recognition ability. These findings suggest that accurate recognition of facial emotion relies upon severity of alexithymia, rather than the presence, or severity, of ASD symptoms. Alexithymia, rather than ASD, predicts attention to emotionally relevant areas of the face (Bird, Press, & Richardson, 2011). Similarly, where vocal affect is concerned, alexithymia again predicts one's recognition ability, while ASD does not (Heaton et al., 2012). These results are particularly helpful in disambiguating the inconsistent literature on emotion recognition in ASD; clearly, impairment should not be treated as a core feature of the disorder. Instead, it is likely that, at a group level, individuals with ASD exhibit emotion recognition deficits due to this subset of individuals suffering severe co-occurring alexithymia. Previously inconsistent findings are therefore likely explained by variation in alexithymia severity across ASD samples; in samples where alexithymia is more severe in the ASD than typical groups, due to the higher incidence in this population, impairments are likely to be observed, while in samples inadvertently matched for alexithymia, group differences are unlikely.

Empathy in Autism Spectrum Disorder

Beyond impairments recognizing others' emotions, it is also often assumed that individuals with ASD struggle to empathize with others (Baron-Cohen & Wheelwright, 2004; Minio-Paluello, Baron-Cohen, Avenanti, Walsh, & Aglioti, 2009; Shamay-Tsoory, Tomer, Yaniv, & Aharon-Peretz, 2002). Empathy is referred to as the ability to share others' emotional states (Decety & Lamm, 2006; Eisenberg, 2000; Preston & de Waal, 2002; Singer et al., 2006; de Vignemont & Singer, 2006) and involves both an affective component (emotion contagion, involving sharing the affect of other individuals) and a cognitive component (involving the distinction between the self and the other). Intuitively, affective empathy is likely to be atypical in individuals who struggle to process their own and others' emotions. Shared-network models of empathic processing posit that neural networks involved in the recognition of one's own emotions, such as the AI and ACC, are also relied upon for the representation of others' emotion (Cheng et al., 2007; Gu & Han, 2007; Jackson, Meltzoff, & Decety, 2005; Lamm, Decety, & Singer, 2011; Lamm, Nusbaum, Meltzoff, & Decety, 2007; Saarela et al., 2007; Singer et al., 2006). If the ability to represent one's own emotions is deficient, therefore, the ability to empathize with others' emotions should also be hampered (Singer & Lamm, 2009; Singer et al., 2004). Similarly, if one does not possess well-defined representations of emotional categories, identifying emotion accurately should be impossible, regardless of whether this is in the self or another, ultimately impacting on empathic accuracy.

Although some studies have reported decreased self-reported empathy in individuals with ASD (Baron-Cohen & Wheelwright, 2004; Johnson, Filliter, & Murphy, 2009; Lombardo et al., 2007), others have found affect-sharing abilities to be comparable with those in control samples (Dziobek et al., 2008;

Rogers, Dziobek, Hassenstab, Wolf, & Convit, 2007). Experimentally, individuals with ASD have been reported to exhibit less inhibition of corticospinal excitability during observation of others in pain than do typical individuals (Minio-Paluello et al., 2009), and decreased sharing of affect with characters in emotional vignettes (Yirmiya, Sigman, Kasari, & Mundy, 1992). As has been typical in the study of ASD, however, these studies failed to measure and account for alexithymia severity, making it difficult to determine the independent contribution of ASD symptom severity to these findings. As alexithymia is known to be closely associated with atypical empathy, its co-occurrence with ASD may account for these findings.

Silani et al. (2008) observed that, when alexithymia is measured, it is alexithymia, rather than autism itself, which predicts both self-reported empathy and anterior insula activity when one's own emotion must be represented, suggesting that atypical empathic responses arise in association with alexithymia, and therefore poor emotional awareness, rather than being a core feature of ASD. Alexithymia severity could predict anterior insula activity during this task to the same extent in both ASD and control groups, and individuals with ASD without co-occurring alexithymia exhibited typical insula responses, suggesting ASD itself does not impact upon empathic processes. These findings were extended in a study of empathy for others' pain, which limited demands on the emotion recognition and mentalizing processes often confounded with affective empathy in experimental paradigms. Bird et al. (2010) explicitly matched ASD and control groups according to alexithymia severity, in order that the two conditions were not confounded. Results indicated that both self-reported empathy and anterior insula activity when observing the pain of a close partner were predicted by alexithymia but not ASD symptom severity itself. Similarly, the ASD and control groups, having been matched according to alexithymia levels, exhibited comparable levels of insula activity; ASD does not, therefore, impact upon this empathic response itself.

Morality in Autism Spectrum Disorder

As alexithymia explains atypical empathy and emotion recognition in individuals with ASD, it follows that any process relying on these abilities should also be predicted by alexithymia, rather than ASD itself. Moral judgments appear to rely upon the human capacity for empathy (Bzdok et al., 2012); in order to determine whether a behavior is acceptable, it is first necessary to identify the emotion likely to be evoked in another in response to that behavior, and share this hypothetical affective state with the other. One's own aversive affective reaction to a victim's distress therefore leads to a judgment that any deliberate action which caused that distress is immoral (Avramova & Inbar, 2013; Haidt, 2001). In line with this view, automatic emotional reactions to victims' emotional states influence moral judgments (Haidt, 2001), and lead to condemnation of moral violations (Decety & Cacioppo, 2012; Hoffman, 2001; Pizarro, 2000). Neurological evidence also suggests that moral reasoning relies on empathy networks (Bzdok et al., 2012; Greene, 2003; Greene, Nystrom, Engell, Darley, & Cohen, 2004; Greene, Sommerville, Nystrom, Darley, & Cohen, 2001; Moll et al., 2002). That empathy deficits are a defining feature of psychopathy (Hare, 1991), and contribute to morally unacceptable behavior, or atypical condemnation of harm in these individuals (Blair, 2007; Soderstrom, 2003; Young, Koenigs, Kruepke, & Newman, 2012), further supports the association between empathy and morality. It is therefore likely that conditions associated with empathy deficits are also associated with atypical moral reasoning.

As the literature on empathy deficits in ASD is equivocal, it is unsurprising that findings concerning moral reasoning ability in this population have also been mixed. While some evidence suggests that moral judgments are atypical in ASD (Gleichgerrcht et al., 2013; Moran et al., 2011), this finding is far from consistent, with numerous reports of typical moral judgments in this population (Li, Zhu, & Gummerum, 2014; Schneider et al., 2013; Shulman, Guberman, Shiling, & Bauminger, 2012; Zalla, Barlassina, Buon, & Leboyer, 2011). As evidence now suggests that empathy deficits in ASD are, in fact, due to co-occurring alexithymia (Bird et al., 2010; Silani et al., 2008), it is likely that individual differences in alexithymia may again be responsible for previously inconsistent findings concerning morality. Indeed, in typical individuals, alexithymia is associated with utilitarian tendencies in moral decision-making tasks, due to reduced empathic concern for victims, as well as increased moral acceptability of accidentally harming others (Patil & Silani, 2014a, 2014b).

In order to determine whether atypical moral judgments are predicted by alexithymia, rather than ASD per se, Brewer et al. (2015b) again matched groups according to alexithymia severity, ensuring a broad range of alexithymia scores in typical and ASD samples. Participants judged the moral acceptability of saying emotionally evocative statements to another individual, and identified the emotion they would feel in response to each statement. While neither ASD diagnosis nor symptom severity affected judgments of moral acceptability, or ability to infer the emotion one would feel in given situations, increased alexithymia in the typical sample was associated with atypical moral acceptability judgments and emotion identification. Individuals with more severe alexithymia considered it more morally acceptable to anger, disgust and frighten others than those with low levels of alexithymia, likely due to their decreased comprehension of the negative state associated with these emotions. Interestingly, this relationship was not observed in the ASD group alone, suggesting that moral judgements in ASD may be based on information besides emotional understanding, such as social norms.

As well as increasing understanding of morality in ASD, these findings add to existing literature on the impact of alexithymia on moral reasoning in non-clinical populations (Patil & Silani, 2014a, 2014b). It seems that difficulties empathizing with others, due to poor identification of emotions in general, not only alter identification of others' emotions, but may also affect the emotions one elicits in others; increased alexithymia may lead to an increased tendency to cause distress to others during social interactions. Behaving in a morally acceptable manner is crucial for the development and maintenance of social relationships, meaning atypical moral judgments may add to the social difficulties experienced by individuals with severe alexithymia.

Emotion Recognition in Eating Disorders

While the findings discussed so far strongly implicate co-occurring alexithymia in emotion-related impairments in individuals with ASD, they do not allow conclusions to be drawn concerning the impact of alexithymia across multiple disorders. The fact that alexithymia co-occurs with numerous disorders besides ASD, however, as well as the fact that the literature on emotion processing is inconsistent in these disorders, suggests that alexithymia may account for atypical performance in these areas in numerous clinical populations.

Eating disorders (EDs) are characterized by disturbed and inappropriate patterns of eating (American Psychiatric Association, 2013), and are characterized as either anorexia nervosa (AN; associated with emaciation, distorted body image and a fear of gaining weight), bulimia nervosa (BN; associated with periods of bingeing, followed by inappropriate compensatory behavior), or binge eating disorder (BED; characterized by binge eating in the absence of the inappropriate compensatory behaviors associated with BN). Although not a diagnostic criterion, it is also widely believed that EDs are associated with atypical social and emotional functioning (Harrison, Sullivan, Tchanturia, & Treasure, 2010; Oldershaw et al., 2011). In particular, several authors have reported deficits of facial emotion recognition in individuals with AN and BN (Harrison, Sullivan, Tchanturia, & Treasure, 2009; Kucharska-Pietura, Nikolaou, Masiak, & Treasure, 2004; Legenbauer, Vocks, & Ruddel, 2008; Pollatos, Herbert, Schandry, & Gramann, 2008) and in non-clinical samples of women with high levels of ED symptomatology (Jones, Harmer, Cowen, & Cooper, 2008; Ridout, Thom, & Wallis, 2010). This evidence is disputed, however, by several reports of typical emotion recognition (Kessler, Schwarze, Filipic, Traue, & Wietersheim, 2006; Mendlewicz, Linkowski, Bazelmans, & Philippot,

2005; Zonnevylle-Bender, van Goozen, Cohen-Kettenis, van Elburg, & van Engeland, 2004). Two recent meta-analyses of emotion recognition in EDs (Caglar-Nazali et al., 2014; Oldershaw et al., 2011) highlighted the discrepancies between studies, noting that, where observed, group differences in the recognition of basic facial emotions are often small. Beyond methodological differences (Oldershaw et al., 2011), it is possible that differing levels of co-occurring alexithymia present in ED samples have again contributed to this inconsistent literature.

Alexithymia co-occurs with all ED subtypes (Carano et al., 2006; Rozenstein, Latzer, Stein, & Eviatar, 2011), and is associated with non-clinical ED symptoms (De Berardis et al., 2007; Ridout et al., 2010). As with ASD, despite high co-occurrence between EDs and alexithymia, these constructs are distinct (Quinton & Wagner, 2005). Interestingly, emotion recognition deficits and severe alexithymia have been reported in the same ED sample (Zonnevijlle-Bender, van Goozen, Cohen-Kettenis, van Elburg, & van Engeland, 2002), raising the possibility that alexithymia is responsible for emotion recognition difficulties in EDs. In order to determine whether difficulties recognizing facial emotion experienced by ED patients are not a symptom of EDs, but are instead due to alexithymia, Brewer Cook, Cardi, Treasure, and Bird (2015a) determined the ability of individuals with EDs and alexithymia-matched control individuals to recognize facial emotion, estimated by tolerance to high-frequency visual noise.

Consistent with the alexithymia hypothesis, the ED and alexithymia-matched control groups demonstrated comparable recognition of facial emotion and identity. Crucially, however, as in ASD samples, alexithymia, rather than ED symptom severity, predicted emotion recognition ability; severe alexithymia was associated with impaired emotion recognition, whereas ED diagnosis was unrelated to emotion recognition ability. Interestingly, this pattern of results held for recognition of facial happiness, as well as of negative emotions. Previous reports of intact positive emotion recognition in individuals with alexithymia (McDonald & Prkachin, 1990) may therefore reflect the ease with which happiness may be discriminated (happiness is often the only positive emotion studied, and happy expressions have highly distinctive local features; Calvo & Marrero, 2009). Having avoided ceiling effects for happiness recognition, these findings suggest that alexithymia is associated with affect recognition across all emotions. These findings suggest that, rather than being a core feature of EDs, emotion recognition impairment is explained by alexithymia. As seems to be the case in the ASD literature, heterogeneity of ED samples, with respect to alexithymia, is likely responsible for many of the contradictory findings reported previously. Where impaired emotion recognition has been observed, ED groups may have contained a greater proportion of individuals with severe alexithymia than control groups (e.g. Zonnevijlle-Bender et al., 2002).

As in ASD populations, the influence of co-occurring alexithymia in EDs may extend beyond expression recognition, potentially explaining a wide range of emotion-processing difficulties in this population. Indeed, alexithymia, rather than ED diagnosis, was associated with atypical performance in a validated empathy for pain paradigm (Brewer, Cook, Catmur & Bird, under review). Similarly, alexithymia was associated with impaired performance when judging protagonists' emotions from vignettes, in ED participants (Bydlowski et al., 2005) and individuals with non-clinical disordered eating (Ridout et al., 2010). While the independent contributions of ED and alexithymia were not addressed, these findings suggest that the impact of co-occurring alexithymia in ED samples may extend to broader socio-emotional abilities.

Impact of Alexithymia in Other Clinical Populations

While discussion thus far has focused on ASD and EDs, the alexithymia hypothesis (Bird & Cook, 2013) predicts that alexithymia has a similar impact in the numerous other clinical conditions with which it co-occurs, such as panic disorder, schizophrenia, post-traumatic stress disorder and substance abuse (Grynberg et al., 2012). The high levels of co-occurrence across a range of disorders, and the fact that alexithymia has already been shown to influence emotion processing in a similar way in individuals with ASD and EDs, as well as in typical populations, highlights the importance of screening for alexithymia in clinical settings. It is necessary to measure and account for alexithymia levels in order to independently determine the contributions of alexithymia and psychiatric diagnostic status to emotion recognition, empathy and moral reasoning atypicalities. If, as the alexithymia hypothesis predicts, alexithymia has a similar effect on these processes in all disorders, the need for emotion recognition and empathy interventions may be determined quickly and easily using standardized alexithymia questionnaires. Where the relationship between alexithymia and morality is concerned, such measures may contribute to decreasing the proportion of individuals with mental health issues currently in the criminal justice system (Singleton, Gatward, & Meltzer, 1998).

Selectivity of Impairment: Specific to Emotion, or General to Interoception?

Thus far, discussion has focused solely on the representation of emotional states, as has been typical in the domain of alexithymia research. Recent evidence suggests, however, that individuals with alexithymia may, in fact, misrepresent all interoceptive states. Alexithymia severity predicts, for example, the extent to which individuals report difficulty interpreting bodily states that do not involve emotion, such as hunger, temperature, proprioception and heart rate (Brewer, Cook, & Bird, under review). Further, while some emotional and bodily states share common interoceptive signals, such as anger and heat, individuals with severe alexithymia report more extreme degrees of overlap between these states than do individuals with low alexithymia, indicative of difficulty discriminating between affective and non-affective states (Brewer et al., under review). Similarly, alexithymia is associated with decreased awareness of one's own heart rate (Herbert, Herbert, & Pollatos, 2011), increased caffeine consumption (Lyvers, Duric, & Thorberg, 2014) and delayed seeking medical treatment in response to acute myocardial infarction (Carta et al., 2013; Kenyon, Ketterer, Gheorghiade, & Goldstein, 1991), suggestive of decreased awareness of internal states. Together, these findings suggest that alexithymia may be better characterized as a general deficit of interoceptive awareness than as an affective disorder. If this is the case, its relevance may be great among diagnoses associated with impaired awareness of interoceptive states besides emotions, for example in developmental coordination disorder. Indeed, the co-occurrence with EDs (both bingeing and restricting types) may be better understood by the fact that individuals with alexithymia may struggle to register signals of hunger or satiety, the association between alexithymia and substance abuse by poor recognition of signals of intoxication or reward, and the link between alexithymia and diabetes by the association between alexithymia and poor glycaemic control in these individuals (Abramson, McClelland, Brown, & Kelner, 1991), likely due to decreased interoceptive awareness. Indeed, recent work suggests that alexithymia predicts awareness of one's own heart beat in those with ASD (Shah, Hall, Catmur, & Bird, 2016). If it is the case that alexithymia is associated with a general interoceptive deficit, it is likely to have a significant impact on individuals' physical, as well as mental, health, through decreased the awareness of internal signals. Reduced identification of disease-related information, as well as difficulty communicating this information, is likely to lead to delayed seeking of medical attention, allowing diseases to progress, increasing disease severity and, in many cases, mortality rate.

The Association between Emotion Identification in the Self and Others

While it makes intuitive sense that difficulties representing one's own emotions (alexithymia) should be related to atypical representation of others' emotion, in the form of emotion recognition and empathy, little evidence thus far has enabled the mechanism linking these processes to be determined. Although it is clear that one's own and others' emotions are processed using the same neural networks (Etkin et al., 2011; Singer et al., 2009), suggesting emotional representations are activated in a similar way during both processes, evidence concerning the causal link is absent. One possibility is that individuals develop emotional categories based not only on their own visceral sensations, but also on interactions with the environment (e.g. Mesquita & Fijda, 1992). For example, caregivers may suggest likely interpretations of a child's emotional state. Similarly, information from the social situation, physical context and cues present in others' facial and vocal affect may also shape the emergence of emotional categories. Once acquired, these emotional categories may inform our interpretation of others' emotional states. Bird and Viding's (2014) learning model of affective representation, for example, suggests that differentiated affective states in the self must be acquired before these states can be associated with cues to the same states in others. Conversely, it may be the case that individuals observe others' emotional expressions, in combination with information concerning the emotion being experienced, and eventually map emotional concepts developed through observation onto the internal states of the self. Determining the mechanisms underlying the connection between the representations of own and other emotional states is a priority for future work, as it is necessary to understand the causal nature of the relationship in order to intervene appropriately; identifying the direction of a causal relationship means that impairment in the causal domain may be targeted, and should lead to improvement in the affected domain.

Origins of the Co-Occurrence between Alexithymia and Disorders

Despite recent findings disambiguating the inconsistent literature on emotion processing in ASD and EDs, and potentially across numerous disorders, it remains to be seen *why* alexithymia co-occurs so frequently with clinical disorders. It is of note that, although emotion recognition and empathy deficits in these populations may be attributed to the co-occurrence of alexithymia, individuals suffering from these disorders are more likely to exhibit these impairments, purely due to the fact that alexithymia rates are elevated among these groups relative to typical individuals. Whether alexithymia and clinical disorders share common causes, or whether one leads to the other is yet to be determined. Moreover, whether the relationship between alexithymia and disorder symptomatology is identical across the different disorders is also unclear.

It is clear that neurodevelopmental disorders frequently co-occur (Leyfer et al., 2006; Pauc, 2005), but the underlying causes of this co-occurrence are thus far unclear. Similarly, the origins of co-occurrence between alexithymia and clinical disorders remain to be determined. In the case of ASD, it has been speculated that a genetic vulnerability to suboptimal neural connectivity may characterize several disorders, and that different phenotypes arise depending on the locus of such poor connectivity (Bird & Cook, 2013). If, for example, affected networks are involved in social cognition and cognitive control, a 'pure' ASD phenotype may emerge, while if limbic structures are affected specifically, a 'pure' alexithymia phenotype may emerge. More typically, however, poor connectivity may affect numerous networks, leading to the co-occurrence of ASD and alexithymia. When other disorders emerge due to decreased connectivity within particular regions, a similar pattern may emerge. Although empirical evidence is lacking, this speculation is consistent with evidence for reduced neural connectivity in ASD (Frith, 2003; Geschwind & Levitt, 2007), as well as schizophrenia (Cook, Barbalat, & Blakemore, 2012; Fitzsimmons, Kubicki, & Shenton, 2013).

The 'reduced connectivity' explanation may not be relevant for all disorders, however; different theories have been proposed concerning the link between alexithymia and EDs. Many researchers have proposed that the symptoms of EDs, such as bingeing, purging, restricting food intake and excessive exercise, are used as strategies to regulate and suppress negative affective states (Cooper, Wells, & Todd, 2004; Overton, Selway, Strongman, & Houston, 2005; Schmidt & Treasure, 2006). As individuals with alexithymia are likely to struggle to regulate emotional states in a typical manner, through limited ability to identify the emotion that requires regulation, they may resort to atypical strategies, such as disordered eating behaviors. It is therefore possible that alexithymia precedes EDs, and contributes to their development. Indeed, cognitive models of anorexia nervosa identify decreased awareness of one's own emotions as a significant risk factor (Connan, Campbell, Katzman, Lightman, & Treasure, 2003). Of note here is the fact that, if alexithymia is characterized as a general deficit of interoception, it may be relatively easy for individuals with alexithymia to develop and maintain ED behaviors, due to decreased awareness of signals of hunger, satiety and exhaustion. Interestingly, social functioning deficits, which are likely to arise in individuals with alexithymia, may maintain ED behaviors (Fairburn & Harrison, 2003). It has also been argued that alexithymia may contribute to ED development and maintenance through lowering mood and self-esteem, which in turn leads to body dissatisfaction and therefore ED behaviors (Eizaguirre, Saenz de Cabezon, Ochoa de Alda, Olariaga, & Juaniz, 2004). Conversely, while little evidence has investigated this possibility, it is possible that alexithymia emerges as a consequence of EDs, due to the fact that individuals attempting to restrict food intake must suppress signals of hunger, and negative affect associated with this state, potentially causing reduced interoception, and, in turn, alexithymia. Finally, alternative factors may lead independently to the development of alexithymia and EDs, whether these are genetic factors, or environmental factors such as decreased expression of emotion in families of ED patients (Esparon & Yellowlees, 1992).

While studies have attempted to characterize the relationship between alexithymia and disorder symptoms, debate remains as to whether alexithymia develops alongside, contributes to or develops as a consequence of clinical disorders, and the relationship is not necessarily identical in all clinical populations. Research concerning the genetic and environmental contributions to alexithymia and all relevant disorders, as well as longitudinal work, is therefore necessary in order to determine the nature of the relationship.

Conclusion

Despite inconsistent findings concerning emotion recognition and empathy in ASD and EDs, recent findings suggest that co-occurring alexithymia can account for previous equivocal results; alexithymia, rather than disorder symptom severity itself, predicts the ability to represent others' emotional states. While replication in other clinical populations is clearly necessary, as well as research into the reasons for co-occurrence, it is likely that alexithymia contributes towards these impairments across all disorders with which it co-occurs. Consistent with the concept of shared representations, it seems that difficulties representing one's own emotions are intrinsically linked to difficulties representing those of others. In order to independently determine the contribution of a specific disorder and alexithymia to any process relying on emotion processing, it is imperative that researchers match clinical and control groups according to alexithymia severity, and separately investigate the relationship of each with emotion-processing abilities. Beyond generalizing the impact of alexithymia to other clinical groups, it seems likely that its presence extends to difficulty understanding and identifying all interoceptive states, rather than simply affective states. It is therefore crucial that research concerning the ability to identify these states, as well as emotions, takes alexithymia into account in order to accurately interpret results. If it is the case, as we suggest, that alexithymia accounts for all interoceptive difficulties, its impact will be significant across a broad range of medical research and practice.

References

Abramson, L., McClelland, D. C., Brown, D., & Kelner, S. (1991). Alexithymic characteristics and metabolic control in diabetic and healthy adults. *Journal of Nervous and Mental Disease*, 179(8), 179.

Adolphs, R., Sears, L., & Piven, J. (2001). Abnormal processing of social information from faces in autism. *Journal of Cognitive Neuroscience*, 13(2), 232–240.

American Psychiatric Association. (2013). *Diagnostic and statistical manual of mental disorder* (5th edition). Arlington, VA: American Psychiatric Publishing.

Ashwin, C., Chapman, E., Colle, L., & Baron-Cohen, S. (2006). Impaired recognition of negative basic emotions in autism: A test of the amygdala theory. *Social Neuroscience*, 1(3–4), 349–363.

Avramova, Y. R., & Inbar, Y. (2013). Emotion and moral judgment. *Wiley Interdisciplinary Reviews: Cognitive Science*, 4(2), 169–178.

Baron-Cohen, S., & Wheelwright, S. (2004). The empathy quotient: An investigation of adults with Asperger syndrome or high functioning autism, and normal sex differences. *Journal of Autism and Developmental Disorders*, 34(2), 163–175.

Berthoz, S., & Hill, E. L. (2005). The validity of using self-reports to assess emotion regulation abilities in adults with autism spectrum disorder. *European Psychiatry: The Journal of the Association of European Psychiatrists*, 20(3), 291–298.

Bird, G., & Cook, R. (2013). Mixed emotions: The contribution of alexithymia to the emotional symptoms of autism. *Translational Psychiatry*, 3(7), e285.

Bird, G., Press, C., & Richardson, D. C. (2011). The role of alexithymia in reduced eye-fixation in autism spectrum conditions. *Journal of Autism and Developmental Disorders*, 41(11), 1556–1564.

Bird, G., Silani, G., Brindley, R., White, S., Frith, U., & Singer, T. (2010). Empathic brain responses in insula are modulated by levels of alexithymia but not autism. *Brain: A Journal of Neurology*, 133(Pt 5), 1515–1525.

Bird, G., & Viding, E. (2014). The self to other model of empathy: Providing a new framework for understanding empathy impairments in psychopathy, autism, and alexithymia. *Neuroscience & Biobehavioral Reviews*, 47, 520–532.

Blair, R. J. R. (2007). The amygdala and ventromedial prefrontal cortex in morality and psychopathy. *Trends in Cognitive Sciences*, 11(9), 387–392.

Brewer, R., Cook, R., & Bird, G. (under review). Alexithymia predicts general deficits of interoception across clinical disorders.

Brewer, R., Cook, R., Cardi, V., Treasure, J., & Bird, G. (2015a). Emotion recognition deficits in eating disorders are explained by co-occurring alexithymia. *Royal Society Open Science*, 2(1), 1–12.

Brewer, R., Cook, R., Catmur, C., & Bird, G. (under review). Alexithymia explains atypical empathy in eating disorders.

Brewer, R., Marsh, A. A., Catmur, C., Cardinale, E. M., Stoycos, S., et al. (2015b). Judgments of moral acceptability in autism are predicted by co-occurring alexithymia. *Journal of Abnormal Psychology*, 124(3), 589–595.

Bydlowski, S., Corcos, M., Jeammet, P., Paterniti, S., Berthoz, S., et al. (2005). Emotion-processing deficits in eating disorders. *International Journal of Eating Disorders*, 37(4), 321–329.

Bzdok, D., Schilbach, L., Vogeley, K., Schneider, K., Laird, A. R., et al. (2012). Parsing the neural correlates of moral cognition: ALE meta-analysis on morality, theory of mind, and empathy. *Brain Structure & Function*, 217(4), 783–796.

Caglar-Nazali, H. P., Corfield, F., Cardi, V., Ambwani, S., Leppanen, J., et al. (2014). A systematic review and meta-analysis of 'systems for social processes' in eating disorders. *Neuroscience and Biobehavioral Reviews*, 42, 55–92.

Calvo, M. G., & Marrero, H. (2009). Visual search of emotional faces: The role of affective content and featural distinctiveness. *Cognition & Emotion*, 23(4), 782–806.

Carano, A., De Berardis, D., Gambi, F., Di Paolo, C., Campanella, D., et al. (2006). Alexithymia and body image in adult outpatients with binge eating disorder. *International Journal of Eating Disorders*, 39, 332–340.

Carta, M. G., Sancassiani, F., Pippia, V., Bhat, K. M., Sardu, C., & Meloni, L. (2013). Alexithymia is associated with delayed treatment seeking in acute myocardial infarction. *Psychotherapy and Psychosomatics*, 82(3), 190–192.

Castelli, F. (2005). Understanding emotions from standardized facial expressions in autism and normal development. *Autism: The International Journal of Research and Practice*, 9(4), 428–449.

Cheng, Y., Lin, C.-P., Liu, H.-L., Hsu, Y.-Y., Lim, K.-E., et al. (2007). Expertise modulates the perception of pain in others. *Current Biology*, 17(19), 1708–1713.

Connan, F., Campbell, I. C., Katzman, M., Lightman, S. L., & Treasure, J. (2003). A neurodevelopmental model for anorexia nervosa. *Physiology and Behaviour*, 79, 13–24.

Cook, J., Barbalat, G., & Blakemore, S.-J. (2012). Top-down modulation of the perception of other people in schizophrenia and autism. *Frontiers in Human Neuroscience*, 6, 175.

Cook, R., Brewer, R., Shah, P., & Bird, G. (2013). Alexithymia, not autism, predicts poor recognition of emotional facial expressions. *Psychological Science*, 24(5), 723–732.

Cooper, M. J., Wells, A., & Todd, G. (2004). A cognitive model of bulimia nervosa. *British Journal of Clinical Psychology*, 43(Pt 1), 1–16.

Craig, A. D. (2009). How do you feel now? The anterior insula and human awareness. *Nature Reviews Neuroscience*, 10(1), 59–70.

De Berardis, D., Carano, A., Gambi, F., Campanella, D., Giannetti, P., et al. (2007). Alexithymia and its relationships with body checking and body image in a nonclinical female sample. *Eating Behaviors*, 8(3), 296–304.

Decety, J., & Cacioppo, S. (2012). The speed of morality: A high-density electrical neuroimaging study. *Journal of Neurophysiology*, 108(11), 3068–3072.

Decety, J., & Lamm, C. (2006). Human empathy through the lens of social neuroscience. *Scientific World Journal*, 6, 1146–1163.

Di Martino, A., Ross, K., Uddin, L. Q., Sklar, A. B., Castellanos, F. X., & Milham, M. P. (2009). Functional brain correlates of social and nonsocial processes in autism spectrum disorders: An activation likelihood estimation meta-analysis. *Biological Psychiatry*, 65(1), 63–74.

Dziobek, I., Rogers, K., Fleck, S., Bahnemann, M., Heekeren, H. R., et al. (2008). Dissociation of cognitive and emotional empathy in adults with Asperger syndrome using the Multifaceted Empathy Test (MET). *Journal of Autism and Developmental Disorders*, 38(3), 464–473.

Eisenberg, N. (2000). Emotion, regulation, and moral development. *Annual Review of Psychology*, 51, 665–697.

Eizaguirre, A. E., Saenz de Cabezon, A. O., Ochoa de Alda, I., Olariaga, L. J., & Juaniz, M. (2004). Alexithymia and its relationships with anxiety and depression in eating disorders. *Personality and Individual Differences*, 36, 321–331.

Esparon, J., & Yellowlees, A. J. (1992). Perceived parental rearing practices and eating disorders. *British Review of Bulimia & Anorexia Nervosa*, 6(1), 39–45.

Etkin, A., Egner, T., & Kalisch, R. (2011). Emotional processing in anterior cingulate and medial prefrontal cortex. *Trends in Cognitive Sciences*, 15(2), 85–93.

Fairburn, C. G., & Harrison, P. J. (2003). Eating disorders. *Lancet*, 361(9355), 407–416.

FeldmanHall, O., Dalgleish, T., & Mobbs, D. (2013). Alexithymia decreases altruism in real social decisions. *Cortex*, 49(3), 899–904.

Fitzsimmons, J., Kubicki, M., & Shenton, M. E. (2013). Review of functional and anatomical brain connectivity findings in schizophrenia. *Current Opinion in Psychiatry*, 26(2), 172–187.

Frith, C. (2003). What do imaging studies tell us about the neural basis of autism? *Novartis Foundation Symposium*, 251, 149–166.

Geschwind, D. H., & Levitt, P. (2007). Autism spectrum disorders: Developmental disconnection syndromes. *Current Opinion in Neurobiology*, 17(1), 103–111.

Gleichgerrcht, E., Torralva, T., Rattazzi, A., Marenco, V., Roca, M., & Manes, F. (2013). Selective impairment of cognitive empathy for moral judgment in adults with high functioning autism. *Social Cognitive and Affective Neuroscience*, 8(7), 780–788.

Golan, O., Baron-Cohen, S., Hill, J. J., & Rutherford, M. D. (2007). The 'Reading the Mind in the Voice' test–revised: A study of complex emotion recognition in adults with and without autism spectrum conditions. *Journal of Autism and Developmental Disorders*, 37(6), 1096–1106.

Greene, J. (2003). From neural 'is' to moral 'ought': What are the moral implications of neuroscientific moral psychology? *Nature Reviews Neuroscience*, 4(10), 846–849.

Greene, J. D., Nystrom, L. E., Engell, A. D., Darley, J. M., & Cohen, J. D. (2004). The neural bases of cognitive conflict and control in moral judgment. *Neuron*, 44(2), 389–400.

Greene, J. D., Sommerville, R. B., Nystrom, L. E., Darley, J. M., & Cohen, J. D. (2001). An fMRI investigation of emotional engagement in moral judgment. *Science*, 293(5537), 2105–2108.

Grossman, J. B., Klin, A., Carter, A. S., & Volkmar, F. R. (2000). Verbal bias in recognition of facial emotions in children with Asperger syndrome. *Journal of Child Psychology and Psychiatry*, 41(3), 369–379.

Grynberg, D., Chang, B., Corneille, O., Maurage, P., Vermeulen, N., et al. (2012). Alexithymia and the processing of emotional facial expressions (EFEs): Systematic review, unanswered questions and further perspectives. *PloS One*, 7(8), e42429.

Grynberg, D., Luminet, O., Corneille, O., Grèzes, J., & Berthoz, S. (2010). Alexithymia in the interpersonal domain: A general deficit of empathy? *Personality and Individual Differences*, 49(8), 845–850.

Gu, X., & Han, S. (2007). Attention and reality constraints on the neural processes of empathy for pain. *NeuroImage*, 36(1), 256–267.

Haidt, J. (2001). The emotional dog and its rational tail: A social intuitionist approach to moral judgment. *Psychological Review*, 108(4), 814–834.

Hare, R. D. (1991). *The Hare psychopathy checklist – revised*. North Tonawanda, NY: Multi-Health Systems.

Harms, M. B., Martin, A., & Wallace, G. L. (2010). Facial emotion recognition in autism spectrum disorders: A review of behavioral and neuroimaging studies. *Neuropsychology Review*, 20(3), 290–322.

Harrison, A., Sullivan, S., Tchanturia, K., & Treasure, J. (2009). Emotion recognition and regulation in anorexia nervosa. *Clinical Psychology and Psychotherapy*, 356(16), 348–356.

    (2010). Emotional functioning in eating disorders: Attentional bias, emotion recognition and emotion regulation. *Psychological Medicine*, 40(11), 1887–1897.

Heaton, P., Reichenbacher, L., Sauter, D., Allen, R., Scott, S., & Hill, E. (2012). Measuring the effects of alexithymia on perception of emotional vocalizations in autistic spectrum disorder and typical development. *Psychological Medicine*, 42, 2453–2459.

Herbert, B. M., Herbert, C., & Pollatos, O. (2011). On the relationship between interoceptive awareness and alexithymia: Is interoceptive awareness related to emotional awareness? *Journal of Personality*, 79(5), 1149–1175.

Hill, E., Berthoz, S., & Frith, U. (2004). Brief report: Cognitive processing of own emotions in individuals with autistic spectrum disorder and in their relatives. *Journal of Autism and Developmental Disorders*, 34(2), 229–235.

Hoffman, M. L. (2001). *Empathy and moral development: Implications for caring and justice*. Cambridge: Cambridge University Press.

Humphreys, K., Minshew, N., Leonard, G. L., & Behrmann, M. (2007). A fine-grained analysis of facial expression processing in high-functioning adults with autism. *Neuropsychologia*, 45(4), 685–695.

Ihme, K., Dannlowski, U., Lichev, V., Stuhrmann, A., Grotegerd, D., et al. (2013). Alexithymia is related to differences in gray matter volume: A voxel-based morphometry study. *Brain Research*, 1491, 60–67.

Jackson, P. L., Meltzoff, A. N., & Decety, J. (2005). How do we perceive the pain of others? A window into the neural processes involved in empathy. *NeuroImage*, 24(3), 771–779.

Jessimer, M., & Markham, R. (1997). Alexithymia: A right hemisphere dysfunction specific to recognition of certain facial expressions? *Brain and Cognition*, 34(2), 246–258.

Johnson, S. A., Filliter, J. H., & Murphy, R. R. (2009). Discrepancies between self- and parent-perceptions of autistic traits and empathy in high functioning children and adolescents on the autism spectrum. *Journal of Autism and Developmental Disorders*, 39(12), 1706–1714.

Jonason, P. K., & Krause, L. (2013). The emotional deficits associated with the Dark Triad traits: Cognitive empathy, affective empathy, and alexithymia. *Personality and Individual Differences*, 55(5), 532–537.

Jones, C. R. G., Pickles, A., Falcaro, M., Marsden, A. J. S., Happé, F., et al. (2011). A multimodal approach to emotion recognition ability in autism spectrum disorders. *Journal of Child Psychology and Psychiatry, and Allied Disciplines*, 52(3), 275–285.

Jones, L., Harmer, C., Cowen, P., & Cooper, M. (2008). Emotional face processing in women with high and low levels of eating disorder related symptoms. *Eating Behaviors*, 9(4), 389–397.

Kano, M., Fukado, S., Jiro, G., Kamachi, M., Tagawa, M., et al. (2003). Specific brain processing of facial expressions in people with alexithymia: An H215O-PET study. *Brain*, 126(6), 1474–1484.

Kenyon, L. W., Ketterer, M. W., Gheorghiade, M., & Goldstein, S. (1991). Psychological factors related to prehospital delay during acute myocardial infarction. *Circulation*, 84(5), 1969–1976.

Kessler, H., Schwarze, M., Filipic, S., Traue, H. C., & Wietersheim, J. von. (2006). Alexithymia and facial emotion recognition in patients with eating disorders. *International Journal of Eating Disorders*, 39(3), 245–251.

Kucharska-Pietura, K., Nikolaou, V., Masiak, M., & Treasure, J. (2004). The recognition of emotion in the faces and voice of anorexia nervosa. *International Journal of Eating Disorders*, 35(1), 42–47.

Lamm, C., Decety, J., & Singer, T. (2011). Meta-analytic evidence for common and distinct neural networks associated with directly experienced pain and empathy for pain. *NeuroImage*, 54(3), 2492–502.

Lamm, C., Nusbaum, H. C., Meltzoff, A. N., & Decety, J. (2007). What are you feeling? Using functional magnetic resonance imaging to assess the modulation of sensory and affective responses during empathy for pain. *PloS One*, 2(12), e1292.

Lamm, C., & Singer, T. (2010). The role of anterior insular cortex in social emotions. *Brain Structure & Function*, 214(5–6), 579–591.

Lane, R. D., Ahern, G. L., Schwartz, G. E., & Kaszniak, A. W. (1997). Is alexithymia the emotional equivalent of blindsight? *Biological Psychiatry*, 42(9), 834–844.

Legenbauer, T., Vocks, S., & Ruddel, H. (2008). Emotion recognition, emotional awareness and cognitive bias in individuals with bulimia nervosa. *Journal of Clinical Psychology*, 64(6), 687–702.

Leyfer, O. T., Folstein, S. E., Bacalman, S., Davis, N. O., Dinh, E., et al. (2006). Comorbid psychiatric disorders in children with autism: Interview development and rates of disorders. *Journal of Autism and Developmental Disorders*, 36(7), 849–861.

Li, J., Zhu, L., & Gummerum, M. (2014). The relationship between moral judgment and cooperation in children with high-functioning autism. *Scientific Reports*, 4, 4314.

Linden, W., Wen, F., & Paulus, D. L. (1995). Measuring alexithymia: Reliability, validity, and prevalence. In J. Butcher & C. Spielberger (Eds.), *Advances in personality assessment*. Hillsdale, NJ: Lawrence Erlbaum, 51–95.

Lombardo, M. V., Barnes, J. L., Wheelwright, S. J., & Baron-Cohen, S. (2007). Self-referential cognition and empathy in autism. *PloS One*, 2(9), e883.

Loveland, K. A., Tunali-Kotoski, B., Chen, Y. R., Ortegon, J., Pearson, D. A., et al. (1997). Emotion recognition in autism: Verbal and nonverbal information. *Development and Psychopathology*, 9(3), 579–593.

Lyvers, M., Duric, N., & Thorberg, F. A. (2014). Caffeine use and alexithymia in university students. *Journal of Psychoactive Drugs*, 46(4), 340–346.

McDonald, P. W., & Prkachin, K. M. (1990). The expression and perception of facial emotion in alexithymia: A pilot study. *Psychosomatic Medicine*, 52(2), 199–210.

Mendlewicz, L., Linkowski, P., Bazelmans, C., & Philippot, P. (2005). Decoding emotional facial expressions in depressed and anorexic patients. *Journal of Affective Disorders*, 89(1–3), 195–199.

Mesquita, B., & Fijda, N. H. (1992). Cultural variations in emotions: A review. *Psychological Bulletin*, 112(2), 179–204.

Minio-Paluello, I., Baron-Cohen, S., Avenanti, A., Walsh, V., & Aglioti, S. M. (2009). Absence of embodied empathy during pain observation in Asperger syndrome. *Biological Psychiatry*, 65(1), 55–62.

Moll, J., de Oliveira-Souza, R., Eslinger, P. J., Bramati, I. E., Mourão-Miranda, J., et al. (2002). The neural correlates of moral sensitivity: A functional magnetic resonance imaging investigation of basic and moral emotions. *Journal of Neuroscience*, 22(7), 2730–2736.

Moran, J. M., Young, L. L., Saxe, R., Lee, S. M., O'Young, D., et al. (2011). Impaired theory of mind for moral judgment in high-functioning autism. *Proceedings of the National Academy of Sciences of the United States of America*, 108(7), 2688–2692.

Moriguchi, Y., Decety, J., Ohnishi, T., Maeda, M., Mori, T., et al. (2007). Empathy and judging others' pain: An fMRI study of alexithymia. *Cerebral Cortex*, 17(9), 2223–2234.

Nemiah, J. C., Freyberger, H. J., & Sifneos, P. E. (1976). Alexithymia: A view of the psychosomatic process. In O. W. Hill (Ed.), *Modern trends in psychosomatic research*, Volume 3. London: Butterworths, 430–439.

Oldershaw, A., Hambrook, D., Stahl, D., Tchanturia, K., Treasure, J., & Schmidt, U. (2011). The socio-emotional processing stream in anorexia nervosa. *Neuroscience and Biobehavioral Reviews*, 35(3), 970–988.

Overton, A., Selway, S., Strongman, K., & Houston, M. (2005). Eating disorders? The regulation of positive as well as negative emotion experience. *Journal of Clinical Psychology in Medical Settings*, 12(1), 39–56.

Parker, J. D. A., Taylor, G. J., & Bagby, R. (1993). Alexithymia and the recognition of facial expressions of emotion. *Psychotherapy and Psychosomatics*, 59, 197–202.

Parker, P. D., Prkachin, K. M., & Prkachin, G. C. (2005). Processing of facial expressions of negative emotion in alexithymia: The influence of temporal constraint. *Journal of Personality*, 73(4), 1087–1107.

Patil, I., & Silani, G. (2014a). Alexithymia increases moral acceptability of accidental harms. *Journal of Cognitive Psychology*, 26(5), 1–18.

(2014b). Reduced empathic concern leads to utilitarian moral judgments in trait alexithymia. *Frontiers in Psychology*, 5, 501.

Pauc, R. (2005). Comorbidity of dyslexia, dyspraxia, attention deficit disorder (ADD), attention deficit hyperactive disorder (ADHD), obsessive compulsive disorder (OCD) and Tourette's syndrome in children: A prospective epidemiological study. *Clinical Chiropractic*, 8(4), 189–198.

Pizarro, D. (2000). Nothing more than feelings? The role of emotions in moral judgment. *Journal for the Theory of Social Behaviour*, 30(4), 355–375.

Pollatos, O., Herbert, B. M., Schandry, R., & Gramann, K. (2008). Impaired central processing of emotional faces in anorexia nervosa. *Psychosomatic Medicine*, 70(6), 701–708.

Preston, S. D., & de Waal, F. B. M. (2002). Empathy: Its ultimate and proximate bases. *Behavioral and Brain Sciences*, 25, 1–71.

Prkachin, G. C., Casey, C., & Prkachin, K. M. (2009). Alexithymia and perception of facial expressions of emotion. *Personality and Individual Differences*, 46(4), 412–417.

Quinton, S., & Wagner, H. L. (2005). Alexithymia, ambivalence over emotional expression, and eating attitudes. *Personality and Individual Differences*, 38(5), 1163–1173.

Ridout, N., Thom, C., & Wallis, D. J. (2010). Emotion recognition and alexithymia in females with non-clinical disordered eating. *Eating Behaviors*, 11(1), 1–5.

Rogers, K., Dziobek, I., Hassenstab, J., Wolf, O. T., & Convit, A. (2007). Who cares? Revisiting empathy in Asperger syndrome. *Journal of Autism and Developmental Disorders*, 37(4), 709–715.

Rozenstein, M. H., Latzer, Y., Stein, D., & Eviatar, Z. (2011). Perception of emotion and bilateral advantage in women with eating disorders, their healthy sisters, and nonrelated healthy controls. *Journal of Affective Disorders*, 134(1–3), 386–395.

Rump, K. M., Giovannelli, J. L., Minshew, N. J., & Strauss, M. S. (2009). The development of emotion recognition in individuals with autism. *Child Development*, 80(5), 1434–1447.

Saarela, M. V, Hlushchuk, Y., Williams, A. C. D. C., Schürmann, M., Kalso, E., & Hari, R. (2007). The compassionate brain: Humans detect intensity of pain from another's face. *Cerebral Cortex*, 17(1), 230–237.

Salminen, J. K., Saarija, S., & Rela, E. A. A. (1999). Prevalence of alexithymia and its association with sociodemographic variables in the general population of Finland. *Journal of Psychosomatic Research*, 46(1), 75–82.

Schmidt, U., & Treasure, J. (2006). Anorexia nervosa: Valued and visible. A cognitive-interpersonal maintenance model and its implications for research and practice. *British Journal of Clinical Psychology*, 45(3), 343–366.

Schneider, K., Pauly, K. D., Gossen, A., Mevissen, L., Michel, T. M., et al. (2013). Neural correlates of moral reasoning in autism spectrum disorder. *Social Cognitive and Affective Neuroscience*, 8(6), 702–710.

Shah, P., Hall, R., Catmur, C., & Bird, G. (2016). Alexithymia, not autism, is associated with impaired interoception. *Cortex*, 81, 215-220.

Shamay-Tsoory, S. G., Tomer, R., Yaniv, S., & Aharon-Peretz, J. (2002). Empathy deficits in Asperger syndrome: A cognitive profile. *Neurocase*, 8(3), 245–252.

Shulman, C., Guberman, A., Shiling, N., & Bauminger, N. (2012). Moral and social reasoning in autism spectrum disorders. *Journal of Autism and Developmental Disorders*, 42(7), 1364–1376.

Silani, G., Bird, G., Brindley, R., Singer, T., Frith, C., & Frith, U. (2008). Levels of emotional awareness and autism: An fMRI study. *Social Neuroscience*, 3(2), 97–112.

Singer, T., Critchley, H. D., & Preuschoff, K. (2009). A common role of insula in feelings, empathy and uncertainty. *Trends in Cognitive Sciences*, 13(8), 334–340.

Singer, T., & Lamm, C. (2009). The social neuroscience of empathy. *Annals of the New York Academy of Sciences*, 1156, 81–96.

Singer, T., Seymour, B., O'Doherty, J., Kaube, H., Dolan, R. J., & Frith, C. D. (2004). Empathy for pain involves the affective but not sensory components of pain. *Science*, 303(5661), 1157–1162.

Singer, T., Seymour, B., O'Doherty, J. P., Stephan, K. E., Dolan, R. J., & Frith, C. D. (2006). Empathic neural responses are modulated by the perceived fairness of others. *Nature*, 439(7075), 466–469.

Singleton, N., Gatward, R., & Meltzer, H. (September 23, 1998). *Psychiatric morbidity among prisoners in England and Wales*. London: Stationery Office.

Soderstrom, H. (2003). Psychopathy as a disorder of empathy. *European Child & Adolescent Psychiatry*, 12(5), 249–252.

Swart, M., Kortekaas, R., & Aleman, A. (2009). Dealing with feelings: Characterization of trait alexithymia on emotion regulation strategies and cognitive-emotional processing. *PloS One*, 4(6), e5751.

Uddin, L. Q., & Menon, V. (2009). The anterior insula in autism: Under-connected and under-examined. *Neuroscience and Biobehavioral Reviews*, 33(8), 1198–1203.

Vignemont, F. de, & Singer, T. (2006). The empathic brain: How, when and why? *Trends in Cognitive Sciences*, 10(10), 435–441.

Yirmiya, N., Sigman, M. D., Kasari, C., & Mundy, P. (1992). Empathy and cognition in high-functioning children with autism. *Child Development*, 63(1), 150–160.

Young, L., Koenigs, M., Kruepke, M., & Newman, J. P. (2012). Psychopathy increases perceived moral permissibility of accidents. *Journal of Abnormal Psychology*, 121(3), 659–667.

Zalla, T., Barlassina, L., Buon, M., & Leboyer, M. (2011). Moral judgment in adults with autism spectrum disorders. *Cognition*, 121(1), 115–126.

Zonnevijlle-Bender, M. J. S., van Goozen, S. H. M., Cohen-Kettenis, P. T., van Elburg, A., & van Engeland, H. (2002). Do adolescent anorexia nervosa patients have deficits in emotional functioning? *European Child & Adolescent Psychiatry*, 11(1), 38–42.

Zonnevylle-Bender, M. J. S., van Goozen, S. H. M., Cohen-Kettenis, P. T., van Elburg, A., & van Engeland, H. (2004). Emotional functioning in adolescent anorexia nervosa patients: A controlled study. *European Child & Adolescent Psychiatry*, 13(1), 28–34.

22 Mirror Neuron Formation via Associative Learning

Caroline Catmur

Abstract

This volume discusses the evidence for – and implications of – the existence of shared representations in the human brain. When we perceive another person's actions, emotional states or even tactile sensations, we activate the same motor programs, emotional circuitry and somatosensory networks that would be active if we were to perform those actions, or feel those emotions or sensations. Thus our own representation of an action, emotion or sensation becomes 'shared': activated not only by our own action, emotion or touch, but also by the perception of the same events in other people. There is now extensive evidence, discussed in earlier chapters, for the presence of such 'shared representations'; in contrast, what this chapter addresses is *how* the brain acquires these shared representations. In this chapter, I focus on shared representations of action, as instantiated by mirror neurons. This is because historically it is shared *action* representations that have been subject to the most investigation; however, I will conclude with some thoughts on how this work may generalize to other types of shared representation.

Mirror neurons fire when the individual performs an action and also when they perceive the same, or a similar, action being performed by another individual. Neurons with these 'mirror' properties have been recorded in the macaque in both ventral (Gallese, Fadiga, Fogassi, & Rizzolatti, 1996; Kraskov, Dancause, Quallo, Shepherd, & Lemon, 2009; di Pellegrino, Fadiga, Fogassi, Gallese, & Rizzolatti, 1992) and dorsal (Tkach, Reimer, & Hatsopoulos, 2007) premotor cortex; in primary motor cortex (Dushanova & Donoghue, 2010; Tkach et al., 2007; Vigneswaran, Philipp, Lemon, & Kraskov, 2013); and in parietal areas (Bonini et al., 2010; Fogassi et al., 2005). Neurons with similar sensorimotor

I would like to thank Cecilia Heyes, who proposed the Associative Sequence Learning account of mirror neurons, and who guided the work described in this chapter; and Geoff Bird, Richard Cook, and Clare Press, who helped develop the associative account. My research is supported by the Economic and Social Research Council (ES/K00140X/1).

matching properties have also been found in the swamp sparrow (Prather, Peters, Nowicki, & Mooney, 2008). Although single-cell recording studies in humans are rare, similar properties have been found in neurons in the supplementary motor area and medial temporal lobe in patients undergoing monitoring prior to surgery (Mukamel, Ekstrom, Kaplan, Iacoboni, & Fried, 2010).

More widespread evidence of mirror-neuron-like responses in humans comes from a variety of sources. Functional magnetic resonance imaging (fMRI) studies have identified overlapping responses to the observation and performance of actions in a range of brain areas including, but not limited to, premotor and parietal cortex (Aziz-Zadeh, Koski, Zaidel, Mazziotta, & Iacoboni, 2006; Buccino, Vogt, Ritzl, Fink, & Zilles, 2004; Iacoboni et al., 1999; Tanaka & Inui, 2002; Vogt et al., 2007). This technique cannot determine whether the motor representations activated by the observation of an action are the *same* as those which would be required to perform that action; more recently, however, new fMRI analysis techniques have provided support for the existence of *matching* shared representations of action in several brain areas (Chong, Cunnington, Williams, Kanwisher, & Mattingley, 2008; Kilner, Neal, Weiskopf, Friston, & Frith, 2009; Oosterhof, Tipper, & Downing, 2012).

Two additional techniques provide the specificity necessary to conclude that *matching* shared action representations are being activated by the observation of others' actions. This specificity is crucial if one considers that the defining property of a mirror neuron is that it is responsive to the *same* perceived and performed actions. Even without this strict definition, techniques that can demonstrate specificity are important, because otherwise an increased motor response to the observation of another's action could be due to non-specific factors such as attention or arousal. However, see Box 22.1 and Sartori (this volume, Chapter 19) for more discussion of the importance of non-matching shared representations. The first of these additional techniques is another neuroscientific measure. A motor-evoked potential (MEP) is produced in peripheral muscles when a single transcranial magnetic stimulation (TMS) pulse is applied to the skull over the primary motor cortex representation of those muscles. The size of the MEP in a particular muscle reflects the activity in the primary motor cortex representation of that muscle at that time. During action observation, MEP size is modulated in a matching muscle-specific fashion (see Figure 22.1a) : the muscle that would be involved in performing the observed action shows greater amplitude MEPs than when an alternative action is observed, and the opposite pattern is found in the muscle that would be involved in performing the alternative action (Catmur, Walsh, & Heyes, 2007; Fadiga, Fogassi, Pavesi, & Rizzolatti, 1995; Strafella & Paus, 2000). This pattern of responses is the result of connections from premotor mirror neuron areas to primary motor cortex (Catmur, Mars, Rushworth, & Heyes, 2011; Koch et al., 2010), suggesting that mirror responses to the sight of others'

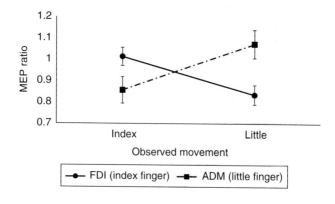

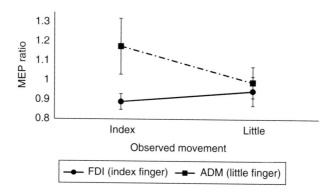

Figure 22.1 Muscle-specific patterns of MEP responses to the observation of others' actions, before training and after counter-mirror sensorimotor training.

Notes: A. MEPs are larger in each muscle during observation of the action which would involve that muscle than during observation of the alternative action. B. MEP responses to the observation of others' actions after counter-mirror sensorimotor training. MEPs are now larger in each muscle during observation of the action with which that muscle was paired during training: thus, for example, MEPs in the little finger muscle are now greater during observation of index finger actions, indicating a counter-mirror shared action representation. FDI: first dorsal interosseous (index finger muscle); ADM: abductor digiti minimi (little finger muscle).

Source: Data reproduced with permission from Catmur et al. (2007).

actions propagate from premotor cortex to the primary motor representation of the matching muscle.

A third technique to measure the activation of shared action representations in humans is behavioral measurement of imitation (also see Obhi, this volume,

Chapter 9). In the laboratory, this is most commonly achieved by measuring participants' response times to perform particular actions, while observing the same or a different action. Participants are faster to perform the same action as that observed than to perform a different action. Known as automatic imitation (Heyes, 2011) or imitative compatibility, this pattern of behavioral responses is evidence that the observation of an action activates the observer's motor representation of that action, speeding matching actions and slowing non-matching actions (Brass, Bekkering, Wohlschläger, & Prinz, 2000).

Box 22.1 Defining shared representations: do they have to be the *same* to be 'shared'?

Two important features of shared representations are their *specificity* and the extent to which they *match* representations of the other onto representations of the self. Which is the more crucial feature of a shared representation: its specificity or whether it involves a *matching* self–other mapping?

Specificity refers to the extent to which there is a one-to-one mapping between the representation of the other and that of the self. For example, if my motor representation of a precision grip is activated by the sight of a precision grip but not by the sight of a whole-hand grip, then I have a highly specific shared representation of a precision grip. However, if the sight of any kind of grasp – e.g. with the hand or mouth – activates my motor representation of a precision grip, then this is not a particularly specific shared representation. What if the sight of many different actions – e.g. grasp, place *and* throw – activates my motor representation of a precision grip (or equally, if the sight of a precision grip activates my motor representations of many different actions)? It would be difficult to argue that such a shared representation permits me to map another person's action on to my own. Yet much of the human neuroimaging literature, in particular that which uses standard fMRI and EEG techniques, cannot distinguish this kind of broad activation of motor representations during action perception from a more specific mapping. Those techniques demonstrate some level of motor activation during action observation but fail to demonstrate its specificity. That is, there is no evidence that one particular motor program is activated by the perception of a particular action. This is problematic because, in this case, motor activation during action observation could result not from the activation of shared representations but instead from more general factors such as increased arousal or attention. Thus, as discussed in the main text, techniques which demonstrate the *specificity* of shared representations are particularly important when investigating shared representations in the human brain.

Often, however, the emphasis on ensuring specificity of shared representations has focused on those representations which are not only specific but also *matching*: that is, a shared action representation is often defined as one in which the perception of an action activates the motor representation of the *same* action. Is this necessarily the case? Shared representations can be specific but non-matching. For example, the sight of a whole-hand grip can activate a precision grip in the observer when the context demands a complementary action be performed (Sartori, Cavallo, Bucchioni, & Castiello, 2012). Additional examples are discussed in this chapter; for instance, as a result of 'counter-mirror' sensorimotor training, the sight of a particular action activates the motor representation of the trained action, rather than the matching motor representation. These are examples of non-matching or complementary shared representations, and they demonstrate the context-sensitivity of shared action representations (Cook et al., 2012). Should these examples still be classed as shared action representations? In these situations, the perception of an action activates a motor representation in the perceiver, although it is not the *same* motor representation. If what is important about a shared action representation is that the observed action produces a specific motor response in the observer, then complementary actions would appear to satisfy this definition. As discussed in the text, further work is required to elucidate the psychological functions of shared action representations. Such work may shed light on whether the matching properties of shared action representations are as crucial as their specificity.

Thus there are various ways of measuring the activation of mirror representations in humans. The key question of this chapter is, how do mirror neurons acquire these intriguing matching properties? Why does the observation of a kick activate the motor program for the performance of a kick, and the observation of a wave activate the motor program for the performance of a wave, and not the other way around?

There are two broad possible answers to this question. The first is that mirror neurons were the product of positive selection pressure during the evolutionary history of the common ancestor of macaques and humans (and – possibly independently – of the swamp sparrow, and any other species subsequently found to possess mirror neurons). Such an argument (e.g. Gallese & Goldman, 1998; Rizzolatti & Craighero, 2004) tends to be based on the assumption that mirror neurons allow 'action understanding', a socially important trait, and that individuals with such an ability would have a reproductive advantage over those without (for a further discussion of this view, see Cook et al., 2014). The alternative is that mirror neurons' matching properties arise as a result of learning during the developmental history of the individual.

Various versions of the learning hypothesis have been proposed (Heyes, 2001, 2010; also see Keysers & Perrett, 2004; Westermann & Miranda, 2002, 2004; and Box 22.2). However, most have in common the assumption that there is nothing inherently special about the *matching* nature of shared action representations; that instead, whether matching or non-matching shared action representations are formed depends on the experience received during development.

Box 22.2 Modeling mirror neurons: alternative versions of the learning hypothesis

Several authors besides Heyes (2001, 2010) have suggested that mirror neurons' matching properties may arise as a result of learning. Westermann and Miranda (2002, 2004) proposed a model of auditory–motor integration by which mirror neurons for speech could develop as a result of hearing one's own voice during development. Although this model was proposed to explain auditory mirror neurons, it can be extended to encompass other sensory domains, similar to Heyes' (2001) model. To my knowledge, this model has not been tested explicitly, but it makes similar predictions to Heyes' associative sequence learning model.

A series of models which make slightly different predictions are those of Keysers and colleagues (Del Giudice et al., 2009; Keysers & Perrett, 2004). These propose, as does Heyes' model, that mirror neurons develop as a result of sensorimotor experience during development. However, they also suggest that such experience is 'canalized': that evolution has placed constraints on the type of experience available to infants during development, in order that mirror neurons preferentially encode others' actions. An example of a constraint which might comprise canalization is a preference for observation of one's own actions (Del Giudice et al., 2009). However, as discussed in the text, research from our lab and others has not found any evidence of constraints on the type of stimuli which can form associations with motor representations (for example, see Press et al., 2012). Note, though, that it is possible that cultural, rather than evolutionary, processes could provide similar constraints; see final discussion in this chapter.

Another model which makes alternative predictions to the associative hypothesis is that of Casile and colleagues (2011), who have proposed a model in which two different mechanisms produce mirror neurons. They suggest that mirror neurons for hand actions are acquired during development as a result of self-observation, but that mirror neurons for facial gestures are 'pre-wired'. This former suggestion again makes similar predictions to Heyes' model. In contrast, the suggestion of hard-wired shared representations for facial gestures predicts that such representations are present at birth and not easily altered by experience. Therefore, one possible approach to test this suggestion would be to adapt the counter-mirror training experiments described in this chapter for facial gestures.

A final approach to the problem of how shared representations are acquired is based on a theory with a long history in experimental psychology. James' (1890) ideomotor theory (also see Greenwald, 1970; and Dolk & Prinz and Bardi & Brass, this volume, Chapters 1 and 8, respectively) precedes the modern idea of shared representations. It suggests that, through learning, all motor codes are associated with their sensory outcome(s): thus the act of switching on a light is associated with tactile feedback, and also with the room becoming illuminated (Hommel, Müsseler, Aschersleben, & Prinz, 2001). The ideomotor theory suggests that, for those actions where I can perceive the outcome of my own movement, my motor representation of that action will become associated with my sensory representation of that action through learning (e.g. during self-observation), producing a shared action representation. The ideomotor theory shares many similarities with Heyes' theory (see Brass & Muhle-Karbe, 2014) but it does not specify how shared representations are formed for those actions where I cannot perceive the outcome of my own movement (Brass & Heyes, 2005). In contrast, Heyes' associative sequence learning theory (2001, 2010) provides suggestions for how shared action representations can be acquired for these types of action (see Figure 22.2).

In that case, what kind of experience is important? Unimodal (sensory *or* motor) experience could fine-tune existing shared representations (see Box 22.3), or increase sensory or motoric expertise, but purely sensory or motor experience cannot *produce* shared action representations. All versions of the learning hypothesis propose that mirror neurons are produced through some form of *sensorimotor* experience in which the perception and performance of matching actions is reliably correlated. Here, I focus on the Associative Sequence Learning theory (Heyes, 2001, 2010) because this is the version of the learning hypothesis which has been tested most extensively. For further discussion of the common ground and differences between the various learning hypotheses, see Box 22.2 and Catmur, Press, Cook, Bird, & Heyes (2014).

Box 22.3 What kind of learning? Effects of unimodal experience on shared representations

Is it only sensorimotor experience which can produce shared representations, or could unimodal sensory or motor experience suffice? Pure sensory or pure motor experience could fine-tune existing shared representations. Imagine that an individual has some limited sensorimotor experience of particular actions, for example a novice in a martial art involving kicks. Due to this limited sensorimotor experience, the sight of any of those kicks may activate the motor representations of all kicks. If the individual then repeatedly observes various different kicks, this purely sensory experience could fine-tune the individual's visual representations of kicks, for example by increasing lateral inhibition between the sensory representations of each type of kick. Such increased lateral inhibition would make it less likely that multiple visual representations of different kicks could be active simultaneously. At the perceptual level, this would mean that the individual is better able to discriminate one type of kick from another (however, it would not necessarily lead to an improvement in the ability to *perform* the different kicks). If, after such unimodal experience, the sight of one kick results in fewer visual representations being activated, this could lead to a reduction in motor activation during subsequent action observation. This can perhaps explain some paradoxical results whereby unimodal expertise can lead to a *reduction* in mirror neuron responses during subsequent action observation (Babiloni et al., 2010; Balser et al., 2014; Liew, Sheng, Margetis, & Aziz-Zadeh, 2013). Purely motoric experience could produce a similar effect. However, neither purely sensory nor purely motor experience could provide the initial link between sensory and motor representations that comprises a shared action representation.

Heyes' Associative Sequence Learning theory (2001, 2010; see Figure 22.2) suggests that mirror neurons develop in the following way. Initially, the brain develops with neural circuits for the control of action, including neurons in parietal and premotor areas; and with neural circuits for the processing of perceptual information. In the case of vision, this would include striate and extrastriate visual areas, pathways for the identification of visual stimuli, and pathways for the visual guidance of action. For simplification, we can consider just two types of action representation: motor representations of the commands required to perform one's own actions; and visual representations of what actions look like when performed. Initially (Figure 22.2A) the pattern of connectivity between visual and motor representations of actions is random, with every visual representation weakly connected to every motor representation.

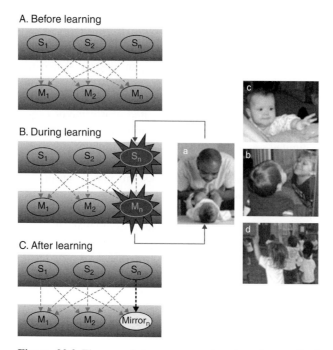

Figure 22.2 The associative sequence learning theory of mirror neuron development.

Source: Reproduced with permission from Heyes (2010).

However, during the course of development, we receive correlated experience (Figure 22.2B) in which the performance of an action is reliably paired with the observation of that action: for example, when observing our own actions (Figure 22.2C); when performing actions synchronously with others (such as during dance or sport; Figure 22.2D); or when being imitated by others (Figure 22.2A; a particularly rich source of experience during development; see Ray & Heyes, 2011). This experience strengthens the connections between neurons coding for the observation and performance of the same actions (Figure 22.2B). Subsequently, the observation of an action results in the propagation of activity along the strengthened connection to the neuron coding for the performance of that action, causing it to fire: a motor neuron has become a mirror neuron (Figure 22.2C).

There are several important things to notice about the associative theory. The first is that it is not denying the importance of genetic information. Most biological traits are the result of interactions between genes and environment, and the associative theory does not deny that genes have an important part to play in allowing mirror neurons to develop: by specifying sensory and motor areas of the brain, and by laying down initial non-specific connections between the two. What the associative theory seeks to explain is the specific pattern of connections between these areas which results in the systematic pattern of shared representations, both matching and non-matching, found in the adult brain; as opposed to a random pattern of connectivity between any visual and any motor representation. The second thing to notice is that the associative theory explains the proportions and properties of mirror neurons as a function of the environment in which the individual has developed. If an individual's environment provides experience in which the performance of a precision grip, say, is more consistently paired with the sight of a precision grip than with the sight of any other action, the individual will develop a matching mirror neuron for precision grip. If, in contrast, the individual's environment provides systematically non-matching experience (e.g. the performance of a throw is consistently paired with the sight of a catch), the individual will develop a non-matching shared representation in which the sight of a catch activates the motor program for a throw.

Finally, it should be noticed that, following standard associative learning theory, the contingencies between perceived and performed actions do not have to be *perfect* in order for a mirror neuron (or a non-matching equivalent) to develop. Associations will be formed between a motor representation and the sensory representation with which the highest contingency is experienced. Thus in order to acquire a mirror neuron coding for the observation and performance of a precision grip, it is not necessary that every time we perform a precision grip we see a precision grip; it is sufficient that, during performance of a precision grip, the *most frequent* sensory representation activated is that of a precision grip. If the probability of observing a precision grip while (or within close temporal proximity to) performing a precision grip is greater than the probability of observing another action, (e.g. a release action), then a mirror neuron coding for precision grip will be formed. However, if the probability of observing a release action while performing a precision grip is greater than the probability of observing a precision grip, then a non-matching shared representation will be formed in which the sight of a release action activates the motor program for a precision grip (see Box 22.1).

How can the associative theory be tested? There are two complementary ways to test this account. The first is to look for evidence that could falsify the theory: in particular, evidence that an individual has mirror neurons for a particular action before that individual has received sufficient correlated sensorimotor experience of that action that could have produced those neurons.

Testing for mirror neurons in individuals with limited sensorimotor experience is understandably difficult, as it generally involves very young infants. Due to ethical and practical considerations, there is no direct (i.e. single-cell) evidence of mirror neurons in neonatal macaques or any other species; nor is there any evidence using the more indirect techniques of fMRI or TMS-evoked responses to observed actions. As discussed in more detail elsewhere (Cook et al., 2014), limited attempts have been made to measure motor responses to observed actions in neonates using the technique of electroencephalography. However, this technique can only indicate whether action observation produces sensorimotor responses in the brain; crucially, it cannot indicate whether the *matching* motor program is activated when infants view an action. Notwithstanding, the results from those experiments are not inconsistent with the associative account: they indicate that sensorimotor responses to others' actions develop over the first few years of life (Marshall, Young, & Meltzoff, 2011; Southgate, Johnson, Osborne, & Csibra, 2009; also see Turati et al., 2013). An alternative is to investigate neonatal imitation. If neonates can imitate a range of actions, then this would suggest that they have a non-learned ability to match the sight of an action onto the matching motor program. However, a recent meta-analysis indicates that the only action for which there is consistent evidence of neonatal imitation is tongue protrusion (Ray & Heyes, 2011); and this appears to be an arousal response to any interesting stimulus (Jones, 1996, 2006) rather than being determined by a mechanism that matches observed behavior onto the relevant motor program.

The second way of testing the associative theory is to test its predictions. The theory makes two strong predictions: first, if mirror neurons arise through experience, then it should be possible to modify their properties relatively easily. In contrast, if mirror neurons' matching properties were the result of positive evolutionary selection pressure (i.e. they provided their possessor a reproductive advantage over individuals without mirror neurons), we would not expect their properties to be easily modified by the type of experience that was present in the environment in which they evolved (Catmur et al., 2014; Cook et al., 2014). Second, if mirror neurons arise through correlated sensorimotor experience, then there is no *a priori* reason to predict that there should be any constraints on the type of sensory stimuli which can be associated with motor responses to produce neurons with mirror or 'mirror-like' properties. In contrast, some accounts (e.g. Del Giudice, Manera, & Keysers, 2009) have suggested that, if mirror neurons' matching properties evolved as a result of positive selection pressure because of their importance for social cognition, then mirror responses should be 'canalized', thus allowing only socially relevant stimuli to be associated with motor responses. Therefore, we have carried out a series of experiments testing whether mirror neurons can be modified by experience, and whether there is any evidence of canalization in terms of the type of stimuli which can be associated with motor responses.

Catmur et al. (2007) tested whether the muscle-specific pattern of MEP responses to action observation can be easily altered through sensorimotor experience in which the observation of an action is paired with the performance of a different action. Participants' MEP responses to the observation of index and little finger movements were measured (Figure 22.1a) and participants were then divided into two groups, both of which received 1–2 hours of sensorimotor training. The 'counter-mirror' training group performed an outward movement of the index finger whenever they saw a little finger abduction movement, and moved their little finger whenever they saw an index finger movement. The 'mirror' training group performed the same movement as that which they observed, receiving the same kind of experience that they would have obtained from a lifetime of observing their own actions. Thus, both visual and motor experience were matched across the two groups; the only difference between the groups was the sensorimotor contingency between the observed and the performed movements. Twenty-four hours after this training, participants' MEP responses to observation of index and little finger movements were again measured. The responses in the mirror training group were unchanged; but the counter-mirror group showed reversed responses: observation of a little finger movement now produced greater MEPs in the index finger, and seeing an index finger movement produced greater MEPs in the little finger (Figure 22.1b). Thus, the 'mirror' response to observed movements can be easily changed with a short period of sensorimotor training, suggesting that mirror neurons' matching properties arise through sensorimotor learning.

Two objections have been made to this conclusion. The first is that the counter-mirror responses may have reached primary motor cortex from a different brain area, i.e. via different neural pathways than the original mirror responses. The second is that the counter-mirror responses may have followed the same pathway but may take longer; that they may have been the result of a more effortful process (e.g. the result of participants consciously rehearsing the previously learned rule during the action observation testing session that took place after the training). In response, however, two subsequent experiments have demonstrated that the counter-mirror training effect relies on the same neural pathways between premotor and primary motor cortex as the original matching responses (Catmur et al., 2011); and that it follows the same time-course as the original responses (Cavallo, Heyes, Becchio, Bird, & Catmur, 2014).

Counter-mirror training also reverses brain responses to observed actions in premotor and parietal cortex (measured using fMRI; Catmur et al., 2008) and abolishes imitative compatibility effects (Cook, Dickinson, & Heyes, 2012;

Cook, Press, Dickinson, & Heyes, 2010; Gillmeister, Catmur, Liepelt, Brass, & Heyes, 2008; Heyes, Bird, Johnson, & Haggard, 2005; Wiggett, Hudson, Tipper, & Downing, 2011). Thus, there is extensive evidence that a relatively short period of sensorimotor training can alter shared action representations, fulfilling the predictions of the associative account.

Additionally, there do not appear to be any constraints on the types of stimuli which can become associated with motor responses: sensorimotor experience in which participants mirrored a robotic hand produced increased imitation of that hand (Press, Gillmeister, & Heyes, 2007); and sensorimotor training with arbitrary color and shape stimuli produced mirror-like MEP and fMRI responses to those stimuli (Landmann, Landi, Grafton, & Della-Maggiore, 2011; Petroni, Baguear, & Della-Maggiore, 2010; Press et al., 2012). These results are difficult to reconcile with the idea that the matching properties of shared action representations arise as a result of selection pressure, because if there were strong evolutionary pressure for individuals to develop *matching* shared action representations, then it should not be possible easily to alter the properties of these representations. Instead, they should be 'buffered' – protected against alterations which could arise due to the kind of experience that would have been available in the environment in which they evolved (Cosmides & Tooby, 1994; Pinker, 1997).

If the sources of the kind of sensorimotor experience that could produce shared action representations are readily available in the environment, as suggested above, then it should be easy to find examples of naturalistic effects of experience on mirror responses, and indeed this is the case. Many studies of this type investigate the effects of *expertise* on mirror responses. For example, dancers who have received sensorimotor experience of a particular type of dance demonstrate greater mirror responses to the observation of the dance genre in which they have been trained, and these effects are not due to visual experience (Calvo-Merino, Glaser, Grèzes, Passingham, & Haggard, 2005; Calvo-Merino, Grèzes, Glaser, Passingham, & Haggard, 2006; Cross, Hamilton, & Grafton, 2006; Cross, Hamilton, Kraemer, Kelley, & Grafton, 2009; Orgs, Dombrowski, Heil, & Jansen-Osmann, 2008; also see Cross & Calvo-Merino, this volume, Chapter 26). Similar results have been found for people with expertise in particular sports (Aglioti, Cesari, Romani, & Urgesi, 2008; Balser et al., 2014; Kim et al., 2011; also see Urgesi & Makris, this volume, Chapter 27). In addition, musicians demonstrate greater mirror responses to the sight or sound of their own instrument being played (Bangert et al., 2006; D'Ausilio, Altenmüller, Olivetti Belardinelli, & Lotze, 2006; Haslinger et al., 2005; Margulis, Mlsna, Uppunda, Parrish, & Wong, 2009; Vogt et al., 2007) – further evidence that mirror responses are not canalized for social stimuli, as an association between, for example, the sound of a piano and a motor response is not something that could have been learned in evolutionary history. Finally, macaque monkeys who have had extensive sensorimotor experience in which they observe tools being used to handle food and respond by grasping the food themselves, develop mirror neurons which respond to the sight of actions being performed with tools (Ferrari, Rozzi, & Fogassi, 2005). All of these examples are consistent with the associative theory.

Thus, a wide range of evidence both from our lab and others supports the claim that sensorimotor experience can alter shared action representations, providing strong evidence for the Associative Sequence Learning hypothesis of mirror neuron formation. This work raises a number of interesting considerations.

The first of these relate to the renewed emphasis on experience as a driver of mirror neuron formation. Under this emphasis, disorders relating to social interaction can be seen in a new light. If mirror neurons arise as a result of experience, then any deficits in mirror neuron responses, rather than being a cause of social difficulties, may instead be their result – for example, due to a lack of attention to social stimuli (Bird, Catmur, Silani, Frith, & Frith, 2006).

This emphasis can also lead us to ask interesting questions about the sources of sensorimotor experience in our developmental environments. For example, what are the best sources of *matching* sensorimotor experience and are these present universally, or do they differ cross-culturally? Is there any evidence that there has been any selection at a cultural level for the types of practice (e.g. synchronous rituals, dance, imitation of infants) that would encourage the formation of matching shared action representations during development?

Additionally, and importantly, if shared action representations are *not* the result of evolutionary selection pressure, then we have to look more closely at what psychological functions shared action representations *are* involved in. The associative theory means that there is no longer a need to assume that shared action representations are the outcome of positive selection pressure because of their contribution to social interaction. That means instead that we need stronger evidence from lesion, intervention and brain stimulation studies to demonstrate which – if any – social abilities they do contribute to (Cook et al., 2014).

The second considerations relate to other types of shared representation. Do emotional and tactile mirroring also arise through experience? There are certainly commonalities in the way that the brain *controls* the tendency to mirror actions, perspectives, emotions and touch (Santiesteban, Banissy, Catmur, & Bird, 2012a; Santiesteban et al., 2012b; Spengler, von Cramon, & Brass, 2009). But more work is needed to demonstrate whether these types of mirroring are also the result of experience. Examples of the types of experience, which could produce these other types of mirroring, would be situations in which we observe others' emotions while feeling the same emotions ourselves; or in which we observe ourselves being touched while feeling touch.

In conclusion, shared action representations arise as a result of experience in which the individual performs actions while perceiving the sensory consequences of those actions. This simple statement can explain the existence of both matching and non-matching shared representations of action, and has the potential to explain other types of shared representation as well.

References

Aglioti, S. M., Cesari, P., Romani, M., & Urgesi, C. (2008). Action anticipation and motor resonance in elite basketball players. *Nature Neuroscience*, 11(9), 1109–1116.

Aziz-Zadeh, L., Koski, L., Zaidel, E., Mazziotta, J., & Iacoboni, M. (2006). Lateralization of the human mirror neuron system. *Journal of Neuroscience*, 26(11), 2964–2970. doi: 10.1523/JNEUROSCI.2921-05.2006.

Babiloni, C., Marzano, N., Infarinato, F., Iacoboni, M., Rizza, G., et al. (2010). 'Neural efficiency' of experts' brain during judgment of actions: A high-resolution EEG study in elite and amateur karate athletes. *Behavioural Brain Research*, 207(2), 466–475. doi: 10.1016/j.bbr.2009.10.034.

Balser, N., Lorey, B., Pilgramm, S., Stark, R., Bischoff, M., et al. (2014). Prediction of human actions: Expertise and task-related effects on neural activation of the action observation network. *Human Brain Mapping*, 8(568). doi: 10.1002/hbm.22455.

Bangert, M., Peschel, T., Schlaug, G., Rotte, M., Drescher, D., et al. (2006). Shared networks for auditory and motor processing in professional pianists: Evidence from fMRI conjunction. *NeuroImage*, 30(3), 917–926. doi: 10.1016/j.neuroimage.2005.10.044.

Bird, G., Catmur, C., Silani, G., Frith, C., & Frith, U. (2006). Attention does not modulate neural responses to social stimuli in autism spectrum disorders. *NeuroImage*, 31(4), 1614–1624. doi: 10.1016/j.neuroimage.2006.02.037.

Bonini, L., Rozzi, S., Serventi, F. U., Simone, L., Ferrari, P. F., & Fogassi, L. (2010). Ventral premotor and inferior parietal cortices make distinct contribution to action organization and intention understanding. *Cerebral Cortex*, 20(6), 1372–1385. doi: 10.1093/cercor/bhp200.

Brass, M., Bekkering, H., Wohlschläger, A., & Prinz, W. (2000). Compatibility between observed and executed finger movements: Comparing symbolic, spatial, and imitative cues. *Brain and Cognition*, 44(2), 124–143. doi: 10.1006/brcg.2000.1225.

Brass, M., & Heyes, C. (2005). Imitation: Is cognitive neuroscience solving the correspondence problem? *Trends in Cognitive Sciences*, 9(10), 489–495. doi: 10.1016/j.tics.2005.08.007.

Brass, M., & Muhle-Karbe, P. (2014). More than associations: An ideomotor perspective on mirror neurons. *Behavioral and Brain Sciences*, 37(2), 195–196. doi: 10.1017/S0140525X13002239.

Buccino, G., Vogt, S., Ritzl, A., Fink, G., & Zilles, K. (2004). Neural circuits underlying imitation learning of hand actions: An event-related fMRI study. *Neuron*, 42, 323–334.

Calvo-Merino, B., Glaser, D. E., Grèzes, J., Passingham, R. E., & Haggard, P. (2005). Action observation and acquired motor skills: An fMRI study with expert dancers. *Cerebral Cortex*, 15(8), 1243–1249. doi: 10.1093/cercor/bhi007.

Calvo-Merino, B., Grèzes, J., Glaser, D. E., Passingham, R. E., & Haggard, P. (2006). Seeing or doing? Influence of visual and motor familiarity in action observation. *Current Biology*, 16(19), 1905–1910. doi: 10.1016/j.cub.2006.07.065.

Casile, A., Caggiano, V., & Ferrari, P. F. (2011). The mirror neuron system: A fresh view. *The Neuroscientist*, 17(5), 524–538. doi: 10.1177/1073858410392239.

Catmur, C., Gillmeister, H., Bird, G., Liepelt, R., Brass, M., & Heyes, C. (2008). Through the looking glass: Counter-mirror activation following incompatible sensorimotor learning. *European Journal of Neuroscience*, 28(6), 1208–1215. doi: 10.1111/j.1460-9568.2008.06419.x.

Catmur, C., Mars, R. B., Rushworth, M. F., & Heyes, C. (2011). Making mirrors: Premotor cortex stimulation enhances mirror and counter-mirror motor facilitation. *Journal of Cognitive Neuroscience*, 23(9), 2352–2362. doi: 10.1162/jocn.2010.21590.

Catmur, C., Press, C., Cook, R., Bird, G., & Heyes, C. M. (2014). Mirror neurons: Tests and testability. *Behavioral and Brain Sciences*, 37(2), 221–241.

Catmur, C., Walsh, V., & Heyes, C. (2007). Sensorimotor learning configures the human mirror system. *Current Biology*, 17(17), 1527–1531. doi: 10.1016/j.cub.2007.08.006.

Cavallo, A., Heyes, C., Becchio, C., Bird, G., & Catmur, C. (2014). Timecourse of mirror and counter-mirror effects measured with transcranial magnetic stimulation. *Social Cognitive and Affective Neuroscience*, 9(8), 1082–1088. doi: 10.1093/scan/nst085.

Chong, T. T.-J., Cunnington, R., Williams, M. A., Kanwisher, N., & Mattingley, J. B. (2008). fMRI adaptation reveals mirror neurons in human inferior parietal cortex. *Current Biology*, 18(20), 1576–1580. doi: 10.1016/j.cub.2008.08.068.

Cook, R., Bird, G., Catmur, C., Press, C., & Heyes, C. M. (2014). Mirror neurons: From origin to function. *Behavioral and Brain Sciences*, 37(2), 177–192. doi: 10.1017/S0140525X13000903.

Cook, R., Dickinson, A., & Heyes, C. (2012). Contextual Modulation of Mirror and Countermirror Sensorimotor Associations. *Journal of Experimental Psychology. General*, 141(4), 774–787. doi:10.1037/a0027561

Cook, R., Press, C., Dickinson, A., & Heyes, C. (2010). Acquisition of automatic imitation is sensitive to sensorimotor contingency. *Journal of Experimental Psychology: Human Perception and Performance*, 36(4), 840–852. doi: 10.1037/a0019256.

Cosmides, L., & Tooby, J. (1994). Beyond intuition and instinct blindness: Toward an evolutionarily rigorous cognitive science. *Cognition*, 50(1–3), 41–77.

Cross, E. S., Hamilton, A. F. D. C., & Grafton, S. T. (2006). Building a motor simulation de novo: Observation of dance by dancers. *NeuroImage*, 31(3), 1257–1267. doi: 10.1016/j.neuroimage.2006.01.033.

Cross, E. S., Hamilton, A. F. D. C., Kraemer, D. J. M., Kelley, W. M., & Grafton, S. T. (2009). Dissociable substrates for body motion and physical experience in the human action observation network. *European Journal of Neuroscience*, 30(7), 1383–1392. doi: 10.1111/j.1460-9568.2009.06941.x.

D'Ausilio, A., Altenmüller, E., Olivetti Belardinelli, M., & Lotze, M. (2006). Cross-modal plasticity of the motor cortex while listening to a rehearsed musical piece. *European Journal of Neuroscience*, 24(3), 955–958. doi: 10.1111/j.1460-9568.2006.04960.x.

Del Giudice, M., Manera, V., & Keysers, C. (2009). Programmed to learn? The ontogeny of mirror neurons. *Developmental Science*, 12(2), 350–363. doi: 10.1111/j.1467-7687.2008.00783.x.

Dushanova, J., & Donoghue, J. (2010). Neurons in primary motor cortex engaged during action observation. *European Journal of Neuroscience*, 31(2), 386–398. doi: 10.1111/j.1460-9568.2009.07067.x.

Fadiga, L., Fogassi, L., Pavesi, G., & Rizzolatti, G. (1995). Motor facilitation during action observation: A magnetic stimulation study. *Journal of Neurophysiology*, 73(6), 2608–2611.

Ferrari, P. F., Rozzi, S., & Fogassi, L. (2005). Mirror neurons responding to observation of actions made with tools in monkey ventral premotor cortex. *Journal of Cognitive Neuroscience*, 17(2), 212–226. doi: 10.1162/0898929053124910.

Fogassi, L., Ferrari, P. F., Gesierich, B., Rozzi, S., Chersi, F., & Rizzolatti, G. (2005). Parietal lobe: From action organization to intention understanding. *Science, 308*(5722), 662–667. doi: 10.1126/science.1106138.

Gallese, V., Fadiga, L., Fogassi, L., & Rizzolatti, G. (1996). Action recognition in the premotor cortex. *Brain*, 119(2), 593–609.

Gallese, V., & Goldman, A. (1998). Mirror neurons and the simulation theory of mind-reading. *Trends in Cognitive Sciences*, 2(12), 493–501.

Gillmeister, H., Catmur, C., Liepelt, R., Brass, M., & Heyes, C. (2008). Experience-based priming of body parts: A study of action imitation. *Brain Research*, 1217, 157–170. doi: 10.1016/j.brainres.2007.12.076.

Greenwald, A. G. (1970). Sensory feedback mechanisms in performance control: With special reference to the ideomotor mechanism. *Psychological Review*, 77, 73–99.

Haslinger, B., Erhard, P., Altenmüller, E., Schroeder, U., Boecker, H., & Ceballos-Baumann, A. O. (2005). Transmodal sensorimotor networks during action observation in professional pianists. *Journal of Cognitive Neuroscience*, 17(2), 282–293. doi: 10.1162/0898929053124893.

Heyes, C. (2001). Causes and consequences of imitation. *Trends in Cognitive Sciences*, 5(6), 253–261.

(2010). Where do mirror neurons come from? *Neuroscience and Biobehavioral Reviews*, 34(4), 575–583. doi: 10.1016/j.neubiorev.2009.11.007.

(2011). Automatic imitation. *Psychological Bulletin*, 137(3), 463–483. doi: 10.1037/a0022288.

Heyes, C., Bird, G., Johnson, H., & Haggard, P. (2005). Experience modulates automatic imitation. *Brain Research: Cognitive Brain Research*, 22(2), 233–240. doi: 10.1016/j.cogbrainres.2004.09.009.

Hommel, B., Müsseler, J., Aschersleben, G., & Prinz, W. (2001). The theory of event coding (TEC): A framework for perception and action planning. *Behavioral and Brain Sciences*, 24, 849–878.

Iacoboni, M., Woods, R. P., Brass, M., Bekkering, H., Mazziotta, J. C., & Rizzolatti, G. (1999). Cortical mechanisms of human imitation. *Science*, 286(5449), 2526–2528.

James, W. (1890). *The principles of psychology*. New York: Macmillan.

Jones, S. S. (1996). Imitation or exploration? Young infants' matching of adults' oral gestures. *Child Development*, 67(5), 1952–1969.

——— (2006). Exploration or imitation? The effect of music on 4-week-old infants' tongue protrusions. *Infant Behavior and Development*, 29(1), 126–130. doi: 10.1016/j.infbeh.2005.08.004.

Keysers, C., & Perrett, D. I. (2004). Demystifying social cognition: A Hebbian perspective. *Trends in Cognitive Sciences*, 8(11), 501–507. doi: 10.1016/j.tics.2004.09.005.

Kilner, J. M., Neal, A., Weiskopf, N., Friston, K. J., & Frith, C. D. (2009). Evidence of mirror neurons in human inferior frontal gyrus. *Journal of Neuroscience*, 29(32), 10153–10159. doi: 10.1523/JNEUROSCI.2668-09.2009.

Kim, Y.-T., Seo, J.-H., Song, H.-J., Yoo, D.-S., Lee, II. J., et al. (2011). Neural correlates related to action observation in expert archers. *Behavioural Brain Research*, 223(2), 342–347. doi: 10.1016/j.bbr.2011.04.053.

Koch, G., Versace, V., Bonnì, S., Lupo, F., Lo Gerfo, E., et al. (2010). Resonance of cortico–cortical connections of the motor system with the observation of goal directed grasping movements. *Neuropsychologia*, 48(12), 3513–3520. doi: 10.1016/j.neuropsychologia.2010.07.037.

Kraskov, A., Dancause, N., Quallo, M. M., Shepherd, S., & Lemon, R. N. (2009). Corticospinal neurons in macaque ventral premotor cortex with mirror properties: A potential mechanism for action suppression? *Neuron*, 64(6), 922–930. doi: 10.1016/j.neuron.2009.12.010.

Landmann, C., Landi, S. M., Grafton, S. T., & Della-Maggiore, V. (2011). fMRI supports the sensorimotor theory of motor resonance. *PLoS One*, 6(11), e26859. doi: 10.1371/journal.pone.0026859.

Liew, S.-L., Sheng, T., Margetis, J. L., & Aziz-Zadeh, L. (2013). Both novelty and expertise increase action observation network activity. *Frontiers in Human Neuroscience*, 7, 541. doi: 10.3389/fnhum.2013.00541.

Margulis, E. H., Mlsna, L. M., Uppunda, A. K., Parrish, T. B., & Wong, P. C. M. (2009). Selective neurophysiologic responses to music in instrumentalists with different listening biographies. *Human Brain Mapping*, 30(1), 267–275. doi: 10.1002/hbm.20503.

Marshall, P. J., Young, T., & Meltzoff, A. N. (2011). Neural correlates of action observation and execution in 14-month-old infants: An event-related EEG desynchronization study. *Developmental Science*, 14(3), 474–480. doi: 10.1111/j.1467-7687.2010.00991.x.

Mukamel, R., Ekstrom, A. D., Kaplan, J., Iacoboni, M., & Fried, I. (2010). Single-neuron responses in humans during execution and observation of actions. *Current Biology*, 20, 1–18. doi: 10.1016/j.cub.2010.02.045.

Oosterhof, N. N., Tipper, S. P., & Downing, P. E. (2012). Viewpoint (in)dependence of action representations: An MVPA study. *Journal of Cognitive Neuroscience*, 24(4), 975–989. doi: 10.1162/jocn_a_00195.

Orgs, G., Dombrowski, J.-H., Heil, M., & Jansen-Osmann, P. (2008). Expertise in dance modulates alpha/beta event-related desynchronization during action observation. *European Journal of Neuroscience*, 27(12), 3380–3384. doi: 10.1111/j.1460-9568.2008.06271.x.

Pellegrino, G. di, Fadiga, L., Fogassi, L., Gallese, V., & Rizzolatti, G. (1992). Understanding motor events: A neurophysiological study. *Experimental Brain Research*, 91(1), 176–180.

Petroni, A., Baguear, F., & Della-Maggiore, V. (2010). Motor resonance may originate from sensorimotor experience. *Journal of Neurophysiology*, 104(4), 1867–1871. doi: 10.1152/jn.00386.2010.

Pinker, S. (1997). *How the mind works*. Harmondsworth: Penguin.

Prather, J. F., Peters, S., Nowicki, S., & Mooney, R. (2008). Precise auditory–vocal mirroring in neurons for learned vocal communication. *Nature*, 451(7176), 305–310. doi: 10.1038/nature06492.

Press, C., Catmur, C., Cook, R., Widmann, H., Heyes, C., & Bird, G. (2012). fMRI evidence of 'mirror' responses to geometric shapes. *PLoS One*, 7(12), e51934. doi: 10.1371/journal.pone.0051934.

Press, C., Gillmeister, H., & Heyes, C. (2007). Sensorimotor experience enhances automatic imitation of robotic action. *Proceedings of the Royal Society B: Biological Sciences*, 274(1625), 2509. doi: 10.1098/rspb.2007.0774.

Ray, E., & Heyes, C. (2011). Imitation in infancy: The wealth of the stimulus. *Developmental Science*, 14(1), 92–105. doi: 10.1111/j.1467-7687.2010.00961.x.

Rizzolatti, G., & Craighero, L. (2004). The mirror-neuron system. *Annual Review of Neuroscience*, 27, 169–192. doi: 10.1146/annurev.neuro.27.070203.144230.

Santiesteban, I., Banissy, M. J., Catmur, C., & Bird, G. (2012a). Enhancing social ability by stimulating right temporoparietal junction. *Current Biology*, 22(23), 2274–2277. doi: 10.1016/j.cub.2012.10.018.

Santiesteban, I., White, S., Cook, J., Gilbert, S. J., Heyes, C., & Bird, G. (2012b). Training social cognition: From imitation to Theory of Mind. *Cognition*, 122(2), 228–235. doi: 10.1016/j.cognition.2011.11.004.

Sartori, L., Cavallo, A., Bucchioni, G., & Castiello, U. (2012). From simulation to reciprocity: The case of complementary actions. *Social Neuroscience*, 7(2), 146–158. doi: 10.1080/17470919.2011.586579.

Southgate, V., Johnson, M. H., Osborne, T., & Csibra, G. (2009). Predictive motor activation during action observation in human infants. *Biology Letters*, 5(6), 769–772. doi: 10.1098/rsbl.2009.0474.

Spengler, S., von Cramon, D. Y., & Brass, M. (2009). Control of shared representations relies on key processes involved in mental state attribution. *Human Brain Mapping*, 30(11), 3704–3718. doi: 10.1002/hbm.20800.

Strafella, A. P., & Paus, T. (2000). Modulation of cortical excitability during action observation: A transcranial magnetic stimulation study. *NeuroReport*, 11(10), 2289–2292.

Tanaka, S., & Inui, T. (2002). Cortical involvement for action imitation of hand/arm postures versus finger configurations: An fMRI study. *NeuroReport*, 13(13), 1599–1602.

Tkach, D., Reimer, J., & Hatsopoulos, N. G. (2007). Congruent activity during action and action observation in motor cortex. *Journal of Neuroscience*, 27(48), 13241–13250. doi: 10.1523/JNEUROSCI.2895-07.2007.

Turati, C., Natale, E., Bolognini, N., Senna, I., Picozzi, M., et al. (2013). The early development of human mirror mechanisms: evidence from electromyographic recordings at 3 and 6 months. *Developmental Science*, 16(6), 793–800. doi: 10.1111/desc.12066.

Vigneswaran, G., Philipp, R., Lemon, R. N., & Kraskov, A. (2013). M1 corticospinal mirror neurons and their role in movement suppression during action observation. *Current Biology*, 23(3), 236–243. doi: 10.1016/j.cub.2012.12.006.

Vogt, S., Buccino, G., Wohlschläger, A. M., Canessa, N., Shah, N. J., et al. (2007). Prefrontal involvement in imitation learning of hand actions: Effects of practice and expertise. *NeuroImage*, 37(4), 1371–1383. doi: 10.1016/j.neuroimage.2007.07.005.

Westermann, G., & Miranda, E. R. (2002). Modelling the development of mirror neurons for auditory–motor integration. *Journal of New Music Research*, 31(4), 367–375. doi: 10.1076/jnmr.31.4.367.14166.

(2004). A new model of sensorimotor coupling in the development of speech. *Brain and Language*, 89(2), 393–400. doi: 10.1016/S0093-934X(03)00345-6.

Wiggett, A. J., Hudson, M., Tipper, S. P., & Downing, P. E. (2011). Learning associations between action and perception: Effects of incompatible training on body part and spatial priming. *Brain and Cognition*, 76(1), 87–96. doi: 10.1016/j.bandc.2011.02.014.

Glossary

fMRI Functional magnetic resonance imaging, a technique for measuring the relative levels of oxygen usage in the brain during cognitive tasks of interest, and hence inferring brain responses to those tasks.

Imitative compatibility A stimulus–response compatibility effect in which the stimuli are visual representations (videos or still frames) of actions, and the same actions are performed as responses. When observing a particular action, we are faster to perform that action and slower to perform a competing action. The difference in response times between the performance of the competing (incongruent) and that of the same (congruent) actions is a measure of the magnitude of the imitative compatibility effect.

MEP Motor-evoked potential, a small electrical potential in a particular muscle produced by stimulation of the motor cortical representation of that muscle.

Mirror neuron A cell that fires during both the performance of an action and the perception of the same or a similar action.

Sensorimotor experience Experience in which the performance of an action is reliably correlated with a particular sensory event, e.g. the sight of that action; the sight of a different action; an action-related sound; or indeed an arbitrary visual or auditory stimulus.

TMS Transcranial magnetic stimulation, a non-invasive technique for stimulating cortical areas of the brain. It has excellent temporal and relatively good spatial resolution and can be used in two different ways: either to probe or to disrupt temporarily the activity in a particular area of cortex.

23   Disorders of Shared Representations

Jennifer Cook

Abstract

This chapter will begin with a focus on a particular subtopic within the shared representations research domain: imitation. Imitation occurs when the perception of another's actions causes the activation of the corresponding motor representation in the observer. Thus imitation relates to *shared representations* in that it concerns the activation of a self-related representation by an other-related representation. In this chapter, I will use examples from the autism spectrum conditions (ASCs) literature to argue that if either the self- or other-related representation is atypical this can result in atypical imitation. In other words, if action observation or action execution mechanisms are atypical, then imitation will be affected. I will conclude this chapter by drawing on research that extends this logic to other socio-cognitive domains such as empathy and to conditions such as schizophrenia and alexithymia.

Imitation

The Importance of Imitation

Imitation is intricately linked with social interaction. Being imitated increases rapport (Chartrand & Bargh, 1999), altruistic behaviour (Van Baaren, Holland, Kawakami, & van Knippenberg, 2004) and trust (Bailenson & Yee, 2005). Furthermore, individuals imitate more when in possession of a positive social attitude (Cook & Bird, 2011, 2012; Lakin & Chartrand, 2003; Leighton, Bird, Orsini, & Heyes, 2010). For example, Leighton and colleagues (2010) asked participants to arrange five words such that they formed a grammatically-correct sentence; these sentences either comprised positive social words (e.g. friend, team, assist) or anti-social words (e.g. rebel, obstinate, distrust). Individuals who had rearranged the positive social sentences exhibited significantly higher levels of automatic imitation compared to individuals who had rearranged the anti-social sentences. Thus, imitation is bi-directionally

480

associated with positive social interaction and is a key component in building social relationships with others (Lakin & Chartrand, 2003; also see Lakens, Schubert, & Paladino this volume, Chapter 13). This tight link between imitation and social interaction has prompted speculation that imitation may be a core difficulty in ASC, which impacts the wider social functioning of individuals with this condition.

Defining Imitation

Automatic imitation, also known as 'simple imitation' (Heyes, 2011) and 'mimicry' (Hamilton, 2008; Tomasello, 1996), is 'a type of stimulus–response compatibility effect in which the topographical features of task-irrelevant action stimuli facilitate similar and interfere with dissimilar responses' (Heyes, 2011, p. 463). For example, Brass, Bekkering and Prinz (2001) instructed participants to perform an index or middle finger lifting movement in response to the appearance on a computer screen of either a 1 or 2. The number was superimposed over a movie of a hand that showed either the same action or the alternative action. Brass and colleagues found that finger movement reaction speeds were slow when participants observed a non-matching action and faster when the matching action was observed. This reaction time (RT) difference is considered an index of the effect of observed action congruency on action selection, i.e. there is conflict between task instruction mediated action selection and imitation mediated action selection on incongruent, but not on congruent, trials. Such automatic imitation effects have been replicated many times and can be found irrespective of effector (Bach & Tipper, 2007; Cook & Bird, 2011, 2012; Gillmeister, Catmur, Liepelt, Brass, & Heyes, 2008; Leighton & Heyes, 2010; Bardi & Brass, this volume, Chapter 8). Such 'interference effects' can also be observed for action control. When a participant is required to execute an action (e.g. horizontal sinusoidal arm movements) and simultaneously observe an incongruent action (e.g. vertical sinusoidal arm movements), the participant's movements are more variable in the direction of the observed incongruent movement compared to when she observes a congruent movement (Figure 23.1; Bouquet, Gaurier, Shipley, Toussaint, & Blandin, 2007; Chaminade, Franklin, Oztop, & Cheng, 2005; Gowen, Stanley, & Miall, 2008; Kilner, Hamilton, & Blakemore, 2007; Kilner, Paulignan, & Blakemore, 2003; Oztop, Franklin, Chaminade, & Cheng, 2005; Stanley, Gowen, & Miall, 2007). Action observation can therefore be said to 'interfere' with ongoing action execution.

This interference effect, defined as variance in the plane orthogonal to the participant's movement (the error plane) for incongruent compared with congruent movement observation, is greater when the observed action is made by an actor with human, rather than robot, form and motion characteristics (Kilner

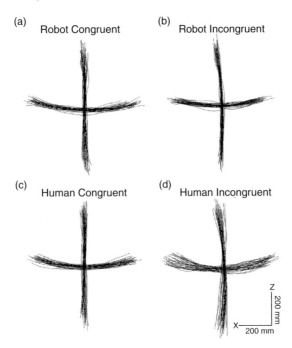

Figure 23.1 Greater interference effect for human compared to robot movements.

Notes: Data from a motion tracker on the hand of a participant whilst she conducts vertical and horizontal sinusoidal movements whilst observing (A) congruent movements conducted by a robot, (B) incongruent robot movements, (C) congruent movements conducted by a human and (D) incongruent human movements. The interference effect (variance in the plane orthogonal to the participant's movement) was greatest when the participant observed human incongruent movements (D).

Source: Image reproduced with permission from Kilner, Paulignan, and Blakemore (2003; Figure 2).

et al., 2003, 2007). With respect to form, Kilner, Paulignan and Blakemore (2003) showed that participants exhibit a greater interference effect when watching actions conducted by a real human compared to actions conducted by a robot (Figure 23.2). Similarly Press and colleagues (2005) demonstrated a greater automatic imitation effect (RT difference between incompatible and compatible actions) for human hand compared to robot hand actions. Interference effects therefore appear to be greater for observed stimuli with human form and human motion compared to stimuli with robot form (for further discussion on the biological specificity of automatic imitation, see Press 2011; see also Press, this volume, Chapter 16)).

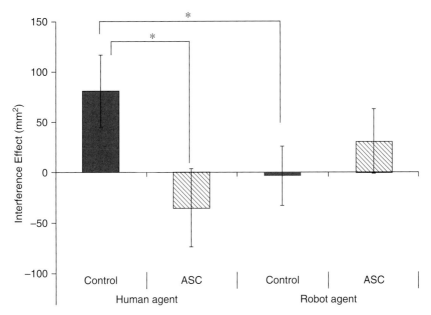

Figure 23.2 Adjusted mean (+/–SEM) interference effect (incongruent minus congruent variance) is displayed. *See Plate 10.*

Notes: The control group exhibited a significant interference effect in the human agent biological motion (BM) and human agent constant velocity (CV) conditions but not in the robot agent BM or CV conditions. In contrast, individuals with ASC did not exhibit a significant interference effect for any condition. * $p < 0.05$.

Source: Image modified from Cook, Swapp, Pan, Bianchi-Berthouze, and Blakemore (2014, Figure 3b; CC BY).

In sum, the observation of an incongruent action can result in effects on both action selection and action control. These effects are stronger for human compared to non-human stimuli.

Is the MNS Involved in Imitation?

Mirror neurons, which were originally discovered in the monkey brain (di Pellegrino, Fadiga, Fogassi, Gallese, & Rizzolatti, 1992), fire both for execution of an action and observation of that same action. Research using a range of neuroimaging methods provides evidence for similar responses to action execution and action observation in the human motor system (e.g. Buccino et al., 2001; Chong, Cunnington, Williams, Kanwisher, & Mattingley, 2008; Iacoboni et al., 1999; Kilner, Neal, Weiskopf, Friston, & Frith, 2009; Press, Cook, Blakemore, & Kilner, 2011).

Since imitation is the execution of observed actions and the mirror neuron system (MNS) responds to both action execution and observation it can be hypothesised that the MNS plays a part in imitation. This hypothesis was supported by a functional Magnetic Resonance Imaging (fMRI) study by Iacoboni et al. (1999) and by transcranial magnetic stimulation (TMS) studies that have demonstrated that applying repetitive TMS to disrupt activity in mirror neuron regions results in reduced imitation (Catmur, Walsh, & Heyes, 2009; Heiser, Iacoboni, Maeda, Marcus, & Mazziotta, 2003).

Imitation Summary

Imitation, the copying of the body movements of others, is bi-directionally linked with positive social attitudes: being imitated increases positive social attitudes and, in turn, being in possession of a positive social attitude makes a person more likely to imitate. Imitation can occur automatically, resulting in online interference with action execution. Such online interference may be a consequence of the automatic motoric simulation of observed action. Brain regions associated with the human mirror neuron system are active both for the execution and observation of actions, and disrupting activity in these regions can lead to imitation impairments.

Imitation in Autism Spectrum Conditions

ASCs are pervasive developmental disorders characterised by difficulties with social communication and interaction and restricted repetitive patterns of behaviour (American Psychiatric Association, 1994). A number of studies have demonstrated reduced imitation and/or MNS activity in individuals with ASCs compared to control participants (Williams, Whiten, & Singh, 2004). We employed virtual reality to investigate the integrity of interference effects (e.g. Kilner et al., 2003, 2007) in ASCs. High-functioning adults with ASCs and age- and IQ-matched healthy controls performed horizontal sinusoidal arm movements whilst observing arm movements conducted by a virtual reality agent with either human or robot form, which moved with either biological motion or at a constant velocity. In another condition, participants made the same arm movements while observing a real human. Arm movement kinematics were recorded with a motion tracking device. Observed arm movements were either congruent or incongruent with executed arm movements. An interference effect was calculated as the average variance in the incongruent action dimension during observation of incongruent compared with congruent movements. Control participants exhibited an interference effect when observing real human and virtual human agent incongruent movements but not when observing virtual robot agent movements. In contrast, individuals with ASCs showed no interference effect for real human, virtual human or virtual robot movements, thus suggesting a disrupted effect of action observation on action execution in ASCs (Figure 23.2).

In 1991 Rogers and Pennington suggested that, along with emotion sharing and theory of mind, a deficit in perception–action matching might be a primary difficulty in ASCs. It was subsequently suggested that the MNS may function atypically in ASCs and that early MNS dysfunction might lead to a cascade of developmental impairments (Ramachandran & Oberman, 2006; Rogers & Pennington, 1991; Williams, Whiten, Suddendorf, & Perrett, 2001). This 'broken MNS' hypothesis of ASCs provides a possible explanation for the atypical interference effect that we observed: in other words, if motor neurons comprise the overlap between action observation and action execution, and if this overlap is disrupted in ASCs, this could explain the absence of an effect of action observation on action execution in our virtual reality paradigm. However, experimental evidence for a broken MNS is mixed, with studies both supporting (Avikainen, Wohlschläger, Liuhanen, Hänninen, & Hari, 2003; Dapretto et al., 2006; McIntosh, Reichmann-Decker, Winkielman, & Wilbarger, 2006; Oberman et al., 2005; Rogers, Hepburn, Stackhouse, & Wehner, 2003) and opposing (Bird, Leighton, Press, & Heyes, 2007; Dinstein et al., 2010; Gowen et al., 2008; Hamilton, Brindley, & Frith, 2007; Leighton, Bird, Charman, & Heyes, 2008; Press, Richardson, & Bird, 2010; Spengler, Bird, & Brass, 2010) this hypothesis. Furthermore, clinical observations of high levels of echolalia (automatic repetition of speech patterns) and echopraxia (automatic imitation of observed actions) in individuals with ASCs (Russell, 1997; Rutter, 1974; Williams et al., 2004) are incompatible with the hypothesis that the mechanisms mediating mapping from perception to action are impaired. The broken MNS hypothesis has thus received much criticism (e.g. Southgate & Hamilton, 2008).

It is important to consider that imitation and interference effects can be decomposed into their constituent parts and that an atypicality in one component can affect the whole process. In other words, since imitation concerns the automatic activation of motor representations upon observation of another's action, atypical imitation could be the result of atypical action observation and/or atypical motor execution. For example, an atypical interference effect could be due to atypical visual processing of the sinusoidal arm movement (i.e. atypical biological motion processing). If this arm movement is not processed typically it may not result in activation of the corresponding motor representation and thus an interference effect would not be observed. In the following section we will review the evidence for atypical biological motion processing in ASCs.

Is Biological Motion Processing Impaired in ASCs?

'Biological motion' refers to the movements of other animate beings. Biological motion processing has been studied using a variety of stimuli from animations of moving people (e.g. Pelphrey et al., 2003) to single dots moving with a velocity profile that matches human movement (Dayan et al., 2007). The most common stimulus employed is the 'point-light display' (PLD) developed by Johansson (1973), whereby he attached 10 light bulbs to the joints of an actor and filmed his movements in a dark room. A number of studies employing PLD stimuli have reported difficulties with biological motion processing in children with ASCs compared to typically developing (TD) children. In a single case study, Klin and Jones (2008) showed children upright or inverted PLD videos accompanied by soundtracks. They found that, whereas TD children preferentially looked at the upright over the inverted PLD, a child with an ASC did not. In a follow-up study, Klin, Lin, Gorrindo, Ramsay, and Jones (2009) found that, whereas a TD group of two-year olds preferentially looked at the upright PLDs, an ASC group of two-year olds preferentially looked at points of audio–visual synchrony (e.g. the simultaneous collision of two dots and presentation of 'clap' sound) irrespective of the orientation of the PLD. Klin and colleagues suggest that toddlers with ASCs spend less time than TD toddlers attending to biological motion. However, it is not clear whether this study indexes a lack of attention to biological motion or a particular attentional engagement with points of audio–visual contingency in ASCs. Furthermore, the PLD videos employed in this study depicted social games (e.g. pat-a-cake); the Autism Diagnostic Observation Schedule (ADOS; Lord et al., 1989) assessment considers disinterest in these types of game a marker of ASC, hence it can be assumed that toddlers with ASCs (who have been pre-selected on the basis of ADOS assessment) spend less time than TD toddlers attending to these types of game.

A study by Annaz, Campbell, Coleman, Milne, and Swettenham (2012) investigated attention to biological motion in young children with ASCs using a task that did not feature audio–visual contingency or overtly social stimuli. They used non-social PLDs (person walking) without an accompanying soundtrack. In two separate conditions this biological PLD was presented alongside a scrambled version of the PLD (scrambled condition) or a PLD of a spinning top (spinning condition). Whereas three- to seven-year-old TD children preferentially attended to the biological PLD in both scrambled and spinning conditions, children with ASC showed no preference for the biological PLD over the scrambled PLD and they preferentially attended to the spinning top PLD over the biological PLD. Together with the work of Klin and colleagues (2009), this finding suggests that, unlike TD children, those with ASCs do not demonstrate a preference for biological motion. The spinning condition suggests that, unlike TD children, those with ASCs exhibit a preference for non-biological motion.

Reduced attention to biological motion from an early age may be causally related to atypical development of biological motion processing. Annaz and colleagues (2010) have demonstrated that between the ages of 5 and 12 TD children improve in their ability to (1) judge whether a PLD 'moved like a person' and (b) pick, from a choice of two, the PLD in which they could see 'dots that look like a person walking'. Children with ASCs did not show this developmental improvement. In line with this, Blake, Turner, Smoski, Pozdol, and Stone (2003) report a reduced sensitivity in judging which dots 'move like a person' in 8–10-year-old children with ASCs. Koldewyn, Whitney, and Rivera (2010) have suggested that this atypical sensitivity to biological motion extends into adolescence. They used a 'direction discrimination task' in which participants were required to determine the direction of a PLD walking left or right within a field of noise dots. It is more difficult to recognise the direction of a PLD when it is embedded in a field of randomly moving noise dots compared to noise dots that move coherently. Thus the coherence of the noise dots can be adjusted to regulate the difficulty of the task. Koldewyn et al. found that, compared to TDs, adolescents with ASCs demonstrated significantly poorer direction discrimination. That is, to accurately discriminate the direction of the PLD walker, individuals with ASCs required significantly higher levels of noise dot coherence compared to controls. Atypical biological motion processing in ASCs has also been reported in adults. Kaiser, Delmolino, Tanaka, and Shiffrar (2010a) asked participants to watch scrambled or unscrambled versions of PLDs of a human actor and to say if the dots moved as if they were 'stuck' to a person; in a control condition, participants had to say whether the dots moved as if they were 'stuck' to a tractor. Whereas the control group exhibited greater visual sensitivity to human motion compared to tractor motion, individuals with ASCs exhibited equivalent sensitivity to human and tractor motion. Therefore, unlike controls, individuals with ASCs did not exhibit an enhanced sensitivity for human motion.

Behavioural reports of atypical biological motion processing in ASCs have been supported by neuroimaging studies. Freitag and colleagues (2008) used fMRI to scan adults with and without ASCs while they viewed PLDs of a walking actor and scrambled versions of these stimuli. Significant differences were found between control participants and individuals with ASCs in terms of fMRI signals relating to biological motion versus scrambled motion. In the right hemisphere reduced (hypo) activation in ASC individuals was found in the middle temporal gyrus, close to the superior temporal sulcus (STS), postcentral gyrus, inferior parietal lobe (IPL), right occipital regions and middle frontal gyrus. In the left hemisphere, hypoactivation in ASCs was found in anterior STS and fusiform gyrus, postcentral gyrus, IPL and claustrum. Similarly, Herrington and colleagues (2007) used fMRI to scan adults with and without Asperger's syndrome (AS) whilst they judged the direction of motion of PLD walkers and scrambled PLDs. Again, no behavioural differences were found. However, in the right hemisphere hypoactivation in ASC individuals was found in a large cluster spanning the cerebellum, fusiform, middle temporal, superior temporal, middle occipital and superior occipital regions. A similar cluster was found in the left hemisphere but this cluster also included inferior temporal gyrus and the cuneus region. Hence both Herrington et al. (2007) and Freitag et al. (2008) demonstrate that, even when behavioural performance is matched, individuals with ASC exhibit hypoactivation in posterior areas, including STS and fusiform gyrus, during biological motion processing.

Work by Kaiser and colleagues (Kaiser, Delmolino, Tanaka, & Shiffrar, 2010a; Kaiser et al., 2010b) demonstrates that atypical neural responses to biological motion can also be found in children and adolescents with ASCs. This group used fMRI to scan TD participants, individuals with an ASC and unaffected siblings while they viewed scrambled and intact versions of PLD movies that were similar to those employed by Klin et al. (2009). Compared to TD participants and unaffected siblings, those with an ASC exhibited hypoactivation in the left ventrolateral PFC, right amygdala, right pSTS, ventromedial PFC and bilateral fusiform gyri, hence replicating previous reports of hypoactivity in ASCs in posterior areas such as the pSTS and fusiform gyrus.

In sum, a growing body of behavioural studies suggests there is atypical attention to biological motion in ASCs in early infancy, and that this is followed by atypical biological motion processing in childhood, adolescence and adulthood (however, for conflicting findings, see Koldewyn et al., 2010; Murphy, Brady, Fitzgerald, & Troje, 2009; Saygin, Cook, & Blakemore, 2010). These behavioural findings have been supported by neuroimaging studies showing atypical neural responses to biological motion in children, adolescents and adults.

PLDs indicate motion information with degraded form information (Johansson, 1973) and are thus often considered as 'motion' stimuli; however, they are not completely bereft of form cues. At a global level, integrating the motion of the dots that comprise a PLD provides configural human form information. In addition, at a local level, the individual point-lights follow characteristic laws of human motion. Examples of these laws of human motion include the minimum-jerk (MJ) velocity profile (Flash & Hogan, 1985) and the two-thirds power law (Lacquaniti, Terzuolo, & Viviani, 1983). The MJ velocity profile describes the bell-shaped speed profile of a straight point-to-point movement (e.g. when drawing a straight line across a page, an individual moves the pencil tip slowly at the beginning of the movement, speeds up through the middle and slows down to a stop (Abend, Bizzi, & Morasso, 1982; Flash & Hogan, 1985)). Movements that obey the two-thirds power law slow down at curved relative to straight parts of motion (Lacquaniti et al., 1983). Both the MJ velocity profile and two-thirds power law agree with observations of human movement (Abend et al., 1982); for example, if an individual makes

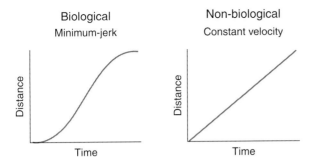

Figure 23.3 Minimum-jerk and constant velocity profiles. *See Plate 11.*
Notes: The MJ velocity profile describes the bell-shaped speed profile of a straight point-to-point movement. For example, if an individual makes a vertical sinusoidal arm movement the velocity of their hand movement will comply with MJ. This stands in contrast to something like a traditional mechanical robot arm that would move at a CV.

a vertical sinusoidal arm movement (i.e. moves her arm up and down in front of her body) her movement will comply with both the MJ velocity profile and the two-thirds power law.[1] In contrast, a traditional mechanical robot arm would move at a constant velocity (CV; Figure 23.3).

In addition to biological motion perception problems, individuals with ASCs exhibit difficulties with global motion processing. A typical global motion processing task comprises a stimulus depicting a large number of randomly moving dots, of which a proportion move coherently in a given direction; participants are required to state the direction of motion (Newsome & Paré, 1988). The dependent variable is the motion coherence threshold (MCT), which represents the percentage of incoherence in dot motion directions at the point at which participants can determine the direction of global motion (left or right) on 75 percent of trials. In three independent studies, Spencer et al. (2000), Milne et al. (2002) and Pellicano et al. (2005) found that children with ASCs had significantly higher MCTs than chronological aged-matched controls: they require about 10 percent more coherent motion than do controls to report motion direction reliably. Atkinson (2009) demonstrated a correlation between MCTs and emotion recognition from PLDs in adults with ASCs (that is, high MCTs were associated with reduced accuracy in identifying emotions). Koldewyn and colleagues (2010)

---

[1] Due to the structure of the human shoulder joint, sinusoidal arm movements follow a more curved trajectory at the start and turning points relative to the midpoints and hence would comply with both the MJ velocity profile and the two-thirds power law.

observed a similar finding in adolescents: high MCTs were associated with poor direction discrimination from PLDs. It is therefore possible that individuals with ASCs are less able to pool motion signals across space than controls (Bertone, Mottron, Jelenic, & Faubert, 2003) and that this may relate to difficulties in biological motion processing when stimuli such as PLDs are employed.

To investigate whether biological motion processing deficits in ASCs are distinct from global motion difficulties, we investigated the integrity of the perception of simple sinusoidal hand movements that require only local, not global, motion processing. We employed stimuli in which the minimum-jerk (MJ) velocity profile was manipulated, and a novel paradigm in which participants watched pairs of animations that showed a biological stimulus (a moving hand) or a non-biological stimulus (a falling tennis ball) moving across the screen. On each trial, the velocity profile with which each animation moved was either 100 per cent natural motion (MJ in the biological condition; gravitational in the non-biological condition), or 100 per cent constant velocity (CV), or some linear combination of the two extremes. In each trial, participants were shown a 'reference' animation, which was always a combination of 85 per cent natural motion and 15 per cent constant velocity, and a 'target' animation, in which the ratio of constant velocity to natural motion varied according to performance. The task was to judge which animation was 'less natural'. A two-interval forced-choice adaptive staircase paradigm was employed to generate separate thresholds for the biological (MJ) and the non-biological (gravitational) condition. We found that, whereas typical controls were more sensitive to perturbations to biological compared to gravitational motion, individuals with ASCs did not show this same enhanced sensitivity to biological motion. Further, within the biological condition, thresholds for the ASC group were significantly worse compared to those generated by controls (Figure 23.4; Cook, Saygin, Swain, & Blakemore, 2009).

In conclusion, this section documents a growing body of evidence that suggests atypicalities in biological motion processing in ASCs. Such difficulties with processing the movements of other individuals are present both with stimuli that require global motion processing and with stimuli that require only local motion processing – such as sinusoidal arm movements. The difficulties those with ASCs experience in processing the kinematics of sinusoidal arm movements raise a potential explanation for atypical interference effects in these conditions: individuals with ASCs do not process the sinusoidal arm movements in the same way as typical controls, thus the observation of these movements does not lead to the activation of the corresponding motor representation. This hypothesis also provides a potential explanation for wider difficulties with imitation and MNS hypoactivation in ASC.

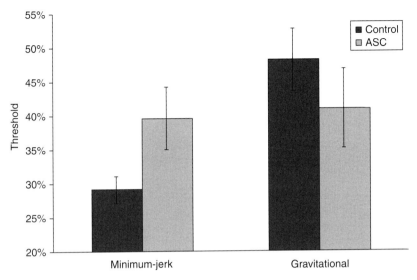

Figure 23.4 Interaction between group and condition. *See Plate 12.*

Notes: There was a significant interaction between group and condition driven by lower thresholds in the MJ condition than in the Gravitational condition for the control group but not for the ASC group. Standard error bars are shown.

Source: Image modified from Cook, Saygin, Swain, and Blakemore (2009, Figure 2; CC BY).

Action Perception in ASC Summary

A growing body of studies suggests there is atypical attention to biological motion in ASCs in early infancy, and that this is followed by atypical biological motion processing in childhood, adolescence and adulthood (however, conflicting findings are described by Koldewyn et al. 2010; Murphy, Brady, Fitzgerald, & Troje 2009; Saygin et al., 2010). Such results have been reported both with point-light display stimuli, which require global motion processing, and with stimuli that require only local motion processing (Cook et al., 2009). Behavioural reports of atypical biological motion processing have been supported by neuroimaging studies showing atypical neural responses to biological motion in children, adolescents and adults with ASCs.

Is Action Execution Atypical in ASCs?

In the previous section it was suggested that action observation may be atypical in ASCs, resulting in a 'knock-on' effect on imitation. This section examines the other component of imitation: action execution.

A number of studies have reported motor atypicalities in children and adults with ASCs. For example, individuals with autism exhibit difficulties controlling the force and direction of a ball when throwing (Staples & Reid, 2010) and differ from typical individuals with respect to handwriting (Beversdorf et al., 2001). Furthermore, when executing motor tasks, they demonstrate atypical activation in motor-related brain areas such as the cerebellum and supplementary motor area, as well as reduced connectivity between motor nodes (Mostofsky et al., 2009). Motor difficulties in autism can be identified at both the level of gross and fine motor control (Beversdorf et al., 2001; Gowen & Hamilton, 2013; Mostofsky et al., 2006), suggesting a possible underlying problem with fundamental movement kinematics.

In a recent study, we used motion tracking technology to record kinematics (velocity, acceleration and jerk) whilst adults with ASCs and a matched typical control group performed simple sinusoidal arm movements of the sort that participants are required to observe in an interference effect experiment. We found that individuals with ASCs produced horizontal sinusoidal arm movements that were more jerky than those of controls, and which proceeded with greater acceleration and velocity (Figure 23.5). The magnitude of these atypicalities was significantly correlated with autism severity, as measured by the ADOS semi-structured questionnaire (Lord et al., 1989).

Though little is known about the aetiology of atypical kinematics in ASCs, one can speculate that a lack of typical kinematics might be a consequence of peripheral factors (Todorov, 2004) such as abnormal muscle tone in autism (Maurer & Damasio, 1982) or central nervous system factors. One putative central nervous system factor is poor anticipation of the subsequent part of a motor sequence (Cattaneo et al., 2007; Fabbri-Destro, Cattaneo, Boria, & Rizzolatti, 2009). For instance, one study examined the time taken to reach for an object when it was to be subsequently placed on a large (easy condition) or small (difficult condition) target (Fabbri-Destro et al., 2009). Controls exhibited the typical pattern of a slower reach phase when the subsequent placing phase was more difficult, but the reaching movements of children with ASCs were not modulated by task difficulty. The authors concluded that, instead of translating their goal into a chain of motor acts, children with ASCs executed these acts independently. One possible explanation for the atypical kinematics that we observed is that individuals with ASCs have a compromised ability to predict the point at which they must change the direction of their movement, or they have difficulties with using this prediction to modulate current action kinematics. Another, potentially related, putative central nervous system factor that may contribute to atypical kinematics in ASCs is cerebellar neuropathology (Rogers et al., 2013). ASCs have been associated with cerebellar abnormalities including reduced Purkinje cell numbers (Bauman, 1991; Courchesne,

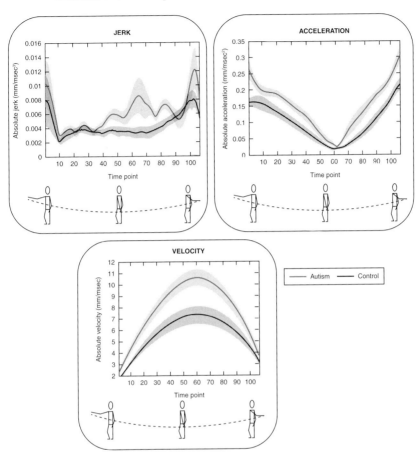

Figure 23.5 Basic kinematics of arm movements for controls and individuals with ASCs. *See Plate 13.*

Notes: When executing simple sinusoidal arm movements, individuals with ASCs made more jerky movements (upper left panel) and travelled with faster absolute acceleration (upper right panel) and velocity (lower panel). Mean movement vectors are plotted in red for the ASC group and blue for the control group. Shaded regions indicate the standard error of the mean.

Source: Image reproduced from Cook, Blakemore, and Press (2013, Figure 3; CC BY).

1997; Courchesne, Yeung-Courchesne, Press, Hesselink, & Jernigan, 1988; DiCicco-Bloom et al., 2006; Palmen, van Engeland, Hof, & Schmitz, 2004), lower cerebellar vermal volumes (Webb et al., 2009), reductions in the size and number of cells in the cerebellar nuclei, excess Bergmann glia and active neuroinflammatory processes within cerebellar white matter (Bailey et al., 1998; Bauman & Kemper, 2005; Vargas, Nascimbene, Krishnan, Zimmerman, & Pardo, 2005). A number of accounts suggest that cerebellar atypicalities play a key role in the development of the cognitive and behavioural profile that characterises ASCs (Gowen & Miall, 2007; Mostofsky et al., 2009; Rogers et al., 2013). Further studies are necessary to assess the contribution of peripheral and central factors and to investigate whether they have specific or general effects on velocity, acceleration and jerk.

Given the importance of kinematics in both gross and fine motor control, atypicalities in movement kinematics could be one reason for the difficulties with everyday motor control commonly experienced by individuals with ASCs (Beversdorf et al., 2001; Gowen & Hamilton, 2013). Such atypicalities may also impact upon imitation and interference effects. For example, imagine you are a participant in the interference effect experiment. Let us suppose that you execute sinusoidal arm movements in a different way from the actor you are observing: he maintains a steady pace whereas you accelerate and decelerate more, thus producing more jerky movements. You have had a lifetime's experience with simultaneously observing and executing your jerky movements so, for you, these visual and motor representations are tightly associated (Heyes, 2010; also see Catmur, this volume, Chapter 22). If you were to observe jerky vertical sinusoidal arm movements it would automatically activate your associated motor representation for vertical movements, which would create an interference effect if you were trying to execute horizontal movements. However, in this example you are watching an actor who produces smooth, minimum-jerk, movements. You have had very little simultaneous experience with observing smooth movements and executing your own movements, thus when you watch the smooth vertical movements of the actor they fail to activate your motor representation for vertical movements and there is thus there no interference effect. As demonstrated in this example, when assessing the integrity of imitation or interference effects, it is important to know whether the population of interest demonstrates imitation-independent motor difficulties.

In sum, this section presents a body of work suggesting that ASCs are associated with motor execution difficulties. Such findings raise (1) an alternative explanation for the atypical interference effect in ASCs, and (2) the hypothesis that an interference effect would be present if individuals with ASCs were shown movements that proceeded with kinematics that match their own.

Action Execution in ASC Summary

Motor difficulties in ASCs can be identified at both the level of gross and fine motor control (Beversdorf et al., 2001; Gowen & Hamilton, 2013; Mostofsky et al., 2006). Such difficulties may be underpinned by atypicalities in the basic kinematics of movements in ASCs (Cook, Blakemore, & Press, 2013). Neuroimaging studies have shown that, when executing motor tasks, individuals with ASCs demonstrate atypical activation in motor-related brain areas such as the cerebellum and supplementary motor area (e.g. Mostofsky et al., 2009).

Summary and Further Directions

This chapter began by presenting an experiment in which we failed to find an interference effect of action observation on action execution in adults with ASCs (Cook, Swapp, Pan, Bianchi-Berthouze, & Blakemore, 2014). This result is compatible with the broken MNS hypothesis of ASCs. However, the broken MNS hypothesis is highly controversial given that behavioural studies have demonstrated typical imitation effects in ASCs, and clinical observations have even documented hyper-imitation in individuals with this condition. The current chapter focuses on two alternative explanations: (1) action observation is atypical in ASC, and (2) action execution is atypical in ASCs. We conclude that there is a growing body of evidence to support problems with both action observation and action execution in ASCs. Thus, even if the MNS (the link between action observation and action execution) is intact in ASCs, such individuals may demonstrate atypical performance on imitation and interference effect paradigms due to their action observation and/or execution difficulties.

Extending the Argument to Other Sociocognitive Processes

The current chapter argues that imitation relates to *shared representations* in that it concerns the activation of a self-related representation by an other-related representation. This conceptualisation can be applied to other sociocognitive processes such as empathy. Empathy occurs 'when the perception of another's emotional state causes the empathizer to experience that state' (Bird & Cook, 2013, p. 2). Thus, like imitation, empathy concerns the activation of a self-representation (this time, emotion related) by the representation of another individual. In a recent article, Bird and Cook (ibid) argue that empathy deficits in ASCs may be due to the co-occurrence of alexithymia, which is characterised by difficulties in identifying and describing one's own emotional state. Bird et al. (2010) find a lack of empathic responses only in individuals who have this alexithymic atypicality in representing their own emotions. Individuals who have ASCs without co-mordid alexithymia exhibit intact empathic responses. Here, we have argued that, with respect to imitation, impairments may be due to atypical representations of one's own actions (i.e. atypical kinematics); similarly Bird and Cook argue that, with respect to empathy, impairments may be due to atypical representations of one's own emotions. They note that alexithymia has a high prevalence rate in many clinical conditions, including schizophrenia and eating disorders; thus atypical empathic responses may also be common in these conditions.

References

Abend, W., Bizzi, E., & Morasso, P. (1982). Human arm trajectory formation. *Brain*, 105(Pt 2), 331–348.

Annaz, D., Campbell, R., Coleman, M., Milne, E., & Swettenham, J. (2012). Young children with autism spectrum disorder do not preferentially attend to biological motion. *Journal of Autism and Developmental Disorders*, 42(3), 401–408. doi: 10.1007/s10803-011-1256-3.

Annaz, D., Remington, A., Milne, E., Coleman, M., Campbell, R., et al. (2010). Development of motion processing in children with autism. *Developmental Science*, 13(6), 826–838. doi: 10.1111/j.1467-7687.2009.00939.x.

Atkinson, A. P. (2009). Impaired recognition of emotions from body movements is associated with elevated motion coherence thresholds in autism spectrum disorders. *Neuropsychologia*, 47(13), 3023–3029. doi: 10.1016/j.neuropsychologia.2009.05.019.

Avikainen, S., Wohlschläger, S., Liuhanen, S., Hänninen, R., & Hari, R. (2003). Impaired mirror-image imitation in Asperger and high-functioning autistic subjects. *Current Biology*, 13(4), 339–341.

Baaren, R. van, Holland, R., Kawakami, K., & van Knippenberg, A. (2004). Mimicry and prosocial behavior. *Psychological Science: A Journal of the American Psychological Society*, 15(1), 71–74.

Bach, P., & Tipper, S. P. (2007). Implicit action encoding influences personal-trait judgments. *Cognition*, 102(2), 151–178. doi: 10.1016/j.cognition.2005.11.003.

Bailenson, J., & Yee, N. (2005). Digital chameleons: Automatic assimilation of nonverbal gestures in immersive virtual environments. *Psychological Science: A Journal of the American Psychological Society*, 16(10), 814–819. doi: 10.1111/j.1467-9280.2005.01619.x.

Bailey, A., Luthert, P., Dean, A., Harding, B., Janota, I., et al. (1998). A clinicopathological study of autism. *Brain*, 121(5), 889–905. doi: 10.1093/brain/121.5.889.

Bauman, M. L. (1991). Microscopic neuroanatomic abnormalities in autism. *Pediatrics*, 87(5), 791–796.

Bauman, M. L., & Kemper, T. L. (2005). Neuroanatomic observations of the brain in autism: A review and future directions. *International Journal of Developmental Neuroscience*, 23(2–3), 183–187. doi: 10.1016/j.ijdevneu.2004.09.006.

Bertone, A., Mottron, L., Jelenic, P., & Faubert, J. (2003). Motion perception in autism: A complex issue. *Journal of Cognitive Neuroscience*, 15(2), 218–225. doi: 10.1162/089892903321208150.

Beversdorf, D. Q., Anderson, J. M., Manning, S. E., Anderson, S. L., Nordgren, R. E., et al. (2001). Brief report: Macrographia in high-functioning adults with autism spectrum disorder. *Journal of Autism and Developmental Disorders*, 31(1), 97–101.

Bird, G., & Cook, R. (2013). Mixed emotions: The contribution of alexithymia to the emotional symptoms of autism. *Translational Psychiatry*, 3, e285. doi: 10.1038/tp.2013.61.

Bird, G., Leighton, J., Press, C., & Heyes, C. (2007). Intact automatic imitation of human and robot actions in autism spectrum disorders. *Proceedings of the Royal Society B: Biological Sciences*, 274(1628), 3027–3031. doi: 10.1098/rspb.2007.1019.

Bird, G., Silani, G., Brindley, R., White, S., Frith, U., & Singer, T. (2010). Empathic brain responses in insula are modulated by levels of alexithymia but not autism. *Brain*, 133(Pt 5), 1515–1525. doi: 10.1093/brain/awq060.

Blake, R, Turner, L., Smoski, M., Pozdol, S., & Stone, W. (2003). Visual recognition of biological motion is impaired in children with autism. *Psychological Science*, 14(2), 151–157.

Bouquet, C. A., Gaurier, V., Shipley, T., Toussaint, L., & Blandin, Y. (2007). Influence of the perception of biological or non-biological motion on movement execution. *Journal of Sports Sciences*, 25(5), 519–530. doi: 10.1080/02640410600946803.

Brass, M., Bekkering, H., & Prinz, W. (2001). Movement observation affects movement execution in a simple response task. *Acta Psychologica*, 106(1–2), 3–22.

Buccino, G., Binkofski, F., Fink, G. R., Fadiga, L., Fogassi, L., et al. (2001). Action observation activates premotor and parietal areas in a somatotopic manner: An fMRI study. *European Journal of Neuroscience*, 13(2), 400–404.

Catmur, C., Walsh, V., & Heyes, C. (2009). Associative sequence learning: The role of experience in the development of imitation and the mirror system. *Proceedings of the Royal Society B: Biological Sciences*, 364(1528), 2369–2380. doi: 10.1098/rstb.2009.0048.

Cattaneo, L., Fabbri-Destro, M., Boria, S., Pieraccini, C., Monti, A., et al. (2007). Impairment of action chains in autism and its possible role in intention understanding. *Proceedings of the National Academy of Sciences of the United States of America*, 104(45), 17825–17830. doi: 10.1073/pnas.0706273104.

Chaminade, T., Franklin, D., Oztop, E., & Cheng, G. (2005). Motor interference between humans and humanoid robots: Effect of biological and artificial motion. *Proceedings of the 4th IEEE International Conference on Development and Learning*, 96–101. doi: 10.1109/DEVLRN.2005.1490951.

Chartrand, T., & Bargh, J. (1999). The chameleon effect: The perception–behavior link and social interaction. *Journal of Personality and Social Psychology*, 76(6), 893–910.

Chong, T. T.-J., Cunnington, R., Williams, M. A., Kanwisher, N., & Mattingley, J. B. (2008). fMRI adaptation reveals mirror neurons in human inferior parietal cortex. *Current Biology*, 18(20), 1576–1580. doi: 10.1016/j.cub.2008.08.068.

Cook, J., & Bird, G. (2011). Social attitudes differentially modulate imitation in adolescents and adults. *Experimental Brain Research: Special Issue on Joint Action*, 211(3–4), 601–612. doi: 10.1007/s00221-011-2584-4.

(2012). Atypical social modulation of imitation in autism spectrum conditions. *Journal of Autism and Developmental Disorders*, 42(6), 1045–1051. doi: 10.1007/s10803-011-1341-7.

Cook, J., Blakemore, S., & Press, C. (2013). Atypical basic movement kinematics in autism spectrum conditions. *Brain*, 136(Pt 9), 2816–2824. doi: 10.1093/brain/awt208.

Cook, J., Saygin, A., Swain, R., & Blakemore, S. (2009). Reduced sensitivity to minimum-jerk biological motion in autism spectrum conditions. *Neuropsychologia*, 47(14), 3275–3278. doi: 10.1016/j.neuropsychologia.2009.07.010.

Cook, J., Swapp, D., Pan, X., Bianchi-Berthouze, N., & Blakemore, S. (2014). Atypical interference effect of action observation in autism spectrum conditions. *Psychological Medicine*, 44(4), 731–740. doi:10.1017/S0033291713001335

Courchesne, E. (1997). Brainstem, cerebellar and limbic neuroanatomical abnormalities in autism. *Current Opinion in Neurobiology*, 7(2), 269–278. doi: 10.1016/S0959-4388(97)80016-5.

Courchesne, E., Yeung-Courchesne, R., Press, G., Hesselink, J., & Jernigan, T. (1988). Hypoplasia of cerebellar vermal lobules VI and VII in autism. *New England Journal of Medicine*, 318(21), 1349–1354. doi: 10.1056/NEJM198805263182102.

Dapretto, M., Davies, M. S., Pfeifer, J. H., Scott, A. A., Sigman, M., et al. (2006). Understanding emotions in others: Mirror neuron dysfunction in children with autism spectrum disorders. *Nature Neuroscience*, 9(1), 28–30. doi: 10.1038/nn1611.

Dayan, E., Casile, A., Levit-Binnun, N., Giese, M. A., Hendler, T., & Flash, T. (2007). Neural representations of kinematic laws of motion: Evidence for action–perception coupling. *Proceedings of the National Academy of Sciences of the United States of America*, 104(51), 20582–20587. doi: 10.1073/pnas.0710033104.

DiCicco-Bloom, E., Lord, C., Zwaigenbaum, L., Courchesne, E., Dager, S., et al. (2006). The developmental neurobiology of autism spectrum disorder. *Journal of Neuroscience*, 26(26), 6897–6906. doi: 10.1523/JNEUROSCI.1712-06.2006.

Dinstein, I., Thomas, C., Humphreys, K., Minshew, N., Behrmann, M., & Heeger, D. (2010). Normal movement selectivity in autism. *Neuron*, 66(3), 461–469. doi: 10.1016/j.neuron.2010.03.034.

Fabbri-Destro, M., Cattaneo, L., Boria, S., & Rizzolatti, G. (2009). Planning actions in autism. *Experimental Brain Research*, 192(3), 521–525. doi: 10.1007/s00221-008-1578-3.

Flash, T., & Hogan, N. (1985). The coordination of arm movements: An experimentally confirmed mathematical model. *Journal of Neuroscience*, 5(7), 1688–1703.

Freitag, C. M., Konrad, C., Häberlen, M., Kleser, C., von Gontard, A., et al. (2008). Perception of biological motion in autism spectrum disorders. *Neuropsychologia*, 46(5), 1480–1494. doi:10.1016/j.neuropsychologia.2007.12.025

Gillmeister, H., Catmur, C., Liepelt, R., Brass, M., & Heyes, C. (2008). Experience-based priming of body parts: A study of action imitation. *Brain Research*, 1217, 157–170. doi: 10.1016/j.brainres.2007.12.076.

Gowen, E., & Hamilton, A. (2013). Motor abilities in autism: A review using a computational context. *Journal of Autism and Developmental Disorders*, 43(2), 323–344. doi: 10.1007/s10803-012-1574-0.

Gowen, E., & Miall, R. (2007). The cerebellum and motor dysfunction in neuropsychiatric disorders. *The Cerebellum*, 6(3), 268–279. doi: 10.1080/14734220601184821.

Gowen, E., Stanley, J., & Miall, R. (2008). Movement interference in autism-spectrum disorder. *Neuropsychologia*, 46(4), 1060–1068. doi: 10.1016/j.neuropsychologia.2007.11.004.

Hamilton, A. (2008). Emulation and mimicry for social interaction: A theoretical approach to imitation in autism. *Quarterly Journal of Experimental Psychology*, 61(1), 101–115. doi: 10.1080/17470210701508798.

Hamilton, A., Brindley, R., & Frith, U. (2007). Imitation and action understanding in autistic spectrum disorders: How valid is the hypothesis of a deficit in the mirror neuron system? *Neuropsychologia*, 45(8), 1859–1868. doi: 10.1016/j.neuropsychologia.2006.11.022.

Heiser, M., Iacoboni, M., Maeda, F., Marcus, J., & Mazziotta, J. C. (2003). The essential role of Broca's area in imitation. *European Journal of Neuroscience*, 17(5), 1123–1128.

Herrington, J. D., Baron-Cohen, S., Wheelwright, S. J., Singh, K. D., Bullmore, E. T., et al. (2007). The role of MT+/V5 during biological motion perception in Asperger syndrome: An fMRI study. *Research in Autism Spectrum Disorders*, 1(1), 14–27. doi: 10.1016/j.rasd.2006.07.002.

Heyes, C. (2010). Where do mirror neurons come from? *Neuroscience and Biobehavioral Reviews*, 34(4), 575–583. doi: 10.1016/j.ncubiorev.2009.11.007.

———(2011). Automatic imitation. *Psychological Bulletin*, 137(3), 463–483. doi: 10.1037/a0022288.

Iacoboni, M., Woods, R., Brass, M., Bekkering, H., Mazziotta, J., & Rizzolatti, G. (1999). Cortical mechanisms of human imitation. *Science*, 286(5449), 2526–2528. doi: 10.1126/science.286.5449.2526.

Johansson, G. (1973). Visual perception of biological motion and a model for its analysis. *Perception and Psychophysics*, 14, 201–211.

Kaiser, M., Delmolino, L., Tanaka, J., & Shiffrar, M. (2010a). Comparison of visual sensitivity to human and object motion in autism spectrum disorder. *Autism Research*, 3(4), 191–195. doi: 10.1002/aur.137.

Kaiser, M., Hudac, C., Shultz, S., Lee, S., Cheung, C., et al. (2010b). Neural signatures of autism. *Proceedings of the National Academy of Sciences of the United States of America*, 107(49), 21223–21228. doi: 10.1073/pnas.1010412107.

Kilner, J., Hamilton, A., & Blakemore, S. (2007). Interference effect of observed human movement on action is due to velocity profile of biological motion. *Social Neuroscience*, 2(3–4), 158–166. doi: 10.1080/17470910701428190.

Kilner, J., Neal, A., Weiskopf, N., Friston, K., & Frith, C. (2009). Evidence of mirror neurons in human inferior frontal gyrus. *Journal of Neuroscience*, 29(32), 10153–10159. doi: 10.1523/JNEUROSCI.2668-09.2009.

Kilner, J., Paulignan, Y., & Blakemore, S. (2003). An interference effect of observed biological movement on action. *Current Biology*, 13(6), 522–525.

Klin, A., & Jones, W. (2008). Altered face scanning and impaired recognition of biological motion in a 15-month-old infant with autism. *Developmental Science*, 11(1), 40–46. doi: 10.1111/j.1467-7687.2007.00608.x.

Klin, A., Lin, D., Gorrindo, P., Ramsay, G., & Jones, W. (2009). Two-year-olds with autism orient to non-social contingencies rather than biological motion. *Nature*, 459(7244), 257–261. doi: 10.1038/nature07868.

Koldewyn, K., Whitney, D., & Rivera, S. M. (2010). The psychophysics of visual motion and global form processing in autism. *Brain*, 133(Pt 2), 599–610. doi: 10.1093/brain/awp272.

Lacquaniti, F., Terzuolo, C., & Viviani, P. (1983). The law relating the kinematic and figural aspects of drawing movements. *Acta Psychologica*, 54(1–3), 115–130.

Lakin, J., & Chartrand, T. (2003). Using nonconscious behavioral mimicry to create affiliation and rapport. *Psychological Science*, 14(4), 334–339.

Leighton, J., Bird, G., Charman, T., & Heyes, C. (2008). Weak imitative performance is not due to a functional 'mirroring' deficit in adults with autism spectrum disorders. *Neuropsychologia*, 46(4), 1041–1049. doi: 10.1016/j.neuropsychologia.2007.11.013.

Leighton, J., & Heyes, C. (2010). Hand to mouth: Automatic imitation across effector systems. *Journal of Experimental Psychology: Human Perception and Performance*, 36(5), 1174–1183. doi: 10.1037/a0019953.

Leighton, J., Bird, G., Orsini, C., & Heyes, C. (2010). Social attitudes modulate automatic imitation. *Journal of Experimental Social Psychology*, 46(6), 905–910. doi: 10.1016/j.jesp.2010.07.001.

Lord, C., Rutter, M., Goode, S., Heemsbergen, J., Jordan, H., et al. (1989). Autism diagnostic observation schedule: A standardized observation of communicative and social behavior. *Journal of Autism and Developmental Disorders*, 19(2), 185–212.

Maurer, R. G., & Damasio, A. R. (1982). Childhood autism from the point of view of behavioral neurology. *Journal of Autism and Developmental Disorders*, 12(2), 195–205.

McIntosh, D., Reichmann-Decker, A., Winkielman, P., & Wilbarger, J. (2006). When the social mirror breaks: Deficits in automatic, but not voluntary, mimicry of emotional facial expressions in autism. *Developmental Science*, 9(3), 295–302. doi: 10.1111/j.1467-7687.2006.00492.x.

Milne, E., Swettenham, J., Hansen, P., Campbell, R., Jeffries, H., & Plaisted, K. (2002). High motion coherence thresholds in children with autism. *Journal of Child Psychology and Psychiatry, and Allied Disciplines*, 43(2), 255–263.

Mostofsky, S. H., Dubey, P., Jerath, V. K., Jansiewicz, E. M., Goldberg, M. C., & Denckla, M. B. (2006). Developmental dyspraxia is not limited to imitation in children with autism spectrum disorders. *Journal of the International Neuropsychological Society*, 12(3), 314–326.

Mostofsky, S. H., Powell, S. K., Simmonds, D. J., Goldberg, M. C., Caffo, B., & Pekar, J. J. (2009). Decreased connectivity and cerebellar activity in autism during motor task performance. *Brain*, 132(Pt 9), 2413–2425. doi: 10.1093/brain/awp088.

Murphy, P., Brady, N., Fitzgerald, M., & Troje, N. (2009). No evidence for impaired perception of biological motion in adults with autistic spectrum disorders. *Neuropsychologia*, 47(14), 3225–3235. doi: 10.1016/j.neuropsychologia.2009.07.026.

Newsome, W. T., & Paré, E. B. (1988). A selective impairment of motion perception following lesions of the middle temporal visual area (MT). *Journal of Neuroscience*, 8(6), 2201–2211.

Oberman, L., Hubbard, E., McCleery, J., Altschuler, E., Ramachandran, V., & Pineda, J. (2005). EEG evidence for mirror neuron dysfunction in autism spectrum disorders. *Cognitive Brain Research*, 24(2), 190–198. doi: 10.1016/j.cogbrainres.2005.01.014.

Oztop, E., Franklin, D., Chaminade, T., & Cheng, G. (2005). Human–humanoid interaction: Is a humanoid robot perceived as a human? *International Journal of Humanoid Robotics*, 2(4), 537–559.

Palmen, S. J. M. C., Engeland, H. van, Hof, P. R., & Schmitz, C. (2004). Neuropathological findings in autism. *Brain*, 127(12), 2572–2583. doi: 10.1093/brain/awh287.

Pellegrino, G. di, Fadiga, L., Fogassi, L., Gallese, V., & Rizzolatti, G. (1992). Understanding motor events: A neurophysiological study. *Experimental Brain Research*, 91(1), 176–180.

Pellicano, E., Gibson, L., Maybery, M., Durkin, K., & Badcock, D. R. (2005). Abnormal global processing along the dorsal visual pathway in autism: A possible mechanism for weak visuospatial coherence? *Neuropsychologia*, 43(7), 1044–1053. doi: 10.1016/j.neuropsychologia.2004.10.003.

Pelphrey, K., Mitchell, T., McKeown, M., Goldstein, J., Allison, T., & McCarthy, G. (2003). Brain activity evoked by the perception of human walking: Controlling for meaningful coherent motion. *Journal of Neuroscience*, 23(17), 6819–6825.

Press, C. (2011). Action observation and robotic agents: Learning and anthropomorphism. *Neuroscience and Biobehavioral Reviews*, 35(6), 1410–1418. doi: 10.1016/j.neubiorev.2011.03.004.

Press, C., Bird, G., Flach, R., & Heyes, C. (2005). Robotic movement elicits automatic imitation. *Brain Research. Cognitive Brain Research*, 25(3), 632–640. doi: 10.1016/j.cogbrainres.2005.08.020.

Press, C., Cook, J., Blakemore, S., & Kilner, J. (2011). Dynamic modulation of human motor activity when observing actions. *Journal of Neuroscience*, 31(8), 2792–2800. doi: 10.1523/JNEUROSCI.1595-10.2011.

Press, C., Richardson, D., & Bird, G. (2010). Intact imitation of emotional facial actions in autism spectrum conditions. *Neuropsychologia*, 48(11), 3291–3297. doi: 10.1016/j.neuropsychologia.2010.07.012.

Ramachandran, V., & Oberman, L. (2006). Broken mirrors: A theory of autism. *Scientific American*, 295(5), 62–69.

Rogers, S., Hepburn, S., Stackhouse, T., & Wehner, E. (2003). Imitation performance in toddlers with autism and those with other developmental disorders. *Journal of Child Psychology and Psychiatry, and Allied Disciplines*, 44(5), 763–781.

Rogers, S., & Pennington, B. (1991). A theoretical approach to the deficits in infantile autism. *Development and Psychopathology*, 3(02), 137–162. doi: 10.1017/S0954579400000043.

Rogers, T. D., McKimm, E., Dickson, P. E., Goldowitz, D., Blaha, C. D., & Mittleman, G. (2013). Is autism a disease of the cerebellum? An integration of clinical and pre-clinical research. *Frontiers in Systems Neuroscience*, 7, 15. doi: 10.3389/fnsys.2013.00015.

Russell, J. (1997). *Autism as an executive disorder*. New York: Oxford University Press.

Rutter, M. (1974). The development of infantile autism. *Psychological Medicine*, 4, 147–163.

Saygin, A., Cook, J., & Blakemore, S. (2010). Unaffected perceptual thresholds for biological and non-biological form-from-motion perception in autism spectrum conditions. *PloS One*, 5(10), e13491. doi: 10.1371/journal.pone.0013491.

Southgate, V., & Hamilton, A. F. de C. (2008). Unbroken mirrors: Challenging a theory of autism. *Trends in Cognitive Sciences*, 12(6), 225–229. doi: 10.1016/j.tics.2008.03.005.

Spencer, J., O'Brien, J., Riggs, K., Braddick, O., Atkinson, J., & Wattam-Bell, J. (2000). Motion processing in autism: Evidence for a dorsal stream deficiency. *NeuroReport*, 11(12), 2765–2767.

Spengler, S., Bird, G., & Brass, M. (2010). Hyperimitation of actions is related to reduced understanding of others' minds in autism spectrum conditions. *Biological Psychiatry*, 68(12), 1148–1155. doi: 10.1016/j.biopsych.2010.09.017.

Stanley, J., Gowen, E., & Miall, C. (2007). Effects of agency on movement interference during observation of a moving dot stimulus. *Journal of Experimental Psychology: Human Perception and Performance*, 33(4), 915–926. doi: 10.1037/0096-1523.33.4.915.

Staples, K. L., & Reid, G. (2010). Fundamental movement skills and autism spectrum disorders. *Journal of Autism and Developmental Disorders*, 40(2), 209–217. doi: 10.1007/s10803-009-0854-9.

Todorov, E. (2004). Optimality principles in sensorimotor control. *Nature Neuroscience*, 7(9), 907–915. doi: 10.1038/nn1309.

Tomasello, M. (1996). Do apes ape? In C. M. Heyes & B. G. Galef (Eds.), *Social learning in animals: The roots of culture*. New York: Academic Press, 319–346.

Vargas, D. L., Nascimbene, C., Krishnan, C., Zimmerman, A. W., & Pardo, C. A. (2005). Neuroglial activation and neuroinflammation in the brain of patients with autism. *Annals of Neurology*, 57(1), 67–81. doi: 10.1002/ana.20315.

Webb, S. J., Sparks, B.-F., Friedman, S. D., Shaw, D. W. W., Giedd, J., et al. (2009). Cerebellar vermal volumes and behavioral correlates in children with autism spectrum disorder. *Psychiatry Research*, 172(1), 61–67. doi: 10.1016/j.pscychresns.2008.06.001.

Williams, J., Whiten, A., & Singh, T. (2004). A systematic review of action imitation in autistic spectrum disorder. *Journal of Autism and Developmental Disorders*, 34(3), 285–299.

Williams, J., Whiten, A., Suddendorf, T., & Perrett, D. I. (2001). Imitation, mirror neurons and autism. *Neuroscience and Biobehavioral Reviews*, 25(4), 287–295.

24 Learning by Diffusion: Using Diffusion Experiments and Social Network Analysis to Understand the Dynamics of Cultural Evolution

Cameron R. Turner and Emma Flynn

Abstract

Culture arises from the interaction of many individuals sharing knowledge and collaborating over time, and, because of this, culture must be studied using different methods to those that are commonly employed in many areas of psychology. The majority of our understanding of the social learning underpinning culture is generalised from 'dyadic' experiments, in which a single participant observes a single model, and as a result leaves questions about the relationship between the individual- and group-level unaddressed. Such questions include how different forms of cultural information spread across the population and how individuals work together to produce cultural products. Diffusion experiments present a method for such dynamics to be examined. This chapter reviews the varieties of diffusion methods available and the strengths and weaknesses each type of diffusion design provides in answering questions about cultural evolution. It also reviews recent innovations in studying the spread of culture via social relations using social network analyses. We argue that social network analyses could be especially useful for examining a dynamic which has hitherto not been widely considered in studying cultural evolution; that is, the feedback relationship between social structure (relations) and social learning, with copying behaviour fulfilling both a role of information exchange and a role of affiliation.

Humans exhibit remarkable biological success as a species; we have undergone an extraordinary demographic shift, and inhabit every corner of the globe (Hill, Barton, & Hurtado, 2009). Yet this success cannot be solely attributed to inborn cognitive abilities; highly intelligent and well-resourced explorers have failed to survive in new terrains, where indigenous populations thrive (Henrich & McElreath, 2003). Human's biological success must also be understood with reference to culture, which is fundamental in constructing the cognition of individual humans. Culture arises out of the interaction of individuals and is a group-level phenomenon, which means that it is particularly difficult to investigate using traditional methods of experimental psychology. Yet as culture plays such an important part in our cognition, as well as our ultimate success as a species, it is essential to develop techniques that allow the interplay between individuals and groups to be explored to address the central questions of how culture is acquired, how it is transmitted and how it changes or evolves. By allowing an experimenter to control and measure both group and transmission processes, diffusion experiments offer a powerful experimental method for addressing these questions. This chapter reviews the diffusion method, and points to a necessary area of extension: namely, the feedback relationship between social structure and culture. Additional methods which offer promise in addressing the complexity in these dynamics are highlighted.

Culture and Human Cognition

Human life is predicated on the successful acquisition of cultural knowledge (Boyd, Richerson, & Henrich, 2011; Hill, Barton, & Hurtado, 2009; Richerson & Boyd, 2005; Sterelny, 2003). While non-human animals (henceforth, 'animals') possess abilities for culture and traditions, even in our most closely related relative, the chimpanzee (Whiten, 2011), the diversity and elaboration of cultural products pales in comparison to that found in humans. Further, human culture has the distinctive attribute of being cumulative: with cultural products and knowledge accruing advantageous modifications over generations, allowing increasing adaptive-fit with the environment over time (Dean, Vale, Laland, Flynn & Kendal, 2014; Tomasello, 1999; Tomasello, Kruger, & Ratner, 1993). Because of the cumulative properties of human culture, it has been argued that – for humans – culture constitutes a second inheritance system working in parallel with genetic inheritance and undergoing its own evolutionary change (Boyd & Richerson, 1985; Cavalli-Sforza & Feldman, 1981; Flynn, Laland, Kendal, & Kendal, 2013; McElreath & Henrich, 2007). That is, along with the genes passed down by parents to offspring, humans also pass down a store of knowledge and artefacts to their children, who will then improve these cultural products, transmitting the modified versions to their own children, and so on.

Fundamental to culture is the transmission of information between individuals. The cognitive abilities and proclivities for social learning, known as 'social learning mechanisms', are key to understanding culture (Flynn & Whiten, 2013; Hoppitt & Laland, 2013; Zentall, 2006, 2012). As children are 'cultural magnets', the development of these special capacities for social learning are especially important (Flynn, 2008). The development of these cognitive capacities early in childhood allow humans to learn the distinctive cultural knowledge of their group; knowledge which has been accrued over generations to allow success in their particular environment (Tomasello, 1999; Tomasello et al., 1993). Cumulative culture in particular requires high fidelity transmission of information across generations (Lewis & Laland, 2012), and as children are the link between generations, studying children's capacities for high fidelity transmission sheds light on how human culture emerged out of the cultural capacities possessed by other apes (Horner, Whiten, Flynn, & de Waal, 2006; van Schiak & Burkart, 2011; Tomasello, 1999; Tomasello et al., 1993, Whiten, 2011).

Indeed, many studies now affirm a substantial difference in the abilities and motivation of young children and other closely related species in the domain of social learning. For instance, Herrmann, Call, Hernàndez-Lloreda, Hare, Hare and Tomasello (2007) compared the performance of children (two-year-olds) to that of chimpanzees and orangutans on a range of behavioural tests of intelligence. On tests which were within the physical domain, such as reasoning about space and causality, all groups performed equally. However, in tests within the social domain, such as following gaze, children outperformed non-human primates. Dean, Kendal, Schapiro, Theirry, and Laland (2012) compared children, chimpanzees and capuchin monkeys on the ability to extract rewards from a complex apparatus which required problem solving to advance through three stages, where each stage provided an increasingly desirable reward. It was found that children more often reached the later stages of this apparatus than the chimpanzees or the capuchin monkeys, and this was shown to be attributed to their greater use of social learning.

Early theorists in developmental psychology highlighted the situated nature of the development of human cognition within a cultural history, and the manner in which cognition is substantially constructed by social learning to acquire this cultural knowledge (Bandura, 1977; Vygotsky, 1978). Contemporary research confirms culture can have pervasive effects on cognition, with differences existing between groups, not only regarding beliefs and attitudes, but also basic processes like visual perception and spatial cognition (Henrich, Heine, & Norenzayan, 2010). The cultural intelligence hypothesis captures the argument of early theorists, and forwards that adult humans have a range of cognitive abilities not possessed by other animals, which are specially developed for their ways of life, and learned by an elaborated social learning process in development (Herrmann et al., 2007; van Schaik & Burkart, 2011). In addition to cognitive differences measurable in humans and animals, paleoanthropological evidence supports the extension of the childhood lifestage within humans compared to other apes (who have a comparatively quick juvenile period), consistent with the emergence of increasingly elaborate culture (Nielsen, 2012).

For these reasons, to understand cognition it is necessary to understand individuals as situated in their cultural context, and to understand the dynamics of culture: how it evolved, how information is transmitted between individuals and how modifications accumulate on cultural products. Acquiring such understanding poses methodological challenges as it requires examining both individual psychology and dynamics that arise from interactions between people. This chapter first reviews the current thinking on how to analyse both individual abilities for social learning and culture. It then reviews the diffusion experimental method, which allows an investigation of the relation between the individual and their culture, as well as the dynamics of cultural transmission. Finally, the chapter highlights a further area of complexity in cultural evolution research: the dynamic nature of social structure and culture. New approaches, and specifically new analytic methods, have recently been used to take into account the way in which culture flows through social relations. We propose that a bi-directional relationship between social learning and social relations also needs to be taken into account; as not only does social learning occur through social relations, but social learning in-and-of-itself creates and strengthens social bonds.

Analysing Culture: Social Learning Strategies

Laland (2004) laid out the social learning strategies framework, which seeks to understand how biases in what is learned might affect which cultural knowledge or products get propagated, and the adaptive basis of social information use (also see Rendell et al., 2011). This framework has become widely used in analysing social learning and culture. Laland (2004) draws on evidence showing that, while using social information can confer adaptive benefit over information the individual learns themselves, unconstrained use of social information (in the form of copying the behaviours of conspecifics) is not adaptive (Giraldeau, Valone, & Templeton, 2002). For instance, evolutionary modelling shows that unconstrained social information use can lead to the use of maladaptive out-of-date information within a population (Rogers, 1988). This begs the question: How did the widespread use of social information observed across species evolve? And specifically: How did the intensive use of social information seen within human culture evolve?

Social learning strategy research seeks to answer these questions by examining the factors which might contribute to the reliability of social information (often via modelling), and testing whether animals and humans adhere to these predictions. For instance, seeing a majority of individuals performing a behaviour may strengthen the reliability of that information – thus a 'copy-the-majority' bias in using social information may be adaptive (Pike & Laland, 2010). Prestigious individuals or dominant animals may be higher in the social hierarchy because of their more adept ability to use information – and thus copying the behaviour of these individuals may be adaptive (Chudek, Heller,

Birch, & Henrich, 2012; Flynn & Smith, 2012; Henrich & Gil-White, 2001). It is posited that humans and animals may have adapted learning rules that confine social information use to instances where it is reliable. These learning rules help to explain how social information use arises and shed light on the differential transmission of information based on the architecture of our preferences in learning social information.

The social learning strategy framework aids in using these evolutionary constraints and dividing questions about social learning and cultural transmission into the logical components of 'what, whom, when and how?' *What* concerns the kind of information that is transmitted; *whom* examines the kinds of model that are preferred; *when* examines situations that promote social information use; and *how* addresses the mechanism of social learning, whether that be through imitation, language or other means.

Social learning strategies research has so far focused on several key avenues as best candidates for areas where social information may be useful (Rendell et al., 2011). The first is aspects of the source of social information or the model: such as their relation to the learner (Henrich & Henrich, 2010), their attributes such as age and/or knowledge state (Wood, Kendal, & Flynn, 2012), and their previous success (Mesoudi, 2008; for a review of whom-based biases, see Wood, Kendal, & Flynn, 2013). Second, frequency-based copying has also been investigated, including copying frequently observed behaviours (Toelch, Bruce, Meeus, & Reader, 2010) versus copying rare behaviours (Griskevicicus, Goldstein, Mortensen, Cialdini, & Kenrick, 2006). Attributes of the learner, such as their age, knowledge (van Bergen, Coolen, & Laland, 2004) or reproductive state (Webster & Laland, 2011), have also been shown to affect social learning. Certain informational content is especially likely to be transmitted – known as 'content biases' – such as information that causes a disgust reaction (Heath, Bell, & Sternberg, 2001) or draws on social rather than non-social information (Stubbersfield, Tehrani, & Flynn, 2014). The social learning strategy framework has been a productive way to organise research in cultural evolution. We now review the diffusion experiment method, which offers a particularly useful tool to investigate the link between individual cognition and culture, and measure the use, or not, of specific social learning strategies under certain contexts.

The Diffusion Experiment Methodology

Culture is a group-level phenomenon; it arises out of the action of many individuals, sharing and improving on information over time. Such dynamics produce methodological challenges for those interested in the psychological mechanisms and interpersonal processes which allow for culture. In many areas of psychology, participants can be tested in a laboratory setting individually or be surveyed *en masse*. However, to properly understand the relation between psychology and culture, it is necessary not only to understand the psychology of the individual, but also the interaction between individuals and group-level dynamics. There has been a plethora of studies examining social learning and information use in both humans and animals (Hoppitt & Laland, 2013; Zentall, 2006, 2012), but often this research has followed a 'dyadic' design. While this work has been essential in elucidating the capacities of different species and age groups of children in their ability and proclivities to use social information, it is limited in generalising about the dynamics of multiple individuals and how group-level behaviour gives rise to cumulative culture.

Previously, naturalistic observations either of populations of human cultural groups (DeWalt, Dewalt, & Wayland, 1998) or animals (Kawai, 1965) have been the most prominent method used to study cultural change. In naturalistic observation, a researcher attempts to describe how certain cultural products arise, how they are used, modified and spread through a natural population (e.g. a village or a troop of monkeys). However, naturalistic observation, being non-experimental, has limitations in identifying causality and discounting alternative explanations. Diffusion studies move the examination of the interactions of individuals and how they give rise to cultural processes into the laboratory, allowing greater experimental control and the possibility of manipulation (Flynn & Whiten, 2010; Mesoudi & Whiten, 2008; Whiten & Mesoudi, 2008). It should be noted that diffusion research, and the use of designs involving small groups, has its roots in social psychology and particularly research on group dynamics (Forsyth, 2006; Tajfel & Turner, 1986), which faces the same problem of examining the dynamic interaction of the individual and the group. In the case of social psychological research, the general concern is how groups influence the attitudes and behaviour of their members; whereas for research investigating 'cultural evolution', there is greater interest in how information spreads and changes. Although there are many iterations of experimental design and procedure which can be used in diffusion research, there are two overarching approaches: open diffusion and diffusion chains.

Open-diffusion designs (sometimes called the 'closed-group method'; Mesoudi & Whiten, 2008) are similar to the observation of cultural transmission in natural populations; however, the context in which the transmission occurs is controlled. Initially, a behaviour is seeded in a population, either by a pre-trained individual or by the experimenter creating the opportunity for the behaviour to arise and waiting until an individual discovers it. All individuals in the experiment have the opportunity to observe the interactions between other individuals and the task, and in principle to demonstrate this knowledge by acting on the task themselves. For instance, Flynn and Whiten (2010), in an initial phase, allowed children to play individually with an apparatus for which two discrete methods could be used to retrieve a reward. In a second phase, all children were allowed to interact in a single group. Variation in the use of the two methods by the children decreased over time within the group, compared to when they interacted with the apparatus individually. By videotaping the experimental session, Flynn and Whiten were able to examine the interactions between children, specifically how their history of observations of success and/ or failure lead to this effect (see Figure 24.1).

In contrast to open-diffusion experiments, in diffusion chain experiments, the transmission process is controlled. The design works similarly to the 'Chinese Whispers' or 'Broken Telephone' games, such that an individual (A) is trained (or has the proclivity) to perform a certain type of behaviour, and then performs that behaviour in the presence of individual (B), and then individual (B) has an opportunity to perform the behaviour in the presence of another individual (C), and so on. Different chains are run to examine the fidelity of transmission along the chain of the seeded information according to their different characteristics – which can be manipulated, such as age or type of participant, content of behaviour or context. This design was first employed by Bartlett (1932), who seeded chains of adults with short stories which varied in their content. While details in the stories were often misconstrued or lost during transmission, by the end of the chain the essential idea or 'gist' of the story was retained. Bartlett further concluded that the distortions which occurred were based on the participants' prior knowledge.

Diffusion chain experiments can also involve a group of individuals in which certain individuals are removed and replaced, and in this way can attempt to replicate the process of cultural 'evolution' over several laboratory 'generations'. Groups perform a task, or are seeded with a behaviour or information, and then members are systematically withdrawn and replaced with new members. Jacobs and Campbell (1961) used this approach to extend Sherif's (1935) classic research on the 'autokinetic effect'. He had groups of three individuals judge the distance a dot of light moved in a darkened room, finding that the groups converged and agreed upon a common distance, thus demonstrating the effect of conformity. Jacobs and Campbell (1961) took the extra step of replacing one group member with a naïve participant, measuring the change in estimates over generations. It was found that norms persisted for several generations but eventually regressed back to the estimates of naïve individuals (also see von Zimmerman & Richardson, this volume, Chapter 12).

Using diffusion experiments allows control over many factors of the experimental design, but the most crucial for answering questions about cultural evolution is control over the manipulation of the group composition (which individuals are present) and the transmission or interaction over time (by controlling aspects of the generations within the experiment). How these aspects of design are varied provides different strengths and weaknesses, and the use of open diffusion and diffusion chains are suited to different questions regarding cultural evolution.

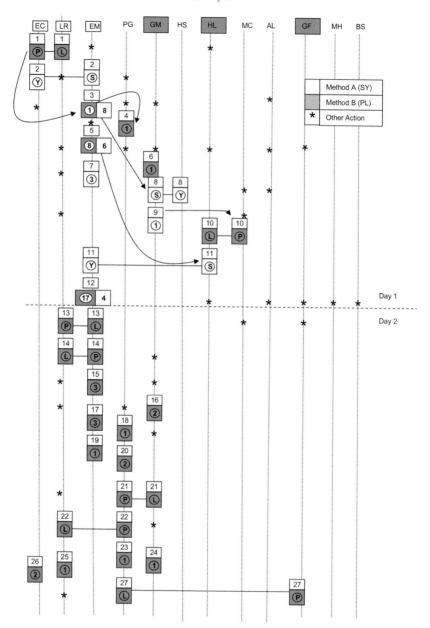

Figure 24.1 Open diffusion over two days.

Notes: The ordered columns are children's successes at extracting a reward from a puzzle box during the open diffusion. The initials in rectangles across the top are those children who were successful in an initial asocial phase;

Figure 24.1 (*cont.*)

white rectangles represent use of method 'A', and dark rectangles represent use of method 'B'. No rectangle means that the child was not successful in the asocial phase. Rows represent successful bouts, sometimes using different methods to complete a series of successful extractions within the same bout. Arrows represent witnessing and adopting a new method, either for a child who had never been successful, or a change in method use in a previously successful child. Some attempts were joint attempts, represented by joining horizontal lines, with two children completing different parts of the extraction (P, turn pink knob; Y, turn yellow knob; L, push long lever; S, push short lever). An asterisk represents a child's interaction with the SB during another child's successful bout; these interactions included wiggling a door, attempting to turn an already turned knob, push an already pushed lever and/or switching on lights.

Source: Taken from Flynn and Whiten (2010).

In open diffusion, group composition is controlled by the experimenter, primarily by influencing the number and knowledge state of the individuals, while the interactions between these individuals unfold naturally over time. Comparisons across several such groups also allow specific research questions to be addressed. Open diffusion has been particularly useful in comparing the spread of social information to the effects of individual (asocial) learning. For instance, Flynn and Whiten's (2010) study, mentioned above, allowed comparison between children's use of behaviour acquired individually in the first phase and the behaviour that was observed in a group setting. Thus it could be established that there was homogeneity of behaviour within the group due to social learning, as is characteristic of culture. Open-diffusion designs have, therefore, often been used in animal experiments where the focus is on whether behaviour can spread and be maintained by social learning at all (Whiten & Mesoudi, 2008). How the interactions between individuals lead to changes in the frequency of a behaviour in a group can be measured, but as they arise organically analysing this is often 'messy' and difficult; yet, open diffusion has an advantage in terms of generalisability because of the natural spread of information it allows (Flynn & Whiten, 2010, 2012; Whiten & Flynn, 2010).

In basic diffusion chain designs where individuals interact sequentially over generations, the group composition is held constant (usually at dyads of two individuals), and the research question is generally the differential spread of information through chains or the specific interaction (the social learning mechanism) between individuals that leads to this information transmission. By seeding different forms of information in separate chains and measuring the fidelity or speed of information flow along the chain, the linear transmission chain method is particularly useful in examining biases which might exist in the spread of information (i.e. relate to which types of information are preferred and therefore spread quickly and faithfully). For instance, Mesoudi, Whiten, and Dunbar (2006) seeded chains of individuals with either information about a third-party ('gossip'), an individual's actions or the physical environment. Information about third parties was retained with the greatest accuracy, supporting a bias for content about social relations, and shedding light on culture by evidencing a hypothesis that humans have specialised social intelligence, for monitoring social relations.

In diffusion chain experiments in which the composition of groups is changed over time by withdrawing and replacing members, the experimenter exerts control both over the group composition and the generations within the experiment. These designs allow for both the study of intragroup dynamics, and how these intragroup dynamics affect the formation of cultural traditions, as well as the successfulness of these traditions. In this way, replacement chain experiments offer a powerful means by which to test hypotheses about cumulative culture. In the method used by Jacobs and Campbell (1961), the experimenter was able to observe how different intragroup processes, such as adherence to norms, contribute to the formation of knowledge within any generation, and how new members either influence or are influenced by these intragroup processes. Replacement experiments also allow the examination of the effect such processes have on the quality of the cultural products produced. For instance, Caldwell and Millen (2008) found that paper aeroplanes flew further and spaghetti towers were taller, over the course of multiple generations, due to the accumulation of information within groups. And Caldwell and Millen (2009) were able to test directly the association between different forms of available social information and learning, and the resulting effect these had on the transmission and accumulation of modifications on culture across generations. In Caldwell and Millen's (2009) study the amount of information available in separate chains within a paper aeroplane constructing task was varied; participants variously (1) had access to the products (paper aeroplanes) of the previous generation, (2) were able to view the previous generation creating their products, or (3) were taught by the previous generation – or combinations of these processes. All forms and combinations of the social information led to cumulative culture, challenging previous assumptions that only certain social learning mechanisms lead to cumulative culture (Tomasello et al., 1993). By using a diffusion design the link between social learning interactions and the generation of culture could be tested directly rather than only conjectured.

Diffusion experiments are increasingly being employed in studies of social learning and culture to offer empirical tests of hypotheses about the evolution of culture, how culture arises out of social learning and the factors which affect the differential spread of cultural information. According to two 2008 reviews, 34 diffusion studies were conducted with adults (Mesoudi & Whiten, 2008) and 33 with animals (Whiten & Mesoudi, 2008); a 2010 review identified 5 studies with children (Flynn & Whiten, 2010). This number has subsequently grown. By allowing control and close measurement of group composition and the transmission of information, diffusion experiments offer a flexible and powerful method linking dyadic research on social learning with research on the group processes underlying culture.

Dynamic Social Networks and Cultural Diffusion

While diffusion experiments offer a critical method for testing the relation between social learning and culture, social structure and social relations are important to culture in natural populations, and this creates a further level of dynamism. Social information flows between individuals, and therefore the relationship between individuals is key to understanding the transmission of information and culture. In fact, it has been argued that changes in social structure were important in allowing the development of cumulative culture; it is reasoned that greater population density leads to greater retention of cultural information, allowing it to persist across generations and accumulate modifications (Powell, Shennan, & Thomas, 2009; Sterelny, 2011). This insight, that social structure impacts cultural transmission, has opened up the recent use of network-based modelling, a promising method that allows the relationship between social structure and information flow to be investigated statistically (Cantor & Whitehead, 2013; Hoppitt & Laland, 2011). However, in examining the transmission of information between individuals along with the social structure, there is further complexity which must be accounted for: social learning, the exchange of information between individuals, itself changes the social structure. That is, there is a feedback loop between social structure and social learning. Copying others' behaviour serves both an informational function, of acquiring knowledge, and an interpersonal function, increasing affiliation and liking between the model and learner (van Baaren, Janssen, Chartrand, & Dijksterhuis, 2009; Chartrand & Bargh, 1999; Over & Carpenter, 2012; also see Oostenbroek & Over, this volume, Chapter 7). We suggest that this second 'affiliatory' function of social learning likely remodels the social network and can be implicated in the clustering of like individuals observed in social network research (Cantor & White, 2013; McPherson, Smith-Lovin, & Cook, 2001). To understand the evolution and dynamics of culture it is, therefore, necessary to investigate not only the effect of social structure, but the change in social structure and relations over time. We call attention to the developing method of social network analyses to be used in concert with diffusion experiments as a further way of investigating the dynamics of culture (a further method which might be fruitful, especially within the developmental literature, is the 'microgenetic' method, reviewed by Flynn & Siegler, 2007).

Social learning has a social role. In both developmental psychology (Over & Carpenter, 2012; Užgiris, 1981) and social psychology with adults (van Baaren et al., 2009; Chartrand & Bargh, 1999), the dual role of social learning as a method to gain accurate information and to increase affiliation has been a source of interest. Matching or conforming behaviour, which sends the message 'we are alike' (whether intended or unintended and unconscious), has been shown in a range of domains with both children and adults to increase affiliation (van Baaren et al., 2009; Chartrand & Bargh, 1999; Over & Carpenter, 2012; also see Lakens, Schubert, & Paladino, this volume, Chapter 13).

A demonstration of the social role of copying for children was shown by Nielsen and Blank (2011). Four- and five-year-old children observed two models using an apparatus, one who included an obviously causally redundant action when retrieving a reward from inside the apparatus, and one who used only causally necessary actions. The researchers then manipulated which one of the models left the room. During the children's opportunity to retrieve the reward, they were more likely to include the causally redundant action when the model who demonstrated it was present, as opposed to absent; suggesting that children were including that action for interpersonal reasons. Similarly, Over, Carpenter, Spears, and Gattis (2013) showed children two models, one of whom mimicked the children's choices in selecting which animal she liked best (depicted on photographs shown to the child), the other selecting a different choice. Children were more likely to endorse both the later preferences and factual claims of the model who mimicked them, rather than the model who did not.

For adults, the use of copying to promote 'alikeness' has been shown to be quite subtle (van Baaren et al., 2009). When individuals engage in interactions with a partner they copy the posture, emotions, mannerisms and speech patterns of that person, and this mimicry increases when the goal is to create affiliation with a partner (Lakin & Chartrand, 2003). This, indeed, has the effect of increasing liking (Chartrand & Bargh, 1999). Participants, naïve to the goal of the experiment, interacted with a partner who either mimicked or did not mimic their behaviour. Participants rated the partner who mimicked them as more likable, and the interaction as more smooth and harmonious than that with partners who did not mimic them.

The liking of individuals who are similar to you, and the copying of their behaviour holds for more abstract domains than just immediate behaviour. For instance, people are more attracted to confederates with similar birthdays and surnames as their own (Jones, Pelham, Carvalo, & Mirenberg, 2004). Group identification is an especially important and powerful level at which this relation between 'acting alike' and 'being liked' occurs; individuals are both pulled to conform to the behaviour and attitudes of their group, and showing these group behaviours increases liking among group members (Deutsh & Gerard, 1955; Tajfel & Turner, 1986).

'Homophily', the clustering together of individuals who are alike, has been well attested to in the social network literature (McPherson, Smith-Lovin, & Cook, 2001). Individuals with similar attributes, such as educational attainment, class background, preferences and beliefs, are more tightly connected, interacting with each other more often, than those to whom they are dissimilar. We propose that the dual role of copying, as both an information transfer mechanism and an affiliation-increasing mechanism, has a role in creating this clustering, and further highlights the necessity of examining (1) the social structure underlying social learning, and (2) the dynamic way in which this might change over time. Homophily is present in animals and predicts their interactions (e.g. Kutsukake, Suetsugu, & Hasegawa, 2006; Madden, et al., 2011; Sundaresan, et al., 2007), increasing interest in the question of the evolutionary basis of the phenomenon (Fu, Nowak, Christakis, & Flower, 2012). Below we review recent research that has employed network-based analyses as an innovative method to examine the relation between social learning and social structure.

Analysing the social network and the spread of social learning. Social network analyses are new methods being imported from the area of network theory to study how culture spreads through social learning within a social network (Cantor & Whitehead, 2013; Hoppitt & Laland, 2011). The analytic methods depict individuals as nodes in a network, with the connecting edges being the relationship between individuals. Edges can be weighted according to the closeness of those individuals, which, for example, may be measured by the proportion of time individuals spend together. This creates the network's topology. Social learning is then assumed to occur along edges, and thus learned traits to be transmitted quickly between closely linked individuals (see Figure 24.2 for an illustration). Networks, therefore, encode both the relation between individuals and the spread of transmission of information, and can in theory be used to model their interaction. In the area of cultural evolution, this method has so far been largely restricted to research on animals, yet these experiments demonstrate the promise of extending this method to other areas of 'culture'. For example, Mann and colleagues (2012) applied social network analysis methods to the spread of a tool-use behaviour within bottle-nosed dolphins. Within a population of dolphins in Shark Bay, Australia, there is differential use of sponges by individuals in foraging; while some dolphins hold the sponges on their beaks as they feed in rocky substrate, others do not. Using information about the time individuals spent together showed that sponge-using dolphins preferentially associate with other sponge users, supporting the hypothesis that the behaviour is related to social structure. Similarly, Allen, Weinrich, Hoppitt, and Rendell (2013) examined the foraging behaviour of humpback whales in the Gulf of Maine where two different foraging techniques exist: 'bubble-feeding' and a method that was an innovation in the population called 'lobtail feeding'. In bubble-feeding, whales blow bubbles below and around schools of prey fish forcing them together, allowing easier capture, but in lobtail feeding the tail is smacked on the surface of the water, and can be combined with bubble-feeding, to create the same effect. Using social network analyses, Allen and colleagues (2013) tested, and found support for, the hypothesis that association between individuals accounted for

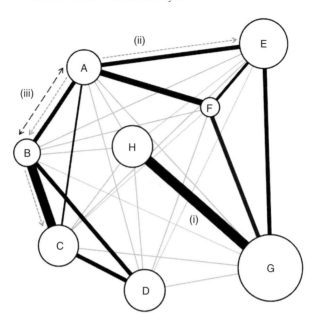

Figure 24.2 An illustration of a social network topology, as analysed by social network analyses.

Notes: Individuals appear as nodes (A, B, C...), which are connected by edges. Edges can be weighted to encode information about level of association (i). Culture/information spreads through edges (ii), and more quickly between more tightly associated individuals. We posit that the spread of social information/social learning itself has an interpersonal role, increasing affiliation, and therefore itself should rearrange network typology in a dynamic feedback process (iii).

the spread of the behaviour, finding that a model in which social transmission was responsible for the spread of lobtail feeding was the strongest supported.

Claidiere, Messer, Hoppitt, and Whiten (2013) combined open-diffusion and social network analyses in an experiment with squirrel monkeys. Two separate populations of monkeys were seeded with different techniques to retrieve a food reward from an apparatus and the amount of time individuals spent together at the site of the apparatus was measured. Group differences emerged, which were characterised by monkeys copying the seeded behaviour, and the behaviour was diffused through social learning. The eigenvector centrality, a measure of how connected an individual is to all other individuals, had a positive association with the speed at which an individual would acquire the foraging method seeded in their group, thus demonstrating how a position in a network influences social learning. It was further found that the initial group differences in traditions maintained by using the behaviour of the model eventually degraded over time, as individuals used non-seeded methods. This fits with a picture of cultural evolution wherein high fidelity transmission and close replication of individuals' actions is important in sustaining culture – abilities which are lacking in monkeys (Whiten, 2011).

These experiments begin to show how network analyses can help in linking together social relations and transfer of cultural knowledge, and testing theories about cultural evolution. They can also begin to tell us about mechanisms. For instance, Atton, Hoppitt, Webster, Galef, and Laland (2012) used network-based analyses to show that, while social network did predict three-spine sticklebacks' likelihood of finding a solution to a task, the social network did not predict the spread of the solution to the task. This suggests that the mechanism of transmission was, in fact, indirect, with individuals simply being present and more likely to discover the solution to the foraging task by being associated with knowledgeable fish and *not* direct observational learning.

The use of network-based analyses with animals has been developed largely because of the difficulty of evaluating hypotheses about social learning in natural animal populations – and has been employed generally in hope of discovering if social learning is present at all, and, if so, to what degree this leads to traditions or culture (Cantor & Whitehead, 2013; Hoppitt & Laland, 2011). The use of similar network-based statistics has not been readily employed within research into culture with humans, although there has been some modelling research investigating the relation between culture and social structure in systems displaying attributes similar to human populations (e.g. Centola, González-Avella, Eguíluz, & San Miguel, 2007). This modelling work suggests that, with humans, these methods could be used to examine subtler questions about the transmission of information, and the relationship between individuals, social structure and the adaptiveness and efficiency of the entire network (Cantor & Whitehead, 2013). Two studies, described below, give examples of the way in which network modelling can be used in the human case to elucidate answers to questions about culture.

First, Kunst and Kratzer (2007) examined the diffusion of an online product through groups of primary school-aged students in The Netherlands. They surveyed the relationships between children in these groups using questionnaires, and measured the uptake of the on-line product over time. Employing social network-based statistics, they were able to determine that children's centrality to their network (their strength of connection to all other individuals) was a strong determinant of their uptake of the product.

Second, Wisdom, Song, and Goldstone (2013) had groups of participants play a computer-based task where they were required to combine virtual pets into teams to compete in leagues. Within this game, participants received information about the various payoffs of combinations of virtual pets and had to attempt to maximise this payoff. Participants also had access to the solutions of other individuals in the group. This created a situation in which there was a complex problem space, where each individual was able to use social information, but also wished to increase her own payoff. Participants used social information in a range of ways, but specifically they used peers' solutions which were similar to their own. By imitating these solutions it was possible for further incrementally improved solutions to be developed, a signature of cumulative culture.

Culture is transferred via social learning through the social relations within a group's social network. Both humans and animals group together based on their likenesses and similarities. We have strong evidence within humans that social learning, including copying the behaviours of and adopting the preferences of others, has an interpersonal function of increasing liking, as well as the function of providing accurate information about the world. Together these points suggest that both social structure and its change over time are fundamental in understanding culture, and that there is a feedback-like relation in which social information transfer itself remodels the topology of the social network (Cantor & Whitehead, 2013). The use of social network analyses has already begun to prove successful in examining the relation between social structure and information flow within animals, and holds promise for similar investigations in humans. Especially promising are designs which couple social network analyses with the use of diffusion experiments, given the control they provide.

Conclusion

Cognition, especially human cognition, must be understood with reference to its situated nature within development, within a culture. The analyses of culture and social learning via social learning strategies have helped frame research into areas of logical investigation, and our knowledge of the situations in which social information is used and the mechanisms which allow this transmission is growing. However, much of this research has employed a dyadic design. To properly investigate culture it is necessary to examine the interactions between multiple individuals and how they give rise to the dynamics of culture. Diffusion experiments allow the direct testing of hypotheses about such dynamics by allowing the experimenter to manipulate the group composition and transmission of information over time. Further, the dynamic bi-directional relation between social network structure and the flow of cultural information must be explored. There is now substantial evidence that social learning provides functional information about one's environment *and* has an interpersonal function, ultimately changing social relationships. It is essential that we study this feedback relationship to establish how social learning restructures the social network. Social network analyses offer promise in investigating this process, being especially useful when combined with diffusion experiments.

References

Allen, J., Weinrich, M., Hoppitt, W., & Rendell, L. (2013). Network-based diffusion analysis reveals cultural transmission of lobtail feeding in humpback whales. *Science*, 340, 485–488.

Atton, N., Hoppitt, W., Webster, M. M., Galef, B. G., & Laland, K. N. (2012). Information flow through threespine stickleback networks without social transmission. *Proceedings of the Royal Society B: Biological Sciences*, 279, 4272–4278.

Baaren, R. van, Janssen, L., Chartrand, T. L., & Dijksterhuis, A. (2009). Where is love? The social aspects of mimicry. *Philosophical Transactions of the Royal Society B: Biological Sciences*, 364, 2381–2389. doi: 10.1098/rstb.2009.0057.

Bandura, A. (1977). *Social learning theory*. Upper Saddle River, NJ: Prentice Hall.

Bartlett, F. C. (1932) *Remembering*. Oxford: Macmillan.

Bergen, Y. van, Coolen I., & Laland, K. (2004). Nine-spined sticklebacks exploit the most reliable source when public and private information conflict. *Proceedings of the Royal Society B: Biological Sciences*, 271, 957–962.

Boyd, R., & Richerson, P. J. (1985). *Culture and the evolutionary process*. Chicago, IL: University of Chicago Press.

Boyd, R., Richerson, P. J., & Henrich, J. (2011). The cultural niche: Why social learning is essential for human adaptation. *Proceedings of the National Academy of Sciences*, 108, 10918–10925. doi: 10.1073/pnas.1100290108.

Caldwell, C. A., & Millen, A. (2008). Experimental models for testing hypotheses about cumulative cultural evolution. *Evolution and Human Behaviour*, 29, 165–171.

(2009). Social learning mechanisms and cumulative cultural evolution: Is imitation necessary? *Psychological Science*, 20(12), 1478–1483.

Cantor, M., & Whitehead, H. (2013). The interplay between social networks and culture: Theoretically and among whales and dolphins. *Philosophical Transactions of the Royal Society B: Biological Sciences*, 368, 1471–2970.

Cavalli-Sforza, L. L., & Feldman, M. (1981). *Cultural transmission and evolution: A quantitative approach*. Princeton, NJ: Princeton University Press.

Centola, D., González-Avella, J. C., Eguíluz, V. M., & San Miguel, M. (2007). Homophily, cultural drift, and the co-evolution of cultural groups. *Journal of Conflict Resolution*, 51, 905–929. doi: 10.1177/0022002707307632.

Chartrand, T. L., & Bargh, J. A. (1999). The chameleon effect: The perception–behavior link and social interaction. *Journal of Personality and Social Psychology*, 76, 893–910.

Chudek, M., Heller, S., Birch, S. & Henrich, J. (2012). Prestige-based cultural learning: Bystander's differential attention to potential models influences children's learning. *Evolution and Human Behaviour*, 33, 46–56.

Claidiere, N., Messer, E., Hoppitt, W., & Whiten, A. (2013). Diffusion dynamics of socially learning foraging techniques in squirrel monkeys. *Current Biology*, 23, 1251–1255.

Dean, L. G., Kendal, R. L., Schapiro, S. J., Thierry, B., & Laland, K. N. (2012). Identification of the social and cognitive processes underlying human cumulative culture. *Science*, 335(6072), 1114–1118.

Dean, L., Vale, G. L., Laland, K. N., Flynn, E. G., & Kendal, R. L. (2014). Human cumulative culture: A comparative perspective. *Biological Reviews*, 89, 284–301.

Deutsch, M., & Gerard, H. B. (1955). A study of normative and informational social influences upon individual judgment. *Journal of Abnormal and Social Psychology*, 51, 629–636.

DeWalt, K. M., DeWalt, B. R. & Wayland, C. B. (1998). Participant observation. In H. R. Bernard (Ed.), *Handbook of methods in cultural anthropology*. Walnut Creek, CA: AltaMira Press, 259–299.

Flynn, E. (2008). Investigating children as cultural magnets: Do young children transmit redundant information along diffusion chains? *Philosophical Transactions of the Royal Society B: Biological Sciences*, 363(1509), 3541–3551.

Flynn, E., Laland, K. N., Kendal, R. L., & Kendal, J. R. (2013). Developmental niche construction. *Developmental Science*, 16(2), 296–313.

Flynn, E., & Siegler, R. (2007). Measuring change: Current trends and future directions in microgenetic research. *Infant and Child Development*, 16, 135–149.

Flynn, E., & Smith, K. (2012). Investigating the mechanisms of cultural acquisition: How pervasive is overimitation in adults? *Social Psychology*, 43, 185–195.

Flynn, E., & Whiten, A. (2010). Studying children's social learning experimentally 'in the wild'. *Learning & Behavior*, 38, 284–296.

(2012). Experimental 'microcultures' in young children: Identifying biographic, cognitive, and social predictors of information transmission. *Child Development*, 83(3), 911–925.

(2013). Dissecting children's observational learning of complex actions through selective video displays. *Journal of Experimental Child Psychology*, 116, 247–263.

Forsyth, D. R. (2006). *Group dynamics*. Belmont, CA: Thomson-Wadworth.

Fu, F., Nowak, M., Christakis, N., & Fowler, J. (2012). The evolution of homophily. *Scientific Reports*, 2, 845.

Giraldeau, L.-A., Valone, T., & Templeton, J. (2002). Potential disadvantages of using socially acquired information. *Philosophical Transactions of the Royal Society B: Biological Sciences*, 357, 1559–1566.

Griskevicius, V., Goldstein, N., Mortensen, C., Cialdini, R. B., & Kenrick, D. T. (2006). Going along versus going alone: When fundamental motives facilitate strategic (non)conformity. *Journal of Personality and Social Psychology*, 91, 281–294.

Heath, C., Bell, C., & Sternberg, E. (2001). Emotional selection in memes: The case of urban legends. *Journal of Personality and Social Psychology*, 81, 1028–1041.

Henrich, J., & Gil-White, F. J. (2001). The evolution of prestige: Freely conferred deference as a mechanism for enhancing the benefits of cultural transmission. *Evolution and Human Behaviour*, 22, 165–196.

Henrich, J., & Henrich, N. (2010). The evolution of cultural adaptations: Fijian food taboos protect against dangerous marine toxins. *Proceedings of the Royal Society B: Biological Sciences*, 277, 3715–3724.

Henrich, J., & McElreath, R. (2003). The evolution of cultural evolution. *Evolutionary Anthropology*, 12, 123–135.

Henrich, J., Heine, S., & Norenzayan, A. (2010). The weirdest people in the world? *Behavioral and Brain Sciences*, 33, 61–135.

Herrmann, E., Call, J., Hernàndez-Lloreda, M. V., Hare, B., & Tomasello, M. (2007). Humans have evolved specialized skills of social cognition: The cultural intelligence hypothesis. *Science*, 317, 1360–1366. doi: 10.1126/science.1146282.

Hill, K., Barton, M., & Hurtado, A. M. (2009). The emergence of human uniqueness: Characters underlying behavioral modernity. *Evolutionary Anthropology: Issues, News, and Reviews*, 18, 187–200. doi: 10.1002/evan.20224.

Hoppitt, W., & Laland, K. (2011). Detecting social learning using networks: A user's guide. *American Journal of Primatology*, 73, 834–844.

(2013). *Social learning: An introduction to mechanisms, methods, and models.* Princeton, NJ: Princeton University Press.

Horner, V., Whiten, A., Flynn, E., & de Waal, F. (2006). Faithful replication of foraging techniques along cultural transmission chains by chimpanzees and children. *Proceedings of the National Academy of Sciences of the United States of America*, 103(37), 13878–13883.

Jacobs, R. C., & Campbell, D. T. (1961). The perpetuation of an arbitrary tradition through several generations of a laboratory microculture. *Journal of Abnormal and Social Psychology*, 62, 649–658.

Jones, J. T., Pelham, B. W., Carvallo, M., & Mirenberg, M. C. (2004). How do I love thee? Let me count the Js: Implicit egotism and interpersonal attraction. *Journal of Personality and Social Psychology*, 87, 665–683.

Kawai, M. (1965). Newly-acquired pre-cultural behavior of the natural troop of Japanese monkeys on Koshima islet. *Primates*, 6, 1–30.

Kunst, L., & Kratzer, J. (2007). Diffusion of innovations through social networks of children. *Young Consumers*, 8(1), 36–51.

Kutsukake, N., Suetsugu, N., & Hasegawa, T. (2006). Pattern, distribution, and function of greeting behavior among black-and-white colobus. *International Journal of Primatology*, 27, 1271–1291.

Lakin, J. L., & Chartrand, T. L. (2003). Using nonconscious behavioural mimicry to create affiliation and rapport. *Psychological Science*, 14, 334–339.

Laland, K. (2004). Social learning strategies. *Learning & Behavior*, 32, 4–14.

Lewis, H., & Laland, K. (2012). Transmission fidelity is the key to the build-up of cumulative culture. *Philosophical Transactions of the Royal Society B: Biological Sciences*, 367, 2171–2180.

Madden, J. R., Drewe, J. A., Pearce, G. P., & Clutton-Brock, T. H. (2011). The social network structure of a wild meerkat population: 3. Position of individuals within networks. *Behavioral Ecology and Sociobiology*, 65(10), 1857–1871.

Mann, J., Stanton, M., Patterson, E., Bienenstock, E., & Singh, L. (2012). Social networks reveal cultural behaviour in tool-using dolphins. *Nature Communications*, 3, 980.

McElreath, R., & Henrich, J. (2007). Dual inheritance theory: The evolution of human cultural capacities and cultural evolution. In R. Dunbar & L. Barrett (Eds.), *Oxford handbook of evolutionary psychology*, Oxford: Oxford University Press.

McPherson, M., Smith-Lovin, L., & Cook, J. (2001). Birds of a feather: Homophily in social networks. *Annual Review of Sociology*, 27, 415–444.

Mesoudi, A. (2008). An experimental simulation of the 'copy successful individuals' cultural learning strategy: Adaptive landscapes, producer–scrounger dynamics, and informational access costs. *Evolution and Human Behavior*, 29, 350–363.

Mesoudi, A., & Whiten, A. (2008). The multiple roles of cultural transmission experiments in understanding human cultural evolution. *Philosophical Transactions of the Royal Society B: Biological Sciences*, 363, 3489–3501.

Mesoudi, A., Whiten, A., & Dunbar, R. I. M. (2006). A bias for social information in human cultural transmission. *British Journal of Psychology*, 97, 405–423.

Nielsen, M. (2012). Imitation, pretend play and childhood: Essential elements in the evolution of human culture? *Journal of Comparative Psychology*, 126, 170–181.

Nielsen, M., & Blank, C. (2011). Imitation in young children: When who gets copied is more important than what gets copied. *Developmental Psychology*, 47, 1050–1053.

Over, H., & Carpenter, M. (2012). Putting the social into social learning: Explaining both selectivity and fidelity in children's copying behavior. *Journal of Comparative Psychology*, 126, 182–192.

Over, H., Carpenter, M., Spears, R., & Gattis, M. (2013). Children selectively trust individuals who have imitated them. *Social Development*, 22, 215–425.

Pike, T. W., & Laland, K. N. (2010) Conformist learning in nine-spined sticklebacks' foraging decisions. *Biological Letters*, 6, 466–468.

Powell, A., Shennan, S., & Thomas. M. (2009). Late Pleistocene demography and the appearance of modern human behavior. *Science*, 324(5932), 1298.

Rendell, L., Fogarty, L., Hoppitt, W., Morgan, T., Webster, M., & Laland, K. (2011). Cognitive culture: Theoretical and empirical insights into social learning strategies. *Trends in Cognitive Sciences*, 15, 68–76.

Richerson, P. J., & Boyd, R. (2005). *Not by genes alone: How culture transformed human evolution.* Chicago, IL: University of Chicago Press.

Rogers, A. (1988). Does biology constrain culture? *American Anthropologist*, 90, 819–831.

Schaik, C. P. van, & Burkart, J. M. (2011). Social learning and evolution: The cultural intelligence hypothesis. *Philosophical Transactions of the Royal Society B: Biological Sciences*, 366, 1008–1016. doi: 10.1098/rstb.2010.0304.

Sherif, M. (1935). A study of some social factors in perception. *Archives of Psychology*, 27(187).

Sterelny, K. (2003). *Thought in a hostile world: The evolution of human cognition.* Hoboken, NJ: Wiley-Blackwell.

(2011). From hominins to humans: How sapiens became behaviourally modern. *Philosophical Transactions of the Royal Society B: Biological Sciences*, 366, 809–822.

Stubbersfield, J., Tehrani, J., & Flynn, E. (2014). Santa crucified, Walt Disney and death by lollypop: Do urban legends exhibit cognitive biases on cultural transmission? *British Journal of Psychology,* 106(2), 288–307.

Sundaresan, S. R., Fischhoff, I. R., Dushoff, J., & Rubenstein, D. I. (2007). Network metrics reveal differences in social organization between two fission-fusion species, Grevys zebra and onager. *Oecologia*, 151, 140–149.

Tajfel, H., & Turner, J. C. (1986). The social identity theory of intergroup behavior. In S. Worchel & W. G. Austin (Eds.), *Psychology of intergroup relations.* Chicago, IL: Nelson-Hall, 7–24.

Toelch, U., Bruce, M. J., Meeus, M. T. H., & Reader, S. M. (2010). Humans copy rapidly increasing choices in a multiarmed bandit problem. *Evolution and Human Behavior*, 31(5), 326–333.

Tomasello, M. (1999). *The cultural origins of human cognition*. Cambridge, MA: Harvard University Press.

Tomasello, M., Kruger, A., & Ratner, H. (1993). Cultural learning. *Behavioural and Brain Sciences*, 16, 495–552.

Užgiris, I. C. (1981). Two functions of imitation during infancy. *International Journal of Behavioral Development*, 4, 1–12.

Vygotsky, L. S. (1978). *Mind in society: The development of higher psychological processes*. Cambridge, MA: Harvard University Press.

Webster, M., & Laland, K. (2011). Reproductive state affects reliance on public information in sticklebacks. *Proceedings of the Royal Society B: Biological Sciences*, 278, 619–627.

Whiten, A. (2011). The scope of culture in chimpanzees, humans and ancestral apes. *Philosophical Transactions of the Royal Society B: Biological Sciences*, 366, 997–1007.

Whiten, A., & Flynn, E. (2010). The transmission and evolution of experimental microcultures in groups of young children. *Developmental Psychology*, 46, 1694–1709.

Whiten, A., & Mesoudi, A. (2008). Establishing an experimental science of culture: Animal social diffusion experiments. *Philosophical Transactions of the Royal Society B: Biological Sciences*, 363, 3477–3488.

Wisdom, T. N., Song, X., & Goldstone, R. L. (2013). Social learning strategies in a networked group. *Cognitive Science*, 37, 1383–1425.

Wood, L., Kendal, R., & Flynn, E. (2012). Context-dependent model-based biases in cultural transmission: Children's imitation is affected by model age over model knowledgeable state. *Evolution and Human Behavior*, 33(4), 387–394.

Wood, L.A., Kendal, R., & Flynn, E. (2013). Whom do children copy? Model-based biases in learning. *Developmental Review*, 33, 341–356.

Zentall, T. (2006). Imitation: Definitions, evidence, and mechanisms. *Animal Cognition*, 9, 335–353.

(2012). Perspectives on observational learning in animals. *Journal of Comparative Psychology*, 126, 114–128.

Glossary

Culture An amalgamation of socially-learned behaviour (traditions), which is often operationalised as behaviour that varies between groups but which is not attributed solely to differences in genetics or ecology.

Cumulative culture Culture exhibited by modern humans, in which learned information is modified or improved on, generation after generation, to allow ever increasing adaptive fit with the environment.

Dyadic design Experiments in which dyads (groups of two) interact. In the study of social learning, dyadic experiments often involve the interaction between a model and a learner.

Homophily The tendency for individuals to affiliate with similar others.

Social information Information that is produced by conspecifics and is available. 'Social information use' refers to learning and using this information, and so social information use can be used synonymously with 'social learning'.

Social learning The process of learning from another individual; this can be through simple processes such as observation or more complex teaching.

Social learning mechanisms The specific process which allows the social learning to occur, such as 'imitation', where a learner watches and copies the actions of a model to produce the same outcome, or 'local enhancement', where simply being near another individual makes more likely the discovery of a behaviour.

Social learning strategy A rule regarding the particular circumstances under which social information is used that is evolutionarily adaptive, such as learning from reliable individuals.

Transmission The process of information being passed between individuals. In the context of the current chapter 'transmission chain' refers to information being passed from individual to individual, to individual, and so on.

25   Observational Motor Learning

Heather McGregor and Paul L. Gribble

Abstract

To survive, we must interact with an ever-changing world. Our capacity
to move accurately in a range of environments lies in the brain's ability to
flexibly modify our motor behavior. For example, simply holding an object
in the hand changes the arm's dynamic environment. That is, the additional
weight of the object changes the relationship between applied forces and
motion such that the brain's motor commands and muscle forces no longer
result in the intended arm movement. In order to skillfully manipulate the
object, the brain must alter its motor commands to compensate for the
object's weight and achieve a desired movement. Subsequent movements
are improved with time and practice; this process is called motor learning.
While many of our motor skills are acquired and refined through active
physical practice, we can also learn how to make movements by observing
others. This is referred to as observational motor learning. This chapter will
begin with a brief overview of modern studies of human motor learning, followed by a discussion of how these concepts relate to observational motor
learning.

Motor Learning

Two broad categories of motor learning have been the focus of recent
research: sequence learning and sensorimotor adaptation. Here, we will focus
on sensorimotor adaptation.

In a typical experiment, participants are provided with altered sensory inputs
or motor outputs and must modify their movements in order to regain a normal
level of performance. Even before moving, the brain makes predictions about
the sensory consequences of the planned movement (e.g. how the intended
movement should look and feel). When sensory inputs or motors outputs are
altered (as in an adaptation task), the actual sensory outcomes of a movement
do not match the brain's predictions. The brain's adaptation of movements is

driven by systematic movement errors. Visual and somatosensory feedback, in particular, inform the brain of how the executed movement differs from the intended movement and guides the brain's modification of motor commands during the planning of subsequent movements (Shadmehr, Smith, & Krakauer, 2010).

This chapter will discuss three well-studied adaptation paradigms commonly used in the study of motor learning: visuomotor adaptation, fingertip force adaptation and force field adaptation.

In a visuomotor adaptation task, participants are provided with altered visual feedback such that there is a discrepancy between the actual trajectory of the hand and the visual consequence of the movement. Visuomotor adaptation has been studied extensively using a range visual manipulations. For example, visual feedback can be shifted laterally using prism lenses (e.g. Martin, Keating, Goodkin, Bastian, & Thach, 1996), inverted using mirrors (e.g. Imamura et al., 1996), rotated in a virtual environment (e.g. Krakauer, Ghez, & Ghilardi, 2005), and so on. When first exposed to the novel visuomotor environment, executed movements do not result in the predicted visual outcome. Based on prediction errors, the brain implicitly updates its motor predictions to account for the visual perturbation. Once adapted, participants aim their movements in the opposite direction of the visual perturbation and successfully complete the task. Figure 25.1 shows an example of adaptation to a rotated visuomotor

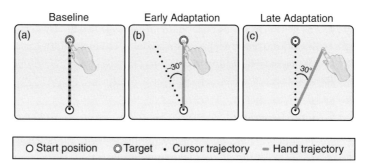

Figure 25.1 Visuomotor rotation. *See Plate 14.*

Notes: Participants are instructed to guide an on-screen cursor to the target. (a) Under the baseline condition, the cursor corresponds to the actual position of the hand. Executed movements result in the predicted visual outcome. (b) Visual feedback is then altered such that the cursor's position is rotated 30° counterclockwise to the hand's trajectory. Moving the hand to the target now results in visual error. (c) With practice, the brain incorporates the visual rotation into its predictions and movements are aimed 30° clockwise to the target so that the cursor hits the target. Executed movements once again match the predicted visual outcomes.

environment. Studies of visuomotor adaptation suggest that the brain predicts the visual outcome of movements. If there is a mismatch between the predicted and actual visual feedback of a movement, the brain will adapt its planning of movement direction in order to bring the motor prediction and actual visual outcomes back into alignment.

Participants are instructed to guide an on-screen cursor to the target. Under the baseline condition, the cursor corresponds to the actual position of the hand and executed movements result in the predicted visual outcome. Visual feedback is then altered such that the cursor's position is rotated $30°$ counterclockwise to the hand's trajectory, and moving the hand to the target now results in visual error. With practice, the brain incorporates the visual rotation into its predictions and movements are aimed $30°$ clockwise to the target so that the cursor hits the target; executed movements once again match the predicted visual outcomes.

In studies of fingertip force adaptation, participants learn to adjust their force output when lifting objects of varying weights. Before lifting an object, we make a prediction about the object's weight based on its visual characteristics, such as its size or material (Ellis & Lederman, 1999; Johansson & Westling, 1984, 1988). This prediction influences our lifting behavior in terms of the force applied by our fingertips (grip force) and the force with which we lift the object (load force) (Gordon, Forssberg, Johansson, & Westling, 1991). For example, individuals tend to grip and lift objects with slightly more force than is necessary to keep an object from slipping; this is particularly true when preparing to lift heavy or slippery objects. Participants also apply vertical load force that slightly exceeds the weight of the object in order to achieve lift off and a smooth lift to the intended height. Immediately before lifting the object, participants increase their grip force and load force in parallel according to the anticipated weight of the object. If the prediction is inaccurate, participants will generate inappropriate forces and the object may be lifted sooner than expected or not at all (see Figure 25.2, for example). In such cases, grip force and lift force are quickly adjusted based on sensory feedback (Johansson & Westling, 1984). The brain's motor predictions are rapidly updated, fully adapting forces to the object's actual weight in as little as one trial (Johansson & Westling, 1988). In fact, we learn to predict the sensory consequences of our movements even before we learn to correctly execute them. Participants were instructed to grip an object with novel dynamic properties and move it along a straight path. The participants rapidly learned to scale their grip and load forces (an indication of accurate prediction) well before they were able to accurately move the object along the desired path, again emphasizing the role of prediction in learning (Flanagan, Vetter, Johansson, & Wolpert, 2003). Fingertip force adaptation studies demonstrate that the brain predicts the force requirements for lifting objects and, if the prediction is inaccurate, motor commands

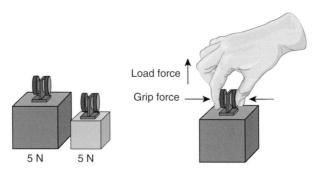

Figure 25.2 Fingertip force adaptation. *See Plate 15.*

Notes: Participants grip the object-mounted handle between the thumb and index finger. The object handle contains force sensors to measure grip force (force applied between the fingertips) and load force (vertical force applied to lift the object). In one version of the object-lifting task, participants are instructed to lift large and small cubes that have identical weights. Based on its size, participants predict that the smaller cube will be lighter. This prediction is incorrect and, when lifting the smaller object, the applied load force is insufficient to lift the object at the predicted time. Based on this mismatch between predicted and actual sensory feedback, the motor system increases its load force output until the object is lifted as intended. Knowledge of the smaller cube's weight is used to update the motor prediction for lifting that object in the future.

for force production are rapidly modified such that the object can be lifted in the intended manner.

Participants grip the object-mounted handle between the thumb and index finger. The object handle contains force sensors to measure grip force (force applied between the fingertips) and load force (vertical force applied to lift the object). In one version of the object lifting task, participants are instructed to lift large and small cubes that have identical weights. Based on its size, participants predict that the smaller cube will be lighter. This prediction is incorrect and, when lifting the smaller object, the applied load force is insufficient to lift the object at the predicted time. Based on this mismatch between predicted and actual sensory feedback, the motor system increases its load force output until the object is lifted as intended. Knowledge of the smaller cube's weight is used to update the motor prediction for lifting that object in the future.

Another widely used task is force field adaptation in which participants adapt their reaching movements to a novel force environment (see Figure 25.3). Participants grasp the handle at the end of a robotic arm and are instructed to perform straight reaching movements to on-screen targets. The robotic arm can apply force to the hand during movement, creating a novel dynamic

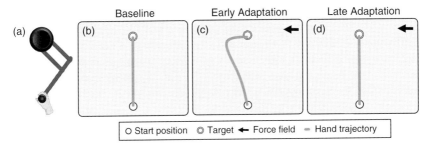

Figure 25.3 Force field adaptation. *See Plate 16.*

Notes: Participants hold the handle at the end of a robotic arm (a) and perform reaching movements to an on-screen target. (b) Under the baseline condition, the robot applies no force and reaches are straight, as predicted. (c) The robotic arm applies a leftward force field, perturbing movements from their intended trajectory. (d) With practice, the brain learns to predict the external forces and modifies its pattern of muscle forces to compensate for the force field. Movements once again become straight despite the continual application of force on the hand.

environment ('force field'). For example, in a leftward force field, the robotic arm pushes the hand to the left as it is moved. Participants' initial movements in a force field are highly curved, but based on prediction errors, the brain quickly acquires a representation of the novel force environment. With practice, the brain updates its motor predictions to account for the external forces imposed by the robot. Subsequent motor commands are modified so as to generate compensatory muscle force patterns that will result in straight, accurate reaches. Studies of force field adaptation indicate that the brain predicts the force requirements for arm movements and, if inaccurate, it can rapidly learn complex muscle force patterns in order to execute the desired movements (Shadmehr & Mussa-Ivaldi, 1994).

Participants hold the handle at the end of a robotic arm and perform reaching movements to an on-screen target. Under the baseline condition, the robot applies no force and reaches are straight, as predicted but when the robotic arm applies a leftward force field, movements are perturbed from their intended trajectory. With practice, the brain learns to predict the external forces and modifies its pattern of muscle forces to compensate for the force field. Movements once again become straight despite the continual application of force on the hand.

Observational Motor Learning

Motor learning can be achieved not only through physical practice, but also by observing the movements of another individual ('a tutor'). As is the case with physical practice, observational motor learning is likely driven by prediction errors. The observer generates predictions about the sensory consequences of the tutor's movements. Presumably, these predictions are generated under the assumption that the tutor intends to move her hand to a target location in a straight path (Morasso, 1981) or to lift an object in a smooth manner (Johansson & Westling, 1984). Any deviation from these predictions would indicate a movement error. The observer lacks the full range of sensory feedback typically associated with physical practice, and must rely solely on visual information of kinematic errors (see Box 25.1). Observers could compare the actual visual outcome of the tutor's movement with their own prediction and use systematic errors to update their own motor predictions for use in subsequent performance (e.g. Blakemore & Decety, 2001).

Observation has been shown to facilitate the learning of novel visuomotor environments. Participants observed a tutor learning to reach for targets in a novel visuomotor environment in which the cursor was rotated 30° clockwise with respect to the tutor's actual hand position. Upon subsequent exposure to that same rotated visual environment, observers' movements were more accurate in guiding the cursor to the targets (by aiming counterclockwise) compared to those participants who had not previously observed a tutor. While the observer's movements did not fully compensate for the visual rotation, their physical performance was significantly facilitated by the observation of the tutor (Ong & Hodges, 2010; Ong, Larssen, & Hodges, 2012; Lim, Larssen, & Hodges, 2013). This indicates that individuals can learn how to adapt to a novel visuomotor environment, at least to some extent, through observation.

Action observation can also facilitate the adaptation of forces when lifting objects. Participants repeatedly lifted an object in turn with a tutor such that the participants observed the tutor lifting the object before lifting it themselves. In some trials, the object's weight was unexpectedly changed; for instance, if the object became lighter, the tutor overestimated the load force and overshot the target lift height. Participants acquired information about the object's new weight by observing just one of the tutor's lifts. Participants were able to use this new weight information to adapt their own load force when subsequently lifting the new weight (Reichelt, Ash, Baugh, Johansson, & Flanagan, 2013). Similarly, Buckingham, Wong, Tang, Gribble, and Goodale (2014) examined the consequences of observing a tutor making load force errors when lifting small and large objects of identical weights. Participants watched either a novice tutor making lifting errors (i.e. overestimations of load force for the large object and underestimations for the small object) or an expert tutor who performed fully adapted, error-free lifts. After observation, the participants lifted the objects seen in the videos. The participants who had observed the novice's lifts outperformed those who had observed the expert's lifts. Specifically, they were less likely to commit load force overestimations when lifting the larger object and needed smaller force adjustments during their lifts. Based on observing the novice's errors, participants were able to update their motor predictions and thus more accurately scale their fingertip forces when they lifted the objects themselves (Buckingham et al., ibid). Therefore, observers are able to use visual information of others' movement errors in updating their own motor predictions and adapt their fingertip force output.

Individuals can also learn to move in novel force environments by observing a tutor's movements (Mattar & Gribble, 2005). Participants watched a video of a tutor performing reaching movements in a force field imposed by a robotic arm. Participants who observed the tutor gradually adapting their movements to a force field performed better (straighter) movements when they later encountered that same force field compared to those participants who did not observe (ibid). While this study assessed the generation of predictive force from the participants' kinematic performance (i.e. movement straightness), this was later confirmed through the direct measurement of participants' generated forces after observing motor learning. Wanda, Li, and Thoroughman (2013) showed that observers indeed change their lateral force output in a predictive manner so as to oppose the observed force field. These studies suggest that we can learn how to execute movements at the level of muscle forces through observation. Furthermore, Mattar and Gribble (2005) found that the beneficial effect of observing motor learning persisted even if participants performed a cognitive distractor task while watching the video, indicating that observational motor learning is likely not dependent on the use of explicit cognitive strategies. However, observational learning was impaired if the motor system was engaged with an unrelated movement task during observation, suggesting that the availability of the observer's motor system plays a key role in this effect. Taken together, these results demonstrate that observational learning of novel force environments occurs through implicit engagement of the observer's motor system (ibid).

Box 25.1 Observing error

Is it more beneficial to observe the large errors of a novice tutor or the accurate performance of an expert tutor? There is some evidence that observing both low and high error movements promotes the most learning. In this study, participants observed either a novice, an expert or a combination of expert and novice tutors performing a simple timed movement task. Regardless of the tutor's level of performance, all observers later outperformed control participants who did not observe a tutor. Furthermore, those participants who observed both the novice and the expert tutors showed the greatest performance benefit (Rohbanfard & Proteau, 2011). Similarly, Brown, Wilson, and Gribble (2009) showed participants high error, low error or a mixture of high and low error movements in a force field. Participants learned best from watching high error movements, but they also benefitted (to a lesser extent) from observing both high and low errors. These studies emphasize the important role of using sensory error signals for updating predictions in observational motor learning (see Box 25.2 for consideration of the generalizability of observational motor learning).

Box 25.2 Generalization of observational motor learning

Generalization refers to our ability to transfer what we have learned to different contexts. While learning through physical practice results in limited generalizability (e.g. Gandolfo, Mussa-Ivaldi, & Bizzi, 1996), there is some evidence that motor skills acquired through observation may be more generalizable. For example, there is evidence that motor learning through observation can be transferred between limbs. Participants observed a tutor reaching in a force field using either the right arm or the left arm. Regardless of the arm observed in the video, participants were able to learn the force as indicated by their improved performance when reaching in the observed force field with the right arm (Williams & Gribble, 2012). Moreover, observational motor learning can also be generalized across tutor–observer visual perspectives. Participants observed a video of a tutor learning to reach in a force field. The video was presented in one of four orientations: 0° (as if it was the participant's own arm), 90°, 180° or 270°. Regardless of the video orientation, participants' subsequent performance in the force field benefitted from observation compared to participants who did not observe (McGregor, Belbeck, Whyte, & Gribble, unpublished). These studies indicate that information acquired about novel force environments through observation can be generalized to different limbs and different orientations from what was observed.

The Neural Basis of Action Observation

Insights into the neural mechanisms underlying observational motor learning come from the discovery of 'mirror neurons' in the premotor and parietal cortices of the macaque. These cells fire while the monkey performs a goal-directed action and while it observes a similar action being performed by another individual (Gallese, Fadiga, Fogassi, & Rizzolatti, 1996; di Pellegrino, Fadiga, Fogassi, Gallese, & Rizzolatti, 1992; Rizzolatti, Fadiga, Gallese, & Fogassi, 1996). There is growing evidence for a mirror neuron system in humans. Neuroimaging studies report a common temporo–parieto–premotor circuit activated by both action execution and action observation (Buccino et al., 2001; Gallese, Fogassi, Fadiga, & Rizzolatti, 2002; Grafton, Fadiga, Arbib, & Rizzolatti, 1997). This putative human mirror neuron system is part of a broader 'action observation network' (AON), which is involved in the visual processing of actions. The AON consists of many of the same brain areas involved in action execution, including the supplementary motor area, premotor cortex, primary somatosensory cortex, primary motor cortex, superior and inferior parietal lobules, and visual area V5/MT (Caspers, Zilles, Laird, & Eickhoff, 2010).

Transcranial magnetic stimulation studies have shown that the observer's motor system is activated in a somatotopic manner during action observation (Strafella & Paus, 2000; Watkins, Strafella, & Paus, 2003). Transcranial magnetic stimulation (TMS) is a non-invasive neurophysiological technique that can be used to depolarize cortical areas to evoke motor potentials (MEPs) as a measure of corticospinal excitability. Strafella and Paus (2000) applied TMS pulses to the primary motor cortex while participants observed hand movements and arm movements. While watching hand movements, the MEPs recorded from the observer's hand muscle were larger whereas, while watching arm movements, the MEPs recorded from the observer's arm muscles were larger. This suggests that the excitability of the observer's primary motor cortex increases in a muscle-specific manner during action observation. Alaerts et al. (2010) demonstrated that the primary motor cortex encodes not only which muscles others are using, but also the predicted force requirements of the observed movements. Participants watched tutors lift objects of different weights while TMS pulses were applied over primary motor cortex and MEPs were recorded from various hand muscles. They showed that primary motor cortex excitability was greater when observing heavy objects compared to light objects, particularly for those hand muscles that were most involved in the lifting movement. Therefore, watching the movements of others activates the observer's motor system in a muscle-specific manner in accordance with the predicted forces requirements of the task.

Action observation can also affect motor memories encoded in the primary motor cortex. Participants performed repetitive thumb movements and then observed a video of a tutor performing thumb movements in the opposite direction. Following observation, the experimenter applied TMS to the observers' primary motor cortex and found that the elicited thumb movements were biased in the direction of the observed movements (Stefan et al., 2005, 2008). These findings suggest that motor memories encoded in the primary motor cortex are subject to modification via action observation.

The direct matching hypothesis posits that the activation of cortical sensorimotor areas during action observation reflects the engagement of the observer's motor representation as it covertly simulates the observed movement (Rizzolatti, Fogassi, & Gallese, 2001). There are numerous proposed roles of covert simulation within the AON, including action understanding, action prediction, inferring intentions, imitation and various functions related to social cognition (e.g. communication, emotional empathy, perspective taking, and so on) (e.g. Gallese, Keysers, & Rizzolatti, 2004; Rizzolatti & Craighero, 2004). Of particular importance to observational motor learning is the AON's proposed function in action prediction.

Flanagan and Johansson (2003) provided behavioral evidence in support of covert motor simulation and prediction during action observation. Participants' eye movements were tracked both while they performed a block-stacking task and while they observed a tutor performing the task. When watching the tutor, participants' eye movements were very similar to those produced when they performed the task themselves. Their eye movements were proactive in both conditions, fixating on the grasp sites of the blocks before the hand picked them up and fixating on the landing sites before the blocks were placed. This consistent gaze–hand coordination suggests that participants were not simply assessing the tutor's movements at a visual level, but rather were predicting the tutor's upcoming movements through activation of their own motor representations.

Collectively, these studies demonstrate that observed actions are represented by the motor system of an observer in such a way that can contribute to the prediction of others' actions. It follows that such a neural mechanism linking action observation and action execution may also underlie motor learning through observation.

The Motor System and Observational Motor Learning

There is growing evidence that observing motor learning indeed engages the observer's motor system. Using transcranial magnetic stimulation, Brown et al. (2009) demonstrated that the primary motor cortex (M1) plays a key role in observational motor learning. Transcranial magnetic stimulation can be used to modulate the excitability of cortical brain areas. When TMS is applied repetitively (rTMS), neurons beneath the TMS coil are temporarily hyperpolarized, dampening excitability so as to create a 'virtual lesion' of the target brain area. In this study, rTMS was applied after participants observed a video of a tutor learning to reach in a force field. Observational motor learning was compromised for those participants who received rTMS to M1 such that their subsequent performance in the observed force field was comparable to participants who had not observed a tutor. In contrast, observational motor learning was not affected by the application of rTMS to a control brain area not involved in motor function. These findings suggest that action observation engages learning mechanisms in the observer's primary motor cortex.

Furthermore, observing movement errors during motor learning engages a network that is also involved in processing our own movement errors (Malfait et al., 2010). Participants underwent fMRI while observing videos of a tutor performing reaches in a force field, which depicted the typical progression from curved to straight movements during learning. During observation, activity in the intraparietal sulcus, dorsal premotor cortex and cerebellum was modulated by the magnitude of the tutor's reach errors. Interestingly, this network shows considerable overlap with a network engaged in processing one's own movement errors during physical practice. This study provides evidence that the observer's motor system is activated when processing visual information about movement errors, particularly when the tutor commits large reach errors. This finding is consistent with the idea that the observer's motor system covertly simulates observed action as a means of detecting movement errors and updating motor predictions.

The neural basis of observational motor learning was recently assessed using resting-state fMRI. Resting-state fMRI is a neuroimaging technique in which the blood-oxygen-level-dependent (BOLD) signal is measured while a participant is in a state of wakeful rest. After performing a task, the brain areas engaged in that task show altered activity while at rest (e.g. Albert, Robertson, & Miall, 2009). McGregor and Gribble (unpublished) assessed changes in resting-state activity after observing motor learning in order to gain insight into the brain networks underlying this phenomenon. Resting-state fMRI (rs-fMRI) is a powerful technique for studying motor learning. As we learn a motor skill, the learning process is accompanied by changes in task performance (e.g. our movements become more automatic). Traditional task-based fMRI paradigms cannot distinguish those changes in brain activity that are due to learning from those changes that are due to such performance differences. Since there is no task performed during rs-fMRI scans, any changes in brain activation are due to learning itself. In this study, participants underwent rs-fMRI both before and after observing a video of a tutor learning to reach in a force field. Participants then performed reaches in a force field and a motor learning score was calculated based on the straightness of their movements. This study revealed a new network consisting of visual area V5/MT, which is involved in motion perception (Zeki et al., 1991), the cerebellum, dorsal premotor cortex, primary motor cortex and somatosensory cortex. Activity in this network was modulated by the participants' motor learning scores, such that those participants who learned more through observation showed greater functional changes in this network (McGregor and Gribble, unpublished). This study provides evidence of a link between visual systems involved in motion perception and sensory-motor circuits involved in motor learning. This network forms the basis by which visual information of others' movements is transferred to the sensory-motor system for learning new motor skills.

Sensory Changes Accompanying Observational Motor Learning

The effects of motor learning are not restricted to changes in motor performance and neural plasticity within motor circuits; there is evidence that learning new motor skills can also bring about changes in somatosensory perception. Somatosensory perceptual changes have been reported following physical practice (Ostry, Darainy, Mattar, Wong, & Gribble, 2010) as well as following the observation of motor learning. Bernardi, Darainy, Bricolo, and Ostry (2013) examined somatosensory function before and after participants observed a video of a tutor learning to reach in a force field. Somatosensory function was assessed by having participants grasp the handle of a robotic arm, close their eyes and make judgments about the position of their arm. Consistent with previous findings, observing motor learning facilitated participants' motor performance when they later encountered the observed force environment. Observational motor learning also affected participants' somatosensory perception such that their judgments of limb position reliably changed depending on the force field they had observed. Those participants who watched a tutor learning to reach in a rightward force field subsequently perceived their arm to be positioned more rightward than it actually was. In contrast, those participants who watched a tutor learning to reach in a leftward force field subsequently perceived their arm to be positioned more leftward than it actually was. These results suggest that observational motor learning promotes plasticity not only in the motor system, but also in the sensory domain.

Conclusions and Applications

The brain can learn to alter its movement planning and force output through observation of others' movements, a process that is driven by prediction errors and relies on brain networks common to those involved in physical practice.

Numerous fundamental questions still require investigation; for example, we know little regarding the duration and generalizability (see Box 25.2) of observational motor learning. Studying the performance benefits and neural basis of observational motor learning is interesting not only from a research perspective, but also for its potential clinical applications. Observational motor learning could serve a role in the treatment of motor deficits following stroke. Current stroke rehabilitation strategies require patients to undergo intensive physical practice aimed at promoting plasticity and reorganizing damaged sensorimotor networks. However, this strategy may not be an effective option for stroke patients with poor or absent voluntary movement control. Observational motor learning may serve as a supplement or alternative to traditional rehabilitation techniques. Through vision, we may be able to promote adaptive plasticity in sensorimotor circuits and restore motor function in stroke patients. While action observation training is a promising option for stroke rehabilitation, recent investigations of the effectiveness of this technique have used inconsistent methods and have yielded mixed results (Garrison, Winstein, & Aziz-Zadeh, 2010). Continued basic research is required to assess whether observational motor learning would be an effective and feasible stroke rehabilitation technique.

References

Alaerts, K., Senot, P., Swinnen, S. P., Craighero, L., Wenderoth, N., & Fadiga, L. (2010). Force requirements of observed object lifting are encoded by the observer's motor system: A TMS study. *European Journal of Neuroscience*, 31(6), 1144–1153.

Albert, N. B., Robertson, E. M., & Miall, R. C. (2009). The resting human brain and motor learning. *Current Biology*, 19(12), 1023–1027.

Bernardi, N. F., Darainy, M., Bricolo, E., & Ostry, D. J. (2013). Observing motor learning produces somatosensory change. *Journal of Neurophysiology*, 110(8), 1804–1810.

Blakemore, S. J., & Decety, J. (2001). From the perception of action to the understanding of intention. *Nature Reviews Neuroscience*, 2(8), 561–567.

Blandin, Y., & Proteau, L. (2000). On the cognitive basis of observational learning: Development of mechanisms for the detection and correction of errors. *Quarterly Journal of Experimental Psychology A*, 53(3), 846–867.

Brown, L. E., Wilson, E. T., & Gribble, P. L. (2009). Repetitive transcranial magnetic stimulation to the primary motor cortex interferes with motor learning by observing. *Journal of Cognitive Neuroscience*, 21(5), 1013–1022.

Buccino, G., Binkofski, F., Fink, G. R., Fadiga, L., Fogassi, L., et al. (2001). Action observation activates premotor and parietal areas in a somatotopic manner: An fMRI study. *European Journal of Neuroscience*, 13, 400–404.

Buckingham, G., Wong, J. D., Tang, M., Gribble, P. L., & Goodale, M. A. (2014). Observing object lifting errors modulates cortico-spinal excitability and improves object lifting performance. *Cortex*, 50, 115–124.

Caspers, S., Zilles, K., Laird, A. R., & Eickhoff, S. B. (2010). ALE meta-analysis of action observation and imitation in the human brain. *NeuroImage*, 50(3), 1148–1167.

Ellis, R. R., & Lederman, S. J. (1999). The material-weight illusion revisited. *Perception & Psychophysics*, 61(8), 1564–1576.

Flanagan, J. R., & Johansson, R. S. (2003). Action plans used in action observation. *Nature*, 424(6950), 769–771.

Flanagan, J. R., Vetter, P., Johansson, R. S., & Wolpert, D. M. (2003). Prediction precedes control in motor learning. *Current Biology*, 13(2), 146–150.

Gallese, V., Fadiga, L., Fogassi, L., & Rizzolatti, G. (1996). Action recognition in the premotor cortex. *Brain*, 119 (Pt 2), 593–609.

Gallese, V., Fogassi, L., Fadiga, L., & Rizzolatti, G. (2002). Action representation and the inferior parietal lobule. *Attention and Performance*, 19, 247–266.

Gallese, V., Keysers, C., & Rizzolatti, G. (2004). A unifying view of the basis of social cognition. *Trends in Cognitive Science*, 8, 396–403.

Gandolfo, F., Mussa-Ivaldi, F. A., & Bizzi, E. (1996). Motor learning by field approximation. *Proceedings of the National Academy of Sciences of the United States of America*, 93(9), 3843–3846.

Garrison, K. A., Winstein, C. J., & Aziz-Zadeh, L. (2010). The mirror neuron system: A neural substrate for methods in stroke rehabilitation. *Neurorehabilitation and Neural Repair*, 24(5), 404–412.

Gordon, A. M., Forssberg, H., Johansson, R. S., & Westling, G. (1991). Visual size cues in the programming of manipulative forces during precision grip. *Experimental Brain Research*, 83(3), 477–482.

Grafton, S. T., Fadiga, L., Arbib, M. A., & Rizzolatti, G. (1997). Premotor cortex activation during observation and naming of familiar tools. *NeuroImage*, 6, 231–236.

Iacoboni, M., Woods, R. P., Brass, M., Bekkering, H., Mazziotta, J. C., & Rizzolatti, G. (1999). Cortical mechanisms of human imitation. *Science*, 286(5449), 2526–2528.

Imamura, K., Onoe, H., Watanabe, Y., Andersson, J., Hetta, J., et al. (1996). Regional activation of human cerebral cortex upon an adaptation in mirror drawing. *Neuroscience Letters*, 209(3), 185–188.

Johansson, R. S., & Westling, G. (1984). Roles of glabrous skin receptors and sensorimotor memory in automatic control of precision grip when lifting rougher or more slippery objects. *Experimental Brain Research*, 56(3), 550–564.

(1988). Coordinated isometric muscle commands adequately and erroneously programmed for the weight during lifting task with precision grip. *Experimental Brain Research*, 71(1), 59–71.

Krakauer, J. W., Ghez, C., & Ghilardi, M. F. (2005). Adaptation to visuomotor transformations: Consolidation, interference, and forgetting. *Journal of Neuroscience*, 25(2), 473–478.

Lim, S. B., Larssen, B. C., & Hodges, N. J. (2013). Manipulating visual–motor experience to probe for observation-induced after-effects in adaptation learning. *Experimental Brain Research*, 232(3), 1–14.

Malfait, N., Valyear, K. F., Culham, J. C., Anton, J.-L., Brown, L. E., & Gribble, P. L. (2010). fMRI activation during observation of others' reach errors. *Journal of Cognitive Neuroscience*, 22(7), 1493–1503.

Martin, T. A., Keating, J. G., Goodkin, H. P., Bastian, A. J., & Thach, W. T. (1996). Throwing while looking through prisms I. Focal olivocerebellar lesions impair adaptation. *Brain*, 119(4), 1183–1198.

Mattar, A. A. G., & Gribble, P. L. (2005). Motor learning by observing. *Neuron*, 46(1), 153–160.

McGregor, H., Belbeck, B., Whyte, N., & Gribble, P.L. (unpublished). Does motor learning by observing depend on observer–tutor visual perspective?

McGregor, H., & Gribble, P. L. (unpublished). Neural basis of motor learning by observing.

Morasso, P. (1981). Spatial control of arm movements. *Experimental Brain Research*, 42(2), 223–227.

Ong, N. T., & Hodges, N. J. (2010). Absence of after-effects for observers after watching a visuomotor adaptation. *Experimental Brain Research*, 205(3), 325–334.

Ong, N. T., Larssen, B. C., & Hodges, N. J. (2012). In the absence of physical practice, observation and imagery do not result in updating of internal models for aiming. *Experimental Brain Research*, 218(1), 9–19.

Ostry, D. J., Darainy, M., Mattar, A. A., Wong, J., & Gribble, P. L. (2010). Somatosensory plasticity and motor learning. *Journal of Neuroscience*, 30(15), 5384–5393.

Pellegrino, G. di, Fadiga, L., Fogassi, L., Gallese, V., & Rizzolatti, G. (1992). Understanding motor events: A neurophysiological study. *Experimental Brain Research*, 91, 176–180.

Reichelt, A. F., Ash, A. M., Baugh, L. A., Johansson, R. S., & Flanagan, J. R. (2013). Adaptation of lift forces in object manipulation through action observation. *Experimental Brain Research*, 228(2), 221–234.

Rizzolatti, G., & Craighero, L. (2004). The mirror-neuron system. *Annual Review of Neuroscience*, 27, 169–192.

Rizzolatti, G., Fadiga, L., Gallese, V., & Fogassi, L. (1996). Premotor cortex and the recognition of motor actions. *Cognitive Brain Research*, 3, 131–141.

Rizzolatti, G., Fogassi, L., & Gallese, V. (2001). Neurophysiological mechanisms underlying the understanding and imitation of action. *Nature Reviews Neuroscience*, 2(9), 661–670.

Rohbanfard, H., & Proteau, L. (2011). Learning through observation: A combination of expert and novice models favors learning. *Experimental Brain Research*, 215(3–4), 183–197.

Shadmehr, R., & Mussa-Ivaldi, F. A. (1994). Adaptive representation of dynamics during learning of a motor task. *Journal of Neuroscience*, 14(5), 3208–3224.

Shadmehr, R., Smith, M. A., & Krakauer, J. W. (2010). Error correction, sensory prediction, and adaptation in motor control. *Annual Review of Neuroscience*, 33, 89–108.

Stefan, K., Cohen, L. G., Duque, J., Mazzocchio, R., Celnik, P., et al. (2005). Formation of a motor memory by action observation. *Journal of Neuroscience*, 25(41), 9339–9346.

Strafella, A. P., & Paus, T. (2000). Modulation of cortical excitability during action observation: A transcranial magnetic stimulation study. *NeuroReport*, 11(10), 2289–2292.

Wanda, P. A., Li, G., & Thoroughman, K. A. (2013). State dependence of adaptation of force output following movement observation. *Journal of Neurophysiology*, 110(5), 1246–1256.

Watkins, K. E., Strafella, A. P., & Paus, T. (2003). Seeing and hearing speech excites the motor system involved in speech production. *Neuropsychologia*, 41(8), 989–994.

Williams, A., & Gribble, P. L. (2012). Observed effector-independent motor learning by observing. *Journal of Neurophysiology*, 107(6), 1564–1570.

Zeki, S., Watson, J. D., Lueck, C. J., Friston, K. J., Kennard, C., & Frackowiak, R. S. (1991). A direct demonstration of functional specialization in human visual cortex. *Journal of Neuroscience*, 11(3), 641–649.

Glossary

Dynamics The relationship between force and motion.

Kinematics Spatial and temporal characteristics of motion (e.g. timing, position, velocity, acceleration).

Motor-evoked potentials (MEPs) Electrical potential recorded from muscles elicited by stimulation of primary motor cortex.

Repetitive transcranial magnetic stimulation (rTMS) A variant of TMS in which stimulation is applied repeatedly to temporarily dampen excitability of a cortical brain region.

Resting-state functional magnetic resonance imaging (rs-fRMI) Neuroimaging technique used to measure the blood-oxygen-level-dependent signal while participants are in a state of wakeful rest.

Transcranial magnetic stimulation (TMS) A non-invasive neurophysiological technique that can be used to temporarily depolarize or hyperpolarize cortical areas.

26   The Impact of Action Expertise on Shared Representations

Emily S. Cross and Beatriz Calvo-Merino

Abstract

Expertise in the motor domain is something we recognize almost instantane-ously in other people, whether a gymnast performing a double layout with a twist, a basketball player slam dunking the ball, a Super-G skier descending a steep course at 80 mph, or a dancer executing 11 consecutive spins on one leg without stopping. While we might be able to readily recognize exper-tise in others, the degree to which action experts can coordinate or move their bodies in profoundly different ways to non-experts raises intriguing questions for those interested in shared representations between self and other in our social world. Namely, how does an observer's ability to embody an action impact how she perceives that action, and how might perception change as further experience with the observed action is acquired? In this chapter, we address these questions by considering empirical research that explores the relationship between an actor and an observer's motor abilities, and how expertise impacts this relationship.

Introduction

When Mikhail Baryshnikov, one of the most celebrated ballet dancers of all time, takes the stage to perform the lead role in the ballet *Apollo*, observers are instantly aware that, though they also embody a human form that is ostensibly similar to Baryshnikov's, there is a fundamental difference between the body sitting in the theater seat and the body moving on stage. That difference lies in the way Baryshnikov can coordinate his limbs to execute soaring leaps or a diz-zying succession of pirouettes, moves which, if most observers were to attempt them, would bear little resemblance to Baryshnikov's. Expertise in the motor domain is something we recognize almost instantaneously in other people, and entire industries rely on some individuals being able to execute sometimes extreme feats of motor control, such as what might be seen in professional sport or performing arts domains. While we might be able to readily recognize expertise in others, the degree to which action experts can coordinate or move their bodies in profoundly different ways to non-experts raises intriguing questions for those interested in shared representations between self and other in our social world. Namely, how does an observer's ability to embody an action impact how she perceives that action, and how might perception change as further experience with the observed action is acquired?

In this chapter, we address these questions by considering empirical research that explores the relationship between an actor and an observer's motor abilities, and how expertise impacts this relationship. As many of the chapters in this volume illustrate (see Catmur; Dolk & Prinz; Hamilton; Press, this volume, Chapters 22, 1, 15 and 16, respectively), the idea that perception and action share a common cognitive architecture dates back at least to the time of William James (1890). Over recent years, since the discovery of mirror neurons within the premotor and parietal cortices of rhesus macaques, psychology and cognitive and social neuroscience have witnessed a surge in interest in the mechanisms supporting coupling between action and perception (Gallese, Fadiga, Fogassi, & Rizzolatti, 1996; di Pellegrino, Fadiga, Fogassi, Gallese, & Rizzolatti, 1992). The discovery of mirror neurons in the monkey brain provided critical evidence in support of a direct matching or common coding account of how the primate brain navigates between perception and action (Gallese, Rochat, Cossu, & Sinigaglia, 2009; Hommel, Musseler, Aschersleben, & Prinz, 2001; Prinz, 1990, 1997). Moreover, this discovery has inspired hundreds if not thousands of studies into the existence, properties and functionality of such neurons or neural mechanisms in the human brain (for a critical review, see Gallese, Gernsbacher, Heyes, Hickock, & Iacoboni, 2011).

The present chapter focuses on shaping the relationship between action and perception at behavioral and neural levels by different kinds of sensorimotor experience. Due to the fact that much of our own research on action experience and expertise uses dance as a model system for exploring complex action competency, we focus on studies from this domain. However, work from sports, martial arts, music and other relevant domains also informs our understanding of the relationship between expertise and social perception, and other chapters in this volume provide detailed analysis of expertise in these domains (in this volume, for sporting expertise considerations, see Urgesi & Makris (Chapter 27) and Collins & Hill (Chapter 28); for more on music expertise, see Keller, Novembre, & Loehr (Chapter 14) and Waclawik, Watson, & Grah (Chapter 29)). To build the most comprehensive understanding of how sensorimotor expertise impacts perception, we first examine how the brains and behavior of individuals who are recognized as experts in a specific domain (such as professional dancers) differ from those with no such expertise during task performance. Next, we explore what controlled training paradigms reveal in terms of emergence of action expertise among expert and novice dancers. After we consider how longstanding and newly acquired sensorimotor expertise impact perception, we consider how individuals lacking motor expertise perceive actions performed by an expert mover. The penultimate section takes a slightly broader view of what kinds of action representation are or are not likely to change based on acquired experience. Finally, we conclude with a framework of how shared representations are shaped by sensorimotor experience, and discuss a number of open questions and possible future directions.

The Impact of Longstanding Expertise on Perception

This section elaborates on how longstanding motor expertise is reflected at behavioral and neural levels. The concept of expertise can be described as in-depth knowledge of a particular field. The domain that concerns this chapter is acquired knowledge in the motor domain. The summary or storage of all motor knowledge an individual has acquired during his lifetime is known as a motor repertoire. A motor repertoire is like a vocabulary of actions where each action representation contains information related to a specific action (how to perform the action, how it feels to perform it, what it looks like, what it means, and so on; see Box 26.1 for more information on action representations). Each person's motor repertoire is unique and defined by the movements he has learnt. At the same time, an individual's motor learning is constrained by two factors. First, learning is constrained by general features and limitations of human anatomy. We are prisoners in our bodies, with fixed degrees of freedom for how we can move, mainly guided by the flexion and extension capacities of the joints (i.e. I only can bend my knee or fingers in one direction). Second, our motor repertoires are defined by our own individual physical experience profiles, which might be quite limited for some people, while others spend thousands of hours training in sport, dance, music, martial arts or other specialized physical activities. Nearly every person naturally acquires the ability to perform common motor patterns, such as walking, running, grasping or gripping. On top of these basic actions, however, we can train to perform far more complex and precise actions. For example, in order to execute the perfect arabesque on stage, the prima ballerina has undergone long hours of training, facilitating the acquisition of a large set of motor commands related to this action (flexibility, timing, balance, rhythm and proprioception), which are stored in a distributed network that composes her motor repertoire.

As with any other kind of experience, motor experience is likely to modulate behavior via modified neural responses. In the following section, we describe how longstanding expertise modulates perception of actions at the neural and behavioral levels.

Box 26.1 Action representations

An *action representation* holds information about a motor act. Depending on the context, this idea has also been termed motor representation, motor repertoire or motor schema. These alternative names may refer to the whole action representation or to just some of its components. Jeannerod's (1997) concept of action representation is similar to Arbib's (1981) motor schema concept. The latter was introduced as a concept to integrate information from perception, action and memory and described how knowledge from these domains was stored and applied. For other authors, such as Schmidt (1975), this schema is the core of complex connections between action's motor and sensory components. Interestingly, Schmidt's schema idea moves away from classical views that consider the motor program as a centralized and predetermined reflex chain, towards a definition that links past action memories and current action effects in a time–experience interaction.

From a cognitive perspective, goal-directed actions are internally guided. They can each be described as a sequence of stages that includes goal identification, intention, planning towards that goal, motor programming and motor execution. Motor representations hold information about processes associated with movements we have learned to execute. Besides these purely motor processes, we store related information that has been associated with particular actions via learning, either during execution or other learning modalities. In this way, motor patterns may be very well linked with information from other modalities, such as vision (e.g. how the action looks), audition (e.g. a clapping action is associated with a particular sound), proprioceptive information (how it feels to perform a specific action), semantic information (action meaning, e.g. a waving movement means 'bye'), intention (e.g. grasping a glass means he wants to drink), and so on. Therefore, action representations are multimodal. When an action representation is activated, an individual has access to action information from all these modalities related to that particular action.

The individual motor repertoire

Each person's motor repertoire is unique, comprising the motor acts she has learnt. While some actions are very common (i.e. grasping, walking) and can likely be found in the motor repertoire of most people, others are more idiosyncratic and can be found only in motor repertoires of those individuals who have learnt them via training (i.e. riding a bike, juggling, performing a pirouette). While action representations are multimodal in general, one may acquire action information from only a selection of modalities. For example, blind individuals' action representations lack visual information about how an action looks, but still retain other related information linked to the motor commands (auditory, proprioceptive, meaning, and so on).

Equally, one can have a good visual representation of how an action looks and its associated sound and meaning without having performed it (lacking the motor component; i.e. an avid diving spectator watching the high dive competition in the Olympics).

Since the discovery of the mirror neuron system, evidence has emerged to suggest that an action representation is activated in an observer when she watches the same action performed by another agent. This suggests a shared mechanism that links the observer (me) with the executor (other). To investigate what sensory components are shared during observation, researchers have compared brain responses in participants who differ in the information stored in their individual motor repertoire (see main text of this chapter; also see Urgesi & Makris, this volume, Chapter 27).

The figure illustrates an action representation schema, including information from different sources. Please note that other action cognitive information such as goals and intentions are not represented in this schema. This diagram aims to represent the possibility of storing multisensory information about any given action. For example, with motor training, information from all the modalities can be stored. The section circumscribed by the red dotted line represents information from an action that has been acquired only through observation, but whose motor programs have never been learnt. Similar segregations can occur excluding other modalities (visual, auditory, verbal/semantic).

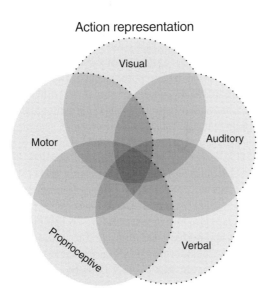

Action representation

Box 26.1 Action representation schema, including information from different sources. *See Plate 19.*

Neuroimaging Evidence

Thanks to the discovery of mirror neurons in the ventral premotor and parietal cortices of the primate brain (Gallese et al., 1996; di Pellegrino et al., 1992; Rizzolatti et al., 1996), we know that overlapping neural codes are recruited whether watching or performing the same action. This discovery provided neural evidence for a *shared* neural system for action observation and execution in the primate brain. Early fMRI action observation studies used paradigms modified from the original electrophysiological work performed with non-human primates involving observation of simple goal-directed actions such as grasping and reaching. These studies consistently reported activation in the ventral premotor cortex, parietal cortex and superior temporal sulcus (a region often associated with perception of social stimuli and biological motion (Allison, Puce, & McCarthy, 2000; Grossman, Battelli, & Pascual-Leone, 2005) during action observation (Decety et al., 1997; Grafton, Arbib, Fadiga, & Rizzolatti, 1996; Grèzes & Decety, 2001). These early fMRI studies provided a strong foundation for understanding which regions of the human brain are engaged during observation of simple goal-oriented actions. However, this early work could not discriminate between a general sensorimotor response during observation and a specific internal motor simulation of the observed action.

Calvo-Merino and colleagues were interested in exploring the extent to which brain activation during action observation truly reflects resonance between an observed action and one's specific motor repertoire. To do this, they designed a series of studies using longstanding expertise. Their expertise model is based on the *individuality* of one's motor repertoire (based on individual learned movements), and the *similarity* of the motor repertoire of those individuals who received similar training. In a first fMRI study, they chose two groups of participants (dancers) who were trained in different movement vocabularies that were kinematically similar: classical ballet and capoeira (a Brazilian martial art that features dance and acrobatics). Having two expert groups was important to ensure that putative effects were not due to a simple experience effect (i.e. larger repertoire and motor abilities in the expert group than in the control, non-expert group). The researchers compared brain responses of ballet and capoeira dancers, as well as non-expert controls, in an action observation paradigm where all participants watched three-second video-clips of ballet and capoeira movements (Figure 26.1a). Participants were asked to watch the videos and perform a dummy task to ensure they were paying attention to the stimuli. Considering the action–execution matching theory associated with mirror neurons (cf. Rizzolatti & Craighero, 2004), the authors predicted stronger brain responses in mirror system regions when participants observed a movement that has previously been learnt (i.e. it resides within the

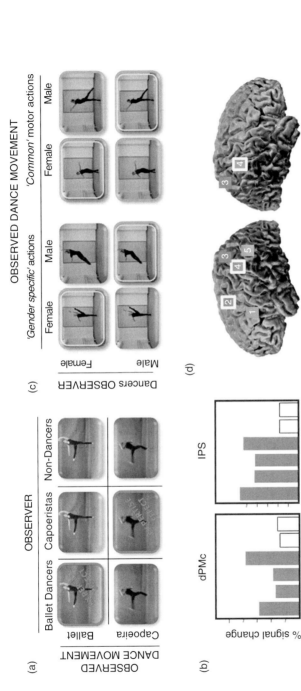

Figure 26.1 Results from Calvo-Merino et al. (2005, 2006) concerning longstanding dance expertise and brain engagement. *See Plate 17.*

Notes: (a) Schema of 2x3 design using expert observers. The expertise effect is determined by interaction group (observer: ballet dancers, capoeristas, non-dancers) and type of observed movement (ballet movements, capoeira movements).

(b) Parameter estimates for the expertise effect during action observation in left precentral gyrus/dorsal premotor cortex (−24 −6 72), left intraparietal sulcus (−33 −45 54). In both brain regions, parameter estimates show that the effect of expertise is driven by a crossover interaction between the two groups of observer expert dancers and the two types of observed action. Movement

547

Figure 26.1 (*cont.*)

type has minimal effects in non-dancers. BB: ballet dancers viewing ballet; BC: ballet dancers viewing capoeira; CB: capoeira dancers viewing ballet; CC: capoeira dancers viewing capoeira.

(c) Schema of 2x2x2 design using experts with visual and motor familiarity (green outline) and only visual familiarity (no outline). Yellow outline indicates the effect of seeing a performer of your own gender. This effect is canceled out by subtracting a similar version from common motor acts, where all dancers have equal visual and motor experience.

(d) Schema of standard brain activations significant at (1) ventral premotor, (2) dorsal premotor, (3) SPL, (4) IPS, and (5) pSTS. Red squares show activations sensitive to the expertise effect (modified from Calvo-Merino et al., 2005). Areas in a yellow square are also significantly active for the purely motor expertise effect (modified from Calvo-Merino et al., 2006).

observer's acquired motor repertoire), compared with an unlearned, unfamiliar movement.

The interaction between group (ballet, capoeira and controls) and type of observed movement (ballet, capoeira) revealed a specific effect of expertise (Figure 26.1d). This was manifest as an effect of watching familiar movement (ballet dancers watching ballet, and capoeira dancer watching capoeira) compared to activations while watching unfamiliar movement (ballet dancers watching capoeira, and capoeira dancer watching ballet). Specifically, this interaction showed significant activation in the premotor cortex (ventral and dorsal sections), superior parietal lobe, intraparietal sulcus and posterior superior temporal sulcus (Calvo-Merino, Glaser, Grèzes, Passingham, & Haggard, 2005). This pattern of findings suggests that neural responses during action observation are modulated by the relationship between the observed action and the observer. The control group of non-dancers did not show differentiated responses within the described areas while watching ballet or capoeira moves. Overall, these results suggest that neural engagement of these regions during observation of familiar actions may provide access to a form of shared action representation, at the neural level, between the observer and the performer.

However, an intriguing question was raised by this work. This question concerns *which* component of an action representation is retrieved during observation. More specifically, does action observation predominantly engage purely motoric mechanisms, over and above the visual representation of the action or semantic knowledge of the action (also see Box 26.1)? In order to answer this question, it is necessary to disentangle an observer's experience associated with different components of an action representation. After several interactions with dancers and choreographers, Calvo-Merino and colleagues became aware of an important factor through which classical ballet movements are classified that served their research purposes exceptionally well.

Classical ballet features gender-specific movements (i.e. movements that are trained and performed by only one gender) and gender-common movements (i.e. movements trained and performed by both genders). Therefore, female dancers trained in classical ballet will have acquired motor training of female-specific moves, and vice versa for male dancers. However, as female and male dancers train and perform together, both genders acquire visual familiarity and semantic knowledge about all the movements, regardless of gender specificity. As such, Calvo-Merino and colleagues designed a subsequent experiment that enabled the dissociation of visual and motor familiarity, to test for brain regions that might respond to an internal simulation of the action in specifically *motor* terms, over and above any associated visual or semantic representations (Calvo-Merino, Grèzes, Glaser, Passingham, & Haggard, 2006).

Similar to the Calvo-Merino et al. (2005) study, the follow-up experiment again used an action observation task. Now female and male classical ballet dancers served as participants and watched three-second video-clips of gender-specific dance movements. These movements were performed by a female dancer and a male dancer, dressed in black clothes (Figure 26.1c). The dancers also watched a set of dance movements commonly performed by both genders, to rule out any possible effects related to observing a female or a male dancer. In order to dissociate purely motor and visual representations during observation of gender movements, it was essential that only classical ballet dancers trained *specifically* in their respective gender movement vocabulary (and not in the opposite gender moves) participated in the study. To ensure that dancers' prior motor training adhered to gender-defined conventions, all dancers completed a preliminary questionnaire enquiring about how often they performed and watched the individual movements used in the experiment in their professional training. The questionnaire showed that male dancers were visually familiar with both male and female movements, but only motorically familiar with the male-specific movements, and the opposite was true for the female dancers. This control was particularly important as it is becoming increasingly common for the 'rules' of classical dance to be broken in order to create novel performances.[1] The neuroimaging results from this study were straightforward and conclusive (see Figure 26.1d). In order to find areas tuned by purely motor resonance with the observed action, rather than other action-related information (such as visual or semantic knowledge), the authors compared brain activity related to gender-specific movement (controlling for visual or semantic knowledge) with classical ballet movements common to both genders in two female and male dancers and a control group. They found that, during observation of motorically familiar movements, brain activity was

[1] For examples, see Les Ballets Trockadero de MonteCarlo, www.trockadero.org, or Matthew Bourne's *Swan Lake*, www.swanlaketour.com, in which male dancers perform typically female ballet vocabulary.

stronger in three brain regions: the premotor cortex in the left hemisphere, and the bilateral superior parietal lobe and cerebellum. Again, because the experimental design controlled for visual familiarity and other information associated with the actions, it was possible to relate the activation in these areas to direct internal motor resonance.

It is of note that brain responses in both studies by Calvo-Merino and colleagues (2005, 2006) shared a common set of areas classically identified as core nodes of the human mirror system (the premotor and parietal cortices). These regions, jointly with the cerebellum (Calvo-Merino et al., 2006), are involved in making motor responses and also coding observed actions. Activations related to general expertise were also found in the STS (Calvo-Merino et al., 2005), but this region did not show significant responses for purely motor experience (Calvo-Merino et al., 2006). This confirms that STS may play an active role during observation of familiar movements, but its response must be related to features of the action such as visual or semantic familiarity rather than strictly motor familiarity. When truly motor resonance is isolated, STS does not appear to participate (ibid). Subsequent work by Orgs, Dombrowski, and Jansen-Osmann (2008), using a similar expertise paradigm in which dancers and non-dancers watched dance sequences and everyday movements, showed reduced desynchronization when expert dancers watched familiar movements compared to non-dancers observing the same stimuli.

Overall, the above studies employing individuals with longstanding expertise suggest specific neural substrates are responsible for a shared representation between observer and performing agent based on the type of action information that both individuals have in common. As psychological scientists, we need to further explore if this differentiated neural response associated with expertise has implications at the behavioral level. This matter is addressed in the following section.

Behavioral Evidence

There are myriad examples of expert observers being able to spot nuances in skilled performers' actions that those of us watching from home could never spot, such as judges of diving, gymnastics or ice skating in the Olympic Games. How is it that expert judges are able to see small details that the couch potato observer cannot? Visual sensitivity enhancement by experience has been demonstrated in other domains using expertise (e.g. car experts, bird experts; Gilaie-Dotan, Harel, Bentin, Kanai, & Rees, 2012; Kirsch et al., 2013; Seligman & Reichenberg, 2009). However, this type of expertise is due simply to high levels of visual exposure. As we have seen in the previous section, expertise in the action domain is multisensory. Is Olympic judges' visual acuity impressive due to the fact that many of them have been practitioners of the same sport they are judging, or is this simply a matter of extensive visual practice, which implies that any of us could reach that level of perception? (For deeper consideration of this question, also see Urgesi & Makris, this volume, Chapter 27).

A study by Calvo-Merino, Ehrenberg, Leung, and Haggard (2010) sought to address this question. This question was precisely evaluated by comparing dance experts' performance in a simple visual discrimination task of dance movements. Four groups of participants took part in this study; female and male expert dancers, and female and male non-experts. The gender factor was important as participants observed two types of dance movement: female gender-specific and gender-common movements (following the gender specialization existing in classical ballet described in the previous section). Therefore, while no differences were expected between the female and male non-experts, any interaction between gender and the type of movement in the expert dancer group would indicate that motor and visual expertise play separate roles in perception of action. To facilitate a broad spectrum of performance across expertise levels on the behavioral task, the authors created a set of stimuli using point-light displays (PLDs), a technique commonly used to study biological motion, whereby points of lights are attached to the main joints of a performing agent while actions are recorded in a dark room (Johansson, 1973). PLDs were created of several female dancers performing the same dance movements. The task consisted of watching pairs of dance videos depicted as PLDs and judging whether the pairs depicted the same or different videos. Video pairs always depicted the same movements, which were performed by either the same dancer or two different dancers. This was a difficult task, as classical ballet dancers are trained such that their performance minimizes any possible idiosyncrasies that could be used to differentiate between the dancers.

As expected, the control group performed the task significantly worse than experts, and no interaction with gender was found. Interestingly, both the female and male dancers performed the task with a similar accuracy. This result suggests that visual sensitivity to others' actions significantly improves with expertise; however, once it reaches a specific level of expertise (motorically and visually) there appears to be little room for behavioral improvement.

Other studies have addressed the effect of expertise or familiarity in the visual domain from a different perspective. For example, in an interesting set of experiments, Loula, Prasad, Harber, and Shiffrar (2005) compared performance on action recognition and agent identification tasks while participants observed PLDs of unknown people (strangers) and friends. Performance was significantly better during observation of a friend performing idiosyncratic movements (e.g. free dancing) as compared to the other conditions (i.e. a stranger performing actions or a friend or stranger performing common movements). This visual familiarity effect represented in the ability to recognize our friends' actions highlighted the effect that mere visual exposure may have on action discrimination. To rule out whether purely motor experience makes an additional unique contribution to action perception, Casile and Giese (2006) performed an elegant training study whereby only motor patterns were learnt in the absence of any associated visual response (participants were blindfolded while they underwent motor training). This study demonstrated significantly better visual discrimination of physically trained (without vision) motor actions. To date, these results provide the best evidence to support the additional behavioral role of motor codes during action perception (in addition to any ongoing visual effects).

The Impact of Experimentally-Induced Expertise on Perception

Another way to explore how motor (or visual) experience with complex action shapes perception is to induce expertise in an experimental context. The benefit of probing the impact of experience on perception in the laboratory is that the actual amount of time a person has spent rehearsing or watching an action can be carefully manipulated and measured, which in turn enables researchers to take a closer look at how the specific amount of experience (or actual performance ability) impacts perception. Naturally, this approach is not without its limitations, as the kind of expertise for the actions being studied has not built up over a lifetime of deliberate practice, or at least 10,000 hours spread over 10 years (the time required for achieving skilled professional status in a motor skill; Ericsson, Krampe, & Tesch-Romer, 1993). However, when studies using such approaches are considered in tandem with those examining perception of experts who have considerably more, and varied, practice with a motor skill (such as those described the 'Neuroimaging Evidence' and 'Behavioral Evidence' sections above), a more complete picture of how visuomotor experience shapes perception begins to emerge. This section first considers the neuroimaging evidence of how experience shapes perception before moving on to discuss the limited behavioral work investigating the impact of *de novo* action representations on perception.

Neuroimaging Evidence

While a growing number of studies have investigated the impact of complex action training manipulations on action perception, the body of evidence is still modest. The first study that reported such a manipulation was performed by Cross, Hamilton, and Grafton (2006), and followed a company of expert contemporary dancers as they learned a new 25-minute work of dance across a six-week rehearsal period. The dancers were invited into the laboratory each weekend across the rehearsal period, where they underwent fMRI whilst watching short video segments of the choreography they were rehearsing as well as kinematically similar movements that they never physically rehearsed. The dancers' task whilst in the scanner was to watch each movement and imagine themselves performing it, and at the end of each video assign a rating based on how well they thought they could reproduce the particular movement segment at present. When the authors compared brain activity across all scanning sessions when the dancers watched rehearsed movement compared to the kinematically similar non-rehearsed movement, they found a pattern of activity comprising parietal, premotor and superior temporal cortices that was very similar to that reported by Calvo-Merino and colleagues (2005) when they compared ballet experts watching ballet compared to capoeira or capoeira experts watching capoeira compared to ballet. The novel discovery by Cross and colleagues emerged when the dancers' ratings of their own performance ability were added to the neuroimaging data as parametric modulators, designed to reveal which brain regions showed increasing levels of activity the better the dancer could perform the observed movement. This analysis revealed activity increases in the two core mirror system regions, namely, the left ventral premotor cortex and inferior parietal lobule (Figure 26.2a). The authors suggest that this finding shows that the more adept an observer becomes at performing an action, the more he simulates that action when observing it.

Shortly after Calvo-Merino and colleagues reported on the impact of visual compared to physical experience on perception among expert ballet dancers (Calvo-Merino et al., 2006), Cross and colleagues conducted a training study to address a complementary question. This question pertained to how visual and physical experience with complex, full-body actions impacts brain and behavior. Cross and colleagues (2009) started with a group of dance-naïve participants and trained them to dance a number of sequences over five days of training using a popular dance video game similar to 'Dance Dance Revolution'. During each day of physical practice, participants spent an equivalent amount of time watching a different (but similar) set of dance sequences that they never physically practiced. A third set of dance sequences remained untrained. In this study, participants underwent fMRI scanning on the very first day of the study (before any training procedures began) and after the fifth and final day of training concluded. During scanning, participants watched and listened to the soundtracks of each of the sequences from the (to-be) physically trained, (to-be) observationally trained and (to-be) untrained sequences. After all scanning and training procedures were completed, participants returned to the laboratory to perform all sequences (from the danced, observed and untrained conditions) with the dance video game, which enabled objective scoring of physical performance across all training categories.

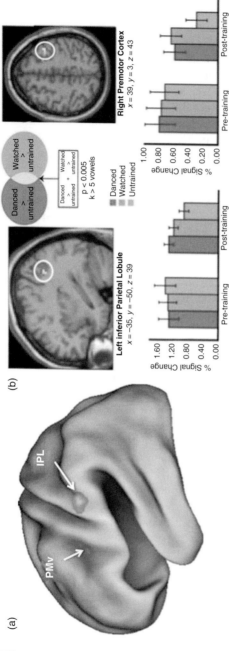

Figure 26.2 Results from Cross et al. (2006) concerning physical expertise and action embodiment. *See Plate 18.*

Notes: (a) Using parametric analyses that took dancers' ability ratings into account, the authors found that left ventral premotor cortex (PMv) and inferior parietal lobule (IPL) showed an increasingly robust response when dancers watched movements they were most expert at physically performing.

(b) Brain regions emerging from the conjunction analysis evaluating overlap between physically practiced > untrained sequences (red activations/bars) and watched > untrained sequences (blue activations/bars) from the training study performed with novice dancers. The parameter estimate plots beneath the brains illustrate the response within the left inferior parietal lobule (left) and right premotor cortex (right) during the pre-training and post-training scans when participants observed music video-clips from the different training sequences during fMRI.

Sources: (a) Modified from Cross et al. (2006). (b) Modified from Cross et al. (2009).

After the five days of physical and observational training, participants performed the physically practiced sequences the best, the untrained sequences the poorest, and performance for the observed sequences was at an intermediate level between practiced and untrained sequences (ibid). It is of note that participants were never explicitly told to try to learn the sequences they observed during daily training, and were not told until the final day of the study they would be asked to perform these sequences. Participants were simply told to sit and watch a few sequences in between physical training bouts to reduce their heart rate. Thus, the evidence of performance gains from visual experience alone likely represents incidental learning from passive observation. This fact is more striking in light of the imaging findings (Figure 26.2b). In a conjunction analyses performed to reveal brain regions that respond to practiced compared to untrained sequences and observed compared to untrained sequences in a similar way, two sensorimotor brain regions emerged: the left inferior parietal lobule and the right premotor cortex. It is of note that the parameter estimates from this analysis (illustrated by the bar plots below the brain images in Figure 26.2b) show that, after the five days of training, neither of these brain regions discriminated between sequences that were physically practiced or visually experienced (see red and blue bars from the post-training plots). In a noteworthy counterpoint to what Calvo-Merino and colleagues showed with expert male and female ballet dancers, Cross and colleagues showed that, in dance-naïve participants, a week of physical practice with one set of movements and visual experience with another set leads to similar responses within parts of the parietal and premotor cortices. However, in the direct contrast of physical > observational practice, Cross et al. (2009) found greater activity in the right dorsal premotor cortex. While not the extensive network of brain regions found by Calvo-Merino et al. (2006) to be more responsive to physical compared to visual experience (also see Figure 26.1d), some correspondence between the two studies did emerge, and in particular revealed a role for dorsal premotor cortex in specifically *physical* action experience.

Together, these studies demonstrate the utility of combining behavioral training with neuroimaging measures to explore the impact of action expertise on action perception (see Box 26.2 for more detail on training studies). As highlighted in the 'Neuroimaging Evidence' section above, the imaging work provides important insights into the neural signature of expertise, but behavioral work is every bit as crucial for developing and exploring these insights. In the following section, a brief overview of some of the laboratory-induced action expertise work is presented that underscores this point.

Box 26.2 Training expertise

Training studies help to build a more complete picture of how action expertise shapes perception through rigorous experimental control of participants' exposure to trained versus untrained tasks. Moreover, training studies afford the opportunity to quantify the impact of a training intervention per se, by comparing behavioral performance or brain activity before and after training. The figure illustrates one approach to running training studies where identical fMRI sessions are separated by a period of several days of identical behavioral training sessions. In some studies, particularly those investigating training experience in the non-motor domain (such as visual/observational or auditory experience with actions), participants return to the laboratory to physically perform all actions experienced during training (testing day 7 in the timeline figure; Cross et al., 2009; Kirsch et al., 2013; Kirsch, Dawson, & Cross, 2015). Such training paradigms have also been used to examine the impact of training visual expertise for actions an observer cannot physically execute, such as those performed by expert gymnasts or non-human agents (Cross et al., 2013).

Another benefit of implementing identical pre- and post-training fMRI sessions when examining the impact of laboratory-based training experience is that they enable precise quantification of how behavior has changed due to the training intervention. In other words, by evaluating the interaction of greater brain activity during the post-training scan in the trained > untrained condition, compared to the pre-training scan to be trained > to remain untrained conditions, it is possible to identify where in the brain the BOLD signal change is *specific* to the training intervention, and not due to spurious differences between stimuli or actions that were trained compared to those that remained untrained. The figure illustrates this – if data were collected during a post-training scan only, it would be impossible to rule out the possibility that some differences existed in terms of how the brain responded (or, indeed, how participants physically performed) to stimuli in the red (trained) and blue (untrained) groups. However, the combined use of targeted training interventions with pre- and post-training fMRI measures enables a closer look at (and elimination of) this possibility when done correctly.

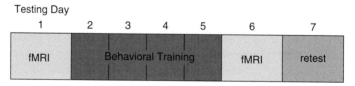

Box 26.2 An approach to running training studies where identical fMRI sessions are separated by a period of several days of identical behavioral training sessions. *See Plate 20.*

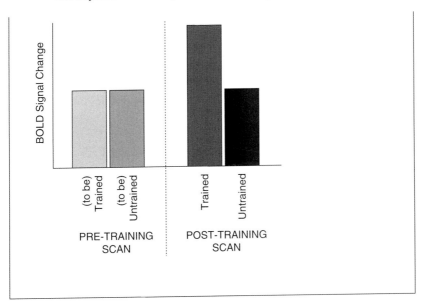

Neurophysiology and Behavioral Evidence

Laboratory-based training experiments have helped to illuminate how experience shapes perception in a number of ways. Elegant work linking training experience with mirror neuron activity comes from work with non-human primates. The researchers who originally discovered mirror neurons described how, after long periods of experimentation, they noticed that mirror neurons seemed to generalize their responses to actions performed by non-biological effectors, such as tools (Arbib & Rizzolatti, 1999). Ferrari, Rozzi, and Fogassi (2005) empirically followed up on this anecdote by training monkeys to perform actions with the hand, arm or mouth, and to observe actions performed by a hand, mouth or tool. The authors found that, after two months of training, a certain subset of neurons in premotor area F5 responded most strongly when the monkeys observed actions performed by a tool. The authors conclude that the training experience enabled the monkeys to extend their action understanding capacity to actions for which they lack a strict corresponding motor representation, thus speaking to the flexibility of neural circuitry underlying action understanding (ibid).

A rich literature of training studies with human participants has also yielded important insights into how behavioral training shapes perception (for a review of some of this work, see McGregor & Gribble, this volume, Chapter 25). One study discussed above bears particular mention, in terms of its innovative approach and the importance of its findings. This was the study by Casile and Giese (2006), where participants learned to perform a novel upper-body movement while blindfolded, with only verbal and haptic feedback. After this non-visual learning, the authors asked the participants to visually identify non-visually learned actions. The authors found that not only were participants able to identify the visual test pattern of the non-visually learned movement after training, but also that the accuracy with which participants could execute the performed movement correlated positively with visual recognition performance. As such, this training study provided another critical piece of support for the notion that changes in one's motor repertoire result in changes in perception (ibid).

A more recent line of work has investigated how training manipulations might impact another side of perception, namely, an observer's *affective* response to a perceived action (Kirsch et al., 2013, 2015; Kirsch, Snagg, Heerey, & Cross, 2016). In these studies, participants learned to perform complex dance sequences in a video game context that uses whole-body motion tracking to quantify performance. The authors were interested in assessing how participants' affective responses when watching these dance sequences changed after they had spent time physically practicing them, simply observing them or only listening to the music that accompanies them. Using both between-subjects (Kirsch et al., 2013) and within-subjects (Kirsch et al., 2016) designs, the authors found that participants enjoyed watching dance movements more after they had spent time either physically practicing them or passively observing them. Listening to the soundtrack only had no impact on the enjoyment participants derived from watching the movements. These studies demonstrate that an observer's affective response to watching others in action presents yet another avenue for exploring the impact of laboratory-induced training experience on perception (also see Orgs, Caspersen, & Haggard, this volume, Chapter 30, for a more detailed discussion of the relationship between an actor, an observer and aesthetics).

As highlighted in Box 26.2, laboratory-based behavioral training studies provide a rich opportunity for inducing *de novo* experience in the visual, motor or visuomotor domains to explore how newly acquired experience shapes perceptual or motor behavior. Naturally, a limitation of this approach is that it is often not possible to train the level of expertise in participants that is possible with studies looking at longstanding expertise, such as those discussed earlier in this chapter. However, taken together, both the longstanding expertise and the laboratory-induced training experiments provide complimentary approaches for probing how experience shapes perception.

Summary and Future Directions

When watching others in action, whether Mikhail Baryshnikov performing on stage or a jogger crossing the road, an observer's prior experience with these actions profoundly shapes how he perceives them. Over the past decade, research from both our laboratories has used dance as a model to explore how observers' longstanding or newly acquired motor repertoires influence perception. This work has demonstrated that sensorimotor regions of the brain associated with the human mirror system are more engaged when dancers watch movements they are experienced in performing (Calvo-Merino et al., 2005), and that the better they are at performing an observed action, the more the left inferior parietal and ventral premotor cortices are engaged (Cross et al., 2006). Moreover, work with expert male and female ballet dancers demonstrates that actual physical experience with particular actions engaged these brain regions above and beyond visual experience only (Calvo-Merino et al., 2006). However, a training study with novice dancers learning a fast-paced dance video game demonstrates that a week's worth of visual or visuomotor experience with dance sequences shows similar impact on parts of parietal and premotor cortices (Cross et al., 2009). In the behavioral domain, evidence has been found with expert and novice dancers that the differentiated neural signatures for expert and non-expert actions reported in the neuroimaging studies are further borne out behaviorally, with evidence showing that action expertise increases visual sensitivity to others' actions (Calvo-Merino et al., 2010) as well as impacts an observer's enjoyment when watching an action (Kirsch et al., 2013, 2016).

It is perhaps unsurprising that the research discussed in this chapter raises many more questions than it answers. Two substantial outstanding questions concern whether *all* action representations are malleable based on experience, and the extent to which embodiment (or 'embodiability') of an observed action matters for how it is perceived and understood. Recent work with amputees (Aziz-Zadeh, Sheng, Liew, & Damasio, 2012; Liew, Sheng, & Aziz-Zadeh, 2013a; Liew, Sheng, Margetis, & Aziz-Zadeh, 2013b) and observing actions performed by non-human robots (Cross et al., 2012) or human or artificial agents that move in ways observers cannot (Cross, Stadler, Parkinson, Schütz-Bosbach, & Prinz, 2013) suggests that actions likely do not need to be embodied (or even 'embodiable') in order for experience with them to shape sensorimotor cortical engagement or behavior. However, this line of inquiry remains ripe for further exploration and exploitation, as possibilities for shaping or instilling (physical) action representations via visual input alone are of great interest to those working in stroke rehabilitation (Garrison, Aziz-Zadeh, Wong, Liew, & Winstein, 2013), as well as in physical therapy, sporting, dance and martial arts contexts.

References

Allison, T., Puce, A., & McCarthy, G. (2000). Social perception from visual cues: Role of the STS region. *Trends in Cognitive Sciences,* 4(7), 267–278.

Arbib, M. A. (1981). Perceptual structures and distributed motor control. In V. B. Brooks (Ed.), *Handbook of physiology :The nervous system II. Motor control.* Bethesda, MD: American Physiological Society, 1449–1480.

Arbib, M.A., & Rizzolatti, G. (1999). Neural expectations: A possible evolutionary path from manual skills to language. In P. V. Loocke (Ed.), *The nature of concepts. Evolution, structure and representation.* New York: Routledge, 128–154.

Aziz-Zadeh, L., Sheng, T., Liew, S. L., & Damasio, H. (2012). Understanding otherness: The neural bases of action comprehension and pain empathy in a congenital amputee. *Cerebral Cortex,* 22(4), 811–819. doi: 10.1093/cercor/bhr139.

Calvo-Merino, B., Glaser, D. E., Grèzes, J., Passingham, R. E., & Haggard, P. (2005). Action observation and acquired motor skills: An fMRI study with expert dancers. *Cerebral Cortex,* 15(8), 1243–1249.

Calvo-Merino, B., Grézes, J., Glaser, D. E., Passingham, R. E., & Haggard, P. (2006). Seeing or doing? Influence of visual and motor familiarity in action observation. *Current Biology,* 16(19), 1905–1910.

Calvo-Merino, B., Ehrenberg, S., Leung, D., & Haggard, P. (2010). Experts see it all: Configural effects in action observation. *Psychological Research,* 74(4), 400–406. doi: 10.1007/s00426-009-0262-y.

Casile, A., & Giese, M. A. (2006). Nonvisual motor training influences biological motion perception. *Current Biology,* 16(1), 69–74. doi: 10.1016/j.cub.2005.10.071.

Cross, E. S., Hamilton, A. F., & Grafton, S. T. (2006). Building a motor simulation de novo: Observation of dance by dancers. *NeuroImage,* 31(3), 1257–1267.

Cross, E. S., Kraemer, D. J., Hamilton, A. F., Kelley, W. M., & Grafton, S. T. (2009). Sensitivity of the action observation network to physical and observational learning. *Cerebral Cortex,* 19(2), 315–326.

Cross, E. S., Liepelt, R., de C. Hamilton A. F., Parkinson, J., Ramsey, R., et al. (2012). Robotic movement preferentially engages the action observation network. *Human Brain Mapping,* 33(9), 2238–2254. doi: 10.1002/hbm.21361.

Cross, E. S., Stadler, W., Parkinson, J., Schütz-Bosbach, S., & Prinz, W. (2013). The influence of visual training on predicting complex action sequences. *Human Brain Mapping,* 34(2), 467–486. doi: 10.1002/hbm.21450.

Decety, J., Grezes, J., Costes, N., Perani, D., Jeannerod, M., et al. (1997). Brain activity during observation of actions: Influence of action content and subject's strategy. *Brain,* 120(Pt 10), 1763–1777.

Ericsson, K. A., Krampe, R. T., & Tesch-Romer, C. (1993). The role of deliberate practice in the acquisition of expert performance. *Psychological Review,* 100, 363–406.

Ferrari, P. F., Rozzi, S., & Fogassi, L. (2005). Mirror neurons responding to observation of actions made with tools in monkey ventral premotor cortex. *Journal of Cognitive Neuroscience,* 17(2), 212–226. doi: 10.1162/0898929053124910.

Gallese, V., Fadiga, L., Fogassi, L., & Rizzolatti, G. (1996). Action recognition in the premotor cortex. *Brain,* 119 (Pt 2), 593–609.

Gallese, V., Gernsbacher, M. A., Heyes, C., Hickock, G., & Iacoboni, M. (2011). Mirror neuron forum. *Perspectives on Psychological Science,* 6, 369–407.

Gallese, V., Rochat, M., Cossu, G., & Sinigaglia, C. (2009). Motor cognition and its role in the phylogeny and ontogeny of action understanding. *Developmental Psychology*, 45(1), 103–113. doi: 2008-19282-002 [pii] 10.1037/a0014436.

Garrison, K. A., Aziz-Zadeh, L., Wong, S. W., Liew, S. L., & Winstein, C. J. (2013). Modulating the motor system by action observation after stroke. *Stroke*, 44(8), 2247–2253. doi: 10.1161/STROKEAHA.113.001105.

Gilaie-Dotan, S., Harel, A., Bentin, S., Kanai, R., & Rees, G. (2012). Neuroanatomical correlates of visual car expertise. *NeuroImage*, 62(1), 147–153. doi: 10.1016/j.neuroimage.2012.05.017.

Grafton, S. T., Arbib, M. A., Fadiga, L., & Rizzolatti, G. (1996). Localization of grasp representations in humans by positron emission tomography. 2. Observation compared with imagination. *Experimental Brain Research*, 112(1), 103–111.

Grézes, J., & Decety, J. (2001). Functional anatomy of execution, mental simulation, observation, and verb generation of actions: A meta-analysis. *Human Brain Mapping*, 12(1), 1–19.

Grossman, E. D., Battelli, L., & Pascual-Leone, A. (2005). Repetitive TMS over posterior STS disrupts perception of biological motion. *Vision Research*, 45(22), 2847–2853.

Hommel, B., Musseler, J., Aschersleben, G., & Prinz, W. (2001). The theory of event coding (TEC): A framework for perception and action planning. *Behavioral and Brain Sciences*, 24(5), 849–878.

James, W. (1890). *Principles of psychology*. New York: Holt.

Jeannerod, M. (1997). *The cognitive neuroscience of action*. Oxford: Wiley-Blackwell.

Johansson, G. (1973). Visual perception of biological motion and a model for its analysis. *Perception and Psychophysics*, 14, 201–211.

Kirsch, L. P., & Cross, E. S. (2015). Additive routes to action learning: Layering experience shapes engagement of the action observation network. *Cerebral Cortex*, 25, 4799–4811.

Kirsch, L. P., Dawson, K., & Cross, E. S. (2015). Dance experience sculpts aesthetic perception and related brain circuits. *Annals of the New York Academy of Sciences*, 1337, 130–139.

Kirsch, L., Drommelschmidt, K. A., & Cross, E. S. (2013). The impact of sensorimotor experience on affective evaluation of dance. *Frontiers in Human Neuroscience*, 7, 1–10. doi: 10.3389/fnhum.2013.00521.

Kirsch, L. P., Snagg, A., Heerey, E., & Cross, E. S. (2016). The impact of experience on affective responses during action observation. *PLoS One*, 11(5), e0154681.

Liew, S. L., Sheng, T., & Aziz-Zadeh, L. (2013a). Experience with an amputee modulates one's own sensorimotor response during action observation. *NeuroImage*, 69, 138–145. doi: 10.1016/j.neuroimage.2012.12.028.

Liew, S. L., Sheng, T., Margetis, J. L., & Aziz-Zadeh, L. (2013b). Both novelty and expertise increase action observation network activity. *Frontiers in Human Neuroscience*, 7, 541. doi: 10.3389/fnhum.2013.00541.

Loula, F., Prasad, S., Harber, K., & Shiffrar, M. (2005). Recognizing people from their movement. *Journal of Experimental Psychology: Human Perception and Performance*, 31(1), 210–220. doi: 10.1037/0096-1523.31.1.210.

Orgs, G., Dombrowski, J.-H., Heil, M., & Jansen-Osmann, P. (2008). Expertise in dance modulates alpha/beta event-related desynchronization during action observation. *European Journal of Neuroscience*, 27(12), 3380–3384. doi: 10.1111/j.1460-9568.2008.06271.x.

Pellegrino, G. di, Fadiga, L., Fogassi, L., Gallese, V., & Rizzolatti, G. (1992). Understanding motor events: A neurophysiological study. *Experimental Brain Research*, 91, 176–180.

Prinz, W. (1990). A common coding approach to perception and action. In O. Neumann & W. Prinz (Eds.), *Relationships between perception and action: Current approaches*. Berlin: Spring-Verlag, 167–201.

———. (1997). Perception and action planning. *European Journal of Neuroscience*, 9(2), 129–154.

Rizzolatti, G., & Craighero, L. (2004). The mirror-neuron system. *Annual Review of Neuroscience*, 27, 169–192.

Rizzolatti, G., Fadiga, L., Matelli, M., et al. (1996). Localization of grasp representations in humans by PET: 1. Observation versus execution. *Experimental Brain Research*, 111, 246–252.

Schmidt, R. A. (1975). A schema theory of discrete motor skill learning. *Psychological Review*, 82, 225–260.

Seligman, L., & Reichenberg, L. W. (2009). *Theories of counseling and psychotherapy: Systems, strategies, and skills*: New York: Pearson.

Part VI

Shared Representations in Applied Contexts

27 Sport Performance: Motor Expertise and Observational Learning in Sport

Cosimo Urgesi and Stergios Makris

Abstract

The ability to form anticipatory representations of on-going actions is crucial for effective interactions in dynamic environments, especially in time-demanding sports. Earlier studies have shown that we use previous motor experience for predicting the future of on-going actions, thus building internal anticipatory models. Indeed, previous research with elite athletes has shown that they possess a unique ability to predict the future of opponents' actions compared to novices. This chapter reviews studies providing this evidence, and clarifies associations between these superior perceptual abilities and differential activations in the motor cortex and in body-related visual areas. Hence, achieving excellence in sport implies not only superior motor performance but also the ability to read body kinematics and predict others' actions ahead of their realization. However, motor and visual expertise may make a differential contribution to the development of elite action perception abilities. In sum, while we need to simulate others' actions to anticipate their future behavior, in some circumstances, for example when faced with deceptive intentions, we may need to flexibly inhibit such shared representations to favor a more abstract aspect of social perception based on visual models of others' actions. These findings point to the need for complimentary use of motor and visual modeling strategies in sports training.

Introduction

During the past few decades, the domain of sport has undergone massive development, with elite athletes constantly challenging the limits of human physical performance. Sport performance has been the focus of studies for many

We acknowledge the contribution from the Ministero Istruzione Università e Ricerca [Futuro In Ricerca, FIR 2012, Prot. N. RBFR12F0BD; to CU], and from Istituto di Ricovero e Cura a Carattere Scientifico 'E. Medea' [Ricerca Corrente 2014, Ministero Italiano della Salute; to CU].

different fields, including cognitive psychology and, more recently, cognitive neuroscience. Most of these studies have tried to investigate the cognitive and neural basis of expert performance in sport and how this is grounded in superior perceptuomotor abilities. However, neuroscience research is constrained by laboratory-based experiments that do not necessarily assess how sport skills, acquired over a long period of time, are related to specific neural processes. In that sense, research in the field has mainly focused on behavioral experiments, confirming the superiority of professional athletes over novices in motor and sensory skills. Important aspects of elite athletes' performance, however, are related not only to their ability to execute complex actions, but also to superior perception of the actions of opponent or confederate players. In this regard, the research stream related to the neural bases of perception and action coupling has recently boosted the interest of researchers in investigating not only the behavioral aspects of sport expertise, but also their neural underpinnings. In particular, studies have shown that the activity of the action observation network (AON), which includes both visual (occipitotemporal) and motor (frontoparietal) areas and seems to be responsible for the observation and simulation of perceived actions (Caspers, Zilles, Laird, & Eickhoff, 2010; Fadiga, Craighero, & Olivier, 2005; Grafton, 2009; Rizzolatti & Craighero, 2004; Van Overwalle & Baetens, 2009), depends on the familiarity of actions. In other words, the more familiar the observer is with a given action sequence, the greater the neural response magnitude in premotor and parietal areas seems to be (see Catmur, this volume, Chapter 22; Cross & Calvo-Merino, this volume, Chapter 26). In view of this, it has been suggested that the recognition and simulation of ongoing actions depends on subjective experience (Aglioti, Cesari, Romani, & Urgesi, 2008; Casile & Giese, 2006; Urgesi, Savonitto, Fabbro, & Aglioti, 2012), and that covert simulation of actions is crucial for both imitative and non-imitative motor learning (Giese & Poggio, 2003; Vogt & Thomaschke, 2007). Sport performance has therefore become an important model in cognitive neuroscience to study how perception and action interact and what neural mechanisms support such interaction. At the same time, better understanding of the cognitive processes and neural mechanisms involved in elite athletes' performance will notably contribute to refining and tailoring sport training protocols to the neurocognitive architecture of the human perceptuomotor system.

Effects of Action Observation on Motor Execution in Sport

The notion of common representation for executed and observed actions is notably interesting in applicative fields like sport learning (Holmes & Calmels, 2008). Indeed, together with motor imagery, action observation may offer the possibility to acquire or boost new motor skills despite the limitations to physical learning caused by injury-related immobilization or physical fatigue (see

McGregor & Gribble, this volume, Chapter 25). Furthermore, in contrast to motor imagery, action observation does not require active effort by the trainee to imagine the movements, and is thus not affected by mental fatigue. Another benefit of action observation compared to motor imagery is that observation can be more easily controlled by the trainer, and as such is less susceptible to any given individual's previous knowledge or imagery abilities.

Several behavioral studies in the field of sport performance and motor control have shown that observational learning of movements can lead to subsequent improved performance (Ashford, Davids, & Bennett, 2007), although the extent of benefit may be lower compared to physical practice. Hence, in the absence of actual muscle contraction and perception of sensory feedback, action observation may form a motor memory trace similar to that formed during motor performance (Stefan et al., 2005; also see McGregor & Gribble, this volume, Chapter 25). The involvement of the motor system during observational learning is suggested by the pattern of activation in the AON and is further corroborated by transcranial magnetic stimulation (TMS) evidence that interference with primary motor cortex activity disrupts the consolidation of motor memories acquired after both physical (Muellbacher et al., 2002) and observational (Brown, Wilson, & Gribble, 2009) learning. This suggests that both types of training induce changes of movement representation in the primary motor cortex (Censor & Cohen, 2011).

Importantly, not only is the general coordination pattern of movements acquired during observational practice, specifying 'what' must be performed, but also acquired are the specific parameters, such as timing and force scaling, which specify 'how' to perform the movements. Furthermore, in keeping with the effects of physical training, the observation-related improvements can be transferred to a different motor task (Gruetzmacher, Panzer, Blandin, Shea, & Charles, 2011; Hayes, Elliott, & Bennett, 2010; Mattar & Gribble, 2005; Ong & Hodges, 2010; Porro, Facchin, Fusi, Dri, & Fadiga, 2007; Shea, Wright, Wulf, & Whitacre, 2000). Importantly, however, the mechanism of motor skill acquisition during physical and observational practice seems, at least partially, qualitatively different. Evidence for this can be taken from work showing that their combination results in a greater advantage on transfer tasks (Shea et al., 2000), compared to either kind of training in isolation. In particular, Gruetzmacher et al. (2011) showed that physical practice induced a greater advantage in transfer to motor tasks in which the motor coordinates of the actions were maintained (i.e. using the opposite limb to control the same pattern of muscle contractions and joint angles). In contrast, observational practice induced a greater advantage in the transfer to tasks in which the motor coordinates of the movements were changed, but the visuo-spatial coordinates were maintained (i.e. using the opposite limb to control movements with the same direction in the external space). In a similar vein, and in contrast to action execution, adapting to the repeated observation of reaching movements in a perturbed environment did not induce any after-effects. On the contrary, adaptation to the repeated execution of the same movements induced after-effects, suggesting that observational practice does not allow an update to an internal sensorimotor model of a particular action (Ong & Hodges, 2010). These studies suggest that observational learning may facilitate the development of a representation of the visuospatial coordinates of a given action but not of its specific motor codes (in terms of joint angles and activation patterns). The specific motor codes require direct motor experience. In sum, although action observation can trigger activation of not only visual but also motor areas, and induce the formation of motor memory, the extent of involvement of visual and motor areas and the cognitive processes underlying observational and physical learning do not completely overlap. This evidence points to the need for using complimentary training approaches in applicative contexts.

Effects of Motor Expertise on Action Perception in Sport

There is evidence that motor expertise also affects action perception, especially in allowing anticipatory simulation of action sequences. Undeniably, in a vigorous and constantly changing environment, the full sequence of an action is rarely visible and missing information needs to be completed. Hence, the formation of meaningful and effective interactions in dynamic environments is crucially served by accurate predictions of their future and outcome. This kind of top-down modulation is responsible for optimal interaction with moving objects or living creatures, as it allows for the perceptual system to format anticipatory representations of observed motion sequences on the basis of internal models of the rules that dictate these actions (Hubbard, 2005; Komatsu, 2006; Motes, Hubbard, Courtney, & Rypma, 2008). In sport, the need for anticipatory representations of observed actions is imperative, as athletes have to plan their actions based on predictions of the future of perceived motion sequences executed by their opponents and confederates. In keeping with this view, there is strong behavioral evidence from different sports that elite athletes are equipped with a unique ability to make accurate predictions of the outcome of observed sport actions.

For a long time, studies focusing on sport performance and the relationship between expert perception and action have focused on whether this relationship is direct or indirect (for a review, see Craig, 2013). Proposers of the 'indirect' process have suggested that expertise is grounded in sensory information and internal representations that are stored in memory and recalled during action execution to influence choice and performance (Handford, Davids, Bennett, & Button, 1997). So when it comes to action anticipation and prediction, experts outperform novices in attending to the most relevant source of visual information, verifying it with the information previously stored in memory and thus making better and more accurate predictions of the outcome of time-constraint action sequences (Williams, Davids, & Williams, 1999). This notion has been confirmed by studies in different sports, such as soccer (Savelsbergh, Williams, van der Kamp, & Ward, 2002), volleyball (Kioumourtzoglou, Michalopoulou, Tzetzis, & Kourtessis, 2000) and rugby (Jackson, Warren, & Abernethy, 2006).

For example, in an early study with French boxers, Ripoll, Kerlirzin, Stein, and Reine (1995) investigated the specific visual search strategies, information processing and decision-making mechanisms of expert athletes, intermediates and novices. All subjects were tested in a virtual environment replicating a boxing field and had to respond to maneuvers of an on-screen opponent. Furthermore, the complexity of the environment was divided into two categories: simple and complex. Behavioral data and eye-tracker recordings indicated that expert boxers were better at predicting the maneuvers of the opponent, as well as accurately responding to these, as compared to intermediates and novices. This was more profound in the complex environment. Moreover, it was found that this superiority was reflected in their visual strategies, with expert boxers exhibiting unique spatial and temporal characteristics of visual search activity. Similarly, in a review of studies with soccer players, Williams (2000) reported that skilled athletes are better at recalling and recognizing patterns of play compared to the less-skilled players. Furthermore, skilled soccer players' superior ability in controlling eye-movement patterns for seeking and choosing the most important sources of visual information provides them with the advantage of making more accurate predictions of the outcome of their opponents' actions.

Despite this evidence, criticism of the view that the relationship between action and perception is indirect has been focused on the fact that it cannot account for cases of consistent skilled performance under extreme conditions that would not allow memory recall (Craig, 2013). Hence, a direct approach to the relationship between expert perception and action has been proposed. The Gibsonian (Gibson, 1979) ecological psychology approach to perception has indicated that action processes are deeply grounded in vision and perception, and that the relationship between vision and action is dynamic and mutual. If that is the case, the relationship between the athlete and the environment, the information with which the environment is constantly bombarding the athlete and the ways the athlete actively reacts to it should be focused upon (Handford et al., 1997). In dynamic sports, the environment undergoes continuous change, as relevant actions are constantly altered, and athletes have to account for the uniqueness and variability of any given scenario (Correia, Araújo, Cummins, & Craig, 2012; Craig, Bastin, & Montagne, 2011).

In a seminal study, Craig et al. (2009) investigated how dynamic on-line changes of ball trajectory affected soccer players' predictions of the ball's future arrival position. Unlike previous studies that focused on the perceptual-cognitive strategies of experts making anticipatory judgments in sport, the authors of

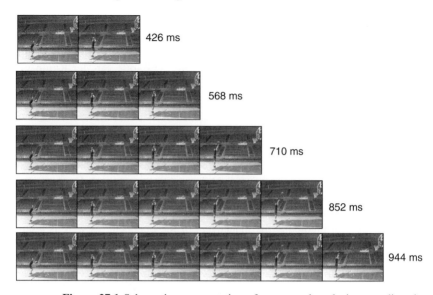

Figure 27.1 Schematic representation of a temporal occlusion paradigm in which presentation of basketball free shots is interrupted at different intervals from onset.

Note: Studies (e.g. Aglioti et al., 2008) have shown that elite athletes, but not expert observers and novices, can predict the outcome of the action for presentation times as short as 426 ms.

this study investigated how expert and novice soccer players are influenced by dynamic visual stimuli, such as a ball's moving trajectory. Their results provided strong evidence that experts are not only superior in recalling previous information for making accurate predictions, but their visual system is also better attuned to visual information invariants. These findings were expanded by further studies (Correia, Araujo, Craig, & Passos, 2011; Correia et al., 2012) with rugby players, which corroborate the finding that in complex, dynamic environments experts are better than novices at attending to or tuning into on-line action-relevant information within the environment, thus achieving superior performance.

Motor Expertise and Reading of Body Kinematics

Using a temporal occlusion paradigm (Box 27.1) it has been found that expert athletes provide not only more accurate but also earlier predictions of the outcome of sport actions, compared to novices. In a seminal study, Aglioti et al. (2008) asked elite basketball athletes, expert observers and novices to predict the fate of basketball free shots (i.e. ball in or out of the basket) whose presentation was interrupted at different time intervals (Figure 27.1). The psychophysical analysis of the acquired data showed that professional basketball players were better at making accurate predictions at shorter video presentation times, compared to both expert observers (such as coaches) and novices. The authors considered this as direct evidence of the role of motor experience in simulating observed actions and predicting their outcome, with expert players being more able to make accurate predictions by basing their judgments on the initial body cues of the model player executing the shots.

Box 27.1 Temporal occlusion paradigm in sport

The temporal occlusion paradigm has been used widely to study predictive perceptual abilities in sport. In a typical temporal occlusion experiment observers are presented with dynamic displays of sport actions that are interrupted at different delays from onset. Domain-specific motor experts and naïve participants are required to predict the direction or the correctness of the actions after viewing only the initial body kinematics of the model player or also the visual consequences of the movements (e.g. ball trajectory). Research in a variety of different sports has shown that motor experts are more accurate than expert observers (e.g. coaches) and naïve participants in predicting the fate of the observed actions after viewing only the initial body movements. This has suggested that elite athletes can 'read' the body kinematics of the observed actions (Abernethy & Zawi, 2007; Aglioti et al., 2008; Smeeton & Huys, 2011).

This temporal occlusion paradigm must be distinguished from the so-called occluder paradigm (Graf et al., 2007; Springer, Parkinson, & Prinz, 2013), in which action video presentation is temporarily masked behind an occluder and then reappears after a variable amount of time, which can be compatible or not compatible with the course of actions during the occlusion period. Observers are asked to judge whether the spatial arrangements of the action kinematics after the occlusion match or do not match those of the action before occlusion. Studies have shown better spatial perception abilities when the temporal dynamics of the action behind the occluder corresponded to the duration of the occlusion. This has been held as suggesting that observers are engaged in mental simulation of the occluded action and present better performance when the state of such simulation processes matches the perceived action phase at reappearance.

In a subsequent study, Urgesi et al. (2012) replicated the aforementioned findings by applying similar experiment paradigms in volleyball. The performance of expert volleyball players was compared to that of expert observers (volleyball team supporters) and novices, in a temporal occlusion paradigm requiring predictions of the fate of volleyball floating services. Crucially, in previous temporal occlusion paradigm studies (Abernethy, Zawi, & Jackson, 2008; Aglioti et al., 2008; Farrow & Abernethy, 2003; Weissensteiner, Abernethy, Farrow, & Müller, 2008), video presentation was interrupted at different instants after the beginning of the action, showing videos of increasing length; thus, the presentation of body- versus ball-related cues was confounded with increasing viewing time and cumulative presentation of more information available on the action. Therefore, it could not be established whether the superior perceptual abilities of motor experts reflected faster processing speed and need of less information to make a decision or were specifically related to their capacity to read body kinematics. Urgesi et al. (2012) used a modified temporal occlusion paradigm, in which only initial body movements or only ball trajectory of volleyball floating services was shown. This procedure allowed them to highlight the complementary roles of motor and visual expertise on the representation of body action and object motion. Similar to previous studies, their data have shown that both expert players and watchers are better than novices at making accurate predictions on the basis of the ball trajectory, but only expert players can also base these predictions on body kinematics.

Developing Elite Action Perception

The aforementioned studies suggest that expert athletes, but not expert watchers, are equipped with fast and generally accurate perceptual mechanisms that allow them to read the kinematics of others' body movements in order to anticipate the future course of observed actions ahead of realization. However, this difference between expert athletes and watchers may reflect either the greater extent of athletes' visual experience with domain-specific sport actions, which is obviously greater than that of any expert watchers, including coaches, journalists or supporters, or the additive combination of visual and motor experience, which allows a better description of movements and their visual consequences. Comparing different groups of individuals with acquired domain-specific expertise enables researchers to test the effects of extensive practice periods, which are seldom used in longitudinal studies. However, such an approach prevents clear disentanglement of the specific roles of motor and visual experience in action perception. Furthermore, studies based on comparison of different groups do not take into account possible pre-existing interindividual differences that may have determined the superior abilities of athletes in sport as compared to novices or watchers. To clarify the specific roles of motor and visual expertise on the fine-tuning of anticipatory perceptual abilities, in a follow-up experiment, Urgesi et al. (2012) used a longitudinal design with adolescents who practiced volleyball and were divided into three groups: (1) those receiving physical training for execution of floating services; (2) those being trained with repeated observation of floating services executed by expert players; and (3) those receiving control training by watching videos of volleyball defense actions, in which the floating services were cut out. Results showed that participants assigned to the physical training condition improved their ability to predict the outcome of domain-specific volleyball floating services by reading the initial bodily cues of the opponent, while participants assigned to the observational training improved in their ability to understand the ball trajectory. Those trained in watching nonspecific volleyball actions did not show any improvement, thus pointing to the selectivity of the training effects. Again, results highlight the distinctive and complementary contributions of physical and observational experience to the development of superior action-prediction skills in elite athletes.

Neural Systems Underlying Superior Action Perception in Sport

As mentioned at the beginning of this chapter, a critical advance made by cognitive neuroscience in sport is the investigation of the neural bases of superior action perception in athletes. In the aforementioned study by Aglioti et al. (2008), the authors ran a second experiment combining a temporal occlusion paradigm with measures of corticospinal excitability by means of single-pulse TMS to study motor facilitation during sport action observation (Box 27.2). During observation of the videotaped basketball free shots, single-pulse TMS-induced corticospinal reactivity of the muscles associated with the observed actions of athletes, watchers and novices – and at different time intervals from action onset – was measured. In line with their behavioral findings, the TMS results showed increased motor excitability in expert players and watchers compared to novices, when they were predicting the outcome of free basketball shots. However, this increase in motor responses was not replicated when the same players and watchers were making predictions in a different sport (i.e. soccer kicks). Conversely, the motor cortex of novice participants was comparably facilitated during observation of basketball and soccer actions. This suggests that both motor and visual expertise allowed greater recruitment of the motor system during observation of domain-specific actions. Notably, however, only players, but not watchers and novices, showed fine-tuned modulation of motor facilitation according to the shot outcome. Among the players, greater facilitation of the little finger motor representation was obtained during observation of erroneous compared to correct throws. This modulation was only obtained when viewing videos showing the ball leaving the hand, thus when the model player could exert final control over the ball trajectory using distal movements of the fingers. Hence, these findings suggest that achieving excellence in sport may be related, in part, to the fine-tuning of specific anticipatory 'resonant' mechanisms that allow for an earlier and more accurate prediction of the future of others' actions, therefore supporting the role of motor expertise in predicting the future of observed actions.

Box 27.2 Single-pulse transcranial magnetic stimulation and motor facilitation

Single pulse TMS is a neurophysiological method that applies single magnetic pulses over the observer's primary motor cortex to record motor-evoked potentials (MEPs) from the targeted muscles. Doing so allows for the assessment of the excitability of muscle corticospinal representation under different experimental conditions. Many studies have shown that observing others' actions increases the excitability of the onlookers' corticospinal motor system (Fadiga et al., 2005), thus inducing motor facilitation that is held as an index of motor simulation processes. Motor facilitation is specific to the muscle involved in the observed action (Alaerts, Heremans, Swinnen, & Wenderoth, 2009; Romani, Cesari, Urgesi, Facchini, & Aglioti, 2005; Urgesi, Candidi, Fabbro, Romani, & Aglioti, 2006a) and is temporally coupled with the action course (Gangitano, Mottaghy, & Pascual-Leone, 2004). Crucially, studies using dynamic and static displays of actions (Borroni, Montagna, Cerri, & Baldissera, 2005; Urgesi, Moro, Candidi, & Aglioti, 2006b; Urgesi et al., 2010) have also indicated that action simulation may be biased toward the future phases of the observed movements, suggesting that the motor system may be involved in the predictive coding of observed actions.

The use of single-pulse TMS to probe motor facilitation should be distinguished from repetitive TMS trains administered to interfere with neural activity in the target area during the performance of perceptual, motor or cognitive tasks. The rationale behind repetitive TMS is that, if an area is necessary for performing the task at hand, interfering with its neural activity should impair performance, thus providing causative evidence that the target area is involved in the task. Accumulating evidence in the field of action perception has demonstrated that stimulation of not only visual areas but also premotor and parietal areas affects action perception (see Avenanti et al., 2013b). Furthermore, a recent study has shown that repetitive TMS of the premotor cortex affects sport action perception only in expert players not in novices (Makris & Urgesi, 2015).

Different nodes of the AON may be more affected by motor and visual familiarity, with the activity of motor and premotor areas being more dependent on motor experience and visual, temporal areas being more dependent on visual experience (Calvo-Merino, Grèzes, Glaser, Passingham, & Haggard, 2006; also see Cross & Calvo-Merino, this volume, Chapter 26). This complementary role of motor-premotor and temporal areas in action expertise is in keeping with single-cell recordings in the monkey's brain, in particular from two critical nodes of the AON, namely, the (STS) and motor and premotor areas. More specifically, neural responses in STS have been found to be more influenced by previous action perception than by execution (Jellema & Perrett, 2003; Rizzolatti & Craighero, 2004). Conversely, neural responses in the premotor cortex seem to occur both during action observation and execution, thus indicating the role of previous motor experience in predicting the outcome of ongoing actions (Avenanti & Urgesi, 2011; Avenanti, Annella, Candidi, Urgesi, & Aglioti, 2013b; Avenanti, Candidi, & Urgesi, 2013b; Friston, Mattout, & Kilner, 2011; Keysers & Gazzola, 2009; Urgesi et al., 2010; Wilson & Knoblich, 2005). These results may suggest that neural activity in STS uses visual information and perceptual experience to form a representation of ongoing actions, while activity in the premotor cortex may function as an internal forward model, enabling us to base our judgments on and predictions for observed actions on our motor expertise.

In keeping with this view, a recent neuroimaging study (Abreu et al., 2012) with expert basketball players has provided strong evidence that superior perceptuomotor skills of elite athletes can also be associated with activation of brain areas not traditionally associated with the motor nodes of the AON. Abreu and colleagues (2012) devised an fMRI experimental paradigm, according to which expert basketball players and novices determined the outcome of free shots performed by model players. Moreover, video-clips of the shots were manipulated in such a way that either forward or backward moving conditions were presented. This allowed the researchers to distinguish pure attentional monitoring from predictive action skills. Blood-oxygenation-level-dependent (BOLD) response results revealed that areas associated with the frontoparietal AON were equally activated in both basketball experts and novices, whenever they had to make an action prediction. Furthermore, in athletes a higher activation of the extrastriate body area (EBA) was observed associated with the observation and reading of the model's action kinematics in the video-clips, as well as an involvement of the inferior frontal gyrus and the anterior insular cortex following response errors in the task. Finally, the fMRI BOLD signal revealed that, in expert athletes, correct action prediction induced higher activity in the posterior insular cortex, whereas this type of activation in novices was observed in areas of the orbitofrontal cortex. On the basis of these new findings, the authors have proposed a functional reorganization of the AON, according to which differences between experts and novices in visual and motor expertise, action anticipation and error awareness are all related to distinctive visual and motor body-related processes, as well as decision-making processes. These data remind us that the neural bases of athletes' superior perceptual and motor capabilities cannot be searched in one area or even a set of areas related to similar function (as the AON), but are related to complex interactions between multiple brain structures.

Motor Expertise and Deception Detection

Bluffing the opponent and detecting others' bluffs are considered crucial components or skills in an athlete's repertoire of sport actions. Researchers have described deception in sports as an exaggeration in body-related cues that induces others to make incorrect action predictions and delays in postural cues that may inform opponents of sudden changes (Brault, Bideau, Craig, & Kulpa, 2010). In that sense, studies looking at the detection of action deception in sport have described it as the ability to identify incongruence between honest and bluffing body-kinematic cues and the flexibility of updating ongoing action representations on the basis of upcoming information. Previous research, however, has reported mixed results concerning the role of experience in detecting bluffing actions and accurately responding to them.

Jackson et al. (2006) investigated the ability to detect bluffing actions both in expert and novice rugby players. The type of detection introduced was simply a change in the observed body direction with and without deceptive movement. All subjects had to predict the direction of the change and it was found that experts' responses were less susceptible to deceptive cues, as compared to those made by novices. Moreover, expert players were more confident than novices in predicting the outcome of the direction change in the case of deception trials. In a similar vein, Cañal-Bruland, van der Kamp, & van Kesteren (2010) studied deception in handball players and novices and found that experts outperformed novices in predicting the outcome of true or fake shots by a penalty-taker. However, they have indicated that, in their findings, neither the degree of motor experience nor visual familiarity could account for successful recognition of deceptive actions.

Using a rather different approach, Dessing & Craig (2010) investigated deception in soccer, especially that involving novice and expert goalkeepers and their judgments about the outcome of free kicks. Instead of looking at how soccer players try to deceive their opponents, they applied an experimental paradigm in which deception was grounded in the bending of free kicks and gravitational acceleration of the ball. In this study, both expert and novice goalkeepers had to decide on the final direction of the ball in relation to the goal line. Their results indicated that, despite extensive visual and motor experience in defending ball kicks, even experts were frequently bluffed when the ball followed a bending trajectory, as they could not account for the spin-induced visual acceleration of the ball. However, the fact that deception in this case depended on the ball trajectory rather than the body kinematics of the players is a limitation in terms of generalizing these findings.

To overcome this limitation, in a more recent study Tomeo, Cesari, Aglioti, and Urgesi (2013) investigated how incongruent body kinematics may affect judgments for the outcome of soccer penalty kicks in expert goalkeepers, outfield players and novices. Applying a temporal occlusion paradigm, the authors presented video-clips of a model player executing penalty kicks. For half of the videos, incongruent kinematic cues were introduced (Figure 27.2). The videos were interrupted at three phases, manipulating the congruence between the kick direction suggested by the initial body movements, the direction indicated by the foot–ball contact and, finally, the initial ball trajectory. At the end of each video-clip, subjects had to indicate whether the ball would end up at the right or left side of the goal post. Their data showed that in the congruent condition expert goalkeepers and outfield players outperformed novices in the task, as they were better in perceiving the body kinematics of the model player and predicting the fate of the kick. However, it was found that outfield players were more susceptible (compared to goalkeepers and novices) to being caught out by the bluffed created by the incongruence between the initial body kinematics and the final direction of the kick indicated by the ball trajectory.

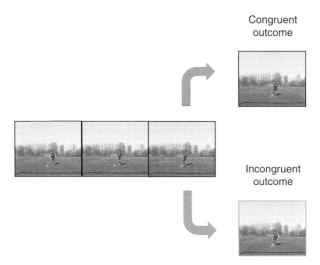

Figure 27.2 Representation of the transitions to congruent or incongruent outcome used in Tomeo et al. (2013) to study athletes' perception of fooling soccer penalty kicks.

This study, which employed rather artificial stimuli to detect the reaction of motor and visual experts to the incongruence between body kinematics and ball trajectory cues, has revealed the 'dark side' of motor expertise for action perception, wherein motor experts cannot refrain from representing actions on the basis of simulative processes and by reading body kinematics even when these last cues are incongruent with upcoming contextual cues. It is, thus, not surprising that goalkeepers need very specific cognitive and visual training in order to be able to update such relatively automatic simulative motor representations and flexibly use other sources of information.

Neural Bases of Deception Detection in Sport

In order to investigate the neural correlates of the aforementioned findings, in a second experiment Tomeo et al. (2013) presented outfield players, goalkeepers and novices with videos showing soccer penalty kicks. This time, however, they were measuring the corticospinal reactivity of the observer during observation of the videotaped penalty kicks. Video-clips were interrupted this time at two phases: after the foot–ball contact or the initial ball trajectory. For half of the trials, incongruent cues were introduced and the corticospinal motor correlates of the subjects for predicting congruent versus incongruent kicks were determined by means of single-pulse TMS. The TMS technique was used to probe excitability of muscles associated with soccer actions (lower leg and forearm) and the results have indicated significant differences in the corticospinal facilitation of the associated muscles between the three expertise groups. More specifically, electromyography measures from the lower limb muscles revealed different levels of facilitation during the observation of incongruent trials as compared to the congruent ones. Furthermore, distinctive differences in muscle reactivity were observed between experts and novices, with outfield players providing comparable measures between incongruent and congruent actions, and goalkeepers and novices showing reduced and increased facilitation, respectively, during observation of incongruent kicks. Although congruent and incongruent actions engendered a comparable facilitation of kickers' lower-limb motor representation, their neurophysiological response correlated with their greater susceptibility to be fooled. Indeed, the greater their motor facilitation during observation of incongruent kicks, the lower their accuracy in predicting the actual outcome of the ball (Figure 27.3). Then again, neurophysiological data in this penalty kick prediction task revealed that neural markers of motor simulation processes were correlated with poorer performance, suggesting that athletes' elite perceptual performance cannot be explained by the use of motor representations alone, but must be ascribed to the fine-tuning of perceptuomotor representations.

These observations have illustrated the need for distinguishing the roles of visual and motor expertise in the simulation and understanding of observed

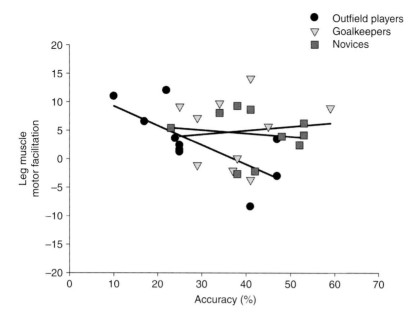

Figure 27.3 Correlation between the facilitation of the corticospinal representation of leg muscles (gastrocnemius) during observation of fooling soccer penalty kicks and accuracy of outfield players, goalkeepers and novices in predicting their actual outcome.

Note: The graph shows that the greater the motor resonance for fooling actions, the lower the accuracy of outfield players in predicting the action outcome.

Source: Tomeo et al. (2013).

action sequences. In a more recent study, Makris and Urgesi (2015) tried to investigate the functional roles of visual and motor action representations in expert athletes' ability to predict the outcome of soccer actions. In an experimental paradigm similar to that of Tomeo et al. (2013), the authors asked expert goalkeepers, outfield players and novices to predict the fate of penalty kicks interrupted at specific time intervals. More specifically, they presented videotaped penalty kicks executed by a model player that were interrupted at the foot–ball contact and contained or did not contain incongruent body kinematics. At the end of each video-clip, subjects were instructed to predict the direction of the ball. Furthermore, in order to investigate the causative roles of visual and motor areas of the AON in the action prediction task, repetitive TMS (rTMS; see Box 27.2) trains were applied over the STS area and the dorsal premotor cortex (PMd) of the subjects while they were observing the action sequences. In this way, a rapid and short interference was induced over the aforementioned brain areas. The results of this experiment have indicated that, for the incongruence condition (incongruent body action kinematics),

STS-rTMS impaired performance in both experts and novices, but this effect was more profound in the subjects with more visual experience in the task (i.e. goalkeepers). Most importantly, PMd-rTMS disrupted performance only in expert players who exhibit strong motor expertise in soccer actions. These results suggest that experts and non-experts seem to use different neural mechanisms to predict others' actions: while both experts and non-experts use visual representations in the posterior temporal cortex, only direct motor experience endows the onlooker's brain with specific motor-resonant mechanisms that allow for the creation of anticipatory representations of ongoing actions ahead of their realization. This was reflected by the fact that, while both experts and novices can access visual action representations in STS, only experts are equipped with and use internal motor representations to predict others' behavior. This suggests that we need to embody others' actions in order to anticipate their future behavior, but also indicates that in some circumstances, for example when facing deceptive intentions, we need to flexibly inhibit such embodied representations to favor a more abstract aspect of social perception based on visual models of others' actions. The implications of these findings are highly important, as for the first time causative evidence is provided of the distinctive and complementary roles of visual and motor expertise in sport. Of course, further studies applying similar experimental paradigms and seeking the same type of causative evidence in a broader selection of sports are necessary to validate and expand on the aforementioned findings.

Conclusions

Overall, skilled performance in sport is a highly relevant topic within the fields of psychology and neuroscience. Researchers intrigued by the superior motor and visual abilities of elite athletes have analyzed their expert performance to attempt to understand the neural basis of this. Elite athletes show increased precision not only in action execution but also on action perception, anticipation and prediction. Simple behavioral studies, as well as neuroimaging and neurophysiological investigations, have provided strong evidence of the differences between athletes and novices in employing distinctive cognitive and neural mechanisms for performing in the field and predicting the future of their opponents' action sequences. Only in the past few years has research provided some insight into the specific neural underpinnings of experts' performance, indicating the distinctive as well as complementary roles of visual and motor areas. Though this type of evidence has to be further evaluated and clarified (Box 27.3), it can provide us with a better understanding of the neural mechanisms that differentiate the motor and perceptual abilities of elite athletes from those of less-experienced athletes and novices. The results of these studies show that motor and visual expertise may provide complementary contributions to the development of the experts' ability to predict the outcome of genuine and deceptive behaviors on the basis of body kinematics and suggest that these differential abilities are reflected by different patterns of motor activation during action observation. In particular, visual experience may foster visual representations of actions that are used to describe and understand the visual dynamics of the actions and of the related contexts (e.g. the ball trajectory). In contrast, motor experience may allow for motor, simulative, body kinematics-based representations that are used to predict and anticipate the future actions of other individuals. Hence, such knowledge should be crucial for developing future training techniques in sport, as well as for identifying and enhancing types of expert skill and performance. The implications are also robust for a repertoire of everyday actions, in which skilled performance is imperative and intentional deception or some level of incoherence are present.

Box 27.3 Critical issues in the cognitive neuroscience of sport

An important issue in the cognitive neuroscience of sport is how informative is cognitive neuroscience research for sport training in real life. In order to control variables involved in motor, cognitive and perceptual tasks, researchers need to reduce the complexity of the experimental set-up, often making it very dissimilar from what people encounter in real life. Furthermore, most techniques for studying brain activity require the subject to refrain from whole-body movements (if not staying completely still, as for fMRI), thus making the study of sport-related functions particularly problematic. How can findings derived from laboratory-based experiments on participants comfortably sitting on a chair or lying down in an MRI scanner be generalized to outfield sport practice? How can reports of subjects judging videotaped actions inform us about the motor behavior of a goalkeeper who needs to intercept a penalty kick, rather than making an explicit judgment on its outcome? A few studies in the field of motor control (Craig et al., 2011; Mann, Abernethy, & Farrow, 2010; Ranganathan & Carlton, 2007) have shown that elite, but not novice, players make more accurate predictions of others' actions when they are required to intercept it than when they provide a verbal response. These results were taken to suggest that perceptual prediction in sport is based on the fine-tuning of perception–action links and that optimal athletes' performance is elicited in the natural environment. This issue is crucial for the cognitive neuroscience of sport, because using visual information to plan a proper motor reaction may involve different pathways (the so-called dorsal stream) than using visual information to make an explicit prediction (Milner & Goodale, 2006, 2008).

This urges caution in generalizing the results of laboratory-based experiments to real-life situations and calls for integrative collaboration between motor control and cognitive neuroscience research fields in order to elucidate which aspects of real-life situations are crucial for triggering naturalistic processing of sport-related actions and to then use this information in neuroscientific studies. Such an investigation is crucial to avoid the simplistic criticism that, since cognitive neuroscience study can hardly test athletes in natural environments, it cannot provide any helpful information for applicative disciplines. In a similar vein, the use of virtual reality environments (Craig, 2013) may notably expand the potential for simulating naturalistic situations without losing control of involved factors.

References

Abernethy, B., & Zawi, K. (2007). Pickup of essential kinematics underpins expert perception of movement patterns. *Journal of Motor Behavior*, 39, 353–367.

Abernethy, B., Zawi, K., & Jackson, R. C. (2008). Expertise and attunement to kinematic constraints. *Perception*, 37, 931–948.

Abreu, A. M., Macaluso, E., Azevedo, R. T., Cesari, P., Urgesi, C., & Aglioti, S. M. (2012). Action anticipation beyond the action observation network: A functional magnetic resonance imaging study in expert basketball players. *European Journal of Neuroscience*, 35, 1646–1654.

Aglioti, S. M., Cesari, P., Romani, M., & Urgesi, C. (2008). Action anticipation and motor resonance in elite basketball players. *Nature Neuroscience*, 11, 1109–1116.

Alaerts, K., Heremans, E., Swinnen, S. P., & Wenderoth, N. (2009). How are observed actions mapped to the observer's motor system? Influence of posture and perspective. *Neuropsychologia*, 47, 415–422.

Ashford, D., Davids, K., & Bennett, S. J. (2007). Developmental effects influencing observational modelling: A meta-analysis. *Journal of Sports Sciences*, 25, 547–558.

Avenanti, A., Annella, L., Candidi, M., Urgesi, C., & Aglioti, S. M. (2013a). Compensatory plasticity in the action observation network: Virtual lesions of STS enhance anticipatory simulation of seen actions. *Cerebral Cortex*, 23, 570–580.

Avenanti, A., Candidi, M., & Urgesi, C. (2013b). Vicarious motor activation during action perception: Beyond correlational evidence. *Frontiers in Human Neuroscience*, 7, 185.

Avenanti, A., Urgesi, C. (2011). Understanding 'what' others do: Mirror mechanisms play a crucial role in action perception. *Social Cognitive and Affective Neuroscience*, 6, 257–259.

Borroni, P., Montagna, M., Cerri, G., & Baldissera, F. (2005). Cyclic time course of motor excitability modulation during the observation of a cyclic hand movement. *Brain Research*, 1065, 115–124.

Brault, S., Bideau, B., Craig, C. M., & Kulpa, R. (2010). Balancing deceit and disguise: How to successfully fool the defender in a 1 vs. 1 situation in rugby. *Human Movement Science*, 29, 412–425.

Brown, L. E., Wilson, E. T., & Gribble, P. L. (2009). Repetitive transcranial magnetic stimulation to the primary motor cortex interferes with motor learning by observing. *Journal of Cognitive Neuroscience*, 21, 1013–1022.

Calvo-Merino, B., Grèzes, J., Glaser, D. E., Passingham, R. E., & Haggard, P. (2006). Seeing or doing? Influence of visual and motor familiarity in action observation. *Current Biology*, 16, 1905–1910.

Cañal-Bruland, R., van der Kamp, J., & van Kesteren, J. (2010). An examination of motor and perceptual contributions to the recognition of deception from others' actions. *Human Movement Science*, 29, 94–102.

Casile, A., & Giese, M. A. (2006). Nonvisual motor training influences biological motion perception. *Current Biology*, 16, 69–74.

Caspers, S., Zilles, K., Laird, A. R., & Eickhoff, S. B. (2010). ALE meta-analysis of action observation and imitation in the human brain. *NeuroImage*, 50, 1148–1167.

Censor, N., & Cohen, L. G. (2011). Using repetitive transcranial magnetic stimulation to study the underlying neural mechanisms of human motor learning and memory. *Journal of Physiology*, 589, 21–28.

Correia, V., Araujo, D., Craig, C., & Passos, P. (2011). Prospective information for pass decisional behavior in rugby union. *Human Movement Science*, 30, 984–997.

Correia, V., Araújo, D., Cummins, A., & Craig, C. M. (2012). Perceiving and acting upon spaces in a VR rugby task: Expertise effects in affordance detection and task achievement. *Journal of Sport & Exercise Psychology*, 34, 305–321.

Craig, C. M. (2013). Understanding perception and action in sport: How can virtual reality technology help? *Sports Technology*, 6, 161–169.

Craig, C. M., Bastin, J., & Montagne, G. (2011). How information guides movement: Intercepting curved free kicks in soccer. *Human Movement Science*, 30, 931–941.

Craig, C. M., Goulon, C., Berton, E., Rao, G., Fernandez, L., & Bootsma, R. J. (2009). Optic variables used to judge future ball arrival position in expert and novice soccer players. *Attention, Perception & Psychophysics*, 71, 515–522.

Dessing, J. C., & Craig, C. M. (2010). Bending it like Beckham: How to visually fool the goalkeeper. *PloS One*, 5, e13161.

Fadiga, L., Craighero, L., & Olivier, E. (2005). Human motor cortex excitability during the perception of others' action. *Current Opinion in Neurobiology*, 15, 213–218.

Farrow, D., & Abernethy, B. (2003). Do expertise and the degree of perception–action coupling affect natural anticipatory performance? *Perception*, 32, 1127–1139.

Friston, K., Mattout, J., & Kilner, J. (2011). Action understanding and active inference. *Biological Cybernetics*, 104, 137–160.

Gangitano, M., Mottaghy, F. M., & Pascual-Leone, A. (2004). Modulation of premotor mirror neuron activity during observation of unpredictable grasping movements. *European Journal of Neuroscience*, 20, 2193–2202.

Gibson, J. (1979). *The ecological approach to human perception*. Hillsdale, NJ: Lawrence Erlbaum.

Giese, M. A, & Poggio, T. (2003). Neural mechanisms for the recognition of biological movements. *Nature Reviews Neuroscience*, 4, 179–192.

Graf, M., Reitzner, B., Corves, C., Casile, A., Giese, M., & Prinz, W. (2007). Predicting point-light actions in real-time. *NeuroImage*, 36(Suppl 2), T22–T32.

Grafton, S. T. (2009). Embodied cognition and the simulation of action to understand others. *Annals of the New York Academy of Sciences*, 1156, 97–117.

Gruetzmacher, N., Panzer, S., Blandin, Y., Shea, C. H., & Charles, H. (2011). Observation and physical practice: Coding of simple motor sequences. *Quarterly Journal of Experimental Psychology*, 64, 1111–1123.

Handford, C., Davids, K., Bennett, S., & Button, C. (1997). Skill acquisition in sport: Some applications of an evolving practice ecology. *Journal of Sports Sciences*, 15, 621–640.

Hayes, S. J., Elliott, D., & Bennett, S. J. (2010). General motor representations are developed during action-observation. *Experimental Brain Research*, 204, 199–206.

Holmes, P., & Calmels, C. (2008). A neuroscientific review of imagery and observation use in sport. *Journal of Motor Behavior*, 40, 433–445.

Hubbard, T. (2005). Representational momentum and related displacements in spatial memory: A review of the findings. *Psychonomic Bulletin & Review*, 12, 822–851.

Jackson, R. C., Warren, S., & Abernethy, B. (2006). Anticipation skill and susceptibility to deceptive movement. *Acta Psychologica*, 123, 355–371.

Jellema, T., & Perrett, D. I. (2003). Perceptual history influences neural responses to face and body postures. *Journal of Cognitive Neuroscience*, 15, 961–971.

Keysers, C., & Gazzola, V. (2009). Expanding the mirror: Vicarious activity for actions, emotions, and sensations. *Current Opinion in Neurobiology*, 19, 666–671.

Kioumourtzoglou, E., Michalopoulou, M., Tzetzis, G., & Kourtessis, T. (2000). Ability profile of the elite volleyball player. *Perceptual and Motor Skills*, 90, 757–770.

Komatsu, H. (2006). The neural mechanisms of perceptual filling-in. *Nature Reviews Neuroscience*, 7, 220–231.

Makris, S., & Urgesi, C. (2015). Neural underpinnings of superior action prediction abilities in soccer players. *Social Cognitive and Affective Neuroscience*, 10(3), 342–351.

Mann, D. L., Abernethy, B., & Farrow, D. (2010). Visual information underpinning skilled anticipation: The effect of blur on a coupled and uncoupled in situ anticipatory response. *Attention, Perception & Psychophysics*, 72, 1317–1326.

Mattar, A. A. G., & Gribble, P. L. (2005). Motor learning by observing. *Neuron*, 46, 153–160.

Milner, A. D., & Goodale, M. A. (2006). *The visual brain in action*. Oxford: Oxford University Press, 297.

(2008). Two visual systems re-viewed. *Neuropsychologia*, 46, 774–785.

Motes, M. A., Hubbard, T. L., Courtney, J. R., & Rypma, B. (2008). A principal components analysis of dynamic spatial memory biases. *Journal of Experimental Psychology: Learning, Memory, and Cognition*, 34, 1076–1083.

Muellbacher, W., Ziemann, U., Wissel, J., Dang, N., Kofler, M., et al. (2002). Early consolidation in human primary motor cortex. *Nature*, 415, 640–644.

Ong, N. T., & Hodges, N. J. (2010). Absence of after-effects for observers after watching a visuomotor adaptation. *Experimental Brain Research*, 205, 325–334.

Porro, C. A., Facchin, P., Fusi, S., Dri, G., & Fadiga, L. (2007). Enhancement of force after action observation: Behavioural and neurophysiological studies. *Neuropsychologia*, 45, 3114–3121.

Ranganathan, R., & Carlton, L. G. (2007). Perception–action coupling and anticipatory performance in baseball batting. *Journal of Motor Behavior*, 39, 369–380.

Ripoll, H., Kerlirzin, Y., Stein, J. F., & Reine, B. (1995). Analysis of information processing, decision making, and visual strategies in complex problem solving sport situations. *Human Movement Science*, 14, 325–349.

Rizzolatti, G., & Craighero, L. (2004). The mirror-neuron system. *Annual Review of Neuroscience*, 27, 169–192.

Romani, M., Cesari, P., Urgesi, C., Facchini, S., & Aglioti, S. M. (2005). Motor facilitation of the human cortico-spinal system during observation of bio-mechanically impossible movements. *NeuroImage*, 26, 755–763.

Savelsbergh, G. J. P., Williams, A. M., van der Kamp, J., & Ward, P. (2002). Visual search, anticipation and expertise in soccer goalkeepers. *Journal of Sports Sciences*, 20, 279–287.

Shea, C. H., Wright, D. L., Wulf, G., & Whitacre, C. (2000). Physical and observational practice afford unique learning opportunities. *Journal of Motor Behavior*, 32, 27–36.

Smeeton, N. J., & Huys, R. (2011). Anticipation of tennis-shot direction from whole-body movement: The role of movement amplitude and dynamics. *Human Movement Science*, 30(5), 957–965.

Springer, A., Parkinson, J., & Prinz, W. (2013). Action simulation: Time course and representational mechanisms. *Frontiers in Psychology*, 4, 1–20.

Stefan, K., Cohen, L. G., Duque, J., Mazzocchio, R., Celnik, P., et al. (2005). Formation of a motor memory by action observation. *Journal of Neuroscience*, 25, 9339–9346.

Tomeo, E., Cesari, P., Aglioti, S. M., & Urgesi, C. (2013). Fooling the kickers but not the goalkeepers: Behavioral and neurophysiological correlates of fake action detection in soccer. *Cerebral Cortex*, 23, 2765–2778.

Urgesi, C., Candidi, M., Fabbro, F., Romani, M., & Aglioti, S. M. (2006a). Motor facilitation during action observation: Topographic mapping of the target muscle and influence of the onlooker's posture. *European Journal of Neuroscience*, 23, 2522–2530.

Urgesi, C., Maieron, M., Avenanti, A., Tidoni, E., Fabbro, F., & Aglioti, S. M. (2010). Simulating the future of actions in the human corticospinal system. *Cerebral Cortex*, 20, 2511–2521.

Urgesi, C., Moro, V., Candidi, M., & Aglioti, S. M. (2006b). Mapping implied body actions in the human motor system. *Journal of Neuroscience*, 26, 7942–7949.

Urgesi, C., Savonitto, M., Fabbro, F., & Aglioti, S. (2012). Long- and short-term plastic modeling of action prediction abilities in volleyball. *Psychological Research*, 76, 540–562.

Van Overwalle, F., & Baetens, K. (2009). Understanding others' actions and goals by mirror and mentalizing systems: A meta-analysis. *NeuroImage*, 48, 564–584.

Vogt, S., & Thomaschke, R. (2007). From visuo-motor interactions to imitation learning: Behavioural and brain imaging studies. *Journal of Sports Sciences*, 25, 497–517.

Weissensteiner, J., Abernethy, B., Farrow, D., & Müller, S. (2008). The development of anticipation: A cross-sectional examination of the practice experiences contributing to skill in cricket batting. *Journal of Sport & Exercise Psychology*, 30, 663–684.

Williams, A. (2000). Perceptual skill in soccer: Implications for talent identification and development. *Journal of Sports Sciences*, 18(9), 737–750.

Williams, A., Davids, K., & Williams, J. (1999). Visual perception and action in sport. Abingdon: Taylor & Francis.

Wilson, M., & Knoblich, G. G. (2005). The case for motor involvement in perceiving conspecifics. *Psychological Bulletin*, 131, 460.

Glossary

Action observation network (AON) A set of brain areas comprising the superior temporal, posterior parietal and premotor areas, which are selectively activated during observation of actions. Some of these areas, which are thought to contain cells with similar characteristics to mirror neurons described originally in the monkey and, more recently, human brain, respond also during action execution, thus coupling motor and visual action representations.

After-effects Effects of repeated presentation of a stimulus on motor and perceptual processes that outlast the duration of the stimulus itself; they may refer to unwanted persistence of compensatory movements when transferring to an environment that does not require such compensations or to alterations of perceptual processing in the direction opposite to the adapting stimulus.

Anticipatory simulation Use of our own motor knowledge to create models of ongoing actions that allow anticipating their future course. This ability is crucial for compensating for hidden information as well as for the intrinsic delays of our motor reactions (i.e. we may take more than 100 ms to initiate a non-discriminative response and after such delay the moving entity will change its position).

Deception Behaviors intended to decrease the information available or to provide misleading information that makes the observers error prone regarding the real intentions of the actor.

Ecological psychology A specific psychological approach to the study of perceptuo-motor processes that refers to the work of James J. Gibson and his associates and stresses the importance of environmental variables and, in particular, how the environment of an organism directly affords various actions for the organism. The main implication of this emphasis on environmental variables versus information-processing factors is the preference for 'real world' studies of behavior as opposed to the artificial environment of the laboratory.

Motor expertise Ability in performing specific actions that has been acquired during extensive direct experience with performing the actions as compared with visual familiarity with the same stimuli. It may refer to either general ability of people in performing everyday actions or domain-specific skills of musicians, dancers or athletes in performing actions that other people are less or not able to perform. In cognitive neuroscience studies, domain-specific expertise is investigated either for its interest per se or as a model of more general expertise in everyday actions.

Observational learning Acquisition of specific perceptual, motor, cognitive or affective behaviors through observation of the behaviors of other individuals who serve as models.

Temporal occlusion paradigm A psychological paradigm for the investigation of perceptual processing in which the presentation of a dynamic stimulus is interrupted at different delays from its onset, thus probing the capability to create anticipatory representation of the perceived stimulus.

Transcranial magnetic stimulation A technique for the study of the brain which applies short-lasting magnetic fields over the scalp locations corresponding to given brain areas. These magnetic fields induce changes of the electrical status of neurons below the stimulating coil, thus altering their functions. These alterations can be revealed by evoked muscular contractions (measured with electromyography), altered brain states (measured with other neuroimaging or electrophysiological methods) or modification of behavioral responses (measured as variation of accuracy or reaction times while performing given tasks).

28 Shared Mental Models in Sport and Refereeing

Dave Collins and Andy Hill

Abstract

Shared representations and coordinated action, in both team sports and for individuals with specific roles, have a big impact on performance outcomes in a wide range of sporting domains. Within team sports, perceptual and decision-making issues are key; performers must both see things in similar ways *and* make similar or mutually compatible decisions if appropriate action is to be taken and performance optimised. To do this, an athlete must interpret perceptual information effectively, applying an implicit 'weighting scale' to determine the pertinence of key factors. Such a commonality of perception across a team allows the formation of a shared mental model (SMM) through a process of both time-pressured and deliberate thinking and action, along with appropriate feedback. As individuals, referees and match officials must apply a consistent weighting scale to both formal decision making (i.e. applying the rules of the game) and more informal game management. The implementation of SMMs has been shown to increase consistency and coherence in leading referees, with shared representations resulting from both training and more 'natural' processes. Selection panels have also demonstrated substantial and rapid improvements in coherence, through exposing and agreeing operational definitions of key criteria, developing common weighting scales, monitoring and regular feedback. Such shared representations also carry benefits for support personnel within interdisciplinary teams and for team cultures; common features in high performance sport. It is clear that socially based or developed shared representations are crucial to effective performance in sport, and the various examples considered here offer considerable potential for future research.

Introduction

The necessity for shared representations and coordinated actions is a big factor in sport, more obviously in team sports but also, surprisingly to some, in some individual performers with specific roles. As such, this chapter will consider these cases separately, even though many of the mechanisms may span across them.

In the first case, relating to team sports, we consider the need for shared representations and shared thinking in coactional environments. Coactional environments are those where the outcome performance of both individual and team is dependent upon the actions of others. As will become clear, in such situations performers must both see things in similar ways *and* make similar decisions (or at least mutually compatible ones) if performance is to be optimised. In fact, consistency of representation is crucial for performance; better results can often accrue from consistent but slightly wrong interpretations than cases where some have it right whilst other team members see things differently. Given the importance of these shared representations, we will also cover how these are optimally developed in an applied environment, in both the short and longer term.

The second case also involves gaining consistency across team members, although in this situation the members are usually operating in much smaller sub-groups or even as individuals. The most obvious sporting example of this is in the case of refereeing, where an individual or small group (referee plus linesman/touch judges or refereeing team) must apply a shared representation consistently, week to week. An interesting subtlety here is the extent to which the models to be shared are both explicit (as guided by rules, laws or formally issued guidance notes) and implicit (as in what is generally accepted as the appropriate sanction for a particular penalty offence, depending on game circumstances, score, 'temperature' of the match, and so on). Once again, we will take the space to consider how these shared mental models (hereafter SMMs) are best developed, monitored and, an increasingly important aspect, modified.

Another interesting and increasingly important example relates to all aspects of team/group selection and how this is achieved in a clear and (at least perceived) equable fashion. SMMs are as essential here as in the examples above; the one key difference lies in the time span that usually applies. In sporting action, examples are almost always time pressured, complex and involve high stakes, whilst in this last example, selectors are able to take their time, ponder and offer justification for their decisions; it has to be said, not always a positive circumstance! The powerful messages inherent in such actions more than outweigh this potential advantage, however, making selection (and other aspects of decision making by coaches, administrators, and so on) worthy of consideration. In short, the influence that selectors can have on performance, for good or ill, makes increasing the coherence of their shared representation a key concern. Whilst covering these aspects, we will also touch on other related concepts, such as the establishment and change of organisational culture, which make this such an important consideration.

These three cases of shared representations and SMMs in sport all share common aspects, although the balance of formal (i.e. regulation driven) versus informal (socially evolved and agreed) criteria as the measure of validity/accuracy differs across them. In considering these exemplars (and touching on other parallel environments such as the military), we will certainly take account of mechanisms and some theoretical perspectives. However, our focus has been to elucidate the issues at hand using a variety of quantitative and qualitative approaches. We must stress that we have not yet begun to explore the underlying neurocognitive mechanisms in any detail. Indeed, such consideration remains an important goal for future work in this area, and some of these are covered in other chapters in this volume (see Cross & Calvo-Merino; Urgesi & Makris; Vesper & Sebanz, this volume, Chapters 26, 11 and 27, respectively).

Case 1. Team Games

In this section, we consider all team games that involve coaction and cooperation between team members. This encompasses invasion games (e.g. football, hockey and rugby (in their various guises), basketball, and so on), team net games (e.g. volleyball) and even some other sports (e.g. curling, relay running) which may at first sight seem strange bedfellows. In all cases, shared representations are apparent in two broad but interlinking areas: perception and decision making. Notably, both these are informed in no small part by a player's ability to run a mental simulation of a team mate's actions; in other words, to look into the future and explore the consequences of what I think they will do. This represents an important link to the ideas of 'mirror system' activation which are covered elsewhere.

Perceptual Considerations

Perception is by far the most researched area in the psychology of team sports. Notably for our present purpose, this is essentially what players look at, and the differences apparent between experts and novices. Thus, in a typical study, Williams and Davids (1998) used a life-size projection of a soccer player, dribbling towards the participant, and used eye tracking to detect differences in focus. Unsurprisingly, experts showed different points of focus compared to novices, enabling them to more quickly and accurately predict the direction of play.

Extending these ideas, however, the role of shared representation is extremely pertinent to perception. The point here is a focus on what each player actually perceives (i.e. interprets) in the display rather than merely what features he attends to. As will emerge later in this chapter, this interpretation process involves an implicit 'weighting scale' that not only dictates which

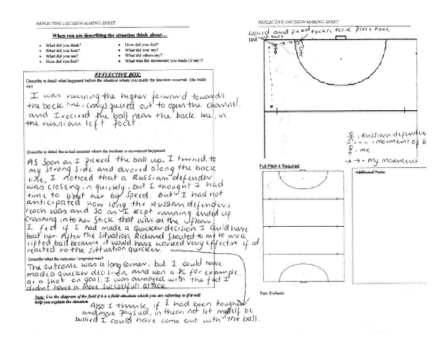

Figure 28.1 One player's notes on critical moments in field hockey and their perceived key factors. *See Plate 21.*

features might convey more or less information than others but also, following the classic work of Norman and his 'pertinence criteria' (e.g. Norman & Shallice, 1986), what these particular display features suggest is going to happen. Based on this approach, therefore, coaches will seek to tease out shared meaning of particular features of the display; a process which is, we suggest, best achieved through a structured questioning approach. Figure 28.1, drawn from the work of Richards, Mascarenhas, and Collins (2009, 2012), presents such an approach; used in this case in women's field hockey.

Players were asked to select critical moments in a game, then asked to explain both what made it critical and, pertinent to our present purpose, what features of the display gave them the best information on what was likely to happen. Through the use of such methods, the coach can develop a shared representation together with 'buy-in' as the players themselves have generated the information. We will return to this approach in the next section.

Decision-Making Considerations

Working on commonality of perception is essential before interventions are attempted to address the decision-making styles of players (cf. von Zimmerman

& Richardson, this volume, Chapter 12). In simple terms, unless we are sure what players are looking at, why and what it means to them, we have no chance of increasing coherence in a team's decision-making structure. Once this is achieved, however, the building of a shared mental model for a team involves a subtle but crucial combination of fast and slow (time pressured versus deliberate) thinking (see Kahneman, 2011). As shown in Figure 28.2, the first step involves the use of the critical moments approach described earlier (shown as Phase 1). This enables both coach and players to reach consensus on what are the key challenges they are likely to meet, what is important to monitor, and the relative weighting scale of these factors in facilitating prediction. What follows is a repeated cycle of fast action simulation drills, combined with slower, often video-facilitated, debrief and refinement (Phases 2 and 3). The actual processes involved in this are still under investigation. Given the ubiquity of team meetings, video debriefs and key point summaries in professional team sport, the suggested process for developing a team SMM holds at least face validity. However this occurs, this cyclic process generates increasingly rapid, accurate and, most importantly, consistent decision making across the team. There are, of course, several key parameters that must be attended to; the quality and accuracy of the simulation is one such factor ripe for research in such fast-action group settings. Nevertheless, as a consequence of using this approach, players' decision making is improved whilst they are also empowered to stay involved in the constant refinement process due to their personal investment in the constructs and methods which have evolved (cf. Bierhals, Schuster, Kohler, & Badke-Schaub, 2007).

As a point of comparison, it is worth mentioning the other epistemological approach that exists towards this goal of team thinking. The dynamical systems approach (e.g. Araújo, Davids, & Hristovski, 2006; Silva, Garganta, Araújo, Davids, & Aguiar, 2013) de-emphasises the shared representation in knowledge ideas described above, focusing more on a commonality in perception (shared affordances). Our own perspective is that this distinction is, at best, artificial, even though it is clear that too much (conscious) tactical thinking is detrimental to performance (see Memmert & Furley, 2007). In short, the differences between the cognitive and dynamical systems descriptions fail to offer advantages in parsimony. Consideration of these two competing views do, however, raise the key question of exactly *how* slow, considered thoughts are internalised into rapid, quick-fire, on-field decision making; seemingly finding resonance with Silva et al.'s (2013) description of the evolution of common affordances from common goals. There is also good evidence that cognitive factors such as shared expectations and concerns co-act with team experience and team chemistry to impact on important factors such as implicit coordination (e.g. in table tennis – Blickensderfer, Reynolds, Salas, & Cannon-Bowers, 2010; in basketball – Bourbousson, Poizat, Saury, & Sève, 2012; in

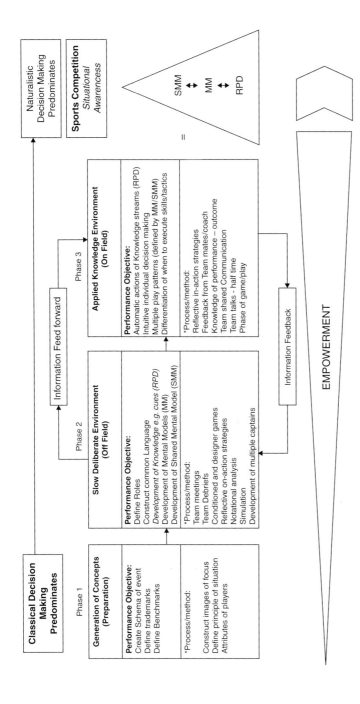

Figure 28.2 A schematic of the development of team SMM for decision making.
Source : Richards et al. (2010).

soccer – Gershgoren, Filho, Tenenbaum, & Schinke, 2013). Once again, the need for further *and* better integrated research is indicated (Ward & Eccles, 2006). Distinguishing between different aspects of the SMM will be essential, as the different components exert different influences on aspects of the team; in simple terms, team processes are related to the knowledge structures apparent whilst these structures and the content are more indicative/causative of team performance. Thus, how SMMs are measured is an important consideration for both research and practice (DeChurch & Mesmer-Magnus, 2010). The use of more sophisticated measuring tools to detect process manifestations of SMMs (e.g. Moura, Martins, Anido, Ruffino, Barros, & Cunha, 2013) will also help.

One other big factor in team performance is the concept of cognitive readiness. Cognitive readiness can be described as 'the state of possessing the psychological (mental) and sociological (social) knowledge, skills and abilities, and attitudes needed to sustain consistent, competent professional performance and mental well-being in dynamic, complex, and unpredictable environments' (Schmorrow, Bolstad, May, & Cuevas, 2012, p. 355). This psychosocial construct, although having a less mechanistic influence on performance, is clearly a shared representation, or at least shared attitude, which is crucial for high-level performance. The construct, which emanates from military environments, sees readiness as adaptability; the team's capacity to be self-adjusting to meet the novel demands of any task rather than just a simple 'we all see this in the same way' model (see Fiore, Ross, & Jentsch, 2012). The bottom line is that an effective team has shared representations on both the task at hand and the processes employed, with team members committed to a specific style of interaction (see Eccles & Tenenbaum, 2004; Eccles & Tran, 2012; Reimer, Park, & Hinsz, 2006) and team leaders showing high levels of coherence in terms of where the team is heading (see Miles & Kivlighan, 2008).

Case 2. Individuals Needing Shared Representations – Referees and Game Officials

The role of referee or match official is a particular example of the use of shared representations. As we stated in the introduction, the necessity is for the referee to present and apply a consistent weighting scale to decision making, based fundamentally on the rules/laws of the game. Once again, as stated earlier, this consistency or coherence must be apparent in both the formal decision making (e.g. Is this a penalty? If so, what sanction is appropriate?) against the rules, but also the informal, game management systems which play an essential part in producing an attractive and flowing game. Examples of this second category would include under what circumstances to 'have a quiet word' with a player, what to say/threaten and, yet again, what weighting scale should be used against the various contributory antecedents in reaching a conclusion.

In researching and supporting officials, similar approaches have been used to those described above with team players. Thus, investigations have focused on the patterning and employment of visual skills, highlighting differences between elite and non-elite officials (Ghasemi, Momeni, Jarfarzadehpur, Rezaee, & Taheri, 2011).

The Role of Cognition, SMMs and Shared Representations

Once again, the role of shared representations or shared skills has emerged as holding greater importance for performance. For example, investigations into the flash lag effect (FLE; e.g. Helsen, Gilis, & Weston, 2006) have looked at the challenge of comparison between two moving objects, as in decisions on offside in soccer (Put, Baldo, Cravo, Wagemans, & Helsen, 2013). When one of these objects is used as a fixed event (e.g. where was the player when the ball was passed), FLE seems to be a more parsimonious explanation of the errors and false positives (offside called incorrectly) observed in elite play. Relevant to our present purpose, it seems that the FLE may be more due to cognitive than purely perceptual reasons (see Catteeuw, Helsen, Gilis, Van Roie, & Wagemans, 2009); in other words, a shared understanding of its implications and how these may be countered underpins the observed effects. The complexity of these effects (it is not as simple as experts are *always* better) shows the importance of bespoke perceptual-cognitive training in developing an appropriate internal representation (e.g. Catteeuw, Gilis, Wagemans, & Helsen, 2010).

As stated earlier, shared representations work in both formal, rule-based situations and informal game management. It is interesting that, when we first started work with England's top rugby referees (Mascarenhas, Collins, & Mortimer, 2005b), this game management factor was both ill-defined *and* acknowledged as crucial for top-end performance. As such, our work to increase the consistency of a shared representation between refereeing teams, and within each referee/touch judge/television match official team, was an important facet in raising consistency in performance. As described earlier, this consisted in large part of exposing the decision weighting scale demonstrated by experts, then developing this in intermediates (Mascarenhas, Collins, Mortimer, & Morris, 2005a): the outcome deliverable from this process clearly being faster-flowing games, less open disagreement from players and coaches, and greater satisfaction for the paying fans. Of particular relevance to the shared representation construct, coherence in leading referees was raised from less than chance (tossing a coin would generate a more consistent result) to better than 90 per cent consistency (Mascarenhas, Collins, & Mortimer, 2005c). Once again, bespoke training did the job, based in this case on video representations from the touch judge's perspective. In a similar fashion, offside accuracy has been improved by web-based exemplars with the weighting scale and logic presented to develop appropriate perceptual-cognitive skills in an SMM (Put, Wagemans, Jaspers, & Helsen, 2013; in basketball, see Schweizer, Plessner, & Brand, 2013).

Of course, shared representations can come from 'natural' processes as well as training. Thus, in judo referees for example, consistent but different judging of certain phases is apparent in referees with actual physical experience compared to those who do not (Dosseville, Laborde, & Raab, 2011). The contrasting impacts on expert dancers of watching dance versus similar movements in non-dance form is another example of this phenomenon (see Cross & Calvo-Merino, this volume, Chapter 26). In this regard, it seems that, unsurprisingly, previous personal experience acts to develop an internal representation shared with other participants. Wherever the data come from, however, it seems that consideration of more information in a reflective manner can drive development of the official's decision-making skills (MacMahon & Mildenhall, 2012). It is perhaps through the communication and mutual consideration of these thoughts that shared representations can be effectively developed; that is, through a cognitive process.

Case 3. Selection and Other Role-Specific Issues

As stated, the first two cases are usually time pressured, and thus have received more research attention pertinent to our topic. There are also other aspects of sport which necessitate shared representations, however, and in this section we consider some of these. We start with the core task of selection; a situation where, if one is to believe the media, representations are often as diametrically opposed as shared!

Selectors

There is little doubt that getting selection issues 'sorted' can have a very positive impact on performance. In the case of England cricket, for example, Bullough, Millar, Ramchandani, and Coleman (2014) showed that central contracting (effectively ensuring a greater consistency in selection) generated greater win ratios and points per match. Couple this with the substantial anecdotal evidence for the advantages of 'settled teams' and the importance of the selector's role is clear. The fact that this role is now almost entirely filled by professionals with clear links to the team/organisation, as opposed to the amateur committees of a few years back, is further evidence. Even in these cases, however, the human subjectivity factors are still a concern. Indeed, even though the selection process is supported by a seemingly exponential plethora of data, many still express dissatisfaction with the process.

Of course, many claim that the human factor can be taken out of selection to good effect, hence the use of mathematical approaches such as binary integer optimisation (Bhattacharjee & Saikia, 2013) data envelopment analysis (Amin & Sharma, 2014) and neural networks (Rama & Sharda, 2009); interestingly, all studies conducted in professional cricket.

Notably, however, all the approaches like this which we have seen are based on retrospective performance information in extremely data-friendly sports. As one of many consequences, we would suggest that the proactive (i.e. predicting who *will* perform) application of these calculation approaches is extremely limited. Indeed, and crucially for this chapter, it is interesting to note that even the most apparently 'hard-core' proponents of objective criteria acknowledge that some crucial aspects are just not capable of objective expression – and this from members of a mathematics faculty (Trninić, Papić, Trninić, & Vukičević, 2008)! The use of such hybrid models involves other issues, relating to the human tendency to put more trust in (or feel able to absolve personal responsibility by) the use of objective data. As a consequence, the objective, number-based data acquires a disproportionate weighting and can serve to unbalance the predictive selection process by a preoccupation with past performance, either the individual performer's or her predecessor's (see, for example, the British Athletics 'Outcome Funnels' 2014). This is an important aspect of shared representations; our seeming preference for, or greater trust in, numbers versus expert opinion.

So how can we develop, and preferably demonstrate/assure, the better shared mental models that underpin valid and effective selection systems? Well, as with the cases described earlier, attention to the declarative knowledge sets of panel members, coupled with the drive for them to meet coherence criteria, will generate the shared representations needed. As before, the 'weighting scale' or relative importance of the various factors under consideration is the issue requiring attention. In evaluating the accuracy of selection in baseball pictures, for example, Lin, Tung, Chen, and Chen (2000) showed that a 91 per cent predictive accuracy could be achieved when different experts' opinions were pooled but against the same provided criteria. So, in simple terms, expose and agree operational definitions of the key criteria, develop the common weighting scale through case-based debate (on actual players rather than as a philosophical discussion), then monitor and provide feedback on the levels of agreement achieved. With well-motivated individuals, this process can be achieved comparatively quickly; for example, our work with first division rugby selection panels took six sessions to achieve a coherence of over 95 per cent, from a starting point of less than 30 per cent (Hale & Collins, 2002). This process can sometimes be accomplished through less structured means (e.g. reflective practice; Roberts & Faull, 2013); so long as the relative importance of different factors is exposed, teased out and made explicit, a greater shared

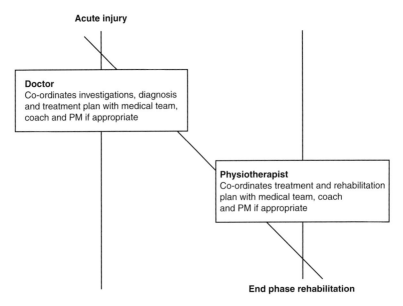

Figure 28.3 Role delineation for injury rehabilitation.

representation will occur. Certainly, doing this as a team activity, especially at developmental level (Couturtier, 2009), is in itself an excellent tool through which the essentials of role clarity and coach expectation may be clarified. Nonetheless, in our applied work, we have always found it best to explicitly address SMM development and maintenance as a specific and separate factor.

Support Personnel

As support teams need to work in an increasingly interdisciplinary fashion, there is a parallel need for SMMs that include clear delineation of roles. In these cases, the shared representation must run across staff, athletes and coaches, with all agreed on who does what and when. Figure 28.3 offers an example of this, using the case of recovery from injury (Collins & Collins, 2011). Note the clear handover of responsibility as recovery progresses. The point is that there is always one specialist in charge, and all others work through him. This avoids mixed messages to the athlete (so no loss of confidence in the process) and maintains a clear common purpose, whilst also encouraging the level of healthy debate away from the athlete, which underpins any high performing environment (see the Zone of Uncomfortable Debate, or ZOUD; Burke, 2011).

Team Culture

As the final example in this case, consider the need for teams or subgroups in organisations to have a shared understanding of what is needed to succeed. We concur completely with Buchanan (2000) that the reward structure inherent in the team system is a major influence on member behaviour. As such, the team manager will use a variety of methods to develop a shared understanding of what team members must do (Cruickshank & Collins, 2012) and a shared reward system which offers mutual but contingent reinforcement. Indeed, the best managers will use a set of communication tools, 'surrounding' squad members with a set of cultural mores and monitoring for conformity. Thus, what we refer to as 'simply' team culture is a carefully designed and nurtured complex system that acts on and through individuals to create a psychosocial set of norms and an associated reward structure, which is increasingly internalised and accepted by squad members. Once again, a shared representation which has important implications for the team/group performance.

Summary

There is no doubt that socially based or developed shared representations are crucial to effective operation in these sport spheres, as well as to the military and emergency services situations on which much of the work is based (e.g. Klein, 1997, 1999; Pascual & Henderson, 1997; Serfaty, MacMillan, Entin, & Entin, 1997). From a research perspective, the various examples considered in this chapter offer considerable potential for future investigation, as they are all complex, high stakes and operationalisable challenges with considerable ego involvement. As such, whilst we have offered some suggestions as to the actual mechanisms of evolution, this is a fruitful area for investigators and practitioners alike. We trust that consideration of this (less neurocognitively-based) chapter with regard to the theoretical material elsewhere in the book will stimulate such.

References

Amin, G. R., & Sharma, S. J. (2014). Cricket team selection using data envelopment analysis. *European Journal of Sport Science*, 14(S1), S369–S376.

Araújo, D., Davids, K., & Hristovski, R. (2006). The ecological dynamics of decision making in sport. *Psychology of Sport and Exercise*, 7, 653–676

Bhattacharjee, D., & Saikia, H. (2013). Selecting the optimum cricket team after a tournament. *Asian Journal of Exercise & Sports Science*, 10(2), 77–91.

Bierhals, R., Schuster, I., Kohler, P., & Badke-Schaub, P. (2007). Shared mental models: Linking team cognition and performance. *CoDesign*, 3(1), 75–94.

Blickensderfer, E. L., Reynolds, R., Salas, E., & Cannon-Bowers, J. A. (2010). Shared expectations and implicit coordination in tennis doubles teams. *Journal of Applied Sport Psychology*, 22, 486–499.

Bourbousson, J., Poizat, G., Saury, J., & Sève, C. (2012). Temporal aspects of team cognition: A case study on concerns sharing within basketball. *Journal of Applied Sport Psychology*, 24(2), 224–241. doi: 10.1080/10413200.2011.630059.

British Athletics. (2014). www.britishathletics.org.uk/world-class/performance-funnels/.

Buchanan, J. M. (2000). Group selection and team sports. *Journal of Bioeconomics*, 2, 1–7.

Bullough, S., Millar, R., Ramchandani, G., & Coleman, R. (2014). The effect of central contracts on the stability and performance of the England Test cricket team. *RICYDE: Revista internacional de ciencias del deporte*, 35(10), 4–15.

Burke, V. (2011). *Organizing for excellence*. In D. Collins, A. Button, & H. Richards (Eds.), *Performance psychology: A practitioner's guide*. London: Churchill Livingstone, 99–119.

Catteeuw, P., Gilis, B., Wagemans, J. & Wagemans, W. (2010). Perceptual-cognitive skills in offside decision making: Expertise and training effects. *Journal of Sport & Exercise Psychology*, 32, 828–844.

Catteeuw, P., Helsen, W., Gilis, B., Van Roie, E., & Wagemans, J. (2009). Visual scan patterns and decision-making skills of expert assistant referees in offside situations. *Journal of Sport & Exercise Psychology*, 31, 786–797.

Collins, D., & Collins, J. E. (2011). Putting them together: skill packages to optimise team/group performance. In D. Collins, A. Button, & H. Richards (Eds.), *Performance psychology: A practitioner's guide*. London: Churchill Livingstone, 361–380.

Couturtier, L. E. (2009). "Why did you cut me?" Preparing coaching education students for the team selection process. *Journal of Physical Education, Recreation & Dance*, 80(9), 39–42. doi: 10.1080/07303084.2009.10598393.

Cruickshank, A., & Collins, D. (2012). "Multidirectional management": Exploring the challenges of performance in the WCP environment. *Journal of Reflective Practice*, 13(3), 455–469.

DeChurch, L. A., & Mesmer-Magnus, J. R. (2010). Measuring shared team mental models: A meta-analysis. *Group Dynamics: Theory, Research, and Practice*, 14(1), 1–14.

Dosseville, F., Laborde, S., & Raab, M. (2011). Contextual and personal motor experience effects in judo referees' decisions. *Sport Psychologist*, 25, 67–81.

Eccles, D. W., & Tenenbaum, G. (2004). Why an expert team is more than a team of experts: A social-cognitive conceptualization of team coordination and communication in sport. *Journal of Sport and Exercise Psychology*, 26, 542–560.

Eccles, D. W., & Tran, K. B. (2012). Getting them on the same page: Strategies for enhancing coordination and communication in sports teams. *Journal of Sport Psychology in Action*, 3(1), 30–40. doi: 10.1080/21520704.2011.649229.

Fiore, S. M., Ross, K. G., & Jentsch, F. (2012). A team cognitive readiness framework for small-unit training. *Journal of Cognitive Engineering and Decision Making*, 6(3), 325–349. doi: 10.1177/1555343412449626.

Gershgoren, L., Filho, E.-M., Tenenbaum, G., & Schinke, R. J. (2013). Coaching shared mental models in soccer: A longitudinal case study. *Journal of Clinical Sport Psychology*, 7, 293–312.

Ghasemi, A., Momeni, M., Jarfarzadehpur, E., Rezaee, M., & Taheri, H. (2011). Visual skills involved in decision making by expert referees. *Perceptual and Motor Skills*, 112(1), 161–171.

Hale, B. D., & Collins, D. (2002). *Rugby tough*. Champaign, IL: Human Kinetics.

Helsen, W., Gilis, B., & Weston, M. (2006). Errors in judging 'offside' in association football: Test of the optical error versus the perceptual flash-lag hypothesis. *Journal of Sports Sciences*, 24, 521–528.

Kahneman, D. (2011). *Thinking, fast and slow*. London: Macmillan.

Klein, G. (1997). An overview of naturalistic decision making applications. In G. Klein & C. E. Zsambok (Eds.), *Naturalistic decision making*. Mahwah, NJ: Lawrence Erlbaum, 49–59.

——— (1999). Applied decision making. In P. A. Hancock (Ed.), *Human performance and ergonomics*, 2nd edition. San Diego, CA: Academic Press, 87–107.

Lin, W.-B., Tung, I.-W., Chen, M.-J., & Chen, M.-Y. (2011). An analysis of an optimal selection process for characteristics and technical performance of baseball pitchers. *Perceptual and Motor Skills*, 113(1), 300–310.

MacMahon, C., & Mildenhall, W. (2012). A practical perspective on decision making influences in sports officiating. *International Journal of Sports Science & Coaching*, 7(1), 153–165.

Mascarenhas, D. R. D., Collins, D., & Mortimer, P. (2005b). Elite refereeing performance: Developing a model for sport science support. *Sport Psychologist*, 19, 364–379.

Mascarenhas, D., Collins, D., & Mortimer, P. (2005c). Assessing the accuracy and coherence of decision making in rugby-union referees. *Journal of Sport Behavior*, 28(3), 253–271.

Mascarenhas, D. R. D., Collins, D., Mortimer, P., & Morris, B. (2005a). Training accurate and coherent decision making in rugby. *Sport Psychologist*, 19, 131–147.

Memmert, D., & Furley, P. (2007). 'I spy with my little eye!' Breadth of attention, inattentional blindness, and tactical decision making in team sports. *Journal of Sport & Exercise Psychology*, 29, 365–381.

Miles, J. R., & Kivlighan, D. M. Jr. (2008). Team cognition in group interventions: The relation between coleaders' shared mental models and group climate. *Group Dynamics: Theory, Research, and Practice*, 12(3), 191–209.

Moura, F. A, Martins, L. E. B., Anido, R. O., Ruffino, P. R. C., Barros, R. M. L., & Cunha, S. A. (2013). A spectral analysis of team dynamics and tactics in Brazilian football. *Journal of Sports Sciences*, 31(14), 1568–1577. doi: 10.1080/02640414.2013.789920.

Norman, D. A., & Shallice, T. (1986). Attention to action. In R. J. Davidson, G. E. Schwartz, & D. Shapiro (Eds.), *Consciousness and self-regulation: Advances in research and theory*, Volume 4. London: Springer, 1–18.

Pascual, R., & Henderson, S. (1997). Evidence of naturalistic decision making in military command and control. In G. Klein & C. E. Zsambok (Eds.), *Naturalistic decision making*. Mahwah, NJ: Lawrence Erlbaum, 217–226.

Put, K., Baldo, M. V. C., Cravo, A. M., Wagemans, J., & Helsen, W. F. (2013). Experts in offside decision making learn to compensate for their illusory perceptions. *Journal of Sport & Exercise Psychology*, 35, 576–584.

Put, K., Wagemans, J., Jaspers, A., & Helsen, W. F. (2013). Web-based training improves on-field offside decision-making performance. *Psychology of Sport and Exercise*, 14, 577–585.

Rama Iyer, S., & Sharda, R. (2009). Prediction of athletes' performance using neural networks: An application in cricket team selection. *Expert Systems with Applications*, 36, 5510–5522.

Reimer, T., Park, E. S., & Hinsz, V. B. (2006). Shared and coordinated cognition in competitive and dynamic task environments: An information-processing perspective for team sports. *International Journal of Sport and Exercise Psychology*, 4, 376–400. doi: 10.1080/1612197X.2006.9671804.

Richards, P., Collins, D., & Mascarenhas, D. (2012). Developing rapid high pressure team decision making skills. The integration of slow deliberate reflective learning within the competitive performance environment: A case study of elite netball. *Journal of Reflective Practice*, 13(3), 455–469.

Richards, P., Mascarenhas, D. R. D., & Collins, D. (2009) Implementing reflective practice approaches with elite team athletes: Parameters of success. *Reflective Practice*, 10(3), 353–363.

Roberts, C. M., & Faull, A. L. (2013). Building a successful Olympic team selection protocol in women's handball: A case study examining the benefits of employing reflective practice. *Reflective Practice: International and Multidisciplinary Perspectives*, 14(5), 648–659. doi: 10.1080/14623943.2013.835719.

Schweizer, G., Plessner, H., & Brand, R. (2013). Establishing standards for basketball elite referees' decisions. *Journal of Applied Sport Psychology*, 25(3), 370–375. doi: 10.1080/10413200.2012.741090.

Serfaty, D. MacMillan, J., Entin, E. E., & Entin, E. B. (1997). The decision making expertise of battle commanders. In G. Klein & C. E. Zsambok (Eds.), *Naturalistic decision making*. Mahwah, NJ: Lawrence Erlbaum, 233–246.

Silva, P., Garganta, J., Araújo, D., Davids, K., & Aguiar, P. (2013). Shared knowledge or shared affordances? Insights from an ecological dynamics approach to team coordination in sports. *Sports Medicine*, 43, 765–772. doi: 10.1007/s40279-013-0070-9.

Schmorrow, D. D., Bolstad, C. A., May, K. A., & Cuevas, H. M. (2012). Editors' introduction to the special issue on exploring cognitive readiness in complex operational environments: Advances in theory and practice, Part II. *Journal of Cognitive Engineering and Decision Making*, 6(4), 355–357.

Trninić, S., Papić, V., Trninić, V., & Vukičević, D. (2008). Player selection procedures in team sport games. *Acta Kinesiologica*, 2(1), 24–28.

Ward, P., & Eccles, D. W. (2006). A commentary on Team cognition and expert teams: Emerging insights into performance for exceptional teams'. *International Journal of Sport and Exercise Psychology*, 4, 463–483

Williams, A. M., & Davids, K. (1998). Visual search strategy, selective attention, and expertise in soccer. *Research Quarterly for Exercise and Sport*, 69, 111–128.

29   Musical Synchronization, Social Interaction and the Brain

Kristina Waclawik, Sarah Watson and Jessica A. Grahn

Abstract

Music production and perception and human social understanding are linked in many ways. Producing and enjoying music appears unique to humans, and debate surrounds the topic of music's function, especially in relation to its evolutionary origins. Here, we discuss links between music and sociality, and how insights from the unique fields of music neuroscience and social neuroscience can be combined to understand this relationship.

Synchronization to Music and Prosocial Behaviour

One feature of music that has implications for social interactions and shared representations is that of synchrony: humans often spontaneously synchronize their movements to music. For example, many of us have been part of a large crowd of people clapping, singing or moving together at a concert. Indeed, this joint active participation in music may be the ultimate raison d'etre of music, as opposed to passive listening or performing for the enjoyment of others (Cross, 2005). In fact, many cultures do not have separate words for music and dance, and even when passive listening is the social norm, such as in a Western concert hall, people may surreptitiously engage in active participation such as foot-tapping (ibid). Therefore, synchronized participation in music appears to be important for both listening and performing music (ibid).

Synchronized music-making and moving to music may possess the social purpose of fostering group cohesion. Indeed, the capacity of music to promote a social connection between people has been proposed as its original evolutionary purpose (see Box 29.1). The tendency for synchronous music-related activity to promote social bonding is part of a larger tendency for people to feel a stronger connection with those who are similar to them or behave in a similar manner as them (de Waal, 2008). This behaviour need not be music-related, and people modify their behaviour to align with that of others in many types of interaction (Bernieri & Rosenthal, 1991). However, music is an effective way of achieving group synchrony because of the natural human ability and tendency to synchronize to music. Music may elicit such uniform synchronization partly because people are accurate at perceiving and synchronizing to auditory rhythms, compared to other modalities such as vision (Glenberg, Mann, Altman, Forman, & Procise, 1989; Grahn, 2012; Repp & Penel, 2002, 2004). Visual stimuli are less conducive to synchronization of large groups because every member must be able to view the stimulus. Synchrony of sensorimotor acts, which often involve music, as in the case of a marching band, dancing to beat-heavy music in a rave, or singing or chanting at a religious ritual, has been proposed to weaken the psychological boundaries between self and other (Hove, 2008). In other words, sensorimotor synchrony may promote psychological synchrony. Along these lines, group dance has been used in warrior societies to promote solidarity and a sense of union within the group prior to going into battle (Hanna, 1977).

Box 29.1 Evolutionary hypotheses of music's origin

Is music the result of evolution?

The finding that music and dance are prevalent in all modern cultures suggests that they may serve such an important purpose that cultures without them did not survive (Kogan, 1997). Furthermore, although there is a somewhat limited distribution of musical ability when narrowly defined as 'talent in musical production', almost all humans are musical, and capable of listening to and 'understanding' music (Cross, 2001). This ability emerges early in life: even before their first birthday infants have music perception abilities on par with those of non-musically trained adults (Trehub, 2003). This early ability is not simply related to exposure, as Western infants respond equally well to non-Western music (Lynch, Eilers, Oller, & Urbano, 1990). However, most non-human animals have not been found to spontaneously synchronize to visual or auditory rhythms, particularly not our closest evolutionary relatives, and to date there has been little success at training them to do so (Patel, Iversen, Chen, & Repp, 2005; Zarco, Merchant, Prado, & Mendez, 2009); therefore this ability appears to be uniquely human among primates, and may be related to the evolution of music-making in humans (Merker, 2000). The evolutionary quandary with music is that it serves no explicit purpose, unlike other universal human behaviours such as eating and sex (Cross, 2001).

Multiple theories of the evolution of music

Various theories exist as to why music evolved. Some, for example, have viewed music as a courtship mechanism, positing that individuals per formed musical displays in order to advertise their capacity to be unpredictable or flexible which is putatively a valuable trait in a mate (Miller, 1997). A simpler mate selection hypothesis suggests that good musical production abilities signify good health (Huron, 2006). Music has also been viewed as a by-product of certain characteristics of the auditory system that evolved for other purposes; for example, music can be viewed as a side effect of the brain's ability to make sense of a cacophony of sounds (Pinker, 1997). Musical behaviour has also been viewed as nonadaptive pleasure seeking; music may stimulate pleasure centres that exist for other, adaptive purposes without actually conferring any adaptive value itself (Huron, 2006). Other theories suggest that musical perception and production provide opportunities for the auditory and motor systems to develop (Huron, 2006). Another theory, more similar to the social cohesion hypothesis discussed below, is that music evolved as a mechanism to promote psychological closeness when physical contact was unavailable (for example, while the mother was preparing food and unable to hold her child; Falk, 2004).

The social cohesion hypothesis

A comprehensive comparison of the many evolutionary theories of music will not be made here, and these theories are not necessarily mutually exclusive, thereby acceptance of one does not require rejection of the others. However, Cross (2005) suggests that many of the above theories rely on the conventional view of music as consisting of two dichotomous parties, performer and listener; this view ignores the importance of active participation in music-related activity for its own sake and does not provide an explanation for the important social effects of synchronization (ibid). The social cohesion hypothesis is most relevant to the current discussion on the relationship between social cognition and music. This theory posits that the human tendency of moving synchronously along with music enhanced cooperative survival strategies for early humans. It is linked to the muscular bonding hypothesis of the evolution of dance, which purports that synchronous movements promoted group identity and even enhanced coordination in other physical activities such as hunting (McNeill, 1995). Experimental evidence demonstrates that synchronized musical activity can increase affiliation for and cooperation with others (Hove & Risen, 2009; Kirschner & Tomasello, 2010; Reddish, Bulbulia, & Fischer, 2014; Valdesolo & DeSteno, 2011; ; Wiltermuth, 2012; Wiltermuth & Heath, 2009), so it is possible that this effect of music resulted in increased selection for musical individuals or groups. Synchronous music-making or movement to music may have contributed to the formation of a group identity and an ability and desire to work as a unit, enabling greater cooperation within the group and thereby enhancing survival (Kogan, 1997). Musical synchronization may have served as a signal for the potential to cooperate in activities other than the musical one currently being engaged in (Cross, 2009). This theory depends on acceptance of group selection as a viable means of evolution, a concept that has fallen under some criticism but is attracting increasing interest (Kogan, 1997). In many societies, such as modern Western society, group music-making may not be as necessary to survival or adaptation, but this evolutionary explanation would explain why the experience of listening to and/or producing music is culturally ubiquitous and why many people devote a significant amount of time to it as either a pastime or a profession (Kirschner & Tomasello, 2010).

A link between synchrony and social cohesion has been demonstrated experimentally. When people sing in synchrony, they feel more similar, cooperate together more effectively, and report feeling more like a team than people who do not sing together, or people who sing simultaneously but not in synchrony (Wiltermuth & Heath, 2009). Similar effects have been found for synchronous versus asynchronous tapping. Affiliation for a tapping partner increases with the extent to which synchronized finger tapping occurs (Hove & Risen, 2009; Kokal, Engel, Kirschner, & Keysers, 2011). People also pay more attention to someone who taps in synchrony with them, as indicated by better memory for interactions with that person and their characteristics (Macrae, Duffy, Miles, & Lawrence, 2008; Woolhouse & Tidhar, 2010). Synchronous tapping results in greater perceived similarity, compassion and altruism toward the synchronous partner (Valdesolo & DeSteno, 2011), and increases prosociality, even toward others uninvolved in the synchronous task (Reddish et al., 2014). Even in preschool-aged children, playing music as a group facilitates cooperation in a later game, compared to another activity with similar levels of social interaction but not involving musical synchrony (Kirschner & Tomasello, 2010). In accordance with anthropological literature on synchronized dance as a preparation for combat (Hanna, 1977), people are more likely to comply with a synchronous partner's request for aggression towards a third party, and this effect is partially mediated by feelings of connection with synchronous partners (Wiltermuth, 2012). Increased affiliation and empathy have also been found in dance partners (Behrends, Muller, & Dziobek, 2012). Therefore, synchronization of music-related activity with another person or group of people promotes feelings of social connectivity, which may result in adaptive behaviours such as cooperation.

The effect of synchrony-mediated social bonding may be achieved at several levels. Joint music-making requires attending to the actions and intentions of others, which may generalize to overall greater understanding of others' emotional states. It also requires imitation, which can also promote sharing of others' mental states (Frith & Frith, 2006; Rabinowitch, Cross, & Burnard, 2012). Cross (2005) has proposed that musical 'communication', unlike verbal communication, can simultaneously contain multiple meanings, and the potential for different players to experience different emotional 'meanings' while maintaining cooperation may promote coordination and understanding between players' mental states. This possibility was examined in a study of children who engaged in a long-term joint music-making programme that emphasized features of music-making that were hypothesized to influence empathy. For example, the group maintained interpersonal synchrony to a constantly changing rhythm to practise synchronization, and composed musical pieces with a specific theme together to promote shared intentionality (Rabinowitch et al., 2012). The children showed an increase in empathy scores on various measures, compared to a control group that engaged in similar types of social game without a musical component (ibid). Thus, specific aspects of joint musical activity may promote understanding of others' actions and intentions, which transfers to a more general understanding of others' psychological states outside music-making contexts (ibid).

The understanding of another person's mental state, which is fundamental to intentional synchrony, may be mediated by mirror neurons, which respond to both the performance of an action by oneself and the observation of that action performed by another (mirror neurons will be discussed in more detail in a later section) (di Pellegrino, Fadiga, Fogassi, Gallese, & Rizzolatti, 1992). The mirror neuron system has been proposed as a plausible neural basis for empathy (Gallese, 2001). For example, synchronous and asynchronous tapping are associated with different patterns of EEG oscillations, which appear to arise from previously established mirror neuron system regions (Tognoli, Lagarde, DeGuzman, & Kelso, 2007). The authors suggest that the EEG oscillations may represent enhancement of the mirror neuron system during synchrony, and inhibition of the same system during asynchrony (Tognoli et al., 2007). Similar oscillations have been identified in pairs of guitarists performing a duet (Lindenberger, Li, Gruber, & Muller, 2009). Brain oscillations are a plausible candidate for a neural mechanism of interpersonal synchronization because they are fast enough to allow for quick adjustments to another person's actions (Roelfsema, Engel, König, & Singer, 1997) and are related to muscle activity (Kilner, Baker, Salenius, Hari, & Lemon, 2000; Lindenberger et al., 2009). Although EEG does not allow for precise spatial resolution, the authors propose that synchronization occurs both in sensorimotor areas and in regions related to social cognition (Lindenberger et al., 2009). Thus, the mirror neuron system may be activated during joint music-making, leading to an understanding of others' actions and promoting a more general understanding of others' mental states that supports empathy.

Somewhat unexpectedly, synchronized activity increases 'team spirit' even when there is no collective musical goal, such as when two people independently move or sing to separate stimuli which happen to have the same beat (Hove & Risen, 2009; Reddish et al., 2014; Valdesolo & DeSteno, 2011; Wiltermuth, 2012; Wiltermuth & Heath, 2009). Perhaps synchronized activity is reminiscent of collective goal-directed musical activity, and therefore produces feelings of unity despite the lack of an explicit collective goal. Synchronized musical behaviour may simply produce thoughts and effects that are similar enough to elicit shared representations (Cross, 2005). Coincidental synchronization may also lead to prosocial bonding by blurring of self–other distinctions (Hove, 2008). For example, when a person does not move, but observes another's movement, her motor areas may activate through the mirror neuron system (Gallese & Goldman, 1998). The absence of expected sensory feedback distinguishes motor activations that result from observing others' movements and motor activations that result from one's own movements. However, during interpersonal synchrony, sensory feedback that is tightly coupled to one's own movement is received from both self and other, potentially weakening the self–other boundary (Hove, 2008). Although mimicking another's actions can also increase social connectivity (Chartrand & Bargh, 1999), its effects are predicted to be weaker than those of synchronization, as mimicking introduces a temporal delay between the shared actions, effectively decoupling sensory feedback from self and other. Thus, increased social connectivity during synchronization may result from two sources: (1) the attention to and understanding of another person's actions and mental states that are necessary for synchronization, and (2) the similarities between one's own actions and the consequences of those actions and those of the other person.

Another explanation for increased social connectivity during synchronization, which is not necessarily mutually exclusive with the explanations described above, is that synchronized music-making activates reward areas in the brain, such as the caudate nucleus. One study found an increase in right caudate nucleus activity when drumming with a synchronous partner compared to an asynchronous one. Moreover, the level of caudate activity predicted prosocial behaviour toward the synchronous, but not asynchronous, partner (Kokal, Engel, Kirschner, & Keysers, 2011). The caudate nucleus has previously been found to be important for synchronization (Repp, 2005; Schwartze, Keller, Patel, & Kotz, 2011), response to rewards (Izuma, Saito, & Sadato, 2008) and decision making that involves taking reward experiences into account (Schonberg, Daw, Joel, & O'Doherty, 2007). The caudate is also involved in prosocial behaviour (King-Casas et al., 2005). Thus, synchronized music-making may be rewarding, which leads to a positive affiliation with the synchronous partner and an increased tendency to help that partner (Kokal et al., 2011). The activation in the caudate, a known reward area of the brain (Izuma et al., 2008), could explain why synchronized music-making is enjoyable (Kokal et al., 2011). Furthermore, the relation of caudate activity to prosocial behaviour (King-Casas et al., 2005) could explain why synchronized behaviour results in group cohesion.

In addition to caudate activity, the release of endorphins might mediate the rewarding effect of synchronous behaviour. Endorphins are related to reward (Dunbar, Kaskatis, MacDonald, & Barra, 2012) and important for social relationships in primates (Curley & Keverne, 2005; Dunbar, 2010). Endorphins are also released during synchronized activity, such as rowing, at levels above those released during physical activity (Cohen, Ejsmond-Frey, Knight, & Dunbar, 2010). Synchronized singing, drumming and danc-ing to music elevate pain thresholds, an effect consistent with an increase in endorphins (Dunbar et al., 2012). Passive music listening does not pro-duce the same effect on pain thresholds, suggesting that it is the active syn-chronization with others that causes this effect (ibid). As endorphins are important for social interactions (Curley & Keverne, 2005; Dunbar, 2010), this finding supports the hypothesis that synchronized activity facilitates social bonding (Dunbar et al., 2012; also see Lakens, Schubert, & Paladino, this volume, Chapter 13). Therefore, activation of neural reward areas and release of endorphins may occur during synchronized musical performance, facilitating social bonding and contributing to the behavioural effects described above.

In summary, physical synchronization in music-making or other music-related behaviours may promote psychological 'synchrony', manifest by increased feelings of unity and empathy and increased cooperation. The mirror neuron system may be active during synchronization and may provide further strengthening of the empathy response. The social effects of synchronization may be mediated by breakdown of the self–other distinction through tight interpersonal coupling of actions, sensory feedback and even oscillatory brain activity. In addition, reward areas in the brain and endorphins respond during synchronization, and may facilitate prosociality.

How Do We Maintain Synchrony?

Understanding the neural mechanism of synchronizing to music is impor-tant for understanding the consequences of musical synchrony. The connec-tion between music and movement can be seen as early as infancy; many young infants spontaneously move to rhythm (Hannon & Trainor, 2007; Hannon & Trehub, 2005; Soley & Hannon, 2010). How can the beat of a drum induce such an automatic reaction in humans, even in those who do not have musical training? The answer may lie in the relationship between movement and beat perception that occurs at the neural level. Even when

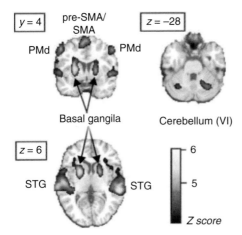

Figure 29.1 Brain areas activated while listening to rhythms. *See Plate 22.*
Notes: Motor areas include the supplementary motor area (SMA), dorsal premotor cortex (PMd), the basal ganglia and the cerebellum. Auditory areas are also activated (superior temporal gyrus, or STG).
Source: Adapted from Grahn and Brett (2007).

people are instructed to remain completely still, listening to rhythms with a regular beat activates brain regions associated with movement. These regions include:

- *The basal ganglia*: a group of structures involved in motor control, action selection and learning (Graybiel, 2005; Graybiel, Aosaki, Flaherty, & Kimura, 1994; Mink, 1996; Redgrave, Prescott, & Gurney, 1999).
- *The cerebellum*: a brain structure involved in the coordination and fine-tuning of movements (Diedrichsen, Criscimagna-Hemminger, & Shadmehr, 2007; Gao et al., 1996; Thach, 1998).
- *Premotor area and supplementary motor area (SMA)*: cortical brain regions that are strongly interconnected with the basal ganglia and cerebellum, and have roles in planning, voluntary control and execution of movement (Boecker et al., 1998; Catalan, Honda, Weeks, Cohen, & Hallett, 1998; Gerloff, Corwell, Chen, Hallett, & Cohen, 1998; Grafton, Fagg, & Arbib, 1998; Picard & Strick, 1996).

These brain regions are commonly activated when listening to rhythms (see Figure 29.1; Bengtsson et al., 2009; Chen, Penhune, & Zatorre, 2008; Grahn & Brett, 2007; Grahn & Rowe, 2009, 2012; Teki et al., 2011).

Although specific functions of each individual brain area that responds during rhythm perception are still unclear, the roles of some regions are beginning to emerge. The basal ganglia seem to be particularly important for 'feeling the beat'. Beat-based rhythms result in higher basal ganglia activation than non-beat-based (irregular) rhythms, suggesting that the basal ganglia may be involved in sensing and tracking the beat (Grahn & Brett, 2007; Grahn & Rowe, 2009, 2012). This finding is supported by research with patients with Parkinson's disease, whose deficiencies in basal ganglia function result in movement impairments such as slow movement initiation, 'freezing' during walking and shuffling of steps (Knutsson, 1972; Nutt & Wooten, 2005; Nombela, Hughes, Owen, & Grahn, 2012). Parkinson's patients also have impairments in discriminating changes in beat-based rhythms, but not non-beat-based rhythms (Grahn & Brett, 2009). The specificity of the patients' deficit to beat-based rhythms indicates that the deficit cannot be accounted for by general problems with timing, working memory or cognitive function. Therefore, overall, the data indicate that the basal ganglia not only activate during beat perception, but are necessary for normal beat perception to occur. The fact that brain regions that control movement are automatically activated during beat perception may account for the universal, spontaneous desire to move when listening to rhythms, although more research is needed to confirm this hypothesis.

Although beat perception enables synchrony in the auditory domain, people are also capable of synchronizing movements using the visual modality, such as when a musician synchronizes his playing to the cues of a conductor. When musicians on stage clap their hands, indicating for the audience to clap along as well, the synchronous movements of the audience involve both the auditory modality (hearing the claps and beat of the music) and the visual modality (watching the musicians clap). Although beat perception occurs for auditory rhythms (such as drum taps) as well as visual rhythms (such as a flashing light), perception and discrimination are more accurate if the rhythm is presented in the auditory modality (Glenberg & Jona, 1991; Grahn, 2012; Guttman et al., 2005; Handel & Buffardi, 1969; Repp & Penel, 2002). For example, people show poorer synchronization performance when tapping with visual than auditory sequences (Repp & Penel, 2002). Therefore, research suggests that visual stimuli do not enable synchronization to the same degree as auditory stimuli. Beat perception appears weaker, or harder to induce, in the visual modality than the auditory modality (Grahn, 2012).

Interestingly, the ability to rapidly identify and synchronize to the beat may be unique to humans among primates (see Box 29.2), but even within humans, individuals differ widely in their beat perception and production abilities. Although most people appear to experience the automatic desire to move or clap along to a song (particularly when not inhibited by social factors), not all individuals can clap along with equal accuracy and precision. Various studies have demonstrated that a wide range of beat perception abilities exist in healthy individuals (Grahn & McAuley, 2009; Grahn & Schuit, 2012; Sowiński &

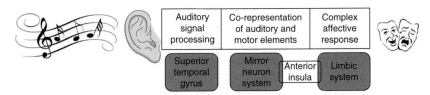

Figure 29.2 Hypothetical model of affective response to music.

Note: The auditory features are processed primarily in the superior temporal gyrus, the mirror neuron system elicits activation of auditory and motor areas, and the anterior insula acts as a bridge between the mirror neuron system and the limbic system which produces the affective response to music.

Source: F rom Molnar-Szakacs and Overy (2006).

Dalla Bella, 2013), although the causes for these differences are unclear. Music training can account for some of these differences, but not entirely: many individuals with no musical training perform well on rhythmic tasks, and musicians sometimes perform poorly. Differences in short-term memory capacity and sensitivity to the beat also account for some variation in rhythm abilities (Grahn & Schuit, 2012). Finally, at the extreme end of the spectrum are healthy individuals who have been diagnosed as 'beat-deaf': they are impaired at perceiving the beat, synchronizing to the beat, detecting when metronome cues are off the beat in music, and visually detecting when a dancer's movements are off the beat (Phillips-Silver et al., 2011).

Box 29.2 Beat perception in non-human animals

Beat perception is often thought to be unique to humans, however studies of some non-human animals seem to suggest otherwise. A dancing cockatiel named Snowball has become a YouTube sensation as a result of his ability to bob his head to a song by the Backstreet Boys, as well as other tunes (see 'Snowball (TM) – Our Dancing Cockatoo' on YouTube) (Patel, Iversen, Bregman, & Schulz, 2009; Schachner, Brady, Pepperberg, & Hauser, 2009; also see Lakens, Schubert, & Paladino, this volume, Chapter 13). Similarly, a sea lion named Ronan has become famous for her ability to bob her head in time to music (see 'Beat Keeping in a California Sea Lion (Ronan)' on YouTube), even to sounds she has never heard before (Cook, Rouse, Wilson, & Reichmuth, 2013).

The exploration of beat perception in non-human animals is growing (Hasegawa, Okanoya, Hasegawa, & Seki, 2011; Patel et al., 2009; Schachner et al., 2009; Cook et al., 2013). One influential hypothesis, known as the Vocal Learning Hypothesis, suggests that beat perception is only possible in 'vocal learning' species. Vocal learning is the ability to modify vocalizations based on exposure to sounds. Vocal learning has only been detected in eight animal

Box 29.2 Snowball, the dancing cockatiel. *See Plate 23.*

groups despite the wide array of vocalizing species; these include humans, bats, cetaceans, pinnipeds (seals and sea lions), elephants, and three bird groups including songbirds, parrots and hummingbirds. Vocal learning species have a tight auditory–motor interface in the nervous system which is proposed to facilitate beat perception abilities (Patel, 2008, Patel & Iversen, 2006). While cockatoos and cockatiels are known to be vocal learners (Emery & Clayton, 2005), sea lions might not be. However, their near relatives, seals, are. Finding a species that is definitively not capable of vocal learning, but can synchronize to a perceived beat, would falsify the Vocal Learning Hypothesis. The proposer of the Vocal Learning Hypothesis, Dr. Ani Patel, has been contacted by several horse trainers who suggest that horses can synchronize to a beat. Horses are not vocal learners, nor are they closely related to a vocal learning species. A protocol has been published for testing beat perception in horses, but to date, no one has tested it, so the Vocal Learning Hypothesis remains viable (Bregman, Iversen, Lichman, Reinhart, & Patel, 2012).

In summary, spontaneous movement to rhythm may be accounted for by automatic engagement of the motor regions of the brain, especially the basal ganglia, induced by beat perception. Music is particularly relevant to this synchronization as people are better able to perceive and thus synchronize to an auditory rhythm than a visual one. This tendency to spontaneously move to the beat may serve the social purpose of creating feelings of cohesion within a group of people moving together, as discussed in the previous section.

Music and the Mirror Neuron System

Earlier in the chapter, we described how synchronous music-making or music-related movement create social connections with others, an effect that may be influenced by the mirror neuron system. First identified in the premotor cortex of the macaque brain, mirror neurons are neurons that respond to both the performance of an action by oneself and the observation of that action performed by another (di Pellegrino et al., 1992). Of particular relevance to music, premotor neurons that respond to an action and the *sound* of that action have also been identified in the monkey brain (Kohler et al., 2002). fMRI studies in humans indicate that a similar mirror neuron network exists: the same regions of premotor cortex respond to observing and hearing an action (Aziz-Zadeh, Iacoboni, Zaidel, Wilson, & Mazziotta, 2004; Buccino et al., 2004). An early function proposed for mirror neurons, that of understanding the intentions of others' actions (Iacoboni et al., 2005), has since been expanded upon to include functions important for human social interaction such as empathy (Carr, Iacoboni, Dubeau, Mazziotta,& Lenzi, 2003; Leslie, Johnson-Frey, & Grafton, 2004), theory of mind (Williams et al., 2006; Williams, Whiten, Suddendorf, & Perrett, 2001), and discriminating between self and other (Uddin, Kaplan, Molnar-Szakacs, Zaidel, & Iacoboni, 2005; Uddin, Molnar-Szakacs, Zaidel, & Iacoboni, 2006). The motor component of the mirror neuron system associated with action and observation and the emotional empathic component associated with attributing emotions in others have both been found to interact with and be affected by musical activity (Molnar-Szakacs & Overy, 2006). It should be noted that the idea of the mirror neuron system involvement in complex behaviours beyond action-observation is controversial, partially due to the less direct evidence available in humans than in other animals (i.e. activity in a single human neuron is not directly measured as it is in a monkey, so one cannot verify that the exact same neurons are responding to the sound or observation of the action and to production of the action). Further research is needed to substantiate the extrapolation of the role of mirror neurons from action-observation to higher-order social cognition. Nevertheless, the potential relationship between music-related mirror neuron activity and empathy is pertinent to the current topic and worthy of discussion.

Music production is necessarily associated with some form of motor activity, whether it be hitting a drum or modulating movements of the vocal tract; this type of motor activity may involve the same sort of mirror neuron activity as the simple reaching and grasping movements with which mirror neurons were first discovered (Molnar-Szakacs & Overy, 2006). Activity in the mirror neuron system also appears to be modulated by musical experience. Greater activity occurs in motor cortex of pianists than that of non-pianists when listening to piano music (Bangert et al., 2006; Haueisen & Knosche, 2001). This system is so specific that even the appropriate finger region is activated when hearing notes that would be played by that specific finger (Haueisen & Knosche, 2001). Pianists also show stronger activation than non-pianists in auditory areas when observing piano movements without auditory feedback (Haslinger et al., 2005) and when making these movements themselves but again receiving no accompanying musical feedback (Lotze, Scheler, Tan, Braun, & Birbaumer, 2003). These findings suggest there is an auditory–visual–motor mirror neuron system that develops with musical training (Haslinger et al., 2005). It is easy to conceive how, during training, repeated coupling of motor outputs and audio-visual feedback establishes a motor representation that can be analyzed for its intended auditory consequences even when another person is performing (ibid).

Indeed, this linking between auditory and motor representations comes online after even a short training period. When non-musicians were trained over five weeks to imitate simple piano key melodies after hearing them, there was increased activation in auditory cortex in response to silent key pressing and activation of motor cortex in response to passive listening, even after the first training session (Bangert et al., 2006). Furthermore, activation patterns differed between the passive listening and silent motion tasks before training, but became more similar over the course of training. This may indicate the formation of a transmodal network that responds to music in the auditory, visual or motor domain (ibid). The formation of audiovisual associations has also been demonstrated by greater activation of the occipital cortex by a presentation of a tone that previously signalled a visual cue (McIntosh, Cabeza, & Lobaugh, 1998). Although in musical training the visual cue (e.g. a musical score) typically precedes or occurs simultaneously with the auditory feedback, this study demonstrates how musical experience may establish associations between visual and auditory inputs.

The existence of common activation associated with listening to, observing and performing music suggests how a music producer and a music listener (particularly a listener who has also produced music) can develop a shared representation of the same musical experience (Molnar-Szakacs & Overy, 2006).

Shared representations may also develop between student and teacher during musical training. In imitation learning of guitar chords, activation occurs in mirror neuron regions such as the inferior parietal lobule and premotor cortex (Rizzolatti, Fogassi, & Gallese, 2001) during both the observation and execution stages (Buccino et al., 2004). This suggests that, even during visual observation, people begin to mentally prepare the motor outputs necessary for imitation (Buccino et al., 2004). Molnar-Szakacs and Overy (2006) propose that a shared representation allows those who listen to music to enter the mind of the producer, in a sense, and to gain an understanding of the intentions behind the actions of the producer.

By extension, shared representation may provide a hypothetical mechanism for musically-induced emotion. Human actions are expressive, to the extent that even footsteps can have an emotion attributed to them (de Gelder, 2006). Therefore, actions lend themselves to interpretation regarding the emotional state of the executor, and listening to music may elicit simple theory of mind interpretations of the mental state of the musician, composer or producer (Molnar-Szakacs & Overy, 2006). The recognition of emotion in music engages the same brain areas that are active during theory of mind processing, or recognizing the emotional states of others, such as the anterior medial frontal cortex, superior temporal sulcus and temporal poles (Frith & Frith, 2003; Steinbeis & Koelsch, 2009). This effect appears to be related to attributions about the mental state of the composer or producer, rather than a different characteristic of the music, as these neural regions are only activated when participants believe the music was composed by another human being, and not when they believe it is computer-generated (Steinbeis & Koelsch, 2009). Not surprisingly, damage in these areas is associated with deficits in both theory of mind abilities and recognition of emotions in music. For example, patients with frontotemporal atrophy consistently display deficits in theory of mind abilities, and recently have been shown to also experience difficulty in attributing emotions to music (Downey et al., 2013; Hsieh, Hornberger, Piguet, & Hodges, 2012; Omar et al., 2011).Thus, when listening to music, people may use theory of mind to identify the emotion in the music, possibly by making judgements about composer agency (Downey et al., 2013).

Music's potential as a therapy to improve theory of mind has been explored; these therapies operate along the same principle as dance movement therapy, which holds that bodily similarity produces psychological understanding and fosters empathy (Behrends et al., 2012). Although children with autism are typically able to attribute emotions to music (Heaton, Allen, Williams, Cummins, & Happe, 2008; Heaton, Hermelin, & Pring, 1999), they do show significant impairments on theory of mind tasks (Baron-Cohen, Leslie, & Frith, 1985; Baron-Cohen, O'Riordan, Stone, Jones, & Plaisted, 1999). This creates a dichotomy between the ability to understand emotional mood and theory of mind abilities which are thought to be related to affective identification in music (Downey et al., 2013). It is unclear whether individuals with autism are able to identify music-induced emotion despite non-typical theory of mind (Heaton et al., 1999) or whether their theory of mind abilities in relation to music are spared. Nevertheless, preserved ability to recognize emotional expression in music despite deficits in recognizing human emotional expression in individuals with autism suggests that music may have potential for improving social cognition.

Coupling of affective and sensorimotor systems may also lead to musically-induced empathy (Carr et al., 2003; Leslie et al., 2004). The posterior inferior frontal gyrus is commonly activated during musically-evoked emotional states (Koelsch, Fritz, Schulze, Alsop, & Schlaug, 2005) and also appears to play a role in sensorimotor affective coupling that occurs in understanding the emotions of others (Carr et al., 2003). The anterior insula is also commonly activated in music-modulated emotion and it has been proposed to be the relay station between the mirror neuron system and the limbic system, which mediates many basic emotions (ibid). Therefore, the mirror neuron system and limbic system may communicate via the insula, adding an emotional interpretation to the perceptual and motor processing of the stimulus (Molnar-Szakacs & Overy, 2006).

In summary, strengthening of a transmodal network that responds to music in auditory, visual or motor domains occurs with musical training. This network may act analogously to a mirror neuron system, whereby hearing music results in the same pattern of activation that occurs when the individual performs the music. This network may provide a basis for shared representations between listener and performer or composer, a phenomenon that may also occur in non-musicians and facilitate the recognition of emotions in music. The idea that sharing of music-related brain activity may transfer to a more general understanding of another's mental states is speculative, but it provides an interesting direction for future research and has many potential applications.

Summary and Future Directions

Music has the capacity to elicit shared representations and to influence social interactions with others. Synchronized musical activity increases liking, cooperation and prosociality toward synchronous partners and promotes a sense of being on the same team. This supports the hypothesis that music evolved because it promoted social bonding and thereby created a group survival advantage. Increased prosociality following music-related synchronization may occur for several reasons. Making music with other people requires an understanding of their actions and intentions. This representation of others' mental states in the music-making context may facilitate a more generalized understanding of others' mental states, thereby promoting empathy and cooperation. The mirror neuron system may mediate synchronization and the prosocial response. The interpersonal coupling of actions and sensory feedback that occurs during synchronization sequences may help break down the self–other boundary, perhaps further explaining the increased empathy and prosociality that occurs with synchronization. Finally, synchronized activity may be rewarding, causing activation in neural regions that also play a role in prosocial behaviour.

Because of people's tendency to synchronize to music, musical synchronization may provide an easy means of joining people together. This tendency may result from the tight relationship between beat perception and movement demonstrated by findings that merely hearing a beat activates motor regions of the brain. Shared representations may also be facilitated by music perception and production, as several studies find that musical training results in activation of motor regions when simply hearing a piece of music one has learned to perform, or activation of auditory regions when one watches silent playing occur. This suggests that musicians may 'put themselves in the shoes' of another musician when hearing her play, resulting in a shared experience between musician and performer. Shared representations may also play a role in the emotional response to music; even in non-musicians there is overlap between the neural regions activated during theory of mind tasks, in which inferences about another's mental state must be made, and during identification of emotions in music.

Existing work could be complemented by future research. For example, there are two interesting findings regarding the effects of synchronized musical activity on third parties uninvolved in the synchronization that remain to be incorporated into the social cohesion theory of musical evolution. First, synchronized musical movement has been found to promote prosocial behaviour even towards an uninvolved third party (Reddish et al., 2014). Second, synchronization increases compliance with a synchronous partner's request to aggress against a third party (Wiltermuth, 2012). Synchronization may promote a generalized prosociality in temporally close interactions with others who could plausibly belong to the same group; however, this effect may be overridden by the request of a synchronous partner who has a much greater likelihood of belonging to the same group. Further work is needed to examine the specificity of the effects of synchronous behaviour in relation to other individuals or groups. In addition, stronger evidence is needed for the mechanisms responsible for the interaction between sociality and listening to, performing or moving along to music.

The development of a strong transmodal network activated in response to music in the auditory, visual or motor domains has been proposed. One possibility is that this network involves mirror neurons and results in a shared representation, as well as greater empathy, between listener and producer. This claim can be further elucidated by future research that more directly examines the relationship between the transmodal network and demonstrations of understanding of another's mental state such as empathy or cooperation. Another interesting line of research would be to explore implications of these findings for contemporary real-world situations in which synchronization occurs, such as synchronized dancing at concerts or synchronized music performance in an orchestra. Humans are social beings, and an important aspect of social interaction is understanding the intentions and emotions of the other. Music may influence how we interact with and think of others in a variety of ways, whether we are performing music with them, synchronously moving to music with them or listening to them perform.

References

Aziz-Zadeh, L., Iacoboni, M., Zaidel, E., Wilson, S., & Mazziotta, J. (2004). Left hemisphere motor facilitation in response to manual action sounds. *European Journal of Neuroscience*, 19, 2609–2612.

Bangert, M., Peschel, T., Schlaug, G., Rotte, M., Drescher, D., et al. (2006). Shared networks for auditory and motor processing in professional pianists: Evidence from fMRI conjunction. *NeuroImage*, 30, 917–926.

Baron-Cohen, S., Leslie, A. M., & Frith, U. (1985). Does the autistic child have a 'theory of mind'? *Cognition*, 21, 37–46.

Baron-Cohen, S., O'Riordan, M., Stone, V., Jones, R., & Plaisted, K. (1999). Recognition of faux pas by normally developing children and children with Asperger syndrome or high-functioning autism. *Journal of Autism and Developmental Disorders*, 29, 407–418.

Batson, C. D., & Powell, A. A. (2003). Altruism and prosocial behaviour. In *Handbook of Psychology*, 19, 463–484. doi: 10.1002/0471264385.wei0519.

Behrends, A., Muller, S., & Dziobek, I. (2012). Moving in and out of synchrony: A concept for a new intervention fostering empathy through interactional dance and movement. *The Arts in Psychotherapy*, 39, 107–116.

Bengtsson, S. L., Ullén, F., Henrik Ehrsson, H., Hashimoto, T., Kito, T., et al. (2009). Listening to rhythms activates motor and premotor cortices. *Cortex*, 45(1), 62–71.

Bernieri, F. J., & Rosenthal, R. (1991). Interpersonal coordination: Behaviour matching and interactional synchrony. In R. S. Feldman & B. Rime (Eds.), *Fundamentals of nonverbal behaviour*. Cambridge: Cambridge University Press, 401–432.

Boecker, H., Dagher, A., Ceballos-Baumann, A. O., Passingham, R. E., Samuel, M., et al. (1998). Role of the human rostral supplementary motor area and the basal ganglia in motor sequence control: Investigations with H215O PET. *Journal of Neurophysiology*, 79(2), 1070–1080.

Bregman, M. R., Iversen, J. R., Lichman, D., Reinhart, M., & Patel, A. D. (2012). A method for testing synchronization to a musical beat in domestic horses (*Equus ferus caballus*). *Empirical Musicology Review*, 7, 144–156.

Buccino, G., Vogt, S., Ritzl, A., Fink, G. R., Zilles, K., et al. (2004). Neural circuits underlying imitation learning of hand actions: An event-related fMRI study. *Neuron*, 42, 323–334.

Carr, L., Iacoboni, M., Dubeau, M., Mazziotta, J. C., & Lenzi, G. L. (2003). Neural mechanisms of empathy in humans: A relay from neural systems for imitation to limbic areas. *Proceedings of the National Academy of Sciences*, 100, 5497–5502.

Catalan, M. J., Honda, M., Weeks, R. A., Cohen, L. G., & Hallett, M. (1998). The functional neuroanatomy of simple and complex sequential finger movements. *Brain*, 121, 253–264.

Chartrand, T. L., & Bargh, J. A. (1999). The chameleon effect: The perception–behavior link and social interaction. *Journal of Personality and Social Psychology*, 76, 893–910.

Chen, J. L., Penhune, V. B., & Zatorre, R. J. (2008). Listening to musical rhythms recruits motor regions of the brain. *Cerebral Cortex*, 18(12), 2844–2854.

Cohen, E. E. A., Ejsmond-Frey, R., Knight, N., & Dunbar, R. I. M. (2010). Rowers' high: Behavioural synchrony is correlated with elevated pain thresholds. *Biology Letters*, 6, 106–108.

Cook, P., Rouse A., Wilson, M. & Reichmuth, C. (2013). A California sea lion (*Zalophus californianus*) can keep the beat: Motor entrainment to rhythmic auditory stimuli in a non vocal mimic. *Journal of Comparative Psychology*, 127(4), 412–427.

Cross, I. (2001). Music, cognition, culture, and evolution. *Annals of the New York Academy of Sciences*, 930, 28–42.

——— (2005). Music and meaning, ambiguity and evolution. In D. Miell, R. MacDonald, & D. Hargreaves (Eds.), *Musical communication*. Oxford: Oxford University Press, 27–43.

——— (2009). The evolutionary nature of musical meaning. *Musicae Scientiae*, 13, 179–200.

Curley, J. P., & Keverne, E. B. (2005). Genes, brain and mammalian social bonds. *Trends in Ecology and Evolution*, 20, 561–567.

Diedrichsen, J., Criscimagna-Hemminger, S. E., & Shadmehr, R. (2007). Dissociating timing and coordination as functions of the cerebellum. *Journal of Neuroscience*, 27(23), 6291–6301.

Downey, L. E., Blezat, A., Nicholas, J., Omar, R., Golden, H. L., et al. (2013). Mentalising music in frontotemporal dementia. *Cortex*, 49, 1844–1855.

Dunbar, R. I. M. (2010). The social role of touch in humans and primates: Behavioural function and neurobiological mechanisms. *Neuroscience and Biobehavioural Reviews*, 34, 260–268.

Dunbar, R. I. M., Kaskatis, K., MacDonald, I., & Barra, V. (2012). Performance of music elevates pain threshold and positive affect: Implications for the evolutionary function of music. *Evolutionary Psychology*, 10, 688–702.

Emery, N. J., & Clayton, N. S. (2005). Evolution of the avian brain and intelligence. *Current Biology*, 15, 946–950.

Falk, D. (2004). Prelinguistic evolution in early hominins: Whence motherese? *Behavioral and Brain Sciences*, 27, 491–541.

Frith, C. D., & Frith, U. (2006). How we predict what other people are going to do. *Brain Research*, 1079, 36–46.

Frith, U., & Frith, C. D. (2003). Development and neurophysiology of mentalizing. *Philosophical Transactions of the Royal Society B: Biological Sciences*, 358, 459–473.

Gallese, V. (2001). The 'shared manifold' hypothesis: From mirror neurons to empathy. *Journal of Consciousness Studies*, 8, 33–50.

Gallese, V., & Goldman, A. (1998). Mirror neurons and the simulation theory of mind-reading. *Trends in Cognitive Sciences*, 2, 493–501.

Gao, J. H., Parsons, L. M., Bower, J. M., Xiong, J., Li, J., & Fox, P. T. (1996). Cerebellum implicated in sensory acquisition and discrimination rather than motor control. *Science*, 272(5261), 545–547.

Gelder, B. de. (2006). Towards the neurobiology of emotional body language. *Nature Reviews Neuroscience*, 7, 242–249.

Gerloff, C., Corwell, B., Chen, R., Hallett, M., & Cohen, L. G. (1998). The role of the human motor cortex in the control of complex and simple finger movement sequences. *Brain*, 121, 1695–1709.

Glenberg, A. M., & Jona, M. (1991). Temporal coding in rhythm tasks revealed by modality effects. *Memory & Cognition*, 19(5), 514–522.

Glenberg, A. M., Mann, S., Altman, L., Forman, T., & Procise, S. (1989). Modality effects in the coding reproduction of rhythms. *Memory & Cognition*, 17(4), 373–383.

Grafton, S. T., Fagg, A. H., & Arbib, M. A. (1998). Dorsal premotor cortex and conditional movement selection: A PET functional mapping study. *Journal of Neurophysiology*, 79(2), 1092–1097.

Grahn, J. A. (2012). See what I hear? Beat perception in auditory and visual rhythms. *Experimental Brain Research*, 220, 51–61.

Grahn, J. A., & Brett, M. (2007). Rhythm perception in motor areas of the brain. *Journal of Cognitive Neuroscience*, 19(5), 893–906.

(2009). Impairment of beat-based rhythm discrimination in Parkinson's disease. *Cortex*, 45(1), 54–61.

Grahn, J. A., & McAuley, J. D. (2009). Neural bases of individual differences in beat perception. *NeuroImage*, 47, 1894–1903.

Grahn, J. A., & Rowe, J. B. (2009). Feeling the beat: Premotor and striatal interactions in musicians and non-musicians during beat perception. *Journal of Neuroscience*, 29(23), 7540–7548.

(2012). Finding and feeling the musical beat: Striatal dissociations between detection and prediction of regularity. *Cerebral Cortex*, 23(4), 912–921.

Grahn, J. A, & Schuit, D. (2012). Individual differences in rhythmic ability: Behavioral and neuroimaging investigations. *Psychomusicology: Music, Mind, and Brain*, 22(2),105–21.

Graybiel, A. M. (2005). The basal ganglia: Learning new tricks and loving it. *Current Opinion in Neurobiology*,15, 638–644.

Graybiel, A. M., Aosaki, T., Flaherty, A. W., & Kimura, M. (1994). The basal ganglia and adaptive motor control. *Science*, 5180, 1826–1831.

Guttman, S. E., Gilroy L. A., & Blake, R. (2005). Hearing what the eyes see: Auditory encoding of visual temporal sequences. *Psychological Science*, 16, 228–265.

Handel, S., & Buffardi, L. (1969). Using several modalities to perceive one temporal pattern. *Journal of Experimental Psychology*, 21, 37–41.

Hanna, J. L. (1977). African dance and the warrior tradition. *Journal of Asian and African Studies*, 12, 111–133.

Hannon, E. E., & Trainor, L. J. (2007). Music acquisition: Effects of enculturation and formal training on development. *Trends in Cognitive Sciences*, 11, 466–472.

Hannon, E. E., & Trehub, S. (2005). Metrical categories in infancy and adulthood. *Psychological Science*, 16, 48–55.

Hasegawa, A., Okanoya, K., Hasegawa, T., & Seki, Y. (2011). Rhythmic synchronization tapping to an audio-visual metronome in budgerigars. *Scientific Reports*, 1, 1–8.

Haslinger, B., Erhard, P., Altenmuller, E., Schroeder, U., Boecker, H., & Ceballos-Baumann, A. O. (2005). Transmodal sensorimotor networks during action observation in professional pianists. *Journal of Cognitive Neuroscience*, 17, 282–293.

Haueisen, J., & Knosche, T. R. (2001). Involuntary motor activity in pianists evoked by music perception. *Journal of Cognitive Neuroscience*, 13, 786–792.

Heaton, P., Allen, R., Williams, K., Cummins, O., & Happé, F. (2008). Do social and cognitive deficits curtail musical understanding? Evidence from autism and Down syndrome. *British Journal of Developmental Psychology*, 26, 171–182.

Heaton, P., Hermelin, B., & Pring, L. (1999). Can children with autistic spectrum disorders perceive affect in music? An experimental investigation. *Psychological Medicine*, 29, 1405–1410.

Hove, M. J. (2008). Shared circuits, shared time, and interpersonal synchrony. *Behavioural and Brain Sciences*, 31, 29–30.

Hove, M. J., & Risen, J. L. (2009). It's all in the timing: Interpersonal synchrony increases affiliation. *Social Cognition*, 27, 949–960.

Hsieh, S., Hornberger, M., Piguet, O., & Hodges, J. R. (2012). Brain correlates of musical and facial emotion recognition: Evidence from the dementias. *Neuropsychologia*, 50, 1814–1822.

Huron, D. (2006). Is music an evolutionary adaptation? *Annals of the New York Academy of Sciences,* 930, 43–61.

Iacoboni, M., Molnar-Szakacs, I., Gallese, V., Buccino, G., Mazziotta, J. C., & Rizzolatti, G. (2005). Grasping the intentions of others with one's own mirror neuron system. *PloS Biology*, 3, e79.

Izuma, K., Saito, D. N., & Sadato, N. (2008). Processing of social and monetary rewards in the human striatum. *Neuron*, 58, 284–294.

Kilner, J. M., Baker, S. N., Salenius, S., Hari, R., & Lemon, R. N. (2000). Human cortical muscle coherence is directly related to specific motor parameters. *Journal of Neuroscience*, 20, 8838–8845.

King-Casas, B., Tomlin, D., Anen, C., Camerer, C. F., Quartz, S. R., & Montague, P. R. (2005). Getting to know you: Reputation and trust in a two-person economic exchange. *Science*, 308, 78–83.

Kirschner, S., & Tomasello, M. (2010). Joint music making promotes prosocial behavior in 4-year-old children. *Evolution and Human Behaviour*, 31, 354–364.

Knutsson, E. (1972). An analysis of Parkinsonian gait. *Brain*, 95, 475–486.

Koelsch, S., Fritz, T., Schulze, K., Aslop, D., & Schlaug, G. (2005). Adults and children processing music: An fMRI study. *NeuroImage*, 25, 1068–1076.

Kogan, N. (1997). Reflections on aesthetics and evolution. *Critical Review: A Journal of Politics and Society*, 11, 193–210.

Kohler, E., Keysers, C., Umilta, M. A., Fogassi, L., Gallese, V., & Rizzolatti, G. (2002). Hearing sounds, understanding actions: Action representation in mirror neurons. *Science*, 297, 846–848.

Kokal, I., Engel, A., Kirschner, S., & Keysers, C. (2011). Synchronized drumming enhances activity in the caudate and facilitates prosocial commitment – if the rhythm comes easily. *PLoS One*, 6, e27272.

Leslie, K. R., Johnson-Frey, S. H., & Grafton, S. T. (2004). Functional imaging of face and hand imitation: Towards a motor theory of empathy. *NeuroImage*, 21, 601–607.

Lindenberger, U., Li, S., Gruber, W., & Muller, V. (2009). Brains swinging in concert: cortical phase synchronization while playing guitar. *BMC Neuroscience*, 10(22). doi: 10.1186/1471-2202-10-22.

Lotze, M., Scheler, G., Tan, H.-R. M., Braun, C., & Birbaumer, N. (2003). The musician's brain: Functional imaging of amateurs and professionals during performance and imagery. *NeuroImage*, 20, 1817–1829.

Lynch, M. P., Eilers, R. E., Oller, D. K., & Urbano, R. C. (1990). Innateness, experience, and music perception. *Psychological Science*, 1, 272–276.

Macrae, C. N., Duffy, O. K., Miles, L. K., & Lawrence, J. (2008). A case of hand waving: Action synchrony and person perception. *Cognition*, 109, 152–156.

McAuley, J. D., & Henry, M. J. (2010). Modality effects in rhythm processing: Auditory encoding of visual rhythms is neither obligatory nor automatic. *Attention, Perception & Psychophysics*, 72(5), 1377–1389.

McIntosh, A. R., Cabeza, R. E., & Lobaugh, N. J. (1998). Analysis of neural interactions explains the activation of occipital cortex by an auditory stimulus. *Journal of Neurophysiology*, 80, 2790–2796.

McNeill, W. H. (1995). *Keeping together in time: Dance and drill in human history*. Cambridge, MA: Harvard University Press.

Merker, B. (2000). Synchronous chorusing and the origins of music. *Musicae Scientiae*, 3, 59–73.

Miller, G. F. (1997). Protean primates: The evolution of adaptive unpredictability in competition and courtship. In A. Whiten & R. W. Byrne (Eds.), *Machiavellian intelligence II: Extensions and evaluations*. Cambridge: Cambridge University Press, 312–340.

Mink, J. (1996). The basal ganglia: Focused selection and inhibition of competing motor programs. *Progress in Neurobiology*, 50(4), 381–425.

Molnar-Szakacs, I., & Overy, K. (2006). Music and mirror neurons: From motion to 'e'motion. *SCAN*, 1, 235–241.

Morris, M. E., Iansek, R., Matyas, T. A., & Summers, J. J. (1996). Stride length regulation in Parkinson's disease: Normalization strategies and underlying mechanisms. *Brain*, 119 (Pt 2), 551–568.

Nombela, C., Hughes, L. E., Owen, A. M., & Grahn, J. A. (2013). Into the groove: Can rhythm influence Parkinson's disease? *Neuroscience and Biobehavioural Reviews*, 37(10), 2564–2570.

Nutt, J. G., & Wooten, G. F. (2005). Clinical practice: Diagnosis and initial management of Parkinson's disease. *New England Journal of Medicine*, 353, 1021–1027.

Omar, R., Henley, S. M. D., Bartlett, J. W., Hailstone, J. C., Gordon, E., et al. (2011). The structural neuroanatomy of music emotion recognition: Evidence from frontotemporal lobar degeneration. *NeuroImage*, 56, 1814–1821.

Patel, A. D. (2008). *Music, language, and the brain*. New York: Oxford University Press.

Patel, A. D. & Iversen J. R. (2006) A non-human animal can drum a steady beat on a musical instrument. In M. Baroni, A. R. Addessi, R. Caterina, & M. Costa (Eds.), *Proceedings of the 9th International Conference on Music Perception & Cognition (ICMPC9)*, 477.

Patel, A. D., Iversen, J. R., Bregman, M. R., & Schulz, I. (2009). Experimental evidence for synchronization to a musical beat in a nonhuman animal. *Current Biology*, 19, 827–830.

Patel, A. D., Iversen, J. R., Chen, Y., & Repp, B. H. (2005). The influence of metricality and modality on synchronization with a beat. *Experimental Brain Research*, 163, 226–238.

Pellegrino, G. de, Fadiga, L., Fogassi, L., Gallese, V., & Rizzolatti, G. (1992). Understanding motor events: A neurophysiological study. *Experimental Brain Research*, 91, 176–180.

Phillips-Silver, J., Toiviainen, P., Gosselin, N., Piche, O., Nozaradan, S., Palmer, C., & Peretz, I. (2011). Born to dance but beat deaf: A new form of congenital amusia. *Neuropsychologia*, 49(5), 961–969.

Picard, N., & Strick, P. (1996). Motor areas of the medial wall: A review of their location and functional activation. *Cerebral Cortex*, 6(3), 342–353.

Pinker, S. (1997). *How the mind works*. New York: W.W. Norton and Company.

Phillips-Silver, J., & Trainor, L. J. (2005). Feeling the beat: Movement influences infant rhythm perception. *Science*, 308(5727), 1430.

Rabinowitch, T. Cross, I., & Burnard, P. (2012). Long-term musical group interaction has a positive influence on empathy in children. *Psychology of Music*, 41, 484–498.

Reddish, P., Bulbulia, J., & Fischer, R. (2014). Does synchrony promote generalized prosociality? *Religion, Brain and Behaviour*, 4, 3–19.

Redgrave, P., Prescott, T., & Gurney, K. N. (1999). The basal ganglia: A vertebrate solution to the selection problem? *Neuroscience*, 89, 1009–1023.

Repp, B. H. (2005). Sensorimotor synchronization: A review of the tapping literature. *Psychonomic Bulletin and Review*, 12, 969–992.

Repp, B. H., & Penel, A. (2002). Auditory dominance in temporal processing: New evidence from synchronization with simultanious visual and auditory sequences. *Journal of Experimental Psychology: Human Perception and Performance*, 28(5), 1085–1099.

Repp, B. H., & Penel, A. (2004). Rhythmic movement is attracted more strongly to auditory than to visual rhythms. *Psychological Research*, 68, 252–270.

Rizzolatti, G., Fogassi, L., & Gallese, V. (2001). Neurophysiological mechanisms underlying the understanding and imitation of action. *Nature Reviews Neuroscience*, 2, 661–670.

Roelfsema, P. R., Engel, A. K., Konig, P., & Singer, W. (1997). Visuomotor integration is associated with zero time-lag synchronization among cortical areas. *Nature*, 385, 157–161.

Schachner, A., Brady, T. F., Pepperberg, I. M., & Hauser, M. D. (2009). Spontaneous motor entrainment to music in multiple vocal mimicking species. *Current Biology*, 19(10), 831–836.

Schonberg, T., Daw, N. D., Joel, D., & O'Doherty, J. P. (2007). Reinforcement learning signals in the human striatum distinguish learners from nonlearners during reward-based decision making. *Journal of Neuroscience*, 27, 12860–12867.

Schwartze, M., Keller, P. E., Patel, A. D., & Kotz, S. A. (2011). The impact of basal ganglia lesions on sensorimotor synchronization, spontaneous motor tempo, and the detection of tempo changes. *Behavioural Brain Research*, 216, 685–691.

Soley, G., & Hannon, E. E. (2010). Infants prefer the musical meter of their own culture: A cross-cultural comparison. *Developmental Psychology*, 46(1), 286–292.

Sowinski, J., & Dalla Bella, S. (2013). Poor synchronization to the beat may result from deficient auditory-motor mapping. *Neuropsychologia*, 51, 1952–1963.

Steinbeis, N., & Koelsch, S. (2009). Understanding the intentions behind man-made products elicits neural activity in areas dedicated to mental state attribution. *Cerebral Cortex*, 19, 619–623.

Teki, S., Grube, M., Kumar, S., & Griffiths, T. D. (2011). Distinct neural substrates of duration-based and beat-based auditory timing. *Journal of Neuroscience*, 31, 3805–3812.

Thach, W. T. (1998). What is the role of the cerebellum in motor learning and cognition? *Trends in Cognitive Sciences*, 2(9), 331–337.

Tognoli, E., Lagarde, J., DeBuzman, G. C., & Kelso, J. A. S. (2007). The phi complex as a neuromarker of human social coordination. *Proceedings of the National Academy of Sciences*, 104, 8190–8195.

Trehub, S. E. (2003). The developmental origins of musicality. *Nature Neuroscience*, 6, 669–673.

Uddin, L. Q., Kaplan, J. T., Molnar-Szakacs, I., Zaidel, E., & Iacoboni, M. (2005). Self-face recognition activates a frontoparietal 'mirror' network in the right hemisphere: An event-related fMRI study. *NeuroImage*, 25, 926–935.

Uddin, L. Q., Molnar-Szakacs, I., Zaidel, E., & Iacoboni, M. (2006). rTMS to the right inferior parietal lobule disrupts self–other discrimination. *SCAN*, 1, 65–71.

Valdesolo, P., & DeSteno, D. (2011). Synchrony and the social tuning of compassion. *Emotions*, 11, 262–266.

Waal, F. B. M. de. (2008). Putting the altruism back into altruism: The evolution of empathy. *Annual Review of Psychology*, 59, 279–300.

Williams, J. H. G., Waiter, G. D., Gilchrist, A., Perrett, D. I., Murray, A. D., & Whiten, A. (2006). Neural mechanisms of imitation and 'mirror neuron' functioning in autistic spectrum disorder. *Neuropsychologia*, 44, 610–621.

Williams, J. H. G., Whiten, A., Suddendorf, T., & Perrett, D. I. (2001). Imitation, mirror neurons and autism. *Neuroscience and Biobehavioral Reviews*, 25, 287–295.

Wiltermuth, S. S. (2012). Synchronous activity boosts compliance with requests to aggress. *Journal of Experimental Social Psychology*, 48, 453–456.

Wiltermuth, S. S., & Heath, C. (2009). Synchrony and cooperation. *Psychological Science*, 20, 1–5.

Woolhouse, M., & Tidhar, D. (2010). Group dancing leads to increased person perception. *Proceedings of the 11th ICMPC*, Seattle, 605–608.

Zarco, W., Merchant, H., Prado, L., & Mendez, J. C. (2009). Subsecond timing in primates: Comparison of interval production between human subjects and rhesus monkeys. *Journal of Neurophysiology*, 102, 3191–3202.

Glossary

Beat A perceived pulse that marks equally spaced points in time.

Empathy Matching of affect with another person; may also include a cognitive component involving understanding the other person's thoughts and feelings (Rameson & Lieberman, 2009).

Mirror neurons Neurons that fire both when an action is performed by oneself and when one watches another perform the same action.

Neural oscillations Synchronized activity of neurons.

Parkinson's disease A progressive disease of the nervous system caused by death of dopaminergic neurons in the substantia nigra. Common physical symptoms include muscular rigidity, slow movements and tremor.

Pro-sociality Tendency to perform actions intended primarily to benefit people other than oneself (e.g. helping, sharing, comforting) (Batson & Powell, 2003).

Rhythm A pattern of (usually auditory) events separated by short time intervals (~200 milliseconds to 2 seconds).

Synchrony Simultaneous action in two or more people; for example, simultaneous clapping in a crowd.

Theory of mind Understanding another person's mental state, including their thoughts, intentions, beliefs and feelings.

30 You Move, I Watch, It Matters: Aesthetic Communication in Dance

Guido Orgs, Dana Caspersen and Patrick Haggard

Abstract

In this chapter we will introduce a new theory of aesthetics in the performing arts that is based on communication via movement. With a specific
focus on dance performances, we propose that movement messages are
communicated from performer to spectator. We suggest that the aesthetic
impact of dance (and perhaps all performing arts) is a result of successful
message-passing between performer and spectator. We show how Grice's
four maxims of successful conversation can be applied to the performance
situation. We propose that communication during a performance is interactive and bidirectional. Information being passed from performer to audience
is primarily communicated through observed movement kinematics and
choreographic structure: we will distinguish between the processing of syntactic information of postures, movements and movement sequences, on the
one hand, and processing of semantics of movement intentions, on the other
hand. Aesthetic processing of the movement message will further depend
on the spectator's visual and motor expertise. In a dimensional model of
aesthetic appreciation of dance, we distinguish between processing fluency
and novelty/complexity of information as two distinct sources of movement
aesthetics that relate to specific brain mechanisms. Aesthetic judgements of
preference and interest will reflect a combination of both implicit processing fluency and the explicit aesthetic strategy of the observer. Our theory
differs from existing accounts of aesthetic experience in that it emphasises

This work was supported by the 'Dance Engaging Science' grant from VW Stiftung, and by a
research grant (F/07 134/DO) from Leverhulme Trust to PH. PH was additionally supported by a
Professorial Fellowship from ESRC and by ERC Advanced Grant HUMVOL. GO was supported
by a transformative research grant from ESRC. We are also grateful to Scott DeLahunta for advice
and encouragement.

627

successful communication as the primary source of aesthetic experience. Appreciation of dance in this context is neither just a function of dance movement features (as an objectivist aesthetics suggests) nor of the spectator's processing fluency (as a subjectivist aesthetics suggests). Instead, our emphasis on communication implies some level of experience-sharing between dancer and spectator.

Performing Arts Aesthetics and Social Cognition

Aristotle argued that the performing arts are based on the human ability to imitate, and that spectators derive pleasure from witnessing imitations of reality (*Poetics*, IV). Aristotle thus emphasises social interactions between performers and between performers and the audience as a prime contributor to the *aesthetics* of the performing arts. The term 'aesthetics', derived from the Greek word *aisthetikos* (I sense, I feel) refers to the science of 'sensual' as opposed to 'rational' cognition and was initially coined by Alexander Baumgarten in the middle of the eighteenth century (Hammermeister, 2002). The first empirical investigations into aesthetic cognition were conducted by Gustav Theodor Fechner (1871), who studied optimal proportions in paintings (the 'golden ratio'). In more recent times, aesthetic perception and its neural basis has been investigated in the visual arts (Leder, Belke, Oeberst, & Augustin, 2004; Zeki & Lamb, 1994) and in music (Koelsch, 2011). In this chapter we will focus on aesthetic perception in the performing arts and its link to social cognition and communication theory. We will argue that aesthetic perception of the performing arts involves successful communication between performers and spectators of a performance. More specifically, we will combine the cognitive neuroscience of how we perceive and interpret other people's actions with knowledge from dance practice to formulate a neurocognitive theory of aesthetics in performing dance.

Dance as a Social Art Form

What is dance? The *Oxford English Dictionary* gives a straightforward definition: Dance is 'a series of steps and movements that match the speed and rhythm of a piece of music'. This simple definition seems appealing at first glance, but regular visitors of dance performances, dancers and choreographers are likely to disagree: a dance performance will very often neither involve a series of steps nor any obvious relation to a piece of music, yet will clearly qualify as dance. Attempts to define core features of an art form are difficult because what qualifies as art constantly changes. The most appreciated art works today were often dismissed when they were created (Gopnik, 2012). To avoid these pitfalls, we will not focus here on trying to define what dance *is*, in the sense of giving minimal necessary and sufficient conditions. Instead, we aim to develop a neurocognitive theory of how dance *works*. That is, *if* anything were to count as dance, we anticipate it would involve the cognitive and neural mechanisms that we describe here. We conceptualise the performing art of dance as a human sociocultural activity where one individual moves and another watches. Our definition differs from the conventional 'movement to music' definition in almost all possible respects, bar one. First, we hold that music is accessory, while one widespread view considers it essential. Second, we hold that the presence of an observer is an essential part of dance as a performing art, yet dance observation barely figures in most dictionary definitions of dance. This is not to say that one cannot dance without being watched; rather, we argue that movement in performing dance serves a communicative purpose; it is *expressive* movement, geared towards exchanging emotions, intentions and ideas between people (Leach, 2013).

In our view, the key feature of dance as a performing art is not so much the dancer, but the dancer–observer dyad. People move all the time. What distinguishes a dance performance from mere movement is that it is intended for and has a receiver. It is movement designed for watching. Performing dance is thus an intrinsically social art form that involves at least two people, the dancer and a viewer. There is often a third person: the choreographer. In collaboration with the dancer, the choreographer designs the movement that is to be watched. We argue that understanding the aesthetic impact of dance involves first and foremost understanding how people see, process and interpret the movements of others.

In a neurocognitive sense, perceiving another's movement involves a perceptuomotor coupling between individuals' brains (Heyes, 2011; Keysers & Perrett, 2004; Rizzolatti & Craighero, 2004). Accordingly, the aesthetic experience of dance can be considered as a communicative process: in its simplest form, the dancer/choreographer is the transmitter of the message, body movement provides the message itself, and the spectator is the receiver of the message (see Figure 30.1). From this perspective, dance is similar to other forms of communication and message-passing. In this chapter, we will investigate how theories of communication deriving from cognitive informatics may help us to understand the aesthetic and cultural impact of dance.

Considering dance as message-passing between bodies has a number of interesting implications. First, it clearly distinguishes dance from other art forms that involve inanimate artistic objects or representations, either visual (such as painting, art or film) or auditory (music). The cardinal activity of communication is the direct contact between two or more people, which is always present in dance. In contrast, cultural activities such as writing or painting may have undeniable artistic value, but the direct contact between artist and audience is not central. Rather, the audience relates to the artist only indirectly,

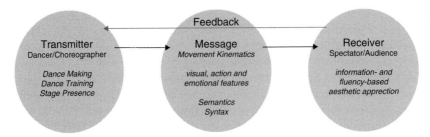

Figure 30.1 Communication during a dance performance.

through an artistic 'work' such as a book or painting. In dance, the communicative situation is the work.

Second, our view focuses on bodily movement as a core feature of all performing arts, including not only dancing but perhaps also acting, miming and singing. Understanding how movement comes to carry aesthetic information therefore provides a basis for understanding how the performing arts work in general. This does not mean that movement is the *only* carrier of information during a dance performance, still less in other forms of performance art. Additional elements (costume, lighting, stage design, music, words, and so on) will substantially contribute to the aesthetic experience of a dance performance. However, we contend that these additional elements are not strictly necessary: observed movement remains the only necessary and sufficient core for dance.

Roadmap

In the first part of this chapter we will characterise the three components of a communication theory approach to dance: the message transmitter (dancer and choreographer), the message (observed movement) and the receiver (the audience). We will then explore the constraints of message-passing by applying Grice's (1989) four cooperative principles of successful communication. These principles relate to the quantity and quality of information that is exchanged and determine the complexity of the movement message in choreography. Finally, we will introduce a dimensional model of the aesthetic experience of dance that will relate the movement message to aesthetic judgement and will identify both implicit and explicit sources of aesthetic appreciation of movement.

The Dancer as Transmitter

In a communication theory approach to dance, the dancer's primary role is to convey a message to the audience by making body movements. This implies a certain level of objectification: the dancer *uses* his body as the *tool* for message-passing. This view clearly distinguishes between performative dance, on the one hand, and other movement practices such as yoga, dance therapy and the martial arts, on the other. The former focuses on successful communication to an audience, while the latter focus more on achieving a desired personal state, or goal. Psychologically, one might say that the goal of dance performance is primarily to induce a state of mind in the spectator. In contrast, the goal of dance therapy, and of some movement practices often associated with dance, is primarily to induce a state of mind in the dancer.

Dance Training Serves to Optimise Message Transmission

The limits of what can be communicated through dance are set by the physical constraints of the human body. In a communication theory approach to dance, the purpose of dance training is to reduce those constraints by expanding and refining the ways in which a body can move. This increases the message-passing capacity of dance, in the same way as expanding and refining the semantic and syntactic capacity increase the communicative capacity of the developing child. The increase in movement repertoire through dance training may involve addition of new movements that were not previously possible (Calvo-Merino, Glaser, Grèzes, Passingham, & Haggard, 2005; Daprati, Iosa, & Haggard, 2009) or may involve perfecting movements that are made every day. In either case, the range of physical and emotional expression is increased. This idea resembles Rudolf Laban's (2011) developments of specific exercises 'to develop the body as an instrument of expression' (Laban, 2011). Interestingly, this definition of dance expertise is not exclusive to any particular dance style or technique (such as HipHop or Indian Kathak), but only refers to a dancer's ability to effectively communicate intentions through movement.

Choreographer versus Dancer

In the case in which dancer and choreographer are not the same person, the dancer will assume an additional role in transmitting not only her own intentions but also the intentions of the choreographer. In this section we will discuss the division of labour between choreographer and dancer in (1) generating messages, and (2) receiving them/reconstructing intentions.

Generating Messages

The division of labour between dancer and choreographer in generating messages is variable and changes according to the methodologies chosen for creating and performing work. The messages communicated in a dance work are affected by numerous elements. Among these are the chosen movement sequences, categories or generation principles, the overall temporal and spatial structures of the work, the relationship of the movement to any sound component and the conditions of the environment within which the performance takes place. According to the method chosen to create the work, these elements may be the work of the choreographer or the performer, or they may be the product of differing levels of collaboration between the two (or more) people involved (Caspersen, 2004).

We illustrate this point with examples from one modern choreographer. William Forsythe's work shows several different divisions of labour between choreographer and performer. In *The Vertiginous Thrill of Exactitude*, Forsythe choreographed set movements in a specific relationship to the music. The audience sees movements that are largely the creative work of Forsythe, which are embodied in the experience and sensibilities of the dancer. On the other hand, in *Sider*, Forsythe and his fellow company members worked together and in parallel, using several different methods to create a body of motion ideas and scenic parameters. These parameters combined allow for the real-time emergence of motion content. In this piece, the dancers wear earpieces and listen to the soundtrack of a film of a Shakespeare play, which acts as a musical entrainment device. At the same time, Forsythe uses the earpieces to communicate with the dancers, directing the temporal and dynamic structure of the scenes. Within this framework, the dancers make decisions that shape the content of the work in performance, according to the strategies that have been established. What the audience sees is movement that results from one indivisible flow of ideas from numerous sources.

There are many ways to make dance, ranging from asking questions – as for example in the work of Pina Bausch (Climenhaga, 2009) – to applying mathematical rules (de Keersmaeker & Cvejić, 2013). Dance pieces often emerge from an extended period of artistic research rather than linearly from a preformed conception. In the process of dance-making, neither dancer nor choreographer may be able to explicitly identify the artistic message that is being created and communicated. In fact, underdetermined, conflicting or ambiguous messages may form an essential part of all art (Jakesch & Leder 2009; Kirk, 2008). Similarly, whereas some choreographic decisions and tools will be deliberately applied, others may be purely intuitive (for a selection of contemporary approaches to dance-making, see motionbank.org). Importantly, however, we argue that dance-making – irrespective of the specific approach taken – ultimately results in a movement message that will prime the spectator to decode both content and the source of the message. Only the dancer can be both carrier and source of the movement message: the choreographer's contribution to the movement message requires the dancer's body as a carrier.

Without the dancer, the choreographer can imagine message-passing, but cannot actually do it.

Receiving Messages

During a dance performance, direct communication occurs only between dancer and spectator. The choreographers' and/or the dancer's contributions to the message are not directly discernible. Rather, the audience must recover the intentions of the message based on what they *see*. A strength of the communication approach to dance aesthetics is that it clearly distinguishes between the message the audience receives, which is based solely on the dancer's movements, and the message that is intended or generated, which is in the mind of the choreographer or dancer. Dance itself is the process of connecting the generative message to the receptive message.

Movement as Message

We have previously introduced a hierarchical model of dance perception that distinguishes three levels of movement representation (Orgs, Hagura, & Haggard, 2013). Based on this model, we will identify body-specific and more general visual features of the movement message. We will show how these contribute to the aesthetic impact of dance, separating at least three distinct levels of movement representation: static body postures, dynamic movement and sequential structure.

Action Features of the Movement Message

Taken together, the building blocks of movement are combined in order to communicate intentions. This is impressively documented in studies showing that people attribute specific and elaborate mental and emotional states to dynamic animations of simple geometric shapes (Heider & Simmel, 1944). Kilner (2011) distinguishes four levels of movement representation: the motor level (neural motor commands), the kinematic level (space, time, force), the goal level and the intentional level. Since the motor commands, goals and intentions of the dancer are not available to the spectator directly, aesthetic communication between dancer and spectator can only occur at the visible kinematic level. In other words,

the dancer consists – at least for his audience – of nothing but what can be seen of him. His properties and actions are implicitly defined by how he looks and what he does. One hundred sixty pounds of weight on the scales will not exist if to the eye he has the winged lightness of a dragonfly. (Arnheim, 1974, p. 403)

Although, auditory cues may play some part in perceived effort of movement (for example, breath, contact with the floor), the primary carrier of the aesthetic impact of dance therefore lies in the visually perceived kinematics of the dancer's movements. The contributions of other levels of movement representation to the aesthetic experience of dance such as goals and intentions can only be inferred from the visually available kinematic level. Importantly, recovering these intentions and goals may require a special processing of the movement message within the motor system of the observer's brain (Calvo-Merino, Urgesi, Orgs, Aglioti, & Haggard, 2010; Keysers & Perrett, 2004; Orgs, Bestmann, Schuur, & Haggard, 2011; Rizzolatti & Craighero, 2004; Urgesi, Calvo-Merino, Haggard, & Aglioti, 2007). Dance traditions have added other elements, such as costume, music and narrative. Nevertheless, the core of performative dance remains sensorimotor coupling induced by observing the dancer's movements and their kinematics.

Emotional Features of the Movement Message

In addition to action goals and intentions, observers readily infer emotional expressions from both static and dynamic displays of the human body (de Gelder et al., 2010). Interestingly, activity in body-specific visual areas of the human brain, such as the superior temporal sulcus (STS) or the fusiform body area (FBA), is increased for expressive (e.g. fearful) compared to neutral (Grèzes, Pichon, & de Gelder, 2007; de Gelder, Snyder, Greve, Gerard, & Hadjikhani, 2004) actions, suggesting a role of these areas in inferring emotions from observed human movement. Emotional body postures additionally activate premotor areas of the brain (Grèzes, Pichon, & de Gelder, 2007). Since these areas are also thought to extract intentions from others' actions, emotion and intention processing may be related. Expressive body postures are also processed faster than neutral body postures, producing shorter latencies in the body-specific N170 event-related potential, relative to neutral postures (van Heijnsbergen, Meeren, Grèzes, & de Gelder, 2007). These findings suggest a direct link between expressiveness of movement and the ease with which the observed action is processed. The ease or fluency of stimulus processing has proven an important predictor of aesthetic processing. We will return to the role of processing fluency when discussing the spectator as the receiver of the movement message.

Visual Features of the Movement Message

Aside from these action-specific features, aesthetic perception of the movement message will also depend on features that are common to all visual aesthetic perception (Palmer, Schloss, & Sammartino, 2013). The best-studied principle of this kind has been composition and balance in visual objects or pictures (Fechner, 1871; McManus, 1980). Aesthetic judgement of dance appears to follow the same rules as for other visual stimuli. Aesthetic judgements of dance postures (Daprati, Iosa, & Haggard, 2009) and of dance movements (Orgs et al., 2013) are governed by principles of symmetry and balance. Visual 'gestalt' principles, such as good continuation of movement, influence aesthetic judgements of movement kinematics. In more complex situations, such as many dance performances, visual attributes, such as the spatial distribution of a group of dancers on stage and interpersonal synchrony, may also be aesthetically relevant (Loeb, 1986).

For example, the use of pointe shoes in classical ballet can be interpreted as a means to enhance the visual features of the movement message. Pointe shoes were introduced at the end of the eighteenth century, to allow dancers to execute movements that involved placing their weight on the tips of their toes. Pointe shoes emphasise the movement message by visually lengthening the legs of the dancer: leg movements become salient.

Similarly, the use of épaulement in classical ballet can be interpreted as a means to enhance the visual features of the movement message. Épaulement is a set of complex relationships between the dancer's eyes, head, shoulders, hips, hands and feet; a series of curvilinear forms, or directed lines or volumes, in angled relationships. Épaulement visually extends the geometric angles within the body, directing attention beyond the body and into the surrounding space. One effect of épaulement is to expand and delineate the audience's sense of the space around the dancers, and the relationships between the dancers, the stage and the audience (Caspersen, 2011).

The Spectator as Receiver

In order to understand the aesthetic impact of movement on the receiver, we need to understand the brain process that underlie movement perception (Allison, Puce, & McCarthy, 2000; Blake & Shiffrar, 2007; Zeki & Lamb, 1994). Aesthetic evaluation of dance inevitably begins with visual perception of body movement. Several recent studies have identified neural processes that underlie perception of static visual bodies (Peelen & Downing, 2007), of human movement kinematics (McAleer, Pollick, Love, Crabbe, & Zacks, 2013) and of inferring intentions from other people's actions (Kilner, 2011). All these processes are potentially relevant to dance perception. Our aim in this chapter is to identify specific neural processes that are essential for the core circumstances of dance: namely, you move, I watch, and it matters. An extensive review of all aspects of the neuroscience of dance is beyond the scope of this chapter (for reviews, see Bläsing et al., 2012; Cross & Ticini,

2011). Here, we focus on the influence of prior experience of aesthetic processing, because this is perhaps the area where existing theories of aesthetic processing are most helpful. In the case of observed movement, the spectator's expertise will depend on both visual and motor familiarity with the movement message.

Visual and Motor Familiarity with the Observed Movement

Aesthetic perception depends on whether movements are familiar to the observer. The influence of familiarity on aesthetic judgement is well documented in the 'mere-exposure effect' (Zajonc, 1968). People like what they know. In the case of movement, we need to distinguish between visual and motor familiarity with the observed movement. Movements that have been frequently observed are preferred to movements that have been seen less frequently (Orgs et al., 2013). The influence of visual familiarity on the spectator can explain why people prefer specific movement styles. This argument is particularly strong if a movement style relies on a relatively restricted movement vocabulary, as in classical ballet. This is because a restricted movement vocabulary will usually imply more repetitions of the same or similar movements, thereby increasing their visual familiarity. Visual familiarity can explain long-term 'Zeitgeist' effects in aesthetic appreciation (Carbon, 2010). Original and unfamiliar choreographies may be initially rejected by the public, but can gain widespread recognition over time. One example is Stravinsky's *Rite of Spring*, first staged by the Ballets Russes in 1913, which caused outrage at its premiere but is now regarded as a masterpiece (Berg, 1988).

We have seen that on the side of the transmitter the vocabulary is limited by what the dancer can do. One important theory of movement perception makes an even stronger prediction: if visual motion perception is an 'embodied process', in the sense of linking the observed actions of others to one's own motor repertoire, then the receiver must have the capacity to make the movement if their brain is to fully respond to it (Aglioti, Cesari, Romani, & Urgesi, 2008; Calvo-Merino et al., 2005, 2006; Orgs, Dombrowski, Heil, & Jansen-Osmann, 2008; Cross, Hamilton, & Grafton, 2006; also see Cross & Calvo-Merino, this volume, Chapter 26). This is because unfeasible movements outside the motor repertoire cannot be mapped onto existing motor representations and are therefore motorically unfamiliar. Movement with low motor familiarity should therefore be less aesthetically pleasant than movements for which the observer has the corresponding motor representation (Beilock & Holt, 2007; Topolinski, 2010). Lack of familiarity should have negative aesthetic impact. Existing studies on perceptuomotor coupling during aesthetic perception of movement, however, have produced mixed findings on the relationship between motor familiarity and preference. Whereas some studies show that knowing how to perform a movement correlates positively with aesthetic preference (Beilock & Holt, 2007; Kirsch et al. 2013; Topolinski, 2010), other studies suggest that novel movements outside of the motor repertoire of the observer are actually preferred to known movements. For example, extreme body postures are preferred to less extreme postures (Cross et al., 2011; Daprati et al., 2009).

Visual and motor familiarity both contribute to the spectator's expertise. Expertise has been shown to have a profound effect on aesthetic judgement (Augustin & Leder, 2006). We will return to the role of expertise in discussing the influence of fluent processing in aesthetic appreciation.

Bidirectionality of Communication

In dance performance, information is exchanged from performer to audience, but also from audience to performer. This bidirectional communication lies at the heart of dance's status as a performing art. Even a 'passive' audience provides continuous feedback that will influence dancers. For example, audience members may spontaneously clap or laugh, or even leave an on-going performance. Even lack of overt audience behaviour may be a signal to the dancer, indicating involvement and concentration. These audience reactions confirm whether the audience receives the message transmitted by the dancer, and further communicate whether the dancer's intentions were understood as intended by the dancer. For example audience laughter provides feedback to the dancer that their intention to be funny succeeded. Or if they had some intention other than being funny, the message of laughter provides feedback that the dancer's intention failed. This information from the audience can then be used by the dancer to modulate timing or expressivity of their movements, so as to either be less or more funny, as appropriate. Accordingly, the feedback provided by an audience is used directly by the transmitter to adjust the communication process. The existence of such a feedback loop supports the view of a performance as mutual communication between performer and audience. This loop is unique to the performing arts, and is absent in other art forms that are not 'live'.

Some choreographers emphasise the bidirectionality of communication between performers and the audience by creating work in which the spectator can become part of the actual performance. A performance may take place among observers or outside the traditional theatre setting, thereby blurring the separation between performers and the audience. Examples for such an

Table 30.1 *Grice's maxims of successful communication applied to dance*

Maxim	Manifestation in dance
Quantity	Movement vocabulary and dance style
Relation	Structural properties of the movement sequence, complexity and novelty of composition
Quality	Congruency between observed movement and inferred movement intentions; stage presence
Manner	Semantic ambiguity and novelty of movement intentions

interactive approach to choreography can be found in the work of Meg Stuart's dance company, Damaged Goods (Peters, 2010).

Dance as Message-Passing or Experience-Sharing?

In this chapter, we use the communication-theory view of dance to sketch an experimental approach to performing arts aesthetics. Defining dance as a communicative act places few constraints on what dance is, other than emphasising the importance of the receiver/audience. A communicative account of how dance works requires more precise constraints if it is to be more informative. A major shift in communication theory occurs if we compare the quantitative, mathematical formulations of Shannon and Weaver (1949), and the pragmatic, behavioural theories pioneered by Grice (1989). The original mathematical theory of information did not restrict in any way the set of messages that might be passed from transmitter to receiver, and required only that the set of messages be known in advance to both parties. In fact, however, human communication typically involves a contextual restriction on what is actually said. Think of the set of messages that you expect to exchange with the person who cuts your hair, for example, and the larger set of messages that you do not expect to exchange. In the next section of this article we show how Grice's cooperative principles for successful conversation can also be used to understand how dancers communicate messages, and how audiences understand them. These cooperative principles relate to (1) the quantity of information, (2) the relation between packets of information, (3) the manner in which information is presented, and (4) the quality of information. Message-passing in dance is highly culturally constrained, and a Gricean approach can help in understanding how these constraints work. Grice's maxims are reproduced in Table 30.1, together with suggestions regarding their possible application to dance.

Quantity: The Size of the Movement Vocabulary

Quantity relates to the amount of information communicated. Messages should contain neither more nor less information than required. In the case of dance, this translates to economy of movement. Quantity of communication would determine how many movements are potentially performed by the dancer, that is, the size of the movement vocabulary. In order for messages to be understood, transmitter and receiver need to share a common vocabulary: he movement vocabulary of dance is constrained by the physical limitations of the human body, on one hand, and by choreographic decisions, on the other hand. In this context, dance styles can be regarded as higher-level constraints on the vocabulary. A small movement vocabulary will facilitate communication between dancer and spectator but will limit the range of what can be expressed. The rise of modern dance in the twentieth century can be interpreted as a deliberate expansion of the message set. A larger vocabulary allows for a greater range of expression. However, some of the extended vocabulary will be (initially) less accessible to the spectator.

Relation: Movement Patterns

Relation refers to the appropriateness of information at a given point of the communicative process. Information should be *relevant* to the specific communicative situation. The most obvious way that this constraint appears in dance involves the sequential structure of the movement vocabulary. Indeed, sequential structure is an important predictor of aesthetic preference in dance (Opacic, Stevens, & Tillmann, 2009; Orgs et al., 2013). On the receiver side, communication of relevant information will fulfil audience expectations, whereas irrelevant information will violate expectations. We propose that the aesthetic impact of dance will depend on balancing when structural expectations are violated or fulfilled. Excessive violation of such expectations is unrewarding (Wunderlich, Dayan, & Dolan, 2012). Equally, excessive conformity to expectation through ordered repetition is monotonous and reduces any sense of involvement. Seemingly irrelevant or unpredictable information may therefore be important to induce an appropriate level of surprise (Berlyne, 1974), and avoid monotony.

The principles of quantity and relation combined determine the *syntactic complexity and novelty* of the movement message. Complexity relates to the amount of information that is communicated through a sequence of movements (ibid): a choreography with few restrictions on the potential movement vocabulary and few or no repetitions (e.g. a dance in which each movement is performed exactly once) is maximally complex and rich in information, but may be hard to follow. Contrastingly, in a choreography that consists of repetitions of a single movement only (such as Sufi whirling), the information is maximally redundant and each individual movement contains only very little information. Compositional rules such as repetition can be applied at the local level and specify transitions between individual movements or body postures. The same compositional rules can also be applied at a more global level, that is, between longer movement phrases or sections of the choreography (Orgs et al., 2013). Berlyne (1974) argued that 'optimal' aesthetic processing occurs at intermediate levels of complexity. We will return to the role of movement complexity in aesthetic experience when introducing our dimensional model of aesthetic experience.

Manner: Ambiguity of Expression

The Gricean principle of manner states that perspicuous messages will be easier to understand than ambiguous messages. Dance movements vary widely in ambiguity. Whereas gestural movements communicate intentions very specifically (e.g. waving or hugging), dance is often characterised by movements that are abstract with no obvious verbal label or specific meaning. While ambiguity is normally considered to impair communication, it has long been considered to have an exceptional, even essential status in art. Indeed, Grice (1989) himself refers to the case of poetry in discussing ambiguity. In poetry, ambiguity can showcase the artistry of the writer by suggesting a number of different though equally plausible interpretations of the same sentence. Similarly, ambiguity of movement meaning may allow the spectator to choose one interpretation with the greatest personal relevance, or to hold a number of possible interpretations in play. In either case, the receiver's choice or evaluation process brings something to the aesthetic process. Alternatively, the spectator may simply enjoy the multitude of possible interpretations. Accordingly, ambiguity of artistic messages is often intentional and part of the message content (Hay, 2000). Messages may be 'perspicuously ambiguous'. In contrast to perspicuous messages, ambiguous messages require that the receiver takes a more active role in recovering intentions from the message (e.g. choosing one interpretation or resolve message conflict).

Whether perspicuous or ambiguous messages are perceived as aesthetically pleasing therefore depends on the spectator's epistemic actions whilst watching dance. We will return to this issue in the next section when we discuss syntactic and semantic processing and the role of cognitive effort in aesthetic appreciation.

Quality: 'Truthful' Movement and Stage Presence

Successful communication requires that messages are genuine and not deceptive. In Gricean terms, this includes two specific rules: (1) 'Do not say what you believe to be false', and (2) 'Do not say for which you lack adequate evidence'. The principle of quality therefore is a prerequisite for the other cooperative principles to come into play (Grice 1989) as its violation collides with the general assumption that communication should be beneficial to both transmitter and receiver. We propose that movement is perceived as genuine if the spectator perceives congruency between a dancer's intentions and his movements. Dance critics and dancers alike speak of performances as 'authentic' or 'compelling' or 'believable' (good) as opposed to 'fake' or 'merely doing the steps' or 'not feeling it' (bad). These comments suggest that an important element of aesthetic evaluation is perceived discrepancy between the observed movements and the intentions that they are supposed to communicate. The importance of congruency between intention and movement execution has previously been emphasised in embodied approaches to acting ('method acting', as developed by Constantin Stanislavski). In his seminal book, *Creating a Role*, he writes:

Scenic action is the movement from the soul to the body, from the center to the periphery, from the internal to the external, from the thing an actor feels to its physical form. External action on the stage when not inspired, not justified, not called forth by inner activity, is only entertaining for the eyes and ears; it does not penetrate the heart, it has no significance in the life of a human spirit as whole. (Stanislavski, 1968, p. 47)

Applying the same principles to dance, we argue that a movement intended to be decisive will not appear genuine if it is performed ineffectively, for example with a hesitant quality. Congruency between performed movement and inferred intention is therefore closely related to a performer's stage presence. In our communicative theory of performing dance aesthetics, stage presence is equivalent to the performer's power to communicate or 'the ability to penetrate the heart of the observer', and results from the performer being perceived as a consistently reliable source of the movement message.

A Dimensional Model of Aesthetic Appreciation of Human Movement

We have emphasised a unique feature of performative art, namely, that the art object is nothing but the kinematics of observed movement. In communication theory, we would say that these kinematics are the sole message. For there to be an artistic *experience*, the receiver must process this message. In Gricean theory, this processing aims to recover the transmitter's communicative intention.

Thus, the act of communication in performative arts involves a performer who provokes experiences in the receiver, the audience. The Gricean principles given above describe some of the constraints and assumptions that are required for this process to work. In this section, we develop a model of the processes within the receiver's brain that operate on the message to generate this artistic experience. At this stage, the transmitter vanishes from our concerns: she has already done her work in generating the message, and it is now up to the receiver to deal with it.

The effect of the stimulus on the receiver ultimately depends on how the receiver's brain processes the message. In the case of dance, we have identified visual, action and emotional features of the movement message. These features are transmitted through movement kinematics and combine to produce both the syntactic structure (quantity and relation of information) and the semantic content (manner of information, ambiguity) of a dance performance. We have further identified the observer's expertise, in particular visual and motor familiarity, as an important factor in how observed movements are processed by the brain. In this section, we consider how processing of the movement message influences aesthetic outcomes.

Dimensions of Aesthetic Experience

How can we relate stimulus processing in the brain to the features of 'dimensions' of aesthetic experience? Osgood's 'semantic differential' method (Osgood, Suci, & Tannenbaum, 1957) purported to identify three cardinal dimensions of all human experience: valence (likable or not), activity or passivity, and potency (strong or weak). Interestingly, many accounts of aesthetic experience recapitulate these general dimensions of all experiences, perhaps reflecting the fact that all experiences have some aesthetic component. Building on Osgood's work, Berlyne (1974) identified two dimensions that played a primary role in the aesthetic aspects of experience. The first dimension is captured by overtly aesthetic judgements, such as beautiful/ugly, pleasant/unpleasant and liked/disliked. The second dimension relates to judgements about stimulus information and structure, such as orderly/disorderly, simple/complex and boring/interesting.

Brain Mechanisms Underlying Aesthetic Processing of Movement

We argue that these two dimensions of aesthetic experience relate to distinct brain processes. Aesthetic valence should strongly depend on processing fluency, whereas aesthetic arousal should primarily depend on brain mechanisms of novelty detection, both in the syntactic and the semantic domains.

Processing Fluency

The effect of the stimulus on the receiver ultimately depends on how the receiver's brain processes the message. The 'fluency' of cognitive processing is a major predictor of aesthetic experience and refers to the ease at which a given stimulus is processed by the cognitive system. A central idea is that a stimulus is fluently processed when brain structures are specifically *tuned* to the features of that particular stimulus. For example, high contrast stimuli are preferred to low contrast stimuli because they are more easily recognised (Reber, Schwarz, & Winkielmann, 2004) and optimally activate primary visual cortex. According to processing fluency theory, it is therefore not objective stimulus features that give rise to aesthetic experience but only how these features are processed by the cognitive system. Zeki and Stutters (2012) show that the amount of activity a simple motion pattern induces in early visual areas is directly linked to its subjective beauty. Stimuli are preferred if they optimally stimulate dedicated brain areas, such as V5 for simple motion patterns.

Fluent Processing of Movement

In the case of watching dance, processing fluency of observed movements will be determined by the neural architecture that mediates movement perception. Several studies identified functionally specialised systems in the human brain for the perception of biological motion (Blake & Shiffrar, 2007) and intentional action (Fogassi et al., 2005). Fluency theories would suggest that the stimuli that readily or optimally activate these brain mechanisms should generate particularly fluent processing, and should therefore be perceived as aesthetically pleasant (Reber et al., 2004). The movement message should induce fluent processing if its visual, action and emotional features optimally excite those brain areas that are specialised for processing these features.

Fluent Processing of Familiarity

In addition, processing fluency strongly depends on the spectator's expertise. We have seen that visual and motor familiarity strongly influence how observed movements are processed by the brain. According to processing fluency theory, familiar stimuli are preferred because they are processed faster and more efficiently (Reber, Wurtz, & Zimmermann, 2004). In contrast to fluency that is based on specialised brain areas for low-level visual parameters (Zeki & Stutters, 2012), processing fluency for familiar movements arises from learning (Orgs et al., 2013). Once new neural connections have been established by a novel stimulus, these connections are more easily activated when the same stimulus is repeated (Hebb, 1949). Fluency theory therefore suggests that familiar movements should be perceived as aesthetically pleasant because they activate existing visual or motor representations automatically and with little cognitive effort. Processing fluency should be largest for movements that are both visually and motorically familiar.

Processing fluency correlates positively with the valence dimension of aesthetic judgement. Fluently processed stimuli are judged to be more pleasant, beautiful and likeable than disfluently processed stimuli (Reber, Winkielmann, & Schwarz, 1998; Zajonc, 1968). From an evolutionary perspective, the experience of fluent processing is perceived as pleasant because it signals safety and a predictable environment. However, fluently processed stimuli may also become more boring since they do not provide new information (Berlyne, 1974).

The Limits of Processing Fluency

Professional dancers have typically undergone years of training and acquired substantial motor skill. In most dance performances involving professional dancers, spectators will not be able to perform what they are observing. Whereas frequent spectators of dance performance may acquire substantial visual expertise with the observed movements, they will not acquire motor familiarity (Aglioti et al., 2008). Acquisition of motor familiarity requires performing and seeing an action at the same time (Heyes, 2010; Keysers & Perrett, 2004). Yet spectators clearly enjoy skill and virtuosity across dance styles, from breakdance to ballet. Indeed, some studies in movement aesthetics suggest an inverse relation between motor familiarity and preference: the more spectacular a movement, the more likely it is to be liked (Calvo-Merino, Jola, Glaser, & Haggard, 2008). Similarly, contorted body postures are preferred to less contorted body postures (Cross, Mackie, Wolford, & Hamilton, 2010). This suggests that fluent processing of familiar movements is not the only relevant process that determines aesthetic appreciation of dance. We suggest that this second aesthetic component is based on novelty and virtuosity of movement. In order to understand how communicating and extracting information will influence aesthetic appreciation of dance, we need to look at brain mechanisms for novelty detection in both movement syntax and semantics.

Novelty of Movement Syntax

Berlyne (1974) emphasises the role of amount of stimulus information in aesthetic experience. He argues that the aesthetic impact of a stimulus crucially depends on an optimal level of arousal that is produced by intermediate levels of stimulus complexity. Stimuli that contain a lot of information are judged as more interesting than stimuli that contain less information. For example, Crozier (cited in Berlyne, 1974) presented sound sequences that varied in information content. Simple sequences that repeated a small number of tones were judged to be less interesting than sequences that consisted of more tones with fewer repetitions.

The brain has dedicated mechanisms that process novelty and predictability of information. In the case of stimulus sequences, this has been studied extensively using the 'oddball' paradigm and event-related brain potentials (ERP) in the human electroencephalogram (Picton, 1992). In the auditory domain, the oddball paradigm involves sequences of identical tones that are interspersed with less frequent tones. These unexpected 'oddball' tones induce a positive deflection of the ERP approximately 300 ms after their presentation. Importantly, this component, which has been termed P300, does not depend on physical stimulus identity but only on whether a stimulus has been predicted or not (Wacongne et al., 2011). The P300 therefore serves as an index of surprise. The experience of surprise is directly related to the amount of information a stimulus provides: Within a sequence of repeated events a novel stimulus contains more information than a previously encountered event (Gottlieb, Oudeyer, Lopes, & Baranes, 2013).

In analogy to these simple sound sequences, appreciating dance involves (implicit) learning of compositional rules (Orgs et al., 2013). Accordingly, the size of the movement vocabulary and the relation between movements determine information complexity and novelty in dance. The same brain mechanisms of sequential information processing that apply to simpler stimulus sequences of sounds will therefore also apply to aesthetic processing of movement and should predict both perceived complexity of the sequence and its interestingness. Choreographies that induce surprise should be more interesting than choreographies that are structurally less surprising, but may not necessarily be perceived as pleasant.

Novelty of Movement Semantics

The second source of information in dance is movement meaning. Whereas meaning of gestures and goals in object-directed actions and gestures is clearly defined, dance often involves abstract movements that are ambiguous with respect to their goal or communicative content. Similarly to processing of meaning in language and music (Koelsch, 2011; Orgs, Lange, Dombrowski, & Heil, 2006), movement semantics have been studied using event-related potential measures (Amoruso et al., 2013). Actions that cannot easily be integrated into an existing semantic context, such as a businesswoman balancing on one foot in the desert (Proverbio & Riva, 2009) induce an 'action-N400', that is, a negative deflection of the ERP 400 ms after action observation. Similar N400 effects can be observed for speech-incongruent gestures, for example saying 'tall' whilst gesturing 'short' at the same time (Kelly, Kravitz, & Hopkins, 2004). These findings show that processing of movement intentions is functionally different from processing of sequential movement structure as described above (P300). Extraction of movement meaning and extraction of movement structure depend on functionally distinct neural mechanisms. Violations of common action semantics and ambiguous movement intentions are common features in choreography. Particularly theatrical styles of performing dance (e.g. choreographer Pina Bausch; Climenhaga, 2009) make frequent use of placing familiar actions in unfamiliar contexts, or alienate gestural actions from their originally clearly defined intentional purpose. We argue that such manipulations of action meaningfulness provide a source of 'conceptual surprise' that is fundamental to the aesthetic impact of dance.

Combined processing of movement syntax and action meaning determine how much information the movement message contains, and how easy it is to extract intentions from it. Accordingly, we propose that these two components should determine complexity and interestingness of observed movement, and should correlate with the second dimension of aesthetic processing (Berlyne, 1974). This dimension can also be linked to a general concept of activity, as in the semantic differential literature (Osgood, Suci, & Tannenbaum, 1957).

Explicit Aesthetic Appreciation and Judgement Based on Two Dimensions of Implicit Aesthetic Processing

The two dimensions of aesthetic *processing* (processing fluency and novelty/ complexity of information) correspond to two dimensions of aesthetic *judgement*, assessing the valence (beauty/likeability/pleasantness) and aesthetic arousal (interestingness/complexity/ambiguity), respectively. Both dimensions are *implicit* sources of aesthetic experience since they depend on the neural architecture for visual processing of human movement. Since the receiver has very little control over the perceptual mechanisms that are triggered by observation of a specific movement, we argue that these implicit mechanisms are primarily under the influence of the transmitter. In creating the movement message, both dancer and choreographer choose how to stimulate the brain of the spectator.

The spectator however deliberately chooses an *explicit* strategy of aesthetic appreciation that may favour either fluency or novelty/complexity. The spectator may enjoy the cognitive challenge that is posed by high levels of movement complexity and ambiguity, or he may enjoy the experience of fluent processing that is induced by watching a familiar dance piece that induces optimal visual

Table 30.2 *The relationship between characteristics of the movement message, aesthetic processing, appreciation and judgement*

Movement message	Aesthetic appreciation	Aesthetic judgement
Clear/simple/familiar	Fluency > novelty/complexity	Pleasant
Complex/ambiguous/ unfamiliar	Fluency > novelty/complexity	Unpleasant
Clear/simple/familiar	Fluency < novelty/complexity	Boring
Complex/ambiguous/ unfamiliar	Fluency < novelty/complexity	Interesting

movement processing. Indeed existing research on the role of expertise in aesthetic appreciation has shown that experts invest greater cognitive effort before making aesthetic judgements (Müller, Höfel, Brattico, & Jacobsen, 2010), and focus on stylistic and compositional features rather than evoked feelings (Augustin & Leder, 2006). A complex choreography of highly unfamiliar movements will only be appreciated if the spectator is prepared to invest considerable cognitive effort. In contrast, simple and familiar movement messages may be considered beautiful because they are easily accessible and communicate intentions clearly and unambiguously, allowing the spectator to relax and be entertained. Ultimately, aesthetic appreciation will therefore depend on how the spectator *weighs* the outcomes of implicit aesthetic processing (valence and arousal) according to his explicit aesthetic strategy (cognitive effort) – see Table 30.2.

Our theory makes the following predictions:

1　At low cognitive effort, aesthetic appreciation will primarily depend on processing fluency. Aesthetic appreciation should therefore strongly correlate with affective aesthetic judgements of preference and likeability. Familiarity of the choreography will be a strong predictor of aesthetic appreciation whereas movement complexity and ambiguity will be less appreciated. Novices will tend to adopt a low cognitive effort strategy of aesthetic appreciation.

2　At high cognitive effort, aesthetic appreciation will primarily depend on surprise that results from both high levels of information complexity and semantic ambiguity. Aesthetic appreciation is strongly predicted by judgements of interestingness, clarity and ambiguity. Experts will tend to adopt a high cognitive effort strategy of aesthetic appreciation.

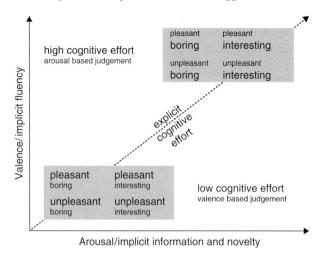

Figure 30.2 A dimensional model of the components of the receiver's appreciation of dance.

Figure 30.2 illustrates our dimensional mode of aesthetic appreciation. It includes two dimensions of aesthetic *processing*: valence and activity. Processing fluency primarily influences aesthetic affect, whereas novelty of syntactic and semantic information complexity primarily influence arousal. The two dimensions of aesthetic *processing* are captured by two distinct dimensions of aesthetic *judgement*. These are based on Osgood's semantic differential and relate to interestingness and pleasantness of the movement message. We further propose a third level that reflects the receiver's strategy of aesthetic *appreciation*. At this level the receiver weighs information from the two sources of aesthetic processing (fluency and information complexity/novelty), depending on how much cognitive effort the spectator is prepared to invest in decoding the movement message.

Is Dance Special?

The analytic structure outlined here partially overlaps with art forms other than dance. Thus, the communicative process that we claim to underlie the aesthetic experience of dance may not be fundamentally different from the communicative processes that occur when attending a live music concert, for example. Existing models of music perception (e.g. Koelsch, 2011) can account for some of the structural aspects of how dance works, such as its composition across time. However, the crucial difference between dance and other art forms, such as music or acting, is that a given musical piece or play can be experienced independently of the human body that initially performed or created it. Dance does not produce anything else but observed movement. In contrast, music and drama *use* movement as a means to produce either sound or spoken text. Their messages can therefore be described based on musical or literary characteristics and independent of the actions that originally produced these messages. Therefore, whereas watching human movement may indeed *contribute* to the appreciation of live music or theatre (Tsay, 2013), it is not essential to appreciate music or a play. Aesthetic perception of music will ultimately depend on the auditory characteristics of the music listened to and not on how the musicians move. In contrast, the unique quality of dance is that human movement is both necessary and sufficient for the key aesthetic experience.

Conclusion

During a dance performance, movement messages are communicated from performer to spectator. The aesthetic impact of dance (and perhaps all performing arts) is a result of successful message-passing between performer and spectator. Existing theories of aesthetic processing focus either on the message (objectivist view) or the receiver (subjectivist view) only. In contrast, we propose that aesthetic processing in dance is interactive and bidirectional. Further, we claim that aesthetic information in dance is primarily communicated by the kinematics of observed movement. We distinguish between the syntactic complexity of postures, movements and movement sequences, on the one hand, and semantic ambiguity of movement intentions, on the other hand. Aesthetic processing of both visual and motor features of the movement message will further depend on the spectator's own visual and motor expertise. In a dimensional model of aesthetic appreciation, implicit processing fluency and information complexity/ novelty of observed movement interact with explicit cognitive effort. Aesthetic judgements of preference and interest will reflect a combination of both implicit aesthetic processing and explicit aesthetic strategy of the observer.

References

Aglioti, S. M., Cesari, P., Romani, M., & Urgesi, C. (2008). Action anticipation and motor resonance in elite basketball players. *Nature Neuroscience*, 11, 1109–1116.

Allison, T., Puce, A., & McCarthy, G. (2000). Social perception from visual cues: Role of the STS region. *Trends in Cognitive Sciences*, 4, 267–278.

Amoruso, L., Gelormini, C., Aboitiz, F., Alvarez González, M., Manes, F, et al. (2013). N400 ERPs for actions: Building meaning in context. *Frontiers in Human Neuroscience*, 7, 57.

Aristotle. (1996), *Poetics*, IV. Harmondsworth: Penguin.

Arnheim, R. (1974*). Art and visual perception: A psychology of the creative eye*. Berkeley, CA: University of California Press.

Augustin, D. M., & Leder, H. (2006). Art expertise: A study of concepts and conceptual spaces. *Psychology Science*, 48, 135–156.

Beilock, S. L., & Holt, L. E. (2007). Embodied preference judgments: Can likeability be driven by the motor system? *Psychological Science*, 18, 51–57.

Berg, S. C. (1988). *Le sacre du printemps: 7 productions from Nijinsky to Martha Graham*. Ann Arbor, MI: UMI Research Press.

Berlyne, D. E. (1974). *Studies in the new experimental aesthetics: Steps towards an objective psychology of aesthetic appreciation*. New York: Wiley.

Blake, R., & Shiffrar, M. (2007). Perception of human motion. *Annual Review of Psychology*, 58, 47–73.

Bläsing, B., Calvo-Merino, B., Cross, E. S., Jola, C., Honisch, J., & Stevens, C. J. (2012). Neurocognitive control in dance perception and performance. *Acta Psychologica*, 139, 300–308.

Calvo-Merino, B., Glaser, D. E., Grèzes, J., Passingham, R. E., & Haggard, P. (2005). Action observation and acquired motor skills: An fMRI study with expert dancers. *Cerebral Cortex*, 15, 1243–1249.

Calvo-Merino, B., Grèzes, J., Glaser, D. E., Passingham, R. E., & Haggard, P. (2006). Seeing or doing? Influence of visual and motor familiarity in action observation. *Current Biology*, 16, 1905–1910.

Calvo-Merino, B., Jola, C., Glaser, D. E., & Haggard, P. (2008). Towards a sensorimotor aesthetics of performing art. *Consciousness and Cognition*, 17, 911–922.

Calvo-Merino, B., Urgesi, C., Orgs, G., Aglioti, S. M., & Haggard, P. (2010). Extrastriate body area underlies aesthetic evaluation of body stimuli. *Experimental Brain Research*, 204, 447–456.

Carbon, C. C. (2010). The cycle of preference: Long-term dynamics of aesthetic appreciation. *Acta Psychologica*, 134, 233–244.

Caspersen, D. (2004). The body is thinking. In G. Siegmund (Ed.), *Denken in Bewegung*. Leipzig: Henschel Verlag.

(2011). Decreation: Fragmentation and continuity. In S. Spier (Ed.), *William Forsythe and the practice of choreography*. London: Routledge, 93–100.

Climenhaga, R. (2009). *Pina Bausch*. New York: Routledge.

Cross, E. S., Hamilton, A. F., & Grafton, S. T. (2006). Building a motor simulation de novo: Observation of dance by dancers. *NeuroImage*, 31, 1257–1267.

Cross, E. S., Kirsch, L., Ticini, L. F., & Schütz-Bosbach, S. (2011). The impact of aesthetic evaluation and physical ability on dance perception. *Frontiers in Human Neuroscience*, 5, 102.

Cross, E. S., Mackie, E. C., Wolford, G., & Hamilton, A. F. D. C. (2010). Contorted and ordinary body postures in the human brain. *Experimental Brain Research*, 204, 397–407.

Cross, E. S. & Ticini, L. F. (2011). Neuroaesthetics and beyond: New horizons in applying the science of the brain to the art of dance. *Phenomenology and the Cognitive Sciences*, 11 (1), 5–16.

Daprati, E., Iosa, M., & Haggard, P. (2009). A dance to the music of time: Aesthetically-relevant changes in body posture in performing art. *PLoS One*, 4, e5023.

De Keersmaeker, A. T., & Cvejić, B. (2013). *En Atendant & Cesena: A choreographer's score*. Brussels: Rosas, Mercatorfonds.

Di Dio, C., Macaluso, E., & Rizzolatti, G. (2007). The golden beauty: Brain response to classical and renaissance sculptures. *PLoS One*, 2, e1201.

Fechner, G. T. (1871). *Vorschule der Ästhetik* [*Preschool of aesthetics*]. Hildesheim: Olms.

Fogassi, L., Ferrari, P. F., Gesierich, B., Rozzi, S., Chersi, F., & Rizzolatti, G. (2005). Parietal lobe: From action organization to intention understanding. *Science*, 308, 662–667.

Forsythe, W. (2010). *Improvisation technologies*. Berlin: Hatje Cantz.

Gelder, B. de, Snyder, J., Greve, D., Gerard, G., & Hadjikhani, N. (2004). Fear fosters flight: A mechanism for fear contagion when perceiving emotion expressed by a whole body. *Proceedings of the National Academy of Sciences USA*, 101, 16701–16706.

Gelder, B. de, van den Stock J., Meeren, H. K. M., Sinke, C. B. A., Kret, M. E., & Tamietto, M. (2010). Standing up for the body: Recent progress in uncovering the networks involved in the perception of bodies and bodily expressions. *Neuroscience and Biobehavioral Reviews*, 34, 513–527.

Gopnik, B. (2012). Aesthetic science and artistic knowledge. In A. P. Shimamura & S. E. Palmer (Eds.), *Aesthetic science: Connecting minds, brains and experience*. New York: Oxford University Press, 129–159.

Gottlieb, J., Oudeyer, P. Y., Lopes, M., & Baranes, A. (2013). Information-seeking, curiosity, and attention: Computational and neural mechanisms. *Trends in Cognitive Sciences*, 17, 585–593.

Grèzes, J., Pichon, S., & de Gelder, B. (2007). Perceiving fear in dynamic body expressions. *NeuroImage*, 35, 959–967.

Grice, P. (1989). *Studies in the way of words*. Cambridge, MA: Harvard University Press.

Hammermeister, K. (2002). *The German aesthetic tradition*. Cambridge: Cambridge University Press.

Hay, D. (2000). *My body, the Buddhist*. Middleton, CT: Wesleyan University Press.

Hebb, D. O. (1949). *The organization of behavior*. New York: Wiley.

Heider, F. & Simmel, M. (1944). An experimental study of apparent behavior. *American Journal of Psychology*, 57, 243–259.

Heijnsbergen, C. C. van, Meeren, H. K., Grèzes, J., & de Gelder, B. (2007). Rapid detection of fear in body expressions: An ERP study. *Brain Research*, 1186, 233–241.

Heyes, C. (2010). Where do mirror neurons come from? *Neuroscience and Biobehavioural Reviews*, 34(4), 575–583.

(2011). Automatic imitation. *Psychological Bulletin*, 137, 463–483.

Jakesch, M., & Leder, H. (2009). Finding meaning in art: Preferred levels of ambiguity in art appreciation. *Quarterly Journal of Experimental Psychology*, 62, 2105–2112.

Kelly, S. D., Kravitz, C., & Hopkins, M. (2004). Neural correlates of bimodal speech and gesture comprehension. *Brain and Language*, 89, 253–260.

Keysers, C., & Perrett., D. I. (2004). Demystifying social cognition: A Hebbian perspective. *Trends in Cognitive Sciences*, 62(3), 501–507.

Kilner, J. (2011). More than one pathway to action understanding. *Trends in Cognitive Sciences*, 15, 352–357.

Kirk, U. (2008). The neural basis of object–context relationships on aesthetic judgement. *PLoS One*, 3, e3754.

Kirsch, L. P., Drommelschmidt, K. A., & Cross, E. S. (2013). The impact of sensorimotor experience on affective evaluation of dance. *Frontiers in Human Neuroscience*, 7, 521.

Koelsch, S. (2011). Toward a neural model of music perception: A review and updated model. *Frontiers in Psychology*, 2, 110.

Laban, R. (2011). *The mastery of movement*. Alton, Hampshire: Dance Books Ltd.

Leach, J. (2013). Choreographic objects. *Journal of Cultural Economy*, 7(4). doi: 10.1080/17530350.2013.858058.

Leder, H., Belke, B., Oeberst, A., & Augustin, M. D. (2004). A model of aesthetic appreciation and aesthetic judgments. *British Journal of Psychology*, 95, 489–508.

Loeb, A. L. (1986). Symmetry in court and country dance. *Computers & Mathematics with Applications – Part B*, 12, 629–639.

McAleer, P., Pollick., F. E., Love, S. A., Crabbe, F. E., & Zacks, J. M. (2013). The role of kinematics in cortical regions for continuous human motion perception. *Cognitive, Affective and Behavioral Neuroscience,* 14(1), 307–318.

McGregor, W. (2013). *Choreographic thinking tools*. London: Hamlyn.

McManus, I. C. (1980). The aesthetics of simple figures. *British Journal of Psychology*, 71, 505–524.

Müller, M., Höfel, L., Brattico, E., & Jacobsen, T. (2010). Aesthetic judgments of music in experts and laypersons: An ERP study. *International Journal of Psychophysiology*, 76, 40–51.

Opacic, T., Stevens, C., & Tillmann, B. (2009). Unspoken knowledge: Implicit learning of structured human dance movement. *Journal of Experimental Psychology: Learning, Memory, and Cognition*, 35, 1570–1577.

Orgs, G., Bestmann, S., Schuur, F., & Haggard, P. (2011). From body form to biological motion: The apparent velocity of human movement biases subjective time. *Psychological Science*, 22, 712–717.

Orgs, G., Dombrowski, J.-H., Heil, M., & Jansen-Osmann, P. (2008). Expertise in dance modulates alpha/beta event-related desynchronization during action observation. *European Journal of Neuroscience*, 27, 3380–3384.

Orgs, G., Hagura, N., & Haggard, P. (2013). Learning to like it: Aesthetic perception of bodies, movements and choreographic structure. *Consciousness & Cognition*, 22, 603–612.

Orgs, G., Lange, K., Dombrowski, J. H., & Heil, M. (2006). Conceptual priming for environmental sounds and words: An ERP study. *Brain Cognition*, 62(3), 267–272.

Osgood, C. E., Suci, G. J., & Tannenbaum, P. H. (1957). *The measurement of meaning*. Urbana, IL: University of Illinois Press.

Palmer, S. E., Schloss, K. B., & Sammartino, J. (2013). Visual aesthetics and human preference. *Annual Review of Psychology*, 64, 77–107.

Peelen, M. V., & Downing, P. E. (2007). The neural basis of visual body perception. *Nature Reviews Neuroscience*, 8, 636–48.

Peters, J. (2010). *Damaged Goods/Meg Stuart. Are we here yet?* Dijon, France: Les presses du réel.

Picton, T. W. (1992). The P300 wave of the human event-related potential. *Journal of Clinical Neurophysiology*, 9, 456–479.

Proverbio A. M., & Riva, F. (2009). RP and N400 ERP components reflect semantic violations in visual processing of human actions. *Neuroscience Letters*, 459, 142–146.

Ramachandran, V. S., & Hirstein, W. (1999). The science of art. *Journal of Consciousness Studies*, 6, 15–51.

Rameson, l. T., & Lieberman, M. D. (2009). Empathy: A social cognitive neuroscience approach. *Social and Personality Psychology Compass*, 3(1), 94–110.

Reber, R., Schwarz, N., & Winkielman, P. (2004). Processing fluency and aesthetic pleasure: Is beauty in the perceiver's processing experience? *Personality and Social Psychology Review*, 8, 364–382.

Reber, R., Winkielman, P., & Schwarz, N. (1998). Effects of perceptual fluency on affective judgments. *Psychological Science*, 9, 45–48.

Reber, R., Wurtz, P., & Zimmermann, T. D. (2004). Exploring 'fringe' consciousness: The subjective experience of perceptual fluency and its objective bases. *Consciousness and Cognition*, 13, 47–60.

Rizzolatti, G., & Craighero, L. (2004). The mirror-neuron system. *Annual Review of Neuroscience*, 27, 169–192.

Shannon, C. E., & Weaver, W. (1949). *A mathematical model of communication*. Urbana, IL: University of Illinois Press.

Stanislavski, C. (1968). *Creating a role*. London: NEL Mentor Books.

Topolinski, S. (2010). Moving the eye of the beholder: Motor components in vision determine aesthetic preference. *Psychological Science*, 21, 1220–1224.

Tsay, C. J. (2013). Sight over sound in the judgment of music performance. *Proceedings of the National Academy of Sciences*, 110, 14580–14585.

Urgesi, C., Calvo-Merino, B., Haggard, P., & Aglioti, S. M. (2007). Transcranial magnetic stimulation reveals two cortical pathways for visual body processing. *Journal of Neuroscience*, 27, 8023–8030.

Wacongne, C., Labyt, E., van Wassenhove, V., Bekinschtein, T., Naccache, L., & Dehaene, S. (2011). Evidence for a hierarchy of predictions and prediction errors in human cortex. *Proclamations of the National Academy of Sciences USA*, 108, 20754–2079.

Wunderlich, K., Dayan, P., & Dolan, R. J. (2012). Mapping value based planning and extensively trained choice in the human brain. *Nature Neuroscience*, 15, 786–791.

Zajonc, R. B. (1968). Attitudinal effects of mere exposure. *Journal of Personality and Social Psychology*, 9, 1–27.

Zeki, S., & Lamb, M. (1994). The neurology of kinetic art. *Brain*, 117, 607–636.

Zeki, S., & Stutters J. (2012). A brain-derived metric for preferred kinetic stimuli. *Open Biology*, 2. doi: 10.1098/rsob.120001.

Index